Paul Trynka is the former editor of *Mojo*. He lives in Greenwich, London, with his wife and son.

STARMAN

DAVID BOWIE

THE DEFINITIVE BIOGRAPHY

Paul Trynka

SPHERE

First published in Great Britain in 2011 by Sphere
This paperback edition published in 2012 by Sphere
Reprinted 2012, 2013 (twice)

A CIP catalogue record for this book
is available from the British Library.

ISBN 978-0-7515-4293-6

Typeset in Palatino by M Rules
Printed and bound in Great Britain by
Clays Ltd, St Ives plc

Papers used by Sphere are from well-managed forests
and other responsible sources.

MIX
Paper from
responsible sources
FSC® C104740

Sphere
An imprint of
Little, Brown Book Group
100 Victoria Embankment
London EC4Y 0DY

An Hachette UK Company
www.hachette.co.uk

www.littlebrown.co.uk

To Kazimierz and Maureen: Heroes

CONTENTS

Genius Steals

Thursday evening, seven o'clock: decadence is about to arrive in five million front rooms. Neatly suited dads are leaning back in the comfiest chair, mums in their pinnies are clearing away the dishes, while the kids – still in school shirts and trousers – are clustered around the small television for their most sacred weekly ritual.

The tiny studio audience, milling around in tank tops and dresses, clap politely as the artist at number forty-one in the charts strums out two minor chords on his blue twelve-string guitar. The camera cuts from his hands to his face, catching the barest hint of a smirk – like a child hoping to get away with something naughty. But then as his friends – Trevor, Woody and Mick Ronson – clatter into action with a rollicking drum roll and throaty guitar, the camera pulls back and David Bowie meets its gaze, unflinchingly. His look is lascivious, amused. As an audience of excited teens and outraged parents struggle to take in the multicoloured quilted jumpsuit, the luxuriant carrot-top hairdo, spiky teeth and those sparkling, mascaraed come-to-bed eyes, he sings us through an arresting succession of images: radios, aliens, 'get-it-on rock 'n' roll'. The audience is still grappling with this confusing, over-the-top spectacle when a staccato guitar rings out a Morse code warning, and then, all too suddenly, we're into the chorus.

From the disturbingly new, we shift to the reassuringly familiar: as he croons out 'There's a star—man . . .' Bowie's voice leaps up an octave. It's an ancient Tin Pan Alley songwriter's trick, signalling a release, a climax. And as we hear of the friendly alien waiting in the sky, the audience suddenly recognises a tune, and a message, lifted openly, outrageously, from 'Over the Rainbow', Judy Garland's escapist, Technicolor wartime anthem. It's simple, singalong, comforting territory, and it lasts just four bars, before David Bowie makes his bid for immortality. Less than one minute after his face first appeared on *Top of the Pops* – the BBC's family-friendly music programme – Bowie lifts his slim, graceful hand to the side of his face and his platinum-haired bandmate Mick Ronson joins him at the microphone. Then, casually, coolly, Bowie places his arm around the guitarist's neck, and pulls Ronson lovingly towards him. There's the same octave leap as he sings 'star—man' again, but this time it doesn't suggest escaping the bounds of earth; it symbolises escaping the bounds of sexuality.

The fifteen-million-strong audience struggles to absorb this exotic, pan-sexual creature: in countless households, the kids are entranced – in their hundreds, in thousands – as parents sneer, shout or walk out of the room. But even as they wonder how to react, there's another stylistic swerve; with the words 'let the children boogie', David Bowie and The Spiders break into an unashamed T. Rex boogie rhythm. For a generation of teenagers, there was no hesitation; those ninety seconds, on a sunny evening in July 1972, would change the course of their lives. Up to this point, pop music had been mainly about belonging, about identification with your peers. This music, carefully choreographed in a dank basement under a south London escort agency, was a spectacle of not-belonging. For scattered, isolated kids around the UK, and soon the East Coast of America, and then the West Coast, this was their day. The day of the outsider.

In the weeks that followed, it became obvious that these three minutes had put a rocket under the career of a man all-too recently dismissed as a one-hit wonder. Most people who knew him were delighted, but there were hints of suspicion. 'Hip Vera Lynn,' one cynical friend called it, in a pointed reference to 'The White Cliffs of Dover' – the huge wartime hit that had also ripped off Judy Garland's best-known song; this *homage* was too knowing. A few weeks later, to emphasise the point, David started singing 'somewhere over the rainbow' over the chorus of 'Starman' – as if to prove Pablo Picasso's maxim that 'talent borrows, genius steals'.

And steal he had, with a clear-eyed effrontery as shocking as the lifted melodies themselves. The way he collaged several old tunes into a new song was a musical tradition as old as the hills, one still maintained by David's old-school showbiz friends like Lionel Bart, the writer of *Oliver!*. Yet to boast of this *homage*, to show the joins, brazenly, like the lift shafts of the Pompidou centre, was a new trick – a post-modernism that was just as unsettling as the post-sexuality he'd shown off with that arm lovingly curled over Mick Ronson's shoulder. This 'appropriation' might have been a hot notion in the art scene, thanks to Andy Warhol, but for a rock 'n' roller to declare 'I'm a tasteful thief' defied a sacred convention – that rock 'n' roll was an authentic, visceral medium. Rock 'n' roll was *real*; born out of joy and anguish in the turmoil of post-war America, and sculpted into the first electric blues. But David flaunted his lack of authenticity with brazen abandon. 'The only art I'll ever study is stuff I can steal from. I do think that my plagiarism is effective,' he told an interviewer. The open lifting of iconic sounds was a disturbing new form of genius. But was rock 'n' roll now just an art game? Was the flame-haired Ziggy Stardust – potent symbol of otherness – just an intellectual pose?

When David Bowie made his mark so elegantly, so extravagantly, that night on *Top of the Pops*, in a thrilling performance that marked out the seventies as a decade distinct from the sixties, every one of those contradictions was obvious; in fact, they added a delicious tension. In the following months and years – as he dumped the band who had shaped his music; when his much-touted influences like Iggy Pop, the man who'd inspired Ziggy, dismissed him as a 'fuckin' carrot-top' who had exploited and then sabotaged him; when David himself publicly moaned that his gay persona had damaged his career in the US – those contradictions became more obvious still.

So was David Bowie truly an outsider? Or was he a showbiz pro, exploiting outsiders like a psychic vampire? Was he really a starman, or was it all cheap music-hall tinsel and glitter? Was he gay or was it all a mask? There was evidence aplenty for both. And that evidence multiplied in the following months and years as fans witnessed – wide-mouthed – astonishing moments like his wired, fractured appearance on *The Dick Cavett Show*, or his twitchy but charming approachability on *Soul Train*. Was this bizarre behaviour also a mask? A carefully choreographed routine?

In the following years David Bowie, and those around him, would struggle to answer this question. He'd emerged from a showbiz tradition propelled chiefly by youthful ambition, his main talent that of 'repositioning the brand', as one friend puts it. That calculation, that 'executive ability', as Iggy Pop describes it, marked him out as the very antithesis of instinctive rock 'n' roll heroes like Elvis Presley. Yet the actions that apparently signalled the death of rock 'n' roll announced a rebirth, too. Maybe this wasn't rock 'n' roll like Elvis had made it, but it led the way for where rock 'n' roll would go. Successors like Prince or Madonna, Bono or Lady Gaga, each seized on Bowie's 'repositioning the brand' as a set-piece example of how to avoid artistic culs-de-sac like the one that imprisoned Elvis. For Bowie himself, though, each brand renewal, each metamorphosis, would come at a cost.

Inevitably, as David Bowie's career moved ever onwards, generations of fans wondered what lay behind those masks. In subsequent years there have been many accounts, either of a flint-hearted rip-off merchant, or a natural-born genius with some minor character flaws. Yet as the hundreds of friends, lovers and fellow musicians who speak within the following pages attest, the truth is far more intriguing.

For the truth is, David Bowie – behind the glitter and showmanship – didn't just change himself on the outside; he changed himself on the inside. Since Doctor Faustus sold his soul, or Robert Johnson found himself at the crossroads, artists and musicians have struggled to transcend the talents they were born with. David Bowie, a youth with ambition and more charm than talent, seemed to have achieved that magical alchemy, the achievement we all dream of: he transformed himself, and his destiny.

PART ONE

I Hope I Make It On My Own

1

When I'm Five

Everything seemed grey. We wore short grey flannel trousers
of a thick and rough material, grey socks and grey shirts. The
roads were grey, the prefabs were grey and the bomb sites also
seemed to be made of grey rubble.

Peter Prickett

It was a cold, wet November in 1991, like the cold, wet Novembers of
his childhood, when David Bowie asked his driver to take the scenic
route to the Brixton Academy. The smoke-filled coach pulled slowly
down Stansfield Road, just a few hundred yards from the venue, and
paused outside a large, anonymous three-storey Victorian house, before
moving on.

Bowie had been chatty, open, almost surprisingly vulnerable in the
last twelve weeks, but remained silent for a few minutes as he gazed out
of the window. Then he turned around, and guitarist Eric Schermerhorn,
sitting next to him, could see tears trickling down his employer's cheeks.
'It's a miracle,' Bowie murmured. He was unashamed of his vulnerability. 'I probably should have been an accountant. I don't know how
this all happened.'

For Schermerhorn, who'd seen Bowie's showmanship and poise from
close-up, the mental image of David Robert Jones inspecting a company
spreadsheet seemed ludicrous. As had the doubts he'd expressed to
Schermerhorn a few days before: he didn't even know if he could sing.
For Schermerhorn, who had seen the man's almost mystical ability to
hold a show together and dominate a crowd, this apparent self-doubt
was bizarre. Over the coming months, Schermerhorn would learn from

Bowie's friends, and his own observations, about the man's organisation, his 'executive abilities', his talent for working the system. Yet here was the man himself, surveying the scene of his childhood, convinced this was some kind of accident. The idea seemed ludicrous. Hadn't someone so eminently glamorous always been fated to be a star?

David Bowie has described himself as a 'Brixton boy' more than once. Although his stay was brief, it's an apt term. Brixton in January 1947 was a unique location: the cultural focus of south London, blessed with its own racy glamour, battered but unbowed by the Luftwaffe and Hitler's terror weapons, whose destruction was visible wherever you walked.

It was natural that David's father, Haywood Stenton Jones, should gravitate towards Brixton, for its music-hall traditions matched his own fantasies. Born in Doncaster on 21 November, 1912, and brought up in the picturesque Yorkshire brewery town of Tadcaster, he had a tough childhood: his father died in the First World War, and his mother soon afterwards. Raised by the local council and an aunt, Haywood Jones came into an inheritance from the family footwear business when he was eighteen. 'So he bought a theatre troupe. What a wise idea!' David recounted years later. The enterprise lost Haywood much of his fortune, and he invested what was left in a nightclub in London's West End that catered to boxers and other exotic characters. It was during this short-lived venture that he also acquired a wife, pianist Hilda Sullivan. When the nightclub burned up most of his remaining cash, Haywood came down with a stomach ulcer. The idea of working for a children's charity came to him in a dream; both an exit route from his own troubles and a way of helping kids who'd suffered fractured childhoods like his own. In September 1935 he started work at Dr Barnardo's at Stepney Causeway, an imposing, sooty complex of buildings in the heart of the East End, which had provided a refuge for homeless children since the 1870s.

When the Second World War broke out, Haywood was among the first to enlist, serving with the Royal Fusiliers, who fought in France, North Africa and Europe. When he returned to a battered but victorious London in October 1945, Haywood immediately rejoined Barnardo's as General Superintendent to the Chief of Staff. Like many wartime marriages, Haywood's didn't last – it was doubtless damaged by an affair with a nurse which produced a child, Annette, born in 1941.

Hayward met Margaret Burns, known as Peggy – a waitress at the Ritz Cinema – on a visit to a Barnardo's home at Tunbridge Wells soon after his return, and his divorce from Hilda only came through in time for him to marry Peggy eight months after the arrival of his second child, David Robert Jones, who was born at the family's new home at 40 Stansfield Road, Brixton, on 8 January, 1947.

In that immediate post-war period, Brixton was cold, damp and soot-blackened and battered by vengeance weapons. Its pre-war raciness and music-hall glamour was only enhanced by its recent history, and in 1947 Brixton looked – to use one of David's favourite words – especially *dystopian*. This part of south London had been judged 'expendable' in the Second World War: Churchill's spymasters had manipulated the press reports of where Hitler's futuristic V1 flying bombs were landing, to ensure they fell short and hit south London, rather than the wealthy West End. Over forty of the pioneering cruise missiles smashed into Brixton and Lambeth – entire streets both behind and in front of the Jones' family home were flattened. Most of the rubble had been cleared away by 1947, but the area retained its foreboding gap-toothed look for decades.

David's first winter was grim. Britain in late 1947 was grim. The Second World War had invigorated American capitalism, but had left Britain tired, battered and near broke. There were no street lights, no coal, gas supplies were low and ration cards were still needed to buy linen, fuel, 'economy' suits, eggs and the scraggy bits of Argentinean beef that were only occasionally available. Christopher Isherwood, the writer who would one day advise David to move to Berlin, visited London that year and was shocked at its shabbiness. 'London is a dying city,' one local told him, advising him not to return.

For parents, life was hard. Yet for the children who scampered around this urban wilderness, it was a wonderland; the abandoned, bomb-damaged houses were playgrounds and museums, full of intriguing treasures abandoned by long-vanished tenants.

In later years, many of Peggy Burns' friends would notice her con-tempt for the Labour Party, who had swept into power in the first post-war election on a platform of radical social reform. Yet given life that winter, her attitude was understandable. The British had been exhausted by the war, but peace had brought no improvement in living standards. In Brixton it was impossible to find soap, the local Woolworth's was lit by candles, Peggy had to constantly scour the local shops to find terry towelling for nappies, and at the end of February the Labour government introduced power rationing, with homes limited to five hours' electricity a day. In the meantime, Haywood Jones and the

Barnardo's organisation wrestled with the problem of thousands of children displaced by the war.

David loved his father – to this day he wears a gold cross given to him by Haywood when he was in his teens – but when asked about his relationship with his mother in 2002, he quoted Philip Larkin's famously bleak 'This Be The Verse' – the poem that starts, 'They fuck you up, your mum and dad.' The occasion was an informal live chat with interviewer Michael Parkinson; the lines drew laughter, as had many of David's quips. As David went on to recite the remaining lines of misery, the titters gave way to uncomfortable silence.

The 'madness' of Peggy Burns' family would one day become part of the Bowie legend, but as far as the young David Jones was concerned, it was remoteness – a simple lack of emotion – that characterised his relationship with his mum. Peggy's sister Pat said of their mother, Margaret Mary Burns, née Heaton, that, 'she was a cold woman. There was not a lot of love around.' Peggy seems to have inherited that coldness. Yet according to family lore, Peggy was good with children in her youth, working as a nanny before falling in love with the handsome Jack Isaac Rosenberg, son of a wealthy Jewish furrier. Rosenberg promised to marry Peggy, but disappeared before the birth of their son, and David's half-brother, Terence Guy Adair Burns, on 5 November, 1937.

There were darker shadows in Peggy's past, too. In 1986 her sister Pat – 'the frightful aunt' as Bowie later termed her – went on the record to detail the troubled history of the Burns family. Peggy and Pat's siblings included three sisters – Nora, Una and Vivienne – who, according to Pat, suffered from degrees of mental instability; what one writer termed the Burns' 'family affliction'. This history later inspired the theory that David Jones was forced to construct alter-egos to distance himself from the madness within. Ken Pitt, David's future manager, knew David, Peggy and Pat as well as anyone, and describes this theory as 'unconvincing'. Although David would later gleefully celebrate his family, announcing, 'most of them are nutty – in, just out of, or going into an institution', most people who knew them considered Haywood friendly and sincere and found Peggy talkative once you got to know her, with many traces of her former vivaciousness.

Peggy had a third child, Myra Ann, born in August 1941, before she met Haywood – the result of another wartime romance. The child was given up for adoption and by the time she met Haywood, Peggy was ready to settle down to a conventional life and agreed to marry the Yorkshireman on the condition that he accept Terence as his son. So for the first nine years of his life, David had an elder brother to look up to; and when Terry left home in 1956 to join the Royal Air Force, he remained the object of David's hero-worship. The messy, confused nature of the Jones household was hardly unusual – illegitimate births had soared in wartime Britain; some historians blame a shortage of rubber and hence a fall in condom production. David's troubled relationship with his mother echoed that of contemporaries like John Lennon and Eric Clapton, both of whom were raised in households that today would have a social worker knocking on the door.

As David grew into a toddler, austerity continued to keep a tight grip, but glimmers of hope started to appear. 1953, a year treasured by many kids, marked an end to sweet rationing and the advent of television. Haywood Jones was one of thousands who bought a new set so the family could watch the coronation of the glamorous young Queen Elizabeth. Just a few weeks later, the six-year-old David snuck downstairs for another TV landmark – *The Quatermass Experiment*, a pioneering BBC science-fiction series that had all of Britain glued to the screen. This 'tremendous series' would leave its mark on David, who remembers how he'd watch each Saturday night 'from behind the sofa when my parents had thought I had gone to bed. After each episode I would tiptoe back to my bedroom rigid with fear, so powerful did the action seem.' The programme sparked a lifelong fascination with science fiction and – through its theme tune: the dark, sinister, *Mars, The Bringer of War* from Holst's 'Planet Suite' – the emotional effect of music.

Brixton was the perfect breeding ground for a future Ziggy Stardust. Waterloo, the Mecca of music-hall artists for a century or more, was just down the road, while Brixton's own Empress Theatre hosted Tony Hancock, Laurel and Hardy, and countless other Variety stars. 'Show business people were scattered all the way from Kennington to Streatham,' says David's near-neighbour, the photographer Val Wilmer. Many locals still talked of Charlie Chaplin, who had grown up just north of Brixton; Sharon Osbourne, five years younger than David, lived on the other side of Brixton Road with her father Don Arden, a failed nightclub singer and comedian, and she remembers being surrounded by 'all the Vaudeville artists'. Kids could look out of the window and see comedians chatting in the corner shop, racy characters in cheap suits and hats, carrying cases that might contain a ventriloquist's dummy, a banjo or a set of knives for their knife-throwing act, on their way to or from a show.

David's home at 40 Stansfield Road was a roomy, three-storey terraced Victorian house, shared, during most of their eight years in Brixton, with two other families. In later years, with conventional rock-star spin, David Bowie described his Brixton youth like a walk on the wild side, with gangs roaming the street. The local kids did indeed wander around the area freely, but their prey was butterflies, tadpoles and other urban wildlife. 'It was unbelievable,' says David's neighbour and schoolmate Sue Larner, 'there were these huge spaces from the bomb sites, and ruined houses, which seemed like mountains to us, covered in buddleia: they were our playgrounds.' Derelict buildings at the bottom of Stansfield Road were sinister, yet fragrant – kids scampered around the sweet-smelling blooms with nets, for there were more butterflies around than before or since, while the many pools and ponds in south London's abandoned bomb sites were packed with tadpoles and newts. Rats also meandered casually through the abandoned buildings, and local kids still remember the sound of mice scurrying around the draughty, un-carpeted Victorian houses at night, as they clutched a hot water bottle for warmth and comfort.

In those early years, the Jones family kept themselves to themselves. Most local kids played out on the street, but David generally remained with his mum, and Haywood spent his days at Barnardo's in Stepney. In 1951, David started school at Stockwell Infants, three minutes walk away from home on Stockwell Road, one of Brixton's main streets. He remembers wetting his pants on the first day; happily, friendly milk lady Bertha Douglas kept a supply of clean knickers for such everyday emergencies. Stockwell Infants' lofty Victorian building looked severe, with its characteristic aroma of disinfectant and rubber plimsolls, but the staff were mostly loving and kind. 'It was a sweet, friendly school; small and cosy,' remembers schoolmate Suzanne Liritis. 'The teachers used to tell us things like, "you're special, Jesus loves you",' says her friend, Sue Larner.

Behind the Victorian primness, things were more exotic than they seemed. The headmistress, Miss Douglas, was tall and thin with severe, scraped-back grey hair. This formidable woman lived with Miss Justin, who taught in the Junior School. Only later did Sue and her friends conclude 'they were obviously a sweet lesbian couple'. If any parents suspected a relationship, they were unconcerned, for as Larner points out, 'Lots of women had lost their beaus in the war.' They took the conventional British attitude: exotic sexuality was fine, as long as it was kept behind closed doors. Don't frighten the horses, as the saying went.

Most of the families around Stansfield Road were large, with kids invariably accompanied on their adventures by brothers and sisters. Maybe it's for that reason that few of them remember David. Sue Larner was one of the only children who did notice him; now a sculptor, she recalls noticing the nice-looking, well-scrubbed boy's skill at art. 'None of us had much to do with boys, but I do remember showing him a few tricks on the drawing board – and he showed me even more. He showed me how to draw a woman's bonnet, with the neck, without having to draw a face first. He was good.'

At weekends, or after school, the five-year-old David's universe was bounded by the bomb sites on Chantrey Road and the far side of Stockwell Road, where all kids played: turning left on Stockwell Road, he'd immediately reach the school playground; turning right, he'd walk past two sweet shops, the nearest overseen by a kindly, camp gentleman. Further down Stockwell Road was the Astoria: later a famed rock venue – the Academy – whose attractions would include David Bowie, in the fifties it was still a thriving local cinema, with morning matinees featuring cowboy movies, Zorro or Laurel and Hardy. On the way to the cinema, a book-shop sprawled out onto the pavement, filled with comics and kids' books. There was a large dairy, with horse-drawn carts, but the main feature that dominated Stockwell Road was Pride and Clarke's, a celebrated motorbike and car showroom that sprawled across a row of maroon-painted buildings, later immortalised in Antonioni's *Blowup*. This was where David, the future petrol-head, could ogle BSAs, Rileys and other legendary British bikes and cars.

As for another intrinsic part of Brixton's appeal, the sound of calypso and the smell of curried goat, these were things David would only have got a whiff of. For in 1954, Haywood Jones and family packed up for suburbia.

It was John Betjeman, the beloved poet laureate, who described the suburbs as the home of 'a new kind of citizen'. As fitting proof of its futurism, David's new home, Bromley, was also the birthplace of H. G. Wells. From the 1950s onwards, the suburbs were an object of both horror and aspiration – the upper classes despised the prim, mock-Tudor houses, while the middle classes flocked to such neatly manicured streets. Today, like many English market towns, Bromley is bland and overrun by chain stores: Wells' birthplace is now a Primark clothing outlet. But in the fifties it was a place in flux – a short train ride from London, but smaller and friendlier. 'It was actually quite charming,' says David's boyhood friend, Geoff MacCormack, 'even soulful.'

The move to Bromley marked Haywood's promotion from board secretary to Public Relations Officer. Haywood's colleagues regarded him as 'unassuming but cheerful – good company'. The Jones' new home, a small but neat Edwardian terraced house in Plaistow Grove – a cul-de-sac near the railway line – was perfectly in keeping with the family's modestly respectable status.

Parts of Bromley were middle-class enclaves –1930s fake Tudor with leaded windows to proclaim their superior status – but poverty was never far away. Children and their parents were encouraged to save 6d a week in the Burnt Ash School Boot Club – to help them buy adequate footwear – and there was no shortage of Dickensian sights. A costermonger, or rag-and-bone man, walked the streets, uttering the 'Any old iron' cry familiar from Victorian times. Several streets still boasted gas lighting, and in most parts of Bromley there was hardly a car to be seen parked at the curbside. United Dairies, which had a yard behind Burnt Ash School, still used horses to deliver milk, which was deposited on everybody's doorstep each morning. Even in the 1950s, electrical supplies were erratic; radios or record players were usually plugged into the light socket in the ceiling, while electric clocks often slowed down in the afternoon, at the time of heavy demand, then would speed up again at night. Few people owned telephones– the Joneses were an exception.

David joined Burnt Ash School a couple of years after most of his classmates and didn't particularly stand out during the first few terms. Within a year or so, however, David was part of a small gang, including Dudley Chapman and John Barrance, who lived nearby and were invited to David's eighth birthday party. Even at this age, many kids noted the cramped interior of the Jones' modest two-up, two-down house. John Barrance thought the family seemed restrained, quiet. 'They were perfectly pleasant, but I think they had a "don't touch this, don't touch that" attitude.' David's friend Max Batten shared more easygoing times with him, enjoying lollipops, chatting with Mrs Jones and, one memorable afternoon, sneaking upstairs and unwrapping Haywood's service revolver. The two boys played with it furtively, before carefully replacing it in the drawer where it had been concealed.

Though few of his contemporaries remember it as being anything out of the ordinary, in later years David's background would be portrayed as dysfunctional – mostly by David himself. In the mid-seventies, when he was in his most flamboyantly deranged phase, he loved to proclaim, 'everyone finds empathy in a nutty family'. Peggy, in particular, was singled out as the perfect exemplar of repression and eccentricity, but the most damning recollection of others is that she was a snob. In general, it was only the more middle-class children were treated to a welcome and a cup of tea at Plaistow Grove, and David seemed to learn which of his friends should be ushered in the front door and which ones were worthy only to wait at the garden gate. In fairness, it's possible Peggy simply preferred boys who, like David, were trained to say 'please' and 'thank you'. John Hutchinson, a well-brought-up Yorkshire lad who enjoyed sitting in the back room with its cosy fireplace and photos on the mantelpiece, maintains that, 'she was nice', remembering how in future years she would knit outfits for his young son, Christian. Some of the tensions between Peggy and David were simply due, says Hutchinson, to the generational shift that would soon grip the country, the advent of the teenager and the fact that, as he puts it, 'it became cool to put down your parents'. In future years, Peggy's sister Pat bore witness to other tensions within the family. In their first year in Bromley, Terry was apparently left behind in Brixton, which was thought to be more convenient for his job as a clerk in Southwark. Later he rejoined David, Peggy and Haywood at Plaistow Grove, but his presence – before he left to prepare for National Service in 1955 – was brief; not one of David's friends remember seeing him at the Jones' house. If parents 'fuck you up', as David put it, then undoubtedly Terry suffered more than his brother.

Peggy's own friends, such as Aubrey Goodchild, maintain David's mum was 'good company. Forthright, though. And conservative in her politics.' And David wasn't the only one who felt frustrated or hemmed in by his family. Compared to America, with its consumer boom, movies and comic-book heroes, Britain was staid and its kids felt suffocated. 'We were shabby,' says Bromley schoolgirl Dorothy Bass. 'Everything seemed grey,' remembers another contemporary, Peter Prickett. 'We wore short grey flannel trousers of a thick and rough material, grey socks and grey shirts. The roads were grey, the prefabs were grey and there were still quite a few bomb sites around in 1956 – these also seemed to be made of grey rubble.' Life was predictable, defined by rituals. Some of them were oddly comforting, like the tiny glass bottles of free milk handed out at school every morning at 11 o'clock, the National Anthem that was played on BBC radio and TV before they closed down for the night, or David's volunteer job at school – putting up the climbing ropes in the playground each morning.

For its time, Burnt Ash was a modern school, with an emphasis on art – particularly in the form of Music and Movement classes, during which the pupils were encouraged to express themselves, dancing around in their underwear. No one owned a PE kit. In other respects it followed fifties norms: a strict uniform policy, formal assemblies with hymns and the cane for misbehaving boys.

Headmaster George Lloyd was, in the words of one pupil, 'interesting'. Slightly portly, and jolly, he took classes in music and reading, individually tutoring his pupils one-on-one. He was 'gentle', affectionate with the children, and often sat alongside boys as they read, putting his arm around the favoured pupil. There were a few boys for whom he seemed to have real affection, 'and one of them,' says a schoolmate, 'was David. He definitely did like David.'

At ten or eleven, David had delicate, almost elfin features, hair cut in bangs, was average in height and slightly skinny. But there was an energy and enthusiasm about him that seemed to win over George Lloyd and others, the beginnings of a knack of charming people. He was a good-looking boy – a fact his female classmates noticed later – and even by his teens he was developing a talent for using charm 'as a weapon', says a later confidante, writer Charles Shaar Murray. 'Even if you'd fallen out, when you met David again you'd be convinced within five minutes that he had barely been able to function in the years he hadn't seen you. I know for a time, I developed a kind of platonic man-love for him.'

It was this charm, this ability to be whoever his confidante wanted him to be, that would be the making of David Bowie; it's what brought him his breaks, the opportunities his ever-active mind worked out how to exploit. In these early days, that charm was not deployed so intensely, or so ruthlessly. Still, 'he was just, somehow, one of the kids you noticed,' says schoolmate Jan Powling, 'bright, quite funny, with oodles of personality.' He was invariably neatly dressed, more so than his classmates: 'always well scrubbed, with clean fingernails,' says Powling. 'In short, the kind of boy that if you were his mum, you would have been really proud of him.'

Well scrubbed, polite, every suburban mother's dream son, the ten-year-old David Jones also stuck to middle-class conventions by enrolling in the local Scout Pack and Church of England choir. 'We were slung in,' says fellow cub scout Geoff MacCormack, 'because that's what parents did with kids then. We didn't kick up a fuss, we just got on with it.' Like Keith Richards, one of Baden-Powell's unlikeliest champions, the kids lapped up the outdoors adventures. The weekly pack meets and services became a crucial part of David's life, because it was there that he met MacCormack and George Underwood, who would prove the most enduring friends of his life. Together, the three donned cassocks, surplices and ruffles for church services, as well as the frequent weddings that would become the future David Bowie's first paying gigs as a singer. 'Not only were you paid five shillings – a princely sum in those days,' says MacCormack, 'but if the ceremony took place in the week you got a day off school.'

George Underwood's family lived on the other side of Bromley, so he was enrolled at a different primary school. Tall for his age, good-looking with an easy, relaxed but passionate air about him, he would become the closest friend of David's youth. Their relationship would go through some rocky patches, but would be a formative one in their lives. For the glue that held their friendship together was rock 'n' roll.

For most of David and George's generation there was a 'Eureka!' moment, the instant when rock 'n' roll exploded into their consciousness: an escape route from their grey world. For both boys, that moment hit in 1955. Towards the end of that year, the movie *Blackboard Jungle* caused a sensation in the UK, generating widespread outrage as politicians denounced the baleful influence of the rock 'n' rollers, like Bill Haley, that it celebrated. Around the same time, Haywood arrived home from Stepney Causeway one evening with a bag full of singles which he'd been given. That night, David played each of the records: Fats Domino, Chuck Berry and Frankie Lymon and The Teenagers. 'Then,' he says, 'I hit gold: "Tutti Frutti" by Little Richard – my heart nearly burst with excitement. I'd never heard anything even resembling this. It filled the room with energy and colour and outrageous defiance. I had heard God.' More than anyone else, Little Richard would be a touchstone, an embodiment of sex, glamour and cranked-up music, of the future David Bowie's career: 'I always wanted to be Little Richard – he was my idol.'

Born Richard Penniman, the most controversial, genre-busting early rock 'n' roller would make a potent touchstone. Many of David's contemporaries, like The Rolling Stones' Keith Richards, would cite Muddy Waters and Chuck Berry as their heroes; they represented authentic blues, forged deep in the Mississippi Delta. Little Richard was a city boy: he had made his name in New Orleans, studying outrageous performers like Guitar Slim and Esquerita, hanging out in a camp, cross-dressing scene where fur-coated queens competed to deliver the best impressions of Dinah Washington or Sarah Vaughan. His records were a far cry from Muddy's deep, soulful songs of yearning or sexual bravado: they were mini-explosions of sound, cranked up using the city's best session men

and designed to pack in the maximum thrills possible within the two
minutes and thirty seconds allowed by the South's jukebox operators.
Richard Penniman didn't only rely on his innate musicianship, or
thrilling voice: he packaged his music in outrageous showmanship and
brightly coloured suits. Later he would come out as gay; eventually he
would find God; much later, David Bowie's wife would buy one of
Richard's suits for her husband. Throughout all those years, David Jones
would treasure the first Little Richard records he bought, on Bromley
High Street. Elvis Presley would be another idol – all the more so when
David discovered he shared a birthday with the ultimate white rock 'n'
roll icon – but Little Richard would be the cornerstone of David's musical identity.

Little Richard's primacy was confirmed when he became the first
American rock 'n' roll star to be beamed into the homes of British television viewers, on 16 February, 1957, when the BBC unveiled its momentous
Six-Five Special, a TV show aimed at teenagers which included segments
of classical music, dance competitions and a short extract from the movie
Don't Knock the Rock, with Richard performing 'Tutti Frutti'. Over the next
few weeks the programme would feature more Little Richard, British rockers Tommy Steele and Adam Faith plus, tellingly, Lonnie Donegan.

Like many British teenagers, David Jones and George Underwood
idolised Little Richard, but copied Lonnie Donegan. Today Donegan's
music is comparatively neglected, but the influence of his DIY ethos lives
on in British music from The Beatles to the Sex Pistols. Donegan's take
on American performers like Lead Belly was gloriously naive – his music
was made on the simplest of instruments and his technical deficiencies
were part of his charm. It could take a schoolboy years of practice to
emulate Little Richard or Chuck Berry, but you could attempt Lonnie's
brand of skiffle after a few afternoons. Donegan's home-grown skiffle
signalled the end of the UK's outdated dance culture and inspired a generation of British rock 'n' rollers, among them the eleven-year-old Jones
and Underwood. For all the kids raised in post-war austerity, this was a
moment they'd somehow anticipated, for years. 'We'd waited and
waited for something fabulous to happen,' says George Underwood.
'And it *did* happen. That was the catalyst. And from then on, music was
the one thing we talked about constantly.'

At Burnt Ash, there were a couple of kids who'd become known as
rock 'n' roll fans – Ian Carfrae, later of the New Vaudeville Band, was
admonished by the headmaster for bringing 'Rock Around the Clock'
into 1955's Christmastime 'gramophone-listening' sessions. But while

David eventually became the better-known, it was George Underwood who got his rock 'n' roll act together before everyone else. He'd already bought a huge Hofner acoustic guitar and formed a duo with a family friend by the time he met David, who owned a ukulele and had a burning desire to be in a band. Roughly a year after they'd first met, the two travelled down to the 18th Cub Scouts Summer Camp on the Isle of Wight, in the summer of 1958. 'We put a washboard bass in the back of the van, and David's ukulele, and between us we managed to conjure up a couple of songs around the camp fire. And that was our first public performance. Neither of us had any claim to virtuosity – but we wanted to sing.'

That tentative first show, with David strumming and George singing, was not the only rite of passage that year. The previous autumn David had sat his 11-plus, the crucial exam that would determine his future school. The Burnt Ash pupils were well prepared, and under the gimlet eye of David's respected and feared teacher, Mrs Baldry, David and most of his friends passed. The rigid pecking order of schools in the area started with Beckenham and Bromley Grammar at the top, followed by Bromley Technical School – which had opened in 1959 and was aimed at future commercial artists and engineers – with Quernmore Secondary Modern languishing in the rear. Later in life, David would advise one of his closest friends to 'do the contrary action' and he first did that himself at the age of eleven. Though David's results were good enough for the grammar school, against all expectations, he opted for Bromley Tech, and talked his parents into supporting his decision.

Some of the inspiration for this precociously unconventional move undoubtedly came from George Underwood, who was also heading for Bromley Tech. The Tech's links with the nearby Bromley College of Art also meant that he would join a wider community, of the art school kids who would ultimately come to define post-war Britain. Contemporaries and near neighbours, like the Stones' Keith Richards and The Pretty Things' Dick Taylor – 'the war babies', as Richards would describe them – were already embarked on the same course. The notion that a generation of kids could make a living via art was novel, born of the radical reworking of the British educational system in 1944. The art college system provided the foundation of Britain's future influence on art, advertising, publishing, movies and fashion. As countless former pupils point out, art college taught them that, rather than working in an office or factory, youths could make a living with merely 'ideas'. This freedom was all the more powerful for being combined with an unrelenting post-war work ethic. 'We understood then,' says David's friend, Dorothy Bass, 'that after your two years at art college, you would have to pay your dues.'

Bromley Tech had moved to a new site alongside Bromley College of Art just one year earlier, and with its airy concrete-and-glass building, it seemed modern and forward looking. Yet its structure aped the English public school, with pupils organised into houses, and some teachers dressed in capes and mortar boards for formal assemblies, to which Catholic or Jewish pupils were not invited. Every morning, David and his friends sang Victorian-era hymns like 'Onward Christian Soldiers' and murmured 'amen' in response to prayers for the Royal Family and other pillars of the establishment.

For all the formality of Bromley Tech, the quality of teaching was variable – with the exception of the art department, which was housed in a custom-designed building with north-facing windows to give better natural light for painting. Owen Frampton, the head of the department, was undoubtedly the school's best-liked teacher. He was enthusiastic – David describes him as 'an excellent art teacher and an inspiration' – but no pushover. Owen, or 'Ossy', not only had a superb eye for art, but could also unerringly spot mischief, says John Edmonds, a student who recalls he once threw a snowball at a teacher, unobserved, only to learn later, when pulled out of class, that the beady-eyed Head of Art had seen the incident. 'I did gain a respect both for his eyesight, and his skills with the slipper,' he recalls, ruefully.

Frampton was a man of eclectic background and tastes: he had served in the Royal Artillery in wartime; designed wallpaper for the Sanderson company; could explain, in inspiring terms, both classical and modern art (David would mention him as the source of his interest in the painter Egon Schiele) and also played guitar, as did his son Peter, who enrolled at Bromley Tech in 1961. Peter, David and George soon became well known around the school. George and David found a spot in the stairwell which had a natural echo and used it as an informal practice space: 'My big hero was Buddy Holly and although David wasn't a big fan we used to do Buddy Holly numbers,' says George. 'David was a great harmoniser, so we used to work on a lot of that material together, by the stairs.' Peter used to sit on the school steps with a guitar, showing kids how to play Shadows or Ventures riffs, and started calling himself Paul Raven.

David paid rapt attention during Owen's art classes, sketching with charcoals or simply hanging out in the art department, but year-by-year his interest in other subjects declined, to the point that, in his third year, his school report described him as 'a pleasant idler'. At fourteen, he had succumbed to the obsessions that would define the years to come: music and girls. He would feed both these addictions after school, in a quintessentially suburban location on Bromley High Street: Medhurst's department store, a huge Victorian building that sold furniture and other household goods and also boasted one of south London's best gramophone departments. Housed in a long, narrow corridor, the gramophone section was overseen by a discreetly gay couple named Charles and Jim. Although they stocked the customary chart hits and sheet music, they were also aficionados of modern jazz music and specialised in American imports. David soon turned up most afternoons after school to check out new releases at their listening booth. His interest in music had become an obsession, and as time went on, his tastes would become more and more eclectic – encouraged by Terry, his record collection expanded to include jazz releases by Charlie Parker and Charles Mingus. Soon he gained the status of a regular and Jim, the younger of the two partners, would let him have records at a discount, as would Jane Green, the assistant. She soon 'took a liking' to David. 'Whenever I would pop in, which was most afternoons after school, she'd let me play records in the "sound booth" to my heart's content till they closed at 5.30. Jane would often join me and we would smooch big-time to the sounds of Ray Charles or Eddie Cochran. This was very exciting as I was thirteen or fourteen, and she would be a womanly seventeen at that time. My first older woman.'

The Medhurst's gramophone booth became a prime hangout for many teenagers seeking glamour on Bromley High Street. In this small world, the arrival of an Indian curry house in the early sixties was an event of seismic importance, as was the opening of two Wimpy coffee bars shortly afterwards, one in north and one in south Bromley. The teenagers would hang out in the library gardens, south of the market square, trying to look cool in their mostly shabby clothes: the girls wore black pullovers from Marks and Spencer – the nearest they could get to a Parisian beat look – while David would take trips into town in search of 'Italian trousers'. These rebels with a cause included David, George Underwood and Geoff MacCormack and they were also occasionally joined by a merchant seaman named Richard Dendy, who brought back obscure records from New York, and Dorothy Bass, who went out briefly with George – their relationship mainly inspired by their shared love of music. George was charming and good-looking remembers Dorothy, and well known around Bromley, 'but not pushy, not "look-at-me". Neither was David . . . really,' she continues, 'but he was really driven. David shows the difference between someone who's good and someone who devotes their life to what they believe in.'

Nearly all the Bromley Tech pupils from this time seem to recall George and David as a pair, and of the two, George is the better remembered. He was ebullient, lovable, expansive; David was cool – people noticed his clothes, his hair, his possessions, mostly, rather than his personality. In later years, when his first band became known around school, he was kind to younger kids, but several of his contemporaries share the impression of Len Routledge, who remembers, 'I think I envied him, or resented him, as kids do. Because he had a better lifestyle than us, and a father who'd bring him things some of us could never expect: a full American football kit, the saxophone etc. I genuinely admired what he achieved . . . but the comfortable circumstances of his life contrasted sharply with me, and many of the other boys.'

The contrast with the Jones' previously modest lifestyle was stark. As Haywood progressed in his career at Barnardo's, the one area where he was generous – profligate, even – with money was David. A few friends remember David's acquisition of his American football gear, but even more of them noticed David conspicuously brandishing a saxophone around the Tech. Originally he'd wanted a baritone sax, but he had to settle for a Grafton alto, a cheaper, but nonetheless glamorous, cream plastic Art-Deco concoction, which Haywood bought him around 1960. For a short time, David managed to 'blag' lessons with baritone player Ronnie Ross, who'd played with the bandleader Ted Heath and other big bands, and lived nearby. Although the musical value of the eight or so lessons was probably negligible, Ronnie's value for name-dropping purposes was incalculable, and probably helped David score a Saturday morning job at Furlong's, the record and instrument store in Bromley South. This little music shop, run by a pipe-smoking, trumpet-playing trad jazz fan, was a Mecca in Bromley's tiny musical landscape, its noticeboard providing a hotline to news of local bands' formation and dissolution, while David's new role – of turning customers on to 'new sounds' – helped fuel a new credibility in the music community and, just as crucially, with local girls.

Even though peers like George Underwood overshadowed David as a musician, his confidence got him noticed. The most celebrated example was when the Tech pupils embarked on what was, for almost everyone, their first foray outside England – a school trip to Spain over the Easter holidays in 1960. Many families couldn't afford the trip, but David was one of the first, and the youngest, to sign up. The small troupe took the ferry to Dieppe, then a coach all the way to Spain. There, they watched a bullfight, goggled at Franco's armed militia and moaned about the spicy foreign food. The other kids exchanged smiles, or played football with the Spanish kids; Jones spent much of the day with the local talent, 'off chatting to the girls,' classmate Richard Comben remembers. David's prowess was commemorated in the school magazine's reference to 'Don Jones, the lover, last seen pursued by thirteen senoritas'.

David describes his behaviour once he'd discovered girls as 'terrible', a quintessential smooth operator. But as far as Bromley's female population were concerned, he was anything but, says Jan Powling: 'He was nice, charming – not at all any kind of show-off.' She knew David from Burnt Ash Junior and, around their third year at secondary school, David asked her out on a date. As was traditional, he phoned Mr Powling to ask for his permission a day or two before the outing, which at some point became a double date. So it was a group of four teenagers who took the 94 bus to the Bromley Odeon cinema: David's moral support was Nick, a Bromley Tech acquaintance, while Jan was accompanied by Deirdre, her friend from Burnt Ash Secondary girls school. It was unfortunate, reflects Jan, that Deirdre was one of the most popular girls in her year, with a blonde bob and trendy clothes. By the end of the evening, David departed arm-in-arm with Deirdre, while Jan had been paired off with Nicholas. 'But I don't blame David,' she adds, generously, 'she was one of the prettiest girls we knew.'

Not everyone was as forgiving of David's emerging jack-the-lad behaviour. One example of David's duplicity would become famous in Bromley Tech folklore, and subsequently in rock 'n' roll history, for it would leave David marked out: an outward sign of what was later taken to be his alien nature.

George Underwood was involved in the celebrated fracas, which is somewhat surprising given that he is the most likeable and mild-mannered of characters. But he was incited to violence by an act of outright skulduggery by his friend in the spring of 1962, when both boys were fifteen. George had arranged a date with a Bromley school girl, Carol Goldsmith, only for David to tell him she had changed her mind and wasn't coming. Soon George discovered that David, who fancied Carol himself, had lied – Carol had waited in vain for George before going home after an hour or so, distraught that she'd been stood up.

David's plan was to swoop in on the abandoned girl, but when Underwood discovered the dastardly scheme there was an altercation. Underwood, enraged, impulsively punched his friend in the eye, and by some mishap scratched his eyeball. 'It was just unfortunate. I *didn't* have a compass or a battery or various things I was meant to have – I didn't even wear a ring, although something must have caught. I just don't know how it managed to hurt his eye badly . . . I didn't mean it to be like that at all.'

The damage was serious. David was taken to hospital and his schoolmates were told he was in danger of losing the sight in his left eye. Underwood, mortified, heard that Haywood and Peggy Jones were considering charging him with assault. With David absent from school for several weeks, George eventually plucked up enough courage to go and see Haywood. 'I wanted to tell him it wasn't intentional at all. I didn't want to maim him, for God's sake!' The injury to David's eye resulted in paralysis of the muscles that contract the iris, leaving the pupil permanently dilated and giving it the appearance of being a different colour from his other eye. His depth perception was also damaged. 'It left me with a wonky sense of perspective,' David explained later. 'When I'm driving for instance, cars don't come towards me, they just get bigger.' It was weeks before David returned to Bromley Tech, and at least a month before he talked to George (Haywood, too, would eventually forgive him, but it took some time). The rift meant that David missed out on a momentous event: the arrival of rock 'n' roll at Bromley Tech, in April 1962. Owen Frampton was one of the key figures in the talent show, overseeing the lights and the PA system. His son's band, The Little Ravens, played the first half, sandwiched between a magician and a dance duo. Underwood's band, George and the Dragons, came on after the interval, a louder, more raucous show than Frampton junior's outfit: 'very avant-garde for the time,' recalls Pete Goodchild, who was in the audience.

Underwood wonders to this day how the gig would have sounded if his friend had appeared on stage with him. By the summer term, their friendship was repaired, although Underwood suffered pangs of guilt for years afterwards. 'I was always looking at him, thinking, Oh God, I did that.' Eventually, David would thank George for the notorious eye injury – 'he told me it gave him a kind of mystique' – although for decades afterwards George would get irritated when David said he had no idea why his friend had punched him. 'He gave the impression he doesn't know why I did it. And he should have known.'

Underwood's disappointment that his best friend missed George and the Dragons' Easter show was as short-lived as the band. George went on to play in both The Hillsiders and The Spitfires over this period, and soon after Easter teamed up with the Kon-Rads, a rather old-fashioned dance-based band formed a few months earlier by drummer Dave Crook and guitarist Neville Wills. Once George was in, he invited David along, too, asking him to join the band on saxophone, with the proviso, 'I'm the singer, but you can do a couple of numbers.' David brought his Grafton down to rehearsals. 'He looked a bit like Joe Brown at the time, so we said you can do "A Picture of You", and "A Night at Daddy G's".'

David Bowie's first public performance took place just a few weeks later, on 12 June, 1962, at the Bromley Tech PTA School Fête. This was the Tech's biggest ever summertime event – the PTA bought a new PA system for the show, and four thousand parents and locals attended. No one got to hear David's Joe Brown impression that afternoon, though – the Kon-Rads set consisted strictly of instrumentals.

David, his hair arranged in a blonde quiff, stood with his cream sax slung to one side, next to George Underwood, who picked out Shadows' riffs on his Hofner guitar. David looked 'cool, well dressed' according to schoolmate Nick Brookes. It was a pretty impressive debut, but there was a clear consensus among most of the audience about who would go on to stardom: David's taller, better-looking, more popular friend. 'It was George who was the singer, who did a great Elvis impression,' says Tech pupil Roger Bevan, who remembers, like many other pupils, Underwood's dark, glossy hair and Elvis sneer. 'Everyone reckoned he was going to be big.'

2

'Numero Uno, Mate!'

I was ambitious. But not like he was.

George Underwood

In late 1962, reputations were fast being made in south-east London, as a new wave of rock 'n' roll young bucks set out to kill off England's staid, suffocating music scene. Kent schoolboys Mick Jagger and Keith Richards were bonding over Chess Records albums and renewing their childhood friendship at Alexis Korner shows, and the future Pretty Things were emerging from the same Kent scene. This was matched by similar setups in west London, Surrey or Newcastle as dozens of musicians, from Eric Clapton to Eric Burdon, Paul Jones to Keith Relf embarked on a fast-lane to fame.

So, what was an under-age kid with a sax to do? David Jones, just a couple of years younger than most of those figures, was marooned, destined to miss the wave that everyone else was catching. While Clapton was becoming God, David was merely the cool kid in class: well liked, noted for his skinny trousers and blond hair, cheerful and indulgent with the younger students who'd follow him around the playground, asking about music or baseball. The damaged eye added a dangerous, disconcerting glamour to his otherwise conventional pretty-boy looks, but as far as native talent goes, David seemed like a supporting act to his friend George Underwood – more relaxed, more masculine – who remained the centre of attention at Bromley Tech.

Most of the kids who saw the Kon-Rads remember few details of their first couple of shows, but that wasn't the point; they were out there, living out the new DIY ethos. Today, their Conway Twitty and Joe Brown covers would sound gauche and naive, but to their peers, they were sweeping away England's suffocating conformity, its smug dance bands and crooners.

Yet before their career had even got going, it turned out that the Kon-Rads were not unified fighters for the cause. Late in 1962, when drummer Dave Crook left their always fluid line-up, a putsch in the ranks saw George Underwood booted out. To this day, the central characters dispute what happened in their schoolboy band. As far as George Underwood is concerned, the new drummer was the villain of the story: 'He just didn't like me for some reason. He was trying to get me out of the band and got one of his friends, not to beat me up, but to give me some kind of warning. It was really intimidating, I was almost crying – it was horrible.' George, for all his talent, was simply too nice – 'a gentleman', he explains. He didn't protest; he even lent them his guitar amp. 'Without it, they were fucked.' It was an early lesson in the ruthlessness of the music industry for Underwood, albeit one he never took to heart.

At first, David was unconcerned by his friend's departure. He was fascinated by the new drummer, David Hadfield, who already seemed like a pro compared to the rest of the Kon-Rads. Hadfield had grown up in Cheshunt, Hertfordshire, where he'd teamed up with Harry Webb, later famous as Britain's first home-grown rock 'n' roller Cliff Richard, at secondary school. Hadfield had hyped his Cliff credentials in a 'Drummer Seeks Work' advert placed in Furlong's music shop. David, along with guitarist Neville Wills, was intrigued, questioning the drummer closely over coffees at the Bromley Wimpy. Rhythm guitarist Alan Dodds joined them for a rehearsal in Neville's front room a few days later, and they all agreed that Hadfield was in. The drummer would become David's closest musical confidant for nearly a year; together, they'd hustle for shows, paint backdrops and update their set list.

Over the following weeks, Hadfield discovered the skinny blond-haired sax player, who looked younger than his fifteen years, was by far the most ambitious band member. 'He was very very boyish, blond, and didn't look his age at all. But he carried himself well – and he just wanted to be part of show business. You could feel it.'

Hadfield was ambitious, too, although he's adamant that he played no part in the ousting of George Underwood, and didn't even know that the Kon-Rads had ever played in public. David would become his main friend but the sax player was also, as far as the other Kon-Rads were concerned, a pain: he didn't understand the way the music business worked. The Kon-Rads were the first musicians to encounter David's restlessness, his urge to keep pushing relentlessly forward. In the main, they resisted his pressure, and the results were a key part of the sax player's musical education, for the Kon-Rads were, in David's terms, a failure. They hit the London scene at a time when the most amazing breaks were available – and they blew every one of them.

Over the end of 1962 and the beginning of 1963, Jones and Hadfield spent every minute avoiding their day jobs. David was supposedly studying for his O-Levels, while Hadfield had recently found a position as an invoice clerk in Borough, but the band rehearsed so intensively at Bromley's St Mary's Church Hall that they were hounded out after complaints about the noise and forced to move to a damp prefab building down the street. Soon the Kon-Rads were playing most weekends in small halls and pubs around south-east London, including Bromley, Beckenham, Orpington and Blackheath.

Over their year-long existence, the Kon-Rads changed line-up continually, with the addition of bassist Rocky Shahan, and later a singer, Roger Ferris, while Hadfield brought in girlfriend Stella Patton and her sister Christine as backing vocalists. Over that year, the two Davids spent nearly all their spare time working together. The younger David was good company, energetic, enthusiastic and practised incessantly on the saxophone. His schoolwork languished, but he became a good sax player, mastering a raunchy King Curtis-style tone on the Conn tenor to which he'd recently switched, and there was something about the way he stood, relaxed on stage, that was effortlessly cool. But his fellow Kon-Rads were unimpressed by many of David's ideas for updating their outfits or their set-list. 'When you've got seven people in the band you can't change things overnight,' says Hadfield. 'Our attitude was, if we go out on a limb we're going to lose all our local bookings – and lose what popularity we have.'

But there was a bigger world out there than local bookings, a world populated by people like Joe Meek, who had scored a huge hit that summer with his space-rock hit 'Telstar'. The pioneering, gay producer had recorded some of the UK's most radical early rock 'n' roll hits in a self-built studio, crammed into a tiny flat above a leather goods store on the Holloway Road. Meek was an obsessive; he recorded day after day without a break, auditioning hundreds of bands, lavishing each session with sonic adornments. Within a few weeks of Hadfield joining the Kon-Rads, the band made their way up to Meek's flat for an audition session. The producer was already known for becoming obsessed with some of the young musicians in his studio, often hassling young, blond lookers – but for the Kon-Rads session he was uncommunicative and surly, unimpressed by their best shot, an MOR version of 'Mockingbird'. The sappy, undistinguished ditty, sung by Roger Ferris, was later consigned to one of Meek's notorious tea-chests full of rejected material. David was the only band member who chatted with the producer for more than a couple of minutes, quizzing him about his productions. But their conversation was cut short when he was called to help carry the band's gear down to their old *Evening News* delivery van, waiting outside. Meek never called them back, and in their postmortem the band acknowledged the possibility they weren't 'original enough'. David's suggestion that they write their own material was ignored by Hadfield and Neville Wills, though, who insisted that their live audience preferred familiar cover songs. (Perhaps the session was not a total dead loss, though, for it's possible the concept of 'Telstar' – a quirky, otherworldly novelty song based on a celebrated spaceshot – lodged in the young David Jones' mind.)

A second failure was harder to stomach, for this time it involved one of David's friends and rivals. After sending a demo recording to the Rediffusion TV company, the Kon-Rads won a slot on *Ready Steady Win* – the talent contest spin-off from the super-hip music show *Ready, Steady, Go!*. There was snickering from the audience and judges during the heat, as the Kon-Rads, in matching suits, set up their lavish backdrop, drum riser and lights, before launching into an impeccably played set of covers. The winning band, The Trubeats, played their own songs and gave a stripped-down performance highlighting their blond, good-looking, teenage guitarist, Peter Frampton – now a student at Bromley Grammar School – who won over boys and girls alike. The Kon-Rads' performance was mocked in a press report, which declared that 'the band has nothing original to offer'.

It was David, the youngest member, still at school, who always rebounded from such setbacks. 'He kept pushing,' says Hadfield. 'He wanted to write more things, change how we dressed, [saying] "We've got to go out on a limb."' The older musicians tried to persuade David that he was being impractical. They were convinced he was addicted to gimmicks – an impression reinforced when he announced one day that he was assuming a new name, 'David Jay'. David persisted in his schemes, persuading Neville to write the music to his lyrics for several songs, including 'I Never Dreamed'. The composition – with dark lyrics inspired by newspaper reports of a train crash, and a poppy tune reminiscent of The Tremeloes – was slotted into their set, alongside their predictable line-up of Chris Montez, Shadows and Beatles numbers. And as he started to influence their material, David also started to make an impression live. 'He looked good, he had a way of standing with his sax slung round his neck – it was very manly, if that's the right word. He was getting noticed more, guys and girls seemed to like him.'

Two breaks had ended in failure, but then, in the summer of 1963, it looked like it might be third time lucky. Bob Knight, a Bromley entrepreneur, managed to interest his friend Eric Easton in the band. Easton was the co-manager of The Rolling Stones – who were on the brink of the big-time – and soon the Kon-Rads were hanging out in his office on Oxford Street, being introduced to Brian Epstein and finally, via Easton, scoring their big break: a trial session for Decca, the Stones' label, on 30 August, 1963.

Determined not to repeat their previous mistakes, the band showcased their own material, including 'I Never Dreamed'. But their first formal studio session, complete with engineers in white coats, was a disaster. Hadfield was 'a nervous wreck', the rhythm tracks were a mess and the results weren't even deemed worthy of a playback. By the time Decca confirmed they weren't interested in the band, David had already announced he was leaving.

David gave little explanation: 'There was no arguing with him. He simply said he wanted to do his own thing,' says Hadfield, who insists that the young sax player, having deserted the band after their first setback, was 'not a band kind of person'. Years later, David explained his defection was inspired by very different reasons. 'I wanted to do a version of [Marvin Gaye's] "Can I Get a Witness" – and they didn't. That was why I left the Kon-Rads.' George Underwood, David's co-conspirator, backs up his version: 'We were determined to do music we enjoyed playing – not copying what was in the Top 10.'

David had coaxed Underwood to make some guest appearances with the Kon-Rads earlier that summer, and the two had spent months sharing their musical obsessions as they plotted their own band. By now David spent all of his free time rehearsing, hanging out at Vic Furlong's, Medhurst's, Bromley's two Wimpy Bars or at George's house – his voracious appetite for music now bordering on the obsessive. The two friends enjoyed a glorious summer, despite the fact that when David's O-Level results arrived, it turned out he'd failed every one but art. He seemed blithely unconcerned; his mother was unsupportive, dismissive of his music, but Haywood seemed, as far as friends could tell, to indulge David's fantasies. Nonetheless, David finally caved in to the pressure to get a 'proper' job, and Owen Frampton used his connections to find him a position as a runner and paste-up artist at the New Bond Street office of Nevin D. Hirst, a small Yorkshire-based ad agency.

The sole nine-to-five job of David Jones' life would enable him, in future years, to pronounce on the world of design, marketing and manipulation as a self-styled expert. In his later career he'd talk about how the advertising industry had been the prime force, alongside rock 'n' roll, in shaping the latter half of the twentieth century, and the fact he'd worked 'as an illustrator in advertising' became a key component of his self-image. Yet as he admits, his involvement with the industry was brief. 'I loathed [it]. I had romantic visions of artists' garrets – though I didn't fancy starving. [Hirst's] main product was Ayds slimming biscuits, and I also remember lots of felt-tip drawings and paste-ups of bloody raincoats. And in the evening I dodged from one dodgy rock band to another.'

Although his commitment to the job was faint, David was lucky to have a hip boss, Ian – an indulgent, Chelsea-booted, crop-haired blues fan – who sent David on errands to the celebrated Dobell's Record Shop, ten minutes' walk away on Charing Cross Road. This was the mother-lode of hip blues, the place Eric Clapton shopped for obscure imports which he'd then replicate, astounding audiences who figured he'd invented the riffs he'd lifted from Albert King or Buddy Guy. David embarked on a similar search for source material; when Ian suggested he pick up John Lee Hooker's *Country Blues* on Riverside, he spotted Bob Dylan's debut on the racks, too. 'Within weeks George and I had changed the name of our little R&B outfit to "The Hooker Brothers", and included both Hooker's "Tupelo" and Dylan's "House of the Rising Sun" in our set.' The pair were so carried away with enthusiasm that they started playing shows as a trio with drummer Viv Andrews before they'd even got a proper band together. Billed as The Hooker Brothers, or David's Red and Blues (a druggy reference to the Mods' favourite barbiturate pills) they guested between sets at the Bromel Club, at Bromley's Royal Court Hotel. Today, as Underwood admits, the notion of two kids from Bromley reinventing themselves as Mississippi Bluesmen seems ludicrous, 'but it was something we needed to get out of our system!' David's first compliment from an 'experienced' musician came from those early shows, when The Hooker Brothers shared a bill with jazzman Mike Cotton at the Bromel Club. It was a brief perform-ance, sandwiched between the two halves of The Mike Cotton Sound's trad jazz-influenced set. 'Well done,' the venerable twenty-six-year-old congratulated the wannabe bluesmen after their set, 'you must be very brave'.

Brave they seemed in the autumn of 1963, when they played several brief shows at the Bromel. Yet by December, when The Rolling Stones cracked the Top 20 with 'I Wanna Be Your Man', a tiny nucleus of British musicians were about to refashion British rock 'n' roll. Two bands emerged in the Stones' wake: The Yardbirds, who'd taken over their residence at the Crawdaddy Club in Richmond, and The Pretty Things, whose Dick Taylor had played with Keith Richards in an early incarnation of the Stones. The Pretties were known around the Bromley scene thanks to Dorothy Bass, David's schoolmate (and, briefly, George's girlfriend), who owned a car and was therefore recruited as the Pretties' roadie.

With the sense that they were about to catch a wave, David and George stepped up their efforts to form a full band. It was David who spotted a classified ad in *Melody Maker* from a Fulham outfit seeking a singer. The trio – guitarist Roger Bluck, bassist Dave Howard and drummer Robert Allen – were, in truth, more in tune with the spirit of Chet Atkins than Muddy Waters, but Jones and Underwood both worked on 'roughen[ing] them up'. Their set was based on songs which countless Brit blues-boomers would cover: Elmore James' 'Early One Morning', Howlin Wolf's 'Spoonful' and 'Howling for My Baby'. The band's name, The King Bees, came from another blues classic, Slim Harpo's 'I'm a King Bee'.

For The King Bees' tiny audience – perhaps a couple of dozen local kids – they were torchbearers for a new music. 'This was a completely different animal from Sonny Boy Williamson's blues,' says Dorothy Bass, 'that was where it came from, this was where it was going. People like us were taking something old, forgotten, and used it to create a new sound, something that spoke to us.'

Bass was probably The King Bees' closest follower, hanging out with them at the Wimpy Bars, coffee shops, parties and gigs. She knew David well: likeable, cheerful, enthusiastic, but almost bland and boring in his single-mindedness. 'All he wanted to do was practise, and listen to tapes or records that he'd got hold of. That was his life. Everybody regarded themselves as an expert in music – but he really was. What made him different was he would pass a party, or anything up if there was something he needed to do for his music. For the other kids, that was inconceivable.'

For David, the lesson of the Kon-Rads ran deep: he was convinced that seeking out new, hip music before the competition was the key to success. When he and George discovered Bob Dylan's debut album at Dobell's, David remembers how, 'we added drums to "House of the Rising Sun", thinking we'd made some kind of musical breakthrough. We were gutted when The Animals released the song to stupendous reaction.' The Animals, of course, had learned their trade playing night after night at Newcastle's Club A-Gogo; David would never pay his dues in such a yeoman's fashion. For a start, although he, rather than George, had taken on the role of lead singer, he was still reticent as a front man. When Dorothy Bass was roped in to drive The Pretty Things to their shows in south-east London, David would often come up and chat to singer Phil May and the band's founder, Dick Taylor, who says, 'We did like him. Skinny little blond fella. Though I don't think I ever saw him sing.'

As a singer, skinny and likeable was about it. 'He was very self-contained,' says Bass, who saw most of The King Bees' shows. 'I didn't think he reached out to the audience very much, maybe he was concentrating on what he was singing. He didn't actually seem sexy to me. George was gorgeous . . . I wouldn't say I dismissed David, he was blond, he was OK, but I didn't see him as a sex symbol. There was no interacting or giving anything to the audience. Not that that bothered us. They were people on stage, our age, and that's all that mattered.'

On stage, David hadn't mastered the swagger of contemporaries like Mick Jagger or Phil May. Off stage, though, he was a natural, a hustler. Aided by his father, who'd now worked in PR for nearly a decade, he also had an innate understanding of the fact that a hustler loves another hustler. For this reason, the letter that helped him score his debut single became better-known than the single itself.

History would have it that David Bowie grew up estranged from his parents. Peggy certainly became irritated by his musical ambitions, and given that David was firmly attached to the family purse-strings for the next half-decade, her intolerance would have been shared by most parents. Haywood's reaction was more complex: he was conventional, but indulgent. He and David were more alike than many realised; calm, but both with a nervous fizziness. The most obvious sign of this in Haywood was his chain-smoking, which David soon imitated – to the extent of using the same brand, Player's Weights. There was the conventional generation gap between father and son yet Haywood's youthful obsession with the entertainment world had not been entirely extinguished. So it was Haywood and David who, in January 1964, 'concocted' a sales pitch for David's new band. Shameless and 'over the top' according to George Underwood, Haywood and David's joint 'sales pitch' would kick off David's career.

Around Christmas 1963, David had noticed news headlines generated by John Bloom, an aggressive entrepreneur who'd blazed a famously fiery trail through Britain's white-goods industry, starting with washing machines, then moving on to dishwashers and refrigerators. He seemed to have a financial Midas touch, and father and son typed out a letter suggesting he put his golden touch to work in the most up-and-coming industry of all, pop music. 'If you can sell my group the way you sell washing machines,' David suggested, 'you'll be on to a winner.'

Before sending the letter, David showed it to George, who protested. 'His dad helped him concoct the letter – and it *was* concocted in that it said things like that famous quote, "Brian Epstein's got The Beatles and you should have us".' Undeterred, David assured him, 'don't worry. It will be all right.' His instincts were on the money. Bloom, amused by the youngster's chutzpah, passed the letter on to Les Conn, a friend from the Jewish scene in Stamford Hill. Within a couple of days, a telegram arrived at David's house, instructing him to call Conn's Temple Bar number.

It was a lucky happenstance. Invariably described as a small-time manager, Les Conn was, in fact, neither small-time, nor a manager. His connections were impeccable, including Beatles publisher Dick James, movie star Doris Day, and emerging music moguls like Mickie Most and Shel Talmy; he played vital roles in advancing the careers of The Shadows, Clodagh Rodgers and The Bachelors. However, to describe him as a manager would imply some degree of organisation, or of the ability to oversee someone's career – qualities which were noticeable by their absence in this charming, supremely scatty man.

Musician Bob Solly, who also met Les that spring, remembers the aspiring mogul proclaiming, 'Conn's the name, con's the game!' before showing off his credentials in the form of a suitcase full of parking tickets he was hoping to evade. A short, slightly pudgy bundle of energy, he'd shoot out rapid-fire yarns and schemes in a cheeky, vaguely posh voice, often punctuated by sudden pauses as he searched for the vital document or press cutting he'd been brandishing just a few seconds earlier.

Conn epitomised the charming amateurism of the British music scene.

He had set up Melcher Music UK for Doris Day before being recruited by Beatles publisher Dick James as a song plugger. He was a moderately successful publisher, a dreadful songwriter, and a genius at spotting talent. In just a few short months he would take on both the future David Bowie and the future Marc Bolan, giving both of them their first career breaks.

Bloom had asked Conn to check out The King Bees to see to whether it was worth booking them, cheaply of course, for his upcoming wedding anniversary party, on 12 February, 1964. Conn remembers The King Bees playing in his flat. 'They were a nice bunch,' he remembers. 'It wasn't commercial music they played, it was underground, really. But David had charisma, George too.' And that was enough to get them the gig.

Their debut, though, was a disaster. Some of The King Bees' blues evangelism started to desert them when they turned up at the Jack Club for the party in jeans and suede Robin Hood boots, and noticed disapproving looks from the moneyed crowd, which included Sir Isaac Wolfson and Lord Thomson of Fleet. The King Bees were asked to follow The Naturals, a well-scrubbed Beatles cover band with a pristine backline of Vox amplifiers, which The King Bees plugged into as they launched into their opening song, 'Got My Mojo Workin''. Unfortunately, David's mojo just didn't work with Bloom, who sidled over to Conn and yelled, 'Get them off! They're ruining my party.' The King Bees shuffled off the stage to make way for the highlight of the evening, a duet between rocker Adam Faith and forces sweetheart Vera Lynn. 'David did cry when I told him to leave the stage,' says Conn, 'but I said to him, "Don't worry, one person was impressed – and that was me."'

Conn would become David Bowie's first champion in the music business, and a few weeks later pulled up in his Jag outside Plaistow Grove for a meeting with David's parents, who needed to co-sign their seventeen-year-old son's management contract. Peggy, Conn noted, was the chattier of the two; Haywood was 'friendly – but very serious, a civil-servant type'. Both parents were impressed, that just a few months into his career, David had signed with such a self-styled mogul, with connections to The Beatles, who assured them it would take him little time to conjure up a record deal, and that David was on the brink of the big time.

David, however, showed no surprise at all; he boasted a bright-eyed teenage confidence that meant he reacted to every break as if it was his by right. Years later, he'd claim that much of this apparent confidence was bravado, and that he suffered from low self-esteem. Some of this seems to be fashionable therapy speak, for while he was restrained on stage, when it came to chatting up girls or greeting a room full of strangers his confidence was unshakeable. In later years he'd learn to be more subtle, but the seventeen-year-old David Jones seemed almost ruthless in his self-promotion. Enthusiastic, receptive, with a sometimes brilliant deadpan humour, he was also, say observers like Les Conn, brash. 'He was sure he was going to be big. But the charm came later as he got more success.'

David's attitude was exactly like that of another aspiring singer, whom Conn met later that year at Denmark Street's La Gioconda coffee bar: Mark Feld, who at this point had yet to metamorphose into Marc Bolan. The two were, says Conn, 'very similar. They totally believed in themselves, both of them. It was me that brought the two of them together, and they both had exactly the same attitude, which was, We are going to make it.' The two would practise their far-fetched stories on each other, both becoming masters of bullshit, as David fondly recalls: 'Marc was very much the Mod, and I was a kind of neo-beat hippie. So there's me and this Mod, and he goes, "Where d'you get those shoes man? Where'd you get your shirt?" We immediately started talking about clothes and sewing machines: "Oh, I'm gonna be a singer and I'm gonna be so big you're not gonna believe it." "Oh, right! Well, I'll probably write a musical for you one day, 'cos I'm gonna be the greatest writer, ever!" "No, no, man, you gotta hear my stuff 'cos I write great things. And I knew a wizard in Paris!" And [this was when] we were just whitewashing walls in our manager's office!'

The pair shared a talent for rabid self-promotion and an unabashed flirtatiousness, with both men and women. David's confidence was always tempered by his interest in people and how they ticked; Marc was far more abrasive. Over the next decade, their careers became intertwined; friends, like the DJ and scenester Jeff Dexter, described them as 'like brothers'. Each took pride in, and was sometimes tortured by jealousy of, the other's achievements. For the time being, their relationship revolved around trading grandiose fantasies in La Gioconda, over cups of coffee cadged from Les Conn.

Over the spring of 1964, Conn used his contacts to arrange The King Bees' first West End gigs, including the Roundhouse. When it came to sorting out publishing and record deals he stayed close to home. Dick James Music looked after the publishing, while Conn used his freelance A&R role at Decca to arrange a session at the company's studios in

Broadhurst Gardens, West Hampstead. For the A-side, the band were presented with an acetate of a song by Paul Revere and The Raiders, 'Louie Louie Go Home' – published, naturally, by Dick James Music. 'We were simply given the single and told to learn it,' says Underwood, adding that in the hurried production process the band 'soon started to feel like cogs in a machine'. The band were left to arrange their own B-side, for which David and George reworked the traditional folk song, 'Little Liza Jane', modifying the lyrics and adding a guitar line borrowed from Howlin' Wolf's 'Smokestack Lightning'. 'It took around fifteen minutes, sitting in my mum's kitchen,' says Underwood, 'the big influence was Huey "Piano" Smith's version.'

The recording was brisk, the standard three-hour session. Underwood was nervous; David was unflappable: 'You'd better get used to this!' he told the others, and when it came time for him to do the singing, with the rest of the band adding backing vocals, there was not a hint of nerves. 'He was very confident. Certain he was going to make it,' says Conn.

Yet it was obvious he wasn't going to make it with this record.

There have been few recording debuts as undistinguished as that of David Bowie. Both sides of the single plodded along in drearily conventional beatboom fashion: on 'Liza Jane', the wonderful energy and sprightliness of Huey Smith's famous hit was bowdlerised – where Huey's song was simple, The King Bees' version was trite. David's voice was horribly generic, a John Lennon wannabe with a phoney London accent. The single sounded exactly like what it was: a rushed attempt to cash in on the emerging blues boom. Conn had to call in all his favours even to get Decca to release the single, which came out on their revived Vocalion label. 'Peter Stevens, who was in charge of releases, didn't rate it at all,' says Conn, who nonetheless got to work exploiting all his contacts for radio and jukebox play and overseeing a press release extolling the, 'action-packed disc which features the direct no-holds-barred Davie Jones vocal delivery!'

Conn's press release didn't mention the other King Bees. It also revealed that the single had been flipped to make 'Liza Jane' the A-side. When the band received their copies, they were surprised to see that the writing credit on 'Liza Jane' was assigned to 'Les Conn'. Conn remained adamant that he had written the song, pointing out that, 'if I had done that to David, why would he have continued to work with me?' Yet his memories of the writing were vague, for instance his suggestion the song title 'maybe came from a girl David was going out with'. Although today David says he can't remember anything about how the song was written, Underwood's story of how 'Liza Jane' was cooked up in his mum's kitchen from a Huey Smith recipe is the one that rings true. But as George explains, 'We didn't want to rock the boat, and figured if Les wanted a piece of the action, he could have it.' Ironically, Conn's manipulation of the songwriting credits prevented Dick James Music, which famously owned The Beatles' songs, from securing an option on the future David Bowie's material, too.

June 1964 was the high point of The King Bees' brief existence. David and George spent most of it hanging out in Bromley: talking music, sipping coffees, or being bought drinks at Henekey's winebar on the High Street, while the remaining King Bees stayed in Fulham. There was a show at the Justin Hall in West Wickham on 5 June to mark the record's official release date, and parties throughout the week. Then on Friday 19 June, David Jones returned with his band to the Rediffusion studio – the scene of his humiliation with the Kon-Rads – to celebrate the sweet victory of his TV debut, on *Ready, Steady, Go!*. They devoured the experience like the teenagers they were, overawed by The Crickets – who woke up briefly from a jetlag-induced sleep to acknowledge George's exclamation that he'd witnessed their 1955 show at the Elephant and Castle's Trocadero cinema – and by John Lee Hooker, who was in a nearby dressing room to record another Rediffusion show. 'I've seen him close-up!' David breathlessly informed George. 'Go and look at those hands, those fingers!' The King Bees' performance passed in a flurry of excitement – and then passed into oblivion.

Over the next few days, David and George basked in their temporary fame, wearing new mohair suits and playing more shows. But as they sat in the Bromley South Wimpy Bar, scouring that week's *Melody Maker*, it became obvious that 'Liza Jane' was not going to trouble the charts.

For George Underwood the release of 'Liza Jane' was 'an achievement in itself'. But for David – who had been singing for less than a year, whose voice was mediocre, and who had yet to write a song on his own – this wasn't good enough. There had been some talk about David or George joining other bands even before the single was released, but George was shocked by the way his old school friend, one day in July, simply announced: 'I've decided to break the band up – and I've found another band.'

The guitarist was devastated. 'At the time it was something like, You bastard! Are you just gonna leave us in the lurch?' Only later did he realise how David had been sounding out how committed he was for some months. 'I was ambitious in my head – but not like he was. He'd decided to throw everything into it.' In later years, he'd read about other ambitious types like Neil Young, recognise the same brutality with which they would drop an approach, or a band, that didn't work, and realise how it made sense. 'What's the point of sticking with it, if it's not working?' At seventeen, David was a second-rate singer, but he already boasted first-class ambition.

For George, being in a band was a passion, one to be shared with your friends. Discovering David had an entirely different agenda was a shock. Just as striking was how unapologetic George's bandmate was; David's selfishness was cheerful, instinctive, almost child-like in its lack of malevolence. George was one of the first, but not the last, to hear what would become a guiding philosophy: 'Numero Uno, mate!'

3

Thinking About Me

There'd be six girls at the front of the Marquee – and half a
dozen of us queens at the back, watching his every move.

Simon White

L ondon, 1964, has been immortalised in popular history as swinging,
racy; its joyous heart beating to the throb of Jaguar engines and pill-
popping Mod anthems, buzzing with the illicit thrills of cheap sex and
gangster cool. In reality, this glorious state of affairs was confined to the
tiniest group of insiders. David Jones was one of them. That fateful year,
David Jones sashayed confidently into the epicentre of swinging
London, hanging out with the scene's hippest stars, participating in the
shag-tastic promiscuity, convincing many he had more right to be there
than they did. Within a year, he had become a leading Face in the scene,
distinguished in every respect bar one: the music.

The nerve with which the seventeen-year-old engineered his next career
move illustrated perfectly how he worked. It was on 19 July, 1964, that he
walked into the smoke-filled living room of a suburban semi in Coxheath,
Kent, and surprised its occupants, a six-piece called The Manish Boys,
who'd assumed the 'amazing' singer Les Conn had told them about was
David Jones, a black R&B singer who could give their horn-heavy blues
vital grit and credibility. They were surprised when – accompanied by the
fast-talking Conn – a blond, skinny, suede-booted youth walked in
through the sliding picture windows. They were even more surprised,
around a half-hour later, to realise they'd hired him as their singer.

The Manish Boys worked more closely with David than any outfit
right up to The Spiders from Mars. It was with them that he first

attracted notice as a singer; it was likewise with them that he discovered the cornucopia of sexual options available in a country eagerly unshackling itself from the prurience and dreariness of the fifties. Together they crafted a horn-heavy, versatile R&B, based on one of David's musical obsessions, the band Sounds Incorporated, and together they made David's first decent record. Their achievements were all the more surprising, considering that their first meeting was so sketchy.

After their disappointment at realising that the 'skinny white kid' was from Bromley, rather than an American ghetto, The Manish Boys had only the briefest conversation with him. Les insisted on playing The King Bees' single, which, after the build-up, was 'disappointing. But David wasn't,' says keyboardist Bob Solly. 'He was a good lively personality, an obvious showman. And he looked good.' The band's leaders, Solly and sax player Paul Rodriguez, ultimately decided to recruit their new singer because they liked his clothing and – hilariously – appreciated his punctuality. As Solly points out, 'His appearance struck us more than anything. And the fact he was reliable. Ninety per cent of people who join bands should be working in a cupboard somewhere on their own – because they have no idea about working with other people. From that first meeting, David was absolutely spot-on punctual – like he was working in a theatre. And theatre people, however bizarre they are, tend to be very, very punctual.'

For all his love of anarchic rock 'n' rollers, David Jones was an old-fashioned trouper, with a sense of style, and a sense of timing. The new kid fitted right in to The Manish Boys, for they too were troupers. They were mostly, like David, only children, 'hence more pushy,' says Solly, 'because we only had ourselves to think about'. They were all filled with a child-like obsession with music, which for all of them represented an escape from the austerity of their upbringing.

The band revolved round Solly and Rodriguez, both three years older than David – or Davie, as he styled himself. John Watson played bass and sang. Guitarist Johnny Flux joined the band a fortnight before David, and was another natural-born hustler who had previously sold newspaper advertising space (and went on to create kids' TV robot Metal Mickey). Woolf Byrne, on baritone sax, also drove and maintained the band's rickety Bedford van, while drummer Mick Whitehead had been persuaded to walk out of his job as an apprentice barber.

During that first meeting, the band were impressed by David's statement that he was writing his own numbers, although they thought the only song he played, 'Don't Try to Stop Me', sounded suspiciously like a Marvin Gaye number. David was upfront about suggesting new material, most notably from James Brown's *Live at the Apollo*; The Manish Boys' own set soon included material by Ray Charles ('What'd I Say'), Solomon Burke ('Stupidity') and even Conway Twitty ('Make Me Know Your Mind') and in August they hit the road with their new singer.

A couple of The Manish Boys, including Woolf Byrne, had initially been unimpressed by the new recruit. Yet during that autumn's shows around the south of England, to audiences ranging from a couple of dozen to a couple of hundred, Woolf began observing something curious: 'I had thought that Johnny's voice was better – deeper and growlier. Then we realised, very soon, that when John sang the kids kept on dancing and behaving the way they did before. When David sang a number they stopped to look.'

Byrne observed how, bit by bit, Davie started using the microphone, getting close up to it when singing in a softer, Dylan-esque drawl, or pulling back for a James Brown-style squeal. He sang in an English, rather than a fake American, accent. As they racked up more shows, Jones' delivery became more powerful – occasionally he was so carried away by the music that he'd smash the maracas he used on 'Bo Diddley' into the mike-stand. Eventually, Bob Solly got into the habit of bringing a small knife with him, to pry out the maracas' little ball-bearings from the keys of his Vox Continental organ. 'Then I realised he had changed us completely,' says Woolf. 'We used to simply stand on stage and play, that changed, then the music we played was different, then our dress became different as well.' 'It was simple enough, what he did,' says Paul Rodriguez, 'he simply knew how to grab a microphone and perform.'

Those first months with The Manish Boys were confused, carefree, rarely boring. The band shared each others' clothes, sleeping on friends' floors while cadging off their parents for food, shelter and cash. Over this summer, David redesigned his own life. By now he'd quit his job at Nevin D. Hirst, and seemed to base his new image on the beat novels he was reading. He was the most nomadic of the group; the others might stay away from home for a day, he would bum around friends' for a week. This fitted in with his often-voiced love of Dylan, Jack Kerouac, or J. Saunders Redding's *On Being Negro in America*, one of many books he picked up in paperback at Bromley South Station. Throughout their gigs, practice sessions at Charlie Chester's Casino or a warren of rooms and brothels on Windmill Street, or socialising at the Regency Club – a hangout for the Kray Twins – The Manish Boys developed an intense, jokey bond, like soldiers on a gruelling campaign. Their intimacy extended to the girls who, that autumn of 1964, were omnipresent – their names and phone numbers written in pink lipstick all over the band's green Bedford van. At the end of a show, while his friends packed away amplifiers and equipment, David was out on the dancefloor, chatting up his female audience: 'getting in there first', as the lingo went.

In many respects The Manish Boys' lives were identical to those of teenagers from the first half of the century; they had few clothes; each would walk for miles to see their friends, many of whom didn't own a phone; chatting with their mums for hours over endless cups of tea; waiting ages for buses; eating egg and chips in cheap 'caffs'. But in the most crucial respect, their lifestyles were transformed: along with music, sex became the driving force of their existence. There was a winning charm and jokiness about David's approach, but in his bandmates' opinion he became obsessive in his pursuit of women. Solly cites one time when David tried to interest him in Sue, a blonde he was trying to cast off: 'I tell you Bob,' David assured him earnestly, 'she's clean as a whistle!' They were open about their sexual escapades, such as the time David and Johnny simultaneously shagged two sisters, alongside each other, in their Gillingham B&B – but at times, Davie's friends accused him of being completely out of control. Driving home one foggy evening, the band spotted a woman hitching a lift, pulled over and let her into the van, where David sat next to her, chatting intensely. A short distance down the road, Woolf, who was at the wheel, suddenly shouted out, 'Eeeuurgh, what's that smell?' Realising the woman was a vagrant, he pulled over and, mercilessly, insisted their passenger get out. David's annoyance at this, the others speculated, was nothing to do with sympathy for the homeless woman. 'Would he have?' they asked each other, before responding in chorus, 'Yes, he would!'

After uniting David with The Manish Boys, Les Conn had declined to take his managerial cut of the band's intermittent live earnings, but he still hustled on their behalf. At the end of September he secured an audition with Mickie Most, who, in the wake of The Animals' 'House of the Rising Sun', was probably the biggest independent producer in London. After setting up at one of their regular haunts, the comedian Charlie Chester's casino on Archer Street, the band ran through a couple of numbers. As was his habit, Most made his decision on the spot, asking, 'Do you want to record for me, boys?' In unison, they shouted, 'Yes!'

There was another meeting with Mickie Most to talk through their material on the evening before the recording session at Regent Sound on 6 October, overseen by Decca's Mike Smith. As the band ran through their three songs, 'Hello Stranger', 'Duke of Earl' and 'Love is Strange', David's singing was flawless, but on every take of 'Love is Strange', John Watson and Johnny Flux's backing vocals were ragged and out-of-sync. As Smith played back the song, pointing out the problem, tension mounted and the singers got more nervous. Except, that is, for David; he was 'totally cool and calm', Solly remembers, easing the tension with deadpan jokes, not for a moment betraying any concern as they struggled for a decent take. Their three hours ran out; their big break had turned to dust. 'Don't worry,' David assured the others, his confidence apparently undented. 'We'll get it next time.'

This was the most potent sign that the band's youngest member was 'mature beyond his years', as Woolf remembers. He could astutely work out the politics of a meeting well before his friends. The most notable example was when The Manish Boys auditioned at the London Palladium that winter, hoping for a residency at Hamburg's legendary Star Club.

The set had gone well, and Bob Solly looked on as the Star Club's promoter called David over. The two exchanged a few words and smiles before David returned to the stage. 'What did he say?' Solly asked, eagerly.

'Oh, he asked me, "Which way do you swing, Davie, boys or girls?"' David told him.

'So what did you say?'

'Oh, I told him, "Boys, of course"!'

The story illustrated his growing talent for hustling a deal, and it came as no surprise when they heard the audition was a success and they would be booked into the Star Club the following summer. The same skills came to the fore when Woolf and David were nursing a coffee in La Gioconda – the hip wood-panelled coffee bar in Denmark Street that was a favourite musicians' hangout – and a BBC researcher approached them to ask if their long hair had ever caused them problems. Both of them fancied a TV appearance and five-guinea fee, but it was David who came up with the idea of a 'League for the Protection of Animal Filament' – a support group for oppressed longhairs that existed entirely in his own imagination.

That chance meeting with the researcher led to a ninety-second interview on *Tonight with Cliff Michelmore*, broadcast on 12 November, 1964, which was destined to be one of David's great TV appearances – because he does such a consummate, humorous job of selling nothing. The 'league' that this cool-as-a-cucumber youth was promoting was a convenient fiction, but everyone was in on the joke, and any prejudice the viewer might have felt at such an unashamed self-publicist was dispelled by David's self-mocking complaints: 'We're all fairly tolerant, but for the last two years we've had comments like "Darlin'" and "Can I carry your handbag?" thrown at us. And it has to stop!'

The Manish Boys' other singer, John Watson, was three years older, with a better voice, experience, and education, but was completely invisible in comparison to his upstart colleague. Although in future years, manager Ken Pitt schooled David Bowie in how to deal with the media, this short snippet, now a YouTube classic, shows Pitt was working with a natural. Where Davie Jones' debut as a singer had been forgettable at best, his debut as a self-publicist was unimpeachable.

The TV slot convinced the band they were headed for the big-time, a conviction reinforced when Les Conn negotiated a deal with the Arthur Howes organisation – Britain's leading promoters of package tours – for a string of dates headlined by Gene Pitney alongside Gerry and the Pacemakers, The Kinks and Marianne Faithfull, opening on 1 December, 1964. It was a cheerily intimate affair; the artists shared the same bus which picked them all up one-by-one across London as they started the tour. Pitney was avuncular and good-humoured – the troupe's Alpha male, which sadly sabotaged David's efforts to chat to Marianne Faithfull, who sat alongside Gene throughout the tour, immune to David's charm. The Kinks also kept themselves to themselves – 'hoity toity' recalls Bob Solly – and rarely mingled. David was unoffended, and promptly introduced a cover of 'You Really Got Me' into The Manish Boys' set.

The tour was a perfect opportunity to trial a new number, 'Pity the Fool', picked out as the band's debut single by Shel Talmy, an American producer who shared an office building with Howes. A one-time child prodigy who'd appeared on NBC's *Quiz Kids* programme, Talmy had 'bullshitted' his way into the UK by claiming to have produced The Beach Boys, then backed up his bullshit by producing a string of super-compressed high-energy hits for The Who and The Kinks. Shel was intrigued by the band and their singer: 'Les Conn told me I should listen to this guy – and Les was right, he always had a great ear for talent.'

'Pity the Fool' was perfect for The Manish Boys' dense, horn-heavy sound – although copying the grizzled vocal on the original acetate, by Memphis bluesman Bobby Bland, was an intimidating task for a Bromley teenager. The afternoon before the session the pressure on guitarist Johnny Flux was ratcheted up, too, when the band bumped into Jimmy Page – fast emerging as London's leading session guitarist – at the 2i's coffee bar, and Page mentioned he was playing guitar on the session, and would be bringing his brand-new fuzzbox with him.

For all their bullishness, The Manish Boys were nervous during the session at London's IBC studio, on 15 January, 1965. 'But David was *certainly* not intimidated,' says Talmy, 'that was what I liked about him.' In fact, David's singing was transformed, compared to his forgettable debut. Confident, impassioned, with perfect microphone technique, the vocals demonstrate a man who, like Shel Talmy, bullshitted his way into a job – and then delivered.

Clunky, naive, and all the better for it, the song became an unsung classic of British blues, a fact spotted right away by Jimmy Page. 'Good session,' he complimented the band as he packed away his Fender Telecaster, 'but I don't think it's a hit.' He softened the blow by donating a riff he'd played while warming up, telling David he was welcome to use it in one of his own songs (it turned up years later, as 'The Supermen'). David was already telling people about his work as a songwriter, although on the evidence of 'Take My Tip', the B-side of their single, he didn't have much of a future. Set to a clunky, clichéd chord sequence, distinguished only by intricate lyrics, the song was an undistinguished pastiche of Georgie Fame, one of the band's current obsessions.

The run-up to the release of 'Pity the Fool' on 5 March was filled with more live dates, and more plotting by the irrepressible Les Conn, who hyped the single with his usual brio, once more stoking up the 'furore' over long hair that had kicked off in November. Conn had persuaded an old friend, BBC producer Barry Langford, to feature The Manish Boys on the show *Gadzooks*, but publicly floated the fiction that the BBC had refused to allow the band into the studio until the singer cut his flowing blond locks. 'I had big placards made, "Let's be fair to long hair",' remembers Les Conn, gleefully, 'and we said we'd parade around the BBC building until they relented!' The artificial controversy – which itself was based, shamelessly, on similar media shenanigans arranged for The Pretty Things and The Rolling Stones – helped David win press in the London *Evening Standard*, *Daily Mail*, *Daily Telegraph* and *Daily Mirror*.

Despite the bogus controversy, the record disappeared into oblivion. The Manish Boys hoped that 'Pity the Fool' would catapult them into the big time; instead, their live dates began to dry up, and the Star Club dates fell through, leaving a huge gap in their schedule. There were arguments about billing; David, who invariably had the shows around Bromley advertised as 'Davie Jones and The Manish Boys', expected the single to be released under the same banner. Solly maintains it was a shortage of cash, rather than arguments about the name, that dealt the death blow; the band's van, their most vital asset, broke down and Woolf had already left before the band's split was finally announced in the *Kent Messenger* in April. 'We were dragging it out,' says Solly, 'but we'd all had enough.'

The slow death of The Manish Boys was made more painful for David by the runaway success of his friend George Underwood. Les Conn had continued hustling for George, whom he considered 'just as talented as David. And really, he was a much nicer guy, he didn't have that "I'm the cat's whiskers' [mentality]".' Les had taken both George and David to see Mickie Most, and it turned out that Mickie 'simply liked George better'. Most treated Underwood almost like a son, driving him around town in his Rolls Royce, advising him on life, money and the music business, before deciding he needed a more glamorous name. Underwood was therefore given the *nom de rock* of Calvin James, after Mickie's son Calvin, and was treated like a star every time he dropped into the offices of Most's record label, RAK. David did not seem to take his friend's success well. Every time they bumped into each other on Bromley High Street, George felt David looking at him 'like daggers'.

The last few Manish Boys shows were riotous: at Cromer on 13 March, David and Johnny Flux, who'd started camping it up together more and more after their Gillingham escapade, were banned from the venue. Their final show was at Bletchley, on 24 April, and the band returned to Maidstone on their own, without David, who had disappeared with a female fan who hosted a party in the town. There were no formal goodbyes: the next time Solly and Rodriguez saw David was in Shel Talmy's office building, obviously planning something new. And this time, there would be no doubt about whose name would get top billing.

The Lower Third had formed in 1964 in Margate, a bustling Regency resort on the coast of Kent, then a lively holiday destination with its tea dances, donkey rides and old-fashioned sideshows complete with a headless lady. After propping up the bills at a variety of local shows, guitarist Denis Taylor, drummer Les Mighall and bassist Graham Rivens decided it was time to turn professional. Leaving pianist Terry Boulton and guitarist Robin Wyatt behind, they decided to head for the bright lights, packed up supplies of food and toilet rolls in their converted ambulance, and rented a flat in Pimlico, central London.

The three had been hanging out around Denmark Street for only a week or so when they had their first sight of the young David Jones in La Gioconda. 'Blimey, I thought,' says Denis Taylor, 'there goes Keith Relf of The Yardbirds!' The band had put out word they needed a singer and arranged auditions at La Discotheque on Wardour Street, a regular haunt where they'd played as a five piece. 'But the funny thing was, he came along with an alto sax, so we thought he was a saxophonist.'

David had brought along moral support in the form of singer Stevie Marriott, whom David had first met at a Manish Boys rehearsal earlier that year. A jam session followed, based around a funky version of Little Richard's 'Rip it Up'. 'Steve was great,' remembers Taylor, 'probably a better singer than David.'

Then, puzzlingly, Stevie left and David took the microphone, sounding 'exactly like Keith Relf' on their version of The Yardbirds' 'I Wish You Would'. Soon he'd convinced The Lower Third of his impeccable connections. 'He told us a few tricks of the trade – I got the impression that Shel had taught him a lot. And he looked amazing. So we decided to get him in.'

The meeting took place just as The Manish Boys were falling apart, depressed at their failure. There was no hint of this in David's demeanour – in fact, his confidence had increased. In both The King Bees and The Manish Boys, Davie Jones had shared the singing and the leadership of the band. With The Lower Third, the eighteen-year-old took creative control, pushing Taylor, who was three years older, to learn new songs as well as assisting with David's own compositions. Their cranked-up version of 'I Wish You Would' became a cornerstone of their live set; David aped Keith Relf's vocal style perfectly – he'd started playing the harmonica, too, for an even better carbon copy. Other obvious influences were The Kinks, whose 'All Day and All of the Night' was also pressed into service, and The Who. In his first few months with The Lower Third, David saw them several times and pressured Taylor to adopt a similar bombastic guitar sound. 'That was a learning curve, that was,' Taylor shudders today.

True to form, David had already penned a press release within a few weeks of joining the band, detailing how the new group, Davie Jones and The Lower Third, featured 'TEA-CUP on lead, DEATH on bass and LES on drums'. The one-page document reminded its readers of 'the legendary Banned Hair tale', and promised another appearance on *Gadzooks*, plus a new single, 'Born of the Night', which was 'destined to rush up the charts'. (The song was a demo, cobbled together at a friend's rehearsal space, and was never released.)

Now that he'd taken over leadership of a band, David seemed liberated; there was an irrepressible energy about the way he'd throw himself into a project. Just eight or ten weeks after securing his first songwriting credit with 'Take My Tip', Davie was already describing himself as a songwriter, dropping in at Shel's studio to demo material, and submitting songs to other performers. He'd had his first song covered thanks to Les Conn, who'd arranged a Kenny Miller recording of 'Take My Tip' in February. Most of those early songs were dreadful, but he kept submitting them; stylistically they veered from Dylan imitations to Gene Pitney knock-offs. Talmy noticed David, 'sounded like lots of different people at different times' and that a lot of the material was 'not great' – still, there was something about David that he liked; like many, he was attracted by David's 'energy', the way he kept coming up with ideas. Whereas George Underwood would get depressed by setbacks, David seemed untouched by them; the fleeting taste of success he'd enjoyed so far simply fed his appetite for more. Today, he points out how such setbacks 'never, ever' made him feel pessimistic, 'because I still liked the process. I liked writing and recording – it was a lot of fun for a kid. I might have had moments of, "God, I don't think anything is ever going to happen for me." But I would bounce up pretty fast.'

As David spent more time in the West End around Denmark St, he started to hang out at the FD&H publishing house and record shop on Charing Cross Road, strumming on guitars or chatting with shop manager Wayne Bardell, and the two became friends. Bardell had accompanied David to the first Manish Boys recording date, and, like so many others, he noticed David was 'very confident, without being arrogant – this was not a person who got stressed'. He watched David progress from being a part of the band with The Manish Boys, to being the leader of The Lower Third. Then one day, as David came in to the shop, and sat down behind the counter, he made a 'very curious' remark. 'It was, you know, "Wayne? When I'm famous I'm not gonna speak to anybody – not even the band." It was a strange thing to say – it stuck in my head.' Only then did he reflect how David was always 'friendly. But I suppose he was never really giving much away.'

A few weeks after David teamed up with The Lower Third, drummer Les Mighall went back to Margate for the weekend and never returned. David located a new drummer, Phil Lancaster, who helped complete the band's transformation into a cranked-up, super-violent style heavily influenced by The Who, a sound honed during the band's busy summer, spent gigging in Margate and other south-east resorts.

It was a blissful period for the band and David, working on songs and hanging out together – in their London flat, at Plaistow Grove or in Margate. David seemed a natural band member: up for a laugh, knowing when to take the piss and when to snap into focus. And on the side, David and Denis worked on commercials for Youthquake Clothing and Puritan, both cooked up and recorded in their Who-influenced style at RG Jones Studio in Wimbledon, where David made most of his demos through 1966.

In retrospect, it's slightly bizarre that Talmy, who'd helped define the sound of The Who and The Kinks, should have produced an unashamed pastiche of his own work, in the form of 'You've Got a Habit of Leaving Me', David's next single. The song spliced 'My Generation's' two-chord trick with 'Tired of Waiting for You's' languid melody. Worse still, David had abandoned the vocal distinctiveness he was reaching for on 'Pity the Fool'. Only in the final seconds does the single take off, as Denis Taylor smashes into a heavy, rolling three-chord sequence and the rest of the band freak out. But those final moments, too, are a rip-off, copied almost note-for-note from The Who's 'Anyway, Anyhow, Anywhere'.

The single, according to legend, featured Les Conn's singing on its flip, the Herman's Hermits pastiche, 'Baby Loves That Way'. In fact, says Conn, he didn't attend the session – nor did the single benefit from his consummate schmoozing skills, and it promptly disappeared without trace. By now, Les was disenchanted with the music business; he'd sub-sidised David and Mark Feld for months, his only payback the time the two of them painted his office 'in a shitty green colour', he recalls. 'And it didn't look very good.' Les had also helped Mark score a singles deal with Decca for 'The Wizard' that November. It met with as little success as David's efforts: 'I was going broke looking after them. And I was getting very depressed with the music business – so I had to say goodbye.'

With by now familiar resourcefulness, David had a replacement in mind, another regular at La Gioconda, named Ralph Horton. Horton became a crucial figure over the next year. There was never any doubt about his commitment. 'He would have done anything to further David's career,' says John Hutchinson, who worked with him, 'so he could have made a good manager.' Yet Horton's time with David was dominated by troubles with money and disputes with David's musicians who, like Denis Taylor, 'didn't like Ralph from the start'. Bassist Graham Rivens is even more vehement: 'I hated him. It wasn't just the fact he was a fuckin' poofta – I hated everything about him.'

Ralph Horton was in his late twenties, but the slightly pudgy, invari-ably stressed-out manager seemed older, despite the black leather gloves he usually wore – a rock 'n' roll affectation – combined with dark suit, dark shirt and black-framed Buddy Holly specs. Horton had grown up in Handsworth, just outside Birmingham, where his family ran a butcher's shop. By 1964, he'd built up The Ralph John Agency with John

Singer, booking out local acts including The Tuxedos and Denny Laine, then with The Diplomats. When Denny Laine and the Moody Blues moved to London, Horton came with them, and by 1965 he was working as a booking agent at The Kings Agency at 7, Denmark Street, next door to La Gioconda.

Horton appeared on the scene just as David's progress had hit another road bump, when EMI pressurised Shel Talmy, who had enough on his plate with The Kinks and The Who, to terminate David's singles deal. 'David was good, but not great,' says the producer. 'He was going to get better, but wasn't in the same league as Pete Townshend and Ray Davies. And EMI simply felt the market wasn't buying it.' The split was amicable. David seemed unconcerned, for Horton assured him he could drum up another deal; even so, the aspiring manager did sense his own limitations, for on 15 September Horton called a well-known publicist named Ken Pitt to discuss involving him in David's management. Pitt explained he was too busy to take on another client; he also suggested that Davie Jones' name was a problem – he already knew of the David Jones who would go on to join the Monkees, as well as the south London war poet and painter of the same name.

Horton would not give up on Pitt and continued to call him. He also took Pitt's reservations about David's name seriously. It turned out David already had an alternative in mind. He had already tried out different names for size, including his *nom de saxophone*, David Jay. During his Kon-Rads period he had seen the movie *The Alamo*, and become obsessed with the character played by Richard Widmark: Jim Bowie. 'He called himself Bowie at least once in the dressing room,' says Kon-Rads drummer David Hadfield, 'and started dressing in this tasselled leather jacket.' The day after their initial telephone conversation, Horton wrote to Pitt, telling him his protégé would henceforth be known as David Bowie. All those involved were enthusiastic about the new name, although it would, of course, generate arguments in playgrounds and sixth-form common rooms over its pronunciation over the next decade. David always pronounced the name to rhyme with Snowy, TinTin's faithful terrier, although many Northern colleagues pronounced it 'Bow' to rhyme with 'plough'.

The new name epitomised David's fantasies of glamour and stardom, and also helped consign his earlier, failed single to history. Mark Feld, who recorded his debut single at Decca Studio 2, followed his example. By the time 'The Wizard' was released on 19 November, Mark had christened himself Marc Bolan and concocted, with Les Conn's encouragement, an engagingly ludicrous press release about a wizard-inspired trip to Paris. Friends and rivals, David and Marc kept close tabs on each other's progress.

Throughout the summer and autumn, Horton put his contacts to good use, booking repeat appearances at the Marquee and the 100 Club, a run of shows in Bournemouth, where the band was already building a following, and the Isle Of Wight. The shows saw the band at their peak. 'Brilliant,' says Taylor. 'They were really good,' says musician John Hutchinson, 'a proper band.' David and The Lower Third shared bills with The Pretty Things, Gene Vincent and The Who (whose Pete Townshend remarked to David and the band, 'Shit, was that one of my songs you just played?'). The Lower Third often drew a better response than their guest stars, and built up a rapport with most of them, sailing out on the Isle Of Wight ferry every week, sharing a tiny caravan and hanging out on the beach. Horton's contacts with the Marquee helped score them a string of shows on Saturday mornings at the club, playing live in support to guest artists like The Kinks or Stevie Wonder, who would mime to their own records, which were then broadcast on Radio London complete with audience applause. The optimistic mood brightened further with a trip to Paris in November for dates at the Club Drouot.

Between shows, David worked on songs, often with the whole band crammed into his bedroom at Plaistow Grove. Today, David voices the insecurities that he would never admit back then: 'I didn't know how to write a song – I wasn't particularly good at it. I had no natural talents whatsoever . . . and the only way I could learn was to see how other people did it. I wasn't one of those people who came dancing out of the womb like Marc – I was stumbling around,' he says. But he was persistent, struggling to build a basic musical vocabulary, humming lines and tunes that Denis Taylor had to interpret, varying the chords until they found one that David liked. It was slow work, like feeling their way through a maze in the dark. David 'wanted the music done straight away – but he was very patient, too,' says Taylor, 'and this would go on for days.' On 'You've Got a Habit of Leaving Me', David had simply told Denis to move his hand up and down the fretboard. Now they added new tricks, ninths, sevenths and minor chords, which brought a new complexity to David's material. 'Some of it was morbid. Quite miserable,' says Taylor. During these extended writing sessions throughout the end of 1965, David worked on 'The London Boys', a vignette of pill-popping boys dressed in their finery that was obviously influenced by the wistful feel of Ray Davies' songs like 'See My Friends'.

A little clunky in places – which only adds to its charm – 'The London Boys' was an anthem for a new generation of kids, an obvious ancestor of Bowie epics like 'Lady Stardust' and 'All the Young Dudes': a celebration of otherness, right down to the clothing, the hint of homo-eroticism, and the evocation of Judy Garland in its 'too late now, 'cos you're on the run' climax. Its combination of world-weariness and naiveté embodies the persona that David would inhabit for a decade or more; a man-child, someone who as a youth was strangely calm and mature, and who as an adult seemed waif-like, with a childish earnestness. In future years, David Bowie's androgyny would be widely – and justifiably – celebrated, but this man-child aura was just as important a part of his personal, often devastating charm.

'The London Boys' was a harbinger of another typical Bowie technique: to hitch a ride on a youth movement, and simultaneously to distance himself from it. In the Mod scene, as in others, David was a latecomer, trailing behind pioneers like Marc Bolan, who'd made his mark early in a seven-page feature in *Town* magazine back in September 1962, shot by celebrated war photographer Don McCullin. Late he may have been, but David was instantly accepted by Mod pioneers like Jeff Dexter, the DJ and leading Face who'd been comparing lapels and partings with Marc Bolan for years. 'I checked out David at the Bromel Club in 1964; he was sharp.' Marc and David's obsession with clothes cemented their relationship; together, they ventured down Carnaby Street looking for reject garments in the bins outside the stores.

More significantly, for just a few weeks, David joined forces with the band who would become the leading lights of the Mod movement. In the days following his Lower Third audition, David had also continued hanging out with Steve Marriott at La Gioconda and then, when Marriott teamed up with the future Small Faces, David sat in on their rehearsals and helped them hump their gear around. For the first couple of shows he guested on vocals. 'He was great,' says drummer Kenney Jones. 'He was absolutely one of us. A wonderful Mod, with a great hairdo, a great personality and a great look – really cared about his image.' Over this period, David became the 'fifth Small Face'. Yet he would never mention this intriguing collaboration with the Small Faces – because it foundered thanks to the drawback that had plagued most of his efforts, namely his shameless imitation of others' styles. 'We were not into protest songs,' says Jones, 'and David was. In the end, we decided he was too Dylanish.'

The band's rejection was presumably a crushing blow, for he would never mention it to any of his confidants. To this day, says Jones, who of course went on to play with both the Faces and The Who, 'I still think about David, personally, and hang on to those memories of our misspent youth.' Although David never publicised his involvement with the Small Faces, he remained respectful of Stevie Marriott who, propelled by his glorious voice and his songwriting partnership with bassist Ronnie Lane, would soon achieve the fame for which David yearned.

Despite such setbacks, Bowie's brief career as a Mod was crucial, for the youth movement established all the essential principles with which he outraged Britain in 1972. In most respects, seventies glam was modernism pushed to the max, and it's no coincidence that the founding troika of glam – Bowie, Bolan and Bryan Ferry – were all definitive Mods. (The only difference in philosophy was that the Mod ideal was exclusive, aimed only at peers, whereas glam was designed to be publicised – knowingly pimped, with an ironic giggle.) In 1964, the notion of preening, peacock males, who bonded with fellow males over a side-vent or suit lining, oblivious to the scorn of outsiders, was outrageous – and powerful – in the monochrome backdrop where simply wearing a pink shirt was a provocative statement. There were no famous role models you could point to, to deflect the scorn of the un-hip; apart from your peers, you were on your own. Mod was the domain of the unashamed narcissist; and David Bowie and Marc Bolan became two of the most committed narcissists in London.

There was an obvious gay frisson about Mod, and indeed 'The London Boys'. The city's Mod and gay crowds shared the same clubs and many values. Le Duce on D'Arblay Street was nominally gay, whereas The Scene, in nearby Ham Yard, was nominally Mod, but you could pose or dance to Bluebeat in either one. Plenty of Mod boys experimented with their sexuality, as well as their clothing, around Soho in 1964 and 1965 – it was no surprise to anyone that David was one of them.

Mike Berry was one of many kids who'd somehow fallen into a dream job, working for the publishers, Sparta Music. History has never recorded how this man signed David to his first significant publishing deal, but Mike met him through their mutual music-shop friend, Wayne Bardell, and used to drop in on David when he was earning odd pennies at the publishers Southern Music over the winter, packing up manuscripts to send out to arrangers. They went out for a drink, 'and I fell in love with the boy, in more ways than one'.

For Berry, as for David, this was an electrifying period. 'Life seemed black and white until 1964. Then it suddenly burst into colour.' Like many of his generation, the rebellion against monochrome, strait-laced values included his sex life, too. 'They were incredible times,' he says. 'I knew I was bisexual, I had a girlfriend and fancied other people– then we all suddenly thought, Nobody cares! Anything goes!'

David and Mike's friendship had a sexual element but any such fumblings were brief, he says, 'Mostly, we'd talk about things. At the time he was semi-straight, and semi-gay, we talked mainly about music, or politics, what was happening with the Cuban crisis – none of us were sure we'd be alive the next year. Or we'd talk about, Do we fancy him or her, who's had who, and of course nobody knew who was telling the truth.'

David was cool, playful, funny, 'and there was something waif-like about him. And of course those eyes struck you straight away, they were unforgettable.' David's good looks helped him pass easily in and out of the gay-oriented scene – he flaunted his campness, but it was nonetheless all a bit of a laugh. In fact, the campness helped him to attract more girls. In the main, he was voraciously heterosexual; occasionally he'd go on dates with Dana Gillespie, a sixteen-year-old former public schoolgirl with an unforgettable cleavage, whom he'd met in The Manish Boys' final days; sometimes Dana would bring along her friend Sarah Troupe for a double date. David had also been briefly involved with Annie Howes, the promoter's daughter, but it seemed to his friends that he 'had a girl in every port', as Denis Taylor puts it. 'Wherever we were, some bird would pop up.'

Still, in mid-sixties Soho, a certain rough-trade appeal was great for the career. This certainly applied to Marc Bolan who, according to his one-time manager Simon Napier-Bell, had 'no great hang-ups' about who to sleep with. By late 1965, David was beginning to build up his own following in the West End's gay music–business clique, particularly around the Marquee Club where, says employee Simon White, 'There'd be six girls at the front, and half a dozen of us queens at the back, with Ralph [Horton] hanging on his every move.'

Many of Ralph Horton's connections revolved around the Marquee and Radio London; both places with a strong gay contingent, all of whom loved speculating about David's relationship with Horton. In a characteristically outrageous anecdote, Simon Napier-Bell claimed on his website in 2006 that Horton had offered him David's sexual favours to sweeten a co-management deal. Whatever Horton may have promised, David's confidants, like Mike Berry, insist, 'It would never have happened in a million years. David was always in control of what he wanted.'

Painted by history as a cynical exploiter, Ralph Horton was – he died in 2009 – in fact 'a nice, gentle person, who was completely out of his depth', says Terry King, who gave Horton his first London job, and in turn fired him. Rather than exploiting David, Horton was simply besotted with him and revelled in displaying his handsome client at clubs around town. Horton's obsession, however, meant that the first months of 1966 were dominated by back-biting and dubious financial dealings, for his jealousy and possessiveness inspired a seemingly irrational campaign to separate David from his closest friends, namely The Lower Third.

For Taylor, David Bowie's main musical foil in the group, Horton's influence was negative, right from the start. 'We had good laughs together when we were a group. David was great fun, one of the lads. And we had hard times, too, the van breaking down, but he didn't mind – he mucked in.' After Horton took over, David started to spend less time in the band's converted ambulance, in favour of a cushier, more upholstered existence. 'And so he got himself a nice lazy little job of pissing off with Ralph in his Jaguar Mark X,' says Taylor. 'It was very disappointing.'

Worse still was the air of sleaziness around Horton's financial affairs, typified by a deal he made in November 1965 with a London business-man, Ray Cook, to borrow £1500 – a sum worth roughly £30,000 in today's currency. A vague contract promised return of the money once David was earning over £100 a week. Ken Pitt, who as Bowie's next manager had to unravel these financial tangles, is not alone in believing Cook had been taken for a ride. 'I felt sorry for him. It was not a good situation.'

Horton's one coup was to secure a new recording contract through Tony Hatch, whom he'd originally met via Denny Laine. The house producer for the Pye label, Hatch later became one of the best-known producers in the UK – the Simon Cowell of the seventies – thanks to his role on the *New Faces* talent show. He thought Horton was pleasant enough, 'but I recognised he wasn't "top echelon" – he was still in the junior league. And I suspected if David had a hit, there would be a new manager along soon.'

Hatch was impressed by David, though – primarily because he wrote his own songs. Pye was a strange agglomeration – spliced together from the Polygon and Nixa labels – which Hatch had joined as part-time pro-ducer, arranging A&R meetings in the afternoon so he could fulfil his National Service as arranger for the Coldstream Guards (another Pye act) in the mornings. His workload was immense, so the fact he didn't have to find material for David was crucial. 'The one thing that struck me is

he had a lot of songs – different songs.' Hatch went to see The Lower
Third at the Marquee to check out the material. 'I remember "The
London Boys" – there were a lot of songs about his background. There
was one about the Hackney Marshes which is probably in some archive
somewhere.' (Sadly, David's unreleased Pye material seems to have disappeared.)

With Hatch's numerous distractions, it took some time to tie up a
recording contract; the publishing stayed close to home, with Mike Berry
signing him to Sparta for his planned singles. The deal brought in a small
advance, and together with the money from Raymond Cook, the cash
flow enabled a season of high living at Horton's Warwick Square flat,
with lavish drinking parties. David acquired a guitar during this high-
living period, and although his playing was, at best, rudimentary, he
worked up songs like 'It's Lovely to Talk to You' and 'Maid of Bond
Street'. In the autumn The Lower Third demoed 'The London Boys',
which they considered a standout song, but Hatch and his Pye colleagues turned it down at their weekly sales meeting. According to
Hatch the main reason was not the downbeat subject matter, or references to pill popping, 'It takes too long to get going. It would never make
a single.'

Its replacement was far more concise, with a simple three-chord chorus
once again lifted shamelessly from 'Anyway, Anyhow, Anywhere'. But
while 'Can't Help Thinking About Me' thieved exactly the same three-
chord trick as 'You've Got a Habit of Leaving Me', it makes far better use
of it, with that punchy chorus allied to a subtle verse whose minor-key
chords perfectly match the foreboding lines of a 'question time that says
I brought dishonour'.

The verse alone was a huge leap forward in David's work, but it was
combined with another sophisticated technique, a pre-chorus section
that raises the excitement level ('it's too late now') before we reach the
release of the chorus. This was a song as story, one musical vignette
giving way to another, in a technique that became a cornerstone of David
Bowie's great songs.

The lyrics, too, are subtle, with hints of a crime that had blackened the
family name, and a chorus that slightly subverts expectations, for according to pop convention, the protagonist should have been thinking about
a 'you', not 'me'. In many cases it's simplistic to assume David is the subject of his own lyrics, but here, the accusation of blackening the family
name echoes some of Peggy's complaints. She'd been hospitable to The
Manish Boys, nice well-spoken middle-class lads, but by now she had

lost patience with David's musical ambitions and demonstrated a sneering suspicion of his mates from Margate. 'She didn't like us at all,' says Denis Taylor, ruefully. 'I remember her telling me, "You're leading my boy astray – he was never like this before."'

Hatch realised the song's virtues instantly – 'it was a standout' – and played piano for the session at Pye's Marble Arch Studio on 10 December, 1965. Although Hatch had reservations about the performance, for Graham Rivens' bass part speeds up noticeably halfway through, The Lower Third clatter along with élan, driven by a neat twelve-string acoustic and superb singing. The David Bowie we know and love croons darkly, before losing all restraint in the impossibly thrilling run-up to the chorus. The single betrays some influences – notably Pete Townshend's 'The Kids are Alright', as well as that chorus chord sequence – but transcends them thanks to its innate drama, as the singer, song and band carry the listener along in their headlong rush.

The single was released on 14 January, 1966, a week after David had turned nineteen. Ralph Horton had borrowed more money from Raymond Cook for a launch party and to help buy the single into the charts. There was a party that evening at the Gaiety Bar in Strathearn Place to celebrate the release: the band walked through the nearby Hyde Park to get there, while David took a ride in Ralph's Jaguar, and all the musicians dressed up and mingled with the Pye staff and celebrities – the most famous was Freddie Lennon, John Lennon's incorrigible absentee father, who was enjoying a brief flurry of notoriety. 'It was a really weird party,' says Taylor. 'Freddie Lennon, this peculiar old geezer, a bit inebriated, wandering around saying "Do you know who I am?"'

David was effervescent that night, friendly with The Lower Third – 'like we were a proper band' – meeting and greeting the minor industry figures and mouthing to his band, 'This is it!' Rail-thin, his hair in a Mod bouffant, he loved being at the centre of the hubbub, taking off to charm one huddle of guests after another, flirting with the Pye secretaries, and adopting an obliging, likely-lad persona with the company's suited execs. He had turned nineteen a week before, had made his first great single and was in no doubt that, finally, this *was* it.

4

Laughing Gnome

I had a minor obsession about David. I just thought he was the
most magical person. I think I would have signed him even if
he didn't have such obvious talent.

Hugh Mendl

For a tiny gaggle of fans, men and girls – centred around Soho – David
Bowie was a star. At home in Plaistow Grove, he was anything but.
Although he disappeared often to Ralph Horton's basement apartment at
79, Warwick Square, he was still reliant on Haywood and Peggy for handouts. Haywood sometimes intimidated David's fellow musicians, but they
were often surprised to discover that behind his strait-laced exterior, he
was surprisingly well informed about David's career – and supportive.
With Peggy it was a different matter; by the end of 1965, her tolerance of
David's musical ambitions was exhausted. Yet although his band used to
joke about how they were forced to wait outside David's house in their
converted ambulance while he chatted to his mum, he seemed unconcerned, and would never mention a word of any family hassle.

After the huge build-up for 'Can't Help Thinking About Me', its performance was underwhelming; the single entirely missed the UK's main
chart, the Record Retailer Top 40. Although Radio London pushed the
single heavily, and placed it at number twenty-five, it was probably
Raymond Cook's money that helped grease the song's path to number
thirty-four in the *Melody Maker* chart. Tony Hatch remembers even this
modest success was enough to make David 'very excited', and the producer was mildly encouraged. 'I did see David as a long-term artist. And
I knew we had a lot more material to play with.'

Yet a slightly dodgy Top 40 placing did not help generate live shows, the only reliable means of raising cash, and while Ralph Horton was not good at wheeler-dealing for money – 'too wimpish' according to flatmate Kenny Bell – he was good at spending it. It was Bell who'd first sub-let a room to Horton in the Warwick Square flat, previously home to The Moody Blues, and during the end of 1965 and beginning of 1966, he saw Horton spending 'like a big shot. Cars, booze, you name it. I don't know how much money Ralph got from Raymond Cook, but he certainly fancied himself as a big spender.'

Much of Horton's spending was designed to impress David, who was learning, says Bell, 'to dominate Ralph. Really, Ralph was a bit of a wuss, and I think David ended up controlling him.'

Unable to control his own spending, or his protégé, Ralph decided to pick on people he could control – namely The Lower Third. Even before 'Can't Help Thinking About Me' had been released, Horton was planning the removal of Denis Taylor. 'He decided to pick on one of us to bring us to heel – and he didn't like me,' says Taylor. 'He wanted to get rid of me and the other two could stay.'

The band started to suspect Horton of trying to drive a wedge between them when Horton took David home in his Jag after another run of Paris Drouot shows over the New Year, leaving The Lower Third to struggle back in their old ambulance. During a short layoff in January, the band's income dwindled to nothing. As a short run of shows approached, Taylor asked when they could expect to be paid. 'That's when Ralph made his big mistake,' says Taylor. 'He told us we were not getting any money, as it was all going into advertising.'

Although Horton's hostility was focused mainly on Taylor, the manager's confrontational attitude succeeded in uniting all of The Lower Third. Following a show in Stevenage on 28 January, 1966, the band asked for their share of the take. Horton informed them there was none. 'He told us it had gone on expenses,' says Rivens. 'Like running his Mark X Jag, I guess.'

After a Marquee show the next morning, The Lower Third were booked in at the Bromel Club, David's home venue. The band met Ralph at the club, and Taylor told him it was No Pay, No Play. This time, Horton told Taylor, 'You are *definitely* sacked!' at which point Phil Lancaster weighed in: 'If he goes, we go!' To break the stand-off, Taylor informed the manager, 'You can have half an hour to think about it. When we come back, tell us what you want to do.'

After downing a half-pint of lager in a nearby pub, The Lower Third returned. 'We were convinced he was going to pay us,' says Rivens, 'but he wouldn't. So we simply packed up our gear and walked.' Taylor walked up to David and asked if he'd stick up for them and prevent the walkout. David's response was to burst into tears. 'He didn't want us to go. But he'd probably been listening to Ralph, all the things he'd made up.' By now the club was packed with Bromley art school students, and various friends and fans of David, and The Lower Third were convinced that David or Ralph would run after them and relent. They didn't.

'We thought within a few days [David] would come running back,' says Graham Rivens. 'But of course he couldn't do that, because Mr Horton was pulling the strings.' After a couple of days waiting for David's call, The Lower Third carried on without him for a few shows, before splitting and joining other bands.

The departure of The Lower Third marked a triumph for Ralph Horton; it would also be symbolic in David's own career. His peers and rivals like Jagger, Lennon and indeed Steve Marriott – whose third single with the Small Faces, 'Sha-La-La-La-Lee', had soared to number three in the charts as David's own single languished at the bottom – each shared a commitment to their own band, building up a grassroots following via show after gruelling show. This was an English rock 'n' roll convention that David ignored; his vision was more old-fashioned, something out of the tinselly showbiz conventions of the fifties, where managers nurture their protégés like mother hens. There was something unmistakably square about David's loyalty to 'Numero Uno', rather than the gang mentality of rock 'n' roll. And in the short run, his career would suffer.

Ralph Horton, meanwhile, revelled in the job of finding a compliant backing band for his charge, placing an advertisement for replacement musicians in *Melody Maker* that same week. Bassist Derek 'Dek' Fearnley was among the first to turn up at Warwick Square. Within thirty seconds of walking into the basement apartment he decided he wouldn't take the job. 'I just felt this strange, gay atmosphere – it made me feel very uncomfortable.'

Ushered in by Horton, Derek saw a skinny, camp young man, reclining on a bed; confused, he was trying to assess the situation when David calmly started detailing how he wrote all his own material, before producing a cigarette packet – 'Literally, a piece of card from a fag packet, with some chords written on the back' – and the bassist found himself intrigued, against his better judgement. David picked up his twelve-string and strummed through some chords, humming along. After eight bars or so, Fearnley was transfixed: this was not the predictable R&B

most London musicians were churning out. 'Then by the time we got maybe halfway through I thought, I don't care what's going on here – I want to work with this guy.'

Guitarist John Hutchinson went through a similar process, hearing from Jack Barry at the Marquee that there was a singer looking for a new band, turning up for an audition at the club on the Saturday, and jamming along on a Bo Diddley riff. Hutchinson – 'Hutch' – and David soon established a natural, musicians' rapport, a bond of which Ralph Horton was, says Hutch, jealous. Horton wanted a pliable band of non-entities who wouldn't challenge his own relationship with Bowie. And for that reason, says Hutch, '[This band] were more meek. We did it and we acted like a backing band.'

Drummer John Eager joined up at the same time as Fearnley, and Hutch suggested a keyboard player, Derek 'Chow' Boyes, whom he knew from the Yorkshire club circuit. Radio London DJ Earl Richmond, who introduced their sets at the Marquee, named them The Buzz, and within a couple of days they were filling in for The Lower Third at a string of live dates and, on 4 March, *Ready, Steady, Go!*, miming to 'Can't Help Thinking About Me'. Steve Marriott was on the same show with the Small Faces, jumping around and joshing David as the cameras rolled. It was good-natured fun, but it showed how David was falling behind the Small Faces' singer who 'had a lot more exposure, success, confidence and natural character [than David]. That's the one thing I remember from that show,' says Hutch.

A few weeks later, the effects of The Lower Third's departure became more obvious, when The Buzz turned up at Pye's Marble Arch studios to record a follow-up to 'Can't Help Thinking About Me'. There were no tempo changes or cranked-up guitars on 'Do Anything You Say' – it was neat, and well played, but the Spector-ish gloss and Motown-style on-beat drums couldn't mask a horrible blandness. The thrill had gone – David sounded like a bad Tom Jones imitator.

Released to capitalise on a near-hit, 'Do Anything You Say' stalled; David's career seemed to have done the same. And while David had built up a small following at the Marquee, when they ventured outside of London for a short tour in April to mark the single's release, according to Derek Fearnley their set left audiences confused, which included dates in Scotland where, 'to be honest, the kids didn't really get it'. Realising the audience wanted some familiar songs, David introduced a cover of 'Knock on Wood', and Tim Hardin's 'If I Were a Carpenter'. The Buzz were 'competent, but not dynamic', according to

Hutch. David's musical confusion, without the foil of The Lower Third, would become obvious, to the extent that his period with The Buzz would soon be airbrushed out of history – notably, by himself. Much later he would claim, 'For a number of years I worked with rhythm and blues bands – my participation in them formed my own black ties.' It's understandable that he'd forgotten his most forgettable music.

Many fans and friends of the time remembered David's work with The Lower Third; few of them mention The Buzz, who worked up a funkier, more jazzy style than their predecessors, but were milder and tamer, in both music and mentality. Sacking The Lower Third might have suited Ralph Horton, but it seemed an act of self-sabotage. David appeared unconcerned. As The Buzz observed, he liked hanging out with a band, sharing his obsessions and flights of fancy. But he was fundamentally a loner: his main fantasy was of a 'nomad' lifestyle. This was the primary attraction of hanging out at Horton's flat, for by now he was open about the claustrophobia that living with his mother and father inspired. This claustrophobia also inspired the rapid turnover of people with whom he worked – the moment they started seeing themselves as a permanent fixture, or making demands, David started seeing them as part of the dullness and convention that oppressed him. As Dek Fearnley, the man closest to David in 1966, observed even at the time, 'He wanted to get away from home. And he wanted to get away from being in a band, in exactly the same way, if that makes sense.'

For those close to him, David's 'dreaminess', his desire to escape the humdrum, was his most powerful and charming character trait. He knew how to make boring situations, like waiting for a bus or train, entertaining. 'He was on a higher plane, really,' says Fearnley. 'He wouldn't be talking about the weather or the latest Who single, he was simply off in his own world.' This man-child blend of escapism and hard-nosed careerism was intriguing – there would be constant flights of fantasy or obsessions that he would draw his friends into. In essence, this seemed to be a mind-control technique, to blot out the everyday details of life in Bromley. In other personalities, such escapist tendencies or daydreaming would have been the mark of an ineffectual, Walter Mitty character, but David worked at turning his fantasies into reality, spending long hours working on arrangements, or planning the next step in his career.

In fact, with the failure of 'Do Anything You Say', it seemed that David didn't actually have a career; but that hardly impaired his ability to move on. This time around, it wouldn't be the band that was ditched in order to break the deadlock, but the man who had, just a few months earlier, seen off The Lower Third. According to Kenny Bell, Ralph Horton was aware he was becoming surplus to requirements, 'He came to the end of any money he had to spend on David, and realised David would probably be off. So the best thing he could do was score a deal with somebody else and at least retain something.' Desperate to secure help – and, just as crucially, money – Horton reapproached Ken Pitt.

A crucial character in David Bowie's history, Ken Pitt is also one of the most complex and misunderstood. Generally depicted as a traditional, old-school figure – a gay showbiz manager in the tradition of Brian Epstein – Ken Pitt is in reality far more complicated and intriguing. Born and raised in Southall, Middlesex, Pitt had studied art at the School of Photo-Engraving and Lithography at Fleet Street, and worked briefly for two London print companies before joining the army in March 1941. He worked in signals, landed at Gold Beach on D-Day, was among the first Allied troops to arrive at Belsen, and served briefly in Palestine before returning to the family home in Southall, where he joined the music business as MC for a local dance band. Pitt soon established himself as a key PR figure in the UK's nascent record industry, and by 1956 he was already representing Stan Kenton, Billy Eckstine, Billy Daniels and Liberace. In 1966, Pitt had built a thriving business operating in both management and PR, his major acts including David Anthony's Moods and Manfred Mann. At the beginning of the year, he had turned down a plea from Mike Prustin to co-manage the recently renamed Marc Bolan. But when Ralph Horton came to see Pitt in his office on 5 April, insisting that Pitt 'had the keys to the doors that are being slammed in our face at the moment', Pitt was interested enough to turn up for a show at the Marquee on 17 April, without having heard any of David Bowie's music beforehand.

Winston Churchill, hailed by many as the ultimate Great Briton, once explained his crucial achievement of bringing America into the Second World War with the words, 'No lover ever studied every whim of his mistress as I did those of President Roosevelt.' David Bowie, self-styled Great Briton, showed a similar mastery of political realities. His performance on 17 April was one of the most important in his life – and he delivered. As Pitt puts it, 'if you went to see David Bowie and David Bowie knew you were coming, he would put on a show for you. Which he did for me. And yes, I was greatly impressed. With everything. Everything.'

The band, Pitt says, were forgettable, playing vaguely Mod music. David himself was another matter. Pitt had worked with Sinatra and Bob Dylan and could recognise charisma. David had it. Although Pitt retained few details of the songs David and The Buzz played, he remembered David's beige jumper, with buttons down one shoulder. 'It looked like something your mother had made, but I noticed it fitted him very well. It was . . . different.'

The band ran through their set, without any number particularly registering, before their last song. At which point, says Pitt, the lights went down, with a single spot on David, who launched into an impassioned version of 'When You Walk Through a Storm' – a classic show-business tune, which Ken knew from Judy Garland's version. Pitt was transfixed, 'I had simply never seen anything like that before.'

After the show, David came up to greet Pitt and with Ralph they went back to Ralph's flat, where they chatted for a very long time. Pitt noticed that when he raised a subject that was new to David, the young singer became animated: 'He had this habit, of sitting on one leg and then rocking backwards and forwards in a chair when he got excited. I noticed after I discussed something he would have this look, and his eyes were bright. That impressed me very very much.' Then, taking command of the situation, this man-child, who seemed as eager to learn as he was to take control, turned to Ralph and said, 'Let's do a deal with Ken.'

There is an intriguing footnote to David Bowie's acquisition of the manager who steered his career over the next four years. Ken Pitt ascribes his conversion to David Bowie as being inspired by his performance of a Judy Garland song. But Bowie's MD and bassist Dek Fearnley, who arranged most of the material, is adamant that, at that performance, The Buzz closed their show with an entirely different song, Tony Newley's 'What Kind of Fool am I?'. The discrepancy perfectly illustrates David Bowie's ability to be whatever the object of his attention wanted him to be.

In later years, Bowie fans and writers would make much of the subtext of that night's conversation, which saw Ralph Horton hand control to Ken Pitt, and in some imaginations many of the undercurrents of that evening were comparable to Joe Orton's *Entertaining Mr Sloane*, the play that immortalised London's gay culture. But the participants were more complex than the clichés we've inherited. Ken Pitt, a fan of Judy Garland, devotee of Oscar Wilde, and supporter of the emerging Campaign for Homosexual Equality, was also a married man, who often mentioned his romances with Hollywood glamour models.

Tall and gangly, rather refined and formal-looking, Pitt could expound with equal enthusiasm on the virtue of Keats and The Velvet Underground in his clipped, measured tones, and was a master of the elegantly phrased, slightly waspish letters that were an essential management tool in London's old-school music industry. Pitt 'doesn't believe' in applying labels to sexuality. 'People always have to say now. It was better when people didn't have to say.' His vagueness is consistent with other rock managers like Andrew Loog Oldham, who was straight but loved camping it up to seem more like Brian Epstein or Kit Lambert – the gay managerial archetypes in the swinging London of 1966.

In other respects, Pitt was anything but vague. First of all, he injected some professionalism into David's business affairs, and paid the bills that started to cascade into his office. Pitt's trademark acerbity shows in his comments that Ralph's management of David's affairs, notably using David's income to pay his own bills, 'was not the usual way of doing things'. Over subsequent months, Pitt paid for outstanding phone bills, new shirts and endless running costs for the band van, all marks of his devotion to David's cause.

Pitt's enthusiasm was in stark contrast to the situation at Pye; in June, Hatch started producing 'I Dig Everything' then, dissatisfied with The Buzz's performance, replaced them all with session musicians. The resulting single, with its cheesy, chirrupy organ, and Austin Powers grooviness, bore more of Hatch's production trademarks than any of his previous Bowie sides, and the result, says Hatch himself, was 'that it didn't work at all. We were getting further away from what we had with The Lower Third single, rough as it was.'

Although it was obvious that 'I Dig Everything' was destined for oblivion, David was unconcerned. 'He knew those songs weren't that good, it's just what was needed at the time,' says John Hutchinson, who sensed that Bowie was ready to move on. Hutch, meanwhile, was pessimistic about The Buzz's future and confided to David that he planned to get married and find a conventional job. David found the notion of getting married bizarre and, the night before the wedding, tried to talk Hutch out of it. 'We were in Dunstable, he'd found these two girls, and he wanted me to go off with him and the girls instead.' David was supposed to turn up for the wedding, but was unsurprisingly absent the next day. Hutch left in search of married bliss and a regular paycheck in Yorkshire, and was replaced by Billy Gray.

Despite the attractions of the female fans who turned up at his shows,

David was fast becoming disenchanted with live performances, live audiences and, seemingly, rock 'n' roll in general. By the autumn of 1966, the British beatboom was subsiding. With The Beatles retiring from live shows, and the presence of Frank Sinatra and Tom Jones in the Top 10 alongside David's contemporaries like The Kinks and the Small Faces, the charts were charmingly diverse and kitsch, with none of today's predictable rock conformity.

Much of David's day-to-day existence was similarly kitsch and charming, for over the summer of 1966 he spent many of his afternoons at places like Dek Fearnley's brother's house in Sussex, observing the family comings and goings, playing with Fearnley's nieces and nephews. He was relaxed, soaking up what was a carefree environment compared to his own strait-laced, claustrophobic family home. The silly, or comic, moments were what struck him most – including the moment when a shame-faced Fearnley admitted he'd subtracted seven years from his age when he joined The Buzz, and was in fact twenty-seven. 'You're joking?' asked David, incredulous at the thought that he was hanging out with such an ancient codger – an uncle no less – who hadn't settled down yet. It was three months later, when David started to run through a new song, named 'Uncle Arthur' – about a thirty-two-year-old who 'still reads comics, follows Batman' – that Dek realised he had been immortalised in song.

Alan Mair, whose group The Beatstalkers were managed by Ken Pitt, also spent many afternoons with David, being shown his songs, and later hanging out in the office. He sometimes brought his three-year-old son, Frankie, with him, and the two built up such a rapport that a couple of times Mair left the toddler in his care. Like Uncle Dek, Frankie and his toy soldiers were captured in song, as 'The Little Bombardier'. Again, the situation was altered into a story where 'Little Frankie Mair' is the adult figure who, like David, enjoys hanging out with kids, and attracts suspicion. The song, a playtime waltz, perfectly illustrates David's mindset of cheeky humour, child-like wonder and adult cynicism. This wasn't Bowie's only baby-sitting job, for in quiet times he looked after Lucy, the daughter of Tom Parker, a friend from Kent who played piano with The New Animals. 'Kids just trust and gravitate towards some people,' says Mair. 'David is one of them.'

Mair knew both Pitt and Bowie well, and saw the manager's influence on Bowie at close hand. In later years, Pitt's detractors would contend he wanted to turn Bowie into an all-round entertainer. In fact, Bowie had joined Pitt as a singer in a rock band; soon he would change into a songwriter, with a unique world view. In that respect, Pitt's influence was the making of him. 'His intentions were right. He was saying, Put make-up on, dress flamboyantly – be gregarious!' says Mair. Pitt's role was not so much to educate David as to give him licence to see himself as an artist, at the same time encouraging him to write more, pushing his songs to other artists.

Pitt knew that David was going nowhere with Pye, where Hatch was being pressured by MD Louis Benjamin to drop David's contract, and he already had a new record company in mind. Early in October he funded a recording session with The Buzz, once more at RG Jones in Wimbledon, where David produced a second version of 'The London Boys', plus new songs 'Rubber Band' and 'Please Mr. Gravedigger'. Together, these quirky, observational songs represented a radical about-turn from David's Pye material, and Pitt was confident that they would help him score a record deal. 'What I wanted was an album that would act like a CV,' says Pitt. 'I had not come across another nineteen-year-old who wrote songs like that. I went to Decca determined to get an album deal – although that was theoretically impossible, because they didn't make albums except if you'd had a hit.'

Pitt made his approach to Decca via Tony Hall, the company's Promotions Manager. Hall had become the key figure in the establishment of the label's 'hip' Deram imprint. He was taken with Bowie's songs – 'they sounded like Anthony Newley 2' – and passed Pitt along to Hugh Mendl, who became transfixed. 'I think I would have signed him even if he didn't have such obvious musical talent. But he did have talent. He was bursting with creativity.'

Mendl was one of the most senior executives in the British music industry: in fact, he had literally invented a huge section of it, through his discovery of Lonnie Donegan and Tommy Steele, and he launched many significant careers throughout the sixties, often while battling Decca's innate conservatism. He rated the nineteen-year-old singer, with a string of failed singles behind him, as one of the most inspirational talents with whom he had ever worked. 'I had a minor obsession about David – I just thought he was the most talented, magical person.' Mendl was well aware of the resemblance between Bowie's voice and that of Anthony Newley, another Mendl signing, but was untroubled by it. 'The [resemblance] was purely vocal. They were entirely different. Tony was an actor. David was . . . David Bowie.'

An effusive but rather patrician character, Mendl had been expected to join the diplomatic service after graduating from Oxford, but despite the scepticism of his grandfather, Sir Sigismund Mendl, then chairman of Decca, he worked his way up through the 'family' company. Better educated and more worldly than Tony Hatch, the man who had signed David to Pye, Mendl's near-obsession with David is recognisable as the same 'heterosexual crush' that writer Charles Shaar Murray remembers David Bowie exploiting so potently in the seventies. David's discovery of this power was as significant a breakthrough as his improving skills at songwriting. David Bowie had grasped a fundamental truth: before you can *be* a genius, you have to *seem* like a genius.

Mendl's fascination with Bowie inspired him to release Bowie's self-produced 'Rubber Band' and 'The London Boys' as his single debut, while in-house producer Mike Vernon would oversee the album. Vernon had his own impressive track record, championing acts like Eric Clapton and Fleetwood Mac, and he too was impressed with the young singer's intellect. 'There was talk of a lot of things, concepts and poetry that went right over my head,' he remembers, leaving the impression he wasn't totally convinced by David's young genius persona. But there was no denying Bowie's creativity, for with the prospect of an outlet for the songs and pictures that were flowing through his head, music was pouring out of him.

Over the autumn of 1966, David was writing frenetically; in one early list of contenders for his debut album, he and Pitt itemised over thirty songs including 'Over the Wall', and now-forgotten compositions such as 'Say Goodbye to Mr Mind' and 'Lincoln House'. His ambition extended to abandoning traditional instrumentation in favour of a more orchestral approach, influenced both by Brian Wilson's ground-breaking *Pet Sounds*, released that summer, and by the fact he no longer had his own backing band. Guitarist Billy Gray left The Buzz in late November, and the others were 'let go' a week later. Ralph Horton, still acting as a kind of co-manager, wrote to Pitt, who had left for a trip to America and then Australia, explaining that they had decided to give up live performances, telling him that David 'hates ballrooms and the kids'. Poignantly, Dek, Chow and John 'Ego' Eager offered to stay on without pay after their last show, in Shrewsbury on 2 December, and also to help out with his album, inspiring another flood of tears from David.

Bowie approached this crucial rite of passage with the sense of calm and organisation that had so impressed The Manish Boys, and with two characteristics that would come to define his career: a willingness to take creative risks and a genius for delegation. He had assured Mendl and Vernon that he would oversee all the arrangements for the album – a task usually looked after by a specialist. Then he told bassist Dek Fearnley that the two of them would do this crucial job, together.

Fearnley's sole qualification was childhood piano lessons and he was intimidated by the prospect, but David confidently steered him well beyond his comfort zone. Aided by a dog-eared edition of Frida Dinn's *Observer's Book of Music*, a guide to the principal orchestral instruments, they attacked their task. 'It was bloody hard work,' says Fearnley. 'I knew how to read the staves and that a bar had four crotchets, David had never seen or written a note, so I was the one qualified to write stuff out.'

The two worked for hours at Dek's brother Gerald's piano: David humming, Dek scribbling. The arrangement for 'Rubber Band' was their first experiment with this working method. The quirky, Heath Robinson feel enhanced the song's off-kilter charm, but as work on the album proper started at Decca's Studio 2 in Hampstead on 14 November, 1966, the pressure was ratcheted up. 'We didn't have enough time,' says Dek, 'and it got embarrassing handing over these scribbles to these musicians from the London Philharmonic!' By Christmas, the two were behind schedule, and Fearnley was left to arrange a couple of songs on his own, including 'The Laughing Gnome', and explain the charts to the musicians, while David oversaw proceedings from the control room.

Mike Vernon remembers being handed a pile of papers and helping assemble each song 'like a jigsaw puzzle', but he and engineer Gus Dudgeon enjoyed the challenge of recording comedy voices and miking up gravel. Most of the musicians were supportive, transposing parts written in the wrong key, although one 'absolute bastard' clarinettist did simply hand his manuscript back to Fearnley, saying, 'there are five notes in this bar. There should be four,' and refused to play.

Just before Christmas, Neil Slaven, who oversaw the artwork for many of Decca's sleeves, dropped in on the session. Mike introduced him, briefly. David chatted with Slaven – 'Hello, Mike's told me all about you!' – interrogating the blues fan about his record collection, seemingly fascinated by his expertise on obscure Chess singles. Bowie seemed a world apart from the rock and blues musicians Slaven and Vernon normally hung out with. A slightly bizarre, undeniably impressive young man: slight, with floppy, collar-length hair and somehow schoolboyish, with a fey, 'theatrical' air. And then Slaven watched from the control room, dumbstruck, as Vernon rolled the tapes, seeing this intense but camp apparition shuffling around Decca Studio Two, crunching underfoot some scattered pebbles and stones which he had shaken over the studio floor, apparently to make some kind of backing track for a spoken-word piece.

When Slaven heard a rough mix of the epic that Vernon and Bowie were crafting, he was even more disconcerted: a monologue, in a theatrical cockney voice which sounded nasal, as if he had a bad cold, delivered over found sounds, like the crunching gravel and the rustle of driving rain. The subject was apparently a Lambeth gravedigger, 'a little old man with a shovel in his hand'. Although Slaven heard this 'song' just once or twice, it stuck with him, and he never got the strange spectacle he had witnessed out of his head. What was most striking was the way this studio neophyte delivered this extravagant confection without a trace of embarrassment. It should have been ludicrous, but despite himself, Slaven was impressed. 'I thought, Here is someone who really is an individual talent – someone who truly follows his own ideas.'

The track in question, 'Please Mr. Gravedigger', was, by most objective standards, dreadful. Its description of 'Mary Ann who [was] ten, full of life' obviously refers to ten-year-old Lesley Ann Downey, who was tortured and murdered by Moors Murderers Ian Brady and Myra Hindley. The song was tasteless and exploitative, but it also illustrated how the nineteen-year-old David Bowie had learned to use the recording studio as an instrument in itself, a lesson which was at the heart of his future career. Today, it ranks as both a bad-taste period piece and an example of artistic courage.

The drawn-out sessions – complete with French horns and English whimsy, just like The Beatles' sessions for *Sgt Pepper* recorded over the same timeframe – resumed after the Christmas break, with 'The Laughing Gnome' completed in January, and the final three tracks including a re-recorded 'Rubber Band' finished later in February 1967.

Predictably, most of the personnel involved remembered 'The Laughing Gnome' – which was released as a single on 14 April – as one of their favourite sessions. Vernon forgot his doubts and dived in, suggesting even more varispeeded effects, and engineer Gus Dudgeon 'totally went crazy', says Vernon, suggesting gnome puns and chirpy voices.

In future years, 'The Laughing Gnome' was the early Bowie song especially singled out for ridicule. Yet as long as you're happy to abandon all notions of taste, the song is brilliantly crafted, from Dek Fearnley's opening oboe melody, through to the breakdown after the chorus, as David intones '... said the laughing gnome'. One of the rare songs on the album where the execution matches its ambition, 'The Laughing Gnome' is infectious – like a skin ailment – and charmingly redolent of those summer afternoons spent playing with little Frankie Mair. In the admittedly narrow niche of pseudo-psychedelic cockney music-hall children's songs, it reigns supreme.

When Vernon wrapped up the sessions on 25 February, the producer felt a profound sense of achievement merely to have realised Bowie's kitchen sink epics. But the satisfaction didn't extend to optimism about the album's prospects. 'If I'm honest, I really thought it didn't have any chance of commercial success – whatsoever.'

The end of the album also marked the official end of David's relationship with Ralph Horton, for on 19 January, David's joint manager retired from the music business, later joining the RAC. Haywood Jones was left to deal with the letters from Raymond Cook that arrived at Plaistow Grove, plaintively asking about Horton's whereabouts, in hope of the payback of his 'loan'.

David, meanwhile, was buoyed with the enthusiasm of Deram's executives, most of whom thought 'The Laughing Gnome', plus 'Love You till Tuesday', were sure-fire hits. But even as the biggest artistic achievement of his life approached its release, he was – in what would become characteristic fashion – preparing to move on.

The inspiration arrived via a white-label acetate that Ken Pitt had acquired on his trip to New York. As an art enthusiast, Pitt had engineered a trip to Andy Warhol's Factory on 47th Street. Initially unaware of Warhol's involvement in the music scene, he had nonetheless briefly met Lou Reed and was given an acetate of The Velvet Underground's as yet unreleased debut album. After a promotional trip to Australia with another management charge, Christian St Peters, Pitt returned to London on 16 December, and handed over the acetate to David. The album is still a treasured possession, and a source of pride that 'not only was I to cover [a] Velvets' song before anyone else in the world, I actually did it before the album came out. Now that's the essence of Mod.'

In forthcoming years, David Bowie would become the world's best-known champion for the Velvets; but in 1967, his attempts to assimilate their narco-deadpan thuggery resulted in some of his most ludicrous music.

Some of the inspiration came in the form of The Riot Squad, a London five-piece, which, through various line-ups, had worked with both Larry Page and Joe Meek, led throughout by Bob Flag. The feisty, eccentric sax player had bumped into Bowie during a Buzz show at the Marquee the previous August and renewed his acquaintance over coffees at La Gioconda, mentioning his band were holding auditions for a singer. Bowie volunteered, partly for a laugh, partly to help them out, and partly so he could experiment with some new material – for, although Dek was still on the scene, keyboardist Chow had bailed out halfway through the Deram sessions.

The new band worked through new material at The Swan pub in Leytonstone on 15 and 16 March, readying David for The Riot Squad's support slot with Cream in Basildon on the 17th. Seven shows later, David enlisted the band's help for an after-hours Decca session with Gus Dudgeon, to record his cover version of the Velvets' 'Waiting for the Man', plus David's own 'Little Toy Soldier'.

'Waiting for the Man' would become a touchstone of David's career, and this early version was effective; stripped down and funky, with taut sax and harmonica embellishing the stomping onbeat drums and a rangy bass riff, all neatly underpinning David's carbon-copy Lou Reed drawl. However, it is David's own – using the term loosely – 'Little Toy Soldier' that was truly arresting. A juxtaposition of cockney music hall with the Marquis de Sade, the song is the aural equivalent of a P. T. Barnum fairground monstrosity: a monkey body stitched to a fishtail. David's hearty main melody introducing Little Sadie sounds like cheery English rocker Tommy Steele; then eight bars in, he drops an entire section – 'taste the whip, and bleed for me' – from the Velvets' 'Venus in Furs'. This fascinating curio seemed designed primarily as a provocative live song, where its mix of comedy and sado-masochism echoed some of the art-college craziness of the Bonzo Dog band; this was New York noir, reborn as Victorian music hall. Although David Bowie was the first European musician to appreciate the importance of The Velvet Underground, it would be years before he learned to assimilate it.

Recorded too late for inclusion on the Deram album, the two songs would become a highpoint of The Riot Squad's live set. For 'Little Toy Soldier', David, in psychedelic make-up, his hair back-combed, would brandish a whip and lash Bob Flag, who wore white face and bowler hat – like one of *Clockwork Orange*'s Droogs – plus protective padding. The shows were anarchic, hilarious – like contemporaries The Bonzo Dog Band, whom Flag later joined – and reminiscent of Marc Bolan's chaotic shows with hippie outfit John's Children. Unsurprisingly, the audience were confused. 'But David was always a laugh. He liked us because we'd do anything,' says Flag. The same could be said of David, who occasionally would reach over and fondle Flag's hair; the audience were left unaware this was a shared joke about the wig the thirty-six-year-old sax player wore to disguise his advanced years.

Although The Riot Squad provided back-up to David at his 13 April show at the Tiles club to mark the following day's release of 'The Laughing Gnome', David otherwise remained an anonymous member of the band for their performances right through to the end of May. Although in later years he often mentioned how early he'd picked up on The Velvet Underground, for his own career he stuck to the mainstream in search of a breakthrough. Certainly, there was no connection between The Riot Squad's loveably cranky recordings, and the smug, show-business gloss of 'Love You till Tuesday', which was re-recorded on with an orchestra directed by Ivor Raymonde, best known for 'I Only Want to Be with You'.

With its gelatinous strings, and trite, complacent lyrics, 'Love You till Tuesday' was a naked statement of David's yearning for a hit, without any of the charming eccentricity of *David Bowie*, which was released on 1 June, the same day as The Beatles' rather more successful *Sgt Pepper's Lonely Hearts Club Band*. By the time he'd completed the album, David had jettisoned no less than five bands in his drive for mainstream success. The failure of 'Love You till Tuesday' demonstrated that ruthlessness and ambition alone were not enough.

Yet as just a few people at the time noticed, ambition was not the only thing that drove David Bowie. For over that early summer of 1967 – much of it spent lovingly teaching The Riot Squad his songs line by line, or playing them Frank Zappa records up in his bedroom at Plaistow Grove – his friends grew to appreciate another compulsion: an intoxicating, child-like obsession with music, which had deepened and crystallised in the years since he had since pored over album sleeves at Medhurst's in Bromley. At heart earnest, obsessive, David Bowie was a simple fan-boy, with this compulsion sometimes battling, sometimes complementing, his ruthlessness. Only with failure would the fan-boy part of him be allowed to surface once more. Failure, it turned out, would be the making of David Bowie.

5

I Wish Something Would Happen

> It was a bit like the Warhol Factory if you wanted to hang out
> you had to learn heavy manners. And David came in, learning
> moves. He was clearly absorbing a lot: mutating.
>
> *Mick Farren*

The sudden inactivity following the polite, but restrained reception for David's Deram debut was a shock. He had stalled: 1968 would be a year that David Bowie would sit around Ken Pitt's flat in Manchester Street, his legs tucked under him in trademark fashion, sighing, 'I wish something would happen.'

Despite its negligible sales, the album did win some prominent supporters. *Melody Maker*'s Chris Welch had been turned on to the album by The Nice. Penny Valentine, of *Disc*, was even more influential: a lucid, widely fêted but unpretentious critic, she had an unerring ear both for talent and for a hit. She supported David faithfully over the next five years, celebrating his talent without, for the time being, predicting success. 'She did love him,' says Chris Welch, 'but she did mention how he wouldn't stop ringing her up.'

Haywood Jones, in the meantime, was in regular contact with Ken Pitt. As ever, he was politely grateful for Pitt's efforts on behalf of his son, but David's nocturnal songwriting activities were adding to the stress in Plaistow Grove. It was around this time that Terry, David's half-brother, had reappeared at the house. After his National Service in the Royal Air Force, Terry had lived intermittently with Peggy's sister, Pat, but now he had become reconciled with his step-father Haywood, and the long-absent prodigal son moved in to the tiny, overcrowded house. The eventual solution to the overcrowding was for David to move in with Ken. Bizarrely, this move to his manager's flat in Manchester Street was the first time the twenty-year-old had left home. Now the aspiring nomad would rely on handouts from Ken, rather than Haywood.

Although David had long outstayed his welcome at his parents' cramped two-up two-down, it wasn't just Peggy's suspicions that he was trying to evade. After Terry had arrived back in Bromley, David had started sharing some of his own musical obsessions with Terry, who had turned him on to so many musicians, from Eric Dolphy to John Coltrane. Hoping to reciprocate, David had taken his half-brother to see Cream at the Bromel Club, in February 1967. It was Terry's first encounter with high-volume rock 'n' roll, and the experience was disastrous. According to David, 'about halfway through he started feeling very, very bad. I had to take him out of the club because it was really starting to affect him – he was swaying . . . He'd never heard anything so loud.'

As they emerged from the hotel doorway onto Bromley Hill, Terry collapsed onto the pavement. 'He said the ground was opening up – and there was fire and stuff pouring out the pavement, and I could almost see it for him, because he was explaining it so articulately.' Terry had suffered a schizophrenic fit. During his stay at the house, Terry also told David he regularly had such visions. This revelation was overwhelming, disturbing, but David did not share his reaction with those with whom he spent most time. His characteristic reserve, that urge, noticed by Dek Fearnley, never to discuss the claustrophobia of Plaistow Grove, seemed to apply to Terry, too. David kept his concerns about his half-brother to himself, and those around him continued to believe that he was an only child.

Once Haywood had crammed his books and records into his tiny Fiat 500 and helped install him in Manchester Street, David cocooned himself in the neat, comfortable bachelor pad. Many of his afternoons were spent wandering around Fitzrovia and the other quiet, elegant Georgian streets around Manchester Square. Often he'd return from these magpie trips with a childish enthusiasm, presenting Pitt with his new discoveries: a Victorian children's book he'd bought from Pollack's Toy Museum, brass bells from some swinging clothes shop, or simply chestnuts, flowers, or leaves that he'd found in the street. At other times, David could be found shuffling through the bookshelves either side of the living-room fireplace, pulling out works like Saint Exupery's *Le Petit Prince*, various first editions devoted to Oscar Wilde and Aubrey Beardsley – who was a distant relation of Pitt's –

typographer Eric Gill and German expressionist Egon Schiele. Pitt enjoyed his role as mentor, and in a Pygmalian-esque manner, he would take David to cultural hotspots or the local Italian place, Restaurant Anticapri. It's possible that Pitt exaggerates his education of the nine-teen-year-old, whom he describes as 'not a cultured person' in those early days, but there's no doubt David was soaking up influences.

David enjoyed those months closeted with Ken. On several occasions he frolicked around the flat naked; Pitt noticed his 'long, weighty penis' and concedes that 'David was a tease.' On another occasion Pitt emerged from the bathroom naked and David, laughing, mimed measuring Pitt's penis, acting out an awed expression. The incident was recounted by one writer to illustrate the sexual frisson between them, but Pitt rejects that interpretation: 'it was simply funny. Any sexual undertone was in their minds, not ours.' To this day Pitt, who knows more than anyone of how David would use his sexuality to win people over, professes himself ignorant of his charge's true sexual orientation. 'Is David gay? I honestly don't know.'

Bowie's arrival at the flat confirmed his status as Pitt's main client, and the manager constantly fired off letters, looking for press, song-writing or acting opportunities. Deram had gone quiet after the release of *David Bowie*; Tony Hall, one of David's supporters, had left, while Mendl and his friend Dick Rowe, both responsible for the label, were beset with political problems. Instead, the main focus of David's com-mercial activities started to centre around his publishers, Essex Music.

David had been introduced to Essex by Tony Hall, an old friend of the company's celebrated proprietor, David Platz. Ralph Horton had signed David to Essex during Pitt's trip to the USA, much to Pitt's cha-grin, for he had been chasing a much bigger advance. But this alliance would prove vital over the next couple of years, placing Bowie within a sprawling musical nexus which included production companies, overseen by Denny Cordell and later Gus Dudgeon, plus publishing clients that included Anthony Newley, Lionel Bart, Lonnie Donegan, The Moody Blues and, from the spring of 1967, Marc Bolan. This ensured Marc and David continued to tread similar career paths, although they diverged when it came to songwriting, for while Marc kept his songs to himself, David was evangelistic about pushing his own material and getting it heard.

The motivation was social as well as professional. For David, sharing his songs was how he related to people. In the later days of The Riot Squad he would happily spend hours teaching his songs to Croak

Prebble, who replaced him as singer. The same applied to his involvement with The Beatstalkers, then Scotland's leading live band, a tight-knit
posse of Glaswegians who would have intimidated many outsiders. But
not David. 'He had incredible confidence,' says bassist Alan Mair. 'No
matter where you were, he would pick up a guitar and sing full blast.
Most people would be cagey, even Freddie Mercury was quite humble or
quiet [in a similar situation], but David would flabbergast me.'

David gave The Beatstalkers' 'Silver Treetop School for Boys', a neat,
'Waterloo Sunset'-style short story of a dope-addled boys school. More
significantly, 'Over the Wall We Go' was recorded by a Robert Stigwood
protégé named Oscar, later famous as sitcom actor Paul Nicholas. A playground ditty, settting the line 'Over the wall we go, all coppers are nanas'
to the tune of 'Pop Goes the Weasel', it failed to trouble the charts but
found an entirely different audience: 'I played it all the time at Middle
Earth in the Roundhouse,' says DJ Jeff Dexter. 'It was a perfect record to
play against the Pigs, man, a psychedelic comedy record – and it had this
fer-lum fer-lum fer-lum beat that idiot dancers love.' The single also
became a late-night Radio London favourite, a camp psychedelic classic,
loved by those who'd grown up on Billy Cotton and The Goons and
could cackle along in dope-enhanced hilarity.

None of these modest successes helped to sell David's own recordings, though, and Ken Pitt remembers his frustration at a logjam of
material, recorded at Plaistow Grove or on an open-reel recorder at
Manchester Street, which seemed destined never to be released. One
evening Bowie vented his frustration, says Pitt, by telling him, 'I'm going
to write some Top 10 rubbish,' then proceeded to write a song which was
neither. 'Let Me Sleep Beside You' would be his first collaboration with
Tony Visconti, the producer with whom he's most associated: the finest
song Bowie had written to date, it would also become the cause of his
biggest artistic setback.

Tony Visconti had arrived in London in April 1967 at the invitation of
Denny Cordell, who'd worked with him briefly in New York. Cordell
was overworked, Visconti had production experience and – crucially –
turned out to be a brilliant arranger. Within weeks he was teamed with
Denny Laine and Procol Harum, while his addition of a woodwind quartet to The Move's 'Flowers in the Rain' helped propel it to number two
in the charts. Visconti had already brought Marc Bolan's new project,
Tyrannosaurus Rex, to Essex Music when David Platz played him an
album by another Essex writer, David Bowie.

Visconti was intrigued, mostly by the album's diversity, 'it was like a demo, trying everything: "Look, I can do this, and I can do that, too!"' He was introduced to David in a tiny room at Dumbarton House, Essex Music's Oxford Street headquarters; the two built up a rapport straight away, both of them fast-talking and obsessive, with almost ency-clopaedic musical tastes. The producer listened to a number of David's demos and picked out 'Let Me Sleep Beside You' as much for its coher-ent, folk-rock style as its content. Taking control of the project, Visconti located the musicians and wrote out every note of the music – 'I had to, as we only had three hours for the session' – and produced the record-ing at Advision. The result was David's most coherent, concise song since 'Can't Help Thinking About Me'. Its lyrics – 'I will show you dreams where the winner never wins' – were vaguely Dylanish, its 'ded-edudum dededum' vocalising Bolan-ish. His voice sounded mature and free of affectation, while in the middle eight, his double-track vocals are a foretaste of Ziggy Stardust's rock 'n' roll yell.

'Let Me Sleep Beside You' was a gorgeous track, but it was none-theless rejected by Decca's regular Monday singles selection panel. The decision marked the beginning of a minor crisis for David (and a major crisis for Deram, as Denny Cordell and Platz switched allegiance to EMI). David had so far endured his career setbacks with a character-istic calm, but over these months he started to voice his pain. Steve Chapman was in charge of Essex Music's demo studio, where he'd help David record songs or cut acetates of the 'amazingly creative' demos David crafted at Manchester Street. The studio was tiny, and they spent long hours in conversation; seventeen-year-old Chapman looked up to the worldly, intelligent singer, 'he had this amazing palette of ideas, Tibetan philosophy, mystical concepts'. But late in 1967, shortly before Chapman left to join a band named Junior's Eyes, he noticed, 'David sounded quite depressed. He told me, "I'm thinking of chucking it in. Really, I'd like to become a Buddhist monk."'

Those frustrating afternoons, often spent hanging around with no recordings in prospect, eventually put paid to the youthful arrogance that Leslie Conn remembered. Ken Pitt persevered, sending a copy of the album to Mickie Most to drum up interest – Most didn't reply – and fruitlessly chasing acting and commercials jobs. By spring 1968, the crisis of confidence had extended to Bowie's manager, according to Alan Mair, who after quitting the Beatstalkers had been given the use of a spare office by Ken Pitt. 'I think Ken Pitt had reached the stage where he didn't know what to do with him. One day he said to me, "Do you want to be

David's personal manager?" I wasn't interested – but I think Ken had reached the point where he was pulling his hair out.' The situation deteriorated further in March, when Deram rejected 'In the Heat of the Morning' and 'London Bye Ta Ta'. It was particularly painful for Hugh Mendl. 'It was so hard,' he reflects, sadly, 'he was a wonderful person – but at that time it was me against fate.'

In the Bowie story, Deram have generally been cast as villains, but 'In the Heat of the Morning' – despite its elegant Visconti string arrangement – was undistinguished, its style essentially that of the Deram album minus the cockney vocal. And in the end, it was Bowie and Pitt's decision to walk. 'David came in and said, "I don't think anything's happening for me as a singer,"' says Mendl. 'He told me, "I'm going to go and do dancing – so could I please be released?"'

Mendl had long, tortuous conversations with his friend Dick Rowe, who was in similar straits with Cat Stevens, who left Deram that spring after a bout of tuberculosis. Distressed that the label was about to fall apart, Mendl agreed to let David go, 'but I had the feeling I was being a bit conned'. At the time he thought that the move was perhaps a piece of grandstanding by Bowie, who had some other masterwork up his sleeve. He couldn't have been more wrong.

David's claim that he was planning a new career as a dancer was, for the moment, true. The move seemed bizarre at the time; in retrospect, it marked the transition from an ambitious boy's conventional career progression, to a series of inspired leaps into the unknown. In 1968, with only a couple of decent songs to his name, the twenty-one-year-old David Bowie did not have many of the hallmarks of a great artist. The one that he undoubtedly did have was courage.

This fascinating digression started when a secretary in Ken Pitt's office sent a copy of the Deram album to actor and dancer Lindsay Kemp. Kemp was 'absolutely enchanted by the songs – and by the voice. It was reminiscent of my favourite other singers like Anthony Newley and Jacques Brel; a husky, smokey voice that was plaintive, damaged. And I was able to identify with that.'

The performer started using 'When I Live My Dream' to open his show at The Little Theatre Club off St Martins Lane; David took up Kemp's invitation to come and see a performance, and was 'very flattered' says Kemp. 'And the show fascinated him, with me as Pierrot. And we met afterwards and it was love at first sight.' After the show, David followed Lindsay to his flat in Bateman Street, Soho; there, he beheld a British version of the New York underworld depicted by The Velvet Underground. 'My flat was filled with strippers, hookers, pimps and druggies,' remembers Kemp, fondly. Given the wide-eyed quality of the Deram album, Kemp had assumed Bowie would be 'as innocent as a child' but was proven wrong. 'He looked around, then he sat down – and was completely at home.'

The story of Kemp's life is theatrical, picaresque and rather heroic. Born in Birkenhead, his sailor father was lost at sea when he was two; Kemp's mother encouraged him to dress up and paint his face, then, worried he'd taken to it too well, sent him to Naval College, where he read ballet books and learned to survive by 'enchanting the boys', dancing clad only in red paint and toilet paper. After art college in Bradford, where he was friends with David Hockney, he trained with, and was thrown out by, the Ballet Rambert. Aided by his bald, muscular and blind collaborator Jack Birkett – often billed as The Incredible Orlando – he developed an unconventional hybrid of drag, mime and song and dance, and became one of London's most respected dance teachers, working out of his studio in Floral Street.

Mick Farren, future underground scenester and member of The Deviants, painted backdrops for Kemp along with fellow former students of the Saint Martins school of art. He liked Kemp, but along with many friends, found Kemp's scene intimidating, 'it was a bit like going into the Warhol Factory, if you wanted to hang out you had to learn heavy manners. And David came in, learning moves. He was clearly absorbing a lot – mutating.'

Kemp in person is engaging and sweet rather than intimidating, his natural extravagance revelling in extraordinary yarns that vary with the telling, as he readily admits. Kemp fell in love with David the first afternoon they spent together, when the dancer spent his time enthusing over his passions, which included, 'The theatre, the music hall, silent movies, the Oriental and ritualistic theatre, Kabuki, Jean Genet, the Theatre of the Absurd.' As yet their interests hardly overlapped; it was David's 'great sense of humour' that sealed their relationship, and they would spend much of their time trading impersonations of music-hall stars, or movie icons like Laurel and Hardy.

Kemp says it was a love affair, as well as a working relationship. Within the first few days, David took Lindsay to the Tibetan Society and later David suggested a title for a new work, *Pierrot in Turquoise*, on which they would collaborate: 'Turquoise is the Buddhist symbol for everlasting-ness. And of course I wore turquoise costumes, as a nineteenth-century-inspired clown.'

As plans developed for the Pierrot show, David attended dance lessons at Floral Street. In those days, said Kemp, 'he wasn't a very good mover, but he was equipped with the essential thing: a desire to move. And I taught him to exteriorise, to reveal his soul. And he had all this inside him, anyway.'

Sadly, no complete record exists of the show that Kemp and director Craig Van Roque crafted, based around the ancient tale of Pierrot and Harlequin, with a modern, anarchic slant. The press reviews of the time suggest that the performance was less than the sum of its parts, but that the parts were beguiling. Bowie played 'Cloud', who as well as singing, observed or commented on events in Brechtian fashion: he contributed 'Columbine', one of the finest songs of his folk-rock period, simple and elegant, 'Threepenny Pierrot', a variant of 'London Bye Ta Ta' and, in the early version, 'Maids of Mayfair' – 'A real craftsman's song,' says Kemp's musical collaborator Gordon Rose, who would later take over as MD at the Palladium. 'I can still remember it – it had a theme, a chord sequence and a good hook.'

The plot revolved around Pierrot's unrequited love for Columbine, who is seduced by Jack Birkett's Harlequin. The most memorable scene was 'Aimez-Vous Bach', which depicted Pierrot's despair: the lovelorn character cuts open his belly, throws out his heart and dances away using his entrails as a skipping rope; meanwhile, pianist Michael Garrett improvises around Bach's *French Suites*. Often Kemp would extend the scene well beyond its normal duration, basking in the attention.

The tiny troupe hustled gigs around the country, sending out letters which Kemp and Garrett dictated while the partially sighted Birkett bashed away at a typewriter. Oxford Playhouse on 28 December, 1967, was the first, followed by three nights at Whitehaven's Rosehill Theatre, a jewel-like confection built in a converted barn on the grounds of an eighteenth-century house owned by arts patron Miki Sekers.

Sekers was an Hungarian immigrant who'd founded a celebrated textile company, which made parachutes as well as the silk for Princess Margaret's wedding dress. The textile magnate also donated the silk with which Russian designer Natasha Korniloff crafted the show's brightly hued costumes. Korniloff was also the member of the troupe with a driver's licence; only just tall enough to see over the wheel, she was charged with coaxing their overloaded van, packed with the gang and their costumes, from Oxford up to Cumbria for the run of shows.

According to Lindsay Kemp, Rosehill was also the scene of an hilarious imbroglio that played out in the farmhouse which they took over.

Nestled in a draughty four-poster bed, Kemp heard 'noises through the wall'. Venturing into the cold night, he discovered Bowie cuddling Natasha. 'I was traumatised,' says Kemp. 'Totally destroyed.'

Kemp does admit that a well-publicised subsequent suicide attempt was 'theatrical' – an attempt to slash his wrists which produced only surface wounds. 'Some of those stories *are* exaggerated. And I've given several versions.' One of those stories has his blood drenching his costume in that night's performance, ensuring rapturous applause from the crowd. Pianist Michael Garrett remembers that at one point during the evening, Kemp sat on the edge of the stage, holding the audience rapt with a long soliloquy, inspired by his star-crossed love affair. Kemp and Korniloff were both united in their anger and grief at their two-timing lover, and in their grief: 'We cried on each other's shoulders,' says Kemp. The treacherous Cloud was then forced to sleep on a chaise longue in the hall for the next two nights ('the poor sod'). Despite such backstage shenanigans, says Michael Garrett – who was also besotted with Natasha – the attitude, in sterling showbiz fashion, was always that the show must go on. 'Lindsay was *always* having affairs with a member of the cast, and there were *always* arguments and fights. David was actually a gentleman. In any case, we would always go on-stage sozzled – which helped.'

With the short run of dates finished, the cast dispersed; David would continue to drop in on Lindsay at Floral Street. Time, the great healer, did its work and eventually the dancer's bruised heart 'began to recover' sufficiently for him to continue working with David for more performances in March.

Although he'd largely kept his distance from psychedelia in 1967, David was content to drift along in its slipstream in 1968. He immersed himself in the underground scene, hanging out with characters like Lesley Duncan – the striking, dark-haired songwriter and backing vocalist who later sang on Pink Floyd's *Dark Side of the Moon* – and Jeff Dexter at Lesley's top-floor flat on Redington Road, which offered a breathtaking panoramic view of Hampstead Heath. For a few weeks they had a regular Thursday night flying saucer meditation session where, says Dexter, 'We hoped the flying saucers would come and take us away.'

During such late-night, consciousness-expanding sessions, David would take any spliffs handed around, although he wasn't a committed dope smoker; photographer Ray Stevenson noticed his tendency to 'hold the joint for a bit – and then pass it on'. According to The Lower Third, he'd boasted that he was first turned on to grass by Donovan, and had encountered 'amazing visions', but his drug of choice remained conventional cigarettes, at least a pack a day. During the heyday of acid, David rarely, if ever, turned on – at least, not with the aid of LSD. As Jeff Dexter recalls, he assumed that everyone present at their evening saucer sweeps was into psychedelics, 'but I discovered many years later lots of people who I thought were psychedelicised with me weren't'.

The sessions at Redington Road included meditation based on Tibetan Buddhism, and the participants, including David, had the idea that 'we could all communicate with other worlds', says Dexter. Some observers, including Ken Pitt, suggest David's fascination with Buddhism mainly involved burning a couple of joss sticks; yet David had studied Buddhism with dedication, visiting Tibet House to meet the Lama Chime Rinpoche. His fascination with Tibet also inspired the stately, translucent song 'Silly Boy Blue' which, while obviously influenced by 'Walk on By', boasted one of the most beautiful melodies of his Deram album. While he was never a full-blown devotee, David's Buddhist credentials, says Jeff Dexter, were convincing. 'When I first went to Samye Ling, the monastery up in Scotland, he'd already made an impression with the head monk, Chogyam Trungpa Rinpoche. And he signed the visitors' book before me – so he already had more than a couple of joss sticks.' Other friends, like Ray Stevenson, remember real anger at China's treatment of Tibetan monks. 'He told me all about Chime, and the atrocities that were inflicted – I remember that anger, it stayed with me.'

That year, another key influence entered David's life: Hermione Farthingale. The classy, sweet, red-haired, classically-trained dancer had been hired along with Lindsay Kemp and David for *The Pistol Shot*, part of the BBC drama series 'Line 625', which was recorded in January and broadcast on 20 May, 1968. Much to Kemp's chagrin ('I still had hopes,' he sighs), from the moment they danced a minuet together, the pair were mutually entranced: 'We were twin souls, very alike' says Hermione; 'I was fascinated by him, this fey, elfin creature.' From late January, they were inseparable, and David would frequently frustrate his entourage by 'disappearing.'

David's relationship with Hermione would mark what his friends saw as a transformation in his outlook; he was relaxed, almost playful. Hermione was upper class – her father was a solicitor in Edenbridge – relatively conservative, quiet and 'sensitive', says her flatmate Vernon Dewhurst. 'She was a lovely girl, quite intense, and quite serious, compared to David.' They made a sweet couple; Hermione the more self-consciously intellectual, David the joker. He didn't strike anyone as particularly bookish or highbrow – generally, he was simply a laugh, with a good sense of humour, always joking.

By August 1968, David had moved into Hermione's shared house at 22 Clareville Grove, just off the Old Brompton Road, an elegant street in South Kensington filled with upmarket shops and clubs. The refined but cosy three-storey Georgian house belonged to boutique-owner Breege Collins. Her boyfriend Tom was a literary, 'Henry Miller type'; photographer Vernon Dewhurst shared a back room along with his girlfriend, model and future Bond Girl Zara Hussein, another couple had conventional office jobs and David and Hermione's bedroom was in the attic. The place 'always smelt nice', according to Ray Stevenson. 'You could tell it was mostly girls lived there.' Hermione's sense of style was evident in the Lloyd Loom chair, a vase of dried grasses in the cast-iron fireplace, lace on the bed head, and hessian cushions on the floor.

For nearly six months, in this cosy little setting, David seemed uncharacteristically at ease, content. The songs he played over that time – 'In the Heat of the Morning', 'Karma Man' – were generally elegant, like his surroundings. By sheer hard work and ambition, he had begun to turn himself into a craftsman. Yet David wrote few, if any, new songs that summer; by now it was obvious his career was lagging behind Marc Bolan, who had finally lodged himself in the public consciousness with the Visconti-produced 'Deborah', which reached number thirty-four that May. Bolan kept it basic: rock 'n' roll with some clever word-play and a Donovan yodel. He had achieved something vital; his music was memorable and distinctive. Four years into his recording career, it seemed doubtful that David would ever manage this feat. Although living with Hermione had rubbed off much of his competitive aggression, Marc's success still rankled. 'Oh yeah! Boley struck it big, and we were all green with envy. It was terrible; we fell out for about six months. It was [sulky mutter], "He's doing much better than I am." And he got all sniffy about us who were down in the basement. But we got over that.'

For all his pangs of jealousy, though, David could be proprietorial, happy for his ex-Mod mate, 'they were like brothers', says Ray Stevenson. 'It was a good rivalry,' says Jeff Dexter, 'young blokes' rivalry.' The two were remarkably similar: fey and boyish, confident and flirtatious – and exceptionally talkative. David could expound on a wide variety of subjects compared to Marc, says Stevenson, who points out that Marc's favourite topic was probably himself. David often talked Marc up to his friends, and when Bolan was preparing his debut album, Bowie suggested George Underwood, who'd now turned to art rather than music to make a living, for the artwork. When the album was a hit, Bowie seemed pleased: it marked a calmer, less competitive side of his character, inspired primarily by Hermione.

Bolan, too, enthused about David to his friends, telling them he'd given him an instrument he'd been toying with, the Stylophone, a toy keyboard played with a stylus that features two buzzy synthesiser waveforms and a groovy wood-grained plastic case (Visconti remembers the quirky plastic gadget was actually a gift from Ken Pitt). But there was jealousy there, too; according to Tony Visconti, when David supported Tyrannosaurus Rex at a Middle Earth show on 19 May, Bolan insisted Bowie should not sing; instead, David improvised 'Yet-San and the Eagle', a mime based on China's invasion of Tibet, set to a tape of 'Silly Boy Blue' – a performance that, as MC Jeff Dexter observes, 'takes a lot of front' and was lapped up by the audience, bar a couple of noisy Maoists.

By the autumn of 1968, Ken Pitt was gradually being excluded from Clareville Grove's cosy little scene; his task, it seemed, was fielding letters from Haywood Jones, who was wondering if his son would ever make a living wage from his music. Pitt and Jones had discussed whether the cabaret scene might provide the solution for David's lack of money. The suggestion, says Pitt, came from Haywood and was agreed to by David. Pitt helped Bowie rehearse a routine that included performing some of his own songs to a taped backing, inter-song patter and – in a poignantly ludicrous detail – props in the form of four cut-out Beatles. However, the idea was still-born – one agent who witnessed a run-through told Pitt, 'It's a great act, but where can I book it? It's too good.'

For Bowie and Visconti, the still-born move into cabaret came to epitomise Pitt's out-of-touch, old-school attitude; the growing backbiting between the Pitt and Visconti camps would anticipate many such battles in David's career. In the absence of any clear direction from David himself, Pitt also continued investigating openings for acting jobs, while also hoping to advance Bowie's musical career with a promotional film based around some of his recent material, including 'Let Me Sleep Beside You'. In the meantime, David paid the bills by starting work at Legastat, a photocopy shop frequented by lawyers and barristers near London's High Court.

With the cabaret idea abandoned, David turned his attention once more to the underground movement; after placing an ad in its house journal, *The International Times*, he recruited Tony Hill – previously guitarist with The Misunderstood – to team up with him and Hermione. Named Turquoise, the 'multimedia' trio performed their first show at the Roundhouse on 14 September; for their second show, they renamed themselves Feathers. Hill was unenthused by the trio and left after three shows to form his own band, High Tide.

Fortunately the indefatigable Hutch, David's companion from The Buzz, had left his latest job, in Canada, and returned to London. With a new taste for folk music, a day job as draughtsman for a refrigeration company in Hornsey (which meant he didn't need paying), and his down-to-earth Yorkshire demeanour, he was a better fit for the band than Hill, and found David more congenial than in the old days, too. 'He was happy and relaxed, which I'd never really seen in The Buzz – probably down to Ralph, whose trousers and everything else were too tight. David had come out of that and was happy with Hermione.'

The music, too, was more spontaneous, worked out on the top floor at Clareville Grove, with Hutch on his Harmony six-string acoustic, David on his Gibson twelve-string. David was still searching out new music, absorbing Hutch's new influences, like Leonard Cohen and Joni Mitchell, picked up in Canada, while Bowie turned Hutch on to a new obsession, Jacques Brel.

Bowie had first heard Brel's songs during the period when he was besotted with Lesley Duncan, hanging around her Redington Road flat. They'd briefly enjoyed what David describes as an 'on-again, off-again' relationship; Lesley had recently had a fling with Scott Walker and had the distressing habit of playing Scott's songs whenever David was round at her flat. Initially offended, Bowie became intrigued by the Jacques Brel songs that Walker was singing; once his jealousy subsided he became first a fan of Walker, but more crucially he became obsessed with Brel. When 'Jacques Brel is Alive and Living in Paris' – Eric Blau and Mort Shuman's Greenwich Village show based on Brel's songs – came to London later in 1968, David was in the audience. Hutch spent many evenings at Clareville Grove working out the chords for the Brel songs 'Port of Amsterdam' and 'Next', which they incorporated into their repertoire.

The new trio played their first 'multimedia' show together on 17 November. The common perception of the band, inspired primarily by Ken Pitt, is that their performances were naïve, almost child-like, but Hermione Farthingale points out that 'David is a powerful presence, he's very magical, and I know I have power when I dance. Some of it was obviously youthful stuff, destined to crumble to dust, but there were good parts in there, some of it in embryonic form, of course. It felt exciting – it won't have been everybody's cup of tea, but some of it came off beautifully.' Feathers was the most democratic project of David's career to date. Their set included David and Hermione's dance, to a recorded spoken word piece, Hutch's rendition of Roger McGough's poem 'Love On A Bus', and cover songs like Djinn's 'Life Is A Circus' and a slow, intense version of 'I Am A Man Of Constant Sorrow'. 'The songs were all poignant, a lot of it was actually quite dark, for instance the Jacques Brel songs, which were based on usually unacceptable subjects,' says Hermione. Feathers' sole new recording, 'The Ching-a-Ling Song', was an unrepresentative experiment, an unsuccessful attempt to ape Marc Bolan (the song, says Hermione, was recorded at the suggestion of Tony Visconti, who liked its childish whimsy). Amid the multimedia experimentation, David's songwriting took a back seat that autumn; except, that is, for the song that transformed his career.

David and Hermione's time together had been special. But as the year drew on, the need for money became pressing: 'we were broke, all the time, simply living hand to mouth,' says Hermione, 'my own career as a dancer was put on hold, and it was always a tricky balancing act, constantly paying out for dance classes.' Friends like Hutch speculated the two had a dramatic falling out but the truth was, says Hermione, 'I simply wanted to dance.' In November 1968, Hermione passed through the first round of auditions for the movie *Song Of Norway* – and as she succeeded in each round of casting, their relationship was shot through with 'sadness, and some tension.' David had an 'extraordinary sense of destiny,' Hermione remembers. As pointed out previously, he was a master of positive visualisation, and in this era he began to do so literally, drawing pictures of himself in a new guise or costume to give substance to that imagined future. 'We knew his sense of destiny was there,' says Hermione, 'and I had to tend to mine.' It was in this atmosphere of change, of moving on, that David conjured up a new song, inspired primarily by the sinister, claustrophobic buzz of his Stylophone. Two notes, a semitone apart set up an 'extraordinary wavelength,' says Hermione, that sounded both space-age and spooky, evoking images of astronauts lost in space, inspiring a song that 'just sounded creepy, wonderful, and sent shivers down the spine.'

'Space Oddity' was born fully-formed, and although it has been said that Hutch wrote the opening chord sequence, he points out that he

'Our playground.' Boys playing in cleared bombsites in Lambeth, 1947, ten minutes from David Jones' birthplace. Brixton was a prime target for Nazi terror weapons, thanks to British duplicity. Bombed-out buildings were omnipresent and ideal for adventures.

Below, left: Stansfield Road, David's street. No garden fences, no cars and kids like David's neighbours Graham Stevens, Leslie Burgess and (right) Roger Bolden could wander unhindered. Below, right: 'Always well scrubbed, with clean fingernails'. The polite, neatly dressed David Jones, 1955, a year after the family's move to Bromley.

Burnt Ash Juniors football team with eleven-year-old David Jones (middle row, far left) and his friends Chris Britton (two to his right) and Max Batten (bottom right). 'Bright, with oodles of personality,' he was already a favourite of the school's headmaster and was fast learning how to deploy his charm 'as a weapon'.

David, 1962, in his final year at Bromley Tech (left), and his best friend and bandmate George Underwood – the boy who damaged David's eye in a schoolboy fight. Both aspiring rock 'n' rollers were well known at the Tech, but the dark-haired, outgoing Underwood was more popular: 'Everyone thought he was going to be big,' says school friend Roger Bevan.

The Kon-Rads – initially George Underwood's band – in late 1962 or early 1963. David is on tenor sax, left. 'He just wanted to be part of show business. You could feel it,' says drummer David Hadfield.

The King Bees, May, 1964. David standing with, from left, Roger Bluck, Bob Allen, Dave Howard and George Underwood. Their single, 'Liza Jane', must count as one of the least auspicious debuts by a noted rock star. 'I had real trouble getting it even released,' says manager Les Conn. When it flopped, Davie Jones abandoned George, who went on, initially, to greater success.

The Manish Boys: tough, horn-based blues; nomad lifestyle. From left, Woolf Byrne, John Watson, David Jones, Paul Rodriguez, Mick Whitehead, Johnny Flux, Bob Solly. Their green van was covered with lipstick messages from girls – most of them dedicated to David.

Denis Taylor

David with The Lower Third at the Radio London Inecto show (bassist Graham Rivens is on the left). 'There'd be six girls at the front of the Marquee – and half a dozen of us queens at the back, watching his every move,' says one regular.

Below: The newly christened David Bowie poses with Phil May and Brian Pendleton, singer and guitarist in The Pretty Things, plus Lower Third guitarist Denis Taylor ('me') and drummer Phil Lancaster.

Denis Taylor

Les Conn

'He was brash, sure he was going to make it.' David's first manager, Les Conn, pictured with him in London, April, 1994, was crucial to his first two record deals. Conn was also an early supporter of Mark Feld – the future Marc Bolan.

A rare photo of David's second manager, the elusive Ralph Horton (extreme right, glasses). Devoted to his charge, Horton also set out to split him from his band, The Lower Third.

Denis Taylor

Below: Ken Pitt (in glasses) – the manager who oversaw Bowie's career from obscurity to his first hit – with The Mark Leeman Five (singer Roger Peacock, far right) shortly before he took over David's career. 'He had the right instincts,' says one client, but others considered him too 'gentlemanly' for the cut-throat 1970s.

Ken Pitt

'The most magical person.' David Bowie, June, 1967 – capable of inspiring near obsession in experienced record company execs, but not as inspiring when it came to delivering a hit.

The Riot Squad, April, 1967. Clockwise from top left: Del Roll, David, Butch Davis, Rod Davis, Bob Flag and Croak Prebble. David's short, obscure tenure with the band showed, for the first time, his ability to take risks (and to cover Lou Reed).

merely changed some chord shapes, to add to the ethereal, disjointed feel. The song's distinctive harmonic structure was defined by David's limited guitar style, its lyrics were tightly plotted. The piece was not organised like a song, with verses, choruses and a middle eight: it was more like a work of drama. For the first time, this was a composition that had arrived without conscious effort, or attempt to mimic others – the first song that derived from the unconscious, rather than ambition.

As guitarist Hutch learned the song and worked out a harmony vocal, two points struck him, as they strike today's listener; the simplicity of the melody, and the complexity of the song's structure. The main melody, accentuated by the Stylophone, is two notes, a semitone apart; the most claustrophobic melody possible, the perfect metaphor for the narrator's isolation. Meanwhile, the song's structure is arranged exactly as a play script, with the simplest of chords anchoring the basic opening dialogue, while the melody and chords become more expansive as the story unfolds, and Major Tom steps into the void. As Hutch observes, 'Most musicians make songs with a structure that has been used before – his songs have a structure he dreams up for himself.'

While it's the words that have drawn most attention on this song, it's the harmonic structure that renders it extraordinary. Each chord change manipulates the mood – as Ground Control tells the Major he's made the grade, the chord swerves from the opening line's minor to a cheerily optimistic major, a psychological judder that tells us of the disconnect between ground control and their astronaut. It's a consummate piece of songwriting, the first evidence that Bowie might indeed be the genius he'd said he was, two years before.

'Space Oddity's sense of numbness has also inspired speculation that its genesis involved heroin – rumours encouraged by David in the mid-seventies, when he was playing up his image as a long-term druggie. The idea is ludicrous; David's main tipples at the time were white wine or ginger beer, with a very occasional toke of grass. Instead, the bleakness of the song was primarily inspired by the buzz of the Stylophone, the sadness of an imminent split and a story-teller's imag- ination: 'It's a work of fiction,' says Hermione, 'we were all very caught up in Stanley Kubrick's 2001, and it was a fantasy based on that. A work of the imagination, a poem.' At a time when songs weren't coming in great profusion, 'Space Oddity' was sketched out quickly, an enduring legacy of a period of bliss that was all too brief. Hermione remembers the atmosphere at Clareville Grove as being idyllic, 'an oasis, a beautiful little house shared with people we liked.' That feeling of contentment, unique in David's life so far, would not return for many years. Its loss marked his rise to the star status he'd craved for so long.

According to Ken Pitt, David's new song surfaced after he had asked David to write a 'special piece of new material' for a promotional film he'd been planning for David (the project, says Hermione, was more to do with Ken reasserting control of David as a solo artist). Filmed on Hampstead Heath and at Clarence Film Studio on Deptford Creek, the film featured nine segments, including the trio performing 'Ching-a-Ling' and 'Let Me Sleep Beside You'. The most historically significant section included a studio version of 'Space Oddity', with David contributing a kooky solo on the ocarina. The footage is marvellously camp, all the more so for the wig which David sports, after a hair cut he'd undergone for a tiny TV role in *The Virgin Soldiers*. Bowie puts his Lindsey Kemp training to use simulating weightlessness, before succumbing to the embraces of a pair of space nymphettes.

Without a doubt, the most bizarre curio of the promo film was David's mime of *The Mask*, for which he wears Elizabethan-style white tights, which flatter his pert buttocks and well-packed codpiece. (*The Mask* was always Ken Pitt's favourite,' observes Hutch, tartly.) To his own voiceover, he mimes the tale of a boy who finds a mask in a junk shop, puts it on and finds it holds the secret of fame; and then at the climax, as the hero performs at the Palladium, the mask strangles him.

The short, hilarious film was both gauche and prescient: even as David Bowie attempts to court fame in an almost Variety-style performance, he anticipates its corrosive effects. That ambivalence would be reflected in the months that followed, as he finally achieved the fame for which he'd hungered. As the film revealed, few other artists were as conscious of the duality of fame as David Bowie. Fewer still, once the fame from that first hit had ebbed away, would find themselves even more addicted.

6

Check Ignition

David was adored on all sides. He has to be in that situation,
to get ahead. You could call it manipulation, but what the hell.

Calvin Lee

As 1968 turned to 1969, hippie unity was splintering for ever. Idealism
and whimsy were being shouldered aside by a wave of denim-clad,
blues-riffin' musos preaching a gospel of authenticity. As bands like Led
Zeppelin and Free exploded onto the scene, the elfin, languid 1969 David
Bowie was just as out-of-sync with this new dress-down era as he'd been
in his previous Anthony Newley mode. During that disastrous era he'd
been powered forward by a brash, luminous confidence, and some artful,
unfocused songs. This time around, that youthful confidence had been battered. But he had one crucial factor in his favour: a copper-bottomed classic
song, 'Space Oddity'. It was his ace in the hole, and he played it with a new
subtlety.

Over these months more acquaintances noticed traits that would become
characteristic of the twenty-something David Bowie: the way he'd earnestly
quiz other people, finding out how they ticked, how he'd search out allies
and file them in his mental Rolodex for future use, without mentioning them
to his current friends. Often, he seemed strangely passive, leaving decisions
to others, content to bury his still-bruised ego. As one friend, musician and
International Times writer Mick Farren puts it, 'You got the feeling he didn't
want to show his cards – because he didn't have many to begin with.'

Those who fell out with David in later years often described his behaviour, from this period on, as cold and manipulative; in reality, although
unusually secretive, he was easygoing, following the flow, simply taking

advantage of random opportunities. One such chance came when he was
visiting Barrie Jackson, an old Bromley friend, who'd moved down the road
to Foxgrove Road in Beckenham. Hearing music drifting from the top flat,
Mary Finnigan, another tenant of the same building who was sunbathing
out in the garden, called out, 'Who's playing?'

A few moments later, David came downstairs to share the sunshine
and, says Finnigan, the tincture of cannabis she was enjoying. A week or
so later, in April 1969, David moved in to stay with Mary and her two
children at 24 Foxgrove Road. His friends had only just noticed the absence
of Hermione, who after completing *Song of Norway* had joined the Welsh
National Opera. They missed David's companion, but were impressed
by how quickly he'd lined up a replacement. 'We were very jealous,' says
David's friend Ray Stevenson, 'he never had to pay any rent.'

Mary Finnigan had an impeccably middle-class background, but after a
brush with the law and conviction for drugs possession – ultimately over-
tuned – with a consequent brief stretch in Holloway Prison in 1967, she had
taken up the hippie cause as a writer for *International Times*. She and David
soon became lovers, and the singer became her new cause; within three
weeks she had helped organise a regular Folk Club at the Three Tuns on
Beckenham High Street; by its fourth week, on Sunday 25 May, the venture
was titled the Beckenham Arts Lab, and eventually started drawing in street
musicians, puppeteers, poets and other artists. Working with the eclectic
group of volunteers, David immersed himself in mime and the visual arts,
as well as music. The group became his main focus of activity, soon after his
partnership with Hutch came to an end. The Yorkshireman had spent many
intense evenings throughout the spring working on material with David
after a long day in the office. In April, when a hoped-for deal with Atlantic
for the duo failed to materialise, Hutch returned up north, in search of a
decent salary to support his wife and young son. David seemed unconcerned, but later Hutch heard he'd been telling his friends, 'Hutch thought
we were never going to make it.' It seemed, Hutch thought, that 'David
simply had no grasp of the concept of having a family to feed.'

With Hutch's departure, David immersed himself in Arts Lab meetings.
The group boasted two formidable administrators in the form of Finnigan
and Nita Bowes – later an adviser to Tony Blair, and daughter-in-law to
Tony Benn – who pursued government grants and talked of setting up a
countrywide network of arts organisations. The pair would dominate their
debates; David more quietly spoken but earnest and thoughtful, as happy
talking about puppeteers and street theatre as about music. According to
Keith Christmas, one of the main musical draws along with David, the

audience's motivations were not as high-falutin' as the organisers'. 'It was a terrific gig from day one. Because the pub looked quite normal from the front, but at the back was a large room and conservatory, with its own entrance. So people could get down there and get off their faces in the warm evenings.'

Throughout the Art Lab period, David's talk was peppered with fashionable underground sentiments; yet a few people close to him at the time wondered how profound his conversion to the cause was. Alan Mair is one of several who were 'not 100 per cent sure about the hippie trippie thing. I thought his mind was somewhere else.' But David's hippie collectivism and talk of being 'off his face' did at least signal his independence from Ken Pitt – who viewed such attitudes with abhorrence. Keith Christmas, later a leading light of the folk revival spearheaded by Fairport Convention and others, was certain that Bowie was a fellow traveller, although not necessarily for cynical reasons. 'He recognised there were groovy people – and he liked groovy interesting people. And he knew that most of the big talent was making acoustic music, so he wasn't slow to have a go.'

For David Bowie, the hippie movement represented a seam of inspiration to be mined, rather than a guiding philosophy. Even while he was taking his foot off the career accelerator, at heart he remained a traditional entertainer. 'Space Oddity', a highlight of his Three Tuns set, embodied this contradiction. It would be the perfect sixties anthem, with its trendy sci-fi theme and rejection of materialism. Yet, as friends like Tony Visconti believed, it was a gimmick song, just like Joe Meek's 'Telstar', and to get it released, David would have to indulge in plenty of old-school, music-biz networking.

Fortunately, David had fallen in with one of London's finest networkers back in June 1967, at a party in New Bond Street. Calvin Mark Lee was a doctor in pharmacology, who'd won a grant to pursue postgraduate research under the internationally renowned Professor Arnold Beckett in 1963. Deciding his criteria for meeting people were that they be 'beautiful, creative and intelligent', and that scientists rarely ticked all three boxes, Lee's new project would be Swinging London. Soon the thirty-three-year-old's social circle included Lionel Bart, fashion boutique Dandy Fashions' John Crittle, acid king Stan Owsley, Monkee Mike Nesmith and Jimi Hendrix. The influential, wayward folk singer Anne Briggs was briefly his girlfriend, and a wall of photos, many naked, in his King's Road flat diarised his eclectic social and sexual acquaintances. If that were not enough to mark his exotic status, Calvin Lee wore on his forehead a glittery plastic disk – a diffraction grating, which shimmered in the light like a hologram –

which proclaimed his starchild credentials, as it would Ziggy Stardust's a few years later.

Lee had met David at a reception at Chappell Music Publishers three weeks after the release of his Deram album in 1967. From early 1969, when Lee was given an expense account by Mercury Records and a role as Head of Promotions for the label, he became an integral part of David's social scene, which was now fiendishly complicated. Lee explains, 'David was adored on all sides. You have Ken, you have me, you have Hermione. So there were certain amounts of jealousy.' The two, says Lee, shared a sexual relationship that was remarkable partly for its brevity. He remembers David's incessant, crippling headaches, which he believes were 'brought on by all these various tensions'. Today, he wonders if David's flirtation with him was partly driven by ambition. 'He has to be in that situation otherwise you don't get ahead. You could call it manipulation, but what the hell.'

Still, Calvin understood David's music, and he was one of the first to hear 'Space Oddity'. He considered it 'other-worldly', in every sense, and set about a mission 'to clandestinely push David Bowie'.

Lee had an ally at Mercury named Simon Hayes, who had come to the label's attention as manager of The Fool – the London design collective that Mercury had, in a bizarre move, signed on the basis that they'd painted John Lennon's Rolls Royce and were therefore the next best thing to having The Beatles themselves. Hayes negotiated the band's deal with Mercury before being offered the job of Head of International A&R by the company's co-founder, Irving Green, in January 1969. Hayes and Lee knew each other from the London fashion and art scene, and according to Hayes, 'Lee was really on the case with "Space Oddity", a total convert. He wanted to sign David – and I said, "Fantastic idea."' David Bowie would be his first major signing.

The process, however, was fraught with complications, thanks to the labyrinthine corporate and internal politics of the Mercury Philips empire: an organisation described by Philips manager Olav Wyper as 'a disaster'. The UK arm, Philips, was a joint venture between Mercury USA and the Dutch electronics conglomerate; the American company also retained its own London office, overseen by Lou Reizner.

Reizner had his own musical ambitions; his best-known achievements would be overseeing the soundtrack for The Who's *Tommy* and the disastrous *All This and World War II*, which set Beatles covers to black-and-white wartime cine footage. He also fancied himself as a singer and saw Bowie as a rival, which meant Calvin Lee had to work surreptitiously to advance his friend's career.

Reizner's dislike of Bowie would soon be intensified by another figure in the web of relationships that surrounded the singer. An American girlfriend of the Mercury exec, who was also involved with Calvin Lee, had declared her fascination with David Bowie after accompanying Reizner and Lee to a Feathers show at the Roundhouse in January 1969. Her name was Angela Barnett.

As Mark Pritchett, a long-term friend of David Bowie's, puts it: 'Angela Barnett was a complicated character at the time – let alone now.' Pritchett's description is as apt as anyone's. In future years, Angela Barnett, who had arrived in London in the summer of 1966 to study at secretarial college and later enrolled at Kingston Polytechnic, would claim to be a key figure in securing David Bowie's new record deal. In fact, the key figures in the signing, notably Simon Hayes, remember Angie's involvement as peripheral in this early stage – but she would become a prime mover in almost every aspect of his career for the next four years.

In 1975, David Bowie would tell writer (and later film director) Cameron Crowe that he met his future wife 'because we were both going out with the same man'. The guy was Calvin Lee, and Bowie's boasts about his own bisexuality would become a key element in his public persona. Angie was the co-creator of this persona, yet her contribution to David's career went much further. From the moment she appeared on the scene, following her first 'date' with Bowie on 30 May, 1969, Angela Barnett electrified everyone around her. For, as Ray Stevenson puts it, 'She was a bit of spunk. She was American. The English sit around whining; Americans get out there and do things.'

The couple first met over a Chinese meal with Calvin Lee – and on his expense account – after which the trio carried on partying at the Speakeasy, where King Crimson were playing one of their first London shows. As they sat, talking and flirting, Angie thought the Mercury promotions man was trying to serve her up as a kind of sexual delicacy for the singer he'd helped sign. Angie dominated the conversation, as was her habit, while David's remarks were mostly drily amused, savouring the electric atmosphere; the two even looked quite similar, with their clear skin and almost elfin features. That night, David returned with Angie to her tiny flat above a travel agent's in Paddington.

It was on a morning shortly after this that Angie and David first mapped out the pattern they would follow during their time together. She knew full well from the outset that he was 'like an alley cat' but nonetheless succumbed to a bout of jealousy – or theatricality – when he told her he was leaving, and threw herself down the stairs. According to Angie, David stepped over her on his way out of the door without batting an eyelid, and quietly took his leave.

For the time being, Ken Pitt remained blissfully unaware of Angela Barnett's existence, and exchanged letters with Simon Hayes over April and May 1969, as the Mercury A&R man put together a deal. With Hayes largely absent in New York and Chicago, David Platz and Essex Music took charge of the recording session for the song that had so impressed Hayes and Lee. Earlier in the year, Ken Pitt had tried sending a demo of 'Space Oddity' to George Martin, hoping The Beatles' producer would agree to oversee a Bowie recording. After chasing him for several weeks, Pitt eventually found out from Martin's secretary that he was unimpressed. There was a more surprising knock-back to come – from the man who'd produced all of David's recent material, namely Tony Visconti.

Today, the stripped-down bleakness of 'Space Oddity' gives it a certain purity. Yet that purity belies its origins, for most of those concerned in releasing it considered it a good song, distinguished mainly by the marketing opportunity it represented – namely the Apollo moon landing scheduled for late that July. It was a good gimmick. According to Simon Hayes, the notion that the single would tie in with that July's moonshot was what drove the signing. 'Everybody was always looking for a hook – that was it.'

Even while Tony Visconti threw himself into planning the album that would follow 'Space Oddity', he disliked the song itself. 'I didn't like the idea of capitalising on the man on the moon,' he says today. 'I thought it was a cheap shot.' For a 'principled hippie', Visconti's celebrated distaste for the song made sense at the time, though today he concedes, 'I've grown to like it a bit.' Meanwhile, having rejected the song, he would help ensure its eventual success by suggesting several of the key figures in its recording – a role he would adopt for many subsequent David Bowie works, even ones that did not bear his name.

The imminent Apollo launch meant that contractual negotiations, and the session, needed tying up quickly. Gus Dudgeon, who had recently joined the Essex empire, worked in the next office to Visconti, who called him up and suggest he take over the song. Dudgeon, who knew David well though their work on the Deram album, thought Bowie's demo of the song was 'unbelievable. I couldn't believe my luck. I had to phone Tony just to make sure he wanted me to do it. He claimed there was a lot of better stuff on the album, at which stage Bowie and I sat down and planned the record – every detail of it.'

The session was tightly budgeted and choreographed: Dudgeon sketched out a plan, adorned with squiggles denoting a Stylophone or

Mellotron part, Visconti suggested guitarist Mick Wayne and keyboard player Rick Wakeman, then still at music college, while string arranger Paul Buckmaster was another Essex contact. Only the rhythm section were experienced hands – drummer Terry Cox had played with Alexis Korner and Pentangle, while bassist Herbie Flowers had been working sessions since he'd been talent-spotted by Paul McCartney in 1967.

The recording session for 'Space Oddity', on 20 June, 1969, was one of those rare occasions where everyone involved sensed its historical importance. According to Gus, 'When we hit that studio we knew exactly what we wanted – no other sound would do,' although there were happy accidents that changed the final result. Guitarist Mick Wayne thought he'd finished an early take and was about to retune a bass string on his Gibson ES-335, but Dudgeon liked the effect of the warped note swamped with reverb and told him to repeat the sound on the next take. Rick Wakeman, who played the Mellotron, found that 'it was one of half a dozen occasions [in my career] where it's made the hair stand up on your neck and you know you're involved in something special. "Space Oddity" was the first time it ever happened to me.' Terry Cox remembers the consensus that a breakthrough was finally imminent, 'That excitement definitely did transmit itself to me, too.'

The sense of event was heightened by the presence of Calvin Lee, waiting to hurry the tape off for mastering. 'I remember him coming in and whipping it off to the factory straight away,' says Dudgeon, 'that's how things were on that day.'

Less than three weeks after the session, the single had been pressed and was released to an enthusiastic critical reception; one of the most welcome reviews came from Penny Valentine in *Disc*, who was not only respected, but who also had a nose for a hit and pronounced that the record 'is going to knock everyone senseless'.

Outside the perfection of that single session, though, confusion reigned. In America, Mercury were sufficiently confident of the single's prospects to greenlight work on an album, which started on 20 July. Yet Philips in the UK were disorganised: with UK MD Leslie Gould under notice that he was to be replaced, it was Essex – David's publishers – who took control of the sessions. Planning was nonetheless sketchy; according to Visconti, the album was mapped out at a meeting between him, Bowie and David Platz. 'As David's previous album was all over the place musically, the master-plan was to keep him on course with one style.' Visconti envisaged a folk-rock sound, based around David's twelve-string guitar, and suggested using Mick Wayne's band, Junior's Eyes, whom he'd recently produced; they were likeable, younger and less expensive than the usual session musicians, just 'a bunch of blokes he could hang out with', says guitarist Tim Renwick. The band – which Renwick and drummer John Cambridge had joined only recently – knew little about David, 'only the "Laughing Gnome", so we didn't know what to expect'.

For his Deram album, David had been confident in overseeing the music; this time around, it seemed much of that confidence had been knocked out of him. During their introductory chat the band found him 'kind of nervous and unsure of himself', says Renwick. 'He was a bit of an unlikely solo artist – a lot of solo artists are very pushy and egocentric [but] he wasn't like that at all.' David was strikingly vague about what he wanted. 'There was very little direction,' says Renwick. 'It was odd that there wasn't a figure saying, "That worked – that didn't work."'

John Cambridge would be David Bowie's drummer for the next nine months; crucial months in the singer's musical development. This was a time when David, according to legend, was an 'ice man': battling inner demons, using and discarding musicians like worn-out guitar picks. In contrast, Cambridge found David energetic and jokey, 'but not pushy'. Instead, he was content to be led, most notably by his new girlfriend, who became a permanent fixture that summer.

Visconti, too, while enthusiastic, was reluctant to take control. 'I was not a very good producer yet and I hadn't started to engineer. I had only made the first Tyrannosaurus Rex album and the Junior's Eyes album,' and his inexperience was noticed by the band. They all liked him, but thought he was 'sort of over polite', says Renwick. The album which emerged from these seemingly directionless sessions was not orchestrated; it was busked, cooked up on the spot, which gave it a delicious tension. For even as Bowie was turning his back on hippie values, he was reliant on people like Mick Wayne – who was talented, shambolic and 'very druggy' – to give shape to his vision.

The sessions – at Trident Studios, in a little Soho alleyway – were drawn out over the summer and early autumn. A session would be booked with no pre-warning of the songs they would be working on, and the day would start with David sitting on a high stool with his twelve-string, saying, 'I've got this one.' After playing through the song acoustically a couple of times, he'd smile at the band and ask them, 'Shall we have a go?' For his acoustic numbers, assisted by Keith Christmas, the process was even more basic. And thus David Bowie's second album was pieced together.

The rather shambolic recording – which Visconti describes as 'personal and warm in many ways but often ragged' – would make this album unique in David Bowie's catalogue. His intricately worked words were set against a loose, hobo backdrop where, on songs like 'Unwashed and Somewhat Slightly Dazed', the results are obviously influenced by Dylan's first electric sessions. Other obvious touchstones include Tim Hardin – whose crystalline, descending chord sequences are echoed in both 'Cygnet Committee' and 'Wide Eyed Boy From Freecloud' – or Simon and Garfunkel, snatches of whose 'Mrs Robinson' pop up in 'Letter to Hermione'. The overall effect mirrors the David Bowie that everyone from that time remembers: intense but passive, intriguing but introverted.

The lack of direction afflicting David was entirely explained by his personal life: for as Visconti explains, 'Calvin Lee was besotted with David – and his hidden agenda was to have him as a boyfriend. But Angie, who arrived on the scene during the recording of the album, squashed all possibility of that.' The business backdrop was even more chaotic; Calvin Lee was operating in a semi-official capacity, posting out promo copies of the single after hours and offering encouragement at many of the sessions, which were then interrupted by 'a nerdy American character, Robin McBride, from Mercury', says Visconti. '[He] turned up on our doorstep and we were told that we were all answerable to him. I despised him.'

As weeks elapsed after the single release, the machinations around its creator became more complex. Before the sessions, David had told Visconti that Ken Pitt was too old school. 'After the record,' he stated, 'I'll be dropping him.' Pitt, meanwhile, pushed the single by sending polite letters to BBC Radio, *Top of the Pops*, and other outlets, augmenting his efforts with an attempt at chart-rigging in a deal with a shady character, who offered to massage the single into the Record Retailer chart for £100. Pitt acceded, ultimately handing over £140 in total; but the single languished outside the Top 40. To this day, Pitt remains slightly shamefaced about the episode; according to other figures in the industry, Pitt's distaste for getting down and dirty was a crucial failing. 'Ken was too gentlemanly,' says Olav Wyper, later general manager of Philips. 'He thought the way to make this a hit was to put money in somebody's pocket. Which wasn't enough.'

The American release was even more confused. Simon Hayes had received an early pressing of 'Space Oddity' and played it at Mercury's Wednesday sales conference in Chicago. 'Everyone had been excited about the record. But when they heard it they all said: "This is a sad story about a guy lost in space. And we're gonna release it when there's a space shot happening – and there's a real possibility we could lose a man in space?"'

With Mercury presidents Irving Green and Irwin Steinberg fast losing their nerve, there was a rush edit, says Hayes, which censored most of the references to Major Tom's fate. It must have made for a very short record. The single was eventually released in a modified US edit 'with absolutely no promotion behind it', according to Hayes, 'and it died a slow death, as these things do'.

Blissfully oblivious of all the corporate machinations, David was genuinely excited as the moonshot approached on 20 July. He, Angie and Ray Stevenson stayed up for the TV coverage. Stevenson found it disappointing, 'It was dull, black and white fuzzy footage of people walking slowly,' but observed, 'David was very excited.' David later described his state as 'over the moon! And they used [the single] as part of the background track – I couldn't believe they were doing that. Did they know what the song was about?'

According to Stevenson, the most memorable part of the evening was when Angie announced, 'I'm going out for a walk,' and then, on her return, 'suddenly she's seen them – little green men, and all this nonsense'. Ray was impressed by Angie, but it was at this point that he started to have 'doubts'. If David was sceptical, he concealed it. 'He humoured her – and asked all the questions that a charming person would.'

Amid the mess of people competing for David's attention – 'vampires and predators' as Ken Pitt terms them – Pitt was especially suspicious of Angie's influence, seeing her presence behind disturbing aspects of David's behaviour, including an attempt in June to negotiate an advance with publisher David Platz, behind Pitt's back. Partly to re-establish his pre-eminence, Pitt organised a trip to a pair of music festivals in Malta and Pistoia, Italy, at the end of July. Bowie would sing 'When I Live My Dream', judged sufficiently MOR for such events, against a backing tape but the main purpose of the trip, says Pitt, was merely the prospect of 'a little fun and sun'. Angie dropped in for the Italian leg of the trip – savouring Pitt's suspicious reaction – following which David and Ken returned to London, in David's case directly on to a show at the Three Tuns. It was only when David arrived in Beckenham that he received a message that his father was ill. He seemed to sense the situation was serious. 'Someone else can host tonight,' he yelled at his fellow volunteers, 'just get me home.'

Ray Stevenson was enlisted to drive David to Plaistow Grove, where it was obvious that Haywood's condition was grave; he'd been suffering from lung complaints for some years, probably linked to his heavy cigarette habit, and had now succumbed to pneumonia. Sitting down at the kitchen table with Peggy for endless cups of tea, Ray found David's mum was relatively composed while David was 'Panicky. It was obvious he really loved his dad.'

David spent most of the next two days at Plaistow Grove. On 5 August, 1969, he called Pitt to tell him his father had died. Pitt joined him at the house, where he sorted through Haywood Jones' papers. They had been left in perfect order. 'He was always wonderful,' says Pitt. 'I wish he could have witnessed David's success.'

John Cambridge, the Junior's Eyes drummer, was becoming closer to David as the sessions continued; he speculates that his broad Yorkshire accent and dry humour reminded David of Haywood. A few days after his father's death, David told John that his phone had rung several times at 5.30 a.m. 'I'd pick it up and there was no one there,' he told John. 'I just knew it was my dad seeing if I was all right.'

Poignantly, the most significant live show of David Bowie's life to date came on 16 August, just five days after Haywood's funeral. The Beckenham Free Festival had been planned for several months, and included every member of Bowie's social circle, with the notable exception of Ken Pitt. Mark Pritchett, who was reading his poetry on the day, met David early in the morning, when he was buoyant, fired up by the beautiful weather and the feverish activity. Short of microphones, they drove round to Mark's house in Haywood Jones' tiny Fiat 500 to borrow some. 'Good grief!' David laughed as they pulled up on Southend Road. 'I've just taken the lease on the place opposite – we'll be moving in in three weeks. Come and see us!'

The afternoon was frenzied for all involved. Even those who – like photographer and blues musician Dave Bebbington – thought David's new girlfriend was too pushy were impressed by the way Angie 'made things happen', selling burgers from a stall to raise cash. Every Arts Lab member was busy with some assignment at the Beckenham Recreation Grounds, whether it was PA, moving gear, puppet shows or impromptu street theatre events. The event was endearingly amateurish – DJ John Peel, who was scheduled to MC, was replaced by a medical student from Blackheath named Tim Goffe; local bands playing blues or Chuck Berry numbers dominated the bill, which included Keith Christmas, Bridget St John and The Strawbs.

As David's afternoon performance approached, however, the mood turned sour, 'a combination of stage fright and thinking about his dad', says Pritchett. Dave Bebbington, who photographed David's solo set from onstage, remembers, 'There was little chat in between the songs; you could tell he was thinking, I have to be a trouper, I'm going to play my set and go home.'

For Mary Finnigan, the day had started stressfully with a missing van and PA; it got worse that afternoon, when she remembers David calling her and Lee 'materialistic assholes' as they totted up the day's takings. 'I don't remember him being unpleasant,' says Bebbington, 'just detached. He wanted to go home.' David was absent from the celebratory curry at an Indian restaurant on Beckenham High Street that night; there were complaints from some, says Bebbington, that 'David [was] being really shitty.' Bizarrely, no one seemed to link his mood with the fact he'd buried his father five days earlier. The bickering, and the fact that Mary had been supplanted by Angie as David's lover and muse, signalled the end of David's close involvement with the Arts Lab, which, for David, had become a place where 'everybody wanted a piece of him', says Bebbington.

When David came to commemorate that sunny but overclouded Bromley afternoon a few days later in the recording studio, he was in a sweeter mood. Charmingly homely, with a tiny Woolworth's reed organ carefully miked up by Visconti, 'Memory of a Free Festival' would be, along with 'Cygnet Committee', a highlight of David Bowie's second album. Where 'Cygnet Committee' was complex, having evolved out of an earlier song, 'Lover to the Dawn' – its lyrics a densely argued dissection of hippie values – this song was simple, poignant, and evoked the ambivalence that had enveloped David that year. When he sang, 'Oh to capture just one drop of all the ecstasy that swept that afternoon', the melody sweeps upwards with yearning for a hippie nirvana that others thought they had attained, but which he knew he hadn't. A jewel of a song, it ended in the glitzy tinsel of a chorus borrowed from 'Hey Jude', a comedown perhaps, but as Tony Visconti points out, 'in the shadow of The Beatles it was hard to have an original idea in those days'.

'Memory of a Free Festival', one of the last songs to be recorded, would close David's Philips album, which bizarrely featured the same eponymous title as its Deram predecessor. It was an appropriate farewell, bidding good-bye to the hippie culture – and, in several instances, people – that had nurtured Bowie for the last nine months. Mary Finnigan and Calvin Lee, who left Mercury later that year, were two more people from whom David moved on, as he and Angie settled in to Haddon Hall, the Southend Road house he'd pointed out to Pritchett.

With the confused welter of emotions that surrounded his father's death – which included grief, sympathy for his mother, and irritation at the constant arguments with her – it's hard to decipher Bowie's feelings at the modest success of his purported breakthrough single, for in the wake of the moon landings, 'Space Oddity' slipped into the UK charts at number forty-eight, on 6 September, 1969, before dropping, seemingly, into oblivion.

For most of the Philips staff, that, it seemed, was that. But they had not reckoned on Olav Wyper, the company's newly appointed general manager – young, dynamic and handsome, with an Action Man jutting jaw that signalled his can-do attitude. Before joining Philips, Wyper had discussed the job with his secretary Sue Baxter, whom he planned to bring with him from CBS. Enthused about the move, she remarked, 'That company has been a disaster for two years – but at least by the time we arrive they will have a hit on their hands.' Intrigued, he'd gone out and bought 'Space Oddity'. 'Sue told me it was a sensational record, and she was right,' he says.

On his first day in Mercury's Stannard Place office, Wyper was surprised to notice that the sales, promotion and marketing staff were sitting around with no new releases to work on, 'So I asked, "Well, what happened to that Bowie record?" "Oh, we tried, but it didn't go anywhere."' With nothing else to promote, Wyper set the entire staff on to 'Space Oddity'. 'This never happened before or since,' says Wyper, 'it was purely because we had this three-week window with no major releases.'

In the last week of September, 'Space Oddity' jumped up the charts to number twenty-five, rising steadily to peak at number five in a fourteen-week chart run.

When David's album was released on 4 November, he was up in Scotland for a short series of shows backed by Junior's Eyes. By now the band were at their peak; a 20 October BBC session, with its superb version of 'Let Me Sleep Beside You', easily surpasses their work on David's album, and offers a tantalising glimpse of how that earlier material could have sounded, had it been worked up live first. But they were 'odd gigs', says guitarist Tim Renwick, 'A couple were quite rough – on one there was a cage up front in case the audience got out of control.'

David was nervous, slightly out of place amid the hard-bitten, hard-working band. Most of them were heavy dope smokers, especially Mick Wayne and his wife Charlotte, who were, 'eyes on the wall, very stoned, always'. There were lighter moments – Junior's Eyes singer Graham Kelly remembers Bowie throwing down a gauntlet to him after a few drinks in a vegetarian restaurant, after which they raced through the frozen Edinburgh Streets, Bowie on the bonnet of his car, Kelly on the bonnet of the band's Transit.

After the success of the single, David's second album shuffled out in a rather half-hearted manner. By now, Calvin Lee's relationship with Mercury was troubled, much to Ken Pitt's glee, and Olav Wyper, who'd championed 'Space Oddity', was 'completely underwhelmed' by the album. 'I think

David had too much control of the album, and didn't defer enough to Visconti,' he suggests. Visconti, meanwhile, is 'not particularly proud' of the work, 'I don't think David had settled on who he was as yet.' David, tellingly, says of this period, 'I was looking for myself,' which provides some explanation for his behaviour. One friend describes it as 'weak, almost', mentioning his reliance on people like Angie and, before her, Mary Finnigan, to deal with his disagreements with Ken Pitt or others.

Today, *David Bowie* is unique in its creator's catalogue thanks to its endearing lack of artifice. Yet even at the time it was obvious it lacked the acuity and intensity of folk rockers like Tim Hardin or Simon and Garfunkel. While the *Observer*'s Tony Palmer famously rhapsodised over David's 'quite devastatingly beautiful' looks, the reviews mostly commented on the thoughtful lyrics and suggested that Bowie was a follower, rather than a pioneer. Even Bowie's own pronouncements to writers like *Music Now*'s Kate Simpson betrayed his awareness that he lacked a convincing, coherent worldview, shown by his praise for celebrated right-wing politician Enoch Powell for at least standing up for a cause – 'whether it's good or bad is not the point'.

More worryingly, Simpson's feature mentions her friends' perception that David was a 'one-hit wonder', a dread phrase that would crop up with monotonous regularity over the next few years. Obviously intelligent, he nonetheless lacked the talent of, say, John Lennon for encapsulating an agenda in a song, or a sentence. Six years after he'd formed The King Bees, David had scored his first hit single, yet the underwhelming impact of his album seemed to rob him of all momentum. To many, he simply seemed all over the place.

Yet, for a few key people, David's live shows – notably his showcase at the South Bank's Purcell Room on 20 November – still demonstrated not lack of focus, but bravery. BBC producer Jeff Griffin was about to stake his reputation on an innovative series of 'In Concert' broadcasts the following spring, opening with Led Zeppelin. When he saw Bowie at the Purcell Room, Griffin was 'blown away. I'd read about him working with Lindsay Kemp, but it wasn't until I saw him there that I realised there was far more to him than the average rock star . . . he was doing brave things, singing Jacques Brel songs. He was one of those rare performers who just had that extra dimension to him, something that's hard to describe.'

Fascinated by the fact that Bowie had moved on so dextrously from his 'twee, but fun' Deram debut, Griffin pencilled in a Bowie show for the spring. By which time, David would have moved on again.

7

All the Madmen

It was all a bit of a mess. But in the centre of all this chaos, mayhem and noise, David was extremely relaxed.

Mark Pritchett

It was their Graceland: the ostentatious, rambling and slightly decaying headquarters where David and Angela Bowie enjoyed marital bliss, interior decoration and sexual frolics. Innocent teenage American girls would one day walk in and fondly imagine themselves as imprisoned in some re-imagined Victorian melodrama; cynical journalists would enter its imposing hallway and be overawed by the Bowie mystique. It was a location where the realignment of the musical and fashion values of an entire decade would be hatched.

Angie had spotted Haddon Hall, at 240 Southend Road in Beckenham, back in the summer of 1969. Beckenham, a relatively green and leafy suburb celebrated mainly as the home of *Noddy* author Enid Blyton, was just down the road from Bromley. Angie and David agreed to move into Flat 7 early in September and established themselves there at the end of the month. The building was the epitome of crumbling magnificence, an opulent High-Victorian family house, which even at the time struck resident John Cambridge as reminiscent of Elvis's grandiose Memphis home.

The building, which boasted a magnificent entrance hall, was divided into flats; David and Angie's flat was on the ground floor, but they also had the use of the staircase, which led the visitors up to a small half-landing, dominated by a magnificent Gothic stained-glass window; from there the staircase divided, ascending to a gallery at first-floor level which gave on to a set of sealed-up doorways, later commandeered as sleeping space. Tony Visconti and girlfriend Liz moved into Haddon Hall in December, taking the back bedroom on the ground floor, and sharing a huge living room, complete with lavish open fireplace, with David and Angie; soon Tony had persuaded Mr Hoys, the owner of the house, to let him build a rehearsal space in the basement.

Royalties from the 'Space Oddity' single – which by January had sold 138,656 copies in the UK – trickled in slowly, but the single's success pushed up the fee for David's live bookings up to a magnificent £100 or more. Flush for the first time in his life, David took to spending money like a duck to water. After passing his driving test and returning his father's Fiat to Peggy, he bought a Rover 100, complete with luxurious leather seats and walnut dashboard, while he and Angie became familiar figures at the antique shops on Old Kent and Tower Bridge Roads, acquiring Art Deco lamps, William Morris screens and mahogany chests of drawers.

The establishment of their own palace at Haddon Hall marked the crowning of Angie as queen to Bowie's king. It was an impressively fast rise to power, but even for her most recent acquaintances, it was no surprise. Born in Cyprus in 1950 to an American mining engineer father and a mother of Polish extraction, educated at a British boarding school in Montreux, Switzerland, Mary Angela Barnett was self-sufficient, energetic and irresistibly loud. She revelled in telling listeners of her scandalous expulsion from Connecticut College for Women for a lesbian affair, and to most Brits – in the era before affordable transatlantic travel – she seemed ravishingly cosmopolitan. Brought up in sophisticated, international surroundings, she was as at home scrubbing Haddon Hall's wooden floorboards to erase the smell of cat pee as she was at distinguishing a genuine Art Nouveau light fitting from a reproduction.

From spring 1970 onwards, as John Cambridge puts it, 'You met Angie before you met David.' Their union would always be as public as it was personal, like the celebrity liaisons brokered by Hollywood PRs anxious to maximise their column inches. Cambridge was one of those people who found Angie irritating – 'too domineering and shouting' – and saw at first hand how Angie would force David into decisions he wanted to evade, notably firing Ken Pitt.

The first public statement of their love affair was 'The Prettiest Star', the only new song David wrote over the winter of 1969. (Absence made his heart grow fonder, for Angie disappeared to see her parents in November, partly to flee from Peggy's phone calls accusing her of 'living in sin'.) Languid and uncharacteristically simple, it would be almost unique in Bowie's canon: a conventional love song, its lyrics speculating on their future fame as a professional couple, 'you and I will rise up all the way'.

As an anthem to Angie, it was appropriate that 'The Prettiest Star' also marked the passing of Ken Pitt's influence. Ken Pitt dropped in to Trident for the session – an event that was becoming comparatively rare. It was around 1 a.m. on the morning on 8 January – David's twenty-third birthday – and as Pitt wandered around the control room he exchanged only a few words with Bowie and Tony Visconti, who were chatting to Godfrey McLean and Delisle Harper, drummer and bassist from Gass, a funky Santana-ish band that Visconti recruited for the recording. Photographer David Bebbington watched Pitt tell no one in particular that he'd just dropped in to see another of his clients, Billy Eckstine, at the Talk of The Town club. Bebbington started to feel embarrassed at how Ken was being cold-shouldered. Pitt proudly mentioned how he'd been working with Eckstine for twenty years, and Bebbington briefly admired Pitt's loyalty before wondering what Eckstine – once a cutting-edge bandleader, now a mannered MOR crooner – had in common with Bowie. When Pitt left the studio a few minutes later, no one else seemed to register he'd gone.

A second visitor was, initially at least, more welcome. It was at Tony Visconti's suggestion that Marc Bolan dropped in to play lead guitar on 'The Prettiest Star'; and while mutual friends at the time remember Marc being brotherly to David, on this, their only official joint recording, their rivalry soured the atmosphere. 'He came in and it was daggers,' remembers Visconti. 'Everyone's having a good time, then Marc comes in and the atmosphere chilled up.'

Visconti had spent a good few days vibing up Marc, who was enthusiastic about showing off his newly acquired electric guitar skills and had carefully prepared his guitar melody. David, too, was upbeat, complimenting Marc effusively, when June Bolan suddenly broke into a tantrum, bitching, 'The only good thing about this record is Marc's guitar.' Marc hurriedly packed up his Fender Strat, and the pair left without another word.

The squabble highlighted the tension that would always exist in the relationship between David Bowie and Marc Bolan. Marc had always enjoyed talking up David, but having predicted 'Space Oddity' would be a hit, Marc seemed irritated to be proven right. This was a clear illustration of how the teenage 'arrogance' that Les Conn remembers derived from different causes. David was generally happy when his friends did well; Marc wasn't. What was confidence in Bowie equated to bravado in Bolan – a distinction for which June Bolan had an explanation, which she shared with Ray Stevenson. 'She had this theory, it was because Marc had a small dick and

David had a monster. A lot of their personalities come from this: David can charm the girl and know that through to the conclusion of this encounter he's not going to disappoint. Marc couldn't.'

David made a good show of seeming unconcerned by Marc's petulance – he was cheerful on the drive back to Beckenham in his Rover in the small hours of the morning, buying a huge Chinese takeaway on the way and spreading it over the dashboard. But though he might appear calm in the face of such troubles, his music often suffered from the confused mess of personalities surrounding him during this period; he relied, more than most, on others. That night's show at the Speakeasy typified the confusion. Tim Renwick – now David's preferred guitarist ahead of Mick Wayne – was booked at the last minute, but found David's passivity and lack of direction irritating. 'It wasn't like, "Right, here we go." It was more like "What's next?" and then nothing.' John Cambridge wasn't even told there was a show; he'd turned up for a drink at the 'Speak', along with Junior's Eyes' 'Roger the roadie', only to be asked at the last moment, 'Do you have your drums?' Fortunately, he kept them in the boot of his Mini Minor. The last-minute request marked his debut as Bowie's official drummer.

Soon after the Speakeasy show, Cambridge also moved into Haddon Hall, and came to enjoy the eccentric domesticity. In later years, Haddon Hall would become celebrated for its sexual excesses. Yet the atmosphere was more Bloomsbury Set than Haight Ashbury: Angie made an excellent hostess, greeting visitors effusively, proffering tea or biscuits. At other times there were schoolboy japes – David and John Cambridge chasing each other round with water-pistols or exchanging deadpan Yorkshire banter. Cambridge's humour was celebrated, sometimes witty and so dry it would take the listener several seconds to register. ('Maybe I overdid it,' he reflects today, 'Angie didn't always appreciate all me jokes.')

The deliciously *fin de siècle* ambience at Haddon Hall became even more obvious when Angie found a housekeeper, in the Edwardian shape of Donna Pritchett, who lived across the road and whose son, Mark, a pupil at Dulwich College, had been drawn into the Arts Lab set. Donna ruled the kitchen, cooking up a Sunday roast in an emergency, or dispensing endless cups of tea. She would generally brook no nonsense, chiding David if he burnt the furniture with a cigarette; David and Angie were adept at charming her, sending her greetings cards or little notes written on the back of a ten-shilling note – 'David was cute like that,' observes Mark.

In fact, David proved remarkably chipper over the period, far more resilient to the poor sales of the Philips album than he had been to the fate of his Deram debut – the influx of money from the 'Space Oddity' single helped, of course. But there was a more traumatic source of disquiet in his personal life, one that he voiced publicly in the final days of the Arts Lab. There was a constant flow of new volunteers through the organisation, and during one of their 'getting to know you' meetings, David introduced himself to those sitting around him with the words, 'My name is David. And I have a brother in Cane Hill.'

Most of those present were unaware David had a brother, but nearly everyone was aware of Cane Hill. Built in 1882, the asylum was a huge, purpose-built Gothic complex intended to provide a more sympathetic, modern environment for the 'incurably insane', with extensive grounds and outdoor pavilions from which the inmates could enjoy views of London. Nevertheless, the building, on a commanding hill in Coulsdon, ten miles south-east of Beckenham, was regarded as a terrifying place, famous locally as the insane asylum which had housed Charlie Chaplin's mother, who had been confined to a padded cell and hosed down with freezing water, as a primitive antecedent of electro-shock therapy. The establishment was more enlightened in the 1960s, but there was a justifiable fear for inmates and their relatives that once they'd walked through its imposing gates, they would never return. As Hannah Chaplin told her son when he visited her, 'Don't lose your way – they might keep you here.'

After his National Service in the Royal Air Force and move into Plaistow Grove, Terry had enjoyed a brief period of apparent domestic harmony, which was nonetheless often overshadowed by the effects of his illness. It was during this period that David had taken Terry to see Cream in Bromley, and witnessed the effects of what was later diagnosed as schizophrenia. For a time after this, while he stayed with mother and step-father, Terry's condition was stable, but in the wake of Haywood's death, he deteriorated. Peggy – who was in the process of moving to a flat on Albermarle Road in Beckenham – was unable to cope with her son, precipitating his move to Cane Hill. Peggy, according to friends, found the prospect of visiting Terry at the hospital too traumatic to endure – instead, her sister Pat would attend with her husband, Tony Antoniou.

Around 1969 and 1970 – the first time David had a home of his own – David was also able to provide shelter for his half-brother, and at various times Terry would be seen around Haddon Hall, on release from Cane Hill. He met many of David's closest friends during this period, and was friendly, sometimes chatty – especially about football – and sometimes confused. But in the long term, David proved as unable to cope with Terry's illness as his mother.

Those who saw David and Terry together were never in doubt that, as Mark Pritchett remembers, 'Terry adored his brother . . . and he was a lovely chap.' David obviously loved and respected Terry, citing him again and again as the source of many of his key musical and literary interests. But the principal emotion that Terry inspired in his half-brother was, says Pritchett, 'guilt'.

In the opinion of David's aunt Pat, who publicly chastised David for his lack of attention to Terry in the 1980s, that guilt was justified: in her view, David simply turned his back on his half-brother. In fairness, there was probably little he could have done. Ray Stevenson, who spent a lot of time around Haddon Hall as Terry's mental health deteriorated, points out, 'I've known some schizophrenics and there is not much you can do to help – they are how they are and it's horrible. You have to just not think about it. So I'd never slag him off for it.'

Bowie's fear of the madness in his family would become a common theme – it's the stuff of classical drama, and has been a prism through which many have chosen to analyse his career, despite the lack of evidence to support it. Throughout this period, David was notably calm, controlled: he couldn't have seemed more sane. Yet, as anyone who has been emotionally close to someone suffering from schizophrenia or paranoia will know, 'madness' is contagious; the descriptions of a schizophrenic's visions can be more affecting, seem more convincing, than genuine, banal experiences. When he wrote songs, David's empathised with his half-brother; in everyday life, David felt helpless. Terry's plight was always an issue that David dealt with in song, rather than in reality, with the result that, says Mark Pritchett, 'David built up a lot of guilt about him. And I think the darker songs are actually tributes to him.'

With 'The Prettiest Star' as yet unreleased, few performances to occupy him, grief for his dad, troubles with Ken, and the traumas of Terry and Peggy, it was hardly surprising that Bowie spent much of January 1970 cocooned at Haddon Hall. To make matters worse, his band, Junior's Eyes, was falling apart. Mick Wayne's increasing ingestion of drugs caused most of those around him to agree with singer Graham Kelly, who says, 'I loved the guy – but working with him was a nightmare.' By the end of January, every member of the band knew they would split; the only question, as singer Kelly remembers, was 'Which way would people jump – and who would go with Bowie?' With the BBC 'In Concert' session scheduled for 5 February, David needed to move quickly.

Tim Renwick was the obvious front-runner for guitarist. But John

Cambridge, the first official recruit to David's outfit, had another prospect in mind, a ferociously talented guitarist who'd played in his previous band, The Rats: 'I'd been pestering [David and Tony] to death, so finally I go down to Hull to find Mick Ronson. I knew where he worked, I arrive and he's creosoting this training ground, I'm telling him I've got in with this band in London, David Bowie, it's really good, and it needs a guitarist. And he's going . . . "Oh I don't know, I got in with a band in Sweden and was ripped off and I'm not about to do that again." So I'm thinking, I just pestered them two to let me come down here – and now I've got to pester him to go up there!'

Cambridge's persuasion worked. Ronson turned up for the band's show at the Marquee on 3 February; after the show the guitarist commented enthusiastically on the performance, as was his way. 'Even if it was shite, Mick would still say it was good,' Cambridge explains. The drummer introduced Bowie to Ronson at the venue, but David was distracted; only when they all returned to Haddon Hall and Ronson picked up an acoustic and started to play did Bowie register him. At that moment, as Tony Visconti describes it, 'Everything was starting to click into place.'

Mick Ronson's career had interlaced with Bowie's over the past five or six years, through fellow Yorkshiremen like John Hutchinson, who had shared the bill with The Rats at venues across the north-east. Born and raised in Hull – once a prosperous and confident Victorian city but, by the late sixties, already gripped by a long-term industrial decline – Mick Ronson was a unique musician, cut-throat in terms of his musical ambition, but remarkably laid-back when it came to advancing his own career.

Local musician Keith Herd witnessed one of Ronson's first tentative shows with his band The Crestas, and bumped into the guitarist regularly in the local music shop, Cornell's. In 1967, after Herd set up a tiny recording studio in his front room, Mick turned up with his new band, The Rats, 'and I couldn't believe how he'd come on'. Playing a Fender Telecaster, Ronson had mastered 'heavy guitar – using the amplifier and volume to get incredible sustain. It was the first time I'd ever heard it done.'

The four-minute long mini-opera that The Rats constructed, 'The Rise and Fall of Bernie Gripplestone', was Who-influenced, distinguished exclusively by Ronson's howling guitar. Although there are shades of Hendrix, Townshend and Mick's principal guitar idol, Jeff Beck, Ronson's playing was already unique; concise, tough rhythm guitar one moment, wildly fluid lead the next, made all the more thrilling by Ronson's talent for bending a note to scary extremes – a unique trick that, according to bandmate Trevor Bolder, he'd mastered thanks to a fingernail on his left hand that was so tough and hard it was 'almost deformed'. Nocking the string into a groove on the nail, he could bend it almost clear across the neck of the guitar. By the end of 1968, when he picked up a Les Paul Custom from Cornell's and plugged it into his Marshall stack, he had become Hull's unchallenged guitar hero.

Good-looking, with his flint-sharp face and boney nose, Mick was friendly, a typical muso: his conversation revolved around music and women; if he ever saw someone ogling his guitar he'd nod and encourage them, telling them, 'Go on, have a go.' Then he'd shake the new acquaintance's hand, enthusiastically. He was open-minded musically, as keen on harmony pop like The Move as heavy rock. And like the rest of The Rats, says bassist Keith 'Ched' Cheeseman, 'he was a piss-taker'. Often, the 'piss-taking' was directed at suggestions that The Rats change their 'winning' formula. And by the end of 1969, Cheeseman noticed that although Mick had been indisputably the best musician in Hull when the bassist had first joined the band, one year later younger rivals were gaining on him.

Mick Ronson, with The Rats, had enjoyed staying in his comfort zone. With Bowie and Tony Visconti, though, he was wrenched right out of it. The process started that Saturday, which he spent huddled with the pair, hurriedly learning songs for Jeff Griffin's 'In Concert' on Sunday 5 February. It was a huge coup for Bowie to headline the new series – Marc Bolan, in contrast, was a last-minute substitution for half of a show – and David's use of a guitarist he'd met two days before was a massive risk; an early example of the inspired gambles that would come to characterise his career.

The 'In Concert' show represented another Bowie first: his use of the BBC to prototype the next phase of his work. From its opening moments in front of a small audience at Regent Street's Paris Cinema, with a gritty, solo version of Brel's 'Port of Amsterdam', there is a new toughness and sense of adrenalin. Familiar songs like 'Unwashed and Somewhat Slightly Dazed' sound Dylan-esque and faintly worthy – until Ronson hooks his mutant fingernail under the guitar string and, for the first time in Bowie's career, the listener is in real doubt as to where the song is heading (a feeling shared by Ronson, who gets a couple of chords wrong). Nonetheless, it's his drawn-out, exhausting guitar work that inspires announcer John Peel to pronounce the song 'a bit of a treat'.

'The Width of a Circle', heard here for the first time, shares the sense of danger; Ronson's guitar lines seamlessly interlacing with Bowie's bashed-out acoustic chords, while Visconti's bass guitar is relentlessly fluid and inventive. There are few recordings where we get to hear a band gel, in public, for the very first time; this is one of them. Ronson's influences are apparent – the modal melodies evoking Hendrix, the twin-note Memphis scale taken from country licks – but are instinctively incorporated into a coherent style. In the process, David Bowie's style becomes coherent, too.

After the concert there was muttering about missed endings, wrong chords, the fact that 'it was a bit crap really', says Cambridge. But the fact the performance was 'raw as fuck' was part of the excitement, 'You could see even then that was a lot better. Mick lifted it.' 'It was incredibly exciting,' remembers Tony Visconti, 'because we knew Mick was going to work out – he had something we needed.'

Rickety and sporadic as it was, Bowie's short tour from the end of February, 1970, would be his first with a proper, consistent band since the Lower Third days. Ronson had no second thoughts about joining up, but there were fleeting suggestions of augmenting the line-up with Tim Renwick, who turned up at Haddon Hall to be checked out by David and Angie. 'My girlfriend came with me and Angie was checking *her* out – I remember thinking, Blimey, this is odd.' Angie perhaps didn't approve, but in any case Renwick needed paying – and Ronson was happy to play for free. For days, he and David immersed themselves in practice at Haddon Hall, sitting opposite each other. John Cambridge would drop in to see how it was going. 'It would be just the two of them in the bedroom with the guitar. I'd go in and they'd say, "Hang on John we're just doing this." In other words "piss off".'

Ronson's arrival galvanised the Haddon Hall crew, and the languor that had overcome David since his father's death seemed to evaporate in the run-up to the band's debut at the Roundhouse on 22 February.

While Bowie and Ronson practised, Angie went shopping for their clothes, assisted by Mark Pritchett. 'Tony was working out of Oxford Street and we all met there in the morning but lunchtime and the whole afternoon was spent, Angie and I, scurrying around theatrical costumiers to dress them all up.'

It was in this brief afternoon, spent scurrying around Charing Cross Road and Fitzrovia, that the foundation of David Bowie's image throughout the 1970s would be laid. In the mid-sixties, he'd become a pretty convincing Mod; since that time, his attire had reverted to a vaguely post-hippie style, his hair curled in what Ken Pitt thought was tribute to Bob Dylan; with his flowery shirts and afghan coats, David could have passed for Eric Clapton in his Cream heyday of 1969 or so. In his previous incarnations, David was pretty, tasteful, or cool. It was Angie – and, later, Chelita Secunda – who would push him to be outrageous.

With Pritchett in tow, Angie masterminded the band's flamboyant attire during that afternoon's shopping: a gangster outfit, with fedora, for Ronson, who was given the title Gangsterman; a leotard with an 'H' sewn on the chest for Visconti, the Hypeman; a cowboy outfit for John Cambridge; and a multicoloured, diaphanous concoction, with scarves attached to a lurex shirt, for David – Rainbowman.

Ken Pitt claimed credit for naming the band, remembering that after Bowie had told him, 'This is one big hype,' he said, 'Well, why not call it The Hype?' But it seems David may have got the idea from photographer Ray Stevenson, who suggested the name only for David to respond, 'We can't use it – Led Zeppelin's publishers are called SuperHype.' According to Jeff Dexter, who introduced the show, the name only started being bandied around after the fact. 'They'd just said the name casually – it was only after certain people caught on that it crept into the vocabulary.'

There was no doubt that the Roundhouse show was a major event; the 'In Concert' performance alerted fans that Bowie was unveiling a new work in progress, and many friends from the Three Tuns turned up for the band's support slot to Noel Redding's short-lived band, Fat Mattress. Mark Pritchett was one of them, and actually remembers the performance being 'a bit of a mess'. Ronson was using a 200 watt Marshall amplifier stack that totally overpowered the other musicians. 'People expected quite a lot,' says Pritchett, 'and what they got was much of *Man Who Sold The World* at thunderous volume. A lot of that material suited thunderous volume – and a lot of it didn't. So it sounded a bit of a mess.' Yet there was one thing Pritchett did notice: 'At the centre of all this mayhem, chaos and noise David was extremely relaxed'.

The show later would be seen as a crucial staging post on the way to glam, not least because Marc Bolan turned up and, says Visconti, watched the show in rapt attention, his chin on the stage. The band's theatrical outfits drew ridicule, according to Visconti, but David, who had seen how Lindsay Kemp could carry off the most outrageous outfits, was buoyed up by the reaction. Just as crucially, as Mark Pritchett observed, 'David was moving.' His body language had entirely changed: the costumes, the artifice and the raw power of Ronson's guitar had unlocked the carefree joy of David's early R&B days.

David seemed well aware he'd turned a corner. 'You could tell he knew a band was good for him,' says Pritchett. During the sporadic run of dates that continued through February and March he was relaxed, enjoying his trip to Hull for a show at the university on 6 March, hanging out in the refectory with a tiny group of fans and bemused students. Angie's presence seemed to register with them as much as the band's. 'David and Angie had identical curly hair, similar skinny build, you know how people who look a little similar to each other can fall in love?' remembered one student, who shared a table with them.

For David, the failure of the single celebrating his and Angie's infatuation was the only disappointment of an otherwise idyllic spring. Released the day they sat chatting in the refectory, 'The Prettiest Star' slipped into oblivion with less than 1000 copies sold. For Ken Pitt, the release of the single confirmed his opinion of Angie as a 'predator', and his fears that influence was irretrievably slipping away from him were confirmed in March, as the two planned their marriage.

In later years, as she came to terms with their celebrated and rancorous split, Angie would publicly doubt that David had ever loved her; indeed, some of her accounts of their decision to marry quote him as asking, 'Can you handle the fact that I don't love you?' On another occasion Angie has described how the pair realised they were in love during their separation over Christmas 1969, which Angie spent with her parents in Cyprus, eagerly awaiting letters. After a ten-day postal strike, she received a card on which were written the words, 'We will marry, I promise, this year.'

Today, Angie retains much of the ebullience and enthusiasm that made her so magnetic back in 1970, but the emotional damage she's sustained since that time causes her to ascribe darker, exploitative motives to most of her ex-husband's behaviour. At one point, she tells me, 'I don't know *anything* that David's done that wasn't for his own benefit.' Again and again we return to the topic, only to find her unable to contemplate any other interpretation.

Most of David's own pronouncements over the years support this bleak picture. When David talked about their marriage at the time, he did so as if it were a brand. After their catastrophically nasty split, he could hardly bear to mention Angie at all. Yet those who were emotionally close to Angie and David in their early days ascribe purer motives to their relationship. Ava Cherry, who would later become David's official girlfriend even as he stayed married to Angie – an official position akin to that of the King's mistress in the French Court – concedes, 'I do think he had love for her,' before pointing out, 'I'm giving her props she would never me.' Ava adds, 'She was nurturing, and he needed that,' but more importantly, 'he liked the way she thought.'

Scott Richardson would later occupy a corresponding position to Ava Cherry's, as Angie's official lover and David's music buddy, and he too states, 'It was genuine, a real thing. They tried to have a new kind of marriage, an open marriage, and it was absolutely brilliant what that represented.'

Angie and David's relationship had been an open one from the day they met. Angie, she says, signalled that the same would apply after their marriage, when she arranged for them to spend the night before their 20 March wedding in bed with a stunning dark-haired actress they'd met via Calvin Lee. Ken Pitt had heard about the wedding from Peggy, who disapproved of Angie, but nonetheless decided to turn up uninvited. It was a tiny gathering; John Cambridge was one of just three men, along with Roger the Roadie. Mick Ronson was absent and Visconti was working. David had asked Cambridge to act as witness; but when the registrar called out, Peggy, seated a couple of rows from the front, got up to sign the register. David looked around at John, and shrugged his shoulders. The wedding reception was a drink in a nearby pub.

The unique nature of the Bowies' marriage was brought home to John Cambridge a couple of days later, when he went to the Speakeasy with David and Angie. They were close friends by now, and John had often heard David frolicking with other women at Haddon Hall, but was shocked to see David dancing with 'a bloke'. 'But they only just got married!' John remembers thinking. Seeing him watching, Angie grabbed John's hand and tried to pull him onto the dance floor. 'I turned around, that wa'ant the way I was brought up. I'm only nineteen, still really naive.' Only years later did he wonder whether shocking his young drummer, and enjoying his reaction, was part of the appeal for David. And the intriguing possibility remains that David's enjoyment of the nineteen-year-old's embarrassment inspired 1972's 'John, I'm Only Dancing'.

The chutzpah of David's new wife would have a transformative effect on David's career in several crucial aspects: one of her first acts was to persuade Philips' Olav Wyper to advance £4000 to The Hype to fund living expenses, PA system and new tyres for the van, which had arrived at Haddon Hall along with Rats roadie Roger, also known as Roger the Lodger.

With The Hype now on their way to a semi-official status, it was time to make their studio debut, in this case with a wonderful reworking of 'Memory of a Free Festival', recorded on 3 April and to be issued as the US follow-up to 'Space Oddity'. To hear each instrument warming up, and then to hear Ronson's guitar take the song by the scruff of its neck and thrust it forward is even now a thrilling experience, in which the listener can hear Bowie's career snapping into shape.

The session would also mark an ending, too. There had been a last-minute postponement of the session due to a double-booking with a live show in Scarborough, arranged by Ken Pitt. Ken had sent a note to Haddon Hall confirming the live date, but the confusion crystallised David's dissatisfaction with the man who'd overseen his career for the last three and a half years.

Some time in March, David called Olav Wyper's office to ask if they could meet. 'He was clearly very depressed – at times very tearful,' says the Philips boss. 'He said he's reached this impasse with Ken, and their relationship was getting in the way of where his career should be going. And he asked, What do I think, and how can I help him?' In later years, Wyper wondered whether David's tearfulness was calculated; if so, it had the desired effect, making him side with the vulnerable singer. As general manager of David's record company, he had a duty to avoid a conflict of interest, but after asking David if he had a copy of his contract with Ken – which he hadn't – he gave him the names of three firms who could advise him. The first entry on the list was a pair of people whom Wyper knew well, who had decided to go into business together just a few weeks before. Their names were Laurence Myers and Tony Defries.

In the spring of 1970, Laurence Myers was well known around the London music industry, principally as a management and accounting expert whose clients included Mickie Most. Myers was meticulous, well connected through his role as a show-business accountant, and was in the process of establishing his own management company, to be known as Gem or GTO.

Tony Defries had come to Myers and Wypers' attention as a lawyer with the legal firm of Martin Beston. Wyper had many friends who happened to be photographers, including Terence Donovan, who had called in Martin Beston to help with copyright issues; Tony Defries was the lawyer assigned to their case. Wyper attended the meeting where Defries pitched for their business. 'Tony was very bullish – he had a very firm attitude, and a belief that right was with him. I was very impressed.'

Only later did Wyper happen to meet another solicitor from Martin Beston and discover that the go-getting lawyer he had seen in action was not exactly what he seemed. 'Tony was very clever. He described himself as a lawyer [and I] assumed he was a solicitor. And then I found out later that Tony was a solicitor's clerk. He *was* a lawyer, which is defined as someone working in the field of law, but not what I assumed.' Winning over an audience on first impression, and leaving details until later, was part of Tony Defries' style.

Defries and Myers' position on the list provided by Olav Wyper meant that, fatefully, they were the first to be called. There were several meetings throughout March, and Myers remembers being impressed by David Bowie. 'I liked him – and I knew David was a special artist.' But over their first discussions, it turned out to be Myers' business affairs manager, Defries, who realised the potential of the young singer hoping to discard his manager. As Myers admits, it was Tony Defries who had 'the vision. His great ability was, far more than I did, he knew what a star David was going to be.'

The exact degree to which Defries was convinced by David's potential on their first meeting, in which David poured out his troubles, is hard to gauge. But David's dilemma appealed to Defries' problem-solving abilities. He assured David that he could extricate him from his contract with Pitt. Pitt, in the meantime, had no concrete evidence of David's dissatisfaction, until a meeting at his office on 31 March, when David finally told him, 'Ken, I'd like to have a go at managing myself.' The news came as no surprise, says Pitt – 'I'd heard of at least one other management team who'd offered David something' – but after promising to cut down on the live dates, and giving David a cheque for £200, it seemed the matter was settled, at least as far as Pitt was concerned. He continued to oversee arrangements, like the fast-approaching sessions for the next Mercury album.

The decision to rid himself of Pitt steeled David's resolve in other respects. During a BBC radio session produced by Bernie Andrews on 25 March, a dry-run for the album sessions, John Cambridge found a skipping bass drum part too tricky. David and Ronson were both calm and patient. 'Course you can do it, come on,' Ronson kept repeating, and Cambridge managed to finish the session. But within the next fortnight, John was gone. His replacement was Mick 'Woody' Woodmansey – who had taken John's place in The Rats when Cambridge left after being asked to rehearse on Easter Bank Holiday. A more expansive drummer, and a more serious, forceful personality, Woodmansey's complex rhythm patterns and extravagant rolls suited the band's move to a freer, more improvisational sound. Visconti, though, admired Cambridge's solid, no-frills drumming, and was surprised to see it was Mick Ronson, rather than David, who had instigated the sacking.

When it came to music, it seemed Ronson was every bit as unsentimental as Bowie. And as the album recording began, on 18 April at Trident, it was the guitarist who commanded the sessions, moving into the realm of recording with the same intensity with which he'd mastered the guitar. Visconti, whose studio experience far outstripped Ronson's, fondly remembers that 'It was Mick who was our guru – anything he told us to do, we'd do.' It was Ronson who worked on arrangements, persuading Visconti to switch to a Gibson short-scale bass for a more fluid guitar-like sound, wrote out synthesiser lines for Ralph Mace, or even duetted on recorder with Visconti. Mick was omnipresent, dominating the texture and the mood of the album christened *The Man Who Sold the World* – in stark contrast to Bowie, who was at times, says Visconti, 'just plain difficult to nail down'.

David had been remarkably unassertive during his first Mercury album; this time around, he seemed more confident, but still often surprisingly casual, leaving huge amounts of work to Ronson and Visconti, who points out, 'As a novice producer I just couldn't understand why David wouldn't want to be in the studio every minute with us.' In recent years, David has occasionally seemed needled by Visconti's comments, pointing out his own, dominant role in the writing: 'Who else writes chord sequences like that?' But Ken Scott, engineer on the session, also remembers Ronson and Visconti dominating every aspect of a record from which Bowie was largely absent. 'Tony and Mick did take over. How much it was David not wanting to have anything to do with it, and how much was Tony taking over I don't know. But I think it was more Tony's ideas [on the album] than David's.'

Visconti's frustration with Bowie derived more from 'them and us' divisions than any musical disagreements. David's infatuation with Angie was understandable, but more galling was the fact that 'David was the only one out of all of us who had money in the bank, from "Space Oddity", while we were living on nothing.' These strange, sometimes pleasant but often dysfunctional circumstances were the backdrop for what would be Bowie's first great, albeit flawed, album. In his previous works, there had been little emotional commitment: 'Space Oddity' encompassed simple alienation, and even in a sweet, personal song like 'Letter to Hermione' he'd sounded disappointed rather than distraught. Yet for this album, he could ride on the wave of noise created by Ronson and Visconti, using them as a vehicle to intensify his own emotions.

The recording of *The Man Who Sold the World* encapsulates an issue that would resurface throughout David Bowie's career; how much was his own work, and how much that of his subordinates? For detractors – using arguments which parallel those who criticised contemporary artists like Andy Warhol, who simply mapped out concepts and left associates like Gerard Malanga to produce their screenprints or movies – this reliance on his sidemen was a flaw.

Visconti's own feelings on the subject are complex, but he summarises his own account by stating, 'With a smile on my face, I have to say that Mick and I couldn't have made such a stunning album with anyone else.' The meaning seems simple: that the album is a Ronson and Visconti album, with David Bowie, as opposed to a David Bowie album with Ronson and Visconti. Yet the ownership of the album is complex, for Bowie unlocked a creativity in both Ronson and Visconti that might otherwise have remained dormant. In his Lower Third days, David's songwriting consisted mainly of outright theft. The moral position here was more nuanced. Without Bowie, Visconti and Ronson's collaborations, as the band Ronno, were utterly forgettable. Can one really 'steal' something that, without you, wouldn't exist?

In Bowie's frequent absences Ronson and Visconti laboured over several songs, notably 'She Shook Me Cold', 'Black Country Rock' and the middle section of 'The Width of a Circle', all of which emerged from band jams, with Ronson leading the way. Bowie took the lead for 'The Man Who Sold the World', 'Saviour Machine', 'The Supermen' and 'After All'; but even in these songs, Bowie acquired, almost by osmosis, Ronson's musical aggression, with the guitarist's twisted lead guitar encouraging him to explore the most twisted, dark themes he'd so far attempted.

'All the Madmen' was a touchtone of the album: imposing and disturbing, its theme of madness, and the musical swerves from child-like whimsy to imposing, gothic heavy rock, were taken by many as an illustration of Bowie's alien nature. This interpretation, however, overlooks its unique genius, for it is in fact a work not of alienation, but of empathy. The lyrics, delivered with a Syd Barrett-like childishness, address Terry's move to Cane Hill – 'a mansion cold and grey' – in almost literal terms. Its talk of being 'high' on the 'far side of town', rather than alluding to drugs, or to Christ being tempted by the devil, refers simply to Cane Hill's vantage point over London. There is an almost unbearable sadness about David's declaration that 'I'd rather stay here with all the madmen', alongside Terry, than remain outside Cane Hill's walls, with all 'the sad men'. That this was a wish David proclaimed in song, rather than acting on it in real life, adds to the song's poignancy.

The intensity of the sessions overpowered occasional weaknesses. 'She Shook Me Cold' was a straightforward knock-off of Hendrix's 'Voodoo Chile'. Yet the conviction with which the song is delivered, and the unique timbre of Bowie's voice and Ronson's guitar, make the song gel in a way that David's previous *homages* had never achieved. For the first time, David's material was transcending its origins.

The same applied to David's lyrics. Many of the references were conventional post-hippie fare, from Nietzsche – endlessly name-checked by Jim Morrison – to Kahlil Gibran, whose books Bolan had posed with on *Unicorn*, Tyrannosaurus Rex's third album. Whether David was a true adept of the philosophies he name-dropped is doubtful. Mick Farren was, as much as anyone in 1970, in the London intellectual vanguard, through his work with *International Times* and membership of the band Pink Fairies. A casual friend of Bowie, he describes him as, 'a bit of poser. Everyone was. Except where some people would read a book jacket and bullshit, David would bullshit, then read the book quietly one Sunday afternoon.' Today, David confirms Farren's take, describing his philosophical investigations of the time as mainly consisting of 'keeping a book in my pocket, with the title showing'.

Still, if the scholarship was sketchy, it worked emotionally. 'The Man Who Sold the World' – its title at least surely influenced by Heinlein's celebrated *Man Who Sold the Moon* – is the most poignant. Under- rather than over-written, it is all the more unsettling because of its simplicity. Ronson's insistent opening riff is claustrophobic and vaguely menacing, as is the narrator's meeting with a man: 'although I wasn't there, he said I was his friend'. Over two simple verses, multiple meanings emerge – all of them disturbing, speaking of death or loss of identity. Ronson's guitar line for the chorus is childishly simple, as are the lyrics. But the guitar scales that punctuate the chorus march endlessly upwards, like a never-ending staircase – representing an eternity spent wandering. Like 'All the Madmen', the song is disturbing, with an emotional intensity that was new to Bowie's work.

The complex, emotional environment that gave birth to *The Man Who Sold the World* became murkier still when on 27 April, halfway through the sessions, David wrote to Ken, informing him he now no longer considered him his manager and asking him – in mis-phrased legal jargon – to confirm within seven days that he would cease acting as such. A week later, he and Tony Defries were at Pitt's Manchester Street office. Defries was low-key, but did all of the talking; as would become his style, he confronted the problem head-on but left troublesome details until later – in this case, compensating Pitt for the money he'd invested in David.

For Pitt, the meeting was devastating. In hindsight, the warning signs were obvious, but David's defection came as a cruel, unforeseen blow. All those around him at the time, including Wyper, remember him being obviously traumatised – but also touchingly anxious to ensure David's career wouldn't suffer. Today Pitt details a host of arrangements he had planned for Bowie – which included a trip to New York on a Cunard liner, using all of his Warhol connections – all of which might well have filled out the career limbo in which the singer would still soon find himself. When considering the suggestion that he was too gentlemanly for the music industry, a shadow passes over Pitt's face before he responds, 'Perhaps I wasn't assertive enough. But my God, I put my hand in my pocket and spent the money on David, which they weren't doing over that period.'

In those early post-Pitt days, Defries played a fatherly advisory role: in the main, he simply talked about solving problems. He was not particularly proactive at first, but was an accomplished name-dropper, who seemed to have a unique sympathy with the artistic temperament. He described how he would protect the precious items that they created, their intellectual copyright, as if it were a religious calling, and explained how he was at the cutting edge of such a process, liberating artists from the clutches of incompetent record companies.

The Man Who Sold the World was completed on 22 May, but as the tapes were handed over to Philips, the record company was once again embroiled in problems that seemed to justify Tony Defries' cynicism about record companies. For towards the autumn of 1970, he discovered that Olav Wyper, his champion at the label, was being ousted. David faced being an orphan artist.

The loss of Wyper was soon followed by the disappearance of Tony Visconti and Mick Ronson. Their defection would become a well-known staging post in David Bowie's career. Another setback is, in comparison, obscure. For by the end of the year, the new manager who promised to champion David Bowie had disappeared, too. Just at the point when he'd demonstrated how much he needed supporters to help realise his vision, David Bowie would be at his most alone.

8

Kooks

It will either be a disaster, or everything will be hunky dory.

Peter Shoot

It's the middle of 2007, and Tony Defries is holding forth. It's an impressive spectacle: the way his conversation flits from subject to subject – analysing hidden patterns and trends, switching from science fiction to steel mills, the Second World War to electronic substrates – is enthralling. His voice has an upper-class languor, but he's proud of his street-urchin credentials, and while his talk is grandiose there's an engaging practicality to all of his high-falutin' claims, a delight in the nuts and bolts of contracts, an innate understanding of how companies are organised, and a disdain for those who lack the command of such essentials.

This is the man whose two role models, Colonel Tom Parker and Allen Klein, are two of the most controversial managers in the history of rock music. Fittingly, Tony Defries is the third. Like Parker, he was an integral part of his client's rise to fame. Like Allen Klein, he and his best-known client suffered the most rancorous and public of splits.

Defries is a master of the Big Lie: telling the masses his client was huge, when he was as yet strictly small-time; manipulating the truth on every level to advance his client; creating a fake reality that would have been envied by a Hollywood press agent of the thirties. But then there is the little lie: the notion that Tony Defries took a chance on David Bowie when he was a washed up, one-hit wonder. For as those who were at the centre of it all testify, the reality is rather different.

*

Soon after Wyper's disappearance from Philips, Tony Visconti left Haddon Hall. He and his girlfriend Liz moved out in July for practical, household reasons – Haddon Hall was getting crowded – but it marked a change in Tony's priorities: from David to Marc Bolan. That same month, Marc recorded a song named 'Ride a White Swan'; by its October release he had shortened the band name to T. Rex – famously, so daytime radio DJs could pronounce it – marking his ascension from the underground to stardom.

By September, Defries' ambitions had extended beyond being a mere legal adviser to David, for it was at that time that he officially joined forces with Laurence Myers, using his relationship with Bowie, and Bowie's social acquaintance, Lionel Bart, as leverage. According to Myers, Defries was employed initially as business affairs manager, with a promise that if his signings made money, Defries would have twenty per cent of Myers' new company, Gem.

With Pitt gone, it was time for Defries to eliminate another 'old-school' collaborator: David's publisher, David Platz. Platz – a concentration-camp survivor and a respected but not necessarily loved businessman – considered David still under contract to Essex Music, with more songs to deliver; Defries simply told Platz the contract was terminated, and started looking for a new publisher. This was classic Defries grandstanding, breaking an impasse and sorting out the details later. The deal caused a long-running legal dispute, with David forced to hand over several songs in later years as recompense, but the legal ramifications were irrelevant. The Chrysalis signing represented a fresh start. Defries promised he would deliver a fresh start for David's recording contract, too, once his Mercury deal came up for renewal in June, 1971.

Defries showed plenty of chutzpah with Platz, as he had with Pitt. But when it came to signing deals, rather than terminating them, he seemed less pushy. In those early days it was Laurence Myers, not Defries, who boasted good connections in the music industry. One of them was Bob Grace, who had just joined Chrysalis to set up a publishing division. In September 1970, Myers called to ask if he'd meet one of his new clients.

Unusually, no one from David's new management company turned up for the meeting at Grace's office. Instead, David and Angie arrived unaccompanied; but if David was nervous, he didn't betray his concern for a moment. Instead, he was expansive, ravishing, charming, a natural-born salesman. Angie, too, exuded glamour. Both of them, says Grace, 'really knew to work the system', telling him about the songs David was working on, inviting him down to spend time at Haddon

Hall, drawing him into their web. Before long, says Grace, Bowie was 'sticking to me like a limpet'.

Grace was already a fan of 'Space Oddity', and loved a new song, 'Holy Holy', that David played him. Soon he had agreed to pay what was, for Chrysalis, the unprecedented sum of £5000 for a five-year publishing contract with David. The deal was signed on 23 October, 1970.

Tony Visconti was another insider who, like Bob Grace, was suspicious of David's new manager. Part of this was prompted by the split with Essex, for whom Visconti still worked – his suspicions deepened with what Visconti regarded as Defries' clumsy attempts to recruit him to Gem. Visconti's dislike of Defries was compounded by Bolan and Bowie's rivalry. Marc knew where he was heading, was more focused and seemed on the verge of a commercial breakthrough. 'David and I had a parting of the ways,' says Visconti. 'I felt terrible, but Marc was about to become almost a full-time job for the next two years of my life.'

Visconti's departure left an opening for a producer and bassist; his immediate replacement was studio veteran Herbie Flowers, who oversaw Bowie's next single, 'Holy Holy'. The song was funky, its looseness and vocal sound obviously Bolan-ish, but as Flowers concedes, 'Some records just don't gel.' The single disappeared into oblivion on its release in January, 1971. Even David's supporters seemed to lose hope. 'Maybe there's something about Bowie that doesn't run alongside the path of luck,' declared Penny Valentine, the writer who had kept a close eye on Bowie's career thus far.

By the time 'Holy Holy' was released, Mick Ronson and Woody Woodmansey had disappeared, too. The abiding rumour was that Defries had sent them home, but in fact the pair weren't pushed: they jumped. Mick Ronson was on his way to a Hype show in Leeds when he saw a sign on the A1 that pointed to Hull. The lure of his hometown proved too strong for the guitarist, who asked Woody, 'Do we really want to do this? Or should we go back and do rock music like we've always wanted?' And Woody replied, 'Yeah!' The pair would reunite with Rats singer Benny Marshall and record as Ronno, with Visconti, before recruiting Trevor Bolder on bass for live shows.

Before the failure of 'Holy Holy', Defries had been bullish. But soon London's newest management guru seemed to fade into the background. One reason was that he had to wait out the expiry of David's contract. A second reason was that David was very needy, calling people up at odd hours, turning up at their door-step if they didn't answer the phone, convinced that his own cause was paramount. Defries could be fatherly, but as his later lieutenant, Tony Zanetta, points out, 'He wasn't there to wipe people's ass for them.'

Yet there was a far more crucial reason for Defries' absence: a singer whose fame far outstripped Bowie's, and who was also attempting to extricate himself from his contract. That singer was Stevie Wonder, Motown's one-time child star, who would come of age in May 1971, and would be entitled to all of the royalties he'd accrued over the last eight years, with his contract up for renewal. Both the size of the prize, and the challenge of taking on Motown, became an obsession for Defries, who spent most of the winter planning his assault on the Detroit label.

Saddled with an absentee manager, abandoned by the collaborators he'd relied on so heavily, and with all the momentum of his one truly great song seemingly lost, David Bowie was finally, but for his wife, standing alone. The experience would reveal both of them at their best. However celebrated their relationship during the media satura-tion of the Ziggy years, it was in the obscurity of 1971 that the pair forged a new lifestyle. Abandoned, free, the pair were reborn, rein-vented.

For David, his isolation, in the insulated microclimate of Haddon Hall, brought out shadows of the earnest, punctual, hard-working teenager. If other people weren't going to help him complete his songs, then he'd do so by himself. And all those hard-earned lessons, the songs pieced painfully together with The Lower Third, the home-made arrangements cooked up with the *Observer*'s book of music, the chords he'd worked out alongside Mick Ronson, would finally cohere in the consciousness of David Bowie, showbiz trouper.

With the faint-hearted supporters stripped away, it was Angie who formed the bounds of David's world. The hostess of Haddon Hall min-istered to David's every need: brought him breakfast in bed, made him endless cups of tea, or ran out for cigarettes. She would talk to Defries to keep him interested, and then she would call Bob Grace and tell him, 'Oh you're wonderful, I don't know what we'd do without you,' before con-fiding in him, 'I *hate* this management.' She loved being at the centre of events, planning schemes, such as using Dana Gillespie – David's teenage girlfriend, who had now reappeared on the scene – in the hope of encouraging Defries to visit Haddon Hall.

The departure of The Hype brought another benefit. Tony and Liz's old room was now empty, so David moved a piano into the light and airy space, which looked out on the garden. It was a battered, old upright that sounded like an ancient pub honky tonk; David would sit at it for hours, obsessively working out runs. Compared to writing on the Hagstrom twelve-string that Ken Pitt had bought him, working out new songs on the piano was hard, painstaking work, but it also allowed him to fit together the harmonic elements in an entirely new way. Over days and weeks he laboured, obsessively, working out songs, and in the process completely reworking his own approach to songwriting. 'The writing sessions were legendary,' says Mark Pritchett, whose band Runk would test-drive David's songs. 'They could be *hours* at a time. Angie might say, "We're scheduled to do this." He'd' be, "I'm not doing it. I'm doing this." Just to get the runs right. And when he got it he was crazed. He was on top of the world.'

Today David explains, almost regretfully, how hard he had to work. 'I forced myself to become a good songwriter – and I became a good songwriter. I made a job of work at getting good.' David had been raised on rock stars who, like Elvis, seemed to emerge fully-formed, instinctive geniuses who could pick up a microphone and transform the world. David might have been born on Elvis's birthday, but he wasn't gifted with the same instinctive talent. His regret expresses how gruelling the journey was to be, until he forced himself to become talented.

But being made, not born, also offered boundless opportunities. Having built up a technique from scratch once, he could do it again. The piano was a new beginning: a new channel for the ideas flooding out of Bowie's consciousness. Songs came together differently on a keyboard; more fluid, based on runs rather than static chords. His writing would be dominated by the new instrument for the next six years: the most creative six years of his career. Bowie's piano playing might have been 'bad', in drummer Henry Spinetti's words, but his writing was sophisticated; fragments of Weimar or Sinatra songs were incorporated into the harmonic bonanza, clues that Bowie was driven more by showbiz traditions than by rock 'n' roll. In some respects, this represented a return to the eclecticism and originality of his Deram days. But back then his ambition far outstripped his abilities. This time around, he could realise his most audacious musical ideas with a minimum of help.

Bob Grace was staggered by Bowie's 'sheer graft' throughout this new phase. 'This was the most hard-working guy . . . talk about diligent, he redefined the word.' Grace would hear the results at his office, and found a cheap demo studio at Radio Luxembourg, where they could record the songs fresh, as they came spilling out. Here David would work up songs with Runk – soon to be renamed Arnold Corns – or drummer Henry Spinetti, who still remembers David's charm in talking him into doing sessions for free.

David and Angie's world was tiny, intimate; as far as work went, they latched on to Grace, monopolising him, jealous of others' demands on his time, travelling to and from Beckenham in cabs they sneaked on to the Chrysalis account. When David wasn't closeted at the keyboard, he'd often be found in mechanics' overalls, underneath his car; over this period, thanks to his publishing income, he progressed from a one-and-a-half-litre black fifties Riley, to a two-and-a-half-litre red version, and finally an 1100cc Riley Gamecock, a wood-framed 1930s racer. It was probably this latter machine that rolled into David, impaling his leg on the starting handle. The incident was witnessed by the Lewisham police, who found the sight of the exotic, curly-haired youth skewered by his own car hilarious. David spent a week in hospital recovering.

As David and Angie drew Grace into their world, Grace was as taken by Bowie's wonderfully dry humour as his skills as a motor mechanic. He was also disorientated by their obsession with taking him to celebrated gay clubs like Yours Or Mine, usually referred to as the Sombrero, or gay movies, or to see flamboyantly gay friends like Freddie Buretti and Mickey King, all in an attempt to get him, says Grace, to 'embrace his trip'.

David's 'trip' – his lifestyle – had blossomed, thanks to Angie's encouragement. He'd been hanging out at gay clubs since his Mod days, but by the time he hooked up with Calvin Lee, the scene had moved upmarket to the Kensington and Notting Hill arty set. Although this time has always been painted as his 'Warhol period' Bowie's circle was quintessentially English – straight out of Noel Coward or Quentin Crisp. Americans who came visiting would be disorientated by the bisexual vibe; acquaintances like Ossie Clarke, who briefly shared a boyfriend with Calvin Lee, was married to a woman he adored, Celia Birtwell, whom he suspected of two-timing him with his celebrated gay friend and rival, David Hockney. Lionel Bart was another: famously devoted to Alma Cogan, he would often be seen with a rent boy in tow, or snuggled up to David. In fact, apart from the inferior dental-work, for Americans this scene was far more glamorous than back home. 'Everyone was a dandy, so much better dressed than in New York,' observes one visitor, Tony Zanetta. It was only later that he noticed that nearly every club-goer owned just the one suit, which on inspection was often slightly grubby, like the impressive facade of a country house which conceals the genteel poverty within.

Future commentators would wonder whether David's gay persona was sincere and genuine. Robert Kensell, a good-looking party animal with a passing resemblance to Terence Stamp, was part of the Sombrero scene with his friend Jonathan Barber, one of Calvin Lee's lovers. Kensell later built a thriving business as 'house' cocaine dealer to musicians at Olympic Studios, but in those early days Jonathan and he would bed-hop for food and fun, sponging off hosts like Ossie, Lionel or Kit Lambert. 'Remember, in 1970 you couldn't talk about something, unless you'd done it,' he points out. 'David wasn't just part of the scene. He was at the centre of it.'

David's flings with men were usually short-lived; the thrill was usually in the discovery. His bisexuality was part of his appeal for many Sombrero boys – 'very manly' is how one scenester describes him – and at least some of his obsession with the scene was, says Bob Grace, down to Mick Jagger. 'Jagger was a role model – not an idol,' says Bob Grace, who explains that despite a lack of any supporting evidence, 'David was *convinced* he was bisexual.'

One of the Sombrero clientele that David loved pointing out with the words, 'Look, isn't he gorgeous?' was Freddie Buretti. Freddie was fully six feet tall, with Caravaggio-esque good looks, and worked for a Kensington fashion retailer. One evening in 1971 he had a brush with the law, charged for importuning after, he said, having sex with the arresting officer. Bob Grace was called in to post bail, and despite the aggravation, had a sneaking respect for the way that Freddie insisted on listing his occupation as 'seamstress'. Usually Freddie was seen hanging out with Daniella Parmar, his 'girlfriend'. 'She was the first girl I had seen with peroxide white hair with cartoon images cut and dyed into the back,' David remembers. 'Blessed with absolute style, she unwittingly changed so much of how female Britain looked – after my then-wife copied her sense of style.' The ambiguity of Daniella and Freddie's relationship was part of the vibe. Another of David's protégés was Mickey King – again, David loved to imply Mickey was another bed-mate, it was all part of the confusion. As was the sight of Angie, with scraped-back hair, in an impeccably tailored suit, chatting up women at the Sombrero. Freddie, thanks to his design skills, became a semi-permanent member of the team along with Daniella. Mickey would drop in and out of Haddon Hall, as he did the rent-boy scene; ultimately, he would die in mysterious circumstances – stabbed by a jealous john, say his Haddon Hall friends.

The kinky, noisy buzz around Haddon Hall inspired David's buoyant mood, which was untroubled by the mess at Mercury and Philips. Although the English version of *The Man Who Sold the World* languished in limbo until next April, delayed by the political changes at Philips, the Americans were keen to release the album. Mercury's Robin McBride flew over that winter to collect the masters and artwork directly from Bowie. David handed him two illustrations by Arts Lab regular Mike Weller, which depicted Cane Hill – later to be replaced by a photo of David reclining at Haddon Hall in his Mr Fish dress.

Soon David's London press contacts would be informed that the album was being 'acclaimed in America . . . a sudden holocaust'. The reality was rather more modest. David's American fans were mainly confined to Mercury staff, principally the newly appointed press officer Ron Oberman, who, as 'torch-carrier' for David, arranged a US promotional tour for *The Man Who Sold the World*, from 27 January, 1971.

David arrived unaccompanied for his first trip to the USA – Angie was five months pregnant and decided to remain at Haddon Hall. He was in his element travelling solo, un-phased by his reception at Dulles, where Immigration detained him for an hour, suspicious of his fey manner and flowing pre-Raphaelite locks. 'For some reason, they seemed to think I looked strange,' he informed Ron Oberman, who'd been waiting in the terminal for an hour. He spent the next few days bubbling with the enthusiasm of a child, accompanied by Ron to radio and press interviews in Washington DC and Chicago, partying, or going out for meals with Ron's parents, who found him every bit as charming as the Manish Boys' parents had, a decade before. Oberman soon picked up on David's tastes, taking him up to 54th Street to see Moondog, the poet, musician and outsider who lived on the street, clad in Viking garb. David chatted to him, intently, fetching him coffee and sandwiches. When Ron was busy, David wandered around New York alone and was thrilled to see, the weekend after his arrival, that The Velvet Underground were playing the Electric Circus. He was transfixed by their renditions of new songs like 'Sweet Jane', venturing upstairs to chat to Lou Reed after the show, telling him how he admired his songwriting and had covered 'Waiting for the Man'. Only later did he find out that Lou had left the band the previous autumn, and the man he'd talked to in the legendary 'Dom' was in fact Doug Yule. David found the notion that the Velvets could be duplicated, like a Coke can or a soup tin, enthralling: maybe the fake Lou was as authentic as the real thing? When he wasn't discussing such concepts with Ron, he picked his brains on how the US music industry worked, quizzing him on the company politics of Mercury and other labels.

Where the East Coast was graced by the earnest, purposeful David Bowie, the West Coast was treated to a more decadent version. Writer John Mendelssohn arrived at LAX to meet the singer, who got off the plane wearing a Mr Fish dress, looking disconcertingly like Lauren Bacall. Mick Jagger had helped publicise the kipper-tie designer's dresses for men, most famously at the Stones' Hyde Park show in 1969. David's interpretation of the same look was radically more feminine – his dress was more ornate, while his curly afro had grown out, and now his hair cascaded in waves over his shoulders. Mendelssohn was disturbed to find his chivalrous instincts aroused by this glamorous apparition; soon he and his friend were struggling with David's trunk – so extraordinarily heavy they speculated he was smuggling a piano. David sashayed along behind them, murmuring 'Oh dear!' every now and then; the perfect, helpless fluttery-lashed ingénue. Mendelssohn had agreed to write a story on the English singer for *Rolling Stone*, but was so intimidated by this exotic creature that he could only think of the most inarticulate, mumbled questions, all of which David treated as if they were the most profound example of the inquisitorial arts.

Later that evening, some of Mendelssohn's verve returned when the two arrived at the Holiday Inn and found the hotel's facilities had been augmented with a girl, who'd been provided for Bowie by the future 'Mayor of the Sunset Strip', Rodney Bingenheimer.

Mercury's radio promotions man on the West Coast, Bingenheimer had been abandoned by his mother in Hollywood as a teenager, but his enthusiasm for rock 'n' roll and frank adoration of celebrity soon helped him become sidekick to Sonny and Cher, and later one of the leading scenesters. Rodney was famous as, in friend and rival Kim Fowley's words, 'purveyor of a posse of pussy' – a skill he proved by sending the girl 'like a welcoming present', says Mendelssohn. As Mendelssohn and Bowie reclined in the Holiday Inn lounge, listening incredulously to a hilarious lounge duo called The Brass Doubles – an organist and drummer, who each played their main instrument one-handed while doubling on trumpet – they competed for Rodney's girl. David won out, chatting away relentlessly in a deadpan, Jagger-esque drawl. Finally, she accepted David's offer to 'come up to me room for some guitar lessons?'

*

Like many Englishmen before and since, David discovered the possibilities offered in the new continent of reinventing oneself, aided by an exotic accent. His skills at enchanting and confusing all onlookers blossomed; resplendent in his dress, or other exotic outfits, he perfected the knack of monopolising people's attentions. At one legendary party hosted by Tom Ayers, one of Rodney's innumerable music-biz friends, he hovered by the door, greeting guests, outraging the elderly ladies, enchanting the groupies and Valley girls. In between chatting to Bingenheimer, and working his wiles on a sixteen-year-old called Kasha ('who had certainly the most beautiful breasts on the West Coast', sighs Mendelssohn) Bowie had a short conversation with Ayers, who was a house producer for RCA. David mentioned his problems with Mercury, and Ayers told him to 'look at RCA', saying, 'The only thing they've got is Elvis – and Elvis can't last for ever.'

It was a short, but momentous exchange. The idea of supplanting the King of Rock 'n' Roll, whose birthday he shared, who had inspired him as a kid, would at one time have seemed ridiculous. Now an insider from Elvis's own company was suggesting the company would be lucky to have him. Riding on a wave of energy, of excitement at the sights and sounds of California, and the enthusiasm of the small gaggle of Hollywood insiders, David started contemplating, for the first time, the prospect of conquering America.

Even the mundane promotional visits were enjoyable. He and John Mendelssohn spent an afternoon driving up to San Jose for a radio interview, talking nonsense and singing their own reworking of Edwin Starr's 'War', with the words, 'Tits! What are they good for?' When they arrived at the station and started chatting, they found the West Coast hippie DJ was sneering and suspicious of the camp, obscure English singer. Bowie was cheery, unintimidated, his deadpan humour in full flow, and when the DJ asked him to suggest a track to play, he instantly sealed his decadent credentials with a languid request for 'anything by The Velvet Underground'.

As the show ran on, Mendelssohn was looking through the record racks when he spotted a copy of *The Stooges*, the debut album by Michigan's punk pioneers, notorious for having crashed and burned in a haze of heroin that year. Intrigued, David chose 'I Wanna Be Your Dog' for his next selection. When the song's moronically monumental riff and Iggy Pop's deadpan drawl blared from the studio speakers, David's amused energy seemed to intensify. As they drove back, Mendelssohn told him about The Stooges singer, Iggy, who'd arrived on the West Coast that summer – his only clothing some ripped jeans, one change of underwear and a pair of silver lamé gloves – and shocked crowds: pulling a girl out of the audience by her face, or dripping melted wax on his chest. David hung on his every word.

Iggy and The Stooges became a near-obsession over the following months, part of a cornucopia of influences that he soaked up like a sponge, the more outré or outrageous, the better. In Chicago, Ron Oberman had played him a crazed record called 'Paralyzed' by the Legendary Stardust Cowboy – David loved it and took a copy of the 45" home with him, along with a stack of albums by Kim Fowley, another West Coast eccentric.

When David returned to Britain, he was 'buzzing' with the sounds and the sights he'd encountered, completely re-energised according to his neighbour Mark Pritchett, who was given four Kim Fowley albums from the stash David brought home. The Stooges' two albums were constantly spinning on David's turntable, and had an immediate effect. One of the first songs he wrote after his return was 'Moonage Daydream': stripped-down and less wordy than his recent efforts, its 'put your electric eye on me, babe' name-checked The Stooges' song 'T.V. Eye'. In April, David worked the song up with Pritchett's band, Runk. (For many years, legend would have it they were The Spiders in disguise, thanks to the improbably monikered drummer Timothy James Ralph St Laurent Thomas Moore Broadbent, and bassist Peter De Somogyi, Pritchett's blue-blooded Dulwich College schoolmates.) The song was written on guitar, and when the trio recorded it at Luxembourg Studios with David, he was painstaking about every detail, singing out the middle instrumental section, an homage to one of Kim Fowley's songs with the Hollywood Argyles ensemble, but used here, says guitarist Mark Pritchett, 'for a Berthold Brecht effect – like a funfair with camp overtones'.

When it came to selling the song, it got camper still, when David recruited Freddie Buretti as a 'lead singer', posing with him and Bob Grace for photos as the band Arnold Corns, for a single released on the tiny B&C soul label. In an interview for *Sounds*, David touted Freddie, or Rudi, as 'the new Mick Jagger', despite the fact his voice was barely audible on the record. But that wasn't the point; the music, rushed as the recording was, signalled a new simplicity which was being sold with a new flamboyance. The serious, rather worthy David Bowie who'd extolled the virtues of the Arts Lab was being consigned to history.

'Moonage Daydream', together with 'Hang onto Yourself', written over the same period, were all the more impressive for being kept in reserve. Instead, it was a third song, written just a few weeks before, which signalled the beginning of the most crucial winning streak of David's life.

The new song's origins echoed, almost spookily, two other songs that transformed their composers' careers. Paul McCartney's 'Yesterday' arrived in a dream, marking the point at which he would assume joint leadership of The Beatles. So did Keith Richards' 'Satisfaction', which he woke up humming one night in a Florida motel, and which would become the Stones' first US number one. The song which was lodged in David Bowie's mind when he woke one morning early in January 1971 would stay just two places outside the Top 10. But it was just as pivotal.

Bob Grace was the first person to hear the news, when the phone rang at the start of a busy day. 'I woke up at 4 o'clock,' David told him. 'Had this song going in my head and I had to get out of bed, work it out on the piano and get it out of my head so I could go back to sleep.'

'What's it called?' asked Grace.

'"Oh! You Pretty Things".'

David insisted he needed to demo the song straight away, and Grace worked out that they could piggyback on a session booked for a radio interview at the Radio Luxembourg studios. There was no time to call in Tim Broadbent or Henry Spinetti, so David recorded the song solo, the only accompaniment the jangling of the bracelets he was wearing. Grace had become close friends with Bowie by now, drawn into his web. After pronouncing the song 'stunning', he felt compelled to recruit more supporters to the Bowie cause. The best contender he could think of was Mickie Most, still the UK's best-known independent producer, who he knew would be at that year's MIDEM festival in Cannes, just a few days away.

With the rendezvous organised, Grace played the acetate for Mickie on a tiny Dansette player in a booth at the festival. He was nervous – and would been even more nervous had he known that Most had turned down David Bowie twice during the preceding years. David had not breathed a word about these earlier failures.

Publishers' folklore was that if Most listened to more than ten seconds of a song you had a chance. Grace paced around nervously as the famously opinionated producer listened to the entire song, waited until the fade-out, then announced: 'Smash!' He told Grace the song would be perfect to launch the solo career of Peter Noone, from Herman's Hermits – uncool as they were, the Hermits were one of Most's biggest acts, and this was a huge coup. The fact that the song had arrived, almost fully formed, from David's unconscious demonstrated how, after five years of writing songs, he had bypassed the critical part of his consciousness. Before his writing had been considered; now it was inspired.

Plenty of other songs demoed at Radio Luxembourg showed how the short US trip had provided David with a store of images to draw on. A theme was emerging. David was a pro, a man who knew how to work the system, but had an instinctive sympathy for those who couldn't, those practitioners of what writer Irwin Chusid terms Outsider Music; erratic people like Syd Barrett, Iggy Pop, Moondog or Stardust Cowboy Norman Carl Odam. David would follow their star-crossed careers, and their fate infuses songs like the gorgeous 'Lady Stardust', demoed on 10 March, along with an early version of 'Moonage Daydream', and the wonderfully hokey 'Right On Mother', also destined for Peter Noone.

At the same time that David was laying the bed-rock of his future music, he was focusing just as diligently on reinventing his image, and, more specifically, consigning the past to oblivion. Bill Harry, childhood friend of John Lennon and founder of *Mersey Beat* magazine, was one of London's busiest PRs; Bob Grace called him in, explaining that David's career had stalled, and they were trying to generate some momentum. Harry and Bowie spent days closeted together, talking about science fiction – a mutual obsession – music and photography. Harry knew many rock 'n' rollers, but none of them had as sophisticated a sense of visuals: Bowie brought in mood-boards of photos and glossy magazine cuttings, photos of movie stars and Egyptian pharaohs to illustrate photographic ideas, and together they plotted to airbrush David's past.

Harry helped push *The Man Who Sold the World*, which finally made it to the shelves in Britain that April, but Bowie's eyes were fixed firmly beyond that release. Armed with a stack of glossy photos taken by the Chrysalis photographer Brian Ward, Bowie and Harry did the rounds of Fleet Street and the music press. While Bill sat in the office, chatting, David would go to the filing cabinet, pull out the old shots of the curly-headed 'Space Oddity' Bowie and replace them with the new session, banishing the one-shot wonder to oblivion. 'He was planning ahead. He didn't seem part of the normal culture at all, sitting around in a pub or club and getting boozed up; he was collecting together images for the future,' says Harry.

Their campaign reaped immediate results: a spread in the *Daily Mirror*, plus stories in the *Daily Express* and the music press. The stories paved the way for Peter Noone's single of 'Oh! You Pretty Things' – with David contributing a strident, bouncing piano – which hit the Top 40 on

22 May, peaking at number twelve. The lumpy, pedestrian arrangement failed to hamper the song's gorgeously inventive melody, which was as fleet of foot as *White Album*-era McCartney; Peter Noone went into print praising David Bowie as the finest songwriter since Lennon and McCartney. Suddenly, the one-hit wonder was the new kid on the block.

Bob Grace, the man who had helped engineer this career turnaround, was overjoyed: this was what he'd joined Chrysalis for, to take an artist 'from demo to limo', as the slang had it. When Terry Ellis, his boss, called him in to his office, with the song still at its chart peak, he walked in to the room expecting a promotion and a pay rise. Instead, Ellis was red-faced with rage. 'This is a disaster!' Ellis yelled. 'You've ruined the image of my company. The Chrysalis Music label on a pop record! How dare you? Furthermore I have a manager outside, Tony Defries, who's absolutely furious.'

Defries walked in, and the conversation turned into a heated argument, with Defries accusing Grace of trying to poach his artist, while Grace countered, 'If you did more for him, he'd stop hassling *me* so much!' Bill Harry had a similar encounter, accused of interfering, and when Defries announced, 'From now on, all interviews must be conducted from my office,' Harry quit as David's PR.

Today, Bill Harry insists that Defries could never measure up to other managers he worked with, like Led Zeppelin's famously aggressive Peter Grant. 'I couldn't work with Defries. I found him quite unpleasant, and inflexible.' But Harry and Bob Grace's accusations that Defries had left Bowie to fend for himself would not be repeated, for in the forthcoming weeks, Tony Defries would reinvent himself as completely as his client.

David Bowie had fought his way back into contention, more or less unaided. But Defries was the man who'd build an army behind him.

Tony Defries was already an expert in reinvention and repackaging. Born in 1943, reputedly near a secret airfield in north London, and just five years older than David, he claimed to have had a similar, 'fractured' childhood and viewed his life in a similar, almost mythical sense. His grandparents had fled from Russia, and the young Defries had, he would tell listeners, been put into care for a year when he was just a few months old; a devastating experience, during which he clinically died at one point from an asthma attack. Like David, he was conscious of growing up amid wartime ruins, in his own case as part of a Jewish family living on its wits in Shepherd's Bush, dodging gangs of Irish, Greek and Turkish Cypriots, whilst building a business selling factory-reject china and other oddments. He and his brother Nicholas soon discovered that an average brace of duelling pistols could be transformed into a desirable rarity once packaged in a convincingly antiqued wooden box; they were selling a fantasy, and in much the same way, Defries, who left school at fourteen, would act as a lawyer, and then a manager.

Tony's unique life was carved out in a British society in a state of flux, with the aristocracy trying to pawn its possessions, and European families trying to reclaim their own inheritance, looted by the Nazis. In this chaos, empires could be rebuilt, and Defries planned to be at the head of one. Even his many detractors concede he was shrewd; he was also fearless, and would go straight to the top of whatever company he was dealing with to cut a deal. Just a few years older than many of his clients, he was nonetheless 'a big daddy figure', as Dana Gillespie puts it, who'd look after them and shield them from all earthly worries. Modelling himself on Colonel Parker, he told David that he would make his protegé famous as a 'one-name star' like Elvis or Dylan: a monolithically famous performer, known simply as 'Bowie'.

The nature of Defries' and Bowie's professional relationship would often be misunderstood, not least by David, despite the fact it was legally documented. Defries did not work for David: David worked for him. In David's ten-year contract as a singer and songwriter, signed on 31 March, 1972, with Defries' newly established MainMan empire, the artist is defined as an 'Employee'. The schedule to the contract also includes the details of David's separate management deal with Tony Defries, signed the previous August. The term of the contract, it states in bold black and white, is 'timeless'.

Defries explains his remoteness in the spring of 1971 by the fact he was simply waiting for David's Mercury contract to expire. A more pressing reason was doubtless his involvement with Stevie Wonder. By May, and the 'Oh! You Pretty Things' breakthrough, Defries' Detroit mission had stalled and Wonder had agreed to renew his deal with Motown. David Bowie was therefore back to being his best bet. But if Defries had waited until the last minute to bet on Bowie, when the moment came, he would bet big. And Defries was betting with much more than money (which came, in any case, from Laurence Myers). He bet his professional life. From the moment he fully engaged himself in Bowie's career, there was never any doubt that the fates of these two men were intertwined.

Anya Wilson was the radio plugger who'd helped drive Marc Bolan's 'Ride a White Swan' to number two, and was hired by Defries to repeat her feat for Bowie. 'I had more than one knot in my stomach working for

Tony, believe me,' says Wilson. 'He was very focused on what he wanted. I got fired several times, but he would rehire me a couple of weeks later and pay me back pay. But when he was locked in it was absolute. There was never any doubt. It was very infectious.'

Defries was ready to bide his time until the end of June, when Mercury could exercise their option on David, but from May onwards he worked closely, plotting with Bowie and Bob Grace. It was the publisher, with Anya Wilson, who secured another slot on the BBC's 'In Concert' series, which would be a key signpost of what was to come.

The growing sense of event was heightened with the news that Angie had given birth to Duncan Zowie Haywood Bowie at Bromley Hospital on 30 May, after a drawn-out labour. David was there for the birth, which further sealed Angie's position as queen to Bowie's king. But Angie, who freely admits, 'I was not the maternal type,' would later pinpoint the aftermath of the birth as a dark portent for their relationship. Zowie – named after the Greek word for 'life' – was a chunky eight and a half pounds, and Angie suffered a cracked pelvis, blood loss, exhaustion and what sounds like classic post-natal depression. A few weeks after the birth, Dana Gillespie persuaded Angie to join her for a trip to her parents' summer villa in Italy. Angie recruited the redoubtable Suzi Frost, henceforth an integral part of the household, to look after Zowie during her absence, and remembers David hardly raising an eyebrow at her departure. Years later, though, she'd speculate that David, for all his sexual non-conformity, retained some distinctly old-school family values and regarded the trip as an unforgivable desertion.

Yet for those around them, the birth and surrounding events seemed largely idyllic, with Angie continuing to provide a protective 'cocoon' around David in which he could create. The impression of a domestic idyll was cemented with David's song 'Kooks', which asked their baby, 'Will you stay in our Lovers' story?' Written after David had spent the day listening to Neil Young's *After the Goldrush*, its jiggling piano feel was based on Young's 'Till the Morning Comes', with its central lyric quoting the Young title 'I Believe in You'. Then, as now, it's a delightful song: deft, light-hearted, totally without artifice.

The song made its public debut a couple of days after it was written, at the BBC 'In Concert', on 3 June, 1971. Like most of the key events in David's life, the show was pulled together almost randomly at the last moment. Late in May, David booked bassist Herbie Flowers and guitarist Tim Renwick for the appearance. Renwick had been an occasional visitor to Haddon Hall; David, says Junior's Eyes singer Graham Kelly, was fascinated by the guitarist – indeed, Kelly maintains that David's Lauren Bacall persona derived from the Marlene Dietrich impression that Renwick often performed as a party piece. Renwick appears on at least one long-lost song from that summer – 'Hole in the Ground', with Herbie on bass and George Underwood, who had not completely given up on music, on vocals – but his role as David's sideman evaporated at the last moment, when David phoned Mick Ronson. The two had kept in touch over recent months – David took a small crew of Haddon Hall regulars down to Ronno's London showcase at Lower Temple – and Mick seized the chance, for the band's undistinguished single on Vertigo had sunk without trace. Ronson brought all his musicians down the A1; they arrived on the 5th and had one afternoon to rehearse. For Ronson, Woodmansey and bassist Trevor Bolder – who had joined Ronno only recently – the one afternoon was an impromptu, scary, electrifying start to a journey that would stay that way.

Their nervousness was useful, forcing them to come up with ideas, and most of the off-the-cuff riffs they pulled together would survive on David's upcoming album. David exuded happiness and positivity: over-joyed both with the arrival of Zowie and the thrill of creation. There was no overlooking his nervous energy, but he projected the conviction that this was meant to be; this was his man-child quality, that incredible sense of focus and belief that everything was simple.

The show united Haddon Hall regulars like Mark Pritchett, George Underwood and David's schoolmate Geoff MacCormack, with Ronson's band, whose singer Benny Marshall guested on a cover of Chuck Berry's 'Almost Grown'. The Hull musicians were 'nervous as hell', yet much of the party atmosphere that is audible on the show's recording is genuine. At times, the vibe was surprisingly intimate – as in the rendition of 'Kooks', dedicated to the new Bowie child, and jokey interactions with John Peel – yet from the moment David walked into the dressing room wearing jeans and a t-shirt, and out of it wearing his Mr Fish dress, exud-ing glamour, there was no doubt that this was an accomplished *coup de théâtre*. At the end, David tearfully apologised to producer Jeff Griffin that he'd completely messed up the vocal on 'Oh! You Pretty Things'. 'It hadn't even registered,' says Griffin. Then once the show was over, David forgot this blip, and was consumed by his next project.

In future years, people would refer to Bowie's mindset during that summer as 'positive visualisation'. He announced the title of his next album, *Hunky Dory*, on the BBC at a time when the album was still a pipe-dream, and he was still tied to a record company he hated. The title came from a catchphrase of Peter Shoot, larger-than-life ex-RAF owner of one of Bob Grace's favourite pubs, The Bear in Esher: 'It will either be a disaster, or everything will be hunky dory.'

David loved the phrase. This time around, everything *would* be hunky dory. He talked about producing other acts as if he already had a star's magic touch. And he laid out the future for the band who had been with him for only a few days, telling them about the two albums they would make in forthcoming months, with a new record company, the venues they would play at the start of the coming onslaught, and where they would end up. 'He had it all in his head,' says bassist Trevor Bolder. 'And then he cited each part of where he was going to be.'

Tony Defries was the other master of positive visualisation. He too would lay out the future in front of them as if it were a map. A key part of his strategy was to cut record companies out of the creative loop; Defries had the means to do that, for he would fund David's next album independently before dispensing with Mercury and before approaching RCA – giving David, as opposed to the record company, control of his own music. This was an unprecedented commitment; as his future lieutenant, Tony Zanetta, points out, 'Tony threw the book out the window. He loved to take huge gambles. Although of course it was Laurence's money that he was gambling with.'

For David to realise his vision, he had to have the best. That included the studio, Trident, already familiar to David, but then at its height of popularity after its conversion to a state-of-the-art twenty-four tracks. Trident's main engineer, Ken Scott, was fast becoming, says Grace, 'the hot guy at the time', primarily thanks to his work on George Harrison's *All Things Must Pass*. Scott got on well with David, who decided to share the production role with him. In June, David, Grace, Ken Scott and Mick Ronson assembled at Scott's house in Catford, south-east London to select an album's worth of material from the Radio Luxembourg demos.

Scott had engineered David's last two albums, and agreed to the producer's role, figuring he'd gain useful experience. 'I thought David was good, but he'd never be a superstar. This would be the perfect time to practise production, so if I fucked up it wouldn't really matter. But when we were sitting there listening to those demos, this lightbulb went on. I thought, Bloody hell! This is for real!'

Some kind of floodgate had been unlocked, so much so that 'Star', 'Moonage Daydream' and 'Lady Stardust' were among the high-quality compositions saved for a later day, for there was a conscious decision to build the new album around the piano. The three standout songs – 'Oh! You Pretty Things', 'Changes' and 'Life On Mars?' – all featured broadly similar piano runs, rolling forward with an irresistible momentum, but each boasted distinct, gorgeously memorable melodies.

The contrast with 'Space Oddity' could not be more pronounced; whereas the melody on that song was constrained, claustrophobic, *Hunky Dory*'s standout melodies were fluid, swooping over an octave or more. 'Life On Mars?' is a typical example, cheekily based on the chord sequence of 'Comme d'Habitude', aka 'My Way', a song for which David had once crafted a set of lyrics at the behest of Ken Pitt. His attempts were rejected, and if the setback had rankled, then revenge was sweet, for the new song was grandiose, its melody arguably superior to Jacques Revaux's original. The main tune arrived in Bowie's head on the bus to Lewisham to buy some shoes: he hopped off the bus, 'more or less loped' back to Haddon Hall and completed the song by the late afternoon. The lyrics were enigmatic, a succession of fragmentary images witnessed by the 'girl with the mousy hair', rather in the style of McCartney's 'Eleanor Rigby'. Only when we reach the chorus, with an octave leap over the words 'life on Mars?', do we realise the song is about a yearning for escape, or transcendence. It's a thrilling trick – and a solidly traditional one, drawing on songwriters like Harold Arlen.

David's three previous albums had all been complicated recordings, overshadowed by politics. With *Hunky Dory,* David set out to satisfy himself, not record company executives: a freedom reflected in the album's freshness. The recording process was simple, dominated by David's child-like optimism and focus – much of which came from the reassuring presence of Mick Ronson, who as arranger carried the burden of translating the songs from piano sketches to luscious epics.

Mick didn't share David's sense of calm. He had taken some refresher piano lessons on his return to Hull; nonetheless, the assignment was far scarier than anything David had thrown at him so far. Although David did occasionally lose his composure – shouting, 'Just play the song right!' when the rhythm section messed up a take of 'Song for Bob Dylan' – he was masterful at motivating people, pushing Mick forward, challenging him, 'Go on, do it! If it doesn't work out it doesn't work out – but have a go!' Mick impressed both Ken Scott and Bob Grace with his quiet efficiency, but Ronson's friend Trevor Bolder noticed the guitarist was 'a bag of nerves'. While Bowie sat in the Trident control room, looking down on the recording area, Ronson would be on the studio floor, checking though manuscript pages, nervously dragging on one after another of his trademark roll-ups; close up, you could see his hands shaking. But there was little time to worry, for the sessions were rushed and David was impatient. For the songs where he played piano, there would sometimes be just a couple of run-throughs, and then the band would have to find their own way through, like session musicians, living on their wits. 'It was always on the edge, wondering if they would make it through,' says Scott. Occasionally they would have a rest, watching Rick Wakeman overdub piano parts at Trident's celebrated Bechstein, on which McCartney had pounded out 'Hey Jude'.

At first, the musicians wondered if David's impatience derived from a selfish desire to monopolise the studio time for his own singing, but it turned out he only required a couple of takes to nail a perfect vocal, his microphone technique perfected by years of experience. 'He was unique,' says Scott, 'the only singer I ever worked with where virtually every take was a master.'

The truth was, he was simply burning to download his work from his mind and commit it to tape. 'The Bewlay Brothers', for instance, arrived during an unsettled day and was recorded, solo, later that evening. Its title derived from a cheap old-fashioned pipe Bowie had once briefly owned, and the lyrics were inscrutable even to their creator. 'Don't listen to the words, they don't mean anything,' he told Scott as they prepared for a vocal take. 'I've just written them for the American market, they like this kind of thing.'

The album's lyrics – which were dense with allusions, with both 'Quicksand' and 'The Bewlay Brothers' among his most evocative collection of images – usually came quickly ('I can't remember much redrafting at all,' says Mark Pritchett). The result was a dazzling collection of musical and lyrical imagery. The songs obviously drew from both traditional English and cutting-edge American influences – 'He stole from the best,' as Trevor Bolder puts it, reiterating David's self-proclaimed role as a 'tasteful thief' – but the borrowed riffs and name-checking merely contributed to the simple, child-like radiance. In his days around Haddon Hall, playing with Zowie, tinkering with his Riley, or flirting with Freddie, David had forged a new manifesto, post-modern – where you could pick and choose from the works of Warhol or Lou Reed, leaving the joins showing – and post-sexual, where the singer is free to play the role of man, woman or child. *Hunky Dory* had the unspoilt, overwhelming charm of a new beginning.

*

If David's new record was naive and simple, Defries' means of selling it were hard-bitten – strictly old-school. The sessions were drawing to a close before he ensured he was free to sell the results to the record company of his choice. He and Laurence Myers were already negotiating with RCA, sending them over half of *Hunky Dory*, before Defries set out to rid himself of Mercury.

Vice President Irwin Steinberg and A&R Robin McBride had flown over to London in the happy expectation of extending David's contract to include a third album for the label. Their fate was like that of a general who has lost the battle before his troops even take the field. 'We were totally blindsided,' says McBride, who had arranged what he thought would be a pleasant lunch at the Londonderry Hotel only for Defries, soberly dressed and immaculately groomed, to bypass the normal pleasantries and announce, 'David will never record for you again.' Instantly, Steinberg pointed out David owed one more album under his contract. 'If you insist on a third album, you will get the biggest pile of shit ever seen on a record,' Defries responded. Steinberg was a brilliant, well-read man, McBride explains, but his instinct when faced with an argument was to say 'fuck you' and walk away. Which is exactly what he did. 'If you want a release, you will have to pay,' he informed Defries. 'You will have to refund Mercury for all the recording expenses, all the art expenses, all the packaging and promotional expenses that we have undertaken on David Bowie's behalf.'

This was exactly the response that Defries had hoped for; he assented to those costs, letting Steinberg believe he had won. Only later did McBride and Steinberg discover that David had already recorded an album intended for another label; only later did they realise that by buying back the two Mercury albums at cost, Defries had actually ended up making a huge amount of money. McBride and Steinberg, music fans both, had been taken, in the consummate example of Defries' aggression and brinksmanship. For both, it would represent one of the most humiliating setbacks of their careers.

Although he acknowledges that Defries did not utter an untruth in that fateful meeting, McBride found the encounter detestable, only rivalled by his meeting with Dylan's famously aggressive manager, Albert Grossman. 'They have both helped in the success of some terribly talented people,' he notes. 'But both personalities belonged in the same garbage can.'

As David finished *Hunky Dory* that summer, Defries was developing an almost messianic sense that he could remake the music industry, buoyed up by his coup at Mercury. He and David were hanging out together more and more, at the Sombrero or back at Haddon Hall. Defries disapproved of drug use, the mark of a loser, but rapidly bought into the Bowie lifestyle, savouring the exotic sexual frisson. David also shared Tony's fascination with Americana – and together they became obsessed with the biggest coup: breaking America. When Andy Warhol's play *Pork*, which so flagrantly symbolised this new world, debuted in London that summer, it was natural that David and Tony would come to witness the event. What few could have predicted was how they would adopt Warhol's work, using it to sell America back to itself.

Collaged from hundreds of hours of Andy's phone conversations by Tony Ingrassia – a graduate of the Theatre of the Ridiculous – *Pork* was scheduled to open on 2 August, and promised a healthy dose of outrage. Two gorgeous nude boys, the 'Pepsodent Twins', stood impassively on stage throughout the show, while 'Amanda Pork' – obviously based on Factory regular Brigid Polk – talked incessantly on the phone, frolicked topless, masturbated and engaged in hilariously deadpan conversations with the Andy Warhol character, played with a languid precision by Tony Zanetta. The play caused predictable outrage, inspiring a *Daily Mirror* exposé which ensured the Roundhouse was packed for most performances.

The Warhol troupe were aware of David even before they'd arrived in London. They'd seen a 'titillating' news story complete with photo of David in his Mr Fish dress in an issue of *Rolling Stone* that had also featured *Pork*. Within days of their arrival in London, stage manager Leee Childers and Kathy Dorritie, who played Pork, hit the town, looking for laughs or getting laid by posing as journalists for *Circus* magazine. It was Leee who spotted a tiny ad for a Bowie gig in the *NME*, and set out with Kathy and Wayne County (or 'Vulva Lips') for the Country Club in Haverstock Hill, in search of 'the man in the dress'. Instead, he complained, they found 'a folkie'.

After the show, Leee and Kathy were initially more taken with Angie's energy and enthusiasm than with the unassuming composure of the flaxen-haired 'folkie', but when the Warhol troupe were invited to Haddon Hall after David, Angie and a group of Gem regulars turned up for a performance of *Pork* a couple of days later, they found the 'quiet and almost drab' creature had metamorphosed. Tony Zanetta, a kind of simulacrum for Warhol, was the performer who found himself fixed in David's laser beam. 'He can walk into the room and every single head would turn and it was like a light was shining. It was uncanny.' They spent the evening locked in conversation, talking about artifice, make-up, glamour; Zanetta telling David about the Theatre of the Ridiculous, while David reciprocated with stories of his Lindsay Kemp days. David was warm, unaffected, with an instinctive genius at building rapport. Zanetta and the others were fascinated by the singer; after their nights at the Sombrero, and the spectacle of Haddon Hall, they felt they had found kindred spirits, who shared their almost child-like enthusiasms. Defries was as fascinated as David; by now he luxuriated in the atmosphere at the Sombrero, and the delicious sensuality of being surrounded by Dana Gillespie, whose career he also promised to take in hand.

Beyond his lofty talk, Defries was practical, too. At the Haverstock Hill show on 26 July, David and Mick's sound was lousy, put to shame by the support group, Tucky Buzzard. It turned out their engineer, Robin Mayhew, was working with a new kind of PA system that would allow a singer free-rein to wander around the auditorium. Mayhew was hired and told to build a new system: 'Sort it out,' Defries told him, 'it doesn't matter what it costs.' He hired Mick's old Rats roadie, Peter Hunsley, too, but there was a limit to his generosity with Laurence Myers' money. Whereas the road-crew were kept on retainer, the musicians – Trevor Bolder and Woody Woodmansey – were sent back to Hull, while David and Defries prepared for their trip to the New York offices of RCA in September.

David was calm, self-possessed, free of self-doubt. Defries was positively messianic, eager to walk into the home of the King of Rock 'n' Roll, and tell them how much they needed him and his client. He wasn't afraid to set his sights high. 'You've had nothing since the 1950s, and you missed out on the sixties,' he would tell RCA. 'But you can own the 1970s. Because David Bowie is going to remake the decade, just like The Beatles did in the 1960s.'

9

Over the Rainbow

It was, I'll do anything, play anything, say anything, wear anything to become a star. And there's nothing wrong with that. And there was a tremendous hunger on the part of the audience for it, too. It was that moment in time.

Scott Richardson

Breaking America had been a staple of every ambitious British rock 'n' roller's career plan since the days of The Shadows, in the early sixties. David Bowie and Tony Defries arrived in New York convinced of their ability to conquer the new world. Given both their characters, that was no surprise. But no one could have predicted how, once in the country, their plans would become even more grandiose.

Defries ensured that the September 1971 trip on which he planned to close the RCA deal was heavy with symbolism by staying at the Warwick – the hotel famous for hosting The Beatles – and holding court for a cavalcade of visitors to build up a sense of event. Different people have different perceptions of that week: Lisa Robinson, who was central to the RCA signing, saw David as the star of proceedings, boyish, enthused, with Defries playing the role of Colonel Parker to David's Elvis. Lisa, her husband Richard, and many others were caught in the spotlight of David's charm, which he'd learned to focus with dazzling effectiveness: he'd pick words out of their sentences and repeat them, as if they had crystallised thoughts in his own mind, or when bumping into them again, he'd act as if he was barely able to function in the intervening minutes. Sometimes, talking to him, the objects of his attention would experience that giddy, tingly feeling you get when you're in love.

Others saw Tony Defries as the star of the show: Tony Zanetta was enchanted by Bowie, but found Defries had a unique sense of power emanating from him. '[He was] a magical person, he seemed older than he was and very wise – like a sage.'

Dennis Katz, RCA's head of A&R, was keen to close the deal. As Tom Ayers had told David, the label had seen Elvis Presley's sales in seemingly irreversible decline; Katz desperately needed new talent and had been bowled over by an acetate of the earlier *Hunky Dory* tracks. But it was Richard and Lisa Robinson who would prove crucial to the signing; the couple were arbiters of cool, RCA's 'company heads'. Richard had joined RCA as house producer and Katz's assistant in A&R; his wife Lisa was New York's hippest music journalist; together they would prove David's most potent champions.

History rarely records Laurence Myers' role in the RCA signing; the Gem founder opened negotiations with RCA, and oversaw the contract, he says today. 'I actually did the deal – I have to point that out as it's so rarely recognised!' Yet it was Defries who turned the signing into an event. Defries was adept at homing in on RCA's insecurities, commiserating with them that RCA was best-known for producing washing machines. But he was 'very, very charming' about it, everyone remembers. Even the money wasn't a problem; RCA agreed to a $37,500 advance on signature, a middling sum, 'but that didn't bother Tony,' says Zanetta, 'he always knew he could improve on the deal later.'

The RCA contract was signed on 9 September: a coup for Defries, who'd promised David he would relaunch his career. But that was not enough. For over two days, 8 and 9 September, Defries' ambitions would inflate from securing a single record contract to launching an entertainment empire.

Yet if Defries was the salesman, it was David who masterminded the product. He was a stranger in a strange land, where the main participants were constantly rushing around, calling their friends on the phone, hanging out at Max's Kansas City and trying to out-cool each other, but he was equally in his element, enthralling the New Yorkers just as he had the *Pork* actors. By now, his talent for identifying people who could help him was as finely honed as his songwriting skills.

Over those two days, the entire structure of what would become MainMan was established. Zanetta was already being drawn in – he represented New York cool to David, while to Defries he was both inspiration and sounding board. He would soon be given the title of MainMain President, USA (his first job would be finding and painting an office) and become the dominant figure in the organisation after Defries, with many of his instincts and off-the-cuff remarks becoming company policy.

It was Zanetta who introduced David to Andy Warhol, an event usually described as 'iconic'. The reality was more messy and inconclusive. David was tense, attempting to impress Warhol with a little mime, based on Kemp's Pierrot schtick where he pulled out his own intestines; the little performance went down like a lead balloon, with Warhol remaining on the edge of the conversation. Instead David talked mainly with Alan Midgette and Glenn O'Brien, later editor of *Interview*. Warhol's only fully formed line of conversation was that he liked David's shoes. The meeting was filmed: but apart from the cheesy feel of David's routine, the footage is notable for another reason: between Andy himself, Zanetta, who played Andy in *Pork*, Midgette, who'd famously impersonated Andy on a college tour, and David, who memorably played Andy in the 1996 film *Basquiat*, the footage features four Warhols. Which is, of course, a very Warholian happening.

Having secured his meeting with Warhol, David enlisted Lisa Robinson as a co-conspirator to link up with Andy's musical protégé. Once he'd learned Lisa was friends with Lou Reed, David was 'absolutely intrigued', says Robinson, who arranged for them to meet over dinner at the Ginger Man, a 'really straight' restaurant by Lincoln Park where Lisa would go out for steaks with her friend Fran Lebowitz. Lou and David chatted: Lou was drunk and manic, David whispered flirtatiously, while Lou's wife Betty looked on adoringly.

Enthralled as Lisa was by David, she didn't quite realise the scope of his ambition. Lou explained he was about to record his debut RCA album with Richard Robinson, who had recently produced the Flamin' Groovies' superb *Teenage Head*. Lou's chat with David was friendly enough, an up-and-coming artist paying tribute to one whose career had apparently tanked, but there was no mention that David was thinking of working with Lou; his furtiveness would soon cause 'a bit of a falling out', says Lisa.

Later that evening David's party, plus Richard and Lisa, moved on to Max's Kansas City. This was both viper pit and arcadia, a place where, says Leee Childers, 'Each night was different and each night was proclaimed the last good night of Max's for years – and of course it only got better and better.' The back room had seen endless cultural and sexual unions, many of which seemed hugely significant in later years, none of which seemed so at the time. 'No one, including Andy Warhol, thought that any of this was important, much less that anyone was going to remember it,' says Childers. 'Everything was of itself the minute it was happening and then it was over and that's how the whole back room was. That's how I remember it – in flashes.'

Although most of those involved could not appreciate the wider significance of the scenes played out in the back room at Max's, one unabashed fan from Beckenham could. For the fragile, thrift-store decadence and glamour of Max's would become the raw material of David Bowie's art. Just like the English bluesmen of the sixties, Bowie would be accused of exploiting his influences; without doubt, they did indeed bring him money and fame. Yet his encounter that night with a down-on-his-luck heroin addict who would one day become his closest friend – his 'twin atom' – reveals him more as a fan than exploiter.

In the seven months since David discovered the colourful story of Iggy Stooge, the Detroit singer's life had taken successively more pica-resque turns. Abandoned by his record company, he had suffered heroin overdoses, van smashes, being stranded in the Detroit projects clad in a tutu, and had recently been booted out of guitarist Rick Derringer's house following the apparent theft of Liz Derringer's jewellery by Iggy's underage girlfriend. After hearing snippets of Iggy's recent history from Lisa Robinson, David asked if they could meet. Lisa made more phone calls, and eventually Iggy was persuaded to pull himself away from the TV in his friend Danny Fields' apartment, and walk up to Max's.

In future years, David would be seen as cold and manipulative, eyeing Iggy much as a Victorian collector would a choice hummingbird destined for stuffing. The reality was almost the opposite, for it was Iggy who manipulated the event, 'almost dancing' into the meeting, Zanetta noticed. Bowie and Defries were both enthralled by the cheeky racon-teur. Iggy could turn on the flutter-eyelashed flirtatiousness and build rapport just like David, but there was an *idée fixe* about his manner that fascinated, and slightly unnerved, David.

Their discussions about music, and Iggy's future, continued the next morning, over breakfast at the Warwick, which in Defries' distinctive style could take hours, interrupted by endless phone calls and scheming. Iggy was impressed by Defries – his 'big vision of what he was going to do' – and he liked David. He could see beyond the charm, and judged him 'very canny, very self-possessed and a . . . not *unkind* person. Which you don't usually see in people so self-aware.' David played him *Hunky Dory*, while Iggy made polite noises. 'It wasn't anything to do with what I was trying to do, but I realised, in terms of song-craft, he can do A, B and C.' By the end of the meeting, Iggy had agreed to come over to London, once he'd completed his methadone programme, and sign to Gem.

Bowie and Defries had set out to close a recording deal – and returned with an empire. Within three days in New York, Defries had signed David's contract with RCA, discussed the re-release of David's old Mercury albums, recruited Zanetta to the cause, formed a relationship with Lou Reed and had recruited Iggy to the Gem fold, promising to secure him a new record deal – a promise Defries fulfilled a few weeks later, signing Iggy to Columbia.

By the time David, Mick and Angie – who had spent most of the trip visiting her parents in Connecticut – returned to London, David had become obsessed with the singer he had met at Max's. 'He talked about Iggy for a full week – it was definitely all-consuming,' says Bob Grace, a recollection shared by Ken Scott and Trevor Bolder. 'Iggy and Lou, it was,' says Bolder, 'always Iggy and Lou.'

David was purposeful, clear-headed, in the days following the New York trip, but wired, too, filled with nervous energy as he prepared to unveil his new songs and his new band. The unofficial debut of what would become The Spiders from Mars was planned for Friars Aylesbury, an assembly hall in an ancient market town an hour out of London, known for its enthusiastic audiences. In the middle of September, Ronson called Bolder and Woodmansey back from Hull for their first show as a band. Rick Wakeman, David's first choice as pianist, had joined Yes just a few weeks before, so David phoned an old friend from Kent, Tom Parker, to play piano, jabbering in nervous gratitude when Parker said, 'Of course!'

When David took to the Friars stage on 25 September he was shaking: he had dressed up in baggy black culottes, red platform boots and a women's beige jacket, worn over his skinny, naked chest. 'Does anyone have a heater?' was one of his asides, in a set of rambling song intro-ductions that took in Lou Reed's sense of humour and why New Yorkers felt compelled to stare into subway tunnels. 'We didn't know if he was on drugs, or just nervous,' says Kris Needs, a Bowie fan who'd designed the flyers for the night. The set was a primitive version of what would become a well-honed set, starting out with acoustic songs, including Brel's 'Port of Amsterdam', with the band only joining in halfway through. But as Ronson cranked up his Les Paul and the energy levels increased, David's announcements grew shorter and the applause in the half-empty club grew in intensity. After closing the set with a ruthless version of 'Waiting for the Man', Bowie walked into the dressing room, exultant. 'That was great,' he announced to Needs. 'And when I come back I'm going to be completely different.'

Few people, outside David's immediate circle, realised how soon he'd come back, or how different he'd be. But within the tiny coterie of people – David, Angie and the band, Defries and a small crew of roadies – the activity was feverish, with David and musicians spending most of October crammed in Greenwich's Underhill studio – the polystyrene-lined basement of a down-at-heel Georgian building that also contained a car parts showroom and an escort agency. *Hunky Dory* was not yet released, and David was burning to record its successor. Already, he had eight or nine songs that they'd run through each day, playing each tune just a few times before moving on to the next, to keep the feel loose, un-studied. It felt democratic, 'a band thing', says Bolder.

Several key songs they rehearsed – notably 'Moonage Daydream' and 'Lady Stardust' – dated from David's last bout of songwriting in the spring, yet most of them had been assembled with astonishing speed within the previous few weeks. In the wake of *Hunky Dory*'s writing blitz, this was impressive. Yet that was, literally, only half the story. Bowie's on-stage chatter at Aylesbury showed him struggling to articu-late his obsessions with Americana, figureheads like Dylan, Reed and Warhol, and the 'presumptuousness of the songwriter'. Bowie's inven-tion of Ziggy Stardust, a concept that would encompass all these diverse obsessions was simple, like all great ideas.

In later years, David Bowie would claim the idea of Ziggy Stardust came to him in a dream – gifted by the same god who had told his father to find a job at a children's charity. If so, like 'Oh! You Pretty Things', it was an unconscious embodiment of all the skills that he'd mastered in the last few years.

David had experimented with a 'rock opera' back in 1968, when he'd worked on a sequence entitled 'Ernie Johnson' at Ken Pitt's apartment – a bizarre, camp, cockney epic which culminated in the titular hero's sui-cide. In comparison, *Ziggy Stardust* wasn't really an opera, more a collection of snapshots thrown together, edited later into a sequence that made sense. The notion that Ziggy would be David's own alter-ego emerged only at the last minute; it was a bodge-job, later refined into a concept.

Ziggy was David's homage to the outsider; the main inspiration was undoubtedly Iggy, the singer with whom David was obsessed and whose doomed, Dionysian career path had already built its own myth-ology. David was well aware, though, that Iggy, too, was a mere creation. During their first meeting David had that learned the scary gold-and-glitter-spattered front man hid another persona: the urbane Jim Osterberg, who was disconcertingly reminiscent of Jimmy Stewart. Vince Taylor, the other inspiration, was an 'American' rocker, who was actually born Brian Holden in Isleworth, and had made it big in France. By 1966, he was washed up, and the teenage David had bumped into him during the period when Vince was hanging around La Giaconda, claiming he was the messiah and pointing out UFO sites on a crumpled map. Hence Ziggy was a tribute to artifice, a play on identity, alter-ego placed on alter-ego, a vehicle for rock 'n' roll which would allow David, if everything failed, to announce that this was all ironic, just a pose.

Ziggy's surname, a reference to the Legendary Stardust Cowboy, was just as nuanced. The name encompassed David's enchantment with glamour and glitter, referenced Hoagy Carmichael's best-known song and even the relatively recent realisation that, as Carl Sagan put it, 'we are all stardust', all of our atoms recycled via supernovae. And what was Ziggy Stardust, but old vital rock 'n' roll matter, recycled, but fresh as a new world?

Ziggy wasn't born fully fledged, though. He developed bit by bit. 'It was never discussed as a concept album from the start,' says Ken Scott. 'We were recording a bunch of songs – some of them happened to fit together, some didn't work.' Once sessions started at Trident on 8 November, the work in progress sounded more like fifties rock 'n' roll than The Stooges. A cover of Chuck Berry's 'Around and Around' featured in the early track listing, and songs like 'Hang onto Yourself' featured quotes from Eddie Cochran and Chuck Berry, as well as shades of Gene Vincent and Vince Taylor. David's obsession with rehearsing and recording songs rapidly helped approximate the roughness of the Velvets or The Stooges, yet Ronson and his musicians – David, too – were too competent to summon up anything like The Stooges' moronic inferno.

The straight-ahead rockers – 'Hang onto Yourself' and 'Suffragette City' – took Eddie Cochran's teenage rebellion as a model, with the same mix of acoustic and electric guitars, as well as liberal musical quotes from 'Something Else'. But where Cochran's songs spoke to kids breaking the parental bonds, Ziggy Stardust's message was explicitly about sexual liberation: 'Henry . . . I can't take you this time' and 'The church of man, love'. Images like 'tigers on Vaseline' or the 'mellow-thighed chick put my spine out of place', made up their own manifesto: theatrical, yet sleazy, all delivered with an arched eyebrow.

The two songs that would open and close the album were even less reminiscent of American heavy rock. Both songs were in a slow-burning, triple-time signature, 6/8 – like 'House of the Rising Sun' or Paul

Simon's 'America' – yet are starker, more stripped down. 'Five Years' and 'Rock 'n' Roll Suicide' are masterful, both built on minimal, almost unvarying broken chords, with David's voice alone supplying the drama. Both songs illustrate how Ziggy could stage an emotional onslaught that David had never attempted – the desperation in 'Five Years', the urgency in 'Rock 'n' Roll Suicide', which completed Ziggy's dramatic arc. The ending, 'Gimme your hands . . . you're not alone', is pure show-business artifice, an act of audience manipulation worthy of Leni Riefenstahl, but Bowie's sympathy for Iggy, Vince and all the other doomed rock 'n' rollers is absolutely sincere.

Some figures, notably Angie Bowie, dispute that David Bowie ever truly loved anyone; yet there is no doubt of his deep and enduring love for rock 'n' roll. 'Rock 'n' Roll Suicide' is all the more poignant given that, just a couple of years later, Iggy Pop, abandoned by Bowie, would stab himself on-stage, in an event publicised as a rock 'n' roll suicide that, his manager informed the press, 'will only happen once'.

'Rock 'n' Roll Suicide', along with 'Suffragette City', was among the last songs recorded in the album's main sessions, demonstrating that the album's central concept – Ziggy's rise and fall – arrived late in the day, with Chuck Berry's 'Around and Around' still on the track listing. But in that whirlwind winter, events were moving fast. *Hunky Dory* was released on 17 December, with the single 'Changes' following it on 7 January and immediately picking up radio play. A gorgeous song, based around one of the piano runs painstakingly worked out at Haddon Hall, with a stammered chorus that echoed 'My Generation' and hence emphasised its status as an anthem for a new youth movement, 'Changes' didn't make the British charts this time around but 'it was the breakthrough', says Anya Wilson, who had to hawk it around the radio.

It was in the closing weeks of 1971, as the final details of Ziggy's mythical career were penciled in, that the hero was given his own costume. The aesthetic was half futuristic, half thrift-shop chic, masterminded primarily by Freddie Buretti. Freddie himself cut an exotic figure – with his high-waisted peg-leg trousers, skinny shirts and, occasionally, eighties-style oversize shades – but when he and David cooked up their new look, they based the designs on the Droogs, the futuristic teenage thugs in Stanley Kubrick's legendary, banned film version of *A Clockwork Orange*. 'But to lessen the image of violence, I decided we should go for extremely colourful and exotic material in place of the Droog white cotton,' says David. Freddie designed and did most of the sewing on the skinny outfits, which were fitted with a generous, Tudor-style codpiece, copied from

Britain's popular Mod jeans, Lee Cooper. To complete the look, David searched out cheap, brightly coloured wrestling boots, custom-made by Russell & Bromley, whose showroom was based in North Bromley. These kind of boots could be seen on television every Saturday afternoon on ITV's hugely popular, ludicrously choreographed wrestling shows, and completed the aesthetic of rock 'n' roll danger and Vaudeville camp.

It was Angie who encouraged the next phase of David's makeover; within a few days, the flowing gold locks that David had worn throughout the recording were shorn. Thus, the final link with the 1960s was severed. Many of David's contemporaries – Marc Bolan, and even the Nice's Keith Emerson, who wore a silver lurex jumpsuit as he attacked his Hammond organ with a knife that October – had already glammed themselves up that year. But their outfits, with flared trousers and wavy hair, were in essence an evolution of the hippie look. The Ziggy persona – with its cropped hair and skinny silhouette – marked a ruthless break with the sixties. It was finely calculated, but impromptu; done in a rush. Freddie had hardly finished sewing David's first sand-and-black quilted jumpsuit when David called Mark Pritchett late one night. 'Can I borrow your Les Paul? The red one?'

It was raining the next day when David came to collect it, mentioning he was off to a photoshoot with Brian Ward, the Chrysalis photographer who'd first worked with David the previous spring. In comparison, this was a simple shoot, in black and white; David posing with Pritchett's guitar directly outside Ward's studio on Heddon Street, the tiny U-shaped passage leading off Regent Street, and then in the nearby telephone box. The ghostly post-apocalyptic Droogs feel was enhanced by the cardboard boxes left out on the street, the glare of the street lights and the early evening chill evident in the car windscreens, in what would be London's coldest January for several years.

Although a BBC session on 11 January was booked to promote his current album, 'Queen Bitch' was the only *Hunky Dory* song – its campy New York vibe especially reminiscent of the Velvets' 'Sweet Jane' – in the session, which was dominated by 'Hang onto Yourself' and the newly written manifesto 'Ziggy Stardust'. This was a bold, risky strategy, considering David's ever-changing musical identity, but Defries and Anya Wilson were happy to follow David's instincts. 'He was our golden boy,' says Wilson. 'People knew it was going to happen.'

Over that intense winter, David spent even more time thinking than he did singing. Earnest conversations at Haddon Hall ranged late into the night: freewheeling, philosophical, touching on Chuck Berry, The Velvet Underground, the post-industrial future and Hollywood glamour. Often David would talk to Anya Wilson and her boyfriend, Dai Davies, about 'the pretty things'. They knew he didn't mean his old friends from the blues scene. 'These are the coming generation,' he told them, 'a change is on its way.'

As David developed his theme, they huddled round the huge corner fireplace, the air thick with the haze from his cigarettes, and listened to him develop a manifesto line by line: this was a new era, factory jobs were obsolete, and so were the Victorian values that defined their parents' lives. The coming generation would not be restricted by work or conventional sexuality. This bisexual, glittering generation was the homo superior – and David would be their spokesperson.

As a spokesperson, David needed someone to spread his message. The old, sixties writers, people who'd written about David already, were out. Then Dai Davies, newly recruited as David's press mastermind, told David about the new generation of journalists, writers who were interested in theories, in manifestos, not in a pint and a chat in the pub. Together, they would approach Michael Watts first; he'd read Norman Mailer, and was developing a new, long-form feature style at *Melody Maker*. Next, they'd take David's new manifesto to Charles Shaar Murray at the *NME*.

In later months, Davies wondered about the manifesto. There were gaps in it, bits that didn't make sense, and he wondered if David knew that and decided it didn't matter. Later still he realised what David had been doing. 'He'd read about Elvis, and he'd read about Hollywood in the thirties and forties, And he was building a brand – before that language had even been invented.'

Watts met Bowie upstairs in Gem's Regent Street office. The *Melody Maker* staff were well aware of Bowie's regular presence at the Sombrero; there was a sense that David had 'something to get off his chest', and a hope that Watts would get a scoop, which is exactly what happened.

Watts remembers Bowie being 'slightly flirtatious' all the way through the interview; and indeed there was a delicious coyness about the whole piece, with Watts feigning a worldly, unshocked demeanour, as David holds forth, self-consciously messianic. 'I'm going to be huge,' he tells Watts, 'and it's quite frightening in a way.' In his words, one can sense the teenage brio that so entranced the Deram staff, but here it's augmented with a consummate display of name-dropping (Lindsay Kemp, Lou, Iggy and the Tibet Society) and a new playfulness, a sense that he is playing a game and is a master of it. When he tells Watts, 'I'm gay – and always have been, even when I was David Jones,' Watts comments that there is 'a sly jollity about how he says it'. It was obvious that Watts was transfixed by what Bowie's next interviewer, Charles Shaar Murray, describes as 'a genius for inducing a powerful, platonic man-crush in fundamentally straight guys'.

For all the playfulness, this was a momentous announcement; utterly without precedent, and ravishingly brave. Gay sex had been nominally decriminalised in July 1967, but arrests for 'Gross Indecency' had tripled over the following three years, while many of David's contemporaries would remain firmly in the closet for decades to come. Gem staff attempting to get Bowie airplay at the BBC had already encountered the objection that 'we don't have perverts on this show'. There was a precedent for David's announcement, of which he was almost certainly aware, namely David Hockney's overt declaration of his own sexuality with his *We Two Boys Together Clinging* painting, back in 1961, when gay sex could land a man in prison. Bowie's move was more flagrant, aimed at the mass-market, rather than a coterie of critics. It was a thrillingly high-risk strategy – and one that David had only discussed with Dai Davies, not Defries, who anyway took the view that any publicity is good publicity.

David's sexual and image makeover had already been anticipated by Marc Bolan – who'd glammed up in the spring of 1971 and proclaimed, 'I'll go up and kiss guys if I think they're nice,' in *Sounds*. But Marc lacked David's chutzpah, his willingness to gamble everything, and David, of course, was in second place and needed to outdo him.

In later years, gay-rights activists would criticise Bowie's coming out as mere 'androgyny as chic'. Some of their cynicism was probably justified, given that after David outed himself, he inned himself a few years later, complaining about the commercial damage that his image had caused him in America. Rarely has such a spontaneous act of courage been followed by such a considered act of cowardice. Yet David's later retraction is irrelevant: he had let a genie out of the bottle and it would never fit back in. This was a generational shift. Steve Strange, later of the Blitz club, was twelve when Bowie made his announcement, and for him and his peers, Bowie demonstrated he was not alone. 'I grew up in Newbridge, in Wales – and as a kid I was the freak of the village. I didn't know what being gay meant, there was no sex education, but I knew it wasn't right.' Bowie's appearance was a beacon that would eventually draw a generation of kids to London or to a new life.

David was careful to have his cake and eat it in the interview – pointing out his 'good relationship' with Angie and Zowie, leaving the implication that his gay side was as camped up as the '50,000' sales of *The Man Who Sold the World* in the US. This is the interpretation David would push in the 1990s, claiming that the excitement of hanging out in the Sombrero outweighed anything physical, which was 'something I wasn't comfortable with at all'. This pained recollection seems to confirm the criticisms of those who regard his gay phase as a pose, a marketing stance. Yet for David, the marketing, the pose, was part of his essence.

Witnesses like Tony Zanetta and Leee Childers were integral members of the organisation that painted David as a poster boy for bisexuality; but the pair, put on the spot, conclude that David's gay stance was primarily about culture, rather than sex. 'He *was* bisexual, but what he really was, was a narcissist – boys or girls, it was all the same,' says Zanetta. 'He was attracted to the gay subculture because he loved its flamboyance. Sometimes it was just an expression of communication – sometimes it was a way of . . . assimilating someone. But it was never his primary thing, and once the girls came flocking it didn't matter.' Michael Watts, who once commented 'sometimes, honesty pays' about the revelation he extracted, today says simply, 'He knew exactly what he was doing.'

Within a few days of the *Melody Maker* interview, David had to contend with a much more sceptical audience; his three musicians from Hull. He had primed Mick, Woody and Trevor by taking them to see *A Clockwork Orange* and explaining that the costumes being designed by Freddie Buretti were 'futuristic', rather than something 'poofs' would wear. When the three were presented with their catsuits – blue for Trevor, gold for Woody and pink for Ronson – ready for the debut of their new set, David was faced with one of the trickiest acts of salesmanship of his career. Bolder frankly admits he was not impressed – 'To be honest, it took a lot to wear that stuff' – and remembers Mick, destined for the pink jacket, as the most vociferous objector. 'Mick was not up for it. Not at all.' Worn down by Bowie's pure persistence, 'We just sort of went along with it in the end.'

It was possibly the wardrobe disputes that meant that when it came time to premiere the band's makeover on 29 January, 1972, the backstage area at Friars Aylesbury, now David's favourite warm-up venue, was closed off. The crowd was double the size of September's show, kids from London – among them, Freddie Mercury and drummer Roger Taylor – had taken the train up for the show, and as Walter Carlos' 'Ode to Joy', from *A Clockwork Orange*, struck up, a ripple of excitement passed through the mostly teenage audience. 'Then there was the climax, with the strobe and he was standing there in this blue-grey check jumpsuit and it was, Blimey! Unlike anything I'd ever seen,' says Kris Needs.

The band unleashed their full Ziggy assault, launching into 'Hang onto Yourself', and then 'Ziggy Stardust' – a sonic slap in the face for the kids who expected to see and hear the David Bowie of *Hunky Dory*. Some of those already familiar anthems – 'Life On Mars?', 'Oh! You Pretty Things' – followed, complete with a long version of 'I Feel Free', Bowie disappearing to change his catsuit as Ronson let rip on his Les Paul. 'By the time they hit "Rock 'n' Roll Suicide" the place was in total uproar,' says Needs.

Dizzied by the experience, Kris made his way to the dressing room after the show. David was exultant. 'Told you I'd be different,' he told him, before planting a kiss firmly on the seventeen-year-old fan's lips. 'It was life-changing stuff,' says Needs of that evening. 'That night invented the seventies, and everything that came after, glam or punk – that was the defining moment.' The local newspaper's review of the show was titled 'A Star is Born'.

The sense of manifest destiny and utter confidence – 'I'm going to be huge – it's quite frightening in a way' – that was surging through David would permeate their whole tiny operation over the next few weeks. Over the winter Tony Defries had taken to wearing an enormous fur coat, invariably accompanied by a huge cigar; together with his prodigious nose and halo of frizzy hair he cut 'the weirdest figure' according to RCA's Barry Bethel, who remembers that the entire record company was in awe of this intimidating figure. Defries loved gathering young people around him, enthusiastic teenagers, unconstrained by convention, who enjoyed his mockery of record companies. Defries was a good listener, though, and took note of RCA's concerns when they heard the initial album acetates. 'RCA told us *Ziggy Stardust* was great – but we needed a single,' says Robin Mayhew, 'something they could pull straight off the album – so David went off and wrote what he called "Somewhere Over the Rainbow". His Starman song.'

'It was at that point that the [Ziggy] concept finally happened,' says Ken Scott, 'it was the perfect single.'

In stories of the songwriting of Paul McCartney and John Lennon, the rivals with whom David would soon be compared, 'I Wanna Hold Your Hand' has been singled out as an early peak, a knowing song that packs in so many arresting songwriting devices – a 'joyous energy and invention', as writer Ian MacDonald puts it – that its hit status was inevitable. 'Starman' represents the same euphoric peak in Bowie's writing, a moment of technical supremacy.

The opening minor chords are cheekily self-referential, a quote from David's one hit, 'Space Oddity'; then the story is mapped out like a novel, with supreme economy. 'Didn't know what time it was,' the narrator tells us, to a claustrophobically tight tune. The lyrics are set against the beat, adding to the intrigue, with the last word in each line – 'low-oh-oh' – drawn out, pulling the listener in syllable by syllable, like a fish on a line. Then the key changes from minor to major, Ronson's staccato guitar fires up like a searchlight in the gloom and we hit the chorus – and as David leaps an octave, over the word 'starman', we hit escape velocity, and take off.

As modern as it feels, though, the song is classic, and if it feels like the music has gone from monotone to Technicolor, that's because the starman waiting in the sky so closely matches Judy Garland's evocation of somewhere over the rainbow – note for note. It draws on the same emotion – a yearning for escape, from the depression and monochrome of 1939 or 1972 – and the listener's response is instinctive, drawn in by the familiar, intrigued by the alien.

'Starman' was completed in the last session at Trident on 4 February, and in the following weeks the band grew to share David's belief that 'there was never a doubt that this wasn't going to work', says Bolder. 'Everything was in place.'

In typical Defries grandstanding, the manager was building up his own management empire before David had even hit the charts; Dana Gillespie was already on the Gem payroll, and Iggy – now named Iggy Pop – joined her March 1972. Although signed as a solo artist – Defries was only interested in 'stars' and considered musicians as mere drains on his income – Iggy smuggled in guitarist James Williamson, and then the remaining Stooges, who holed up in Kensington, picking up girls, locating drugs suppliers and ignoring Bowie's suggestions that he produce their album. With Defries' artists descending on London, showing up at parties or T. Rex shows and Iggy's legend already being celebrated in papers including *Melody Maker*, the sense that 1972 would be David's, and Defries', year was inescapable.

As David and the band prepared for a string of live shows running up to the *Ziggy* album's release date, each of them was convinced that 'Everything seemed right,' says Bolder. 'That was the weird thing, we didn't even have to think about it.' Then Woody painted the front of his Ludwig kit with the words 'Spiders' and they were a band.

The short tour opened at a tiny pub named the Toby Jug in Tolworth, Surrey. The stage was just a foot high, and the roadies had crammed a full PA and lighting rig into the room; the audience, numbering fifty or sixty were as transfixed as those at Aylesbury, and in the fourteen shows that followed, David recruited hard-core fans – in their dozens, not in their hundreds – but each of them, like audience member Pete Abbott, who witnessed the show at Imperial College, remember, 'It was like nothing I'd ever seen before. We knew about Bolan, but that was pop music. This was *serious*.'

At Imperial College David attempted to emulate the feat he'd seen Iggy perform, in a short snippet of footage at Cincinnati, of walking into the audience and being held up; he toppled to the floor, one of several tumbles he took in those weeks. 'He would never let the audience know [it had happened],' says Bolder. 'He would just get back up and carry on.' The band roved up and down the country, David, Angie and band in two used Jags, with the crammed one-ton van bringing up the rear. In show after show, David was putting his moves together, expansive gestures that, when he finally played big halls, would reach the back of them. 'He was a really good front man. He knew exactly what he was doing.'

By the time David arrived at Manchester's Free Trade Hall on 21 April, and attempted to crowd surf once more, the audience held him up. Angie's input was 'vital – she drove the whole thing, made it happen', says Robin Mayhew; she operated the lights on the first shows, organising the costumes, the food. But on stage it was Mick Ronson who was king; there was no clue that this was the man who'd pored nervously over studio arrangements, for he was in total control. 'If the thing was getting shaky, he would hold it together,' says Mayhew. 'If Bowie noticed something, say the finish of "Ziggy Stardust" was dragging, it was Ronno would stay and direct things. No shouting or screaming, no egos.'

When *The Rise and Fall of Ziggy Stardust* was released on 6 June, plenty of reviewers were irritated by the audacity of the concept. *Melody Maker* described Bowie as a 'superb parodist'; *Sounds*, which had applauded *Hunky Dory*, declared, 'It would be a pity if this album was the one to make it . . . much of it sounds the work of a competent plagiarist.' Their words illustrated the irrelevance of the music critic, for over the next three or four weeks it became obvious an unstoppable juggernaut was on the move. Early in the month there was the announcement that MainMan would be presenting both Iggy Pop and Lou Reed in concert – recruiting two of America's hippest acts as supporting attractions in the Bowie circus – while just one week after its negative album review *Sounds* decided the Bowie live show 'just needs to be packed with sweating teenagers to pull it off'. Over just a few short weeks, a consensus was emerging; if Ziggy was merely a joke, everybody wanted to be in on it.

There was one wobble, after the Oxford Town Hall show on 17 June. This was an amazing performance, where Mick Rock – the brilliant photographer who'd joined the MainMan cavalcade at the Birmingham show on 17 March – captured David knelt in front of Mick, his arms grasping Mick's thighs as he bites at Ronson's guitar strings with Ronson and the audience transfixed with laughter; instant glam pornography, the 'guitar fellatio' shot would be printed as a full-page ad, purchased by Defries, in the next week's *Melody Maker*. There was a flurry of concern from Ronson – not a fear of the reaction of homophobic gangs in Hull, as has been speculated, 'but because the musicians, Mick and his muso mates, thought bands like Sweet were unbearably naff, manufactured. He was caught in a divide,' says Dai Davies, who spent hours reassuring the guitarist that the music would be taken seriously, despite such gimmickry. Bowie would later explain that he and Marc Bolan were high glam: conceptual. Brickies in satin, like Sweet, were low glam.

As the band toured through the spring, there was the sense both of a groundswell of support, driven through word of mouth, and a potential backlash from critics, who found Bowie and Defries' operation considered and manipulative. The perfect response to such cynicism came with the song that would seal the deal between David and his fans, the ultimate example of the spontaneity that co-existed with his meticulous planning.

Late in March, David had discovered that Mott The Hoople – one of his favourite bands, whom he imagined as 'a heavy biker gang', says singer Ian Hunter – were splitting, and after begging them to reconsider, he invited them down to Gem's Regent Street office, and played them a song which he'd just finished with them in mind. 'He just played it on an acoustic guitar,' says Hunter. 'I knew straight away it was a hit. There were chills going down my spine. It's only happened to me a few times in my life: when you know that this is a biggie. We grabbed hold of it. I'm a peculiar singer but I knew I could handle that.' 'All the Young Dudes' reimagined Mott, in reality well-behaved Hereford boys, as heavy-duty punks, *Clockwork Orange* Droogs. Against a stately, descending chord sequence, the lyrics name check juvenile delinquency, acne, cockney rhyming slang, TV and suicide at twenty-five; 'All the Young Dudes' was a glorious celebration of youth, in all its glamour, ephemerality and heroism. It would be as sincere a love song as Bowie would ever write, to his most enduring love: rock 'n' roll.

Now, having written the definitive anthem of the seventies, David simply gave it away. Some thought that this was a self-serving act, designed to underline his own musical omnipotence. Bob Grace, the man who'd overseen most of Bowie's recent songs, is emphatic that in giving away the song, Bowie paid a price. 'I thought that was a mistake. If David had put out "All the Young Dudes" himself that autumn, he would have been huge beyond our comprehension. It was great he gave [Mott] the song, but I'm convinced it cost him.' Both arguments ignore the fact that Bowie remained, at heart, a fan. This was a simple act of spontaneity, helped by the fact that the music was in any case simply pouring out of him.

Mott The Hoople recorded 'Dudes' on 14 May at Olympic in Barnes, with David producing. Mott, too, had now joined the MainMan empire, and it seemed likely they would provide its first hit, for David's own 'Starman' had now hung around for a fortnight, without troubling the charts. But show by show, in little towns like Torbay or Weston Super Mare, David and The Spiders won over their audiences: a dozen here, a hundred there, before the single made a modest entry into the UK singles chart on 24 June, at number forty-nine. The following day, Dai Davies announced, with only marginal exaggeration, that '1000 fans were turned away' from The Spiders' show at The Croydon Greyhound, where Roxy Music were the support act. But 'Starman' still languished at number forty-one when David and the Spiders walked into the *Top of the Pops* studio on 5 July.

The song had actually made its TV debut on celebrated kids' teatime show *Lift Off with Ayshea* on 15 June – Bowie and his Spiders followed an owl puppet named Ollie Beak – but it was the *Top of the Pops* performance, broadcast on 6 July, that transfixed the nation's youth, and horrified their parents. Bowie was clear-eyed and joyous, his come-to-bed eyes inviting both girls and boys. As Ronson approaches the microphone for the chorus, the sight of David 'casually' draping his arm around the plat-inum-haired guitarist Ronson had a visceral impact. This was the *Melody Maker* cover made flesh.

Marc Bolan – name-checked in the line 'the DJ was playing some get-it-on rock 'n' roll' – had camped it up on *Top of the Pops* first, but he was cute, unthreatening; David and The Spiders were dangerous, a warning not only to lock up your daughters, but your sons, too. The moment David put his arm round Mick Ronson, teenagers around the country shared 'a moment of epiphany', as ballet's *enfant terrible*, Michael Clarke, puts it. 'It was like "Oh my God, maybe other people are a little bit like I feel inside."' In just three minutes, David Bowie laid out his claim as a glam messiah, and propelled his single to number ten, in what would be a twelve-week run in the charts.

David had turned up late at the glitter rock ball – Marc Bolan had famously sprinkled glitter over his face for his 'Hot Love' appearance on *Top of the Pops*, back in March 1971. Yet Bowie's intervention was definitive, it was unashamed, committed, thought through in every detail; besides, many contemporaries remembered that, with The Hype, he had helped inspire Bolan's glitter look in the first place. With their long-running mutual name-checks, Bolan and Bowie were seen as joint creators of what was then known as glitter rock, later renamed glam – in fact, they'd both glittered up at the same time, at the hands of Chelita Secunda, fashion editor of *Nova* magazine and a much-loved (and wayward) rock 'n' roll society hostess. 'She always had David, Marc and Reg – Elton John – over at her place,' says Jeff Dexter. 'She wore glitter herself and one day she put glitter on Marc. David was there and said, "I want some," and Reg had some, too. So the birth of Glam Rock was definitely at Chelita's.'

Just as Judy Garland's dreams of life beyond the rainbow seduced a world gripped by the Depression and threatened by war in Europe, David's own blend of space-age futurism and glamour lodged in the consciousness of a generation in sore need of escapism: glitter sparkles best when set against a grey landscape. In January 1973 a stock market crash finally killed off the sixties boom; the collapse in share prices was followed by an oil crisis and full-blown recession, and the landscape became as grey as anyone could remember since the austerity of David's youth. References to the 1920s Weimar republic, or 1930s Hollywood and Art Deco, and even the threadbare glamour of Edwardian music hall – all images of partying amid the ruins – pervaded David's music, as it did that of emerging rivals like Roxy Music's Bryan Ferry; this was their time. Their ruthless competition added to the excitement, just as it had in thirties Hollywood. 'It was, I'll do anything, play anything, say anything, wear anything to become a star,' says David's friend Scott Richardson. 'And there's nothing wrong with that. And there was a tremendous hunger on the part of the audience for that, too. It was that moment in time.'

Other people who passed within the Bowie orbit underline that sense of mission. Cindy M was a friend of Rodney Bingenheimer, who arranged for her to meet David at Haddon Hall. She was ushered into the most bizarre of environments for a young girl from LA: gothic stained-glass windows, grandiose staircases, Persian rugs, carved elephants, shelves full of art books and a hi-fi playing Roxy Music were some of the kaleidoscope of impressions she retains from that overwhelming afternoon, together with the luminous stars she remembers painted on the ceiling above David and Angie's bed, where she spent much of her time. 'Roxy Music are going to be massive, too,' he told her, but Cindy was already in no doubt that she was in the presence of a hero in the making. When Angie arrived later, says Cindy, she got her face slapped.

Even as 'Starman' ascended into the Top 40, David was setting out a wider agenda, one that marked him as the indisputable curator of all that was hip. As if delivering a ready-made hit to Mott The Hoople was not enough, as well as producing their album – completed in rushed snatches over June and July – Bowie and Defries had by now appointed themselves as saviours of Lou Reed's career too. On a New York trip back in March, Defries had heard Lou's solo album was a disaster and arranged for David to produce its follow-up, before announcing MainMan would present live dates by Iggy Pop and Lou Reed in mid-July. The two shows would form an appetizer for David and The Spiders' most crucial show to date, for which Defries planned to jet over a plane-load of American journalists, ready to preview David's forth-coming US tour.

The venue for the 15 July show was Friars Aylesbury: the one place Defries could guarantee a packed house. By now, *Ziggy Stardust* had hit number five in the UK charts (*Hunky Dory* would soon follow it, up to number three), and it was at this show that all involved knew that David was no longer on the brink of stardom: he had made it, exactly as he and Defries had predicted. 'That night, you knew this had become a move-ment,' said Dai Davies, 'when you looked into the audience and could see a hundred Ziggies.' Many of the US journalists, including Lisa Robinson, Lilian Roxon, Lenny Kaye and *Creem*'s Dave Marsh, knew Ziggy's primary influences first-hand. But even Marsh, a veteran of high-energy shows by the MC5 and The Stooges, thought it 'a good show. The one thing you would be afraid of, that the costumes would outweigh the music, wasn't happening. This was a real songwriter, with real songs and a real band – and Ronson was fabulous.'

Marsh was not alone, though, in wondering if there was something 'vampiric' about Bowie's sponsorship of Iggy and Lou. At the next day's press conference at The Dorchester hotel, Marsh walked in with his old Detroit buddy, 'and it's as if somebody has taken the floor and tilted it in Iggy's direction', as all the New York journalists scurried over to see their old pal. Marsh saw David watching the mêlée with 'eyes like darts. But how was I to know? I was just a twenty-three-year-old greeting a friend.'

Recording on Lou's album began at north London's Morgan Sound in August, proceeding at a whirlwind pace, with three backing tracks recorded in a single day. Like his recruitment of Iggy, Bowie's offer to produce what would become *Transformer* was outrageously presumptuous; it was also a tougher task than anyone could imagine, for Lou was a mess, addicted to bickering and manipulation. Many onlookers would credit arranger Mick Ronson with doing the bulk of the work. Indeed, 'He was the one on the shop floor sorting things out,' says bassist Herbie Flowers, and he worked closely with David to map out the songs. David, however, had the much more difficult task, soothing Lou's frazzled ego, talking him out of his moods and coping with his mind games. 'Lou was extremely messed up, like a parody of a drug fiend,' says Dai Davies, who sat in on the sessions. 'David was incredible, like a much older, mature producer, and would talk Lou down.' Ken Scott, who was engineering, points out, 'It was a team, David, Mick, myself, everyone knew what to do. But David just understood Lou. Which no one else did, in the state he was in.'

David's calm in the studio seemed almost supernatural compared to the frenzy around him, which would soon come to a peak with two elaborate shows at the Rainbow Theatre in north London. He had planned a series of innovations: choreography by Lindsay Kemp, a multi-level set and Warhol-style projections. All of the tiny crew were caught up in the manic preparations: screens were improvised from paper and wood, silver paint for the scaffolding bought cheap from a friend, choreography worked out over a single evening at Haddon Hall. David's focus was unrelenting; he'd selected the venue, the look of the lighting and staging, using techniques he'd seen employed in *Cabaret* and shows by the Living Theatre and filed away in his mental Rolodex for the right occasion. The look seamlessly incorporated Warhol, Jean Genet and *Jailhouse Rock*.

At the centre of it all, David also planned the transformation of his own look, a further distillation of the essence of Ziggy. In his search for more outrageous clothes, he'd already seen the creations of Japanese designer Kansai Yamamoto, and finally managed to score one leotard – red, with cut-off legs and a ludicrous 'bunny' design, that was so outré it was languishing, unsold. The leotard completed the classic later-period Ziggy look, joining an innovation that was just as crucial as David's musical advances.

Along with Elvis's DA and The Beatles' mop-tops, Ziggy's carrot-top makes up the founding triumvirate of definitive rock 'n 'roll 'dos. This creation had been sculpted earlier in July, and according to David was inspired by a model with a Yamamoto haircut – 'It was [in] a slightly girly magazine like *Honey*, not *Vogue*.' Angie called in Beckenham hairdresser Suzi Fussey, who'd long looked after Peggy's hair, to construct the elaborate concoction – razor-cut at sides and back, backcombed into a puffy fluffball, like a tropical bird's mating crest, at the front – and dye his locks an unforgettable flame red. 'I designed the colour and the haircut, but Angie had a lot to do with it – she was the one who gave David the courage to attempt the most exotic things,' says Fussey, who joined the crew as David's personal hairdresser and assistant shortly before the Rainbow concert.

The transformation was electrifying; just a few weeks before David had looked cute, gamine; now he looked like an alien peacock. Yet at the centre of the hubbub around his most ambitious shows to date he remained focused, relaxed, directing rehearsals with deftness and humour, taking time out to show new pianist Matthew Fisher the opening chords for 'Starman', delighted that someone appreciated his songwriting. Behind the alien facade, he remained reassuringly human. Early in the preparations he'd called Fisher's house and the pianist's wife, Linda, had rushed to answer the phone, and got the sweetest of tellings-off: 'You shouldn't be rushing in your condition,' he admonished her. 'When's the happy day?' Linda was shocked to realise he'd remembered Matthew's chance remark of a few weeks back that she was pregnant; soon they were discussing breathing exercises and parenting tips. Few other musicians of that sexist time would have done the same – it was a typical example of how his charm was innate, not purely manipulative.

Those who'd known David for years, though, noticed a new 'distancing' – an exclusion zone opening up around the Bowie persona. When Lindsay Kemp had first met David, the teenager had been convinced of his own talent, 'but he was not starry, by God, no'. By that August, just a few months of genuine stardom, of seeing fans dressed up in his own image had had a subtle effect. Kemp observed that David 'fell for it. You know – he believed in his own iconism – it made it difficult to be close to him.'

This subtle realignment, the sense that David felt himself different, special, was uncomfortable. It didn't seem the result of innate selfishness. More it was a reaction to the sheer intensity, a hysteria which would affect the most stable psyche. 'That Rainbow show was a shock – a big shock,' says Kemp. 'When I saw how he captured an audience of thousands and knew exactly what to do. It was absolutely electric – I was numb from beginning to end.'

The two Rainbow shows were a triumph, the high point of the Spiders era; there was the sense that the ideas had been plucked out of the air, without the formulaic overtones that afflicted some later performances. The audience screamed occasionally, but stayed politely in their seats; for all the glitter, the attention to musical detail was stunning. Fisher, the ex-Procol Harum keyboard player, who had been asked to help out for the two Rainbow shows, was placed behind a screen and was therefore free to walk out into the audience when he wasn't playing the piano. 'His singing was simply incredible. I'd never realised how his voice is 100 per cent, spot in tune, and that if he sings out of tune on his records, it's because he wants to.' The two showcase events, with the presence of two Bowie albums in the charts shortly afterwards, sealed the deal for David. He was no longer a novelty; now he was a phenomenon, just eight weeks since that first sell-out show in Croydon.

The sense of event was heightened two weeks later, in Manchester. Throughout the tour, both band and crew had stayed in tiny hotels and B&Bs; that evening, for the first time, they were checked into an up-market hotel, the Manchester Excelsior, and told they could sign for whatever they wanted on room service. After a night getting wasted on the band's signature cocktail (the Spider Special, made up of brandy, advocaat and lemonade) the assembled MainMan staff were bleary and slightly green-faced the next morning, when they were greeted with a speech almost Churchillian in its scope.

'As far as RCA in America are concerned,' Tony Defries informed his audience, 'the young man with red hair sitting at the end of this table is the biggest thing to come out of England since The Beatles. And if we get this right there's every possibility we *will* be as big as The Beatles, if not bigger. We're relying on all of you – and you all have to learn to look and act like a million dollars!'

Like all great generals, Defries was as concerned with logistics as he was with morale, and he briskly went around the table checking on the status of instruments, amplifier backline and PA. It turned out the band didn't own most of the backline. 'What do you need for this, William?' Defries asked Roadie Will Palin. 'Er, £20,000?' Within a couple of days, all the gear had been purchased, flight-cased, and was on its way across the Atlantic for The Spiders' biggest adventure so far.

10

Battle Cries and Champagne

David was like a lost child, looking for Angie. I'm sure he was very vulnerable and nervous. I didn't think about it at the time – what did I know?

Tony Zanetta

The 22 September, 1972 show in Cleveland that launched David's assault on America felt like a thrilling, surreal, high-cholesterol version of his early British dates. Local radio stations filled the airwaves with Ziggy songs, encouraged by Brian Sands, a friend of John Mendelssohn's who had set up a local Bowie fan club. There was a decent scattering of Ziggy clones in the six-hundred-strong audience, which gave the high-powered show a riotous reception. As David and the band sat drinking during the after-show party at Hollenden House – a huge, 1960s hotel with bleached-wood interiors and space-age fibreglass furniture – the room was fizzing with excitement.

'Oh, don't worry,' said Defries. 'You're coming back to Cleveland at the end of the tour, and we'll be playing the big venue, with 10,000 people.'

The band laughed. 'Yeah, yeah, yeah, Tony,' they all chorused.

'But we did come back,' says Trevor Bolder. 'Two nights, sold out.'

For David, this was the rollercoaster ride of which he'd fantasised; the people, places and the spaces in America would all make their mark on his music. Through the following months, he would be pushed through a schedule more gruelling than that which had brought many tightly-knit bands to grief – and lap it up, devouring the experience. 'He was just completely on it, the ultimate pro – a machine,' says Scott Richardson, one of many who remember David's exuberance and excitement. Yet those heady months would also splinter his relationship with Angie and open up cracks in his own, once sturdy psyche.

For Tony Defries, too, the challenge of conquering America was at the core of all his fantasies. He'd started with one artist, and now had a stable of them. At the beginning of that year he had measured himself against Colonel Parker; now that ambition seemed too prosaic. By the end of the year, he talked of his company as the new Metro-Goldwyn-Meyer. His business was bigger than rock 'n' roll; he traded in stars.

In order to build this lofty edifice, Defries needed a New York base, so during late 1972, Tony Zanetta found a two-bedroom apartment on the Upper East Side, bought furniture and painted it himself. His theatre background meant he was content with the occasional cash handout or gift in lieu of a salary – an important qualification for any prospective MainMan employee. Zanetta was soon joined by Leee Childers – who would become road manager and later advance guard, checking out venues before the band arrived – and Cyrinda Foxe, a charming Marilyn Monroe lookalike beloved of the Warhol crew. The trio were all 'dreamers', with minimal business experience, but Defries loved hanging out with them, absorbing their enthusiasm. Within weeks, they realised Cyrinda's forté was not administration; instead Kathy Dorritie – Cherry Vanilla – replaced Cyrinda and proved to be the only one with any idea of how to run an office. Zanetta was handed day-to-day management of the forthcoming tour, initially accompanied by the sage figure of Gustl Breuer. An elegant fifty-seven-year-old opera expert from the RCA classics department, he had been delegated by the company to oversee spending on the tour, which they had been persuaded to underwrite by the silver-tongued Defries. Gustl joined a cavalcade of exotic characters which included hairdresser Suzi Fussey, photographer Mick Rock, the roadies – including Peter Hunsley and Robin Mayhew – David's friends George and Birgit Underwood, plus a team of three bodyguards led by Stuey George, an old Hull mate of Ronno's with a noticeable limp.

David arrived in New York on 17 September, 1972, with Angie in tow. Their week-long cruise across the Atlantic on the QE2 was well publicised, highlighting their status as eccentric 1930s-style glamour icons. Defries considered David's stated fear of flying an affectation, inspired by one occasion when David wanted to avoid flying with Angie to Cyprus to see her parents. He naturally incorporated David's intermittent phobia into his palette of publicity gimmicks, while David likewise became addicted to the quirky, cosmopolitan charm of travelling by boat and the temporary fear of flying became permanent.

In their first couple of days in New York, Bowie and Ronson set out to find a replacement for the various temporary Brit pianists who'd helped them out so far. Annette Peacock – a delightfully genre-busting artist who was briefly signed to MainMan – suggested her own pianist, Mike Garson, who was scraping a living giving piano lessons. It was Ronson who oversaw the auditions at RCA, sitting in with Garson in the main studio and showing him the chords to 'Changes'. Mick had an amazing ear for detail and fell in love with Garson's playing after just seven or eight bars. David, too, was overwhelmed – 'he was simply extraordinary' – and grew to love sitting alongside the bearded, almost gentle musician on the tour bus, finding out how he ticked. Garson brought a decadent, almost Weimar ambience to the music, which perfectly offset The Spiders' no-nonsense R&B. He made his debut at the Cleveland show, and would quickly become integral to David's music. He would also become a key player in the ultimate dismemberment of the band he augmented so perfectly.

For David, being on the road was the fulfilment of fantasies he'd treasured ever since Terry had turned him on to Jack Kerouac. He loved the long drives along the American highways in their rented bus, and as the band drove from Cleveland to Memphis, and then back to New York, he spent endless hours surveying the landscape and buildings along the roadside, or chatting with George Underwood and Birgit, George's beautiful, dark-haired Danish-born wife, who'd come along for the adventure.

George was as obsessive a Yankophile as David, overjoyed to be in the land of Elvis Presley and Muddy Waters. It was during the drive from Cleveland to New York that he was messing around on an acoustic and started to strum out the distinctive stop-start riff of Muddy's 'I'm a Man'. David started strumming along with him. 'And then he wrote the song,' says Trevor Bolder.

Other passengers claimed to have contributed to that jam too, notably Will Palin, but it was Bowie who appropriated it. David had messed around with some words that afternoon – at least one person remembers a variant of the song that went 'We're bussing, we're all bussing' – but by the time they reached New York, ready for their prestigious slot at Carnegie Hall on 28 September, David had come up with a complete lyric, which he sang in New York for Cyrinda Foxe, with whom he was canoodling – very publicly. The song was called 'The Jean Genie'; everyone recognised its sensuous, reptilian hero as inspired by Iggy.

The Carnegie Hall show was, despite Bowie's forty-eight-hour bout of flu, a triumph, inspiring a deluge of press coverage. Defries particularly loved the *Rolling Stone* cover story, which applauded David's music but commented cynically on how he was invariably flanked everywhere by three security heavies. Defries quipped, with an all-knowing smile, 'Without the security guards, he wouldn't *be* on the cover of *Rolling Stone*, would he?'

For all Defries' big talk, the initial number of confirmed shows booked for David was tiny, but the deluge of press and audience enthusiasm generated a flurry of interest from promoters which allowed MainMan to add another eight weeks of dates. The extra shows seemed to vindicate Defries' genius in promoting David as if he were already America's biggest star, but the empty seats inside many venues would take their toll, both on MainMan's finances and David's psyche. In the UK, David was not yet mainstream, but he had enough fans for the glitter kids to gather in little groups and brave the derision of rockers who hated 'that poof Bowie'. In American cities with a good radio station or a cool headshop, like-minded fans could gather and the venue would be full. But outside of those cosmopolitan enclaves, few fans ventured out, and in the Midwest many of the venues' seats were conspicuously empty. Normally an English band touring the USA could rely on their record company for expertise on the ground. But this was the downside of Defries' obsession with signing to RCA, where David would be the biggest fish in a small pond. 'David was stuck on the worst record label in the world,' says Dai Davies, who was sent out to rustle up more shows. 'And ultimately, the more money they took off RCA to try and make things happen, the longer it would take David to pay them back.'

In the first few weeks, though, the feeling of infallibility was hardly punctured. When the band convened in New York's RCA studio on 6 October, most of them were surprised to find they were going to record their Greyhound bus jam, 'The Jean Genie' – the session was so rushed that co-producer Ken Scott didn't even make it to New York. The song was like a musical collage; the titled blended Jean Genet – Lindsay Kemp's idol – with Eddie Cochran's rocker, 'Jeanie Jeanie Jeanie'. But the sound was a complete lift – how could anyone have the cheek to record it? 'We all looked at each other and just thought, This is "I'm a Man!"' said Bolder, who like Ronson knew the song via The Yardbirds' version. It was recorded in just a couple of takes – the mid-song crescendo of The

Yardbirds' version was moved to the beginning, while the chorus was as simple as could be, with the band merely staying on one chord. It was a consummate example of explicit *homage* in a grand tradition, for as Underwood and Bowie both knew, Muddy Waters had borrowed the riff from Bo Diddley in the first place – as would Mike Chapman and Nicky Chinn a few short weeks later, for the Sweet's hit 'Blockbuster'.

Released on 25 November, 'The Jean Genie' would hit number two in the UK. It was a one-trick pony of a song, but that didn't matter. It kept up the momentum; Lou's 'Walk on the Wild Side' shot up the chart in parallel. Lou's hit was self-consciously cool, David's childishly simple: both contributed equally to David's growing legend.

Meanwhile, the tour dates continued, moving south from Detroit and Chicago to St Louis and Kansas City. There was gossip that David had turned to drink to help cope with the stress of some of the poorly attended shows in the Midwest, notably St Louis. Not true, according to his inner circle, but Ian Hunter, whose own tour with Mott The Hoople criss-crossed the states that autumn, bumped into his mentor several times and noted 'glimpses of sadness'. Some of it was sheer bewilderment; George Underwood remembers David's worries that audiences weren't even reacting to the shows, 'but they were simply open-mouthed, in amazement and shock!'

Despite the niggling worries, there were long periods when David would be 'up', working on songs or enjoying the peaceful train journeys. David, accompanied by George and Brigit, or Ronson, savoured the names of the huge beasts – Texas Chief, San Francisco Zephyr – and vied for a place in the Zephyr's magnificent Vist-a-Dome, a Plexiglas viewing pod which gave panoramic views across the ever-changing landscape. 'A couple of the band or friends, gladly one and the same most of the time, would often come and sit with me on these stretches,' says David. 'Ronson would love it, so too would my old chum George Underwood and his wife Birgit. At about 10 at night we'd creep up there, the air rich with the smell of grass, and laze around with guitars and a bottle of wine, watching the western moon get bigger and shinier into the early hours of the morning.'

The gorgeous 'Drive In Saturday' was inspired by the succession of images he saw on the train to Phoenix, and debuted in the show there on 4 November – but there was a constant conflict between the buzz of ideas and the demands of his schedule, from which he was starting to shrink. 'The work had to be defined by him, but that wasn't necessarily what had to be done when you're on the road. It was always a conflict,' remembers Zanetta. 'If left to his own devices he'd stay in a dark room in bed all day long. You had to force him to do things.' The tour progressed with bursts of activity, then sudden stopovers, a disorientating existence in which many people – Angie most obviously, but David too – seemed almost manic depressive, oscillating between energy highs – business and sexual – and days of utter, exhausted torpor.

The nervous energy carried David through to Los Angeles for a four-day break before two shows at Santa Monica, dates full of promise thanks to the enthusiastic promotion of Rodney Bingenheimer, who by now had opened Rodney's English Disco on Sunset Strip. A mirror-walled temple to English glam, it was laid on with every staple a Brit muso could need: Watney's Bitter, sausage rolls and teenage Valley girls. It was this period that most closely resembled Fellini's *Satyricon*: the streets were full of boys and girls, men and women offering services both sexual and pharmaceutical; Quaaludes were the drug *du jour*, popped like jellybeans by most of the crew, although David rarely, if ever, indulged. Prompted by Lisa Robinson, Leee Childers had booked band, crew and hangers-on into the swanky Beverly Hills Hotel, where the two stars – Bowie and Defries – had their own bungalows. Elton John overlapped with Bowie on their stay; David dropped in on him and found him isolated, dwarfed by a mountain of vinyl records. Cyrinda Foxe was flown over from New York. Andy Warhol, film director Paul Morrissey and Iggy Pop were on the scene, while Rodney's girls descended on the party in a frenzy of what Tony Zanetta called 'kiddie decadence'. 'Cracked Actor', written over that week, was an almost literal depiction of the sleaze on offer; the line 'since he pinned you baby' was a straight lift from the paranoid drug argot developed by Lou Reed and John Cale in the Velvets: 'pinning someone meant they were on drugs – you'd pinned them, you'd got them,' says Cale.

Rodney's regular Nancy McCrado remembers her friends Sable and Queenie, both of them in their early teens, sneaking into Mick Ronson's room, stripping off their clothes and waiting for him, naked. 'Mick was really upset about it – pushed them out and locked the door.' Later, Rodney's girl Lori Madox sneaked with a friend into David's room. According to Madox, David was tired but eventually proved more obliging than his lieutenant.

Roadie Robin Mayhew, like McCrado, remembers that 'Ronno wasn't involved in the dubious scenes – he was more selective.' Ronson's focus was legendary; the perfect example was the afternoon at the Beverly Hill

Hotel that he spent running carefully through a pre-show checklist with the roadies. He asked them a couple of follow-up questions, then the moment that business was concluded and the conversation started to wander, coolly informed them 'That's enough' and ushered them out of the door so he could attend to the blonde who'd been waiting patiently on the bed. Most of the others did take advantage of Rodney's girls – made up of a mix of 'unsupervised rich kids or more desperate street kids', according to regular, Kathy Heller. The girls were part of LA's rich cornucopia of pleasures, which also included Lobster Thermidor, which everyone ordered from room service, or the Quaaludes offered by the young Hollywood boys who were desperate to get access. Even for those who'd seen some of the excesses of the sixties, like Robin Mayhew, 'It was a total eye-opener.'

For The Spiders, the roadies and bodyguards, this was their first experience of Los Angeles; it could never be equalled. The frenetic, confused buzz surrounding them intensified from the moment Mike Garson revealed he was a member of the Church of Scientology. He talked to David first, and was rebuffed ('What a ludicrous idea, expecting David to sublimate his ego to L. Ron Hubbard,' quips writer Mick Farren) before approaching the rest of the organisation.

Bowie, Ronson and Bolder loved Garson's musical input, which offset his religious fervour. For David, the issue became a joke, and he labelled the pianist 'Garson the Parson'. But for the junior members of the crew, Scientology became a serious issue. 'The other guys became obsessed, there was this righteousness about them, that they knew no wrong,' remembers Mayhew. 'It became bizarre, very black and dark.'

Garson's evangelism for Scientology started taking effect when they arrived in LA, where he persuaded most of the entourage to visit the Scientology Center and each musician was assigned his own mentor. 'He tried to get me into it and failed,' says Bolder, who during his visit saw 'all these weird people doing weird things, tests, mind games – I didn't want to know.' Shortly afterwards, Bolder returned to his hotel room after a heavy night's drinking at [famous Hollywood nightclub] the Whisky, only to open the door and see Garson and a woman who'd been assigned to recruit him, sitting on his bed. Bolder threw them out, 'but Mike hounded me for years. But Woody did go back in there. And I think Scientology had a big influence on him.'

Woody Woodmansey became the Spiders' best-known Scientology convert, and from his first sessions with the cult, says Bolder, he was taught to 'be more positive and speak your mind. And if you're a type of person who speaks their mind anyway you're going to speak it even more. He was confident that he was a Scientologist and everything was gonna be wonderful and he couldn't fail.'

Defries took little interest in the details of what was going on backstage, where the atmosphere was turning nasty and Stuey George in particular was becoming 'far too heavy', says Mayhew. 'If there were fans hanging around he'd lay into them. We're saying, "Don't be so heavy" – he'd be shouting at the kids, effing and blinding, and it was very scary for them, this heavy, coloured guy with a limp, who looked like he'd been through it, heading for them.' Tony Frost, the second of David's three bodyguards, became another Scientology convert, adding to the haze of hype and confusion emanating from the MainMan circus.

Much of the edge, intensity and euphoria of that LA week was audible in the Santa Monica shows on 20 and 21 October. They were a triumph, the seventeen-song set offering delight after delight, running across what would be five Bowie albums. Defries had sold the tour as the biggest by an English act since The Beatles; that night's radio recording, for KMET, suggests that if anything he'd undersold his charges, for this set was more adventurous, more visceral and more proficient than anything the Fabs had delivered on stage in America. For years, the recording of the opening night's performance would be a definitive rock 'n' roll bootleg; in the mid-seventies, many English punk bands would admire its high-octane assault, and copy Ronson's modified chord sequence on 'Waiting for the Man'.

In the couple of days before David departed for San Francisco, he was required to sprinkle his magic fairy dust on yet another MainMan album, namely the tracks that Iggy and The Stooges had assembled at CBS studios in London. David's relationship with Iggy was complex; while Lou Reed would always pay due fealty to David, Iggy was already confiding to friends that the Ziggy album sounded 'Mickey Mouse'. When the singer heard 'The Jean Genie', he felt he'd been assimilated. 'I just rolled my eyes and said, "Oh my God – not only has he done The Yardbirds but he's done me too!" That was when I first realised he was taking a lot off me.' The web of mutual respect and distrust was complicated by the fact that Angie had had affairs with The Stooges' Ron Asheton – celebrated for his droll humour, he resembled a young Philip Seymour Hoffman and owned a scarily comprehensive collection of Nazi uniforms – and then James Williamson, the dark, glowering lead guitarist who cordially disliked David but was, says Angie, 'smart. He knew when to keep quiet.'

For all the openness of the Bowies' marriage, it was a messy business, 'a dumb thing to do', admits Williamson. When he had met Bowie back in Haddon Hall, David had been enthusiastic and talkative. During the Iggy mixing sessions at LA's Western Sound he was tense, preoccupied, 'this super-stilted kind of stiff guy', says Williamson. The mix was an exercise in damage limitation: James and Iggy had jumbled up the instruments on the multitrack and all David could do was pull out a few instruments from the sonic holocaust, adding an effect here and there. The results were, a few years later, the prime influence on seventies punk. But at the time it was the first of many half-cocked projects. And soon, Iggy and his Stooges would soon be sent to MainMan's luxurious new house in the Hollywood Hills, where they would be ignored by Defries and return to their old, druggy ways.

The last weeks of that first US tour included several cancellations, poorly attended performances in San Francisco and Seattle, arguments between Defries, Davies and the RCA staff on the ground and friction between the British and American halves of the entourage. None of those problems affected David's songwriting, or his performances, which were riveting, night after night; when he was 'up' he was great company, camping it up with the *Pork* crew, or 'taking the piss' with the Yorkshire crowd. Yet behind the scenes, the relationship that had sustained him for the last two years was splintering.

It's impossible to pinpoint the moment at which David and Angie's marriage was irrevocably doomed. By the autumn of 1972, Defries was gunning for Angie, irritated that she'd used her initiative to rescue the remaining Stooges, who'd been stranded in London without their singer. Although their plane fares, which Angie billed to MainMain, represented a trifling amount compared to the huge sums the company was haemorrhaging on the cancelled US dates, it was Angie's alleged profligacy that Defries fixed on.

For Tony Zanetta, who occasionally found himself miserable and isolated on the bus, a defining moment came during one of the first tour stopovers, in Erie, Pennsylvania. He'd noticed how David would often step out and become the focus of attention – but at other times would withdraw, lost in thought, or nerves. In Erie, David had retreated to his room when Angie started 'fooling around' with a bodyguard, Anton Jones, the two of them skinny-dipping in the motel pool. 'David was like a lost child, looking for Angie,' says Zanetta. 'I'm sure he was very vulnerable and nervous. I didn't think about it at the time – what did I know?'

Angie had been jealous of David's well-publicised affair with Cyrinda

Foxe in New York; making loud remarks about her relationship with Anton seemed to be her way of getting back at him. 'He makes me scream!' she announced to Zanetta and Davies, apparently referring to his sense of humour, but with an obvious double-entendre. 'It was an incredibly unhealthy situation.'

Angie, maybe more than anyone, had helped David get to America. But now they were here, her antics made for one prima donna too many. In reaction, Zanetta sacked Anton Jones, while from now on Defries would try and separate Angie from the touring party. According to Dai Davies, who witnessed Angie and Anton's banishment, Defries' response, however cruel, was the only practical one. 'It's a simple question of management, with thirty-four people and the trucks and everything else, with a tour that wasn't that successful. You can fall in behind one temperamental person. You can't fall in behind two. It becomes a nightmare.'

Angie and David had exchanged wedding wrist-bands rather than the customary rings for their marriage in Bromley; it was during the last days of this tour that David's were snatched by a fan. 'It was highly symbolic, I thought,' said David recently. 'Our marriage was pretty much over in all but name. We were to see less and less of each other as the next year rolled around.'

One can only assume that it was Scott Richardson who unwittingly contributed to the breakdown. The singer – an old friend of Iggy's from the Detroit rock scene – had met Angie when she'd stopped over in Ann Arbor with The Stooges. He joined her for her reunion with David in Cleveland, and soon became her 'official' lover and – he thought – David's friend. Caught in the centre of this unconventional ménage, he regards their open marriage as optimistic, naive: a loving arrangement that also represented a Faustian pact. 'They had this open relationship that the fans and all the world knew about. They utilised all that to seduce the world – and it was incredibly effective. But what they were trying to do with each other ultimately backfired. And my little part, if it did end up causing distress, I apologise.'

If David felt sexual jealousy of Angie he concealed it well. When David took up with Cyrinda Foxe, Angie indulged in a classic defence mechanism, becoming chums with Cyrinda, and copying her haircut. David took on a similar role with Richardson, becoming his rock 'n' roll buddy. Richardson observed that 'David was pulling everybody left and right – and she was doing the same thing. And fantastic as that was for the publicity of the Ziggy Stardust era it was also incredibly destructive.'

David relied on Angie for support – she was the one who encouraged him when his nerve failed: when he worried about wearing the outrageous Kansai Yamamoto 'jockstrap' outfit in Japan, for instance. Yet by the end of the US trip, David seemed to have bowed to Defries' restriction, and demanded Angie obey the old, sexist musicians' rule of 'no wives on tour'.

'David would just get in a furious mood [when Angie was around] because maybe she was too outrageous – or maybe she took over too much of the limelight,' says Suzi Fussey, who now worked as David's PA. 'I honestly don't know.'

Watching David at close hand, and working together with him later, Richardson developed bottomless respect for his abilities. As for Angie, he says, 'I admired her so much as a human being.' Yet he looked on as 'the things that David counted on her for got diminished by the fact that there was so much sex going on. I lived in Haddon Hall and I used to wake under a pile of bodies. I thought having been on the road in America I knew what the rock 'n' roll life was. I didn't have a clue until I went to England.'

By the time David and The Spiders had returned to New York on 3 December, Defries was already planning a Japanese tour, and persuading RCA to co-promote David's return to the States. During the stay, David recorded his own version of 'All the Young Dudes' and a new song, 'Drive In Saturday'. When he met Ian Hunter a few days later, on 10 December, he played him the songs, offering the latter for release; Hunter told him it was 'too complicated' for Mott. By now, Hunter was worried about being regarded as Bowie's creature, but he listened attentively to David's advice, which was incisive, including the observation that it was impossible to run a band as a democracy. Despite his respect for David, Hunter was growing suspicious of the MainMan cavalcade, and kept his MainMan contract in his suitcase; he would never sign it, despite several reminders.

In spite of his concerns, Hunter remained full of admiration for Bowie, who was eight years younger than him, but more worldly and analytical. The Mott singer concluded that David was 'holding up well' under the pressure – which was about to be ratcheted up a few more notches with an imminent short UK tour followed by a return to the US and then a short run of dates in Japan. A few hours after his chat with Hunter, Bowie set sail for London, the boat-trip a welcome relief before the onslaught was renewed.

*

The British press had closely reported the triumphs of the US tour – for all the problems, it was obvious that David had made much more of an impact than Marc Bolan, who'd also toured America than autumn. Two homecoming shows at the Rainbow before Christmas had a celebratory air, with David appealing for donations and, on the 24th, collecting a truckful of cuddly toys to be delivered to children in the Barnardo's homes across London, to which Haywood had devoted so much of his life.

David, Angie and Zowie spent their Christmas together at Haddon Hall, a brief respite before work started again, their family gathering augmented by dozens of fans singing in the street and, according to press reports, camping in the garden. Then it was back to work on the 28th, with a string of shows, starting in Manchester, interrupted by sessions back at Trident.

Completed over December and January, *Aladdin Sane* – its title announced to the camply vague interviewer Russell Harty on 17 January 1973 – bore all the marks of its rushed genesis. Yet this was as much a blessing as a curse, for while songs were at a premium – with a re-recording of 'The Prettiest Star' and a cover of the Stones' 'Let's Spend the Night Together' making up the numbers – there was a freshness and grandeur to the recording, even if the internal logic was not as well developed as *Ziggy*'s. Mike Garson's piano in particular added an anarchic, decadent edge, most obviously on the title track, in a solo which to this day he counts as an amazing moment in his life. 'I played a blues solo and David said, "No, that's not what I'm looking for." Then I played a little Latin solo. "No, that's not what I'm looking for."' David was relaxed, chatting easily to Garson, remembering their conversations on the tour bus. 'Then he said to me, "Well, you told me about playing on the avant-garde scene in New York. Why don't you try something like that?" I said, "Are you serious?" He said, "Absolutely." That whole solo was one shot, one take – boom, that was it. But it came about because he got it out of me.'

Garson was one of many musicians struck by David's growing ability to inspire musicians to reach inside themselves and come up with ideas buried deep within their consciousness. Matthew Fisher, who dropped in on the Trident sessions, was also struck by the way Bowie would communicate ideas. 'He issues very strange instructions to people – not in the prosaic way I would do it. He was talking to the brass players using terms like "renaissance" and "impressionist" – it was very esoteric, but people seemed to understand.'

For Garson, asked to sprinkle his piano, like magic fairy dust, over the album's best songs, David's approach was liberating; soon Mike realised he was expected to bring something new to every track, contributing, for instance, a warped stride piano part to 'Time' that was brilliantly counterpointed by Ronson's perfectly judged guitar. 'That was a great piece; it was a chance for me to play in a whole other way,' says Garson. 'You've got to understand, if the inspiration is given to you – and it was given me – how can you go wrong?'

Garson's bravery in the studio, his willingness to take musical risks on the first or second take, was 'so perfect', says Ken Scott. 'You could see it was pushing the envelope.' However, not every musician was proving so obliging, for reasons not unconnected with Garson – or, rather, his religion.

Drummer Woody Woodmansey had always had 'strong opinions', says Trevor Bolder, but as he fell more deeply under the influence of Scientology he became even more opinionated. Woody had already clashed with Bowie over such trivial matters as the jacket he'd wear on *The Russell Harty Show*; now, his attitude affected the music, too. As they were laying down the backing track for 'Panic in Detroit', David asked Woody to play a Bo Diddley rhythm. 'No way, it's too obvious,' Woodmansey retorted. Ronson had a word; Woody was immovable. 'He wouldn't have any of it,' according to Trevor Bolder. In the end, Woody recorded his drum part much as he wanted – David and Mick asked Geoff MacCormack to overdub congas and other percussion to get the rhythm they'd had in mind.

'Panic in Detroit' was among the last songs recorded for *Aladdin Sane*, the final overdubs laid down as Ronson and Bowie rounded up musicians for a return to America, just a couple of days later. John Hutchinson was sitting in his Scarborough bedsit, when he got a call from Ronson, who asked if he was still playing guitar, then handed the phone to David. 'Are you up for it?' David asked, and he was in. Sax players Ken Fordham and Brian Wishaw were session regulars. Geoff MacCormack, David's old Bromley schoolmate, got the call to join up for backing vocals – and to keep David company on the tour, now that Angie was banished. MacCormack duly packed in his job at *Construction News* and boarded the SS *Canberra* with David, where they settled into the routine of long dinners and nights at the bar, exchanging Oscar Wilde and Bosie witticisms.

Soon after their arrival in New York, David took Geoff down to Max's to see Biff Rose, whose 'Fill Your Heart' he'd covered on *Hunky Dory*;

they were more impressed, though, by a new act, Bruce Springsteen, who was sharing the bill. During rehearsals, David was vibed-up, almost ecstatic as he chatted with his old mate John Hutchinson. There was no hint of reproach that Hutch had left David, back in 1969; instead, David shared his excitement. 'Who'd've thought we'd all get here?' Then back at the Gramercy Hotel, it was straight into one of David's customary bonding sessions, as he gave Hutch a run-through of his latest musical discoveries – 'This is Roxy Music – the singer's a guy from Newcastle, he studied with [the pop artist] Richard Hamilton.'

After rehearsals with the new, bigger band at the RCA soundstage (Harry Belafonte dropped by and politely asked them to turn down the volume) David took Hutch, Geoff and Stuey to see the Rockettes at Radio City Music Hall, where they'd be playing a few days later. Absorbed by their ludicrously camp high-kicking act, David confided to Hutch that he intended to descend from the gods, just like the cabaret they were watching, as part of their act. For a man who now refused to stay in rooms above the hotel's fourth floor, claiming vertigo, this was true devotion to his art.

On the opening night of their second US tour on 14 February, 1973, the show was more grandiose than ever, with five costume changes for David alone; the news that Salvador Dali was in the house generated a special buzz, in a hectic night which culminated in David succumbing to a theatrical fainting fit. Whether this was a Lindsay Kemp-style act of drama, or genuine exhaustion, witnesses like MacCormack are 'still not sure' – but it generated headlines worldwide.

David's recovery was evidently rapid, for by the next night he hit the town again, ending up at a reception for Stevie Wonder at the club Genesis, which was packed with the city's soul talent. Aretha Franklin and Gladys Knight were hanging out, and broke into song, accompanied by Ava Cherry, a striking black model with bleached blonde hair. David walked straight up to Ava and asked, 'Are you a singer?'

'Yeah,' Ava assured him, stretching the truth a little, before a bystander introduced them. 'I've been listening to your albums for a month,' she told him. 'I think they're incredible.' This was not a total exaggeration; Cherry's manager had helped engineer the meeting, hoping it would advance her career. But Ava was fascinated by this outlandish figure: a model of English charm and good manners, buzzing with energy, but content to go with the flow, even when she declined his invitation back to the Gramercy. Within the next couple of days, though – which were packed with a trip to see Charles Mingus, hours spent listening to records and sharing opinions, attendance at rehearsals, and then an informal audition where Defries assessed her singing – they became lovers. 'Then the very next day we're up and getting breakfast,' says Cherry, 'and all of a sudden the door knocks and it's Angie. "Darling! How are you?" So I'm standing there and you can picture the look on my face!'

Once she'd been briefed by David about his open marriage, Ava was shocked, simultaneously intimidated and impressed by Angie, and 'really depressed. I said to David, "Why didn't you tell me?"' Still, she found herself 'a little bit in love with David', as well as entranced by the intriguing cast of characters around him. Just before David left town, he told her he'd like her to join the tour as backing singer. Soon Cherry left her job and apartment, to wait in Chicago where, instead of confirmation, she would receive a telegram saying, 'Sorry, tour has been cancelled.' Informed that David would catch up with her later, Ava concluded, 'Thanks very much. That's completely messed up my life.'

For Cherry, the realisation that she could be taken up then discarded like a child's toy was an unwanted insight into the behaviour of stars and their retinue. It was a lesson that many who passed into the orbit of David Bowie in the forthcoming months would share.

PART TWO

Where Things Are Hollow

11

Star

David acted as if everything was completely normal. I don't know if he was delusional and thought no one knew.

Suzi Fussey

To break up a band like that is astonishing. I have to credit Bowie with having a lot of courage: to say, 'I'm not coming back.'

Scott Richardson

David Bowie's three- or four-day idyll with Ava Cherry in New York marked a new phase his life – an era when he would be surrounded by people using him to advance their careers, when subordinates would overlook every aspect of his working day and when the world's media would pry into every aspect of his life.

David's friends from 1971 and 1972 retain countless, varying impressions of the man, from David the iceman to David the boyish dreamer, but Iggy Pop probably describes it best: 'You're talking about a rather worldly, knowledgeable young buck who was ready to go out into the world and shoot his bolt. But who was focused on a particular target – success.'

That drive for success would cause confusion or resentment from those, like Iggy, Mick Ronson or countless others, who had a different agenda. By 1974 Iggy would be accusing David – 'that fuckin' carrot-top' – of 'sabotaging' his work. Few of those left, damaged and bitter, in David's wake would realise that the newly emerged star was as damaged by the process as they were.

In the heady opening days of 1973, though, David was 'relaxed' and 'sweet' according to his new lover, Ava Cherry. The routine was well established: a morning call from Tony Zanetta or road manager Jaime Andrews, followed by a long bus ride, which for the Spiders was invariably set to the only two tapes they had on the eight-track player: The Stylistics and The Buddy Rich Band. Check-in, soundcheck, a quiet moment as David did his make-up, show, and only then was it time to relax: Geoff MacCormack hanging out with David or other band members; Ronson hanging with Hutch; Woody and Trevor with each other, or occasionally their wives. Once they'd all left New York, Bowie's main social contact with the band was at the aftershow parties, which were usually decorated by the best-looking local girls, selected from all the contenders by David's hairdresser and PA, Suzi Fussey. This was where Hutch first learned the phrase, 'No head, no backstage pass': such transactions were always more explicit and more efficient in America. With Geoff to talk to, Bowie spent less time with Mick, who would chat to Hutch over Irish coffees in the bar. Meanwhile Garson the Parson would be preaching the benefits of Scientology to new band members like Hutch and Fordham.

For this second jaunt around the States, David took in a similar cavalcade of sights: the viewing cars in the trains, the Stetsons in Nashville, the routine at Elvis's favourite hotel, the Peabody Hotel in Memphis, where a trio of ducks waddled through the hotel lobby; each sight shared with the wide-eyed Geoff MacCormack. With a larger crew, and Geoff in tow, David spent less and less time with Trevor and Woody, too. Yet when they did talk, he would reassure them, 'Don't worry, we're all going to be really, really rich.' Trevor and Mick were trusting – until Woody Woodmansey heard from Mike Garson that the new pianist was on a $800 a week salary and, stunned, shared the information with his fellow Spiders. Woody and Trevor were on £50 a week. When they complained to Defries, and asked when they'd get to see the riches David had promised, the MainMan boss was cold as ice. 'Never mind what Bowie told you you're getting – it's what I tell you you're getting.'

It was Mick Ronson who decided he'd had enough of this run-around about pay; a few weeks into the American dates he called Dennis Katz, now managing Lou Reed, to see if he could secure a record deal for The Spiders – without their singer. Katz soon called to say he'd secured a six-figure advance from CBS. The trio were buoyed up, until a traitorous roadie informed Defries of the band's scheme. Characteristically hardball, Defries informed CBS that Katz had no right to negotiate for The Spiders, cutting him out of the deal entirely. Then he called a meeting with the band, and emolliently informed them, 'Why didn't you tell me you wanted a record deal? RCA are willing to sign you – they'll pay you an advance – upfront, if you want some money?' According to Trevor Bolder, Defries then embarked on a textbook divide-and-rule strategy, seeking out Ronson and offering him his own solo deal.

Meanwhile, as he plotted with Ronson, Defries lulled David's rhythm section into a false sense of security. Normally he barely bothered to register their presence, now, when Woody Woodmansey returned to the attack with his usual bluntness, demanding the sidemen receive a rise to £500 a week, Defries was uncharacteristically helpful, assuring them he'd discuss the money situation with RCA. During their last American dates in California, the manager reported back, 'RCA have agreed to pay you £500 a week,' he told them. 'But you can't have that until we get to England – until then, you can have £200 a week, but when we get to England you'll get all the money, upfront [as back-pay].' Delighted that Defries had finally seen sense, the Yorkshire duo chorused, 'That sounds all right.'

On the surface, David remained friendly. He loved Woody's drumming, but it was probably the drummer's bloody-mindedness during the *Aladdin Sane* sessions that marked the turning point. Once Defries had told David of Woody and Trevor's treacherousness – that they'd been planning to cut a record deal behind his back – the question of David's next musical move suddenly became clearer.

David's attitude to Mick Ronson was more complex; the guitarist was stubborn, but he was obliging, a problem-solver and as close a musical friend as he had. Defries wanted a Ronson solo album both to head off The Spiders' revolt and to add another act to his entertainment stable. David had recently discovered a Richard Rodgers' song, 'Slaughter on Tenth Avenue', and saw it as a brilliant vehicle for Ronson's own solo album. He even suggested his friend – and Angie's lover – Scott Richardson as a collaborator. Encouraged by the vision of a glittering solo career, with a musical agenda provided by David, Ronson went along with the plan. As the entire tour party prepared for their most ambitious trip to date – a ten-show stint in Japan: still exotic, unexplored territory for most British musicians – David's rhythm section were content, unsuspecting, for what would turn out to be The Spiders' last ride.

Geoff MacCormack, who kept David company now that Angie was being 'encouraged' to keep her distance, had become an enthusiastic convert to the luxury of international cruising. He was disappointed to find his second trip, from Los Angeles to Yokohama, was on the SS *Oronsay*, a

1940s liner in the twilight of its career that was nicknamed 'SS *Rancid*' by the childhood friends. They spent the trip practising phrases from Geoff's Japanese primer, or treating passengers to Latin records they'd picked up in New York. Finally arriving in Yokahama on 5 April to a five-hundred-strong welcoming crowd, David was resplendent in a wide-lapelled tartan jacket, flanked by frowning matrons irritated at the intrusion, his excitement at the bizarre culture clash equalled only by his exhaustion.

It was during this leg of the tour that many of the contradictions in the MainMan empire were becoming exposed. Endless stories of The Stooges' depredations filtered out of LA in those weeks, with allegations they'd spent company cash on smack and abortions for groupies. Defries, always disapproving of drugs use, ordered them thrown out of MainMain's mansion on Torrenson Drive.

David was upset, but didn't attempt to talk Tony out of his decision. Then, within weeks of Iggy's sacking, another of David's protégés left MainMan, a split resulting from a management meeting where a drunken, impassioned Tony Zanetta proclaimed their business was now based on 'stars, not boring rock 'n' rollers'. The next day, sober, Zanetta was staggered to find his outburst had inspired the sacking of Mott The Hoople, the company's main rock 'n' rollers. (Their career was unharmed, for Ian Hunter, sceptical of Defries, had never signed his management contract.)

MainMan's lack of focus and the way the company was expanding in random fashion was highlighted once the party hit Japan. When David formed a mutual admiration society with Kansai Yamamoto – championing his designs, accompanying his family to the Kabuki theatre – Defries promptly announced that he would now represent the designer in the West, via a Japanese division, MainMan Tokyo. That spring, Defries also floated the notion that David was to star in a movie based on Robert A. Heinlein's *Stranger in a Strange Land*. No names were attached to the announcement, which was suspiciously vague. It's likely the grandstanding was aimed as much at RCA America as the general public, for while David's album sales were phenomenal in Britain – where *Aladdin Sane* debuted at number one in May, bumping The Beatles' 'Red' and 'Blue' greatest hits albums off the top – they were underwhelming in the US.

In Japan, though, David's was the biggest debut tour of recent years; every aspect of his distinctive rock 'n' roll recipe – the clothes, make-up, all the theatrical elements – seemed to strike a chord with the Japanese youth. For all the band, mobbed at stage doors every night, drinking in the deliciously alien Japanese culture by day, the tour was an idyllic experience;

until Woody, outraged that his promised wage rise had not yet materialised, once more set out to confront Defries, with bassist Trevor Bolder in tow.

As ever, Woody came straight to the point. 'This is a joke! We've been promised more money, and now we find the roadies are getting more than us!' Defries, unused to being challenged, momentarily lost his cool. 'Well? I'd rather give the money to the road-crew than to you.'

Woody shot back, 'Well, if that's your attitude – you can stick it up your arse!' before bundling his bassist out of the room. Shortly after the meeting, Woody announced he and Trevor were going on strike. Mick Ronson eventually talked them around. 'Don't make trouble,' he told them, 'not when it's going so well.'

But it was not going well.

Even as David was being vibed up by Defries, who grandly told him how much money they'd make in Japan, the last reserves of that calm, that energy, were being drained. On their last night in Japan, Geoff and David spent the evening dining in an exquisitely peaceful restaurant, with Geoff's newly acquired Chinese girlfriend, and David's companion, a beautiful, blue-eyed French-Japanese woman. 'I knew he was trying to think of some angle that would allow us to stay in Japan,' says MacCormack, 'but there was no way.' The pair had a boat to catch, the *Felix Dzerzhinsky* – named after the notorious founder of the KGB – whose crew and passengers were treated to an impromptu Bowie and MacCormack performance of 'Space Oddity' and 'Amsterdam', followed by a seven-day train journey through Siberia and on to Moscow. MacCormack's photos document the endless steppes, stop-offs for food, and two days in the dog-eared Moscow Intourist hotel. When they finally reached East Berlin, the bombed-out hulks of buildings seemed greyer and more ominous than anything they recalled from 1950s London. The memory would stay with them both.

The entire crew were weary on their return to London. The costumes were frayed, too, held together with home-made repairs. There was a brief respite with a party at Haddon Hall – which Tony Visconti and new wife Mary Hopkin attended – but as if to confirm the unrelenting grind of what was nearly sixteen months of repetitive, gruelling touring, David's Earls Court show on 12 May was famously disastrous. Both lighting and PA were pitifully inadequate for the venue, and the familiar 'jing-jing-a-jing' introduction of 'Rock 'n' Roll Suicide' was transformed into, 'Jing-jing-a . . . oh shit,' as rhythm guitarist John Hutchinson fell off his podium in the stygian gloom. All the extra musicians, including Hutch and the sax section, were still reading charts on manuscript, which they couldn't make out in the dark, while none of the band could hear themselves through the lousy monitoring.

The show was a disaster, but the negative press it generated was forgotten as the tour rolled on into June. Reviewers and audiences alike were transfixed by the spectacle and the smoking music: 'A total success, based on an inspired and uniquely amazing talent,' was *Sounds*' verdict on the Newcastle show. David was on a high; on 6 June, he partied into the night at 'Hallam Towers', a nouveau-riche hotel in Sheffield. Rival singers Lulu and Labi Siffre happened to be in the city, and played an impromptu show at the bar – but their gaze, and that of the audience, was fixed on David. Lulu's own star seemed in the descendant: it was now a decade since she'd first notched up hits like 'Shout', while her Eurovision success of a few years before seemed to signal a permanent move to the lounge, chicken-in-a-basket circuit. But the tiny Scots singer was undeniably charismatic, with an infectious energy. Later that evening she disappeared . . . and so did David, his absence loudly publicised by Angie, who marched up and down the hotel corridors knocking on doors in search of her missing hubby. Witnesses like John Hutchinson thought Angie seemed to enjoy the drama of chasing her husband around, advertising that Lulu had become another notch on the Bowie bedpost. The hilarious episode was enjoyed by all the band and crew; the next morning, David's shaven eyebrow seemed to curl a little, in appreciation of the hubbub of gossip over the previous night's events. But the episode also illustrated the stress and drama generated by his and Angie's supposedly open marriage.

Throughout June, David Bowie's defiantly extravagant cavalcade was a much-needed burst of colour in what was otherwise a grim summer, with unemployment rising, and the UK paralysed by strikes and overshadowed by an IRA bombing campaign. The success of Lou Reed's 'Walk on the Wild Side', a hit in both the US and UK that summer, underlined Bowie's magic touch – hearing Lou drawl how Candy Darling 'never lost her head, even when she was giving head' every few hours on BBC Radio 1 represented a delicious cultural marker for a generation, while David's own unstoppable momentum was illustrated by June's announcement that he would soon be recording a new album in France, with yet another American tour to follow in the autumn. Later in the summer the BBC's *Story of Pop* magazine hit the streets: the 'First Encyclopaedia of Pop', it started with Elvis – and ended with Bowie.

For a generation of kids, the Bowie tour's escapism, his visions of transcending the bonds of earth, represented a vital beacon of hope, of glamour. But on the tour itself, what had started out as thrilling was becoming drudgery. Week by week there was less camaraderie backstage; Bolder and Woody hardly exchanged a word with David over the summer, while David's renewed friendliness with Hutch had evaporated by the time they returned to the UK. Ken Fordham's unflappability endeared him to David, who named him Ken 'Funky' Fordham, because he so obviously wasn't. But with shows at forty venues over fifty days, with sixteen matinee performances, everyone felt that 'Defries was working us to death', says Bolder, who was amazed that David survived without losing his voice. Instead, any damage seemed psychological; during a day's layoff in Torquay, Devon, the band took off to see the sights – promoter Mel Bush lent Hutch his flash green Rover to tour the countryside – but David didn't emerge from his room all day. 'No matter how nice the day was, you wouldn't see him. He was going very pale and thin,' says Hutch. David's charisma still shone through, and still he seemed 'excited and thrilled' in the dressing room before he went on, says Suzi Fussey, but there was a tense, almost hysterical edge to his public persona. Sometimes he seemed shaky, while his skin was stretched over his skull, pale and waxy; the contrast with the previous January's photos for *Melody Maker*, when he looked joyous and gamine, is almost painful to behold. Even Freddie Buretti's costumes, frayed and worn, were obviously at the end of their life. As David recalls, it was during these dates that his enthusiasm finally gave out. 'I really did want it all to come to an end. I was writing for a different kind of project and exhausted and completely bored with the whole Ziggy concept, couldn't keep my attention on the performances with much heart. Strangely enough, the rest of the tour was a success . . . but I was wasted and miserable.'

In the run-up to the Hammersmith show on 3 July, only the roadies, MacCormack, Garson and Ronson had been informed that this endless cycle of euphoria, boredom, excitement and exhaustion was coming to a close. It wasn't just David's stamina that was at breaking point – MainMan's cash reserves were exhausted, too.

Around mid-June, Defries became aware that the forthcoming US dates could expose MainMan to huge losses. That same week, it became obvious that David's unparalleled, amazing streak of creativity was coming to an end, with the announcement that the next single would be a *Hunky Dory* track, 'Life On Mars?'.

Defries had performed an amazing financial sleight of hand over the previous months, by persuading RCA to underwrite his hefty financial losses on the two American tours. With the establishment of MainMan, more or less independent of Laurence Myers, in June 1972, he'd lost access to his ex-partner's cash reserves. From that point the company's financial situation was always on a knife edge. When, early in 1973, RCA finally refused to underwrite the next US tour, Defries decided to tackle the potential crisis head-on: he would 'retire' David. David would stave off exhaustion, Defries would stave off a financial catastrophe, the Bowie enigma would be sustained and, a crucial side benefit, the troublesome Spiders could be eliminated.

As David and Defries' plans progressed, the musicians, bar Ronson, remained oblivious. Zanetta had asked a couple whether they'd like to play with MainMan's latest act, Ava Cherry. 'Why would I want do that?' Hutch had replied, happy in the knowledge a tour of America was imminent, with a possible jaunt to Australia thereafter, 'I'm in David's band!'

As for David, his secretiveness about their imminent disbandment did not derive from sadism; rather, this was theatre, the chance to ensure the tour's Hammersmith finale was a set-piece of the most gripping drama. 'Pure showbiz,' remembers Suzi Fussey. 'He loved that.' Scott Richardson, a confidant of both Bowie and Ronson throughout the final tour, knew what was coming, but still reckoned 'to break up a band like that is astonishing. I have to credit Bowie with having a lot of courage: to say "I'm not coming back."'

On the evening of the Hammersmith show, David gave no clue as to the evening's denouement. Suzi Fussey, ministering to him in the dressing room, had been tipped off by Defries, but had to feign ignorance, as did the roadies and the various MainMan staff. 'David acted as if everything was completely normal,' she says. 'I don't know if he was delusional and thought no one knew.' Despite the imminent drama, he seemed rather more relaxed than normal, grateful for the coming rest. 'Relieved, I think,' says Fussey. 'He had been frightened of becoming a parody of himself.'

Bolder, Woody and Hutch, for all their exhaustion, were fired up to be playing the Odeon and all three of them relished the presence of Jeff Beck, guesting on guitar. Their attention was mainly on Ronson, as Bowie and band rampaged their way through what *Sounds*' Martin Hayman called 'one of the best concerts I have ever seen'.

Hutch was the first one to get a hint that something unusual was happening, when David walked over for a word, the first time he'd spoken to him in weeks. 'Don't go straight into "Rock 'n' Roll Suicide",' David instructed his old friend. 'I'm going to say something there.'

When David announced, 'Not only is it the last show of the tour, but it's the last show that we'll ever do. Thank you!' during the break, Hutch and the others were confused. Then they saw Bolder mouth the words, 'He's fuckin' sacked us!' The moment the closing notes of 'Rock 'n' Roll Suicide' died out, Bowie and Ronson disappeared. Woody and Trevor were left to find their own way home.

Presiding over the glittering gathering marking the tour's close at the Cafe Royal the next night, David posed alongside Mick Jagger; they were the undoubted stars of a party that included Lou Reed, Keith Moon, Barbra Streisand and Elliott Gould. It was a sweet moment, the two of them out-camping the other, equals at last. Woody and Trevor were rock 'n' roll lepers, Trevor desperately questioning Ronson – who was non-committal, not letting on he'd known anything – while Woody's attitude was 'Bollocks. I want to do something else, anyway.' But the news of Woody's sacking was not confirmed until he received a phone call from a MainMan flunky a week later, the day of his wedding to girlfriend June, officiated by Mike Garson at the British Church of Scientology headquarters.

Bolder, meanwhile, had heard nothing, until he was asked up to a gathering at MainMan. Walking in to see MacCormack, Zanetta and others gossiping and pouring themselves drinks, Bolder started to have a go at David – 'What are you up to? How can you treat people this way?' – when he was pulled away by Mick Ronson. 'Keep your mouth shut and don't say anything, otherwise you'll be gone as well. Just cool it and be quiet.' – When Bowie spoke to him again, telling him his next album would be a collection of covers, and started playing some of the songs he intended to record, Trevor did as Ronson advised. 'Only then did I realise how much Mick was looking out for me. I had a wife and kids, nobody else did, Mick had been the best man at my wedding. So he protected me.'

By now, Scott Richardson had been recruited by Bowie as a general rock 'n' roll companion and sounding board, accompanying him to gigs, helping him choose songs for his covers album, and delegated to assist with Ronson's solo album. Richardson was one of a couple of people aware, like Bowie, that Roxy Music's Bryan Ferry was also planning a covers album – the knowledge, if it didn't inspire Bowie's own covers collection, certainly put a rocket under the project. Not only was Ferry a rival, he'd also had the audacity to criticise Bowie in print the previous winter, pointing out how he liked to 'push all [his] band back – like props in their little boxes'.

The recordings at Château D'Hérouville – a glorious, slightly tatty, compact castle just outside Paris where Marc Bolan had recorded *The*

Slider – were cheerful on the surface, with long lunches in the sun, but overshadowed by future portents, each participant conscious this was the end of an era. 'It didn't feel comfortable to me,' says Ken Scott. 'I had other things on my mind, my wife was pregnant and I wanted to fly back to England. My mind was elsewhere, and there were legal problems, because my royalties weren't getting paid. And that seemed to be the general thing.'

The awareness that this adventure was coming to a close imbued the album with a kind of desperate nostalgia. David, Ronson and Richardson simply picked out a bunch of 45s – The Pretty Things' 'Rosalyn', The Kinks' 'Where Have All the Good Times Gone', Syd and the Floyd's 'See Emily Play' – and played a couple of the records to the band each morning; they learned each song in the same key, then bashed it out. David was more obviously disengaged from Angie, at ease in the studio, enjoying the carefree atmosphere of simply playing other people's songs, happy to let Mick Ronson bear most of the musical burden while he honked away on his schoolboy saxophone. He was nevertheless rushed, as always, and keen to lay down his vocals as quickly as possible. Ava Cherry was over in Paris on a modelling job, and after tracking David down to the Château, they spent cosy afternoons together cuddled up before the huge Baroque fireplaces. David was calm, but distracted, and Ava noticed how he would defer his decisions to Tony Defries, reliant on him – almost like a child. For her to become anything more than a temporary fixture in David's life, Tony had to give his approval: he was the gatekeeper to David's personal life, like a father or a priest, and had to be honoured. Her ritual offerings took the form of demo recordings, which David recorded with Ava in the studio.

Over those weeks, Ava also observed Bowie and Ronson's relationship up close. 'Mick seemed very distraught – there was some scuttle about him doing a solo album and David wasn't totally happy about it.' Mick was both a friend who David supported and a rival; just as with Bolan, David wanted him to succeed, but was scared of being overshadowed. Mick himself was enthused by the challenge of a solo album – a 'happy camper' says Ken Scott – but according to Scott Richardson, much as he knew things had to change, Ronson was in mourning for his band and buried himself in work. 'Really, he worked all the time,' says Richardson. 'Looking back on it now and listening back to it, Ronson was the force to be reckoned with musically and I think he was completely at sea about his future because that band had a real integrity. And they were gone.' Bolder was later told that David had only done the album, *Pin Ups*, 'to keep the band happy'. Considering Ronson knew he was leaving, that Trevor had been sacked then recalled, and Woody was gone, happy they weren't. 'It wasn't fun,' says Bolder. 'It was all right. We did it, it was fun playing the songs. And Aynsley Dunbar's a great drummer but he wasn't a Woody Woodmansey.'

Throughout the *Pin Ups* sessions, David was simultaneously busy – dragging on a cigarette and drinking his usual incessant coffees while spinning plans for a new musical, *Tragic Moments* – and bored, sitting apart from the band and reading the paper while they chatted among themselves. For all the poignancy of this event, the musicians had a blast rambling around the Château, or catching a cab into Paris to 'raid the chicks at the Crazy Horse Saloon', says Richardson. 'It was great. It didn't feel like the ship was sinking from my perspective, but it obviously was.'

If, for David and Defries, *Pin Ups* derived from a simple need to deliver more product, the album itself sealed Bowie's status as a phenomenon rivalled only by The Beatles or Elvis; the album entered the charts at number one, with its predecessors sitting nearby at thirteen, nineteen and twenty-six in the UK, while its standout track, 'Sorrow', shipped 147,000 copies before release in the UK. Although today it sounds obviously mannered, Bowie's voice a self-parody, *Pin Ups'* humour and carefree charm emphasised David's humanity; its simple odes to Mod good-times a welcome contrast to the intensity of *Aladdin Sane*. For all that, contemporary critics like *Rolling Stone*'s Greg Shaw were quick to point out its weaknesses, citing its lack of edge and Bowie's over-cooked voice concluding, 'even in 1965, any of a thousand bands could have done better'. At a time of general nostalgia, with TV-advertised fifties and sixties compilation albums hogging the charts, *Pin Ups* was an uncharacteristically predictable move, and even industry friends like John Peel commented, 'I'll be glad when Bryan Ferry and David Bowie get this oldies business out of their normally diverting systems.'

In Bowie's string of successes that summer, there was one minor setback. After abandoning his plan for the musical *Tragic Moments* – for which he'd recorded a fifteen-minute segment at the Château – David switched subjects to George Orwell's *1984*, working briefly on a script with *Pork* director Tony Ingrassia. Unfortunately, Orwell's widow Sonia was no rock 'n' roll devotee, and when MainMan approached her for the rights to a show based on Orwell's novel, she refused, describing the notion as 'bizarre'. Bowie would be forced to refashion his idea into a more amorphous concept, but as he and Defries discussed the possibility of recording a TV show in the hope of finally achieving his mass-market breakthrough in America, David decided to feature a couple of the songs destined for the musical in *The 1980 Floor Show*, a one-off special for NBC to be recorded in October at his old London haunt, the Marquee Club.

Most of David's previous projects had benefited from the adrenalin rush of improvisation that gave birth to them. It seemed natural to assume *The 1980 Floor Show* would be the same. Freddie Buretti crafted the costumes, and Bowie formed a vocal backing trio, The Astronettes, with Ava, Geoff MacCormack and Jason Guess, whom Bowie knew through a friend who owned a soul-food restaurant. Mark Pritchett, who'd worked on the sessions that gave birth to both *Hunky Dory* and *Ziggy*, came in to augment Ronson on guitar. The new material, notably '1984/Dodo', was dense and intriguing, but the show itself was a mess – the settings looked cheesy, and the camerawork uninspired. Even the fans who'd been invited in to make up the audience were mostly underwhelmed. 'It was really disappointing,' remembers writer David Thompson, 'with him doing the same three songs forty times.' For the musicians, the main highlight was the sight of Marianne Faithfull's backside, clearly visible in a perverted nun's costume – it was certainly more pleasing than her singing, in a rather Teutonic version of Sonny and Cher's 'I've Got You Babe', which sees singing partner – and, it seemed, lover – Bowie wincing at her frequent bum notes. Ava Cherry remembers Defries being convinced that the production 'was going to give us the juice to go into America and really be big'. If so, he was wrong. The show was broadcast by NBC on 16 November, with its more intriguing snippets excised – Bowie's costume was declared too provocative, as was the word 'suicide' in 'Rock 'n' Roll Suicide' – and the show, after its initial broadcast, was then sent to languish in the archives, seemingly for eternity.

The half-cocked management of *The 1980 Floor Show* was typical of MainMan's increasing disorganisation. The main breadwinner, Bowie himself, had not as yet generated consistent profits across America, while the European market was, for some reason, completely overlooked. Although Iggy had been sacked and Mott, Lou and Annette Peacock had fled, the MainMan roster continued to grow amoebically, without any logic. Wayne County, later to become the celebrated punk musician Jayne County, was one of many artists who saw their projects – in her case the *Live at the Trucks* film and soundtrack – abandoned or confined to the vaults. 'To this day I hate the man,' she says today of Defries, 'damn his eyes, damn his soul.' Simon Turner – later a cult musician who recorded for the UK's Creation and Mute labels – was another signing lost in the chaos, while guitarist Mark Pritchett remembers going to Sarm Studios in London's East End to make a complete album with 'some exotic South American bird, she was good', which would prove another expensive, unrealised MainMan project.

Defries always had a strangely contradictory attitude towards money, unconcerned about spending it on ambitious projects, yet penny-pinching with smaller amounts. In those autumn months, there was unrelenting office gossip about Defries' investments in the precious-metals market, taking advantage of the abolition of controls on the price of gold. At the time the stories seemed merely to illustrate his Midas-like skills of generating even more profits. By November, Defries had grandly declared that MainMan was now an 'International Entertainment Conglomerate' and put into execution his long-treasured scheme of moving his base of operations to America. Before the year's end he had augmented the original Manhattan apartment with a loft apartment on the Lower West Side, a penthouse on the Upper East Side, several apart-ments for MainMan artists, and finally his pièce de resistance, a MainMan estate of buildings in Greenwich, Connecticut. The vacuum of power this left in London, the location of MainMan's main money-spinner, was initially filled by Hugh Attwooll, who'd been hired as an agent with no experience whatsoever, and was promoted to 'something between office boy, Chief Executive and money juggler'. Most of the income came from RCA advances, publishing income and PRS (Performing Rights Society) income, all of which was generated by David and which then went into 'a big tub', says Attwooll. 'Or, rather a small tub actually. That was the problem.' Attwooll is one of several MainMan executives who believe Tony Defries generally gets 'bad press, which I'm not certain he deserves', but through the course of 1973 it became obvious that 'the whole thing was completely nuts'.

In the meantime, MainMan's only proven source of income had his own eyes on America, a destination that would shape his next musical move, says his accompanist, Mark Pritchett. 'He knew it was a multicultural place – black, Hispanic as much as white. And he wanted that Nile Rodgers, funky type of thing.' This American vibe would inspire David's last session at Trident, on '1984/Dodo' – which would also be his last with both Ken Scott and Mick Ronson. 'Within the first couple of takes, it became fundamentally clear that all of us – but Mick was the lead musician – weren't black funky,' says Pritchett. 'This was not it.'

Given time, it's possible Ronson and Pritchett might have mastered the stripped-down funk that David envisioned. But right back to 'Space Oddity', David had become used to having his ideas put on tape instantaneously. 'David wants it *now*,' says Pritchett. 'He's not exactly first-take Dave, but it's "Can't you hear what I hear?" and if it's take number four he gets frustrated: "I'll get someone who *can* then."'

Those Trident sessions marked the end of Mick Ronson's partnership with Bowie; Mark Pritchett, who'd worked with David since the Arts Lab days, would be replaced later that year. Pritchett's departure was hardly noticed, although Mick's would be pored over for years by fans who knew that Ronson had been a key architect of Ziggy Stardust's success. But such departures, says Pritchett – who would later be given parting gifts including David's Jag and the Hagstrom twelve-string David had used since signing to Ken Pitt – are simply the price of progress. 'Any musician that had any kind of contact with David that he enjoyed, I dare you to name one who would say that when the parting came they were in any way discarded like a spent toy. Not me. And not Mick.'

Mick's own feelings were mixed; he was nervous of occupying the spotlight, but his own ego had been stoked up by the MainMan machine, which finally launched his solo career over the following months, complete with a promotional film to publicise his own album, which was recorded at the Château with Trevor Bolder, Aynsley Dunbar, Pritchett, Scott Richardson and others, directly after *Pin Ups*. Pritchett's last project with David was the sessions that David booked that autumn, when he used Olympic Studios in Barnes – best-known for its Rolling Stones connection – almost as a demo studio.

This would be a creative period for David, although his activity was not confined to music, for Ava Cherry remembers him 'staying up for forty-eight hours learning how to work a video machine, or reading fifty books at a time about one subject, stacking them up and reading them for days.' The Astronettes, his backing group from *The 1980 Floor Show*, were just one of his musical projects, inspiring new songs including 'I am a Lazer' and 'I am Divine' – later reworked as 'Scream Like a Baby' and 'Somebody Up There Likes Me'. Those sessions were later abandoned, for Jason Guess's bland, wavery vocals were hopelessly inadequate, but they served their purpose as David was 'working out how to do a soul thing', says Cherry. They would become part of a host of sessions conducted at Olympic, as David developed new working methods. 'You'd get a call, turn up, it might be just you and a drummer, it might just be you laying down something on your own, David would say, "These are the chords, can you give it a funky feel?" He may use your part, he may decide he doesn't like it, or he might use the idea as part of something else,' says Mark Pritchett.

This cut-and-paste approach – rather than the organised, succinct sessions overseen by Mick Ronson – would become a hallmark of David's post-Spiders style. Soon he adopted a similar approach to writing lyrics, inspired by William Burroughs, whom he met on 17 November for a *Rolling Stone* feature. Writer Craig Copetas bought him all of Burroughs' books – none of which he'd properly read, despite later claims to have discovered the writer 'as a teenager' – and David instantly adapted Burroughs' cut-up technique on songs like 'Sweet Thing/Candidate', writing a paragraph of text, then cutting it up into four- or five-word sections and shuffling them.

Celebrity encounters arranged for magazines are notoriously unenlightening, but the *Rolling Stone* set piece provided a perfect portrait of Bowie at his apogee in London. Copetas noted the contrast between the humble minimalism of Burroughs' Piccadilly flat and Bowie's materialism, recording the extravagance of Bowie's new rock-star house and his coterie of attendants, who dispensed avocados stuffed with shrimp and bottles of Beaujolais Nouveau. The contrast in their intellectual approach was stark, too, with Burroughs' outlook formed by books – he was surprised to hear that Bowie had never read T. S. Eliot – and Bowie's from people, like Lindsay Kemp, Chime Rimpoche and the cast of *Pork*. Nonetheless, there was an obvious rapport, Bowie hopping from Andy Warhol to Cuban musician Joe Cuba like a gadfly, or listening intently as Burroughs rapped about orgone accumulators and infrasound.

David camps it up impressively for Burroughs, discoursing on tribalism and the sex life of kids, in his vitality and enthusiasm he is still recognisably the same teenager who talked about poetry and art when making his unsuccessful debut album. And he exhibits exactly the same competitiveness, allying himself subtly with Mick Jagger, delighting in deconstructing him as 'a white boy from Dagenham trying his damndest to be ethnic'.

Marking his ascent from being a curiosity from Beckenham to a fully fledged rock star, David and Angie had left Haddon Hall in the summer, moving briefly to Maida Vale before installing themselves in the customary rock hangout of Chelsea, at 89, Oakley Street, not far from Jagger's Cheyne Walk home. Freddie Buretti and Daniella Parmar occupied the basement of the four-storey, flat-fronted 1850s house; Ava Cherry, after a month at Oakley Street – which was long enough to outstay Angie's welcome – moved into Daska House, an apartment building one hundred yards up the King's Road. Various Beckenham artists reworked the house as a model of rock-star chic: stairs painted alternately matt and gloss black, a hallway lit by car headlamps, a sunken double bed, airbrushed murals in most of the rooms – a sun rise, based on the Sun Pat peanut butter logo for David, a tropical beach scene for Zowie's room on the top floor, alongside the office. The living room was in white shagpile, dominated by one of George Underwood's paintings and a larger Dali-style work. The sunken central area was surrounded by scatter cushions, with a spherical TV, a state-of-the-art video machine and Polaroids of 'exotic activities', remembers airbrush artist Mick Gillah.

Towards the end of 1973, this sleek, busy household seemed an epitome of domestic bliss, a glossier version of the Haddon Hall ethos. David was once more enthused by his work, occasionally treating visitors to sights of lyrics he'd cut and pasted together from his more bizarre fan letters. Generally busy with her own projects or shopping trips, Angie still operated as a domestic goddess, treating guests to an impeccably turned-out soufflé or quiche. Zowie was now an outgoing two-year-old: dressed in brightly coloured dungarees, with long blond hair, he'd scamper around the house singing songs he'd made up. Only granny was missing from this idyllic scene – although visitors to her flat on Albermarle Street remember Peggy being devoted to Zowie, she was seldom, if ever, seen at Oakley Street, and never featured in David's conversation. Instead, Tony Defries was David's only father figure.

Defries' absence in America was the only disquieting element in David's domestic life. Musicians, producers, girlfriends could be discarded; Defries' inspirational visions, his insights, were irreplaceable. 'It could be anything: business, what people to see, girlfriends, Tony would orchestrate it all,' says Ava Cherry.

At the summit of his career – released from the live treadmill, finally ranked alongside his teenage idols – the close of 1973 should have been a time for David to savour his own success and freedom. Finally, he was given time to relax; fatefully, he was also given time to doubt. And once he'd opened himself up to them, those doubts intensified remarkably quickly. The impact on the psyche of a man who saw himself almost as Defries' son was predictable. 'Devastation is the word,' says Cherry, his closest companion over this period. 'They were great days, till Tony messed David's head up – really messed him up.'

12

The Changing isn't Free

Cocaine is a cruel drug. It makes people behave like absolute bastards.

Keith Christmas

As 1973 drew to a close, with David Bowie in London and Tony Defries in New York, both men basked in their achievements. They had finally beaten the system. But neither of them could wait to join it.

Defries, the man who had derided old-school, bloated record company management, was building an over-staffed empire that mirrored the system he despised. And David, who had constructed a manifesto that positioned him as a new species of human, couldn't wait to become chums with the previous generation of rock stars. Each of them spotted the contradictions in the other's position, but not their own. 'They were a really solid team up to that point,' says Tony Zanetta, who respected – worshipped, even – both men. 'But once everything stopped and they could enjoy the fruits of success, the cracks started to appear.'

Those cracks would fail to damage Defries' serene sense of self-worth; David Bowie, however, could hardly bear to contemplate them, burying his worries so deep that the inevitable crisis would be utterly devastating.

In the meantime, David cast around for role models. Iggy and Lou no longer sufficed; instead he increased his focus on their apparent antithesis, Mick Jagger. Mick was always a rival, rather than an idol. Determined to topple Jagger from his pedestal, David was also fascinated by him to the point of obsession. He and Ava enjoyed several dinners with Mick and Bianca, chatting volubly, with the pair even noodling on a tune together one night, which became the Astronettes song 'Having a Good Time'. But neither one could quite discard their elegant, sophisticated personas. 'It was polite, intellectual – but there was a line they didn't cross,' says Cherry. In later years, Angie Bowie described how she'd caught Bowie and Mick in bed together, which is ludicrous to anyone who saw the two together. Each man was guarded, and even twenty years later would be almost excessively conscious of his relative standing; the notion that one would be completely open with the other, let alone to be 'a bottom' was unthinkable. To Ava, the two personalities seemed similar; bright, competitive, with a similar dry or camp humour, but in reality they were very different. David was always in the grip of some obsession, or enthusiasm. Mick wasn't. 'He was never under the spell of anything,' says Maggie Abbott, later the movie agent for both Mick and David. 'He was always totally under control. He was a typical Leo, much more disciplined than David. He would never be taken in by anything.'

Although David acted otherwise, he was intimidated by his rival, who was an old hand at managing pretenders to his throne. Jagger had led the way for so many of David's obsessions, from recruiting the coolest African-American girlfriends, like Marsha Hunt, to writing lyrics in a Burroughsian cut-up style, as Mick had done for *Exile on Main Street*, back in 1971. Yet at a Rolling Stones show in Newcastle that spring, it finally dawned on Bowie that he was in a position to top the Stones singer. Standing in the wings, he was telling confidant Scott Richardson about the time he'd offered to carry Brian Jones' guitar and been told to piss off. Suddenly, the pair noticed that Jagger was glaring at them from centre stage. Glancing behind, they realised hundreds of fans were ignoring the band, craning their necks to see the carrot-haired presence at the side of the stage.

David and Scott accompanied Jagger and Bianca to a casino that evening, where Scott noticed that Jagger was fascinated by his rival. Thereafter Jagger would stay in regular touch, keeping tabs on David, who relished the accolade – but also found his competitive instincts re-awoken. Until now, he had measured himself against Marc Bolan, who had never made an impact in the States, and whose appeal in Britain would wane that autumn, prompting Marc's final split with Tony Visconti. Jagger would be an altogether more challenging friend and rival.

As was his habit, David approached the task of measuring up to Jagger by moving directly on to his turf, liberally appropriating from him. This helped inspire his choice of Olympic as his working studio, along with Keith Harwood, at that time the Stones' favourite engineer. While the lyrical core of David's next album would be a reworking of his *1984* concept, its chaotic, dystopian edge intensified by his use of Burroughs' cut-up technique, the musical blueprint was unashamedly based on The Rolling Stones.

The core of the album was completed within a few frenzied days at Olympic, according to bassist Herbie Flowers and guitarist Alan Parker, seasoned session men who together made up the UK soul band, Blue Mink. The pair were well used to having their melodic ideas become the basis of someone else's song – Serge Gainsbourg's superb *Melody Nelson* album, for instance, on which they took almost total responsibility for the music, uncredited. 'That was part of what we did,' says Parker, 'so on high-profile sessions we would simply double the fee.'

For the album that would become *Diamond Dogs*, the principal songs were well organised, with five or six backing tracks laid down in roughly three or four days. Parker and Flowers both remember the development of what would become the album's best-known song, 'Rebel Rebel', for David introduced it quite specifically. 'I want it to sound like the Stones,' he told them, before showing them the song, borrowing Parker's black Les Paul. Bowie's riff was uptempo, Stonesy, but it needed honing; Parker picked the main notes out clearly, adding a particular chord shape, rather than the original single note, just before the chord change, and a distinctive 'beeeoonng' in the last line of the chorus, just as David sings the line 'I love you so'.

'David played the riff to Alan, Alan made sure it was good enough to record, and then [Alan] played it,' says Herbie Flowers, who remembers the electric guitar, bass and drums laying down the backing track simultaneously – which accounted for the loose feel, with the song speeding up as Aynsley Dunbar launches into his stomping, on-beat drum pattern, which consciously evokes the Stones' 'Satisfaction'.

A gloriously simple song which marked his farewell to the Ziggy era, 'Rebel Rebel' would become one of Bowie's best-known singles. But Parker was shocked when, a few years later, he realised that, beyond writing the riff, Bowie was credited in the album notes with playing the guitar on the finished version. It would be nigh-on impossible for the most skilled guitarist to replace Parker's work, because of the changing tempo and the sonic spill between the studio microphones. 'I can tell my own playing, and my own sound,' says Parker, 'and I know it's me.'

The emphasis on David's role as guitarist seemed calculated to show

Mick Ronson – whose solo career was flourishing, briefly – how well David could manage without him. 'It's silly . . . I don't know why it would matter so much,' says Parker, who'd chatted with both Ronson and Bowie at previous sessions. The confusion over the credits was all the more pointless, considering the superb job David did of playing guitar on the remaining songs, notably the title track – which with its cowbell and loose backing vocals echoed 'Honky Tonk Women' – and the jagged, New Wave-ish guitar on 'Candidate'.

Look more closely, though, and the pettiness was more easily explained, for in the closing months of 1973, David's world was falling in on him. At the beginning of the sessions, he was relatively optimistic, fired up by the challenge of learning the electric guitar, and enjoying the camaraderie of the studio, dropping in on Mott guitarist Mick Ralph's new band, Bad Company, who were mixing at Olympic. But that cama-raderie was splintered when Bowie was barred from the studio after an argument; by the end of the sessions there was precious little good will remaining.

David's musical isolation, his dependence on session men – yes-men, really – had its upside, bringing a new intensity to his work. Yet outside the studio, his isolation was corrosive, worsened by the growing chaos and back-biting within MainMan. After Tony Defries' departure for New York, MainMan's cashflow problems took a dramatic turn for the worse. One of the company's recent recruits, Corinne Schwab, did a heroic job of controlling the company's UK finances, but even she failed to talk the Château D'Hérouville out of banning all MainMan's acts in a dispute over unpaid bills. In January 1974, Olympic followed suit. Meanwhile, tales filtered back of the profligacy of MainMan New York, where staff had their own credit cards and had limos on call. 'One by one, people were telling us what was happening,' says Ava Cherry. 'Eventually the truth of the matter was the company was spending money like water, while David couldn't get any ready cash.'

As the suspicion that Tony Defries, the father figure who controlled so much of his life, was presiding over a financial meltdown grew, David found the perfect psychological crutch, one that had contributed to the air of glamour and decadence that surrounded the Rolling Stones: cocaine.

It's fitting that cocaine would reach its height as the last vestiges of the 'we' decade were destroyed and the 'me' decade took over. Considered at the time as a safe, non-addictive substance – 'We thought it helped us be smarter and more creative,' says MainMan's Tony Zanetta – cocaine would ravage the psyche of a generation of musicians. New Stones guitarist Ron Wood, and Iggy, would be just two of its victims; Iggy would later be sent to a mental institution as a result. Guitarist Keith Christmas, who'd been part of the optimistic, co-operative Beckenham scene, saw the drug's effects on David and many others, and shudders as he recalls them. 'It's a cruel drug. It makes people behave like complete bastards. Because it takes away a lot of the fearful emotional need we have not to upset other people – it allows you to feel you can upset whoever the fuck you please. I found sometimes at a party, people would be having a good time, then someone would mention coke and the whole party would change completely. "Get some coke in, get some lines in," would be all people could talk about. The compulsive quality of it is horrifying.'

Although a compulsive consumer of coffee and cigarettes, David had been almost virtuous in his avoidance of other drugs. 'It was so peculiar,' says Tony Zanetta, 'he didn't smoke pot, he'd simply drink a couple of glasses of white wine. It was so fast – cocaine was definitely something he incorporated into what a rock star should be.'

Ava Cherry remembers David's 'occasional toot' as overlapping with the apparent financial crisis. 'He was in a dark place . . . saying these people have taken all my money. And at the first stage [cocaine] would be a crutch: "It calms me down."' Angie, too, dates David's obsession with cocaine as starting from these weeks. 'It's what they did to him, my boy,' she laments in a rare outbreak of sympathy, also blaming the drug for the breakdown of their marriage.

David's mental state would also have an obvious effect on his music. Although some of *Diamond Dogs*' songs were languid and melodic – 'Sweet Thing/Candidate' – there was an obsessive quality about the recording, with jagged guitars and saxophones layered ominously on each other. The lyrical imagery, too, was dark, its stories of the Diamond Dogs drawn from Haywood Jones' stories of Dickensian London, when orphan kids crowded the rooftops of the London rookeries. The resulting intensity marked a distinct sonic and spiritual departure from the optimism of his three albums with The Spiders. This new territory was fertile, and marked a progression in David's work, but there was a sacrifice too; in the obsessive regard to sound, texture, an almost physical heaviness, the deftness of *Hunky Dory* and *Ziggy Stardust* – with their swooping melodies and restlessly mobile chord sequences – had gone.

The break with the past was crystallised when Trevor Bolder, who'd been working with Mick Ronson on the guitarist's solo album and tour, answered the phone late one night.

'Oi, Trev!' his ex-singer greeted him. 'What are you doing?'

'I'm doing nowt,' Bolder responded.

'Do you want to come and play on a song?'

Bolder agreed, and turned up at Barnes to find Bowie, Mike Garson and drummer Tony Newman working on a slow acoustic number. It was an uncomfortable experience, sitting in the studio with Bowie but no Spiders. The quartet ran through the song several times before running tape. 'But it was a nothing song,' says Bolder, 'and it obviously got dumped later.' The take complete, Bolder packed away his bass guitar, while Bowie sat with his back to him.

'I'm off now Dave, I'll see you later on,' said Bolder. Bowie didn't say a word. Bolder repeated himself. 'I'm going, then. See you! Bye.' Again, Bowie ignored him. The ex-Spider walked out of the studio, in silence, taking a last look at Bowie's back, silhouetted against the control-room window. It was the last time they would share a studio.

During the same period, Bowie's teenage friend Wayne Bardell bumped into him in Tramp's nightclub. Overjoyed to see his friend, whom he'd last talked to during the first Ziggy tour, he walked up to him.

'Hi, how are you?'

'Hi. Who are you?' was David's response.

'That hurt,' says Bardell, who had sat in on the recording of 'Pity the Fool', and seen David regularly over the last nine years. 'I was taking cocaine too . . . but it didn't stop me *knowing* people. This was cold. Calculated.'

The freezing out of those who'd known him from his days as a struggling musician was conventional behaviour for the 1970s – Marc Bolan exhibited a nastier version of the trait, again bolstered by cocaine use. David wasn't nasty; he would simply cut people off, coldly. With those still in favour, he was considerate and thoughtful: after hearing from Tony Visconti that the home studio he was building was short of furniture, he sent around a Conran Shop van packed with office chairs, plus a dining suite and crockery – later they'd mix the bulk of the *Diamond Dogs* tracks there.

There had always been a child-like element to David's persona – that clear-eyed earnestness was an intrinsic part of his charm. Yet that childishness was not so charming once it was distorted by the flattery of minor MainMan staff, the constant attentions of cooks or maids, and the other corrosive effects of celebrity. As Ava Cherry remembers, 'Children think the whole world revolves round them. And that's the way David was encouraged to think, by everyone.' Certain friends would learn to manage David's moods; notably Ron Wood, whom David knew from his Marquee days. David renewed his friendship with the guitarist once the *Diamond Dogs* sessions moved to Hilversum, in the Netherlands, where the Stones were also working. The two bonded over a mutual love of Peter Cooke and Dudley Moore, memorising and replicating their dialogues. 'Ronny was very good at making you feel that you were having fun,' says Ava Cherry, 'and I always felt good when Ronny was coming over. Because David wasn't angry then – he'd always be laughing.'

David built up a deeper, more enduring relationship over that same period. Corinne 'Coco' Schwab had been hired by Hugh Attwooll in the summer of 1973. MainMan's UK office manager thought her well educated, intelligent and capable. He soon discovered she was 'smarter than me, that's for sure. I hired her and within a month I was gone – and she had my job.' By the autumn of 1973, Corinne was the only person keeping the MainMan UK office afloat, for by then the financial situation was 'intolerable' says Tony Zanetta: 'She was abandoned in the English office, Defries refused to pay almost any bills, David was spending wildly. She certainly earned her position.'

Defries liked Coco's old-school efficiency, her command of languages and her cosmopolitan background; born, she told her friends, during her mother's shopping trip to Bloomingdales, New York, she had been educated in America, Europe and Kashmir. Defries initially encouraged her rise, in order to diminish Angie's influence. By the autumn of 1973, Coco had become David's personal assistant (a job Suzi Fussey turned down, eventually to marry Mick Ronson) and was installed in the top floor of Oakley Street, where she controlled access to David.

Corinne would become a central character in David's life: intelligent, slim, witty, she seemed in other respects almost anonymous. This was part of her charm, and her effectiveness. She was happy to devote herself utterly to David and seemed to have no agenda of her own to impose on him. Many years later David would sing of 'your soothing hand that turned me round' in his song devoted to Coco, 'Never Let Me Down'. The song speaks of her as a lover, but in reality her role was more complex, like a combination mother, sister, lover and – most crucially – all-purpose intellectual confidante, rather like the paid companions hired by refined ladies of a certain age. 'David liked her because she was intellectual and they could have good conversations,' says Ava Cherry, who also points out that Corinne was 'in love with [David] from day one'.

David savoured Corinne's utter devotion to his cause, and would occasionally taunt Ava with stories of how indispensible she'd made herself. In February, Ava was sent over to New York, ostensibly to link up with Tony Defries and prepare David's move to the city, but Cherry soon concluded that Schwab 'systematically did nothing but try and get me out'.

In Ava's absence, David turned to another exotic creature: Amanda Lear. The one-time muse of Bryan Ferry and acquaintance of Salvador Dali, Lear helped celebrate David's twenty-seventh birthday by taking him to see Fritz Lang's 1926 masterpiece *Metropolis*. In the weeks before he left for America, David immersed himself in Lang's work, which along with the staging he'd first planned for Arnold Corns started to form the basis of the imagery for his next American tour. From 1971 on, he'd dreamed of presenting his shows as a three-dimensional spectacle. Now he planned a new, grandiose vision, without any compromises.

David arrived in New York on 1 April, 1974, sailing the Atlantic with Geoff MacCormack on the SS *France*. The one-way journey was laden with symbolism, both positive and negative; David intended to base himself in America, a country he'd long dreamed about, to soak up its vibe and conquer it. And he needed to sort out his problems, in the form of Tony Defries.

As far as soaking up the vibe, the move to New York was perfect. After moving in to the Sherry Netherland Hotel by Central Park, Bowie used Ava Cherry as his guide to the soul scene. Ava suggested they check out Harlem's Apollo Theater, where it turned out there was a show on the 26th topped by Richard Pryor, featuring The Main Ingredient: one of RCA's few cool bands, the Harlem outfit had changed line-up in 1972, recruiting new singer, Cuba Gooding Sr, and scored a huge soul smash with 'Everybody Plays the Fool'. The Apollo's audience was overwhelmingly black, with the red-haired, pasty-faced Bowie sticking out like a white cat in a coal scuttle. 'He loved it,' says Ava. 'He soaked all of it up.'

There was another joyful source of Americana to be explored in 1974, in the charismatic form of Norman Fisher, a stockbroker turned art collector, famous for the lavish parties he'd throw in his tiny Downtown apartment. David remembers them as 'the most diverse soirees in the whole of New York. People from every sector of the so and not so avant-garde would flock there – Norman was a magnet.' Fisher turned David on to the most gloriously eclectic art and music: Florence Jenkins, the famously inept opera singer who attracted huge audiences in the 1920s, drawn by her ludicrous costumes and atonal performances, was one typical example. As well as good company, Norman also supplied cocaine for his social circle. '[But] he did not want to,' says Ava. 'Norman just wanted to be friends and hang with people.'

Fisher remained a close friend of David's for years, and epitomised the glamour of New York. But in his role as David's supplier, he unwittingly contributed to a profound transformation. 'I saw David at the NBC Special [in October 1973] and didn't see any cocaine problem,' says Tony Zanetta. 'Then in April 1974, there it was: full-blown.'

David's obviously transformed state would be yet another factor in the breakdown of his relationship with Tony Defries. David thought that moving closer to Defries would invigorate their relationship; instead, they became more estranged. *Diamond Dogs* won mixed reviews on its release in April 1974, but was David's best-performing album in the US to date, peaking at number five. Defries, however, preferred more showbiz concepts, like *Ziggy Stardust*, and the concise songs it contained. Furthermore, he considered David's nascent plans for his next, grandiose tour with disapproval.

This was typical inconsistency from a man overseeing a company that now employed twenty-five full-time staff and had its own travel agency, plus a TV, radio and movie production company. It was all the more galling to David, considering how Defries loved to boast of his own largesse, such as his scheme to fulfil his staff members' 'ultimate fantasy'. (Leee Childers had his teeth done; Cherry Vanilla's bonus was spent on a boob job.)

As ever, Defries' generosity did not stretch to David's musicians. In his first weeks in New York, David had arranged a recording session with Lulu, calling in Main Ingredient founder Tony Silvester to help. Silvester suggested his new guitarist, Carlos Alomar. One-time member of the Apollo house band and a session regular for everyone from Peter, Paul and Mary to Roy Ayers, Carlos Alomar turned up at RCA studios and was struck by Bowie's red hair, and 'mousey skin. It was so translucent. And the black under his eyes was somewhat alarming.' After the session Alomar invited David over to his house in Queens for a decent meal and was impressed when the singer actually turned up, spending the evening talking about soul records, and quizzing Alomar on his work with Chuck Berry and James Brown. 'He's always surprised me like that – he's willing to go right in.'

That evening David asked Carlos to join for his forthcoming tour and, thrilled at the prospect of leaving behind 'the chitlin' mentality' – represented by notoriously cheapskate employers like James Brown or Chuck

Berry – Carlos found himself a white manager to negotiate the deal. Only then did Carlos discover that MainMan would only pay half of the weekly $800 he was getting from The Main Ingredient. Regretfully, he returned to his session work and left David to find some cheaper musicians.

In his quest for a new band, David phoned Keith Christmas, who'd played acoustic guitar back on the *Space Oddity* album. A virtuoso musician, with a distinctly English folk style, Christmas was out of place in Bowie's new surroundings. Arriving in New York he found David surrounded by 'a punch of pretentious fucking posers, so full of themselves with their dyed white hair and shaven heads. There was something distinctly sleazy and unpleasant about it.'

The audition itself was a non-event – Christmas was an acoustic guitarist, and his playing on the electric was barely competent – but the surroundings were bizarre: the cavernous RCA studios on the Avenue of the Americas, empty but for Bowie, Christmas and an engineer rolling tape. Whenever David wanted 'a toot' he would beckon Christmas down the corridor, to huddle together furtively in the toilets. 'So this is all strangely paranoid. I'll never forget he had this double-sided razor blade with which he's chopping out lines. When he stuck his finger on a little bindle of coke and held it up to my nose I saw how much his hand was shaking; and the meaning was, I want this stuff so much, I will risk severe personal injury for it.'

The experience was disturbing. Yet, behind the paranoid, scary facade, Christmas believes, on reflection, this was exactly the same person he'd known in 1969. 'David actually seemed like he was completely in his element. It was a continuation of the Art Lab days in terms of who he was as a person; the people had changed, the drugs might have changed. But the actual person might not have changed at all.' In Beckenham, David asked Christmas to embrace his hippie trip, just as he asked Bob Grace to join the sexually ambivalent Sombrero scene. The furtive ritual of sniffing cocaine in a toilet was a new trip, for a new persona; but it was not a persona he would lay aside so easily.

Within the first few days of arriving in New York, David contacted an old friend of Ossie Clark, Michael Kamen – another talented, transplanted Brit with a hefty coke habit with whom David hung out. Kamen ran a rock 'n' roll band with sax player David Sanborn and recently recruited guitarist Earl Slick, but was also a formidably trained classical musician. Kamen had recently written the music for a ballet based on the life of Auguste Rodin; Bowie and MacCormack attended the New York premiere and were transfixed. Kamen's cross-cultural connections echoed David's own ideas on dance and staging, and the composer was engaged as musical director.

The grandiose staging for David's new show, novel as it seemed, was in fact based on ideas he'd toyed with since May, 1971. When constructing fantasies of how to present Arnold Corns, he'd imagined the band playing in an open-sided boxing ring, surrounded by huge pillars, each of which supported a single white spot: 'Remorseless, it has to be,' he told a bemused Freddie Buretti. 'I don't want any colours, I want it all stark.' Later, his ideas for the Rainbow shows were restricted by budget and time; now he raided MainMan's fast-dwindling coffers to realise his fantasies. A huge stage backdrop represented Hunger City, a decaying future metropolis, with thirty-foot-high skyscrapers, augmented by a motorised bridge, a remote-control mirrored module, and a cherry-picker in which David would descend from the heavens. For 'Rebel Rebel', Bowie would perform in the boxing ring, with a couple of over-sized leather boxing gloves; even the mask he used harked back to the mime he'd filmed for Ken Pitt.

For many fans, the remodelling of David himself was far more dramatic than the new, mechanised backdrop. He had arrived in New York with his spiky carrot-top essentially intact; now it was consigned to history, in favour of a forties-style 'do, with parting and floppy fringe, while the Yamamoto outfits were ditched for a double-breasted suit with high-waisted trousers, a skinny jumper and braces. The style was obviously influenced by 1940s Harlem, as well as Sinatra, another hero. Yet in essence David's consciously 'cool' image came from closer to home, namely Roxy Music's Bryan Ferry, whose stage movements he studied closely; David practised Bryan's gestures, including a distinctive movement which the Roxy singer made with his index finger, and incorporated the wiggle into his own repertoire of stage mannerisms.

When the tour opened in Canada on 14 June – less than a year after Bowie's 'retirement' – the sight of goggle-eyed Ziggy clones aghast at David's new earthly manifestation, and overwhelmed by the visual smorgasbord – which included loose 'street' dancing, choreographed by Toni Basil – was a vindication of the weeks of preparation. Yet there was chaos with the equipment which meant David was in constant danger of electrocution. The set blended conservatism – an emphasis on the hits, and some self-consciously bombastic arrangements – with subtlety and risk; 'The Jean Genie's' verse was turned into an urban rap, like Lou's 'Walk on the Wild Side', while The Ohio Players' 'Here Today and Gone

Tomorrow', delivered at later shows, was delivered straight, show-casing the soul pipes David had been developing ever since 'Pity the Fool'. Old-school session hands Herbie Flower and Tony Newman ensured the rhythms were slick and relentless; the show 'rocked real hard', as Detroiter Robert Matheu, a veteran of shows by the MC5 and Stooges, remembered.

Yet the first run of shows, the product of such intense work and obses-siveness, would become famous as a beacon of cynicism, thanks to the ill-will surrounding the recording of the Philadelphia shows between 8 and 12 July. Bassist Herbie Flowers was the prime mover in a threatened strike by the musicians who arrived at the venue and noticed extra microphones: these were the first indication they'd received that MainMan intended to release an album of the night's performance, without paying any extra fees. Guitarist Earl Slick recalls benefiting from Flowers' staunch performance as a shop steward in a stand-up row between MainMan and the musicians. Today, Flowers insists the row 'was blown up out of all proportion. We did ask, "Do we get any money?" and we were told we would get the American Musicians' Union rate.' Only a trace of dis-dain remains in his remark about the tour's staging. 'I've always liked opera,' he remarks. 'But this was pantomime.'

John Peel, David's old champion, was less generous in his assessment of David's prosaic cover of 'Knock on Wood', which trailed the live album in September, proclaiming it 'lazy, arrogant and impertinent'. The same would apply to the *David Live* album when it followed in October: despite many creative moments, the performances were bombastic, sounding like the output of a leviathan corporation, rather than a singer. Still, it would be one of David's most successful US releases to date, peaking at number eight; in the UK, it was held off the top slot by the Bay City Rollers. Many early Bowie uptakers, the people who'd first championed Bowie in the press or looked him out at tiny clubs like Friars Aylesbury saw it as mere filler, a sign of a creative drought. Yet within a few months, they'd be forced to rethink.

From the moment he'd seen The Main Ingredient back in April, David had embarked on an obsessive exploration of cutting edge R&B, which soon extended beyond the obligatory Aretha Franklin to boxes of soul vinyl obtained for him by LA writer Harvey Kubernick, including Philly International singles by Harold Melvin and the Bluenotes and Patti Labelle, and MFSB, the Philly soul band who recorded the theme tune to *Soul Train*. David watched the celebrated music show every week, usu-ally in a party atmosphere, along with fellow soul obsessives like Geoff

MacCormack. Part of David's fascination with Ava Cherry was the fact that she epitomised US soul culture. As with so many of his confidantes, he pumped her for information, all of which fed into his life and work. 'My dad was a musician in the forties [in Chicago] – black guys used to wear baggy pants and they called them gousters. I told David once, "My dad has got a couple of pairs of ties and suits." He was, "Really? Where? Can you bring some over?" So I ended up bringing over a couple of my dad's silk ties and a pair of gouster pants that had suspenders [braces] on them.'

Many of David's previous stylistic swerves had taken months of preparation; manifestos worked out at Haddon Hall, musicians persuaded down from far-flung spots like Hull. In America, things could move more quickly. The new line-up of musicians took a single phone call. The new look was based on a pair of pants. David put on his gouster outfit, with silk ties and suspenders, and then told his girlfriend, 'I'm going to record a session now.'

13

Make Me Break Down and Cry

This was so fast. When it came time to do a song we were like,
Cool, let's go! Boom, boom, boom!

Carlos Alomar

During a brief stopover in New York, David phoned Carlos Alomar,
the guitarist he'd met back in Queens but been unable to hire, thanks
to MainMan's stinginess. 'Look, Carlos,' he told him, 'I'm going to be
coming to Philadelphia, to Sigma Sound.' He employed a persuasiveness
honed over years of working with musicians. 'I know you've just finished
working there and I really want you to come down.' The guitarist appreciated David's charm, but needed little persuasion to leave the chitlin'
circuit, once he'd established David would match his existing salary.

Born in 1951 in Puerto Rico, and brought up in New York, Alomar had
worked relentlessly – applying what he calls 'due diligence' to both his
music and his schoolwork – ever since his father, a minister on 109th
Street, died when Carlos was just fourteen. Being fined by James Brown
(for missing his 'hit me' cue), or hanging out with Chuck Berry– rock 'n'
roll poet and notorious skinflint – helped shape Alomar's Buddha-like
calm but cutting-contest competitive persona. Alomar brought his
wife, session singer Robin Clarke, to the sessions at Sigma Sound in
Philadelphia; together with their friend Luther Vandross, the couple
were probably the key influence in the genesis of what would become
Young Americans – 'They glued it all together,' as Ava Cherry remembers.
'Carlos was very even-tempered, never got mad; and he made David feel
he could bridge the gap between soul and where he was.'

Tony Visconti, called back for a proper production job at last after a

brief reunion with David, to mix *Diamond Dogs* and *David Live*, was overjoyed to be back in the creative pressure cooker. But he was worried
about the singer's obviously fragile state. When the pair discussed his
condition, David assured him he was fine. 'And I kind of believed him.
In retrospect,' says Visconti, 'it's hard to know exactly why, but I did.
Whereas Phil Lynott told me much the same thing and I didn't.' But
Visconti's souvenir photo of David at the Sigma Sound desk shows him
as skeletal, his skin grey and papery. As one of those in the studio with
him remarks today, 'David must have had an angel watching over him.
That photo says it all – but in person, it was even *more* horrible.'

Inside the cocooning safety of Sigma Sound – a studio he'd first tried
out with Ava Cherry, on 9 July – David was in his element. The basic routine was established from the first day, recognisable as the same routine
from his first album with Visconti: David would strum through the song
on guitar or piano, the musicians would pick it up and go for a take after
a few run-throughs. But this time he dictated the feel he wanted, insisting that he lay the vocals down live along with the backing track;
Visconti set up a dual microphone array to cut out some of the instrumental spill onto the vocal track and the tapes rolled. 'But this was fast,'
says Alomar, 'Remember, I brought most of the band so when it came
time to do a song we were like, "Cool let's go." Boom boom boom. Our
music was out in a week and he was like, "Holy shit!" These sessions
were going so hard and so fast.'

In a blitz of recording, the title track, 'Young Americans', was first
to go down, on the first day; in essence, the song comprised a succession
of TV-style images, from Nixon's resignation – announced just three days
earlier on the 8th – to Afro Sheen, the hair-care product whose adverts
bookended *Soul Train*. The song's story of a newly married couple
echoes Bowie's own planned seduction of America: like 'Oh! You
Pretty Things', the song name-checks its audience.

It's impossible to miss the musical change signalled by 'Young
Americans', but the song's lyrics are just as emblematic of his magpie
tendencies. A complete about-face from *Diamond Dogs*' fractured
imagery, 'Young Americans' is observational – musical reportage that
even includes dialogue: 'They pulled in just behind the bridge. He lays
her down, he frowns, "Gee my life's a funny thing" . . .'. The backing
might have been funky, but the lyrical style was a straight lift from Bruce
Springsteen, whom David and Geoff had seen back at Max's. To make
the *homage* even more specific, David had laid down a cover of Bruce's
'It's Hard to Be a Saint in the City', which he delivered in his new, baritone

croon, a kind of cross between Elvis, Sinatra and Bryan Ferry. During the session, Tony Visconti discovered Bruce lived nearby – in a caravan, he remembers – and they invited the New Jersey singer down to the studio. Bruce was puzzled, confused that this English glam singer was covering one of his songs and praising him so extravagantly; in the end David's enthusiasm won him over, and they talked about music late into the night.

Although on many other songs the soul element was low-key and understated, the title track of *Young Americans* was self-consciously funky, a statement of intent. Exactly as he had done with Ziggy, David was 'repositioning the brand', as Dai Davies put it. But the move was intuitive, not calculated, says Ava Cherry. 'He was so happy doing this – it was simply living out what he wanted to be, living out a dream.'

Several tracks from those sessions illustrated that Bowie's love for the music he was channelling was deep and heartfelt, notably the astonishing 'It's Gonna Be Me'. It's a gloriously stark, slow eight-bar blues, backdropped by Mike Garson's minimal piano. David cajoles, sketching out image after image of regret and his own sexual addiction. His voice is breathy, pitch-perfect – Aretha meets Judy Garland – in one of the most accomplished vocal performances he would ever commit to tape. 'Can You Hear Me?', recorded in the same early sessions, is equally subtle, the final mix benefiting from a typically haunting Visconti string arrangement. 'Win', started but not completed at Sigma Sound, is an almost spiritual meditation which represents a neat antithesis to the white man's conventional take on R&B. Where Surrey bluesmen like Eric Clapton expressed a faux-empathy with the downtrodden, David Bowie uses soul to celebrate success: 'All you got to do is win – that's all ya gotta do.'

In the coming months, many critics, notably *Creem*'s Lester Bangs, would tear into Bowie's assimilation of R&B; it was brazen, unashamed. Yet Bowie's unapologetic overnight makeover was a triumph compared to his friend and rival, Marc Bolan. Influenced by girlfriend Gloria Jones, Marc had dabbled with R&B for over a year, even playing with Ike and Tina Turner on the B-side to 'Nutbush City Limits'. But Bolan could not bear to totally abandon his trademark style; his R&B was a compromise, buried under those familiar languid vocals. Bowie, in contrast, turned funky late, but went all the way. More self-secure than Bolan, he would not hedge his bets, and his confidence in the studio was not fuelled by the cocaine; it was innate. As confirmation of his imminent success, a small group of fans gathered round the studio each night. They were given the title of 'the Sigma kids', regarded as a kind of lucky charm, and were finally invited in to listen to the rough mixes – perhaps predictably, they were wildly enthusiastic.

The sense of focus around the Sigma sessions provided a powerful contrast to David's chaotic private life. Ava, his girlfriend, had helped inspire his work in the city; but during the recordings he'd frequently disappear, a cat on the prowl. 'I knew the party was going on somewhere else,' says Cherry of his nocturnal escapades. When Angie arrived in Philadelphia there was yet more drama, when she heard Ava was on the scene and ran off towards a hotel window, threatening to throw herself out.

Angie's behaviour was all the more extreme in that she was one of the few at the time who didn't drink or do drugs. David and Angie were caught in a bizarre cycle where David would decide he needed her and call her up; Angie would arrive, only to be ignored, which provoked a crisis. 'It was a very odd relationship, very weird to be around,' concluded Zanetta, who realised during these weeks that David was considering finally ridding himself of Angie. The timing was significant, for it followed, by only a few days, David's belated understanding of his relationship with MainMan.

The devastating conversation took place in a New York hotel at the end of July. Coked out of his mind, as was Zanetta, Bowie poured out his woes: 'Did I work this hard, to have nothing?' The pair were discussing the money that was pouring out of MainMan, when Zanetta realised that David thought he owned half the organisation. 'It was odd,' says Zanetta. 'He didn't understand that he didn't own [half of] MainMan. We were sitting there, going over what had gone wrong and trying to keep it all together. I adored both David and Tony, so this was more than heartbreaking – it felt like the end of the world.'

Traumatic as the situation was for Zanetta, for David it was far worse. He'd simply always assumed he owned his own company, his own music; the situation, as mapped out by Zanetta, was so horrifically different, he seemed incapable of comprehending it. Zanetta tried to explain to him that he owned half his own revenue, less expenses, but had no share in the other MainMan enterprises. The obvious next step, if David wanted to ensure he had received everything he was entitled to, was to hire an accountant and go through the books, where every penny of expenditure was documented. But David had no interest in analysing his predicament. Defries had created a magical aura, a cocoon where David could create. Now the magic bubble had popped. Over subsequent weeks, David made no effort to investigate his contract with MainMan;

he was only interested in terminating it. 'It was coming to an end between them,' says Zanetta, their conflicted go-between. 'Part of that was money. Part of it was Defries' megalomania. In fact, they were both megalomaniacs'.

'Tony had been a total father figure,' adds Ava Cherry. 'David would do everything Tony said, would listen to his every word. When he heard about the money he was simply . . . afraid.'

The ramifications of David's deal with MainMan were complex; there were indeed advantages to the way David's contract was set up, for it gave him control of his masters – as long as he remained with MainMan. Defries himself maintains that MainMan's unique position as owner of David's master recordings increased his royalties from the industry standard 10 per cent to 16 per cent, a cut that was, in the early 1970s, unusually generous. But one crucial aspect of their relationship is beyond debate. David believed he was a partner in MainMan; in reality, he was an employee. His failure to even question his own status displayed staggering naiveté.

This discovery was a devastating blow to David's self-esteem. As he saw it, his father figure had betrayed him. Ava Cherry, and Coco, comforted him throughout the distraught crying jags that overcame him whenever he thought about his situation, but most of the time, his problems were too bleak to contemplate. Instead, David fixed on Angie, deciding he could no longer cope with her outbursts. For months to come, he would continue to play his public role with his wife – maintaining the image that, as Scott Richardson puts it, 'had made the world fall in love with them' – but David's emotional detachment from Angie was part of his detachment from MainMan. Angie, more than David, had defined MainMan's image; it was she who had established the company's cradle at Haddon Hall, who had formed the relationship with the *Pork* crew. As Leee Childers points out, 'MainMan had been created in Angie's image.' For David, both were now encumbrances. But in the short term he would keep his counsel, while he worked out how to cut himself loose.

The summer of 1974 was temperate and balmy, and when David resumed his tour – the band now augmented with Carlos Alomar, Ava Cherry and most of the Sigma crew – his personal traumas were briefly forgotten in the excitement of creation. For the time being, David informed Defries, via Tony Zanetta, that he was planning a new stripped-down production, and wanted to ditch the Hunger City set and play against a white backdrop. Defries affected nonchalance at the news that the $400,000 construction was destined for the trash-heap.

Over seven nights at Hollywood's Universal Amphitheatre, David's claim to bona fide superstar status was laid out in the most convincing fashion. His previous 'retirement' seemed only to add to his unpredictability and glamour. The Hollywood aristocracy turned out; Diana Ross made a conspicuous appearance in a silver gown, as did her fellow Motown stars The Jackson Five.

Marc Bolan was another attendant on the triumphant hero. He had bitched about David in print earlier that year, deriding his American success as all marketing gloss. Now, pudgy and nervous, he paid due fealty to the man who had so often paid tribute to him. 'David was obviously at a high point and Marc at a low point,' says Zanetta, who sat with the two of them at the Beverly Wilshire hotel. 'But David did not gloat at all, he was very kind.' Later that year, Marc would tell *Melody Maker* how he would be directing David in his first movie. By then, with David being courted by Hollywood's biggest stars, Marc's bravado seemed unbearably sad. Iggy Pop eventually turned up, too. After his split with MainMan, and well-publicised attacks on 'that fuckin' carrot-top' for sabotaging his *Raw Power* album, he had finally split from The Stooges following a legendarily disastrous last tour. His last public performance had been a pathetic affair at Rodney's English Disco, which culminated in him stabbing his chest with a blunt steak knife. Now mocked around Hollywood as a trashcan drug user, Iggy missed David's show after being beaten up by a bunch of surfers in the parking lot. He turned up later to cadge food.

Burying himself in musical preparations throughout the LA shows, David seemed genuinely happy; over successive nights he coached Ava Cherry, ready for her solo number, which was Luther Vandross's 'Maybe It's Love'. He was the perfect mentor: rehearsing and encouraging her. 'He walked me through the whole thing, the movement, the way I would enter the stage. He was very nurturing, it was wonderful.'

David had even seemed gracious and hospitable when a young BBC director, Alan Yentob, appeared in Hollywood, explaining that Tony Defries had, in a momentary lapse, agreed to give him access. Impressed by Yentob's explanation of the theme of the documentary – that this would be an exploration of a significant, serious artist in his new, American setting – David agreed to grant him an interview.

Yentob's documentary would be unforgettable, a gripping depiction of a fractured, dislocated existence. One of the main contributors to that fractured aura was a local celebrity who introduced himself to David after one of the first Hollywood shows. Freddy Sessler, concentration camp survivor and rock 'n' roll fan, was 'the kind of guy who can make a party happen', says Iggy Pop. Sessler is one of those characters whose existence is rarely acknowledged in the wider world, despite the influence he had behind the scenes. For decades he acted as companion to Keith Richards and Ron Wood, loved for his Chico Marx-style gruff humour and for his ability to source the best drugs in the West. With customary ease, Freddy gained admission to the Beverly Wilshire, his pockets bulging with vials of pure 'Merck' – medicinal cocaine, far more powerful than anything available in New York. This was the mother lode, the drug lauded by Sigmund Freud as 'this magical substance'. From then on, Freddy would be David's companion, too.

Over those weeks in Hollywood, David was also being courted by the UK's most glamorous movie icon: Elizabeth Taylor. Their first meeting was awkward – Terry O'Neill, who photographed David for the *Diamond Dogs* sleeve, invited David to a shoot at director George Cukor's house, for which David arrived 'two hours late – dishevelled and out of it. Liz was pretty annoyed and on the verge of leaving, but we managed to persuade her to stay.' Liz's irritation with David was outweighed by her own instinct for publicity. A huge star in the 1960s, Taylor had fared less well in the 1970s and was eager to be associated with Bowie: O'Neill's photos showed the two frolicking like teenagers, Liz embracing David, holding his cigarette suggestively.

Within days she was making high-profile visits to David's rehearsals, and floating the idea that David would star in *The Blue Bird*, a remake of Maurice Tourneur's 1918 movie, in the press. Her adoption of David as an up-and-coming superstar was made official during a party for Ricci Martin – Dean's son – in Beverly Hills, where they sat close to each other, chatting softly.

There was another star in the cavalcade of celebrities gathering around David and Liz that evening: John Lennon, then in the midst of his so-called 'Lost Weekend' with May Pang. John was 'saucer-eyed', according to Pang, at seeing so many of his movie heroes in LA and was soaking up the vibe at the party, chatting with Elton John. Taylor called John and May over, introducing them to David in her sing-song, almost childish voice. John was chummy, 'But David was odd,' remembers May Pang. After a few seconds he told them, 'I have to go now.' A few minutes later they walked into another room to see David and Liz, still huddled together. 'It was strange – David was very thin, I remember he seemed stand-offish. John didn't know what to think. Me, him and Elton were looking at each other: what was *that* about?' Lennon was not offended, merely puzzled.

As the tour moved on to the Midwest, and then the east, early in October, the soul vibe became more obvious, and Hunger City's skyscrapers finally met the wrecking ball. These shows were mocked by some observers as a patronising wannabe soul revue, but for band and crew these were thrilling dates, with the set evolving from one night to the next. Received wisdom would have it that David's cocaine habit reduced him to such a state of dehydration that his lips adhered to his gums: Ava Cherry, who stood close to him on stage, remembers no such event. But there were many moments of crisis, in particular a show in Boston that November. Before the show started, he demanded a gramme of cocaine. 'I'm not going on unless I get it.' After scurrying around, a flunkie came up with the goods. But when David walked out on stage the first two rows stayed immobile. For some reason, most of them had dressed up in Halloween costumes for the occasion. 'Skeleton masks, scary masks,' says Cherry.

'Why are they doing that?' David appealed to his backing singers. 'Why the masks?' He was terrified, offended that his fans saw him simply as a freak. Then, as he made his way out of the Music Hall, he was handed a poster-sized sheet. On it were tombstones bearing his name. The poster troubled him for days. Later he mentioned it to Ava, when trying to explain his own behaviour: 'If you don't like some of the things I do, that's why – I don't live a normal life.'

Writer Mick Farren had been sent to report on the tour for the *NME*, and found himself relishing the weird culture clash, 'like a crazed Funkadelic tour, with added cocaine, paranoia and Scientology', he says. Farren loved the 'James Brown vs Elvis vibe – obviously they'd cobbled it together on the fly, but it was kinda cool'. Photographer Robert Matheu remembered the same seedy glamour in Detroit. 'The drugs were apparent in so many ways – they actually seemed to add to the overall vibe, there was a darkness to it. You know, an Ike Turner thing: Ike always had that vibe, you knew he was holding.' The culture clash was reflected in backstage friction between the band: Kamen's crew seemed at odds with the Main Ingredient players; Coco Schwab was lined up against Ava Cherry, or Angie when she turned up; the Scientology vibe was still present thanks to Mike Garson, plus there were 'monstrous amounts' of cocaine in evidence. 'Piles of the shit everywhere,' says Farren. 'They must have been carrying half-ounce bags. This was about as excessive as it got – in a period of excess.'

When he wasn't on stage, David, whom Farren knew back from his Lindsay Kemp days, looked lost and, as in the later stages of his previous American tour, 'lonely'. Most of the time he walked around in an overcoat with his hood up, nose dripping, twitchily rejecting any attempts at conversation. When anyone got in the lift with him, he looked terrified. Many outsiders remember the cut-throat, paranoid atmosphere, with different cliques trying to entice outsiders back to their room 'for some blow', each accusing the others of being drug-fiends, even of stealing money. But on-stage, David was always in command; the backstage friction gave the music an edge. 'David had people playing against each other on stage, to make them better,' says Ava Cherry, 'like the James Brown thing, always that pressure of, You're in, You're out. Sometimes it was brilliant. Me and Diane [Sumler] would fight harder to be better than each other – 'cos we were opposites.'

The atmosphere was all the more bizarre because the darkness and paranoia were offset by the mood of 'the kids', as Zanetta called them: Carlos, Robin and Luther were wholesome and loving, relishing their big break. Although guitarist Earl Slick had his own 'mindless' moments, as he recalls, he too seemed like a carefree child, in his element, and Ava Cherry, innocent and luscious, was 'adored' by most of the crew. In another bizarre touch, Zowie and his nanny Marion Skene were around for several dates. While David was generally distracted, when he made time for his son he was 'absolutely attentive – focusing on him completely,' says Zanetta. Likewise, David's boyish enthusiasm was obvious when he concentrated on the music, and at soundchecks the whole crazy family would come together and unite, with a wired optimism.

In the afternoons when the troupe remained in the city, at the Michigan Palace or Chicago's Crown Theatre, there would be extended jam sessions where David would be filled with energy, pointing out riffs and directing arrangements, and over the October dates, new songs were added one by one: the devotional, gospelly 'It's Gonna Be Me', and a funked-up version of The Flares' 1963 Doo Wop hit, 'Foot Stompin''.

The autumn and winter of 1974 was the period most marked by a cocaine blitz, one in which David would famously describe himself as permanently 'out of my gourd'. Yet even outsiders, although shocked by David's physical deterioration, were somehow convinced that this was simply another phase, one which would pass. 'He's such a survivor,' Mick Farren points out, 'plus we weren't all dropping dead back then.' Only in retrospect, says Farren, did he reflect on the psychological burdens David had assumed. 'It's like what Lennon said about Elvis: "I don't know how he did it, 'cos there were four of us and it nearly killed us." And of course there were only two of David.'

David's performance on *The Dick Cavett Show*, taped on 2 November, 1974, during the New York dates, was the high watermark of his 'out of my gourd' period, and the perfect embodiment of the tour's prickly, paranoid energy. Sniffing loudly, with his eyes flitting from side to side, David bares his teeth several times in a grimace almost like those of the skeleton masks that had freaked him out in Boston. As if in reaction, Cavett mentions black magic and how 'some people said they're scared to sit and talk to you'. David's main response is to fiddle obsessively with his cane, and for a moment Cavett looks truly worried, as though his guest is drawing a pentagram on the studio floor. At odd moments – a little chuckle here, his statement that when he's on stage 'that's it, [I'm] complete' – he still manages to impersonate a normal human being, but mostly he revels in his fractured condition. Together with Alan Yentob's *Cracked Actor*, screened by the BBC on 26 January, 1975, this would be the definitive depiction of Bowie in his most alien state. But in the sense that he is exploring the limits of his mental condition, he is also recognisably David Bowie, in exactly the same way that the coked-out David witnessed by Keith Christmas was merely another manifestation of the person he'd known in 1969.

As if in tribute to David's newly minted image as an icon of excess, the police raided the end-of-tour party at Atlanta's Hyatt Regency on 1 December. Backing singers Geoff MacCormack and Gui Andrisano had noticed a couple of 'strange guys with bad taste in clothes and suspiciously short haircuts' hanging out in the hotel suite and warned their fellow musicians. When the police broke in, none of the crew was holding, but the suite contained nine phials of cocaine, ten lumps of hashish, five bags of grass and three roaches. Tony Zanetta, who had booked the suite, was dragged off for an overnight stay in the cells, but finally released without charges.

After an exhausting drive back to New York, David had booked studio time to complete *Young Americans* at the Hit Factory, around 3 December. After David added more overdubs and completed 'Fascination' – based on a Luther Vandross song – and 'Win', Tony Visconti flew over to London with the tapes, to mix them at his home studio, happy at finally completing the thrilling, but gruelling sessions.

In his first few days back in New York, David had also called up John Lennon and May Pang; he was nervous about meeting the ex-Beatle again, and at one point called Tony Visconti over to the Sherry Netherlands hotel to help ease the conversation along. Although their meeting in LA had gone nowhere, David and John had a huge amount in common. Bowie would talk about John frequently; John was interested in David, friendly, but invariably slightly puzzled. 'David was still very nervous, John was happy to hang out,' says May Pang. The atmosphere remained slightly awkward, all the more so when Paul and Linda McCartney – who had just bumped into John and May – entered the picture in mid-January.

The four of them went over to the Sherry to meet David, who repeatedly played the various mixes of his new album for them, 'and we had heard it already. In lots of different states,' says Pang. David was about to replay the acetate for John for at least the second time when John told him, 'David it's great, a great album . . . is there anything else we can listen to as well?' David looked devastated; John hadn't noticed Paul had made almost exactly the same remark a few minutes earlier, and when the couple returned to their apartment on 52nd Street that night, the phone was ringing as they came through the door. 'Yes David, sorry man, I didn't mean that,' John consoled his offended, cocaine-fuelled friend.

May Pang remembers that Lennon was taken aback by the size of David's coke habit, remarking to May, 'I've never seen such mounds of the stuff!' But John enjoyed his company, and although he was puzzled when David told him that he was planning to add a cover version of 'Across the Universe' to the album, he instantly agreed to turn up at Electric Lady studio around 15 January, for he was a studio hound. 'He loved being in on the recording,' says renowned engineer Eddie Kramer, who worked the session, 'and just playing guitar – he was a ridiculously good rhythm player. '

In the studio, the environment they both loved, John's empathy with David was obvious, Kramer observed. David too was obviously having a blast: 'Whatever stimulants he was taking didn't affect his ability to be creative,' says Kramer, who was present when Carlos Alomar started playing the riff, adapted from a Rascals song, 'Jungle Walk', that he'd added to the band's live version of 'Foot Stompin''. 'David said, "I'll have that," or words to that effect – and he took the riff that Carlos played and made a song out of it.'

Lennon was playing around on the acoustic in the lounge, singing a couple of lines from Shirley & Company's disco hit 'Shame, Shame, Shame' over the top of the same one-chord vamp. 'So he was working it, and David walks in and hears that,' says Pang, who remembers David leaving the room and returning with a complete set of lyrics within twenty minutes.

David had misheard 'shame' as 'fame' – a subject he'd been discussing with John earlier – and also the title of yet another disastrous MainMan project, a Tony Ingrassia play launched just a few weeks before. The misheard word would give him his biggest hit to date. Although some key recollections vary as to whether Carlos started the vamp first and John joined in, or vice versa, Bowie 'was very much in charge, he knew exactly what he wanted', says Kramer, who watched David work the elements into a song once John had left the studio. Part of Lennon's own guitar vamp survived in the three acoustic chords – F minor, C minor, and B flat – that open the song and punctuate the main theme before the last verse. Carlos's riff, effective on 'Foot Stompin'', was the killer element on 'Fame'; but it's Bowie who makes sense of it – he plays the crunchy ascending guitar riff at the end of each line.

Restricted mostly to a single chord, 'Fame' is obsessive, monotonous and claustrophobic. On *Hunky Dory*, David had worked with piano chords; here he was playing with sound itself, using the studio as a giant cut-and-paste machine. Yet the emotional impact was just as powerful, for the song was an almost literal rendition of his life, jump-cutting from his omnipresent worries about money – 'what you need you have to borrow'; to his loneliness – 'takes you there where things are hollow'.

'Fame's' last-minute addition to the album, which had already been trailed in the press as *Fascination* in December, would be the making of *Young Americans*; it would also arguably break it, too, for David felt compelled to include his version of 'Across the Universe', the song that had inspired Lennon's arrival in the studio. The cover version was a horrible mess, marred by David's warbling vocal, the most extreme example so far of his mimicking of Bryan Ferry and Scott Walker's style, and an obvious flaw that the album's detractors would latch onto. (Lennon was just as puzzled as everyone else: 'Why *that* song?' he asked May Pang.) When 'Fame' became David's first US number one, the following September, John was as delighted as David. 'He had that competitiveness with the others guys [i.e. Paul McCartney] – and he thought it was great,' says Pang, who disappeared from John's life in February, as the ex-Beatle returned to Yoko and The Dakota. May would later marry Tony Visconti, whom she'd met at the Sherry that winter.

The excitement around the recording was one of the few high spots in a bleak winter. Much of David's Christmas was spent in a coke-fuelled haze with Tony Zanetta at the Sherry Netherlands. David had lost his very last vestige of faith in Tony Defries, and in all of MainMan, on 18

November, the day that the company made its grand entrance – and its ignominious exit – on Broadway. *Fame* was a chaotic, confused comedy based on the life of Marilyn Monroe, written by Tony Ingrassia, the mastermind of *Pork*. *Pork* had launched the MainMan circus; *Fame*, which closed after one performance, was its death-knell, for Bowie deeply resented the reported $250,000 that had been lost on its production, money his hits had generated. David's conversations with John Lennon at Electric Lady confirmed his decision. John had just divested himself of Beatles manager Allen Klein, commemorated by one of his last great songs, 'Steel and Glass', which mocked Klein's LA tan and his infamous BO ('you leave your smell like an alley cat'). Defries frequently claimed to have learned his trade from Klein; if John had had enough of Klein, David had had enough of Defries.

Over Christmas, David attempted to contact Defries, who was away on his favourite island hideaway of Mustique, without success. The two finally met up in January. The encounter was strangely dysfunctional, as far as those close to them can tell, with neither man coming to the point. David told friends Defries had accepted his decision to leave MainMan; Defries believed he'd smoothed over David's concerns and persuaded him to stay. In later months, when their split became increasingly ill-tempered, Defries would tell his friends how 'disappointed' he was in David. He was let down by his ingratitude, his lack of understanding of commercial realities, his addiction to drugs (for added drama he speculated David was on heroin, too).

Later, when friends asked Defries, the supreme negotiator, why he had failed to negotiate a settlement at his meeting with David, he would coldly ask, 'David had been working for me. Why would *I* want to work for *him*?'

Defries also seemed to astutely judge Michael Lippman, the lawyer David had found to represent him. Previously an agent for CMA, Lippman had pitched film work to both David and Angie; he'd been a fully qualified partner in a law firm rather than a mere clerk like Defries, and was liked and trusted by those around David, but could never match his opponent's aggression. Defries told his friends that Lippman was a very junior agent with not much to offer, and that he'd advised Bowie to retain a more high-powered lawyer.

MainMan would be dismembered in David's wake, all its artists subsequently dropped; Defries' subsequent management career failed to make headlines. One singer did approach him for advice a few years later, Defries confided to his friends. Her name was Madonna.

*

In later years, Defries would be painted as cynical and manipulative; but speak to anyone who worked with him, and a trace of the magic still lingers. For Defries 'was never the demon figure he's made out', says Hugh Attwooll, one-time head of MainMan England. 'He's a man without care. He knew he could beat the system and he did it. All he said to David was that he'd make him a star. He didn't elaborate and say, "I'll use a lot of your money to make it work." My view is that he gets rather a bad press. Because it *did* work – without it, David wouldn't be as famous as he is.'

Over the next year, David would be dogged by disputes with Defries, who would retain a share of David's future records for the remainder of the MainMan contract term, right up to 1982, with the right to reject any album should Defries deem it uncommercial. Such onerous conditions naturally made most observers side with David. But those who were there testify that, not only was Defries was the key figure in helping Bowie rise to fame, he was also an integral part of that period's unforgettable magic.

'What entertained him was the intellectual challenge of doing it – taking the risk and making it work,' says Attwooll. 'He spun a web of magic, which no one had ever done before, and persuaded RCA to spend huge amounts of money both in the UK and US. He was a very nice bloke, but what line he stepped over in achieving what he achieved is probably an argument that will never be satisfied.'

David, meanwhile, spent years dealing with the ramifications of the split with the figure who'd overseen his rise to fame. He'd put off his confrontation with Defries for months; David's friends, including Coco Schwab and Ava Cherry, hoped the split would finally produce some resolution. But there would be none.

David Jones had embarked on a long, gruelling, ruthless journey in pursuit of fame and success; many of his peers had shown similar ambition, but few had transformed themselves so painstakingly from a mediocrity into an inspirational songwriter. Soon, he'd discover, the very stuff he'd created, at such personal cost, was lost to him. David's friends hoped that his final split with his one-time father figure would bring 'closure'. Instead, it brought crisis.

14

White Stains

> He – and this is glamorising it – did use the drugs to enlarge his capabilities in every dimension. It really magnified his intelligence, if you will. But it had its way with him.
>
> *Glenn Hughes*

David believed that cutting his ties with Defries promised mental freedom; independence in his business affairs seemed almost secondary. 'Forget about the money,' he had told a couple of people, 'that's all in the past.' Above all, he had confidence in his music; his new album would finally bring him mainstream success in America, and represented the ultimate bargaining chip in his relationship with RCA who, early in January, confirmed that they were prepared to deal with David directly, effectively cutting Defries out of the deal.

But by February 1975, the awful truth dawned that the freedom might be illusory; that although David had left MainMan, MainMan – and Defries – retained control of his existing masters. During his conversations with John Lennon – whose business savvy he admired – he discovered that Lennon had lost his own publishing, and at times despaired of escaping Allen Klein's clutches. David's contract with Defries, as an employee, was even more restrictive. 'That was when David's whole mood changed,' says Ava Cherry, who witnessed David's conversations with John. 'He was always irritated after that, quick to get angry. David was a little bit naive – and he couldn't believe he'd really signed so much away.'

While David was mired in his financial worries, the extent of his physical deterioration was revealed in gripping fashion, on 26 January, when

Alan Yentob's *Cracked Actor* was screened on the BBC. In later years, it would be acclaimed as one of the greatest music documentaries ever made. With the minimal interview time he'd been given, Yentob lingered over every shot, capturing perfectly the emptiness and loneliness in which David was sealed. Defries' predecessor, Ken Pitt, was one of many disturbed by David's fractured, disconnected state. He concluded simply that David 'was ill. That was what all the Defries big talk had done for him. This was not the David I knew. It was very disappointing.'

An interview with Bruno Stein published in February's *Creem* was even more alarming, indicative of what seemed classic cocaine-induced paranoia. David was obsessed with UFO cover-ups. 'And I made sightings [of UFOs] six, seven times a night for about a year when I was in the observatory,' he confided to the astonished writer, before pronouncing that Adolf Hitler was 'a perfect figurehead'. In reality, these proclamations reflected an old obsession, dating back to when he was hanging out with Lesley Duncan at Redington Road. All those who had gone UFO-spotting with him around 1967, like Jeff Dexter and Wayne Bardell, confirm, 'We *did* see UFOs – absolutely.' Equally, Adolf Hitler was an old, favourite topic for debate, for David used to eulogise the work of Albert Speer back in Arnold Corns days. Yet what had been cheery, hipsters' chat in the sixties became ominous and disturbing in 1975.

While onlookers' reactions to David's state varied from horror to fascination to cynicism, one woman saw a solution to a movie casting problem. Maggie Abbott was an agent at CMA who'd been crucial in uniting her clients Mick Jagger and writer Donald Cammell with Nicolas Roeg for *Performance* – the definitive celluloid depiction of late sixties decadence. She'd first heard of David through a friend who trained with him at Lindsay Kemp's studio – now he was, thanks to CMA, her client. Yentob's documentary convinced her that he would be perfect for the lead role in Roeg's upcoming project, *The Man Who Fell to Earth*. Abbott's tenacity played a crucial part in the genesis of the film, not least because the BBC refused to release a video of *Cracked Actor* for Roeg and producer Si Litvinoff to watch, and she had to use 'cunning charm' to smuggle out a copy. 'Nic and Si didn't take any convincing, they knew as soon as they saw *Cracked Actor*, especially the sequence with David in the back of the limo.' The pair, and Abbott, were struck by how, as Bowie gazed out of the car window, he seemed totally isolated, disconnected from the world – alien.

Roeg had planned to cast Michael Crighton, Mick Jagger and later Peter O'Toole to play Newton, the alien who comes to earth in search of

water and is corrupted by earthly vices. Crighton and O'Toole were
unavailable; Abbott talked Roeg out of using Jagger, her other major
client. Watching the documentary, Roeg noticed countless facets of
Bowie that resonated with the part. But the most important one was 'that
curious artificial voice. It wasn't absolutely definable as a brogue or
accent. Like, did it really exist?' Today, Roeg admits that while the
decision to cast Bowie was obvious in retrospect, 'I don't know if it
was immediate.' Likewise Maggie Abbott – who flew to New York in
February, 1975 to show David the script – remembers his initial response
as 'cautious . . . cool'. His reserve was not so striking as his physical
state, which was even worse than *Cracked Actor* had suggested; his
hip bones jutted through the jump suit he was wearing, his skin was
white, and his teeth grey. 'Ghastly,' is Abbott's description. But he was
astute: he understood the logic of her case, asked the correct questions,
and was obviously intrigued by Abbott's connections with Roeg and
Mick Jagger. She, in turn, had no doubt about whether he would rise to
the task. 'He could sleep-walk through it,' she told Roeg, who arranged
to meet David a couple of days later.

Convinced that signing David was crucial to his movie, Roeg won
him over by his gentle persistence, for David had forgotten their meeting and was busy, says Roeg, in a recording session. Roeg waited for
most of the day, and when Bowie eventually arrived late that evening the
pair talked for only a few minutes before David agreed to sign up.

Roeg was an undeniably impressive character, and his assiduous
courting of David together with the completion of 'Fame' both represented hope, for the thought of Defries' control over his work – which
culminated in attempts by MainMan to injunct the release of *Young
Americans* – made David feel like a helpless, naive child. David's encounters with John Lennon, through January and early February, brought out
the best in him – his unaffected joy and enthusiasm – for he was
impressed with how down to earth and 'un-starry' Lennon was, and
acted the same in his company. John, too, had come to genuinely like
David; for all his quirks, he was a committed rock 'n' roller, like John,
and once the stand-offishness had faded away, he seemed simply like a
younger brother who needed counselling.

But the influence of other stars was far less benign. Cherry Vanilla had
left MainMan before David's split, and kept in regular touch; she had
introduced him to Norman Fisher when he'd first moved to New York,
and would have brief chats with David quite regularly, the two of them
gossiping away before David got to the point – which was usually a

request if he could 'borrow' her apartment for sex sessions, away from the watchful eye of Ava, or Angie, who lived briefly nearby before returning to London. Then, one evening, Vanilla saw David hurrying down the street, asked if he was OK, and he blurted out that he'd just been to see Lou Reed. 'Don't ever go near him,' he warned her. 'He's the devil.'

Vanilla was only briefly worried. 'He was on this trip, whatever Lou had done to him had freaked him out that day.' By then it was well known that David was living solely on a diet of 'coke and milk' but like most of her circle, she was convinced that cocaine had no downside. 'We didn't think of it as ill then. We thought of it as fashionable.'

David's encounter with Led Zep guitarist Jimmy Page in February was even more unsettling. Their acquaintance went back to The Manish Boys days, but during a night with Ava at Bowie's house, the atmosphere was strained, and then when Page spilt wine on some silk cushions and tried to blame Ava, Bowie turfed him out, spitting out, 'Why don't you take the window.' The two glared at each other; Page seemed to be invoking dark forces against David, who in turn, says Ava Cherry, 'wanted to show Jimmy that his will was stronger. Then all of a sudden, after that night, David has all these books around and is reading them.'

David's battle of wills with Page helped inspire a deeper investigation of the works of 'the wickedest man in the world'. Jimmy Page's devotion to the work of occultist Aleister Crowley was well known – he had bought and restored Crowley's famed magical headquarters, Boleskine House, in 1971. Crowley's work was popular in hippie circles from 1969; Graham Bond, Elton John's old employer, released *Holy Magick*, an album devoted to Crowley, in 1970; Sombrero regular Robert Kensell was another devotee. David himself had name-checked Crowley in 'Quicksand', and possibly 'Holy Holy', too; those close to him in 1971, like Dai Davies, believe that back then Bowie had a 'fashionable, but fleeting interest' in dropping Crowley's name, as he did with Nietzsche. The meeting with Page seemed to convert what had been shallow name-dropping into a full-blown obsession.

Over the course of 1975, David embarked on a journey that would take him into the heart of psychic darkness. One key text in this journey was – according to Gary Lachman, an acquaintance of Bowie who has written on the occult – Trevor Ravenscourt's *The Spear of Destiny*. Published in 1973, the book explored Hitler and Himmler's harnessing of occult powers, notably the Holy Grail and its partner artefact, the lance that pierced Christ's side. Other Bowie influences almost certainly included the hugely fashionable *Morning of the Magicians*, by Louis Pauwels and Jacques Bergier. Together with works by Crowley and his acolytes, these formed the core of Bowie's reading list. Lachman debated such subjects as the occult interests of *Outsider* author Colin Wilson with Bowie, and believes 'he is interested in lots of such ideas, and can speak intelligently about them. Jimmy Page went into it more deeply and was a serious devotee – Bowie picked lots of different elements, and gave them a twist.'

By the time Bowie met Page, the Led Zep guitarist had spent over six years investigating Crowley's work; David's immersion was comparatively brief. Rather than seek to harness dark powers, he would embark on a coke-addled quest for meaning. In 1993, Bowie would explain his fascination with Himmler's search for the Holy Grail and Spear of Destiny as an 'Arthurian Need – this search for a mythological link with God. But somewhere along the line it was perverted by what I was reading and what I was drawn to.'

Like The Rolling Stones, who'd danced with the devil in the guise of Crowley disciple Kenneth Anger, Bowie's new, dangerous aura would take a heavy toll on him, and those around him. Obsessed and scared by the ominous forces he saw gathering around him, David started planning his escape from New York. It wasn't just people like Jimmy Page or Lou Reed he wanted to flee; even normally well-behaved musicians seem to resent his presence. Aretha Franklin had mocked him at the Grammys ('I'm so happy I could kiss David Bowie'), ruining his mood for weeks, and at a party thrown by Alice Cooper's manager, Shep Gordon, Bob Dylan had delivered one of his trademark put-downs: 'Glam rock isn't music,' he had sneered, before turning his back on David, as the watching industry heavyweights and their flunkies gasped.

A move to LA, ready for *The Man Who Fell to Earth* shoot – later delayed as Roeg and producer Si Litvinoff looked for backers – represented a clean break with such nastiness. It meant he'd be closer to his new, Hollywood manager, Michael Lippman; it also meant he could escape Ava Cherry and her complaints about his obsessive womanising. (Angie, in comparison, had given up, and seemed content to pursue a mostly separate existence.)

The move also meant David would be close to LA's raconteur and coke dealer *par excellence*, Freddy Sessler. Geoff MacCormack, who flew over to join David a couple of weeks later, would characterise this period in LA as a time when 'a common form of greeting was for someone simply to say, Hi, and stick a silver spoon under your nose'. Freddy ·

would arrive, not with a vial of cocaine, but a plate. The potency and quantity of Sessler's wares were unrivalled: they would contribute towards David's marked mental deterioration over the summer of 1975.

Glenn Hughes, a twenty-three-year old English bassist and singer who'd recently joined Deep Purple, had become fast friends with Bowie in LA the previous year. During their long phone conversations, Glenn – then about to start on Deep Purple's last tour with guitarist Ritchie Blackmore – had offered David refuge at his house in Beverly Hills. With a sizable coke habit himself, Glenn was well aware of David's increasing problems; staggered to hear that David planned to make the train trip on his own, he arranged for his driver to pick up David from Union Station, when he arrived in LA around 16 March, 1975. He wanted to make sure that David wasn't left alone – but it was a vain hope. 'David was on his own a lot over that period,' says Hughes. 'He could be in a room of five or six people, with a book, and be on his own.'

Over the following months, Glenn's relationship with David would be deepened and tempered by their mutual obsession with cocaine: 'It was a dark year – for him, and for me. I know he doesn't like to think about it now, but this is the service we have to give back to people. We have to acknowledge the dark side of what happened.'

Throughout their friendship Bowie and Hughes would have, at fleeting moments, the time of their lives: rapping wildly about music, arguing about clothes, mapping out the future. They were both still young, 'invincible', and Bowie was a good friend, advising Hughes, teaching him how to use his influences but to keep moving on. He was also 'a funny son of a bitch' – unusually for coke addicts, they'd spend some of their time laughing uproariously. But the enduring image of their time together is the two of them, sitting alongside each other, isolated, Glenn obsessively working out riffs on the guitar, and David watching the same dark, disquieting movies, over and over, both of them lost in their own world: 'It was miserable. It always is miserable.'

Within a couple of days of his arrival in LA, David re-encountered a paradigm of the West Coast lifestyle's corrosive effects, in the subdued shape of Iggy Pop. Since he'd last seen David, an attempted partnership with ex-Doors keyboard player Ray Manzarek had fallen apart, and Iggy had been abandoned by his self-proclaimed manager, Danny Sugerman. Late in 1974 he'd ended up at the Neuropsychiatric Institute (NPI) at UCLA's Westwood complex, after being forced to choose between jail and hospital by a cop who'd found him drooling aggressively at the customers in Hamburger Hamlet.

When David arrived at NPI to visit, Iggy was in a pathetic condition, withdrawing from the cocktail of drugs that had permeated his system for the last year. During his stay on the wards he had fascinated the psychiatrists, who diagnosed an excess of narcissism and, more seriously, an underlying bipolar condition. Ex-Stooge James Williamson had visited, but friends like Sugerman, who had publicised his descent into oblivion, stayed away. 'Nobody else came, nobody,' Iggy recalled two years later. 'Not even my so-called friends in LA. But David came.'

Even Iggy was surprised at David's opening words: 'Hey, do you want any blow?' Being Iggy, he took a toot. On his first visit, David was accompanied by actor Dean Stockwell; later, Dennis Hopper tagged along, as did Ola Hudson, the clothes designer who became David's main companion over the summer. She was accompanied by her son, Saul – aka Slash, later the top-hatted, guitar-slinging founder of Gun N' Roses. The nine-year-old was still distraught at his parents' separation, and understandably disorientated by his recent move from Stoke-on-Trent, the homely centre of England's pottery industry, into the mental wildlands of Los Angeles: seeing his mom with Bowie was, says Slash, 'like watching an alien land in your back yard'.

In truth, David was equally adrift in an alien landscape. The city fascinated him – 'LA is my favourite museum,' he had quipped to writer Cameron Crowe while driving him on a mad jaunt around the city in a borrowed yellow VW bug – but in the weeks between April and June 1975 his mental condition deteriorated from excitable but rational, to near-delusional. Glenn Hughes had regular phone conversations when he was out of LA on tour, and checked in with his house-minder, Phil, who informed him, 'There are birds of every colour, coming and going at all hours of the night.' David's own description of what was going was a good deal less jolly. 'The conversations were scary,' says Hughes. 'This black magic theme crept in; and my house was near where the Sharon Tate murders were, he was convinced the whole Manson family was still around, and I found he's hid all the knives in my house. Though I didn't know it at the time, I was learning all about cocaine psychosis– which I would go through myself soon.'

In May, David took Iggy into Cherokee Studios for a set of later-abandoned recordings. James Williamson, one of the few people who persevered with Iggy, accompanied him to the sessions. By now Iggy was 'pretty far gone', says Williamson. Bowie, in comparison, looked together. 'He always was this reserved, almost aloof kind of a guy – so he just looked like a more wasted version of that.' What struck

Williamson most was the 'dreadful' noise on the recordings, an earth hum that would make them useless. Bowie's obliviousness to the noise was the main clue things weren't well. 'But hey,' points out Williamson, who'd narrowly evaded a smack possession charge that same year, 'everybody was in trouble in LA then.'

Iggy's own recollections of Bowie from that time seemed rather conventional (compared to his own existence, perhaps it was). 'Sometimes I would go over to his house for a couple of days. There would be books all over the floor and Dennis Hopper stopping by – and David always had ideas. He was about to do *Man Who Fell to Earth*, and he had a great book, a slim volume about a group of people for the government who faked a Mars landing in a TV studio, a wonderful little idea for a movie, he was keen on talking about that. Then he had an idea for a rock 'n' roll move in which I would play a character called Catastrophe. I indulged him in that 'cause, well . . . I am open to a lot of things.'

Sadly, no detailed memories of the household antics of Dennis Hopper, Iggy Pop and David Bowie survive, for each of the participants' recollection of this period is patchy. Iggy by now was like a sad child, profoundly depressed at the failure of his own career. Hopper was in his own coke-fuelled professional tailspin: with his non-linear conversation, occasionally profound insights into art and movies, and his fondness for boasting about his acquaintance with Charlie Manson, the actor was another walking embodiment of Hollywood burn-out.

For Ava Cherry, who felt compelled to track David down, her ex-lover too seemed another burn-out – the charming, driven man she'd met at a New York party in 1973 seemed to have 'cracked'. After David's departure from New York, Ava had disappeared to Jamaica with her friend, ex-Playboy model Claudia Jennings, and sometime in June managed to locate David at Michael Lippman's villa, where he'd moved from Hughes' house. Ava instantly recognised 'it was over between us'. Their relationship seemed a relic of the past, and on occasion she was simply scared. For a short time that summer, David came to stay at Claudia Jennings' house; Claudia was always light-hearted and positive, but Ava 'felt kind of afraid. David would talk about ghosts and I didn't know how to take it. One day we were talking, he started to cry and had a glass in his hand. And it suddenly shattered. He is an intense person, there was this energy . . . you read about people who sit in a chair and self-combust. Claudia wasn't afraid – I was.'

Bowie's own fear of occult forces was only equalled by his fascination. His conflicted emotions were epitomised by his visit to Kenneth Anger, the film-maker and friend of Church of Satan founder Anton LaVey. Bowie brought Ava along with him for the meeting, but the pair could only stomach around twenty minutes of Anger's presence. 'I don't remember exactly what happened,' says Cherry, 'I kind of blotted it out. But then David started [to] tell me stories about something that happened with Angie, that there was a ghost in the house when they lived in Beckenham.' It seemed David saw ghosts wherever he looked; later he invited Ava to another house. 'It's Marilyn Monroe's old house, but it's haunted,' he told her. 'Another haunted house. I went there, but it never was the same between us. We made love after I left there but that was it.' Their relationship would peter out a few weeks later.

Around the same time – probably early June, although the date and details vary across different accounts – David phoned Cherry Vanilla at her apartment in New York. His voice was slurred, he skipped halfway through a sentence to the next one, and it was hard to know what he wanted. And then Cherry Vanilla realised that 'He got it in his head that these girls were out to make a devil baby with him, to have him impregnate them. Nothing could convince him that this was fantasy on his part, 'cos he was coked to the gills. So he called me at my apartment and he asked me if I knew any white witches?'

Fortunately, Vanilla's social circle did include one white witch – Wally Elmlark, a fellow contributor to *Circus* magazine. David took Wally's phone number, and then, before he put the phone down, promised he'd produce Vanilla's solo album.

Like many such yarns, the details of David's exorcism vary with the telling; many years later, Angie would describe how she was called in to perform a ceremony at David's house on Doheny Drive, conducted on the phone with Wally Elmlark, who talked her through the ritual, like the control tower guiding in a novice pilot. Ava Cherry remembers David burning a bracelet he'd been given by a singer he'd been dating – another suspected witch. Other tales, including the one of David storing bodily fluids in his refrigerator, look to be myths that exaggerate a situation that was already bizarre. When Cameron Crowe, *Rolling Stone*'s seventeen-year-old star writer, came to interview him at Lippman's house, Bowie lit a black candle and informed him, 'Don't let me scare the pants off you . . . I've been getting a little trouble from the neighbours.'

Paranoia, and ultimately psychosis, is a well-known side-effect of heavy cocaine use, usually found in combination with sleep deprivation; heavy users might well stay up for three days at a stretch, in which case, says Harry Shapiro of the Drugscope organisation, 'heaven knows what you will see'. Beyond visual and auditory hallucinations, heavy users— the wealthy ones, on upwards of one gramme a day – often experience 'ideas of reference': delusions that others are plotting against them, or a narcissistic conviction that they are the focus of worldly, and other-worldy, events. This is the condition in which David spent most of the summer of 1975, a period compellingly sketched by Crowe in his article, published the following February.

The ease with which Bowie flitted from one subject to another in the interview and – most striking – the moment when he pulls down a blind, momentarily convinced he's seen a body fall from the sky, are disturb-ing, classic depictions of a rock-star encounter. Bowie was an old-hand at overawing – or, more accurately, bullshitting – journalists, and any rational person would conclude that much of his bizarre behaviour was motivated by his unerring instinct for good copy. But the crayoned marks on the blinds meant to ward off evils spirits were genuine – Glenn Hughes found them all over his house on his return from Europe. The fractured, disconnected state that Bowie displayed to Cameron Crowe was 'for real' too, according to Ava Cherry.

Crowe was late for their second interview, in June; pacing around anx-iously waiting for the *Rolling Stone* reporter to turn up, David and Ava had snorted up huge lines of Freddy Sessler's finest Merck and by the time Crowe arrived, 'We were flying. We were fucked up, I'm not going to say we weren't.' The Bowie portrayed by Crowe, Ava Cherry and others is a classic, isolated narcissist, his mind racing from scheme to scheme. To Crowe, he dismissed, icily, the subject of MainMan; in real-ity, he was agonising over the fate of his masters: 'the Tony Defries thing was really affecting him', says Glenn Hughes, 'addiction is all about burying your head in the sand. But this was his period of hell.' It was natural that David would construct grandiose, omnipotent fantasies in his conversations with Cameron Crowe, for this was the man who had lost his music, his birthright. He had been emasculated. Dispossessed of a huge part of what had defined his life, he really was rootless and alien.

Glenn Hughes returned to Los Angeles later in May, and was the closest witness to David's desperate condition. Ava was finally off the scene; Angie was staying, briefly, and picked up Hughes from the air-port, and on first impressions David seemed okay. But within days, as Bowie and Hughes stayed up for days at a stretch – four, five or more – their existence became that of lifeless wraiths, cut off from human warmth. Corinne – a source of succour, but also a gatekeeper who enforced his isolation – and driver Tony Mascia were busy with other projects, and Michael Lippman, too, had 'his hands full, there was so much going on'. Over those weeks running up to filming of *The Man Who Fell to Earth*, David was lonely, and mostly alone, but for occasional visitors like Hughes.

It wasn't all darkness; David could be hilariously funny. He christened Hughes 'old big head', presented him with a portrait inscribed with his new title, and spent hours badgering the rock bassist to throw out his flares and blue denim. He'd lose entire days engrossed in painting, and shared his insights on various subjects freely. Hughes, a fellow soul fan, loved Stevie Wonder, and wanted to record with him. 'No,' Bowie instructed him. 'It's too obvious that you're influenced by Stevie; do something with Nina Simone, instead.' Only in later years did Hughes appreciate the depth of Bowie's perceptiveness.

But those moments of clarity and positivity were rare. Mostly, David would sit there, his forehead creased, 'thinking, always thinking', and watching the same movies again and again. From Hughes' perspective, David's involvement with the occult was exaggerated: it was something he was frightened of, rather than drawn to. Yet Bowie's fascination with the Third Reich, often dismissed as publicity-seeking, ran disturbingly deep. 'He would watch a lot of movies. Never-ending Nazi stuff, which he'd watch with this constant frown on his face.' Sometimes Hughes would go home to crash out, and return to David's house a day later to check on him, to see him sitting in the same place, wearing the same clothes, with the same frown, watching the same movies. Faced with the endless black-and-white footage, Hughes could manage little more than a coked-up 'wow'. David showed no evidence of racism, but his fascination with Nazi lore seemed extreme. 'I couldn't analyse what he read or saw, I wasn't capable – his brain was simply on a tangent to everybody else's. It certainly wasn't spiritual – who is spiritual when they're on coke?'

At the time, Hughes assumed David was making some kind of sense of the images and words flooding through his consciousness. In reality, Bowie was like a babbling drunk, convinced he's discovered the secret of the universe. Other conversations that summer made his encounters with Cameron Crowe seem a model of rationality. Talking to the *NME*'s Anthony O'Grady in August, David opined that a fascist dictatorship was on its way, explaining, 'It's like a kaleidoscope – no matter how many little colours you put in it, that kaleidoscope will make those colours have a pattern . . . and that's what happens with TV – it doesn't

matter who puts what in the TV, by the end of the year there's a whole
format that the TV puts together. The TV puts over its own plan . . . Who
says the space people have got no eyes? You have – you've got one in
every living room in the world.' Then, perhaps sensing his interviewer's
realisation that he was talking gibberish, David added, 'That's theoret-
ical, of course.'

Glenn Hughes didn't imagine that aliens were controlling his TV, but
the cocaine would bring similar delusions: by the end of the year he was
hiring guard dogs and security to deal with imagined intruders. Yet, in
his view, David positively revelled in his own world. 'David used to
drive his Mercedes alone through Los Angeles, on blow, the most paranoid son of a bitch in the city, wearing a hat, all the way from Doheny
Drive to Beverly Hills. I tried it once that year, but I was too paranoid,
too loaded. He arrived at my house and I'm, How the *fuck* did you get
here?'

David had undoubtedly learned to use cocaine, savouring the impact
it had on his psyche. 'He – and this is glamorising it – did use the drugs
to enlarge his capabilities in every dimension,' says Hughes. 'It really
magnified his intelligence, if you will. But it had its way with him.'

Ironically, it was playing the part of an alien that would force this damaged creature to abandon his quest and come back to earth. Even as he
started to prepare for the upcoming movie shoot in New Mexico, waiting for the mostly English crew to assemble, David seemed capable of
utter focus and dedication. In a strange way, David's frazzled mental
state seemed to accentuate his almost child-like earnestness. He was
still a showbiz pro. Given direction by Nicholas Roeg in rehearsal, he
was calm, almost pliant; none of those present remember any trace of
nervousness.

Shooting of *The Man Who Fell to Earth* had been delayed by problems
with the intended backers, Columbia Pictures, who withdrew after realising their choice for leading man, Robert Redford, had been supplanted.
The newly formed British Lion company, led by producers Michael
Deeley and Barry Spikings, stepped into the breach. There would be
constant disputes over budgets and other issues, but when filming com-
menced late in June at Lake Fenton, New Mexico, the tight schedule and
budget became an integral part of the movie's feel. When a passing
tramp turned and belched in the opening shot, Roeg incorporated the
scene as a motif. Everyone pitched in: Bowie's limo driver, Tony Mascia,
performed the same function for the character of Newton. Roeg and his

star shared the same instincts. 'During filming, we were close and not close at the same time,' says Roeg. 'We didn't go out for dinner, but we were very close in understanding.'

If, for Bowie, his greatest movie was a depiction of his condition, adrift in LA, the perfect example of the city's emotional blankness was the fate of Maggie Abbott. In February she'd persuaded both Roeg and Bowie to work together. In March she'd negotiated with Michael Lippman, who demanded a large fee but was negotiated down. Around June, she gave a joint party for David and Charlotte Rampling in LA. Then in July, she heard that she had been barred from the New Mexico set. The woman who'd made the movie possible didn't see Bowie for another ten years, when she bumped into him at another movie industry party. In true Hollywood fashion, to avoid losing face, Abbott 'pretended I didn't know him. He did the same.'

Geoff MacCormack accompanied Bowie and Coco Schwab to New Mexico, where he was given a sinecure as David's body double. The three spent a healthy few weeks at the Albuquerque Hilton and later in Santa Fe, relaxing and sightseeing in the run-up to the filming; David used the break to start painting during peaceful afternoons in the conservatory of his rented ranch-style bungalow. Over the course of just a couple of weeks he visibly filled out, and his skin regained some of its natural glow. Roeg was worried about David's weight fluctuating, should he binge on cocaine, and there seems to have been an understanding that David would not indulge during the shoot. When Bowie did succumb, Roeg decided not to react, and to see where the ambiguity of the situation would take them. 'I did not do or say anything. You can't reason someone out of anything. I'm not into the guilt thing or trying to cure anybody of our humanity – everybody has a sense of shame, guilt, secret happiness, accusation or praise. There are certain things I wouldn't want to know about someone anyway, and I wouldn't want them to know certain things about me. It all goes back to this idea of exposing yourself. You have to live with yourself first.'

With its echoes of Howard Hughes, and of David's own life, *The Man Who Fell to Earth* seemed, for all its art-house values and rarefied conceptualising, simple in tone. The movie was totally reliant on Bowie's charisma – and his vulnerability. Leading woman Candy Clarke was Roeg's partner; being directed in her sex scenes with Bowie by Roeg was something she says Roeg 'got a kick out of. You English people can be very kinky.' Clarke's own recollections of her leading man focus exclusively on his physicality. 'He was so perfect for the role that it was very easy to imagine he was from another planet – he was beautiful, really at the height of his beauty. Really thick hair, dyed that lovely colour, and his skin was just gorgeous.' Her memories seem to involve scant sense of Bowie's fragility, but for one instance, when 'he'd drunk some milk, saw something in it – and then got sick'. (His absence meant that Clarke had to record one key scene – where Newton reveals his alien, genital-free body, and Candy's character pisses her pants – solo.) Otherwise, Clarke recalls Bowie's condition as surprisingly robust; when, at the end of the movie, Mary-Lou lifts Newton from the floor and places him gently on the bed, Clarke attempted to lift him up only to find 'he was very heavy – I couldn't budge him'. The crew had to rig up a seat, mounted on to a skateboard, to allow her to move the apparently emaciated entity.

On its release in May 1976, *The Man Who Fell to Earth* would be mostly eulogised by critics. 'Roeg has done it again,' proclaimed the *Guardian*. Bowie's crucial role won a near-unanimously warm reception: *The New Yorker*'s legendary critic Pauline Kael pronounced the plot 'uninvolving', but praised Bowie as 'the most romantic figure in recent pictures'.

David himself was confident, once the movie had wrapped, that it would launch him as not just a movie actor but as a multimedia creative force. The formidable focus with which he approached his next project seemed to vindicate his view, as did the success of *Young Americans* – a slow burner, but a commercial breakthrough in the US, winning gold status from the Recording Industry Association of America for 500,000 sales in July, with the single 'Fame' hitting number one on 20 September. The significance was not lost on David, who was still gently reminding writers of this breakthrough, five months later. And as 'Fame' ascended the charts, David was already crafting a follow-up album.

Station to Station is usually regarded as the climax of David Bowie's love affair with Freud's 'magical substance', as well as his definitive statement on his rootless, confused existence in Los Angeles. Yet it was more complex than that, for the album was an almost scientific experiment in risk-taking: one of its key features, he told those around him, was to walk into the studio with no songs prepared. *Station to Station* was also a love letter to Europe, and would be a remarkably coherent statement from a man whose grip on reality was intermittent. Just a few months later, Bowie would describe the attraction of 'watching artists crack open a bit – and seeing what they're really like inside'. For the first time in years, underneath the clinical precision, the listener would find the real David

Jones, devoid of masks, looking down into the abyss, and upwards in search of 'that Godhead feeling'.

There were brief rehearsals in LA before the album – not to work up material, but 'to get loose', says guitarist Earl Slick – before the small crew of Bowie, Alomar and Slick, bassist George Murray and drummer Dennis Davis convened in Cherokee Studios, a twenty-four-track facility that offered far more scope for experimentation than the sixteen-track set-up at Sigma. And this, Bowie told his musicians, was the ethos of the album: 'Experimentation – and don't worry about how long it takes,' according to Carlos Alomar. This would be a journey into sound.

The consistent reports that the album was recorded amid a blizzard of cocaine do indeed ring true. Bowie later remarked he could remember nothing of its making. These were indeed 'weird times' says Earl Slick, then just twenty-three years old. Slick's tough, gnarly guitar is a centrepiece of the album, winding in and out of Alomar's lithe, complementary melodies. Although most of the band remained in the studio for the early sessions, often they would be parachuted in and out, unsure of precisely what they were contributing to. 'I was at the Rainbow on Sunset – I thought I had the night off,' says Slick, 'and I was in a state as usual. I lived in a state. Then Tony, the maitre d' said, "Somebody is trying to find you," so I got on the phone and they need me in the studio. It's about fucking midnight and I'm trashed and I worked until whenever we finished putting a solo down.'

The state of stretching the mind until it cracked was an intrinsic part of *Station to Station*; but what's surprising, in retrospect, is that this state was conscious. Bowie seemed to weave in and out of it, relishing the effect both of being trashed, and in control. Blues writer and producer Neil Slaven by now had the quintessentially seventies job of star-minder, travelling with Glenn Hughes, charged with the futile task of keeping him off cocaine, and was therefore one of the few 'straight' people on the scene. In the studio, despite the omnipresent huge bag of coke on the mixing desk, David was completely rational. When Slaven mentioned that the topic of their last conversation, back in 1972, was Buddhism, David became enthused. 'Oh, you'll like this then,' he told him, before handing over a sheet of yellow exercise paper with the lyrics of a new song, 'Word on a Wing'. At times, Slaven looked at David, with his striking orange Weimar hair, and got the overwhelming impression of 'I'm hiding behind this. But you can see me, can't you?' For all the decadent veneer, David was obviously the same singer Slaven had seen at Decca in 1967, spreading out gravel on the studio floor, revelling in the attention. If he'd ever worried that his sanity could fracture for ever, like Terry's, then this experiment with his own psyche suggested his mind remained intact, behind the cracked facade. Glenn Hughes, too, recalls that despite all the drugs on display, David was 'running the show. I was blown away by that. My mind would be all over the place when I was doing drugs, but he had total command of the sound – and this understanding of the musicians, it was like watching the greatest football manager in action.'

There were other crucial, perhaps surprising, influences. Carlos Alomar had been back working in New York when he got the call. His lifestyle was essentially wholesome and straight during the recording. Told that the keyword was 'experimentation' with no time limits, one of his key motivations on the self-consciously epic title track was his session-man's knowledge that 'If a song is over three minutes you make double the royalty – Glory Glory!' As he and the rhythm section experimented with the opening section of 'Station to Station', messing around and adding muso tricks ('I was listening to Jethro Tull at the time,' says Alomar), Bowie instantly seized on a disquieting turnaround in the rhythm, with a bar of 3/4 and then 5/4 to disorientate the listener, a prog-rock technique which rendered the introduction jarring and disturbing, preparing the listener for lyrics which are similarly grandiose – but sinister.

The song's mention of 'White Stains' invokes one of Crowley's most obscure works, a collection of pornographic poems he'd written under the pseudonym George Archibald Bishop. 'One magical movement, from Kether to Malkuth' is a reference to the kabbalistic tree of life: Kether is the sphere of Godhead, Malkuth the sphere of the physical world. Some commentators, notably writer Ian MacDonald, believe Bowie's understanding of the kabbalistic system drew on works like *The Tree of Life*, by Crowley's pupil Israel Regardie, and see something of the dark in Bowie's mindset – a plausible interpretation, given Bowie's enduring interest in the Thule Society – a German occultist group – and other esoteric Nazi philosophies. Yet 'Station to Station' is capable of wonderfully diverse interpretations. It could represent absolute megalomania; that Bowie is a God who has chosen to embrace the physical world. The kabbala reference could equally signify that Bowie has renounced the high of chemically derived nirvana in order to savour everyday existence. The song is also capable of being read as a song of sensual love, in which case 'the European canon' becomes a bad pun.

Yet despite the train sounds that open the record, 'Station to Station' also featured Christian imagery at its core, for its title alluded, David would later confirm, to the Stations of the Cross. A similar yearning for salvation pervades 'Word on a Wing'; almost conventionally Christian, it was written at a time when David started wearing a crucifix, given to him by Michael Lippman. Later he would wear one his father had given him in his teens. They weren't just empty symbols; over time he would describe himself as 'not religious – I'm a spiritual person. I believe a man develops a relationship with his own God.'

Glenn Hughes, who has never previously spoken in detail of his deep, but troubled friendship with Bowie, believes that David had sent himself on a journey deep into the cocaine mindset in order to create new territory for his art. Bowie had never really suffered for his music before; not like Iggy, or Vince Taylor – mocked and vilified by the masses. But in LA, he had staked out his soul under the unrelenting California sun. 'His period of hell,' as Hughes puts it. 'Because that stuff did have its way with him. It twisted and turned him inside out.'

Some songs were cooked up in the simplest of fashions: early in the sessions David bashed out the simplest two-chord progression on the piano and told Carlos it was a new song; only then did they realise the simple F sharp–E riff and melody was uncomfortably close to George Benson's version of 'On Broadway'. Alomar transformed the rhythm with a springy, funky riff based on Cliff Noble's classic Philly-soul instrumental, 'The Horse', while David's lyrics and optimistic doo-wop vibe came straight from The Diamonds' 'Happy Years'. Bowie's pitch-perfect, multitracked vocals were added in a quick sequence of mostly first takes, aided by Geoff MacCormack, and that, with the brief addition of a breathy melodica here, and a chirruping vibra-slap there, was that. Beautifully simple, 'Golden Years' transcended its influences, another perfect example of how talent borrows, and genius steals.

With just six songs, *Station to Station* was both sprawling and coherent; it would stand alone in his work, the perfect gateway between American and European music. The turnaround it represented with the David Bowie of *Ziggy Stardust* – the man who arrived in the studio with a dozen songs, written and fully rehearsed – was complete. This was not an exercise in songwriting: this was a sculpture, carved out of sound. In less than three years, David had not just changed genres; he had completely changed his working methods, from start to finish. This was the embodiment of the advice he'd given to Glenn Hughes, earlier that year. 'Do the contrary action – do something you're not used to. Let's not make it comfortable – let's make it *un*comfortable.' *Station to Station*'s chart performance was perhaps the ultimate vindication of this advice, peaking at number three after its release in January 1976: the critical reception, too, was respectful, recognising the bravery with which Bowie had staked out new territory.

Yet the fate of David's next recording showed the downside of his high-risk approach. Since signing up for *The Man Who Fell to Earth*, David had seen the challenge of composing its soundtrack as an intrinsic part of the project's appeal. Around November, he started work on the project, partnered by Paul Buckmaster, who'd arranged the strings on 'Space Oddity'. Alomar, Dennis Davis and George Murray were called in for some of the recording, augmented by J. Peter Robinson on piano. Roughly six pieces were recorded, two of them funky-ish rock instrumentals, a ballad instrumental, later named 'Subterraneans', and 'Wheels', 'which had a gentle sort of melancholy mood to it', says Buckmaster. The recording, however, stretched on. Assembling a soundtrack required focus and discipline. Both were lacking and, according to Buckmaster, 'it just wasn't up to the standard needed'.

According to Buckmaster, Bowie's soundtrack never approached a finished state. Yet Roeg and producer Si Litvinoff considered what they heard 'brilliant', says the latter, 'but [producer Michael] Deeley tried to get David to accept a lesser deal and was told to take a walk. To me this was a large disappointment.' Litvinoff believes the movie would have been a much hotter commercial proposition with David's music and considered the replacement, by John Phillips, only 'adequate'. Bowie, meanwhile, was humiliated and blamed Michael Lippman for the fiasco. Lippman had also made the mistake of building himself an impressive new house that autumn, partly financed with an (agreed) loan from David.

By Christmas, Lippman was out. Most of those who knew him considered him diligent and kind; he lacked the killer instinct of Tony Defries, but would go on to have a more long-term career in management, managing both George Michael and Matchbox Twenty's Rob Thomas. Guitarist Earl Slick, also managed by Lippman, fell foul of the messy split, and was left behind when David left for Ochos Rios in Jamaica to rehearse for *Station to Station*'s upcoming tour.

The preparations provided another reminder, if one were needed, that for all his Third Reich fetishes and pharmaceutical peculiarities, David Bowie remained the consummate pro. Geoff MacCormack saw his friend in January: he'd put on weight, had a personal trainer and a suntan. He was 'not perfect', but he was 'better'. Later that year, in Paris, he would meet Bob Grace, a key architect of his *Hunky Dory* breakthrough. 'I'd missed him, so we had a nice dinner and caught up,' says Grace. 'He told me, "I've got over all my cocaine stuff now." And I said, "How's that?" And he said, "I took that image off. I put it in a wardrobe in an LA hotel room and locked the door."'

Grace saw a man who'd simply decided to abandon his wicked ways, then had done so. Such transformations are rare, and indeed David's second interview with Cameron Crowe, conducted in February 1976, was riddled with megalomaniac statements, such as, 'I'd adore to be prime minister. And, I believe very strongly in fascism . . . I dream of buying companies and TV stations, owning and controlling them.' Complete with approving namechecks for Nietzsche and Hitler, it made for great press to launch his tour. Yet Ben Edmonds, the one-time editor of *Creem*, met the singer in the same week as Crowe, and observed he was 'not fucked up at all, not in the slightest – if anything, he was like a businessman in drag'. The two spent much of their conversation talking about their mutual friend, Iggy Pop. For a few moments, Bowie's professional veneer softened as he discussed his one-time protégé, a man who is 'not so hard and all-knowing and cynical. Every artist always knows the answers of the world. It's nice to see someone who hasn't a clue – but has insights.'

Bowie's comments were more perceptive than anyone could imagine, because at that precise moment Iggy indeed did not have a clue. Since walking out on Bowie, he had deteriorated from being a figure of ridicule on the strip, to a twilight existence, sharing an abandoned garage with a male hustler called Bruce, sleeping on a stolen lounger mattress. Thrown in jail after shoplifting some cheese and apples, Iggy found he'd run out of all his friends but one – Freddy Sessler. And the man who'd helped bring Bowie down, raised Iggy up. Sessler stood bail for the singer, and hired him for a telephone scam he'd cooked up. Then, when Iggy proved a lousy telemarketer, Sessler suggested a solution. 'Look, you better call David. I know he likes you and wants to work with you.'

'But I had too much pride,' says Iggy today. 'Then a few days later Freddy tells me, "I'm going to see David, I told him I was with you – and he said, Bring Iggy along."'

The pair met up in San Diego. David was kind – genuinely so, for there was no hint of condescension in his offer to make an album with Iggy in Europe. In future months, many would comment on the amazing turnaround in Iggy's fortunes. Fewer people would realise that their friendship would mark just as profound a change in Bowie's life. In tending to Iggy, David would heal himself, too.

15

Ghosts in the Echo Chambers

The guy has a lot of psychic stamina – he was perfectly able to go out and do the gigs, drive the entire continent by car, then go out to a club after almost every one until four in the morning, and do all the other things. And he never showed bad form, even once.

Iggy Pop

For all the icy grandiosity of the *Station to Station* tour – undoubtedly the most intense performances David had put on since Spiders days – there was something cosy, almost domestic about the small retinue's daily routine. The tiny group revolved around David and his new best friend, 'Jimmy', as he always called Iggy Pop. Usually, on the long drives between shows, the pair would sit in the back of David's car, the faithful Tony Mascia at the wheel, as David cued up his current musical obsessions on cassette, and the two of them exchanged their reactions and insights. Often they'd talk late into the night; at other times, they'd sit silently, sipping espressos and reading without feeling obliged to chat, like old men who'd been friends for decades.

The two were figureheads of a cosy travelling household. Barbara Dewitt – sister of photographer Bruce Weber, and one-time head of publicity at United Artists – looked after David's press, while Andrew Kent, who'd shot an amazing portfolio of Iggy during his grandiose self-immolation with The Stooges, was in-house photographer. Corinne, and Pat Gibbons, previously with MainMan, looked after most of the administration. This tiny crew would ultimately form the basis of Bowie's management organisation, Isolar. David's focus and attention to detail were simply phenomenal, Iggy observed. 'The guy has a lot of psychic stamina – he was perfectly able to go out and do the gigs, drive the entire continent by car, then go out to a club after almost every one until four in the morning, and do all the other things. And he never showed bad form, even once.'

Asked if David was psychically damaged, Iggy replies, 'Of course he was – but he wasn't gonna show it. There were certain quirky, odd, theatrical, slightly megalomanic ways of, er, relating – but I was used to that, 'cos I got some of that myself.' It was not until a short break in the tour in May that David mentioned any of his troubles. In the meantime, he was relentlessly professional: always enthusiastic, efficiently checking through transparencies to be released to the press, and above all fired up by music, playing his friend pioneering records by Tom Waits, Kraftwerk and even The Ramones – the latter, he told Iggy, was a sign that the world had not forgotten The Stooges. Carlos Alomar saw the two talking and noticed their joint explorations 'somehow had a calming effect'. They were similar, but different, 'just like when you split an atom and it's twins'.

There was something marvellously instantaneous about Iggy and David's new, deep friendship. In some respects it was completely bizarre. 'I really didn't have a reference for why they were friends,' says Carlos Alomar. 'Nor were they musical friends.' Both men were enormously narcissistic, and had proved irredeemably selfish over the previous year, yet each was supportive and kind to the other. Iggy didn't make special claims on David, nor did he abase himself. 'There was no kow-towing, or humbling,' says Alomar. If others complained about David's behaviour, and Iggy could do something, he would. But when necessary, he'd be brutally honest with those who asked for his intercession. 'That's how it is,' he'd tell complainers, 'just deal with it.'

In part, each one's frank admiration for the other was driven by the fact they were almost polar opposites: 'They each want what the other one has,' says a mutual friend, Eric Schermerhorn. Yet each of their characters was widely misunderstood. Bowie was the supposed middle-class intellectual; yet it was Iggy – in the guise of Jimmy Osterberg, school debate champion – who'd been voted 'Most Likely to Succeed' by his Junior High School classmates, and made it to university. And Iggy was the wild man: yet it was Bowie who'd push himself, and others, well outside their comfort zones.

There was a simple reason, beyond the cosy family atmosphere, for the air of relative tranquillity that was evident throughout the thirty-nine

The Thin White Duke on furlough in Moscow: dinner at the Metropol with Iggy Pop and Corinne 'Coco' Schwab, circa 23 April, 1976. The three set up home together in Berlin that summer.

David celebrates his thirtieth birthday with Iggy Pop (standing), Romy Haag and Coco Schwab (just out of view), l'Ange Bleu, Paris, January, 1977. 'This is a guy who a year before was supposedly out of his mind on cocaine,' says one friend from the time, 'and here he was in sensible shoes, jacket . . . flat cap, just open and chatting to everyone.'

'Everything said, "We shouldn't be making a record here".' Berlin's Hansa TonStudio (left) in 1976: set among the ruins that evoked Brixton in 1947.

Below: David Bowie, Tony Visconti and *Ton-meister* Eduard Meyer, completing *Low* at Hansa, October, 1976.

Filming *Marc* with old Mod friend Marc Bolan, 9 September, 1977 (with Bowie's old bassist, Herbie Flowers, behind). Their last public appearance together was marred by a silly tiff that epitomised the pair's intertwined friendship and rivalry. Marc would die in a car crash on Wimbledon Common on 16 September.

Moving on: relaxing at London's Dorchester hotel, September, 1977, after emerging from his Berlin seclusion.

Barry Plummer

David Bowie finally proves himself as an actor on-stage, inhabiting the role of Joseph Merrick in *Elephant Man*, summer 1980. He enchanted his fellow actors – who nonetheless concluded his was 'the most horrible, horrible life.'

16-page pullout on John Lennon's life

DAILY ❂ NEWS
Tonight
25¢
New York
December 10, 1980
TUESDAY NIGHT EDITION
CLOSING STOCKS
Late Racing

Killer stalked him 3 days
Page 2

EXCLUSIVE: Lennon & suspect

New York's *Daily News* shows John Lennon signing Mark Chapman's copy of *Double Fantasy*, 8 December, 1980. Chapman's murder of The Beatles singer, with whom David had recently renewed his friendship, inspired Bowie's flight from New York to Switzerland.

Hobo intellectual: Bowie filming *Baal*, August, 1981, in a rare break from his seclusion in Switzerland. The Brecht play represented a farewell to Berlin and underlined Bowie's newly acquired intellectual credentials – but was destined to be remembered as a flop.

News Ltd Newspix/Rex Features

David Bowie signs on the dotted line for EMI, 27 January, 1983, in a $17m deal that would today, says the A&R who signed him, have record companies 'in a line around the block'.

Barry Schultz/Sunshine/Retna

'You have no idea … it's like they're feeding you the sun, the moon, and the stars.' David Bowie, bona fide superstar, on the *Serious Moonlight* tour.

arena shows of the US leg, which ran through to 26 March, 1976. That reason was illustrated by the fourth date on the tour, in San Francisco. When David had played the city back in October 1972, amid all of MainMan's hype and bluster, the Winterland had been embarrassingly empty. Now, the same city's Cow Palace was filled with 14,000 adoring fans. Speaking to *Melody Maker*'s Robert Hillburn, David described himself as 'at peace', drawing a simple satisfaction from a job well done, rather than the 'false gaiety' of the Ziggy days. In its place was a genuine gaiety, a delight at the after-show-party presence of celebrities like David Hockney and Christopher Isherwood, who came, says Andrew Kent, 'to pay homage' after the LA show. David's conversation with Isherwood inspired a plan for David to base himself in Berlin; he'd already thought about working in Germany, studying the recordings of engineers like Konrad 'Connie' Plank, as well as his current musical obsession, Kraftwerk. Before the tour started, he had agreed to the suggestion of Angie, and his lawyer, to move to Switzerland for tax reasons. By the time the tour reached New York in March, he had confided to all his friends that he was planning to live in Germany, and record there with Iggy. Only Angie was kept in the dark about the scheme.

On the 26 March, the US leg of the *Station to Station* tour concluded with a masterful performance at Madison Square Garden, followed by a star-packed party at the Penn Plaza Club. David and Iggy spent most of the evening huddled together, both of them graciously greeting old friends like John Cale. The pair positively glowed with health – Jimmy wearing a suit which he'd just bought for a court appearance with Bowie the previous day in Rochester, New York, to answer charges following a marijuana bust at the Americana Rochester Hotel. A mug shot of Bowie survives in the Rochester Police Department files, and is a classic of its genre: David impeccably suited, gazing at the camera with clear-eyed *sang-froid*. Perhaps his serenity reflected the irony of the fact that one of the music industry's best-known cocaine-abusers had been 'caught' with a soft drug that rarely figured on his own esoteric menu. The charges were later dropped.

Both Iggy and David had, by this time, agreed that they'd both leave their drug habits behind in LA; the agreement was never formal, and they'd both lapse at various times, but a measure of their success came when Iggy stayed on in New York for a couple of days after David and Coco Schwab sailed for Cannes on 27 March. For the first time, he realised The Stooges' legacy had influenced a new generation of New York bands;

and for the first time, he turned down a sniff of heroin, offered to him by ex-New York Doll, Johnny Thunders.

When the party reunited in early April, David had hatched a rationale for a move to Berlin, in the form of a movie to be scripted by Christopher Isherwood. 'I'm supposed to be living in Switzerland – but I don't know how long that will last,' he told Radio One's Stuart Grundy. 'I've got to come back to Berlin.' Later that same evening, on 10 April, nightclub entertainer Romy Haag turned up for his show at Berlin's Deutschlandhalle.

Nearly six feet tall and drop-dead gorgeous, Romy's deliciously indefinable sexuality embodied the vibrant, fragile glamour of pre-war Berlin that Christopher Isherwood had so compellingly recorded in the books that David had been reading in the last few weeks. Born Edouard Frans Verbaarsschott in The Hague, Romy had opened her own nightclub, Chez Romy Haag, just two years earlier, and established herself as Berlin's most glamorous woman, despite the accident of having been born a man. Romy brought a posse of her dancers and entertainers to the show; they made a dazzling spectacle, and according to Haag, 'We looked at each other and that was that. The next day he had a concert in Hamburg and he was four hours late because he didn't want to leave.' Thereafter, Romy became one of the many friends with whom David would spend hours chatting on the phone late into the night.

The European tour dates were a sensation; the set itself, opening with a grinding, thrilling version of 'Station to Station', was sprawling but tough, seemingly anticipating the musical changes that were in the air in 1976. Yet it was David's emergence from nearly two years in American limbo that was the main attraction.

His arresting, glamorous, 'Thin White Duke' persona was an intrinsic part of his appeal, especially because this was the first time he'd hit the stage in Britain since Ziggy's farewell. The contrast between Ziggy's femininity and the Duke's masculine, 1930s neatness and fetching Weimar haircut could not have been more pronounced. The hint of depravity behind the neat, crisp white shirt and waistcoats was erotic, reminiscent of the thinking woman's forbidden crumpet, Amon Göth in *Schindler's List*. Perhaps his most drop-dead glamorous look to date, Bowie's European superman persona was carefully judged; it signalled his focus over the coming years, which was to build up a fanbase on the continent. David Bowie's previous tours had, incredibly, overlooked the

European market; now the string of shows at huge arenas showed the pent-up demand, all spread by word of mouth.

As the tour moved on from Germany to Bern, Switzerland, on 17 April, there was a short layover in Zurich. Intent on building on his Ziggy-era experiences on the Trans Siberian Express he announced a move into travel writing, yet another project floated and abandoned – David asked photographer Andy Kent to sort out the paperwork for a trip to Moscow, before their next date in Helsinki on 24 April.

The journey was packed with unforgettable moments. On the 21st, there was a little party to celebrate Iggy's twenty-ninth birthday; David presented him with a Polaroid camera to record their three-day trip. Once the small party – David, Iggy, Kent, Corinne and Pat Gibbons – reached Poland, the train clattered more slowly through an increasingly bleak landscape, and the five voyagers spent hours gazing at buildings pockmarked by machine-gun bullets, or the gaunt remains of towns still shattered by bomb damage. The train stopped every now and then to pick up bottles of brown beer, or the soup and peas that were the only food on offer. Pulling up alongside a goods train in Warsaw, they witnessed a grey-clad worker throwing lumps of coal up from a flatcar, piece by piece, while sleet rattled against the windows of their own train. An unforgettably dreary image, it would later be evoked in the haunting instrumental 'Warszawa'.

For most of the trip, the small party managed to evade official scrutiny by travelling as conventional tourists, but when the passengers transferred to a wide-gauge train at Brest, on the Russian border, they were met by the KGB and ordered to pick up two suitcases each and follow the officer to the huge interrogation room. 'Then a guy who spoke English came up and said, and it was bone chilling, "We weren't expecting you,"' says Kent.

Kent had a copy of *Playboy* confiscated; Iggy attracted special suspicion for attempted bribery, because he'd impulsively given away the flowers that decorated their cabin. David had a large trunk full of books which the KGB rifled through, taking 'one, maybe two' away, says Kent. The offending volumes were on 'that subject' – the Third Reich – but their removal did not cause any specific concern; instead, their worries centred on the travel documents that the border guards studied intently – then reluctantly conceded were in order.

The small party breathed a sigh of relief as their passports and forms were handed back to them. Then, ominously, one burly, blond-haired official, who they took to be KGB, closed their encounter with the words, 'Someone will be there to meet you in Moscow.'

They spent the next few hours chatting nervously, wondering what the KGB had in store for them. But, incredibly, once they pulled into Moscow's opulent, marble-lined Belorusskaya station, the platform was empty: Big Brother, as so often, was not as efficient as claimed, and they were free to explore. After dropping their luggage off at the Metropol – a sumptuous, historic Art Nouveau building which was the setting of several key Lenin speeches, as well as Bulgakov's sinister novel *The Master and Margarita* – they wandered across Red Square, posing like happy schoolkids alongside Russian conscripts, then on to a shopping trip at the huge, glass-roofed GUM department store for tourist trinkets, and dinner back at the Metropol.

Their frolic in Moscow lasted just seven hours before they caught the train out but they had not seen the end of Soviet bureaucracy, for on the way to Helsinki, the border guards chose to strip-search both David and Iggy. Both of them were unperturbed by the experience, which was blown up into a manufactured furore about David having disappeared. 'I don't know if it was a publicity stunt or not – but it was a great one if it was,' says Kent. The next publicity stunt was not so easily explained, namely David's quote at a press conference in Stockholm on 24 April that did not surface until 2 May, when the *Station to Station* tour – also known as the Isolar tour – hit the UK and David greeted his fans at Victoria station. Photographs across the media a few days later, including one by Andrew Kent, were printed with David's arm outstretched in what looked like a Nazi salute. In conjunction with his remarks at the Stockholm conference one week earlier – 'I believe Britain could benefit from a fascist leader. After all, fascism is really nationalism' – a media firestorm soon blew up.

Bowie qualified his Stockholm remarks to Jean Rook in the *Daily Express* a couple of days later. 'If I said it – and I've a terrible feeling I did say something like it to a Stockholm journalist – I'm astounded anyone could believe it . . . I'm not sinister. I don't stand up in cars waving to people because I think I'm Hitler.'

Rook found him sincere – there was a schoolboyish earnestness about his demeanour that enhanced his horror at being so misunderstood. Yet this was a mealy-mouthed politician's defence; one he would repeat in later months, when he declared himself upset or hurt that anyone considered him racist. Few people did, certainly none of David's friends. 'There was no trace of that,' says Ava Cherry. 'I'm Jewish and I never [suspected] anti-Semitic reasons. If I'd thought that I would have quit,' says Andrew Kent. Movie footage of David's arrival later revealed his so-called Heil Hitler salute as nothing of the kind. But there were enough quotes sitting on journalists' tape recorders to demonstrate that, while not a racist, David was happy to flirt with fascistic imagery in search of a newspaper headline.

Without doubt, during that sweltering summer of 1976, Bowie's fascist chic chimed with sentiments voiced by some of his rivals. Bromley contingent figurehead Siouxsie Sioux sneered that there were 'too many Jews for my liking' in one of the Banshees' earliest songs, 'Love in a Void', and in August Eric Clapton ranted that Britain should 'get the wogs out, get the coons out'. Most of Britain's youth would, rightly, suspect Bowie of cheap opportunism rather than racism, but that summer Bowie's credibility as a champion of the outsider took its first severe dent.

Yet by the time the tour wound up in Paris on 18 May, celebrated by a party where David spent most of his time canoodling with Romy Haag, those concerns were mostly forgotten, as David turned his attentions to working with his friend Iggy. Up to his stay in Paris, David had intended to work in Munich with his new friend, but a change of plans was prompted by staff at the Château D'Hérouville, the residential recording studio where David had recorded *Pin Ups*. Commercial manager Pierre Calamel and studio manager Laurent Thibault, the new regime at the studio, astutely calculated that Bowie might need a refuge from the French fans crowding around the Plaza Athenée hotel, and invited him back to the eighteenth-century Château, set in the rolling countryside of the Oise valley, an hour's drive out of Paris. Enticed by Calamel's offer of 'some peace – and some French cheese', Bowie arrived that afternoon, wearing a flat cap, accompanied by Iggy, and deployed his natural gentlemanly charm, inhaling deeply to take in the distinctive smell of the grand old building and announcing to Iggy, 'This is a great rock 'n' roll studio.'

After a long lie-in – although David woke up in the night and was found wandering the grounds, confused and naked but for a forties-style Burberry Macintosh – Bowie called a meeting with Laurent Thibault. He'd brought a huge case over full of albums, which he played through, critiquing each of them, including a couple by Thibault's previous band, Magma, before announcing that in a couple of days he was taking a trip to his new house in Switzerland, but he'd return in a matter of weeks to produce Iggy's solo album, and would use Thibault as engineer. Later, it transpired that a crucial sweetener for using the Château was the prospect that David and Iggy's living costs would be picked up by a record company: David had no cash for day-to-day expenses. With the flow of MainMan-era royalties staunched, and imminent legal disputes with Michael Lippman, he was forced to watch every penny. Over subsequent weeks, onlookers would be astonished to see Corinne reprimanding David for spending 100 francs on a new jacket; when he came to settle the bill for Iggy's recording, David's cheque bounced.

In Switzerland, Angie had taken great care in selecting the first marital home the couple would actually own. The move was perhaps an act of self-deception, given that she and David had been living apart for two years, with Zowie under the care of the redoubtable Marion Skene. Yet David had continued to maintain that deception in print, telling Cameron Crowe in February that Angie was 'remarkably pleasant to keep coming back to. And, for me, she always will be.' Believing that her problem-solving abilities would continue to endear her to her husband, Angie had steered her way through the Swiss bureaucracy, investigating the various tax and residency issues, convinced that with this feat, as with so many others, she could prove herself indispensable. Clos des Mésanges was a luxurious house, with seven bedrooms and a caretaker's lodge, set in several acres of land in the village of Blonay, just above Lake Geneva. Her efforts were wasted: the first home she jointly owned with her husband would be the last. When he arrived in Switzerland, David took one look at the house, exchanged only a few vague words, and then disappeared. As so often, Angie swung from exhilaration to near depression, and soon started looking for the villain in the scheme, not for the first time alighting on Coco Schwab. Undoubtedly there was little love lost between the two women; but Corinne was in essence a convenient scapegoat, for David's dissatisfaction with his marriage had predated Coco's arrival on the scene. In any case, Angie's suspicions that her marriage was doomed were correct, for it was during his brief stay in Switzerland that David, who had so far kept remarkably quiet about his problems with both Angie and Michael Lippman, first confided in Iggy, discussing the future without being too specific. 'He's English,' says Iggy, by way of explanation, 'reserved and all that.' Within a couple of days the pair, along with Coco, set off again for the Château, probably stopping off in Berlin for some flat-hunting en route.

By the end of May, David was in the Château for the sessions, concentrating all of his focus on Iggy. The album would be based around 'Sister Midnight', a song he'd written with Carlos Alomar, and had played Iggy within a couple of days of their meeting in February, telling him how he'd love to put together a solo album based on a similar dark, electronic groove. It was a long way from The Stooges, but Iggy instantly responded to the challenge, realising that in its minimal, robotic way, it boasted a unique power. 'For me it was perfect! And I loved it, when I heard it I went whoa. And there wasn't one stinker on that whole period, he only pitched me great balls – and I grabbed every one.'

If there is any period in David Bowie's songwriting that is under-appreciated, it is this one. The music was once again flowing out of him, and behind the twisted, distorted facade of *The Idiot*, the subtlety and deftness of David's craft was at a latter-day peak. Most songs were sketched out with David's electric piano and guitar, augmented by Laurent – 'Tibo' – playing scratch bass. Brittany session-man Michel Santangeli did the same for the drum parts; David would keep whatever bits he liked and augment them with other musicians later. Bowie had explained to Jimmy back in the spring that this would be a chance for him to explore concepts he planned to use in his own work, yet Iggy would also get the benefit of songs, like 'China Girl' and 'Nightclubbing', which were more commercial than anything David had kept in stock for himself.

The pair made an engaging, odd couple: David with his severe, Germanic haircut, focusing intently on the music, sitting in a lotus posi-tion on a chair by the console; Jimmy, blond haired, spreading out like a lizard on the floor amid sheafs of lyrics, or bouncing around the grounds like an enthusiastic puppy when David was busy in the control room. Zowie played in the grounds, accompanied by Marion Skene, or other kids from the studio household. David's old friend Daniella Parmar showed up at one point to add to the family vibe; Angie, of course, was absent. With Corinne following David around – all-purpose factotum, helper and lover – and Iggy sunbathing by the pool, there was an intriguing, warped domesticity about the setup. The impression was heightened by incidents like the time Iggy took a day out to see his old flame, Nico, in Paris. The Velvets chanteuse was known to be a diehard of the Parisian heroin scene, so Iggy or a minder had to call in regularly to reassure Coco he wasn't high, like a teenager calling home.

David was sweet with Zowie, less distracted than in the Ziggy days. For the French staff, his lack of physical affection with Zowie – for he was not a tactile person – raised eyebrows, then was dismissed as typi-cally English – which indeed it was. He didn't cuddle Zowie, but when he was with him, he gave him his full attention. One day in the dining room the staff saw David and his son chatting away; Zowie was drink-ing a coke, when his dad joked, 'You'll get paranoid if you drink that.'

Instantly the five-year old responded, 'Well, no one believes what a para-noid person says, anyway.' Bowie laughed proudly at his son's quip; it sounded as if paranoia was a regular subject for father–son repartee.

In the opulent surroundings of the Château, David took to the role of *le grand seigneur*, politely asking if he could have the largest room, with fireplace, as well as a stereo. His polite requests were invariably repeated, more forcefully, by Coco, who initially irritated the staff – before they realised 'she had no life' and sympathised with her self-imposed 'slavery'. The Château's owner, composer Michel Magne, had let his musician friend Jacques Higelin take up one wing of the building, along with his girlfriend Kuelan Nguyen and three-year-old son Ken. A brief affair between Kuelan and Iggy added to the edge and intensity of *The Idiot* sessions, and within its first few days was immortalised when Iggy re-wrote one of David's songs, 'Borderline', to become 'China Girl' – whose lyrics simultaneously implored Kuelan to come with him to Berlin and warned her away. David seemed to savour the energy and vitality that their affair represented; he, too, focused on Kuelan, rubbing her back flirtatiously, or puffing on the pipe he'd lately taken to smoking, enjoying the ambiguity of the situation: 'It's good for Jimmy's heart to be loved that way,' he told Kuelan, almost like a father giving his consent.

Gossip from this period has David as a cocaine-raddled paranoid wreck – perhaps the best apocryphal story has him abandoning a session after Iggy invoked occult forces by pushing him in the pool – but throughout the recording, David's main vices were beer and women. It was only when rival musicians arrived, say the staff, that the atmosphere soured. There were rows, inspired by old rivalries, when Bad Company prepared to move into the studio; Edgar Froese was also frozen out, after arriving at the Château to add some synthesiser parts. Called up to the control room, Froese listened to a rough mix, then over dinner confided to David, 'At first I didn't really like your record . . . but finally I know you are making very interesting things. I am very proud to be here.' Casually, David told him they'd call down later for him to record. Several hours had passed when Pierre Calamel went to check on Froese, who was still sitting near the pool. 'I came over and said, "Are you OK? Do you want something more to drink?" It was a sunny, very hot day and I moved the parasol because the guy is getting very pink. And they didn't call him up. I was very sorry for him.'

When the time came for Froese's flight back to Berlin, the Château staff ordered a taxi, and the Tangerine Dream founder left without a backward glance.

The surreal atmosphere of *The Idiot* sessions was even more obvious once David and Iggy left the Château to make room for Bad Company. Their next studio, Musicland, had been built in the basement of a Munich hotel and mall; Thin Lizzy were recording there by day, Iggy and David would piece together their gothic soundscapes by night.

Guitarist Phil Palmer was called to the phone late one night by his mum, and spoke to a polite, charming David, who asked him to bring his Telecaster and hop on a plane to Munich. Palmer found the nocturnal, subterranean sessions disconcerting, '"vampiric" would be the word'. David's instructions were more psychological than musical: 'Imagine you're walking down Wardour Street and as you're walking past each club you're inspired to play what's coming out of it.' That would be the most specific instruction he'd get throughout the recording. The sessions were 'experimental on every level', says Palmer, with the pair pushing him for more extreme guitar sounds, asking if he would like to order in any sheep brains to eat, or leafing through monographs by artists such as Egon Schiele and Erich Heckel: 'They were very supportive of each other, and just having fun. And they were . . . obviously experienced in some pretty weird stuff. I wasn't aware they were taking anything – but their minds were a little odd.'

Engineer Thibault relished the experimentation, crafting long tape loops into electronic collages, but the nocturnal existence eventually took its toll as they concluded the mix. One night, frazzled, while David was out of the room, he crafted an Indian head-dress out of strips of red leader tape and attached it to his head. David returned, said not a word at this ludicrous spectacle, but then disappeared to use the phone. It's likely that this was the moment David called Tony Visconti in London to ask him to assist on his own album, which he planned to start work on directly after *The Idiot*.

It was around 20 August, 1976, that Tony Visconti arrived at 155, Hauptstrasse, a typical 'altbau', or period apartment, set on a tree-lined twin-lane avenue in Schöneberg, an anonymous district in the south-west of Berlin. Bowie had told him Iggy was living with him; Visconti knocked on the door, hugged his old friend, said hello to Coco, whom he knew from David's 'skeletoid' *Young Americans* period. 'Then David said, "This is Jimmy." So I shake his hand and look around and say, "Great – where's Iggy?" Everyone laughed, it kinda broke the ice.'

The session had originally been booked for some preparatory work on the *The Man Who Fell to Earth* tapes from Cherokee; when they were

delayed, Visconti helped put the finishing touches to Iggy's album at
Hansa Studio 1, on the Kurfürstendamm. Throughout the process, says
Visconti, 'You could see David evolving and developing his next phase
from this strange record.' Over the same fortnight, Visconti was plunged
into another thrilling, confusing new world. 'One thing about David is
that he's not a workaholic. He really loves to explore his environment.'

In that first stay, Visconti lodged at the Schlosshotel Gerhus, a magnificent, decayed building once owned by art collector Walter Graf von
Pannwitz. They'd work at Hansa Studio 1 in the afternoons, then in the
evenings go to 'Romy Haag's or some dungeon club', says Visconti.
Bowie was keen to share the experience of Haag's club. It was oddly
wholesome: 'It wasn't really a gay thing, there were kids there as well as
grown-ups, it was just part of their cabaret culture. Even if you couldn't
speak German you could get off on the cabaret. Romy was about six-foot
tall and couldn't possibly have been a woman, which added to the mystique, and we'd [always] get the best table.'

Schöneberg embodied the contradictory nature of David's fascination
with Berlin. Five minutes down the road was a huge Nazi bunker on
Pallasstrasse, the site of Goebbels' 'Total War' speech. Another five minutes
away was Christopher Isherwood's old house on Nollendorfstrasse – the
'deep, solemn massive street' he'd immortalised on the opening page
of Goodbye to Berlin, with its description of young men whistling up to
the women on the upper stories in hope of an assignation – a pastime
in which David, naturally, also indulged. It was indicative of David's
mindset that he was as interested in the iconography of Hitler's Berlin
as he was in the gay communities murdered by the Nazis, who were
commemorated by a plaque on Nollendorferplatz, where David and
Jimmy shopped for books or sipped coffee. Equally, David might visit
the Brücke Museum, study works by Heckel or Ernst Ludwig Kirchner
that the Nazis had declared degenerate, then wander into antique
stores and examine tickets and leaflets adorned with the tell-tale
sticker that concealed a Swastika.

Jimmy was relaxed about David's interest in the Third Reich – hardly
surprising, given that Iggy's last new work presented on stage had
involved him being whipped by his old bandmate, Ron Asheton, who
was wearing a Nazi uniform complete with party armband. (Asheton,
incidentally, claimed to have invented the 'Hitler was the first pop star'
line that became a virtual Bowie catchphrase.) Other friends were
equally non-judgemental; one Jewish acquaintance who knew David
through his time in Berlin points out, 'He was always fascinated by it.

But the quote David was stigmatised for, he didn't mean it in a bad way. He meant [the Nazis] knew how to work the media.' Although convinced David was one of the least racist people she'd ever met, the friend does not remember him ever explaining his crass statements – only in the later Berlin days, when David had met pleasant young men whose fathers had served in the SS, did he fully realise the full implications of his fixation. It wasn't until 1980 that he'd describe his flirtation with fascist chic as 'ghastly stuff'. At the same time, in a wide-ranging interview with Angus MacKinnon for the *NME*, he pointed out, quite reasonably, that he'd never shown racism in his personal dealings. But he didn't apologise.

Tony Visconti had first learned that David was starting a new album of his own when he'd been called by David and a man he introduced as his newest collaborator: Brian Eno. 'They said to me, "What are you going to bring to the table?" says Visconti. 'It was the first time I'd heard that phrase, which put me on the spot, so I had to think fast.' Famously Visconti responded that he had discovered a new digital delay unit, the Eventide Harmoniser, that could delay a sound, and change its pitch, independently of each other. His succinct explanation of the novel unit was that 'it fucks with the fabric of time'. And he was in.

One collaborator never made the session. David had wanted to recruit Neu!'s Michael Rother for the project, working title *New Music Night and Day*. Rother and his proto-ambient group Harmonia worked with Brian Eno that September, and the guitarist is "positive" no request arrived, although he did discuss a link-up with David in 1977 which foundered due to a communication breakdown.

When the sessions convened early in September at the Château D'Hérouville, all of the musicians were unsure as to what they'd encounter. Roy Young, Britain's best-known boogie woogie pianist, had received a phone call from David at the Speakeasy. It was the second time David had called – Roy had been unable to make the *Station to Station* sessions – and while David was effusive, Young had no idea how his piano would fit in to Bowie's music. The same applied to guitarist Ricky Gardiner, who, like Phil Palmer, was another Tony Visconti discovery – a replacement for Michael Rother. Young and Gardiner shared a plane out to Paris, nervously picking each other's brains as to what they would be faced with.

As it turned out, the sessions were relaxed, with David sitting on the studio floor, showing Young, Gardiner, Carlos Alomar, George Murray and Dennis Davis little riffs, getting them to add their own feel, open-minded about what they'd come up with. But it felt strange: asked what his plan was, David was frank. 'I'm not sure yet, till we develop it.' Brian Eno, who Visconti had been told would be one of the key collaborators, did not arrive until later in the session, which increased the nervous tension. Visconti recalls, 'We had defined it as an experiment. Before we went in, we said this might be a waste of a month of our lives. And it was three weeks before we knew it was working.'

All those present knew David was dealing with problems, deriving from an imminent legal battle with Michael Lippman; they sensed his preoccupation, but shared in the studio camaraderie. In the early weeks, David was more ebullient. But when Angie briefly arrived at the recording with boyfriend Roy Martin to 'help the session along', as one wit puts it, there was a huge fight in one of the rooms and the sound of glasses being thrown. Iggy and Visconti had to pull Martin and Bowie apart. David seemed to quite enjoy the drama, then worked up a groove with the rhythm section, which became 'Breaking Glass': 'I've been breaking glass in your room again.' The lyrics also warned Angie not to look at the carpet, a reference to his drawing Kabbala symbols on the floor back in Los Angeles. 'Always Crashing in the Same Car' was a reference to the time David crashed his Mercedes in Switzerland; the accident had additional comedy value because David was trying to raise some much-needed cash by selling the mangled vehicle.

As the tape rolled, the musicians relaxed, gamely replaying and revising, happy to be hanging out in luxury for two weeks. Drinks and food were on call twenty-four hours a day, and Roy Young kept the staff busy replenishing the bucket of ice which he kept on top of the piano alongside a bottle of gin and a bottle of tonic. After one take, Young heard a 'rat-tat-tat' in his headphones and looked up to see David at the talkback mic, holding up a glass. 'So I sent him one in, mixed just how I had them,' he says. 'And this happened a few times.'

Some time later, Visconti announced that they had a possible take, and the band trooped in. As the tape rolled, David sat in his characteristic lotus position on a chair by the desk, chin resting on his hands, apparently deep in thought. The assembled musicians waited expectantly for several minutes to hear his verdict until they realised he was fast asleep. 'And I will always remember, he scratched his head exactly like Oliver Hardy when he woke up,' says Young, 'and then Tony said, "David, I think you'd better go for a lie-down."'

As David made his way down the steep stairway that led from the control room, there was a sudden thud, followed by a series of bumps, as he bounced down the wooden steps. The musicians all crowded around to check on their singer, sprawled in a heap on the floor below – all, that is, except for Roy Young. 'I hid under my piano,' he says, 'petrified.' The next morning David pulled up his shirt to reveal dark red weals all the way up his skinny ribcage; the spectacle was accompanied by Visconti's warning that if another gin and tonic made its way into the control room, Young would be on the next plane home.

The lack of a clear outcome to these experiments was confusing, but at its heart was a simple, intuitive, brilliant leap forward. David's intentions on the album that would become *Low* was to combine the glacial electronic instrumentation that he'd heard on Kraftwerk and Tangerine Dream records, and combine them with a boisterous, vibrant R&B rhythm section. In sonic terms, the result was heavily influenced by Neu!, the band founded by Kraftwerk refugee Klaus Dinger – the harmonised, resonant guitar lines of Neu! songs like 'Seeland', from their last great album, *Neu 75*, have echoes throughout *Low*, and *"Heroes"*, too. But where Dinger's drumming was static, a metronomic pulse, Dennis Davis' spirit and energy drives the first half of *Low* ever onward.

A restless improviser, who worked in parallel with Roy Ayers throughout much of his time with Bowie, Davis was as obsessed with the recording process as Bowie and Visconti – who rigged up the Eventide Harmoniser on Davis' snare drum, then fed the results through the drummer's headphones so he could interact with its superhuman clunk. The constant counterpoint between the buoyant optimism of Davis, Alomar and Murray and the contemplative, intellectual clarity of Gardiner and Eno gives the album a delicious tension between optimism and anomie. The music reflected exactly David's mental condition. 'I was at the end of my tether physically and emotionally. But overall, I get a sense of real optimism through the veils of despair from *Low*.'

Throughout the summer of 1976, while the same old financial and legal crises continually menaced him, David's main strategy – along with attempts to seek oblivion through sex or beer – was to find solace in problem-solving, piecing together *The Idiot* and *Low* like giant jigsaw puzzles. Iggy was his main partner in this occupational therapy; and David's unfailing instinct for selecting collaborators had led him to Brian Eno.

David knew Eno vaguely from the very first Ziggy tour, when Roxy Music had shared the bill at The Croydon Greyhound, and later at the Rainbow show. They'd not kept in touch, but when Eno turned up at the

Station to Station Wembley dates in May, David had exerted all his charm, telling him he'd been playing Eno's *Discreet Music* throughout the American leg of the tour: 'Naturally, flattery always endears you to someone,' says Eno. 'I thought, God, he must be smart.'

When he turned up, around ten days into the *Low* session, Eno effected a quiet revolution. Hired initially by Bowie because he represented a one-man entrée to ambient music, a genre he'd created pretty much single-handedly with *Discreet Music* and *Another Green World*, Eno was an inspired choice for accomplice, for his musical twists and turns paralleled David's own journey. A grammar-school boy and art-school student, he had quit Roxy Music in July 1973, frustrated by their abandonment of art-rock experimentation. The cultural battle that took place within Roxy – Ferry's penchant for cover versions and glossy artwork, versus Eno's love for the random – echoed similar conflicts being played out in Bowie's head. In broad terms, Eno was hired to play right brain to Bowie's left brain; in musical terms, he was an inspired, punctilious synthesiser craftsman. In personal terms, he and Bowie were as *sympathisch* as they come, sharing a healthy sense of humour and a healthy streak of pretension, a taste for sexual adventure, and a love of re-enacting Peter Cooke and Dudley Moore comedy routines.

In future years, Eno would often be inaccurately credited as the producer of *Low*; yet he was co-conspirator as well as hired hand. Arriving late in the sessions, he sat alongside Bowie as they briefed the musicians on the next stage of the recording, like a pair of avuncular Squadron Commanders prepared to wave their jittery recruits into the azure. 'They sat us down and played us these tapes of the [*The Man Who Fell to Earth*] soundtrack and told us what they were planning,' says Young. 'It was out of our experience . . . and honestly, quite a few of us didn't really like the idea.' Bowie was acutely conscious that RCA might have a similar reaction. 'We don't know if this will ever be released,' he told Young and the others, 'but I have to do this.'

Eno arrived when the rhythm tracks for side one of *Low* were essentially complete; Murray and Davis flew home, while Carlos, Gardiner and Roy Young stayed on to work up the instrumental lines. Although Eno's more unsettling managerial techniques – like his Burroughsian use of 'Oblique Strategy cards' – were not extensively deployed on this record, he was crucial in motivating both the musicians and Bowie, who was distracted by legal negotiations to extricate himself from Michael Lippman. Eno encouraged a bullish attitude in which, as Visconti puts it, 'Whether the record company was behind it or not did not matter at that point – we simply made the most far-out album we could think of.' Yet the musical discussions weren't exclusively high-falutin': the decision to augment the first batch of recordings with an instrumental side two followed a debate about whether Bowie fans would consider the results decent value for money. 'We felt that getting six or seven songs with David Bowie singing, with choruses and verses, still made for a good album,' says Visconti, 'then making the second side instrumental gave a perfect Ying Yang balance.'

Indeed, the seven songs that made up the first side were all intricately worked, with an impeccable internal logic; David's singing on the main vocal lines was his most honest and unaffected in years, offset by his vibratoed Brechtian yelps for the choruses. Soon a decade's worth of imitators would copy the impressionistic lyrics, the low-key narrative vocal and foregrounded snare drum; yet none of them would share the sense of discovery of the Château sessions.

More low-key than David, happy to share japes with Iggy, Brian Eno often took a similar tack to David, picking people's brains for ideas, quizzing the Château engineers about techniques other studio clients had used, patiently working out how to operate the desk and tape machine before asking to be left alone to painstakingly overdub harmonised parts one line at a time using his EMS AKS suitcase synth – a glorious object which looked like an overgrown Stylophone mated with the TARDIS control panel. Appropriately, Eno pieced together his parts to the sombre 'Warszawa' on the days when David had to drive in to Paris for soul-sapping meetings with Lippman's lawyers at the Hotel Raphael. Once the backing tracks were finished, Visconti's wife, singer Mary Hopkin, arrived at the Château to add her 'doo-doo-doo's to the introduction of 'Sound and Vision', while Tony and Mary's son Morgan played with Zowie and Marion.

One day, Eno heard Morgan picking out three notes on the reception room piano; he used the simple sombre A, B, C as the main melody of 'Warszawa', later augmented with David's devotional, wordless vocals, influenced by one of Eno's favourite recordings of a Balkan boys' choir.

Although Iggy is hardly audible on the *Low* recordings – his voice appears on 'What in the World', a survivor from the *Idiot* sessions – his laid-back humour was vital. He'd huddle with David after his gruelling legal meetings, which went on for days in a row, and use humour to ease him out of his exhausted, emotionally drained, state.

Towards the end of the recording, Iggy's jokes developed into full-blown comedy monologues, based on the endless, hilarious disasters he and his fellow Stooges had suffered. One night he described how Stooges' drummer Scotty used MainMan's cash to buy a huge drum kit, which got smaller and smaller at each show. 'A simple beat is where it's at,' Scotty assured the other Stooges, who soon realised he was selling the kit off, piece by piece, to support his smack habit. Another night, Iggy stripped off his shirt to show the scars on his chest – then mimed out how he was forced to roll in broken glass to end a song, the only fool-proof way of making his fellow Stooges, nodding out on heroin, recognise the final bars. 'We would just fall about, aching with laughter, our sides would hurt,' says Visconti. David would listen to these pica-resque stories for hours, shaking his head, telling Eno or Visconti, 'This is unbelievable, I can't imagine any human being went through this and lived.' The tales of disaster, all true and rendered without any self-pity, were somehow soothing.

There were echoes of more ancient tragedies, too, according to Tony Visconti, who claims the spirits of the previous residents of the Château, star-crossed lovers Frédéric Chopin and George Sand, haunted the building. Bowie, too, considered it 'a spooky place – I did refuse one bedroom, as it felt impossibly cold in certain areas', he says today. Interrogated about the spectral presence, the Château's staff dismiss the stories. 'The ghosts were in the echo chambers,' says Laurent Thibault, 'that's where the odd noises came from.' Yet, delving deeper, it turns out that Visconti and Bowie were not the only ones to sense the pianist and his muse: Deep Purple's Ritchie Blackmore had similar experi-ences; while at one Ouiji-board session, ghostly messages turned out to be rendered in perfect Polish – Chopin's native tongue. In later years, the Château staff attempted to damp down widespread gossip about spec-tral presences, which persisted until the studio closed in the wake of owner Michel Magne's suicide.

David loved the Château – 'It was a joy, ramshackle and comfy' – but as his slot came to an end, his last days at the studio were marked by bickering. Visconti cordially detested rival bassist and producer Laurent Thibault, who was blamed for the presence of a reporter posing as a receptionist (she spent hours in David's room, engaged in 'research'). He also disliked the food and the alignment of the tape machines, and pre-ferred the 'Germanic efficiency' of Hansa Studios. Visconti remembers he and David suffered food poisoning from warm cheese; so David, Tony, Brian and Iggy decamped to Berlin in mid-October, shortly before the news of David's 'exile' in Europe broke in the German press, and then worldwide.

There were more overdubs to come at Hansa; first David, Eno and Visconti reviewed the tapes at Studio 1 on the Ku'Damm, before completing 'Weeping Wall' and 'Subterraneans' at the newly opened studio by the Wall. Their assistant and translator was Eduard Meyer, a qualified *Ton-meister* – sound-master – whom the trio would soon corrupt, subverting his formal training. They went easy on him first: when David discovered he was a skilled cellist, he asked him to add a cello line to 'Art Decade'. 'I am sorry, Mr Bowie,' Meyer replied, 'I am a score-reading musician, not an improvising one.' Remembering the skills picked up from Frida Dinn's *Observer's Book of Music*, David wrote out a part in manuscript. It was among the last instrumental additions to an album that David knew represented the biggest risk of his career.

According to Visconti, when RCA heard the album, one executive told David, 'If you make *Young Americans Two* instead, we'll buy you a mansion in Philadelphia!' David had been prone to occasional doubts when he'd completed albums in the past, but not this time. RCA's confusion simply hardened his resolve. If that were not enough, when Tony Defries heard an acetate of *Low*, he dismissed it as 'a piece of crap that even Nic Roeg turned down' and refused to allow it to count to David's contractual obligation towards him. What could be more perfect? *Low* would be a new beginning, and David Bowie's estranged father figure wouldn't even have a slice of it.

16

Helden

> This was clearly an ex-war zone and now it was an international boundary, which was really scary. We recorded 500 feet from barbed wire, and a tall tower where you could see gun turrets, with foreign soldiers looking at us with binoculars. Everything said, 'We shouldn't be making a record here.'
>
> *Tony Visconti*

Checkpoint Charlie, the fabled gateway between West and East Berlin. Tony Visconti, sitting alongside David Bowie, Iggy Pop and Coco Schwab, watches nervously as the guard scrutinises their passports, while his colleagues cradle their machine pistols ominously, all of them overseen by a low, glass-fronted watchtower. Suddenly, the guard calls for assistance: *Friedrich, kommen sie hier!* The party freezes, looking on as the second guard flips through the passports – suddenly both of the Prussian-Grey-uniformed figures, sidearms at their hips, break into laughter.

Visconti steps out of the Mercedes, and the guards point out the passport photos. 'Iggy had this platinum hair, and Bambi eyes,' says the producer. 'Bowie had that dreadful curly perm from around "Space Oddity".' The two remade, remodelled, crop-haired stars, far from home, are forced to silently endure the ridicule, before finally driving out to the East, with its ruined buildings, derelict train tracks, women sporting fifties-style beehives, and the countryside beyond.

What might have surprised the guards even more, had they known it, was that for both rock stars, abandoning the hedonism, excess and silly haircuts of the West – i.e., exactly those values being kept out at gunpoint at Checkpoint Charlie – had brought David Bowie and Iggy Pop to a new 'joy of life', as David put it. 'It was an education,' says Iggy Pop, 'always there was the idea, we're trying to learn something here. And to be pretty disciplined about it.'

In Berlin, play and so-called work were intertwined. It was a rare week that involved no recording, or administration, but there were plenty of days when they could ramble however they chose. David and Iggy might spend such a day wandering around the antique markets on Winterfeldplatz, or book shops and cafés down by St Matthias Kirche. Iggy would often rise early and walk for five or eight miles; eventually he claimed to have explored every nook and cranny of the city. In winter, they'd sometimes take the S-Bahn train to the Wannsee, a lake resort on the Havel River, for long lunches under the glass roof, not far from the villa where senior Nazis mapped out the Final Solution. David showed Iggy how to prep a canvas, or apply acrylic paint; both of them spent time on artwork. David completed a portrait of Iggy rendered in a convincing expressionist style reminiscent of the works they'd seen at Die Brücke, a tiny, modern museum shaded by the pine trees of the Grünewald Forest. Most of all, they'd simply walk, often dropping in on friends without warning just to say hello, like they used to back in the sixties, before most people owned a phone.

Compared to their previous existence, this was a life of monk-like restraint. But both men were realistic about their regime. Occasional excess was acceptable, but heroin, Iggy's old *bête noir*, was out of bounds. One evening, David took a cab back home to the Hauptstrasse when the taxi driver mentioned he had 'the dooj' ready for his friend. David warned the cabbie, coldly, there would be dire consequences if any of 'the dooj' – heroin – should reach his friend, but didn't mention the incident to Iggy, careful not to appear too controlling. Both men tried every brand of German beer on offer, but in the city, rather than the omnipresent American drug scene, 'There was an artsy-crafty weekend drug culture,' says Iggy. 'So on the weekends we'd go meet an eccentric character who was interested in the arts, and knew other people, and maybe you'd have a little coke and get drunk and go till four in the morning to three or four clubs.'

Many locals knew who Bowie and Iggy were; but, naturally polite, they'd pretend not to recognise Bowie when they saw him in regular haunts, like the city's two Zip record stores. Instead, fans would sneak up to the cashier once David had departed with a carrier-bag full of records, and ask, '*Was hat Bowie gekauft?*'

Visitors came and went regularly over this period, most of them stay-ing at the Schlosshotel Gerhus. Angie was among the first, arriving soon after the completion of *Low*, in November 1976. It's difficult to pinpoint, from her point of view, that point at which she realised her marriage was irrevocably doomed, but her disdain for her husband's and his friend's attempt to sort themselves out indicates their relationship was now poi-soned by indifference and contempt. 'A lot of people love the idea of going and making nice to the people you've defeated so you can treat them like slaves. That was David's going to Berlin story: "Let me lie with you in case there's something we didn't take from you that I haven't learned yet" – it's pathetic.' Angie's distaste extended to *Low*, and *The Idiot*, too, her opinions echoing those of her old patron and nemesis, Tony Defries. Unsurprisingly, the Bowie family Christmas, spent in Switzerland, would be their last together. Bowie was back in Berlin by 8 January, 1977, for his thirtieth birthday, celebrated with Iggy and Romy Haag. *Low* was released the next week, on 14 January.

Low's reception by both the press and Bowie's record company was oddly in context with the record's sleeve – the title and photo, of David in profile, made up a visual pun: *Low* profile. RCA's reaction to the album was simple incomprehension. As Robin Eggar, RCA's press officer at the time, remembers, the company 'didn't really know what to do with *Low* or *"Heroes"*. They only put them out because they were Bowie albums – and the attitude totally was, What are we going to do with this?' Equally, David's failure to promote the album meant press coverage was modest. Yet the myth that *Low* was greeted with wide-spread disdain is just that, for most reviewers realised this was a major event in Bowie's career. Tim Lott, future Whitbread-prize winning novelist, spoke for many in declaring *Low*, 'the most difficult piece of music Bowie has ever put his name to'. The writer ended his preview for *Sounds* with an appropriately fractured procession of adjectives, which ended:

So. This album might be
    Bowie's best ever.
    Eno's best ever.
    A mechanical classic.

Lott cited 'Sound and Vision' as the 'pinnacle' of the album; his verdict anticipated its success as a single, reaching number three in the UK (but stalling at sixty-nine in the US). Its success further confused RCA, who were also, Eggar points out, intimidated by Bowie, accepting his refusal to tour the album without argument, and likewise caving in to his persuasion that the company should release Iggy's *The Idiot*, which came out on 21 March, 1977. From RCA's point of view, David's announcement that he would tour to promote Iggy's album, rather than his own, was perfectly consistent in its complete flouting of commercial logic. David took over all the arrangements for the tour, calling in *Low* guitarist Ricky Gardiner, as well as two brothers who had passed him a demo cassette during David's first US tour, back in October 1972.

Hunt and Tony Sales were the sons of comic Soupy Sales; they'd earned their Musicians' Union cards when drummer Hunt was twelve and bassist Tony was thirteen, hung out with Frank Sinatra, sax legend King Curtis and other hep-cats, and recorded their first album with Todd Rundgren when Hunt was just sixteen. Loud, hell-raising and formidably talented, from the moment they arrived in Berlin in February, they ensured that David and Iggy's weekend debaucheries became seven-day affairs. Their routine normally involved a late breakfast at the Schlosshotel, rehearsals from 11 until 5, goulash for dinner, a quick sleep, then trips to Romy Haag's, or an old bar frequented by the SS where patrons could use the phones on the table to find conversational or sexual partners, or clubs in Kreuzberg where, says Tony Sales, 'I saw a real-life re-enactment of that Doors LP cover, with a midget with an umbrella, standing on the bar.'

In the brief, intense rehearsals at the old UFA film studios, filled with old filing cabinets crammed with film canisters and ancient Weimar and Nazi-era paperwork, through which all the band members rifled, the brothers watched the two oddly complementary singers chat, work and relax. 'It was two schoolboys hanging out, chums,' says Sales. 'It was a very loving relationship in a sense. David was at a place where he needed to recharge and got behind Iggy – and in return that helped him, taking the pressure off being David Bowie.'

The brothers were among the first outsiders to see the two singers in their new hide-out. As word had leaked out in the autumn that David had holed up with the ex-leader of The Stooges, rumours had started to spread. Back in 1976, supporters like Iggy fanzine editor Harald Inhülsen were writing letters to fellow fans, speculating that David had kidnapped Iggy and was keeping him 'under his thumb'. The implication that Iggy was being exploited as David's sex slave was widespread, entertaining, and has made its way into print. Iggy himself laughs, and denies such hanky-panky; even Angie Bowie, always prone to seeing her husband in the role of exploiter, believes otherwise, asking, with her unerring eye for practical detail, 'Who would be on the bottom?'

A more plausible interpretation for cynics was that Iggy's main purpose was to give David credibility: this was probably the case with Iggy's role at MainMan, but by the time of *The Idiot*, there was a self-lessness to David's behaviour that, says Hunt Sales, is rare in the jaded world of rock music. 'David really loved him as a friend. Giving something to someone is not giving something and expecting something in return. You just give it.'

It says much for the zeal with which fans followed Bowie's career that by the time the Iggy tour started, on 1 March, 1977, David's absence from the public eye had become a widespread obsession. For the opening date of Iggy's first ever solo tour, David chose the town that had hosted Ziggy's debut performance over four years before, Aylesbury. He cheerfully greeted old acquaintances, like promoter David Stopps, jokily enquiring, 'What's a clean-cut kid like you still doing in a town like this?' and insisting the crowd not be kept outside waiting when the backline amplifiers were delayed in customs.

Kris Needs, who'd designed the flyer for the Friar's show back in 1971, had seen Bowie in nearly all of his guises. This one was the biggest shock of them all. 'This is a guy who roughly a year before was supposed to be out of his mind on cocaine. And here he was in sensible shoes and a jacket, maybe a flat cap like Iggy's, just open and chatting to everyone.'

When the doors opened, it took a couple of songs before the audience noticed David Bowie, sitting at the side of the stage, playing a Baldwin electric piano. Soon, like the parting of the Red Sea, the audience split in two, as fans in the Civic Hall craned their necks to look at the keyboard player, who was studiously avoiding their gaze. Hard-core Iggy fans – like Johnny Thunders, Sex Pistols bassist Glen Matlock and Damned guitarist Brian James, all part of a London punk posse who'd travelled up for Iggy's comeback – remained at stage centre. The reactions to Iggy's new guise were mixed. Johnny Thunders was dismissive: 'Iggy's gone cabaret,' he whined.

The punk movement had finally exploded into mainstream consciousness with the Sex Pistols' appearance on Bill Grundy's *Today* show the previous December. Bowie's *Station to Station* shows at Wembley the previous May typified the stadium rock that many punks affected to despise; even his patronage of Iggy and Lou, the twin punk figureheads, was regarded as self-serving. But few of the British punks bothered to hide the fact that they'd cut their teeth on Ziggy-era Bowie. Even if the Sex Pistols had stolen Bowie's microphones from the Hammersmith Ziggy farewell, as claimed by guitarist Steve Jones, the theft was partly an act of affection. For those attempting to break out of punk convention, especially out of London, Bowie would be a guiding light; Manchester's Joy Division would take *The Idiot* as a sonic and lyrical template, and Bowie was soon being name-checked by Echo and the Bunnymen, Cabaret Voltaire, Talking Heads and more.

In the meantime, Bowie's low-key, stage-right role alongside Iggy was another object lesson in 'positioning'. Soon, peers like Ray Davies and Pete Townshend would embrace the punk movement, donning skinny ties and losing a little bit of dignity. David's slightly aloof position located him as an insider, not a follower; he was a decent keyboard player, too. But the Iggy tour was harder work than David had anticipated, keeping up with Iggy and the unstoppable Sales brothers. The latter two were phenomenal musicians – they had an almost telepathic musical bond which meant they didn't even need to hear each other in the monitors to stay in sync – but they existed in a blaze of drink, native energy and cocaine. Bassist Tony remembers 'walking through the hallways of hotels naked and stoned . . . it was over-the-top exhaustion and then you'd do more cocaine to cover the exhaustion.'

It was a mark of the new, relaxed David that his fear of flying evaporated over this tour; David boarded a 747 to New York with Andy Kent and was 'perfectly fine', says the photographer. But from the moment the band hit the States, the drug use and manic behaviour intensified. A wonderfully strait-laced joint appearance on *The Dinah Shore Show*, with David letting Iggy occupy the limelight, seemed calm, as if the pair had attained a new maturity, but backstage it was another story. Tour members remember full vodka bottles hitting the rafters in Detroit; a gun pointed at the stage in California; and a walking-talking doll with a Nazi flag marching across the Sales brothers' dressing room. Soon Iggy was overcome by a new megalomania, and things became 'very dark', says bassist Tony Sales. 'I was in real bad shape . . . but I could always stand up.'

David begged off from a subsequent Iggy tour, explaining, quite reasonably, 'The drug use was unbelievable, and I knew it was killing me,' but a few weeks after the first tour concluded in San Diego on 16 April, he threw himself into the fray again, to produce a second Iggy album. These sessions would take place at Hansa in its Köthenerstrasse location, just by the Potsdamerplatz and the Wall. By the time the recording started, says Iggy, 'I think David was pretty sick of my rock histrionics,

and I was probably pretty sick of where he was coming from, so there
was a lot of friction – but on the other hand we were both really into it.'

Bowie's production on what would become *Lust for Life* was, quite
simply, masterful. When he heard guitarist Ricky Gardiner strumming
a catchy guitar riff, he suggested Iggy use it as the basis of what became
'The Passenger'. His own melodies, on 'Lust for Life' and 'Some Weird
Sin', were powerful and muscular. During these sessions Bowie showed
a rare flexibility, ready to change the schedule at any moment if Iggy, for
instance, had a vocal idea he wanted to nail. Iggy describes himself as
'the happiest person in the world' during this period. 'I was living on
red wine, cocaine and German sausage, slept in a cot and only had a cold
shower.' (He adds that other musicians avoided him as, having only a
cold shower, he never used it.)

By now, Iggy had moved into his own flat in the Hinterhof –
servant's quarters at the back of 155, Hauptstrasse – with girlfriend
Esther Friedmann, and was asserting his independence. One perfect
example was the song 'Success': dissatisfied with David's original melody –
'a damn crooning thing', he called it – Iggy arrived at the studio early
to record the song with a simpler, stripped-down tune, over the Sales
brothers' swinging, mid-tempo groove – 'a controlled gallop', says Carlos
Alomar. The song, as the title suggests, proclaims that success is finally
on its way; Iggy's stream-of-consciousness lyrics – a car, a Chinese rug –
were all the more poignant, as events would soon conspire to deny him
the very luxuries he described in song.

Just as with *The Idiot*, David's work on *Lust for Life* served as a dry-run
for his own project, which he started almost immediately after wrapping
up Iggy's album. The centrepiece of his so-called Berlin trilogy, *"Heroes"*
was the only album of the three entirely recorded in Berlin. The city permeated both the sound and the ambience of the album, in a location
which, according to Tony Visconti, was both 'a dream . . . and [a place]
where everything said, "We shouldn't be making a record here."'

It was Hansa Studios that best embodied Berlin's grandeur and
menace. The main building, on the Köthenerstrasse, was built as the
Meistersaal in 1910, a beautiful, stern clubhouse to showcase the skills of
Berlin's master masons. But in 1976, it looked like a forlorn wreck, in a
forgotten sector of the city. Left derelict throughout most of the Second
World War, its elegant Ionic pillars were bullet-scarred, the lofty pedi-
ment blown off, the upper windows bricked up, with pigeons roosting
within; a quarter of its courtyarded block had simply collapsed. All

around, streets retained their gap-toothed look, like Brixton in 1947, and from the second storey the section of the Wall leading up to Potsdamerplatz was clearly visible: 'this was clearly an ex-war zone,' says Visconti, 'and now it was an international boundary, which was really scary. We recorded 500 feet from barbed wire, and a tall tower where you could see gun turrets, with foreign soldiers looking at us with binoculars.'

The tiny crew included Alomar, Dennis Davis, George Murray and Visconti, all of whom would get a taxi in from the Schlosshotel Gerhus every lunchtime. According to the producer, one factor in getting the album done quickly was that 'David was paying my hotel bills – so he didn't want to waste time.' The musicians would therefore work 'an intense eight-hour day, from 12 till 8, and then hit the Berlin clubs', says Visconti. Brian Eno stayed at Hauptstrasse, at least some of the time. Iggy often entertained listeners with a hilarious description of Eno's girlfriend handcuffed to a radiator, a superlative example of art-school sophistication which impressed the posterboy of rock 'n' roll excess, although sadly it's doubtful Eno had the leisure time for such pursuits. Eno loved the ambience; Carlos Alomar was less impressed: 'The hotels were, for an American, very old European, too many back staircases. My first impression of German men was that they were pigs. They ate a lot of pork, they looked a certain way and when it came to treating their women I was appalled . . . maybe it was an age thing, but the overall German experience for me was very "this sucks".'

The difference in atmosphere between the Château and Hansa, sensed by Alomar and the rhythm section, had its effect from the moment the backing tracks went down. Last time around, the beats were funky, spritely; here, four-square rhythms give a solid, dogmatic rock feel, more evocative of Krautrock bands like Neu!. The sound was bigger, literally, for the musicians set up in the wood-floored main hall – Studio 2 – which Visconti miked up to capture an ambient zing and excitement. Working out the songs was an edgier process; the chord changes would be mapped out and endlessly altered, sometimes at random.

In those first few days, Alomar's contribution was vital; mild, almost stately, he was supremely competitive but always remained calm when challenged to deliver. 'The mentality that I had with David was always the same; you ask me for one thing, I will supply you with a million options until you tell me to stop. And that's my claim to fame.' Visconti, too, remembers Alomar's inventiveness at crafting 'subtle melodies, one after another – the ones people don't notice straight away, but they make the song come together'. 'He's quite remarkable,' Eno told writer Ian MacDonald later that year.

And he had to be. As early as 1967, David Bowie would arrive in the studio with a complete set of songs, all of them painstakingly mapped out on manuscript paper. A few years later, by the time of *Hunky Dory*, songs had arrived seemingly by magic, in a dream or on a bus ride. Now, in the culmination of a process that had begun just two years before with *Station to Station*, David walked into the studio without one complete song. He had completely changed the process at the heart of his music, as if he'd abandoned a conventional representational technique for a new kind of aural expressionism.

Yet buried within the abstract shards of the songs that were slowly pieced together – making sense of the random – there were plenty of traces of Bowie's hard-learned traditional skills. 'Sons of the Silent Age', the only song sketched out before the sessions, showed many glimpses of earlier Bowie personae: its opening is delivered in a nasal Tony Newley croon and the agonised swooping melody of its middle section – 'baby I'll never let you go' – is an almost literal restatement of the middle-section theme from 1971's 'Width of a Circle'. Then, suddenly, the melody morphs into multitracked, Lennon-esque vocals; the gloriously naive saxophone evokes a barren future world and the fifties kitsch of the Kon-Rads or Joe Meek.

Similarly, the futuristic gleam of 'V-2 Schneider' – a tribute both to the terror weapons that had landscaped south London and Florian Schneider, the founder of Kraftwerk – was also humanised by the glorious teenage honk of Bowie's sax, while 'Blackout' briefly quotes 'Boney Maroney' by Little Richard acolyte Larry Williams. Like the 1930s futurism that inspired him, the music of *"Heroes"* evokes both past and future. For perhaps the first time, Bowie's long, circuitous route to his present state seemed to make sense.

For Bowie and Eno in particular, the sessions pushed them to a new level of intensity; both had hardly any time to eat, with Bowie subsisting mainly on a rushed raw egg, Eno on cereal. ('Brian would start his day with a cup full of boiling water into which he would cut huge lumps of garlic,' adds Bowie. 'He was no fun to do backing vocals with on the same mike.') Guitarist Robert Fripp, with whom Eno had worked closely since July 1972, would be thrown into the mix for just two days; forty-eight hours in which he would fantasise fondly, in a Somerset accent, of unleashing his 'sword of union' on the locals – but he would never get the chance.

For all of the tiny crew, their time in Berlin during *"Heroes"* would result in a series of unforgettable images: the day that Visconti cropped Iggy and David's hair and they wandered around looking like old men; visits to an antique shop whose proprietor had known Marlene Dietrich; the frenzied warehouse parties with local tearaways like artist Martin Kippenberger; the day Tony Visconti saw a huge black tank rumbling down the Kurfürstendamm; or the time Edu Meyer saw a guard on a DDR machine-gun post surveying them though his binoculars and attempted to dazzle him with an Anglepoise lamp, causing Bowie and Visconti to duck under the control desk, terrified.

For David, these Berlin experiences had 'a calming effect', says Alomar. But even in the act of creation, his joy was always controlled. In this, he was a complete contrast to Iggy, who would swing from euphoria to depression – indeed, just when *"Heroes"* was being completed, Iggy succumbed to a manic-depressive cocaine jag, for which David and Coco arranged an 'intervention', asking Barbara and Tim Dewitt to whisk him away to Capri. David was 'an educated thinker – so that would rescue him from the depressions', says Carlos. But David also thought 'way too much'. His enjoyment of the now was always overshadowed by the thought it wouldn't last.

Likewise, David's trademark futurism was omnipresent in *"Heroes"*, but gained a new poignancy in their Potsdamerplatz outpost. Later, describing this time in Berlin as one of the happiest periods in his life, David would pick up this poignant note. 'In some ways, sadly, [the three albums] really captured, unlike anything else in that time, a sense of yearning for a future that we all knew would never come to pass.'

'Neuköln', the most desolate song of the set, epitomised the bleakness at the centre of this futuristic optimism. Haunting and stately, it played the same role as *Low*'s 'Warszawa', and was inspired by the once-grand, now grim multi-occupation buildings of the Berlin sector– actually called Neukölln – that housed the city's Turkish *gastarbeiters* (guest workers). Workers brought in to supply Berlin's insatiable demand for labour, they were denied citizenship: stateless, temporary residents, like David.

One song was notably simpler than the rest; based on the same, basic G-to-C chord change that David had used for Iggy's song 'Success' just a few weeks before, and taken at a similar stately pace: Alomar's 'controlled gallop'. The song's melody, when it arrived, was based around the same three notes that David had sung on the Iggy song; and as the musicians worked on the backing track, Alomar once again added an insistent, unforgettable guitar line that emphasised the purity of its two-chord sequence; yet it would be Robert Fripp's majestic, yearning guitar that would emphasise the song's monumental quality.

In future years, rumours would persist that David had told Fripp the track was an instrumental, to encourage him to play all the way through; Visconti remembers otherwise, although Eno, who left before it was complete, assumed the track would be an instrumental. He thought it sounded 'heroic'. Fripp recorded his guitar in the huge ballroom, stepping between two taped marks on the floor, which marked the location at which each note would build into a feedback loop. Fripp made three passes at the song; Visconti blended all three, to ensure the guitar line floats serenely overhead, without falling to earth.

When David came to add the vocals after Eno had left, he used the technique he'd seen Iggy harness on *Lust for Life*, improvising words, or finalising them at the last moment. The improvised lyrics, simple and deep, were the making of the album's most famous song. Visconti: 'He would scribble down a few notes on the top of the piano, then say, "OK, drop me in after 'dolphins can swim'." And that way he wrote and sang "Heroes" simultaneously. At the end of an hour and half we had a complete vocal.'

The unique ambience of Hansa, with its view of the Wall, imprinted itself on the sound as well as the imagery of 'Heroes'. The moment he'd walked onto the studio floor, Visconti realised the room itself had a unique sound; when it came time to add the vocals to 'Heroes', Visconti placed one Neumann mike in the normal position, close up, then one fifteen feet away, and one on the back wall. The two distant mikes were routed through a noise gate, a device to switch them on as David's voice filled the space. The effect was magnificent; Bowie's singing was the best he'd committed to tape, fresh and without artifice.

Few lyrics have been created and captured in such quick succession; and this is what gives 'Heroes' much of its immediacy. The lyrics are simple, but shot through with caveats. The song's lovers yearn for transcendence, but will only reach it briefly. Even the brief state of lover's bliss, as they kiss by the Wall, is an act of the imagination. David claimed he had indeed seen two lovers underneath the Wall; later, once Tony Visconti had divorced his wife, Mary Hopkin, it turned out the lovers in question were Visconti and Antonia Maas, a nightclub singer whom he'd met and asked to sing on the album just a few days before. Yet in 2008, Maas stated that the song had been completed before their tryst – and that Bowie could not have seen them.

The six or so minutes that Bowie, Visconti and Eno carved out were all the more precious because they were irreplaceable. To shape the song, Visconti had cut apart the master tape to edit it; to record the vocal, Visconti had mixed the three microphones onto one track on the master – all he had space for. They couldn't revise the effect, or re-arrange the song. This was Bowie's doing. 'He quoted this Buddhist philosophy, how we live in a mire of options,' says Visconti. 'If you commit yourself, you're free.'

Bizarrely, 'Heroes', the song that would become arguably the best-known of David Bowie's career, would hardly set the charts alight. In the UK, it entered the charts in October, peaking at number twenty-four in an eight-week run. David himself would come to treasure the song for the effect on his live audience. 'In Europe, it is one of the ones that seemed to have special resonance.' The song failed as a single in America, but according to Bowie, it would become 'pivotal' in live shows: 'It's a strange phenomenon . . . Many of the crowd favourites were never radio or chart hits; "Heroes" tops them all.'

Resistant as they were to *Low*, RCA summoned up more enthusiasm for its successor, unleashing a memorable print campaign for its release on 14 October, 1977; the press ads featured the *"Heroes"* sleeve photo – the pose based on *Roquairol*, Erich Heckel's portrait of his friend Ernst Kirchner – accompanied by the slogan, 'There's New Wave, there's Old Wave, and there's David Bowie'. It was a masterful piece of positioning which allowed him to remain aloof from a punk movement which, like glam before it, soon turned into a parody of itself.

The new, dressed-down David would do his own share of promotion, spending most of the autumn engaged in press and TV interviews. His first appearance, on 9 September, was his most memorable; like his appearance on *Lift Off with Ayshea*, five years before, this would be in Granada Television's children's slot, designed to catch kids just back from school. From late August, this half-hour slot had also become the venue for the comeback campaign of David's earliest musical friend and rival, Marc Bolan, in his new TV series, simply titled *Marc*.

The reunion with Marc was warm, chatty – relaxed at first, for what was their second meeting that year. In the spring, Marc had been chubby and pasty, thanks to his brandy and cocaine diet – 'people used to call him the glam chipolata', says Marc's PR and confidant, Keith Altham – but a brief reunion with David back in March had helped rebuild his confidence. Marc had played Altham an acetate of 'Madman', a song the pair had recorded together: 'It was avant-garde, quite Eno-ish,' says Altham, 'and Marc said they were going to work on it together as a single. Though you never knew if there was any foundation to some of Marc's stories.'

Since that meeting, though, Marc had been through 'a wonderful, hard-working summer', says his friend Jeff Dexter, who was business partners with Bolan's manager, Tony Howard. Marc cut out the cocaine and booze, instead staying in his room writing, going out in the evening to tap into the vibe of London's punk scene, many of whose leading lights were featured on his show, which was filmed at Granada's Manchester studios and launched on 24 August, 1977. Marc oversaw every aspect of each programme, choosing guests including Generation X, The Boomtown Rats and The Jam, introducing each of them, and playing three or four songs of his own with the latest line-up of T. Rex. Throughout the series 'everything was on a high', according to Dexter. 'And then we came to the last one in the series. The one with David.'

The two men's conversation was affectionate; the only awkward moment was when it turned out David hadn't brought a guitar. Marc handed him a vintage Fender Stratocaster, insisting a little too anxiously that David keep the valuable instrument, still intent on playing the role of wealthy, gracious superstar. Marc's new band was essentially David's old band – Tony Newman and Herbie Flowers – and were greeted like long-lost friends; Jeff Dexter, too, was happy to see his fellow Buddhist and UFO-spotter from the Redington Road days.

Jeff left the studio to pick up Tony Howard, confident the afternoon's show would be a fitting finale to Marc's series. Things began to fall apart soon after Jeff's exit. Anxious to put Bowie at ease, Bolan had asked his own guitar roadie, Cliff Wright, to attend to his guest. 'They all got on OK, absolutely, it was old buddies,' says Wright. 'David was chatting with Herbie and Tony, they'd discussed the new song. And then it became apparent that Marc wasn't going to play on "Heroes".'

This would be the song's TV debut and David, reasonably enough, insisted on overseeing the backing track, sitting down and playing the guitar part himself, as Flowers and Newman picked up the song straight away, playing in a folky, almost Velvets style. 'David just sat on a chair, and somehow got that feedback, it was really cool,' says Wright. 'Herbie and Tony were the kind of players who could pick up the song straight away, Marc's guitar wouldn't have suited – [but] I suppose he wanted to be on TV playing it.'

As the musicians swiftly assembled the backing track, Marc mulled over what he considered a snub; looking 'miffed', he asked Wright to fetch four bottles of wine for David, then retired to his own dressing room – with some of the bottles. 'And he stayed in there,' says Wright. 'He felt he'd been blanked.'

Sitting in his dressing room, Marc got 'a little bit worse for wear', says a staff member. There was worse in store for his fragile ego, as Jeff Dexter discovered. On his return to the studio, accompanied by Tony Howard, Dexter found his way blocked by a burly figure, who informed him, 'You can't come in. This is a closed set.'

After insisting, 'This is our session, and no one's closed it,' Dexter managed to gain entrance, only to find the union floor manager complaining he'd been banned from his own set – the entire studio had been over-run by David's security. Keith Altham, who'd brought journalist Chris Welch down to cover the show, managed to get in, only to find 'there was some daft woman throwing her weight around, upsetting people, being really obnoxious, and this heavy-handed bunch trying to get everyone out. And it was Marc's show!'

Welch hid behind a pillar and watched as Coco Schwab, an RCA executive and other members of Bowie's entourage argued with the crew, Tony Howard, Altham and others. David, occupied with the music, hadn't noticed what was going on. But as the time for the pair came to record their own appearances over the backing tracks, the scene was ugly, says Dexter: 'Right before they went on, both of them were upset, Marc particularly, he was in tears.'

With the programme now running late, David and Marc each taped their own vocal overdub before they tackled a jam they'd worked on earlier. Marc looked slightly forlorn as he introduced 'a new song' in his familiar camp murmur, before the band launched into a chunky riff copped from Bo Diddley's 'Road Runner', with David on Strat and Elvis shades. As Bowie slinks up to the mic and sings 'what can I do' there's a sudden flurry in the corner of the screen, a hand grasping a microphone, a confused smile and a streak of curly hair as Marc Bolan attempts to stand on a monitor wedge, misses, falls off the stage and out of the picture. As the band shudders to a halt, the camera zooms to Bowie's grin, and the credits roll.

Some of the cast members of *Coronation Street*, who'd arrived to record their own show, looked on at Marc as he laughed and picked himself up. Then the union crew, riled by the confrontation with Bowie's minders, refused to go into overtime and reshoot. This would be the last public appearance that Marc Bolan would ever make. 'It was a really shameful end,' says Dexter. 'The whole of that summer we'd been working on the show, making sure they were as good as they could be. It was very sad. I was very affected by it.'

On the train back to London, Bowie was low-key and cheery, chatting happily to the very people, like Keith Altham, that his own security had tried to eject from the studio. 'You must read this book by Kurt Vonnegut, you won't regret it,' he told him, showing him his copy of *Cat's Cradle*. 'He wasn't heavy at all, once you took him away from this suffocating protection,' says Altham. Back in Manchester, there was a hurried, miserable debrief with producer Muriel Young about the fate of the programme, before Bolan, Howard and Dexter returned to London. Later that night, says Tony Visconti, Marc and David went out to dinner and made up their quarrel.

The heavy-handedness that had overshadowed Bolan's show was an example of behaviour that would soon become commonplace in the music industry. For writers like Chris Welch, who'd championed Bowie a decade before, 'It was new in pop terms – that distancing. Mick Jagger would have still been going around on the subway back then; David set this entourage to create a vibe. Really it's just a way to draw attention to yourself.' It was ironic that, having decried the hype of the MainMan years, David would unwittingly replicate the same heavy behaviour.

In this respect, as in so many others, David would establish a new convention. Those who followed in his wake – Madonna, Prince – also employed a protective screen of minders to shield both their person and their image. To this day, friends who send David Bowie packages of photos or records might find they'd been edited or censored, with seemingly random items removed before they reach him. Such behaviour saves time for a busy man, and there were many occasions in the future where David would venture out without minders. But from this period onwards, much of David's reality – the sensory input of people, communications, ideas – would be filtered by other people. His life had changed, irrevocably. At thirty, he'd grown up; that earnest, child-like quality had dissipated, for he was too savvy to attempt to prolong it. And there was a powerful reminder of his mortality to come.

The kerfuffle around the *Marc* show would have been a passing concern, but for the fact that by the time it was broadcast, David's friend and rival was dead. Marc enjoyed a happy, quiet week after the taping of his show, but when girlfriend Gloria Jones returned from America, he stayed up drinking into the small hours at the Speakeasy and then Morton's restaurant on 15 September. Marc had never learned to drive; it was Gloria who took the wheel of the purple Mini GT, which crashed into a tree on the south side of Barnes Common, around 5 a.m. Gloria was badly injured, her jaw broken and foot trapped beneath the Mini's engine, but it was the left side that took the full force of the collision, with Marc's seat crushed into the back of the vehicle. He was killed instantly.

David was devastated by Marc's death. He would be one of the highest-profile stars at Marc's funeral in Golders Green, joined by Tony Visconti and wife Mary Hopkin, Rod Stewart and The Damned. David would pay endless tributes to his friend and there would never be any doubt of his affection for the teenager with whom he'd fished for clothes in Carnaby Street, twelve years before.

Their final appearance together had typified their relationship of interlaced respect and rivalry. It was also a stark illustration of how, where Bolan had rested on his laurels or simply repeated himself, David had now spent a dozen years relentlessly pushing himself forward. With Bolan's life over, it was more obvious than ever that David had won the race for fame they'd both embarked on. It was also more obvious than ever that, despite the companions he'd acquired in Berlin, David was now quite alone.

17

I Am Not a Freak

He just had a tacky T-shirt, a pair of jeans and a cardboard
suitcase. It was the most horrible, horrible life.

Ken Ruta

1977 had been a joyful year, but it was a strange kind of joy, one many people wouldn't recognise. As a teenager, David had avoided proper work, but now it was more obvious than ever that as an adult he enjoyed the worthiness of studying, of good old Yorkshire graft. He'd dug deep into his reserves of psychic stamina during the Spiders era, with compelling results, but this second creative streak was arguably even more impressive. There would never be another twelve months in Bowie's life as productive as those that stretched from the summer of 1976 to the summer of 1977, months in which he recorded four landmark albums: *The Idiot*, *Low*, *Lust for Life* and *"Heroes"*, all of which would have a huge effect on the musical landscape. David knew the significance of these albums – he was filled with 'a special kind of optimism' over that time, as Tony Visconti and others recall, in words filled with a kind of nostalgia. Yet even as he immersed himself in work, David was filled with a sense that this special period wouldn't last.

He had always moved on briskly when he sensed his musicians had nothing more to offer him. Yet he was even more ruthless with himself; and even as he came to the last of his Berlin albums, he was dismantling the lifestyle that gave birth to them.

Immediately after the release of *"Heroes"*, David embarked on an old-school publicity blitz. The single itself was released in three languages, evoking the carefree early days of The Beatles, and David's promotion of the record took him to Rome, Amsterdam, Paris and London and even, in September, to the Elstree TV studios just outside of London, where venerable crooner Bing Crosby was recording a Christmas special for ITV. Swapping scripted jokes before duetting on 'Little Drummer Boy', looking clean-cut and healthy, David seemed strikingly similar to the twenty-two-year-old who'd camped around on Malcolm Thomson's promotional film, back in 1969. But while the dialogue seemed fake, the jokey pleasantries and the engaging politeness were genuine. Many of those who encountered him over those weeks were put off their stride to find that David, while serious, was easygoing and pliant, not the assertive, rather megalomaniacal creature on display early in 1976. He retained his equilibrium even when faced with the most ludicrous questions, like that posed by radio interviewer John Tobler, in January 1978. Tobler pointed out that, with Bing Crosby's death in November, plus Marc Bolan's tragic accident back in September, David's most recent collaborators had both died soon after working with him. 'Do you see anything sinister in that?' Tobler enquired. 'No, I don't,' David replied with commendable restraint, before mentioning that the next act on his list – for production, not termination – was Devo. His championing of the band helped them secure a Warner Brothers deal, although time pressures meant it would be Brian Eno who produced their debut album.

In between the rounds of interviews, David spent a quiet Christmas at Hauptstrasse. Coco cooked goose for a cosy, celebratory get-together, according to the Berlin friends who attended, including Edu Meyer. But it would be their last Christmas break in Berlin, and caused a public spat with Angie, in an outburst that effectively announced their marriage was over. The exchange kicked off with Angie complaining to the *Sunday Mirror's* Tony Robinson on 8 January, 1978, that her husband had 'without my knowledge taken our son' from the Swiss house over Christmas. In fact, she'd left Zowie with Marion Skene while she visited friends in New York. 'I really want David to suffer,' she told Robinson. 'Perhaps the only way he'll suffer is if I do myself in.' Soon after the first interview, she attempted suicide by downing sleeping pills, then smashed all the glassware in the house before throwing herself down the stairs, breaking her nose. According to Robinson, Angie apparently created so much commotion at the Samaritan's hospital that the woman in the neighbouring bed, admitted after a cardiac arrest, suffered a relapse.

Just six months before, David and Angie had been happily playing pool in the Tschungle; both of them with identical haircuts and trench-coats, 'like brother and sister', says Esther Friedmann, Iggy's girlfriend. Angie's outburst in the tabloid, attacking her husband in public for the first time, was an act of war – and of desperation. It was a sign of her isolation. As one German friend put it, 'She was just helpless – she had no one on her side. We'd say "*Die Felle schwimmen weg*" – your furs are swimming away.* Everything is falling apart.' Angie blamed Coco for edging her out of her husband's life, but by now her distaste for David's music and lifestyle could not be concealed: she disliked Dostoyevsky, she detested flat caps, she even hated the food he and Iggy sampled in Berlin – 'They ate offal!' she exclaims today in disgusted tones, as if this alone explains her estrangement from her husband. Such distaste only speeded up the inevitable, given Angie's lack of interest in sublimating her own life to David's. Now, she told Robinson, 'I have to seek a divorce.'

Angie's official exit made little difference to David's romantic life. Since separating from Ava Cherry in the summer of 1975, he'd relied on Coco for many of his needs – conversation, jokes, protection and domestic neces-sities – although by now she'd moved into her own little apartment in the Hinterhof, like Iggy. In Berlin, both he and Iggy developed the habit of disappearing for a couple of days every now and then, 'going where the drugs and girls were', says a friend. 'David had his little muchachas that he would visit and Jim probably had his. Coco would wind up looking for them all over Berlin worried something had happened.'

Bowie would in future years rarely comment on his marriage to Angie; one of his most memorable observations was that the experience was 'like living with a blowtorch'. While his public criticisms were limited, his feelings about Angie eventually verged on mutual hatred; he would rarely mention her by name, and simply referred to her as 'my ex-wife'. Like Tony Defries, her role in David's rise to stardom, as well as her name, would never be mentioned again, as she was airbrushed out of his personal history. Subsequently, the gruelling intensity of life with Angie had a predictable effect on his future liaisons, which he would try and keep casual. Occasionally there'd be the odd obsession. On tour with Iggy in Vancouver, he'd become besotted with a boutique owner named Bessie – 'beautiful, African, just as striking as [David's second wife] Iman', according to Annie Apple, an old friend of Iggy's – and he'd begged her to

---

* This lovely phrase derives from leather tanners who would cure their hides in rivers. If they didn't watch them closely, they'd float away and all their work and money would be lost.

come back to Berlin with him. But after travelling on with him to Seattle, she'd been disturbed by the manic intensity that surrounded David; even eating at a Shakey's Pizza Parlour in the suburbs, Bessie noticed how fans would steal his cigarette butts. Two days of this was thrilling, but the idea of more sounded horrific. Shortly afterwards David would date another striking black woman, an ex-girlfriend of Shep Gordon's who stayed with him in Vevey for a few days before being sent back home. Towards the end of the year, David briefly dated Bianca Jagger – then still married to Mick – with the kind of exaggerated secrecy that ensured the news spread far and wide. They made an attractive couple, but David's courtship of her didn't outlast the forthcoming tour.

Instead, during his last months in Hauptstrasse, away from his tour entourage, David revelled in dressing anonymously, spending time with Zowie, still wandering down to the Kreuzberg clubs, smoking his way through three packs of Gitanes a day, but also cycling on his Raleigh to 'pretty normal places, talking about life and the books he was reading', says Tangerine Dream drummer Klaus Krüger – whom David called up that spring, asking him if he'd like to join Iggy's band, shortly after Iggy had given the Sales brothers their marching orders.

At the end of January, 1978, David started work on the movie that constituted his farewell to Berlin. *Just a Gigolo* was the brainchild of David Hemmings, the *Blow Up* star's second movie as a director. David was at first enthused by the production, which embodied many of his Berlin obsessions and was filmed around his regular haunts, including Café Wien. Hemmings had secured a remarkable coup, which helped draw David into the venture, by signing up Marlene Dietrich for her first film in eighteen years. David had spent hours in Berlin, chatting to antique-store owners who'd known the reclusive star back in the day; the prospect of meeting her was an intrinsic part of the movie's appeal.

Hemmings was ebullient and easygoing – his catchphrase was 'not too shabby, not too shabby' – and David told friends he bonded more with the old-fashioned, hard-drinking luvvie than he had with the more intellectual Nic Roeg. But it wasn't long before the shoot started to go awry. During a celebratory dinner with Bowie, other crew members, Iggy and Esther Friedmann, Hemmings went missing. 'Something weird happened,' says Friedmann. '[Hemmings] went somewhere and never came back, people were looking all over. And then David never got to meet Marlene. It turned out instead of acting with her, he was acting with a chair.'

Hemmings explained later that Dietrich's brief appearance in the movie would be filmed in Paris; her half of the exchange with David was filmed in a set recreating the Café Wien, intercut with his lines, delivered back in Berlin. The scene – like the movie – was disjointed and irredeemably stilted; still, from today's perspective, the movie is a poignant last glimpse of the great German star, while David manages to look fetching, carrying a pig.

The fate of *Just a Gigolo* would typify David's cinematic career, which was more successful than those of rock-star rivals like Jagger and Sting, but never came close to justifying his new job description, which he announced that year was 'generalist' – a term obviously influenced by, but lacking the charm of, Eno's 'non-musician' tag. Picking out a decent script was a crapshoot in which David would never quite beat the odds – and as Hemmings' problems mounted, with finance problems and negative reactions to his first edits all publicised in the movie press, the prospect of David's own biggest tour to date provided a welcome distraction.

Ranging across four continents, with seventy-eight dates, many of them in huge stadia, the *Isolar II* tour would put the flakey, stressful zigzagging improvisation of the Ziggy era to shame. The show was an ambitious, futuristic epic, showcasing the largely electronic soundscapes of *Low* and *"Heroes"*, but it drew deep on David's musical history. Clothes designer Natasha Korniloff was a friend from the Lindsay Kemp troupe; guitarist Adrian Belew was snaffled from Frank Zappa's band. Violinist Simon House had hung out with David and Hermione in 1968 and played in High Tide with Tony Hill, David's guitarist from Turquoise. Pianist Sean Mayes met David through the band Fumble, who'd rehearsed alongside him at Underhill and supported David for March 1973's *Aladdin Sane* tour. Keyboardist Roger Powell came from Todd Rundgren's Utopia; the four joined Bowie stalwarts Alomar, Dennis Davis and George Murray.

Carlos had spent six days running the band through a set based on *Low* and *"Heroes"* – brandishing a baton, like a classical conductor, for 'Warszawa' – at the Showco soundstage in Dallas before David arrived on 19 March after a brief holiday in Kenya and suggested they work up a sequence of Ziggy songs. The seven-piece outfit was competent, not too polished, with Mayes' stomping piano adding a vital roughness for a string of shows that were rapturously received.

Over the three months, the shows settled into a predictable routine. Each night there'd be the desperate race for a good restaurant, or a club that was still open – Sean Mayes often acted as pathfinder, seeking out gay clubs where David or the others could arrive later. Whereas at the time of *Station to Station* the cavalcade had centred around Iggy and David, now Carlos acted as the head of household, with David quiet and humorous but rather distant. Meanwhile, business tensions seemed to fizz around the margins of the little crew, between Coco and Pat Gibbons, or Pat and road manager Eric Barrett – a seasoned pro, famous for his work with Hendrix. The tensions weren't helped by what Simon House remembers as 'mountains of blow'. David rarely participated, although on one memorable occasion in Paris on 24 May, he stayed up for a twenty-hour coke bender after the first show; no one in the band saw him until shortly before the second night's performance. Simon House was chatting in the doorway of a dressing room when he sensed what felt like a kind of psychic vibration behind him. Turning round, he saw the singer, pale and clammy, his whole demeanour transformed – but that night's performance was storming.

It was on stage that the disparate English and American band-members truly came together; an hour and a half of bliss, punctuated by musical communiqués or jokes. Dennis Davis was the key perpetrator, on-stage and off; often he'd attempt to render the whole band helpless on-stage by, for instance, playing a hugely extended drum fill, rolling over every drum in his kit in turn in a kind of mad extended rhythmic monologue that would crease them all up. (Off-stage, he was much the same, taking the mic whenever they were on the bus and delivering a mad, surreal, pseudo tour-guide commentary.) David loved it; he seemed to relish the vibrancy of his band, who would, in turn, occasion-ally watch him, hypnotised by the spectacle. David retained a distance from his musicians – Sean Mayes referred to him as 'his Lordship' – but even today there's a kind of loving fondness in their descriptions of sharing a stage with him: 'He has some power,' says House. 'An aura that helps you transmit to thousands or millions of people. Freddie Mercury had it too. Maybe it's just that they wrote these colossal songs. But the music was always the one good thing on this tour.'

Adrian Belew shared with House the sense that Bowie was 'some-what troubled. Maybe he was still doing some drugs, I don't know, maybe he was tired. I remember him overall as amazing to be around, but I did have a sense he was riding through it, not totally happy.'

Simon House's memories of the tour are much darker, for reasons unconnected with David. The violinist's partner, Sue, was ill with Huntington's disease. Her plight was all the more sad, for she wouldn't acknowledge the problem which eventually left her hospitalised, and insisted on joining the tour. The illness manifests itself in varying guises;

in her case, she'd act as if aggressive or drunk, causing so much racket in Tokyo that the hotel called the police. David, not unreasonably, got upset if he saw Sue while on stage. It made House feel like an outcast. Worse, Bowie didn't address the issue directly so House couldn't even explain Sue's illness first-hand. In those situations, as with most issues, it was Carlos Alomar who brought an almost spiritual, soothing attitude. 'Carlos is a psychologist, a spiritualist, one of the most charming people in the world,' says House. 'We got on really well; I wouldn't have enjoyed the tour without him. He was the one would distract from the problems.'

On the *Station to Station* tour, there was always the sense that David was head of a family; this time around, it seemed that he was head of a business empire. Coco and Pat Gibbons formed the nucleus of Isolar, David's management company, which changed in form over the next few years, but would always have David at its apex. In those early days, the fact that David effectively managed himself marked him out as a maverick; but that would change. The beginnings of the realisation that he was a businessman, as well as an artist, came with the announcement that he would release a live album, recorded primarily in Philadelphia, while the tour was still rolling across Japan. The double album was intended both to scupper the efforts of bootleggers and count towards David's RCA obligation. The album's financial motivations were undoubtedly too obvious – Jon Savage of *Sounds* epitomised the reaction when he described *Stage* as 'a combined summing-up, money-making and time-gaining device' – but the audacity of the live show was obvious, too, even in the album's first version, released with its tracks sliced and diced into chronological order.

By the time *Stage* was released on 8 September, 1978, David was using a short break from his tour to work on the third album in a trilogy that he'd announced back in January. Trilogies, even when rebranded as 'triptychs', as David called this set, risk outstaying their welcome, and *Lodger,* for all the randomness involved in its recording, lacked the sense of risk and excitement that had pervaded *Low* and *"Heroes"*. Some of that was down to the location: Mountain Studio in Montreux was carpeted, comfortable and bland compared to the edgy, unsettling vibe of Hansa. To the session stalwarts, like Carlos Alomar, *Lodger* was a more intellectual, less inspired affair than *"Heroes"*.

For the previous album, Eno had used some of his Oblique Strategy techniques on the instrumental side, notably 'Sense of Doubt'. On this project – working title *Planned Accidents* – they were used for the band tracks, most memorably in an exercise where Brian would point randomly at a chord chart on a wall and ask the musicians to play them. 'And then I'm like, This is not going to substitute for a group chord chart which I can write,' says Alomar, 'and this experiment is stupid.'

'It sounded terrible,' says House. 'Carlos did have a problem, simply because he's very gifted and professional [and] he can't bring himself to play stuff that sounds like crap.'

David encouraged the reluctant guitarist – 'Come on fellas, play along!' – although the experiment was ultimately abandoned. It was indeed 'not Brian's finest idea', according to Tony Visconti. Carlos does admit that on other occasions, Eno's Oblique Strategy cards, which instructed random actions in order to bypass creative blocks, worked as theorised. 'One time Brian asked me something and I was blocked because I didn't understand what he wanted,' says Alomar. 'Then one of the cards said something like, "Remember those silent moments," and then another said, "Think like a gardener." Some kind of eclectic, weird reference. It worked – or let's say you find yourself accepting it. I would have chosen other things to play – but in hindsight it was fun.'

House was one of the few musicians who had played with Eno outside of Bowie – they'd recorded together on Robert Calvert's solo album – and loved Eno's creativity: 'He's always got an idea, is always on the case.' But on this project he thought that Eno's inspiration was ebbing away – and that the prime reason for his own use of Oblique Strategies was to cope with his own artistic block, not the musicians'.

Eno's preference seemed to be to experiment almost endlessly, and on this session it was Bowie who showed decisiveness, seizing on one idea to keep things moving, impatiently overseeing the last few days when the real creativity took place. The real beauty of the album came from the way that random ideas were scattered like confetti over ordinary (and in some cases, repeated) chord structures: Adrian Belew's brilliantly warped guitar on 'Boys Keep Swinging', for which the band all switched to unfamiliar instruments, a trick David and Carlos had first tried on *Lust for Life*; House's Byzantine violin, which influenced the Turkish vibe of 'Yassassin', or the twisted interplay of Alomar's guitar and Visconti's swooping strings on 'DJ'. One night Visconti downed a bottle of Tequila and wrote out an arrangement for three mandolins, which became 'Fantastic Voyage'. 'It was a beautiful moment,' says House, who played the part along with Belew and Visconti.

Once the frustrations of the first few days were over, with the basic tracks montaged from tape edits, the recording sessions were blissful. The songs were sculpted into shape in the setting of an idyllic Indian summer, during which the musicians basked in the gorgeous view over Lake Geneva and enjoyed chats with Eugene Chaplin, Charlie's grandson, who'd bring over trays of beer. 'It was a perfect fortnight,' says House. 'Although the music didn't ever perfectly gel.' The violinist had high standards, though, for he considered *Low* and *"Heroes"* perfect albums, which couldn't be bettered.

Adrian Belew arrived at a later stage of the recording, once the backing tracks had been edited into shape. He was warmed up with a compliment first. 'I walked in, and David, Brian and Tony are all smiling, like they've a shared secret. Soon I ask, "What's going on?" And they said, "When we did all the tracks with Robert Fripp for *"Heroes"* we did them as composite tracks. We took something from each take, edited it all together to make something that was impossible to play. And you didn't know that, and you played it all live!"'

The trio were buttering him up; knowing he had played the impossible, he was expected to deliver the same on the session. Belew was sent upstairs to the recording room, where Bowie, Eno and Visconti watched him through a closed-circuit TV camera, while the guitarist's only contact with the outside world were the instructions that came over his headphones.

Belew had only just plugged in his Fender Stratocaster when he heard someone tell him: 'The drummer will go 1, 2, 3, then you come in.'

'What key is it?' he asked anxiously.

'Don't worry about the key,' he was told. 'Just play!'

There were maybe three passes at the music, which arrived in a torrent over his headphones, then he was told that was it. As the recording went on, that became the pattern: three goes at each song, with the resulting parts edited into one composite track. 'When I heard the final versions, I had no memory of how I came up with these parts. And meanwhile they're going, "This is the first time this guy has been in a recording studio!"' Today, Belew can't remember how any of the individual songs came about, bar 'Boys Keep Swinging', where they told him that Carlos was playing drums. 'It was like a freight train coming through my mind,' he says of his now celebrated solo. 'I just had to cling on.'

Completed in March 1979 at New York's Power Plant, *Lodger* would meet with a respectful, slightly subdued reception on its release in May. Visconti blamed the lack of enthusiasm on a rushed mix. Much of the instrumentation did indeed sound thin next to the ebullient clatter of *"Heroes"*; the same applied to the emotional content, for where its two predecessors were deep, *Lodger* was restless and quirky. The album would attract admiration rather than visceral love or hatred, but its art-rock intellectualism sat neatly alongside emerging bands like Talking Heads – produced by Brian Eno over the same timeframe – or New Romantic bands like Spandau Ballet, whose Germanic name, sound and peg-leg pants were all based on the 1978-model David Bowie.

After the break for the main *Lodger* sessions in September, the tour continued through Australia and Japan. For Belew in particular, the experience was one of the most fulfilling in his career: 'We got to Japan and it was amazing, like the stratosphere of super-fame.' Seven months of touring with David 'really propelled me into being the guitarist I became. He was the first person to give me the freedom to go and explore, in front of 20,000 people. When you have that scenario, you almost transcend yourself – you dig deep and find stuff you didn't know was there. I was on a permanent high.'

Lodger enjoyed a decent chart run, reaching number four in the UK and number twenty in the US, but for all the slackening in his chart momentum, David was positioned perfectly, alongside Eno, as a patron of the late seventies New Wave. Now in his thirties, he seemed to be moving on more quickly, from album to album, than he had in his twenties – and the impressiveness of his achievement was underlined, if it needed to be, by the fate of the two men who were his closest peers as patrons of the New Wave, namely Lou Reed and Iggy Pop.

After the triumph of *Transformer*, and its densely wrought, emotionally gruelling successor *Berlin*, Lou's music had spiralled into self-parody with *Coney Island Baby* and *Rock and Roll Heart*. Reed was short of ideas and money, and by his spring 1979 European tour he was drinking his way through two pints of Scotch every three days, swigged straight from the bottle.

Lou and David had met only occasionally since the MainMan days, but an air of excitement bubbled around Lou and his band in April 1979, when they heard David would be showing up at Lou's Hammersmith Odeon date. The show was a mess. Seeing David sitting on an amplifier case at the side of the stage, Lou started screaming at his musicians and switched the set around. But once he made it through to the last number Lou was ebullient, overjoyed to see his friend. The pair hugged each other at the side of the stage, Lou running his hands lovingly through

David's hair, before the pair climbed into the tour bus, then set off in search of a restaurant.

The dishes were on the table at the Chelsea Rendezvous, when an infamous spat broke out. Lou was flanked by his girlfriend Sylvia; David by another woman and Lou's guitarist Chuck Hammer, who heard Lou ask David if he would produce his next album.

'Yes,' David agreed, 'if you clean up your act.'

Lou slapped David across the face, hard, once on each cheek, screaming, 'Don't you *ever* say that to me! *Never* say that to me!' Lou's manager, Eric Kronfeld, wrestled him away, and for a few minutes peace resumed, until suddenly Lou slapped David again. This time David's bodyguards pulled them apart, and within seconds, Lou and his party were bundled out of the restaurant.

The fracas, witnessed by an astonished Allan Jones of *Melody Maker* and Giovanni Dadamo of *Sounds*, would feature in the respective music weeklies, but neither writer saw the next act of the drama. An hour or two later, Reed's band were back at the hotel and guitarist Chuck Hammer was on the phone, describing the night's events to a friend. Suddenly he heard footsteps in the corridor outside, the sound of fists hammering on a neighbouring door and then shouts of 'Come on Lou – I know you're in there!'

For perhaps the first time in his life since being clocked in the eye by George Underwood, the man who had proclaimed he was 'not much cop at punching' in 'Kooks' was attempting to pick a fight. But the dark prince of New York decadence, if he was in his room (no one found out), remained cowering under his duvet, and after a few more minutes of stomping up and down the hall, David left the building.

Even a month later, when David told Iggy and girlfriend Esther Friedmann about the fight, he was still 'devastated', remembers Friedmann. The incident showed the pitfalls of helping out people you admired. Relations with Iggy, too, were strained. The ex-Stooge had managed one fairly successful album, *New Values*, under his own steam, but since then he'd been growing increasingly depressed. David and Coco had attempted to help, taking him and Esther on holiday with them, including a trip to Kenya, 'but sometimes when people are good to you it's worse', says Friedmann.

By September 1979 Iggy was in a bad way; marooned in a residential studio in Wales, lost in a haze of dope and booze, and seemingly unable to finish the follow-up to *New Values* on his new label, Arista. David drove out, with Coco, to help, cheering up Iggy and the musicians with a long monologue on Johnny Binden, the gangster, hanger-on and owner of a legendarily huge cock which he'd displayed to David's former MainMain stablemate Dana Gillespie and Princess Margaret, among others, on Mustique. The story ended up being turned into a song, 'Play it Safe'. Bowie was dauntingly impressive – 'like a creative playmaster', says keyboard player Barry Andrews – but his visit seemed to highlight Iggy's failure at finding his way through the corporate maze. Both men shared similar demons – egotism, jealousy and a tendency for a kind of musical post-natal depression, once they'd completed a project – but David's competitive nature always inspired him to bounce back with a characteristic zest.

That competitiveness would add a satisfying edge to David's next project, for as Lou Reed hit an artistic block on his next album, *Growing Up in Public* – leaving most of the music to collaborator Michael Fonfara and writing the lyrics drunk, by the studio pool – David was schmoozing Lou's guitarist, Chuck Hammer. 'Lou had really been an asshole [in London],' says Hammer, 'and I was really impressed by David. He was just the perfect gentleman. But I always wondered, later on, if David was trying at get back at Lou, trying to break up his band a little bit.'

Hammer would become a key contributor to what many Bowie fans would regard as their hero's last truly great album. There's much justification for that view, for *Scary Monsters* still sparkles today. Its intense, churning grooves sound remarkably contemporary – in retrospect, it's the obvious source of Blur's angular rock attack from *Park Life* onwards – but despite the complexity of its arrangements, there are many moments of unaffected simplicity.

In a signal that it was a move on from his European albums, *Scary Monsters* was recorded mostly at New York's Power Station, widely regarded as the best-sounding American studio of its time. But for the first time since Ziggy's nod to fifties rock 'n' roll, the album also looked back, both at Bowie's own career and at the 'New Wave kids' who were coming up behind him.

Popular folklore has it that Bowie was intent on scoring a hit record. Certainly that's the impression that Chuck Hammer got, for he arrived to witness a much more focused, almost conventional work ethic compared to the last Eno collaboration. Although now an established artist, David was still recognisably the confident, punctual young buck remembered by teenage friends like The Manish Boys. For the recording David, sporting a moustache, dressed in a full-length leather coat and Japanese sandals, brandished a clip-board, on which he'd tick off items on a

musical 'to do' list. Just as in the Iggy sessions, he was entertaining, with
that trademark flirtatious jokiness, but with a formidable sense of focus.
Tony Visconti was almost scarily 'on it', recording and planning ahead
at the same time. 'They were an absolutely unified team,' says Hammer,
'really impressively organised, there was no chaos – but it was very
relaxed and creative, too.'

Hammer was called in primarily to work on a song titled 'People Are
Turning to Gold'. He had been working on a new technique of building
up synthesised layers, which he called Guitarchitecture, and had sent a
tape of his experiments to Bowie. As he worked on the song, which as
yet had no lyrics, he quickly added distinctive 'choir' parts to the chorus,
before moving on to 'Teenage Wildlife' and the gospelly 'Up the Hill
Backwards' (the latter part didn't made the cut, being replaced by Robert
Fripp's superb, frenzied electric guitar). 'Chuck was very experimental
for us, it was 50/50 whether he would make the cut,' says Visconti, but
as so often, Bowie drew out an inspiring performance from the young
guitarist, to offset the conventional electric guitar parts which Robert
Fripp would record a few days later for the rest of the album. Bowie
would wait another two months before writing lyrics for the song, finally
naming it 'Ashes to Ashes': 'We did love it immensely, and knew it was
one of the major tracks,' says Visconti.

For all the arresting sonic effects laced through 'Ashes to Ashes', it was
the song's melodic inventiveness that underpinned its success: it represented a return to David's old-fashioned songwriting, with a swooping
melody in the verse, and one of his characteristic pre-verse digressions –
'the shriek of nothing is killing me' – as well as a conventional, but
gorgeous middle eight, which even seemed, with its 'never done anything out of the blue', to address the age-old criticism of David that
he was premeditated and calculating.

As a UK number one single, 'Ashes to Ashes' seemed to signal that
Bowie would dominate the 1980s as convincingly as he had the seventies. For the video, an intrinsic part of the single's eventual success, he
commandeered the Blitz club scene – a scene which, of course, took
Bowie's style as a template. In what was one of the first instances of him
interacting with a new generation of artists whom he'd influenced, he
was again the epitome of charm, dropping in for an evening with the
club's host Steve Strange, then inviting him to the next day's 6 a.m. trip
to Southend for the celebrated video shoot, which reprised the Pierrot
style of Lindsay Kemp, again with a costume designed by Natasha
Korniloff. Now thirty-three, he was relaxed, sociable – and, says Steve

Strange with pride, 'when he snogged me, I got some tongue, too'. If David did intend to get back at Lou Reed, he must have considered two-timing him with his guitarist, and scoring a number one in the process, had put him in his place.

For all those involved, the eventual success of *Scary Monsters* was a poignant one. Even as a host of groups copied *Scary Monsters'* gritty electro-funk mélange, most of those responsible, including drummer Dennis Davis and bassist George Murray, were looking for new jobs. But for a brief session in Berlin, Tony Visconti would not work with David again for another twenty-one years. 'It is one of my favourite Bowie albums ever,' the producer points out. 'I considered it going out on a high note.'

For David, the album marked a happy change of setting; he had never officially left Berlin, but he was fired up by his return to New York, where he could hang with a younger generation of arty New Wavers, and also resumed his friendship with John and Yoko, under happier, more relaxed circumstances for both of them. John's respect for David had only increased with the success of 'Fame', which had put the ex-Beatle back in the charts. David still considered John, alongside Mick Jagger, as his closest role model, but his admiration for John was not intermixed with rivalry, as it was with Mick. Lennon brought out a better side of David, and he knew it. Happily, John had started writing again. David admired the unique lifestyle he'd carved out, based around his and Yoko's elegant, white-carpeted, minimally furnished apartment in The Dakota, by Central Park, where John and Yoko could wander, undisturbed.

As David was finishing what would become an enduring classic, he was starting work on another, more transient triumph. The *Scary Monsters* sessions were in full flow when he took a call from Jack Hofsiss, direc-tor of *The Elephant Man*, the play based on the life of Joseph Merrick, which David had seen in New York back in February. Hofsiss needed a replacement for Philip Anglim, who was quitting the title role. Bowie had been bowled over by the play; given just twenty-four hours to make his decision, he agreed to take on the part.

David spent time rehearsing with Hofsiss one-on-one before the cast convened for a fortnight of intensive work in San Francisco. His recruit-ment was quintessential celebrity casting, of the kind still practised today, so when David arrived at the Geary Theater the suspicion might have been that Bowie's fellow actors would have resented being upstaged by an upstart rock 'n' roller. Especially Ken Ruta – stalwart of the American Conservatory Theatre, admirer of Gielgud and Tennessee Williams – who would play opposite him night after night as Doctor Frederick Treves, Merrick's friend and benefactor. But Ruta is unequivocal about his leading man. 'He was incredible. Right on the money.'

As one listens to the recollections of *The Elephant Man* cast, echoes abound of David's time on the road with the Lindsay Kemp company, a dozen years before. Back then, Kemp points out, 'he was not starry at all, by God no.' Ruta is similarly emphatic: 'He was absolutely not a show-off,' an opinion shared by co-star Jeanette Landis. 'He was a very pure actor. In fact, more professional than the actor he replaced.'

For just a few months, the setting echoed Bowie's late teens, when he was soaking up experiences as part of Kemp's tiny crew. With his upbringing among the imposing Victorian edifices of Brixton, or The Lower Third's performances alongside the bearded lady side-shows of Margate, Bowie was well aware that the England that fêted and mocked Merrick still existed. Before rehearsals, David had visited the London Hospital to examine Merrick's bones and the poignant cardboard church he'd constructed, which – in grander form – is a centrepiece of the play, a symbol of Merrick's yearning for beauty and peace. Most of the actors in the play, including David, shared a sympathy for Merrick, heightened by the presence in the audience of people who sufferred from his condition. What they didn't expect was to see such startling parallels between the life of Merrick, circus freak, and that of their leading man.

Parts of David's routine were conventional. On a Sunday, he'd buy the *New York Times* and carefully read through the book reviews. Then, later in the week, he'd lay each of the books that had received raves out on a table in front of him; soon he would have read all of them. At the end of each week, there'd be a modest present, a token of affection, to his fellow actors. 'It depended on your taste in diversion,' says Ruta. 'I usually got a nice bottle of red wine.' Some days, once the play opened in Denver, he'd walk down to a little milk bar he'd found, just to relax or dance with some younger company.

He seemed to master the routine on stage easily, too. At first, there were plenty of little lapses, none of which affected the flow. 'He hadn't acted on a stage, so the acting technique wasn't completely in his control,' says Ruta, '[but], thank God, he had such an imagination, so the integrity was there. There was a basic honesty. And the best gift, to me, of any great actors is that thing about listening. That doesn't happen all the time.' It is an intriguing observation; for when making *Low*, or "*Heroes*", what else had Bowie been doing but listening – picking out sounds and making sense of them?

His fellow actors found Bowie's physical transformation into Merrick equally impressive: 'He seemed to have captured that – better than all the other ones who wanted to be glamorous. He wasn't doing glamour. He was doing Merrick,' says Jeanette Landis. When Ken Ruta later watched John Hurt play Merrick, swamped under a prosthesis, in the movie of *The Elephant Man*, he found the experience far less involving than seeing David.

Even before David's appearance, the play had been a success; US president Jimmy Carter was a fan of the book, and he and his wife had come to meet the first cast. Yet when David took over from Anglim, the upstart replacement lifted the play. 'Whatever that thing is – it was nothing that is practised or manufactured – it was there,' says Ruta. *Variety*'s review of the opening night in Denver bears out Ruta's memories of the performance. 'Bowie takes the stage with authority,' the review commented. 'Vocally, he is both quick and sensitive.'

When David had billed himself as 'the actor' on the sleeve of *Hunky Dory*, it had seemed a pretentious claim. Now he earned that title. In the nomadic world of the theatre, where actors make friendships then move on to the next production, he was a much more sympathetic figure to his colleagues, who rarely – like musicians – expect their working relationships to last. As far as the Denver and Chicago cast members were concerned, Bowie was 'a honey. Kind, good, bright, and he worked for his money.' Jeanette Landis, his leading woman, was equally impressed. 'His talent was bigger than his ego – which is rare.'

Yet there was a divide between David and the other actors. It was a divide that was hardly perceptible in the week they spent in Denver, breaking the theatre's box office record. But from the time the troupe hit Chicago on 5 August, 1980, Bowie's companions were shocked by the conditions in which he was forced to live. Like Merrick, he lived the life of a freak. 'It was fun in Denver, which was more or less the Hinterlands. In Chicago, it was scary,' says Ruta. 'Mobs of people, unrelenting.' Jeanette Landis, too, remembers, 'It was out of control.'

Within days, David was forced to travel to the Blackstone Theatre in a garbage truck, sneaking in and out of the building via a basement window. With fans stalking the city's main hotels, he stayed instead in a flat above a nearby department store. Only a couple of cast members knew its location. At one point during the run, most of his clothes were stolen: 'He just had a tacky T-shirt, a pair of jeans and a cardboard suitcase,' says Ruta. 'It was the most horrible, horrible life.'

The incessant attention from the fans, seen at close quarters, was terrifying because it was relentless. Throughout the Chicago run it would never let up. For the first time in their careers, Ruta and Landis worked closely with security guards, hired to protect the cast. In this context, Coco, seen as intrusive by so many of David's musicians, was 'a protectress', says Ruta. 'Wonderful. She took care of him.'

After the first few days, the cast would look over the first few rows as soon as they walked on stage, wondering who would be there. One night a fan left an object on the stage: 'Leave it, don't touch it,' Bowie told Ruta, as they snatched a few words in the wings. Caught up in the feverish, intimidating atmosphere, Ruta obeyed him.

Towards the end of the Chicago run, Ruta spotted one distinctive gaggle of fans in the front row. 'About six girls, all weird looking, this was before punk became crazy, all with dyed hair, all holding purses in their laps.' They were there throughout the week, for the Saturday matinee, and again for the evening performance. Then, as the actors took the curtain call at the end of the performance, all six girls rose, carrying their purses, and headed for the stage. 'It was instantaneous, they were all tackled from the sides by I don't know how many plain-clothes men. And they were carrying something in their purses, metallic – they were there to do something dirty. It was just coo-coo that night.' The girls were bundled out of the building by security and Ruta never found out their intentions, but he is convinced they had set out to scare David – or worse.

When the show transferred to New York on 23 September, 1980 – after a two-week break for rehearsals and the installation of a higher-profile supporting cast – the media frenzy intensified, and the curtain opened to a star-studded audience including Christopher Isherwood, Andy Warhol, David Hockney, Aaron Copland and David's Montreux neighbour – and supposed lover – Oona Chaplin. The New York reviews were generally effusive or respectful, and with *Scary Monsters* nestled at number one in the UK chart, and twelve in the USA, Bowie finally seemed to have reached the status of cross-cultural figurehead to which, despite too many protestations, he obviously aspired. John, Yoko, Iggy, Esther and May Pang were among the friends who pressed at the dressing-room door after the first performances, enthusing over his theatrical debut. Throughout the month, journalists from weighty tomes, from the *New York Times*, to London papers *The Times* and *Sunday Times*, queued up for their allotted fifteen minutes, invigilated by Barbara and Tim Dewitt. In several of the interviews, he extolled the anonymity of New York; like his friend John, he loved how you could walk the city unmolested. 'The most you get is, "Hi Dave, how's it going?"' he told *The Times'* Patricia Barnes.

It was 8 December, exactly two weeks after *The Times* interview appeared, that May Pang called David Bowie's Chelsea apartment to tell him she'd heard that John Lennon had been shot dead by Mark Chapman. Coco answered the phone. 'David is out, on a date,' she told May. 'Get down here, now. You shouldn't be alone.'

David arrived at the apartment around the same time as May. She remembers him screaming, 'WHAT THE HELL, WHAT THE FUCK IS GOING ON WITH THIS WORLD!' over and over, angry, devastated, numb. At times, for all of them, there were flashbacks, or momentary convictions that this was a prank, and hadn't really happened; again and again they'd tell each other, 'We have to be calm, we can't let our emotions take over.' After he'd screamed himself to a numb acceptance, David sat in front of the TV, absorbed by the news footage of distraught fans milling around The Dakota building and Central Park. He was still up when May Pang left the apartment around dawn. New York was strangely quiet as she walked home.

David played out most of the three remaining weeks of *The Elephant Man*, missing several nights. It was 'awful, just awful', he would explain two years later. 'A whole piece of my life seemed to have been taken away; a whole reason for being a singer and songwriter seemed to be removed from me. It was almost like a warning.' There were rumours, never substantiated, that Mark Chapman had attended a performance of *The Elephant Man*, or that he'd written down a list of targets which included David Bowie and Keith Richards. Whatever the truth, the murder of the one man in New York with whom he most identified left David with only one option: flight.

18

Snapshot of a Brain

I've never worked with an artist like that before or since. It was
all beautiful images. We went to people's houses that he knew
had certain things . . . it was like fact finders, treasure hunters,
conquistadores looking for gold.

Nile Rodgers

Just three years before, the main fixtures in David's life had been rock-
star buddies and *enfant terrible* artists, his main entertainment boozing
and exploring bullet-riddled hotspots. In the summer of 1981, this was
a distant memory. In its place were calm walks in the heights above Lake
Geneva, and civilised drinks with Eugene Chaplin: a cheery, relaxed
character who looked like a rather more rotund version of his celebrated
comedian father. Most novel of all, David's house resounded to the
hubbub of kids.

For several years now, Zowie's social life had revolved around making
friends with the children of musicians or studio staff, all under the devoted
care of Marion Skene, the nanny who'd taken care of him for nearly eight
years. Although Zowie had stayed with David for much of the Berlin
period, he was more than conscious of how his often absentee role affected
his son. Now, in the tiny family's last summer in the house at Corsier-
sur-Vevey, Zowie had unhindered access to his dad – and David's array
of video equipment. Later, he'd vividly recall using his father's broadcast-
quality U-Matic tape recorder, the size of a shopping trolley, for *Star Wars*
parties at which he and his friends would watch George Lucas's films,
with each film spread across two or three tapes. It was the first time the
ten-year-old had enjoyed a proper chance to make friends – although it

turned out the idyllic sojourn would be relatively brief, for David – a conventional father – later enrolled him at the notoriously spartan boarding school Gordonstoun, a favourite of English royalty.

Zowie's education was a typical example of the conservatism hidden behind David's supposedly unconventional exterior; in this respect, as in several others, he seemed to show the influence of his own father. Even in his Haddon Hall days David had surprised friends, like Mark Pritchett, when it turned out Mark had skipped a school athletics event. 'You should have gone to that – it's important,' David had admonished him. As a father, he was definitely of the 'you won't get your pudding till you've eaten your vegetables' school, but not bossy – he'd reason with Zowie, almost like he was a friend. As for real friends, they were few. Iggy would call and ask his advice, but there were no real peers David could call on when he was in the same position. Corinne was the most zealous, but eventually David came to the conclusion he didn't make friends that easily. Later in life, he'd realise that the only friends who stayed with him were those he'd known in Bromley, people like the kind, unflappable George Underwood: 'There are about half a dozen [friends] that I would think of as close in the accepted sense, i.e. would I reach out to them in a time of real crisis?' he would tell his wife Iman, many years later, reflecting on how his males friends in that group 'all go back to my teenage years'.

Isolated, but for Zowie, in Switzerland, David turned to professionals for help. His visceral, encompassing fear in the wake of Lennon's murder was 'not at all an affectation – it was real', according to those who knew him. While Keith Richards started carrying a gun, David hired a new bodyguard, this time one who was literally trained to kill. His main muscle was named Gary, an ex-Navy SEAL. It turned out that in his time with David, Gary never got to demonstrate his talent for despatching people using only a spoon or other household implement, so he'd fill in the time by running flabby, thirty-something rock musos from David's band through fitness routines between overdubs in the studio.

Next, David started to rethink every aspect of his own relationship with his fans. He found and attended a course which trained media figures on how to deal with the public: it showed how to deal with casual encounters on the street, and mapped out danger signs in letters or other communications – code-words that signified latent stalkers or killers. Stars were advised not to respond to some cues; in extreme cases, they were told to change their address.

David's own fan correspondence, it turned out, was packed with the danger signs. One such letter, from several fans writing together, opened with the typical comments about lyrics, make-up and fashion. Several letters later, his correspondents had progressed to informing him of a friend's death – 'We don't blame you,' they informed him. When David showed the letter to his advisers, they told him to move house.

David's new-found awareness of his own mortality not only inspired him to spend more time with Zowie, he also re-established contact with his own mother. He and Peggy stayed together over Christmas 1980, and remained in regular contact from then on. 'I've gotten closer to her,' he remarked later. 'I think the recognition of the frailty of age makes one more sympathetic to the earlier strains of the parent–child relationship.' In contrast, Zowie's interaction with Angie was limited. David and Angie had fought a lengthy battle through the Swiss courts, with Angie represented by celebrated 'palimony' lawyer Marvin Mitchelson, who later claimed to have climbed a Swiss mountain in pursuit of Bowie. It was a tough case, with witnesses like Marion Skene testifying to Angie's maternal shortcomings. Faced with such opposition, Mitchelson secured a settlement of just $700,000 when the divorce was finalised in February 1980: a derisory figure from today's perspective for a woman who was undoubtedly crucial to the creation of Ziggy. Once a ten-year gagging order on discussing the divorce had expired, Angie blamed Corinne for most of her troubles, accusing Schwab of first floating the notion of a move to Switzerland, so David could take advantage of its sexist legal regime.

Angie's anger at Coco seemed to outweigh her grief at losing Zowie, for her contact with him was limited by the terms of the settlement. The years following her divorce were torrid ones. By 1983, twelve-year-old Zowie had taken the name Joey, and in the summer of 1984, after staying with Angie and boyfriend Drew Blood at their Lower East Side tenement, he decided to break off contact with his mother. Angie blamed David – 'he used his millions to poison Zowie against me' – but Tony Zanetta, who was there for Joey and Marion Skene's visit over a sweltering New York summer, witnessed messy scenes culminating in a screaming match. 'It was hard for him . . . maybe if Angie had devoted herself to him that summer . . . It was very sad.' Whether or not David helped inspire Joey's estrangement from his mother, he made little effort to conceal how much he detested his ex-wife, whom he described as having 'as much insight into the human condition as a walnut and a self-interest that would make Narcissus green with envy'.

*

Throughout the first half of 1981, David revelled in his seclusion; now, the focus and dedication that had usually been directed at his music was applied to 'seeing [Zowie] grow . . . and be excited about the future'. There was just one musical venture that summer, for which he only had to stroll down the road: the previous year, he'd agreed to collaborate on the theme song for Paul Schrager's remake of Val Lewton's classic movie *Cat People*. The song was Bowie's first and only collaboration with Giorgio Moroder, whose work he'd discovered back in Los Angeles. The Italian electro pioneer was best-known for the chattering sequencers of songs like Donna Summer's 'I Feel Love', but for this song he constructed a bleak, minimalistic soundscape, based on the simplest of two-chord changes. Bowie recorded his languorous, hypnotic vocal over Moroder's backing track at Mountain Studios; the opening minutes would count among the most magnificent, and restrained, of his career. A modest success on its release the next April, 'Cat People (Putting Out Fires)' would become one of the most overlooked Bowie gems until Quentin Tarantino unearthed it for his Nazi splatter-movie, *Inglourious Basterds*, in 2009.

It was during his visits to Mountain – which eventually became a second home once he negotiated his own, off-peak, David Bowie discount – that David reacquainted himself with a fan-turned-rival who was recording in the main casino studio.

David had met Freddie Mercury back in the summer of 1970, when the Queen singer worked on a stall in Kensington Market and fitted Bowie with a pair of suede boots. Introduced by their mutual friend, ex-Beatstalker Alan Mair, Freddie had shyly mentioned he was rehearsing with a new band. David, then disenchanted with Ken Pitt, had replied, 'Why would you want to get into *this* business?' Fortunately Freddie had ignored him, but over the next few years would take more than a few leaves out of the Bowie book. Queen turned up regularly at Bowie shows, recorded at Trident and hired MainMan photographer Mick Rock, while the influence of Mick Ronson's pioneering work on songs like 'The Supermen' was readily discernible in Brian May's trademark multi-layered guitar style.

According to Mercury's personal assistant Peter Freestone, Bowie only realised Queen were in Mountain working on their R&B-flavoured album *Hot Space* by chance. Asked to add backing vocals on the song 'Cool Cat', David stayed for a marathon session in which Queen's song 'Feel Like' was transformed into 'Under Pressure'. David contributed the bulk of the lyrics, set over drummer Roger Taylor's descending chord sequence. By now, Mercury had developed more of an ego than in his market-stall days, and it was the Queen drummer who was at the heart of the session, interacting with the interloper. 'Roger and Bowie got on very well,' according to Freestone, 'although the lyrics and title idea came from Freddie and David.'

David was charming, polite, sensitive in his dealings with these four relative strangers, but also remarkably confident, just as he had been in his youth, showing his songs to bands like The Beatstalkers, certain they'd accept them. 'It was hard because you had four very precocious boys – and David, who was precocious enough for all of us,' says Brian May. 'David took over the song lyrically. It's a significant song because of David and its lyrical content – I would have found that hard to admit in the old days – but I can admit it now.' David championed the song, encouraging Freddie, and contributing a classic, swooping melody, as well as one of his own distinctive, reflective middle-eight sections ('the terror of knowing what this world is all about').

Queen were uncertain about the track, even after Bowie and Mercury re-worked their vocals and mixed the recording at The Power Station in New York, a fortnight later – John Deacon's distinctive bassline was added at the same session, hummed to him by David. Brian May was particularly unhappy, recalling the 'fierce battles' around the mix, and his own misgivings about the song's release as a single; instead, it was Queen's record company, EMI, that pushed the collaboration, which finally hit the streets that September and would became Queen's second number one, hitting the top of the UK charts on 21 November, and number twenty-nine in the US a few weeks later.

It was a satisfying coup for David, helping craft another hit from behind the scenes, as he had for many others, all the more so given his sudden disappearance from the music scene. He was happy to relinquish 'Under Pressure' to Queen – it would take persistent persuasion to get him to perform the song, decades later – but another incentive for him to take a back seat was the fact that his contractual obligation to Tony Defries wouldn't expire until October 1982; Queen were welcome to take the mechanical royalties on the record, rather than his former manager. Instead, he would lie low for a year, venturing out only to work on a project that was of interest mainly to academics, and would produce one of the quirkiest, most overlooked and – in its own way – perfect records of his career.

The project was the brainchild of Alan Clarke, a brave, gritty director best-known for the controversial movie *Scum*. Early in 1981, he had discussed the notion of a TV version of Bertholt Brecht's first full-length play, *Baal*, with BBC producer Louis Marks. Clarke planned a minimal, studio-based production of the 1918 play, using a pioneering split-screen effect for Brecht's trademark *Verfremdungseffekt* – in which the actor directly addresses the audience, commenting on events.

The play was 'ambitious – bordering on the dangerous', says Louis Marks. 'But I had great confidence in Alan Clarke; he was a great director.' From the start, Clarke, Marks and writer John Willett were preoccupied with the casting of the central character. The three debated Steven Berkoff and Barry Humphries (Willett admired Dame Edna Everage's 'demonic intensity') before the writer suggested Bowie; he knew of his work on *The Elephant Man*, and guessed he 'might be interested in pre-1933 Germany and even in Brecht'. He guessed right: Clarke and Louis Marks went to see Bowie in Vevey in mid-July. 'When they came back, we had our Baal,' says Willett.

The casting was a fascinating one: the notion of an amoral hobo poet shagging his way around the world was appropriately close to David's nomad sex-junky existence with the Manish Boys – a time that, from his safe Swiss retreat, seemed a world away. Bowie didn't hesitate, says Marks. 'The chat at his house was very brief – and then it was simply down to practicalities, him and Alan talking about how they would do it.'

Marks, Clarke and Willett's experience with David closely mirrored that of *The Elephant Man*'s crew. Bowie was a trouper, but the atmosphere around him was disturbing. The project was shrouded in obsessive secrecy; once rehearsals started the crew were ordered not to reveal Bowie's involvement. Two security guards stood by the studio door throughout; the sign on the entrance to BBC Studio 1 read simply 'Classic Play'.

Producer Louis Marks was a Doctor of Philosophy, an Oxford-educated expert on renaissance studies; John Willett was the English-speaking world's foremost Brecht scholar and translator, who'd met the playwright in 1956 – both of them were bona fide intellectuals. Once David had arrived in the rehearsal space in Acton, the trio sat down to discuss the play. Their conversation turned to the look of the play; Willett explained how he saw it as reminiscent of the illustrator Masereel. 'How wonderful!' David replied, before mentioning how he'd tracked down some of his prints in Berlin, part of his growing collection of expressionist art. They discussed the Brecht *recitatif* singing style. 'I think of it rather like plainsong,' Bowie murmured. Willett was shocked; the comparison made complete sense, but had never occurred to him. They continued talking about Brecht and the Neue Sachlichkeit art movement – the stripped-down, austere reaction to expressionism – and Bowie's understanding seemed just as sophisticated.

As they walked away from one discussion, Willett turned to Marks, 'He knows more about Germany as a whole – and Brecht in particular – than anyone we know!' They didn't discuss whether David knew more than the two of them – but it was a distinct possibility.

A decade before, David absorbed his culture from people, whether William Burroughs or Andy Warhol, skipping around different subjects like a gadfly. It was in his cocaine period that he'd learned to focus, spending endless hours pondering alien visitations or Nazi folklore; yet when he'd put that focus to real use, studying in Berlin galleries or poring over artist monographs, he'd transformed himself from a sophisticated name-dropper to a figure who could impress and even intimidate Oxford's finest intellectuals.

As discussions gave way to rehearsals, the pair were impressed by how Bowie took command of Brecht's music, imposing sense and rhythm on the words. Yet, as an actor, he was totally unconventional. An actor would build up a performance from scratch, adding or modifying elements with each rehearsal. David, instead, gave a set of completely separate, different performances. Each version seemed complete, full of ideas: 'Nothing he said was routine,' says Willett.

There were four weeks rehearsal in Acton before the one-week shoot, which reached a climax on the final day, 12 August, when Clarke had to tie up the split-screen shots and the opening 'Hymn', which was crucial both to set up the play and to establish Bowie's credibility as the central character. The pressure was on as Bowie started singing the hymn; then suddenly there was a tremendous banging through the studio wall. Clarke stopped the cameras, and sent a messenger round to Studio 2 to tell them to be quiet; but the door to Studio 2 was locked. With the hammering echoing around the studio, Louis Marks phoned BBC administration, and the noise stopped for a few minutes; only to start again, from a slightly different location. The cycle repeated itself several times, and tempers were frayed, before Bowie announced, 'I know how to stop this!'

He strode into the centre of the studio, put his hands to his mouth, and shouted, 'Lunch!' Suddenly, the tension evaporated. The noise did reoccur, but the filming continued, with actors and crew energised once more, and Clarke wrapped up the shoot, confident he'd pulled off a difficult coup.

By now, Bowie seemed to exert almost a superhuman influence over his distinguished colleagues; but he wasn't poncy, rather he was enthusiastic and sincere. When working on the songs for the TV play, he'd collaborated closely with Dominic Muldowney, a pioneer in interpreting Brecht's music. Towards the end, he'd confided in Muldowney that he'd like to record some of the material in Berlin; would Muldowney like to oversee the arrangements? Muldowney leapt at the chance; writer John Willett volunteered to come along, too. 'Really, you will?' asked David Bowie, with his dazzling charm. 'You'd be doing me a terrific favour!' He went on to explain that he wanted the recordings to serve as his final album for RCA. Muldowney would help not only bring one distinguished era of David Bowie's career to a close, but free him for the next one, too.

A few weeks later, Bowie assembled with Muldowney, Willett, Tony Visconti and Edu Meyer for David's final recording at Hansa Studio 2. It was a relaxed session, relying heavily on the eight-strong band of Berlin musicians assembled by percussionist Sherry Bertram, which included plenty of Brecht old-timers, notably a seventy-five-year-old bandoneonist who'd played in the first productions of *The Threepenny Orchestra*.

Bowie arrived late for the recording, which meant Muldowney and Visconti laid down the bulk of the backing tracks before his arrival. Muldowney had an unrivalled pedigree in classical and Brecht-related music, having studied with composer Harrison Birtwistle, but was staggered at the creativity on display: even as he arranged one string part, Visconti was already compressing and EQ-ing the sound, 'and suddenly these four strings sounded like four tanks'.

With the backing tracks complete they cleared the hall, and Visconti and Meyer set up microphones in each corner so that they could record David filling the Meistersaal with his voice, like the cabaret acts who'd performed there in the 1920s, finishing the entire set within three or four hours. It was a masterclass in technique, says Muldowney. 'The standout was "The Drowned Girl", which is like an Ophelia song, where she dies in the river. He's singing about "Her slow descent" below the water, right down in the bass baritone. Then halfway through he jumps up the octave. I play this song to composers at the Royal Opera House on courses. When he sings up to the word "smoke" it's got smoke all around it, it's cloudy. Then we get to the "k" of smoke and you can see again. It's an absolute tutorial in how to paint a text. The only other person I know can do that is Frank Sinatra.'

After the day's singing masterclass, David spent that night giving Muldowney a cultural tour. While the exhausted Visconti slept, David and Muldowney turned up first at a club in Kreuzberg where the clientele were draped over dentists' chairs; next came a New Wave club, the Dschungel, where David danced with a beautiful, elfin, Ziggyish boy, flirtatiously sharing the same cigarette with him. Later still they were knocking on an imposing basement door: the peephole slid open, David was given a delighted welcome, and he ushered Muldowney into a transvestite bar. Chatting to the stunning creatures serving drinks, he admired the gilt mirror that ran the length of the bar. 'Thank you,' they told him, 'it was made for Hermann Göring.' Around four in the morning, Muldowney returned, spent, to his hotel on the Ku'Damm, and left David going strong, in his own goodbye to Berlin.

David's anonymous exploits in Berlin were in stark contrast to the media frenzy that greeted the crew on their return to London. The news that the star, out of view for a year now, was appearing in an obscure German play inspired headlines and spreads in the *Daily Express*, the *Sun*, and most of the UK press. The *Daily Mirror* explained: 'He plays a singing poet with a huge appetite for sex and wine called Baal by German' – a typographically challenged précis which perhaps did not fully communicate the play's significance.

Clarke and Willett now discovered that the BBC had retitled the play *Bowie In Baal*, and delayed transmission until the spring, when they could showcase Bowie's presence with a cover story in the *Radio Times*. There was 'a spat', as producer Louis Marks tried to fight the decision, but failed. An obscure play, previously of interest only to academics, was now being promoted as a ratings-grabber; Bowie was now overshadowing both Brecht and *Baal*.

The play's transformation into a prestige production brought its own repercussions. A few weeks before the transmission date, 2 March, 1982, Louis Marks discovered ITV had scheduled an equally prestigious play, starting that same evening but a half-hour earlier. *A Voyage Round My Father*, John Mortimer's poignant, funny memoir of the decline of his cantankerous barrister father featured Laurence Olivier in one of his last and best-loved roles. The BBC was comprehensively upstaged; ITV trounced *Baal* both in ratings and press coverage – although the reviews of Bowie's acting were in the main complimentary. Clarke and Willett later agreed the production was hampered by its compromise between naturalism and minimalism – 'it needed more edge and power', according to Willett – yet even today it remains the definitive interpretation of this fascinating, immature work. 'I have no reservations about it today,' says Marks, the figure who more than anyone steered the project through the BBC bureaucracy. 'I was thrilled to be involved.'

Baal was destined to become a lost artefact, often discussed by Brecht scholars. Today, only the album remains to document what was not only one of Bowie's bravest artistic efforts, but would also constitute his final Berlin document. The Hauptstrasse lease had expired in February 1981, so he stayed in his old haunt, the Schlosshotel Gerhus, and went to visit Esther Friedmann, whose relationship with Iggy was splintering as Iggy's own life was falling apart. He'd been booted off Arista Records, was back on cocaine, and stayed drunk most of the time to swamp his awareness that his music, the one thing that had always sustained him, sounded awful. Esther had seen David help Iggy out for years; now he sat playing piano in her new apartment in Kreuzberg, counselling her. 'You know a lot about art,' he told her. 'You should do it for a living.' Friedmann followed his advice, and later built up a thriving gallery business.

The *Baal* EP was David's final RCA release; it reached number twenty-nine in the UK album charts in the spring of 1982. It was now an open secret that David was simply waiting out his contract with RCA – the motive was not just financial, for the company's shortcomings had been obvious from his very first US tour, with their patchy efforts at arranging local airplay and promotion. The label's lack of enthusiasm for *Low* had not eased his disenchantment. David's solution was simply to ignore RCA while he pursued other business.

It wasn't long before other business started to stream in, for after a year in Vevey, David was getting itchy feet. With recording on the backburner, he turned again to acting. It had been Tony Defries who claimed he would make David into a mainstream entertainer, like Liz Taylor, and with two major movie projects in 1982, it looked like David was getting close. Both were quirky concepts, although the one that looked the most commercial turned out to be the bigger failure. Tony Scott, a successful commercials director, was hoping to make a leap into cinema like his brother Ridley – who had graduated from selling Lyon's Maid ice-cream back in 1969, with an ad that coincidentally featured a young David, to directing *Alien* and *Bladerunner*. Tony's first shot at the mainstream was *The Hunger*, a slick, glossy vampire movie based on a novel by Whitley Strieber. With its MTV-influenced visuals, bombastic soundtrack, a guest appearance by Goth band Bauhaus and scenes shot in the nightclub Heaven, it was exactly the kind of film in which you'd expect to see a rock star attempting to cross over into acting, and its combination of sensationalism and dreary predictability ensured this 'sensual classic of perverse fear' was a box-office flop on its release in April 1983. Eventually, however, its Goth glossiness helped the movie build a cult following, inspiring a nineties TV spin-off, which helped hatch a long-standing relationship between Tony Scott and David's son.

Joey – who would eventually revert to his first name, Duncan – was on set for some of the filming of *The Hunger*; it would become a formative experience in his eventual career. For Bowie, though, his longest stay in England since 1973 brought the family skeletons dancing out of the closet. Both his mother Peggy and his aunt Pat had long nursed resentments, feeling that they, and David's half-brother Terry, were being neglected.

Peggy had phoned Charles Shaar Murray at the *NME* back in 1975 to share her grievances, and was at the point of going public again. David's ex-manager, Ken Pitt, had remained in contact with her, and dissuaded her from approaching the tabloids. Although admirably circumspect, Pitt sees Peggy's boredom and constant demand for attention as problems that would never be solved. 'I would be on the phone to her quite often, with some issue or other. In the end I used to say to her, "Peggy, if David were a plumber, you wouldn't even be talking about him, would you?"' Pitt's influence and David's more consistent efforts to ensure Joey remained in touch with his grandmother helped keep Peggy out of the press, but his aunt Pat was not so easily controlled, contacting the *Sun* and the *Star* that July to tell them that David was 'callous and uncaring ... and needs to face up to his responsibilities'.

Pat's anger was prompted by the increasingly sad condition of Terry. David's half-brother's outlook had improved after his marriage to Olga in 1972, but had again deteriorated in recent years. Pat would later accuse David of ignoring Terry and his wife, although her account is challenged by David's friends, including Mark Pritchett, who remembers seeing the couple at Haddon Hall. Pat's anger derived from the belief that she had taken on the lion's share of caring for Terry; her relationship with her own husband, Tony, suffered under the strain of Terry's illness, which had reportedly resulted in fist fights between Terry and his uncle. Although often accused of ignoring Terry's fate, David had wrestled with the issue of his brother, opening up to confidants and even writers such as Timothy White, whom he told, 'I've never been able to get through to [Terry] about how he really feels. I guess nobody has.' David did go to see his half-brother during his stay in London; his visit was followed by an unhelpful headline in the *Sun*, blaring: 'I'm terrified of going mad, says Bowie.'

Pat's attacks on Bowie, over this period and thereafter, ensured his reputation as a manipulative 'ice man', who used and then discarded family and friends without qualm. There were indeed many instances of his unashamed devotion to 'Numero Uno, mate!' Yet his ruthlesness usually had a musical motive – outside of his own career, he was genuinely kind to people like Esther Friedmann, Iggy Pop, Tony Sales and others. Some of David's accusers, notably his ex-wife, insist that each and every example of David's compassion was self-serving, aimed at shoring up his own credibility. Yet there are plenty of examples of help given and not publicised; notably, David continued to pay the school fees of Marc Bolan's son, Rolan, once he realised the Bolan estate would not do so. In other instances, Bowie helped with his time, not money, searching out specialised medical treatment for the son of a writer friend. Angie's depiction of David as a flat, one-dimensional, selfish character does not ring true.

Selflessness and positivity often co-exist with pettiness and grudge-bearing – David was always capable of both. An example of such duality was the way David's artistic bravery and contempt for convention was hampered by his unhealthy habit of reading reviews or features on himself. He could harbour resentment at perceived slights or inaccuracies for years. One issue of *MOJO* magazine featured Mick Ronson on its cover in 1997: two years later, David was still complaining about 'the magazine that said Mick wrote all my songs!' – irritated that colleagues such as Tony Visconti had highlighted Mick's influence on David's early albums.

It was such haughty pronouncements, exacerbated by the flunkies and yes-men who surround most stars, which helped inspire his nickname 'The Dame', first coined by *Smash Hits* writer Tom Hibbert in the early eighties. Yet, once David was liberated from his flunkies, he could often confound expectations. That March, Carol Clerk, then a news editor for *Melody Maker*, spent an afternoon drinking poteen with The Exploited and other assorted acquaintances in Matrix Studios, where they were celebrating finishing their *Troops of Tomorrow* album. Come opening time – in those days pubs closed for a couple of hours in the late afternoon – they hit a few pubs and 'late at night, really plastered', says Clerk, 'we arrived at Gossips [nightclub]. And Bowie was in there, with some discreet security. We took a table and to our amazement, given the terrible state of everyone, Bowie asked if he could join us.'

It turned out that Bowie wanted to know all about The Exploited, thrash punk and Mohican fashion, and he was exactly as earnest and charming as he had been when pumping the *Pork* actors for information, a decade before. He sat with the chaotic, droolingly drunk group for hours, politely buying rounds. The punks were impressed by how the power of stardom ensured the bar staff 'for the first and only time in my life' brought drinks to the table and kept the club open beyond its 3 a.m. closing time. One of the few details Clerk could still recall the next morning was the way Bowie worried about Linc, the bass player from Chelsea, who'd passed out under his leather jacket before David arrived at the table. Throughout the night, Bowie kept lifting up Linc's jacket, checking that Linc was still breathing, like an ultra-cool mother hen, until all the parties finally staggered home.

It was in his guise as fan that David was always the most engaging; any perceived snootiness would evaporate in his boyish enthusiasm. As ever, there was no dividing line between his enthusiasms and his own work; they blended into each other imperceptibly. One perfect example happened during that July, when David returned to Montreux after winding up the shoot for *The Hunger*, just in time for that year's Jazz Festival. This was the year that Stevie Ray Vaughan, then a struggling blues guitarist, had been championed by famed Atlantic producer Jerry Wexler, who persuaded Montreux mastermind Claude Nobs to present Vaughan and his band, Double Trouble.

The unsigned outfit played on the acoustic stage, where Vaughan's clanky, raw Texas blues brought boos and catcalls from an audience expecting cool, quiet jazz. Although their reception 'did kinda hurt our feelings', says bassist Tommy Shannon, the blues trio were so fired up by their first overseas show that they later carried their amplifiers downstairs to the bar, where they jammed until dawn. As the sun came up, they noticed a figure drinking at the counter: they knew it must be David Bowie – 'He just had this look,' says Shannon. Stevie and the band were not starstruck – they hardly knew Bowie's music – but they were impressed by his charm, the way he'd stayed up until dawn to talk to them: 'He was just real nice-looking, and handled himself well.' He sat with them for a while, speaking mostly to Stevie, talking about guitar playing. David's enthusiasm helped banish the memory of the audience's boos, as did the response of singer-songwriter Jackson Browne, who'd also seen the show and offered them free recording time in his home studio.

David's respite in Montreux turned out to be a brief one. Despite having planned to make a single movie in 1982, a project that he'd discussed several years before suddenly spun into action. Director Nagisa Oshima, best-known for *In the Realm of the Senses*, was planning a film based on the memoirs of Laurens Van Der Post. Oshima had approached singer Kenji Sawada to play the role of POW commander Yonoi; Sawada dropped out, to be replaced by Japanese musician Ryuichi Sakomoto, but only after he'd suggested David Bowie for the part of Jack Celliers. Oshima liked casting singers or other performers – 'without the peculiarities actors often acquire' – and approached David during his *Elephant Man* run. He readily agreed. Producer Jeremy Thomas had already worked on two films with Nicolas Roeg; Paul Mayersberg, who wrote the script with Oshima, had scripted *The Man Who Fell to Earth*, and once Bowie was on board, rewrote the part with David in mind. Thomas remembers that 'Bowie knew everything about Oshima. Once he understood Oshima's interest in him, he was interested in the film. It was an ideal situation: he was immediately on board, saying, "Tell me when and where – and I'll be there."'

The film was intriguing, the antithesis of a conventional prisoner of war drama. Three key roles were played by comparative novices: Bowie as Celliers, Ryuichi Sakomoto as Captain Yonoi – the commandant who is obsessed with him – and comedian Beat Takeshi as Sergeant Hara. At the centre of this nexus is Tom Conti, as Laurens Van Der Post, who attempts to bridge the huge cultural gaps between them all. Conti's humanity carries the film; Bowie and Sakomoto's characters are stylised, almost ritualistic – both of them yearn to be archetypes.

Oshima filmed extremely fast, with no rushes, and Sakomoto would later comment that when he saw his own performance, 'I couldn't believe how bad my acting was . . . I was traumatised.' Bowie's portrayal of Jack Celliers – the perfect soldier who is attempting to atone for abandoning his crippled brother – is also variable, most notably the faintly risible flashback to Celliers as a seventeen-year-old schoolboy. Nonetheless, Bowie's physical beauty – all jagged teeth and exquisite cheekbones – and ethereal air is perfect for a character who, as his initials indicate, is a Christ-like figure, human but other-worldly. Flawed but meaningful, engagingly human, Bowie's performance would prove the high watermark of his cinematic career.

In America, the movie – titled *Merry Christmas Mr. Lawrence* – was a box-office failure; as scriptwriter Paul Mayersberg explains, 'US audiences were baffled by a prison camp movie where nobody tried to escape' and roles of this calibre would ultimately dry up. But in Europe and

Japan, the movie's themes of atonement, cross-cultural incomprehension, homo-eroticism and a search for meaning were more resonant and *Merry Christmas Mr. Lawrence* acquired the reputation of a classic. As Jeremy Thomas, who would go on to produce films like *The Last Emperor* and *Sexy Beast*, points out, 'It was my first film that caught the public imagination and was shown all over the world. And it has aged well, because it was set in period – and because Bowie somehow doesn't look any older today than he did then.'

The filming wrapped up with David presenting an impromptu show which was rapturously received by the crew. It marked an unexpectedly intense year, for along with filming in Rarotonga and New Zealand with Oshima, and London with Tony Scott, he'd also shuttled between Montreux and New York, where friends like Anne Wehrer and Esther Friedmann enlisted his help with Iggy, who had returned penniless from Haiti that summer, apparently under the influence of a voodoo curse, still in what seemed like an unstoppable downward spiral.

In the weeks when he wasn't working, David started to base himself in New York, in parallel with the impressive château-style house he'd recently bought in Upper Lausanne, Switzerland. Sometimes he'd venture out of his Midtown loft with bodyguards – one musician who had a disagreement with him remembers being turfed out of the room by two attractive women, 'like Bambi and Thumper, Blofeld's bodyguards in *Diamonds Are Forever*' – but by the summer he felt comfortable enough to hang out solo in musician's haunts like the Continental, in Manhattan. Occasionally this meant chatting politely to coked-out upstarts like Billy Idol – presumably talking about the old days in Bromley, where Billy had grown up, too. Idol was a regular at the club, and arrived around 5 a.m. one morning with a friend in tow: Nile Rodgers, the founder, with Bernard Edwards, of Chic. David and Nile talked till dawn. Just a few days later, David asked Nile to produce his next album.

In hindsight, David's collaboration with Nile Rodgers looked a sure-fire winner. At the time it was anything but. Rodgers' red-hot winning streak with Chic, Sister Sledge and Diana Ross was now a couple of years old, and since then his magic touch had deserted him: Debbie Harry's *Koo Koo* had not delivered one hit single while his own solo album had also failed to set the charts alight. 'To this day, I owe David for his commitment – because at the time I had five flops in a row,' says the celebrated producer. 'I mean it, five! It was really tough for me.'

Rodgers was probably the most experienced producer David had ever teamed up with – but the way he worked with David was utterly unlike anything he'd done before, or since. Yet if their collaboration was unique in Rodgers' experience, for David it marked the summit of a working method he'd established with Dek Fearnley, or Mick Ronson, many years before, where he delegated key tasks, giving his collaborators huge freedom. On the album that would become *Let's Dance*, his delegation was even more extreme, with Rodgers responsible for recruiting key musicians, as well as overseeing the finest details of the arrangements. It was Nile Rodgers who programmed the music. But it was David Bowie who programmed Nile Rodgers.

The process began at David's new house in Lausanne, where they spent days getting to know each other, before one morning David walked into Nile's room with a twelve-string guitar. Or what had once been a twelve-string. 'It had just six strings on it, which was weird. Why not use a six-string guitar in the first place?' says Rodgers. 'And then he played me this song. And told me he thought it was going to be a hit.'

The song was folky; David played it vaguely in the style of the Byrds, and it was called 'Let's Dance'. 'And I was like, "That's not happening man." It totally threw me. And it was not a song you could dance to.' Rodgers simply didn't understand. Was this some kind of mind game? So he called a mutual friend in New York: 'Do you think David is the kind of guy who would play a trick on me?' he asked. 'Is he playing me this song he says is going to be a hit to see if I'm some sort of sycophant?'

'No, he wouldn't do that,' came the reply. 'If he says that, he really believes it.' The information didn't help. 'Oh shit! What do I do now?' Nile asked himself.

Rodgers kept schtum about such worries as his discussions with David continued. For much of the time they'd talk about fifties album sleeves, flipping through David's collection of vinyl albums, some of them venerable originals that he'd bought twenty years before at Medhurst's in Bromley. They played records like 'Twist and Shout', discussing the difference between The Beatles' sweat-drenched version and the Isley Brothers' original; they both fondled the *film noir* sleeve of Henry Mancini's *Peter Gunn* and Nelson Riddle's *Route 66* soundtracks, chatted about the Chicago Art Ensemble and Lester Bowie, and they spent a lot of time listening to and looking at photos of Little Richard, the childhood hero whom David still revered. It was like being inducted via a series of visual and auditory mood-boards.

It was only later that Rodgers realised he was being programmed:

brainwashed, in a musical version of *The Manchurian Candidate*. For many of Bowie's previous records, he had honed the art of briefing musicians, getting them to pull something out of their consciousness that they hadn't known existed. Now he was doing it on a bigger scale.

The simplest illustration of how this worked comes on 'Let's Dance'. Rodgers knew that if this was to be a dance hit, it needed funking up; no problem, this was his forté. But all his previous hits had a memorable opening, too. The solution came from 'Twist and Shout': Rodgers simply lifted the vocal stacking effect – the bit where The Beatles sent teenagers crazy – and put it at the beginning of the song: 'Ah . . . Ah . . . Ah . . . Ah!'

After each line of the verse there was a space, which required some kind of response. The solution was Henry Mancini's *Peter Gunn* horn riff – dropped in directly after David sings the words 'dance the blues'. 'It was taken straight from that record, a thing I never did before,' says Rodgers. 'That [riff] seemed to me so anti-groove, but sticking it on something that was so hard groove it was like, "Shit! This is magic!" And I realised that all that fifties and sixties stuff was a snapshot of Bowie's brain. Then I was like, "Wow! You can do that!"'

Himself a master producer, used to vibing up musicians to get the right take, Rodgers realised that he too was being produced, but given absolute freedom, in a way that no other musician had attempted. 'When we did *Let's Dance* the pre-production was so clear. I've never worked with an artist like that before or since. It was all beautiful images. We went to people's houses that he knew had certain things . . . it was like fact finders, treasure hunters, conquistadores looking for gold and we were going and looking at everything, in museums. "Nile look at this picture. Look at this!" So he was like the world's greatest cook showing you, This is what we want it to be. Once I had that I was clear as a bell. I was unwavering.'

The same process would apply with the other standout songs on *Let's Dance*; David played Nile Iggy's version of 'China Girl', again telling him it was a hit, and he had to work out how to make it one, adapting the opening riff from Rufus's 'Sweet Thing' to give it a Chinese feel. After their extensive discussions, and pre-production at Montreux, the sessions at New York's Power Station were brief; the studio was booked for twenty-one days, and, according to Rodgers, the tracks were recorded and mixed by day seventeen. There was only one artistic disagreement; Rodgers was unimpressed by Bowie's suggestion of Stevie Ray Vaughan for most of the guitar solos, telling him the guitarist just sounded like

Albert King. 'This guy's different,' David told him, 'he's got a whole other thing going on.'

Vaughan was recording his debut album at Jackson Browne's studio using downtime over the Thanksgiving holiday when he got the call. The guitarist was intrigued by the offer. 'It was a challenge – and Steve was always confident about being in the studio,' says Stevie's bassist, Tommy Shannon. Vaughan showed up within a day or two, and added his guitar parts 'instantaneously', according to Nile. Vaughan played an old Fender Strat, plugged straight into an old Fender amp – all the tone coming from the player, with no tricks. The same applied to the rest of the music, for *Let's Dance* was at heart a simple, minimal album, with most of its impact coming not from electronic effects, but from the intuitive musicianship of players like Vaughan, and the consummately funky Tony Thompson – who would later be called in to play drums with Madonna, Robert Palmer and others, but would never surpass the effortless swing of *Let's Dance*.

Over the following months, David Bowie was often be seen in the corridors of EMI, cutting such a refined, elegantly suited-and-booted figure that on first glance the record company execs thought he was a wealthy investor. Although he had financial advisers, he negotiated the deal himself; the story within EMI was that he persuaded the aggressive new American arm of the company to pay a huge advance purely on the basis of hearing the backing tracks. The amount David secured for his services on signing of his contact with EMI America, on 27 January, 1983, was publicised as just under $17 million.

'You know how deals are constructed,' says Gary Gersh, the A&R who, with US chairman Rupert Perry, signed Bowie to EMI. 'That figure would depend on a lot of clauses. But it was a superstar deal – when maybe David's sales so far wouldn't warrant it.' Many other EMI staff agreed it was 'a huge risk', in the words of David's A&R man, Hugh Stanley Clarke; there was debate as to whether EMI would ever make their money back. Even at the time, Gersh agrees, all the company management had their doubts. But today, he points out, 'If you were to say to *any* record company they could have that deal again – you would have a line of people around the block.'

19

On the Other Side

I got the spider built and only saw the first few shows. That was enough.

Chip Monck

It was spring in the northern hemisphere, but there was a streak of autumnal gold to the light in Sydney and Carinda, as David Bowie brandished a guitar in the outback, or bared his backside as the surf spilled over him and his China Girl. Back in Manhattan, Carlos Alomar was assembling the musicians for what would be the biggest world tour of 1983. With a typically consummate grasp of the priorities of the modern pop industry, David was filming videos on the beach.

According to Nile Rodgers, David had been happy to sit in the lounge at the Power Station while many of *Let's Dance*'s tracks were laid down, but when it came to the video, David kept a close eye on every aspect of David Mallett's production. 'Let's Dance' was filmed in an Australian outback village, a transplanted Mississippi Delta. David mimed the song in a shack, with two kids from the Aboriginal-Islanders Dance Theatre acting out a storyline based on the message, Bowie explained, that 'it's wrong to be racist!' For 'China Girl', the song inspired by Iggy's affair with Kuelan Nguyen, Bowie and Mallett cast a student and model, Geeling Ng, who marched around Sydney's Chinatown in a Chairman Mao outfit and re-enacted *From Here to Eternity* on the beach, frolicking with David in the surf. In this idyllic interlude, the two became lovers, hanging out together in David's apartment in Elizabeth Bay.

*

Back in 1967, friends like Tony Visconti had ridiculed Ken Pitt's efforts to mould David as an all-round entertainer. In 1983, the all-round potential offered by the new medium of music video was an intrinsic part of his pitch to EMI. The British company's new American arm was expanding fast, its success bolstered by Brit acts who had been making videos to screen on *Top of the Pops* for decades, and were cleaning up at the newly dominant MTV.

The few American outfits who caught on – principally Michael Jackson, whose 'Billie Jean' video was screened on the lily-white network in March 1983 – would dominate the eighties, and as Bowie's video drove 'Let's Dance', his debut EMI single, to his first simultaneous UK and US number one, in May, the smart money was on him to dominate this decade. In the seventies he'd re-branded himself as the world's first bisexual rock star; now his niche brand was being relaunched as an international multimedia product. His star status was highlighted by a sensational appearance alongside Nagima Oshima and Ryuichi Sakomoto at the Cannes Festival in May to promote *Merry Christmas Mr. Lawrence*: tanned, his hair a mass of blond candyfloss, he joked casually with the admiring press, switching effortlessly from self-deprecation to intellectual earnestness. European critics in particular loved the movie, a strong contender for the Grand Prize – although it was ultimately pipped at the post by Monty Python's *The Meaning of Life*.

Far away from the glitz of Cannes, the rehearsals for David's biggest tour to date had moved to Dallas, overseen by Carlos Alomar, much like David's 1978 tour. The musicians were based around the 'Let's Dance' crew, plus a three-piece horn section and Dave Lebolt (later a senior figure at Apple Computer) on keyboards.

If there was a perfect way to do a modern tour, this was it. Spanning sixteen countries, ninety-six performances, and selling over two-and-a-half million tickets, the *Serious Moonlight* tour would become the definitive stadium event. Every decision in its progress was closely scrutinised by a triumvirate of David (or an Isolar representative), accountant Bill Zysblat and agent Will Forte, each keeping a close eye on the logistics, the money and each other. Its only rival over the early eighties was the Stones' 1981 *Tattoo You* tour, which grossed more in ticket sales, but was confined to the USA and Europe. The Stones outing was a reminder of past glories, promoting a collection of tracks dating back a decade. In contrast, *Serious Moonlight* captured Bowie at his peak.

Guitarist Stevie Ray Vaughan was, at first, thrilled about the tour, and believed that he'd extracted a promise from David that his own band,

Double Trouble, would play support. Once rehearsals shifted from
Manhattan to Dallas, Vaughan's hometown, he started hanging out with
his band again. Only two or three nights in, they'd have to sit and hear
his complaints: 'There was a point in the set where he was supposed to
come down this ramp doing these [dance] steps,' says bassist Tommy
Shannon, 'and that just wasn't in his nature. He'd been pushed into it
anyway by management. He was having a hard time adjusting.'

Vaughan was, says Shannon, focused and hard-working over this
spring, but the guitarist was becoming increasingly isolated in the Bowie
camp. The suggestion that Double Trouble could support was dropped.
Then Vaughan saw the 'Let's Dance' video, which showed David, atop
a mountain, miming Stevie's guitar solo on a Fender Strat. Anyone used
to the ways of showbiz would have accepted such a harmless deception. For a Texas bluesman, it was an outrage: 'The video showed David
faking it – and Stevie was *furious*,' says Shannon. For Stevie, the videos, the
staging and the glitz were a distraction, a sign of fakery. Relations soured
quickly. Lenny Vaughan – a pushy rock wife, says Shannon – interrupted
rehearsals to brandish a newspaper which showed Stevie's photo as
a full page, David a mere single column. Bowie, who remained unruffled for most of the tour, was enraged. 'Don't you ever break up my
rehearsal!' backing singer Frank Simms heard him shout. 'If you were
a man I'd kick your ass.' Lenny was barred from rehearsals and then
Vaughan, says Simms, 'disappeared for five days without telling anyone'
to attend the funeral of Muddy Waters. Vaughan's manager Chesley
Milligan – a good ol' boy who was in over his head – demanded an extra
$500 per week for Stevie and a place on the plane for himself or his client
would walk. Stevie walked.

David, who wasn't actually present, would later describe Vaughan
standing disconsolately by the roadside as the band boarded their coach
and left town. But Stevie cheered up quickly, says Shannon. 'He got in the
car with us and said, "Well, I'm not going." And he was really relieved.
When it comes down to it, Steve wanted to stay with his band.' Vaughan
started his own ninety-date tour that June, racking up 500,000 sales of his
debut album by word of mouth. He and David would never meet again,
according to Shannon.

As one guitarist passed out of David's orbit for ever, another returned.
Earl Slick had fallen out with David after *Station to Station*, thanks to disputes involving Michael Lippman, Pat Gibbons and, says Slick, 'the fact
my head was up my ass'. After calling Slick in for the last two days of
rehearsals, David did what he hadn't done last time around and spoke

to the guitarist face-to-face: 'I showed up and David is going, "Where's the Earl?"' says Slick. 'I said, "Come on!" He goes, "Alright!" Which he wouldn't have done earlier – but we were both different then. So we went out and had lunch and cleared the air because there were a lot of bad feelings. So everything was cool.'

When Slick had joined the *Diamond Dogs* tour, his induction had consisted of having his long hair cropped, like Samson: he was livid, but realised later it was part of a process of being taken out of his comfort zone. For *Serious Moonlight*, Slick had to endure a series of suit fittings, as clothes designed for a lanky Texas cowboy were shortened and taken in to fit his wiry Italian frame. Then Slick sat one-one-on with Carlos and learned the entire set over forty-eight hours, fuelled by coffee after coffee, before setting out on a tour that made his last venture with David seem like amateur hour. 'David was totally on it – the good days, the bad days, it doesn't matter. There was a lot to think about and that made it easy.'

The tour opened in Brussels, and *NME* journalist Charles Shaar Murray – who'd followed Bowie since 1971 – was flown over to the opening show by Bowie's management company, Isolar. In a signpost to the changing times, he'd been commissioned to write the copy for the glossy tour booklet. The 'huge' production he saw was a potent reminder of how the stakes had been raised for live shows, and how they'd continue to rise with Prince and Madonna – but in Brussels and London, says Murray, there was no hint of the flabbiness with which eighties stadium tours later became associated. 'When Tony Thompson nailed a groove down, it stayed nailed down – it was right on the money. Alomar was playing rhythm, and he'd been in the pit at the Apollo, that was all the credentials you needed.'

For those earlier shows, David's voice was superb. 'In a moment of euphoria I described him as the best white singer alive,' says Murray. 'Which I possibly overstated, but he was good enough to be rated against the best. And I'd give him the highest marks for stage-craft, charisma and the dancing, too.'

All those involved in the tour felt they were breaking new ground. 'There was a sense of the magnitude from literally the first day – I thought it would be enormous, and it was,' says Frank Simms. It wasn't merely the size of the venues, or the luxury of the hotels. Simms later played an arena tour to 40,000-strong crowds with Billy Joel: 'They would cheer and clap – but it wasn't the same magnitude, and didn't have the same magic. With *Serious Moonlight*, in the larger cities, you'd have the biggest stars: in England the royal family, in Thailand the King, Queen and Prince, in Australia the Prime Minister, then in LA you'd have movie stars, Michael Jackson – they were all there.'

For a couple of weeks, when Geeling Ng joined the tour in France and Germany, there was a blissful, easy happiness around the organisation. The band loved her – she was unaffected, calm, 'normal as apple pie', says George Simms, who double-dated David and Geeling with his wife. 'It was sweet, as normal as can be, and we managed to find some places where not too many fans would bother us.' George got the sense that Geeling was overwhelmed by the experience and realised 'it was just a short-term thing'. After accompanying David for a fortnight, she caught a plane back to New Zealand and a normal life, just as David and band flew over to San Bernadino to play a one-off show at the US festival for the widely publicised fee of $1 million.

Headlining on an evening that included U2, The Pretenders and Stevie Nicks to a 300,000-strong crowd, they walked out onto a stage that had been completely cleared, at eleven o'clock to a stunned, rapturous reception: 'like Jesus walking on water', says Simms. The festival was a disaster for its sponsor, Apple's Steve Wozniak; losing over $7 million according to the *New York Times*, with one audience member murdered in a drug deal, another dead of an overdose. But for David it was a triumph; the date hugely raised his commercial profile, and helped bring more US promoters on board. But with stories of the $1-million price tag came reports that David considered the tour his 'pension plan' – a sentiment guaranteed to inflame his detractors, who started to speculate that the tour was more about money than music.

David, meanwhile, dealt with the constant buzz of attention and adrenalin calmly and efficiently. He had his little strategies to retain a degree of normality: often, he'd hang with the Simms brothers, enjoying their humorous skits. He had the gift of instantly flipping from such japes, to coming over all regal and refined if, say, Susan Sarandon was in town. He was a 'good boy' throughout; occasionally he'd have the odd social toot of cocaine, but generally showed exemplary self-control. During the eight-month tour, he went on the rampage just once, in London, during a party in Frank Simms' room. There was a glint to his expression, and the sense he'd had a couple of drinks too many, before he hit on one of the girls. 'Then he'd leave the room with her and come back fifteen or twenty minutes later – and hit on another girl. And then it would happen again. And this went on several times.' Finally, one of the party-goers turned him down, complaining to Simms, 'How dare he? Who does he think he is?' But this was an out-of-character lapse in 'a very light tour, as far as drugs and other behaviour. He knew his limits,' says Simms, 'he was under a superior degree of control.'

The dizzy heights to which David's fortunes had risen were in stark contrast to his friend Iggy, who over the same period was touring himself into oblivion. By the spring of 1983, he had lawyers pursuing him after an incident when he'd stamped on a girl's head at a gig in Poughkeepsie. Though this period was worse than his humiliation with The Stooges – for the music was lousy, too – he'd stayed in touch with David. On 20 June, he met fan and future wife Suchi Asano, who'd gone back to retrieve her umbrella after his show in Tokyo; exactly one week later, 'China Girl' hit number two in the UK, promising him the royalties that had eluded him for so long. Iggy abandoned his tour and flew back with Suchi to LA, where they met up with David when the tour reached the Forum on 14 August.

It was a poignant example of how lives can turn around. Iggy – or rather Jimmy, his avuncular alter-ego – was all sparkly-eyed and boyish, with a side-parting that made him look like Bing Crosby. Healthy and, soon, drug-free, he was teaching English to Suchi, which seemed to calm him down. They made a sweet couple. With David and George Simms, they sat around reminiscing about Berlin, before David started enthusing about life in Lausanne: he explained the Swiss legal system, the government, the culture and the citizen militia, as Jimmy nodded attentively. Then David described the twenty-four-seat jet in which they were flying, mapping out its lounge area and seating arrangements on a carpet with the same excitement he might have shared over a Heckel painting, seven years before. David suggested they join the tour, which would soon be heading out to the Far East. 'I've got too much to sort out right now,' Jimmy told him, before they agreed to meet up in December. David's other celebrity visitor at the Forum was Michael Jackson; the two chatted together, so quietly that bystanders could not make out the conversation.

Three weeks later, on 3 September, another old friend showed up. Since Mick Ronson's short, disastrous solo career under the auspices of MainMain, he had retreated to his comfort zone, contributing his tasteful guitar to work by Ian Hunter and Bob Dylan, and building up a solid, unflashy reputation as a producer, most recently for A&M Canada. Mick arrived at David's hotel with Canadian singer Lisa Dalbello, whose career he was helping relaunch; David asked him to return the next night and play. Dalbello remembers Ronson being 'OK, whatever' about the prospect, but the guitarist returned the next night and met the band. 'He was kind of drunk, and I think he was intimidated,' says Frank Simms. Ronson walked on stage after the encore with Earl Slick's blue Stratocaster to a tumultuous welcome: the band launched into a rocking version of 'The Jean Genie' – at one point the strap slipped off Earl's blue guitar and Ronson waved it around his head: 'I thought, That's not necessary! But he was nervous,' says Simms, who was standing nearby.

The Japanese and Australian legs of the tour, over October and November, were again huge events, unrivalled as spectacles until Michael Jackson's *Bad* tour in 1987, and the Stones' *Steel Wheels* in 1989. But by the time they hit the Far East, a sense of being divorced from reality had overtaken all the participants. The tour helped kick off the eighties obsession with size and statistics, but the sheer scale and repetitive drudgery meant that, for David more than anyone, the experience would become routine. Charles Shaar Murray recalls, 'I saw the footage of Bowie in Singapore. And I suddenly thought, He's turned into a rock 'n' roll version of Prince Charles. In a suit, with an old-fashioned haircut like a lemon meringue on his head, talking in this posh accent, and it's very, "Oh, what do you do?"'

For the band the unending spectacle was numbing. 'Night after night, you start to lose touch,' says Frank Simms. 'By the time we got to Australia we would have these tremendous parties every single night – actresses and models, buffets and drinking, then a yacht, with its own caterer. I would go for two weeks without calling home. My wife said, "I wish you'd call, you may be having fun but we miss you." I would apologise and say, "You have no idea . . . it's like they're feeding you the sun, the moon, and the stars." I don't know how David lived with it.'

The closing night of the tour, in Hong Kong, was the anniversary of John Lennon's death, 8 December. During the show, David sat down at one point, talking about John, almost as if in prayer or meditation. And then David and band walked backstage, as if in a daze, hugging each other gently, before the final encore. 'So we ended on this very sombre note,' says Frank Simms. 'We memorialised Lennon, and we memorialised the fact we had been together for this wonderful experience.'

Most of the band went home, feeling subdued. David and Coco – who, as ever, was there to keep him company once his love affairs fizzled out – stayed out in the Far East, meeting up with Iggy and Suchi before disappearing for an extended holiday in Bali and Java. The sights they witnessed, notably the ostentatious villas of oil magnates, each with its own open drain carrying a stream of sewage down the hill into the jungle, would be documented in Iggy's lyrics to 'Tumble and Twirl', one of the few new songs recorded for David's next album, which he started recording in Marin Heights, Canada, just a few months later, in May, 1984.

By May of 1984, David Bowie had made fifteen studio albums; each had been conceived in a burst of creativity and ideas, usually accompanied by a manifesto that was floated around the press, or previewed live. Even *Let's Dance*, for which new songs had been at a premium, was born out of a love for R&B and a yearning to evoke the spirit of Little Richard. Little Richard had scored hit records without compromising himself, without losing his status as an outsider. David thought he'd finally managed the same feat.

In the old days, he had advised his friend Glenn Hughes, 'When everyone turns right, turn left!' Now he himself turned right, without noticing.

A year or so later, David would compare the concept behind album number sixteen, *Tonight*, to *Pin Ups*. He was referring to the album's emphasis on cover versions, but the comparison was also apt in that the main inspiration for *Pin Ups* was to keep a commercial rollercoaster moving. Last time around, of course, it was Tony Defries who was intent on relieving the fans of their cash; in 1984, it was David.

This wasn't the only change in David's philosophy. Just a few years earlier, he had told pianist Sean Mayes he was 'suspicious of virtuosos'. Now, following the example of *Let's Dance*, he surrounded himself with them. David's key assistant for *Tonight* was Derek Bramble, previously bassist with Heatwave – briefly the UK's most successful home-grown funk band and recently famous once more thanks to keyboard player Rod Temperton, who'd crossed the Atlantic to huge success as principal songwriter on Michael Jackson's *Thriller*. Perhaps David thought Bramble would graduate to similar fame; he also valued the fact that Bramble could play 'proper reggae bass lines'.

David's venture into reggae would prove the most bizarre of his stylistic about-turns. He'd fallen for The Velvets before they'd had a record out, and Neu! when they were hardly known outside Germany; now he was experimenting with white reggae just as the smart money – notably The Police – was moving out.

The location for the recording of *Tonight* was suggested by Hugh Padgham, best-known as producer of The Police (and more recently

McFly); he was the man who inspired the simple, yearning piano part on 'Every Breath You Take', which was recorded at Le Studio in Morin Heights, a skiing resort north-west of Montreal. Padgham suggested using the same studio, and volunteered to step down to an engineering role because he wanted to work with Bowie. Well aware of the restless creativity that Bowie had summoned up for a decade or more, Padgham was taken aback to find that the singer seemed simply 'bored' once sessions started. There were similar recollections from some of the studio staff, who remembered 'he was obsessed with the *I Ching*', one of them asserting he even used it to determine if a mix was 'done'. The only traditional aspect of his recording behaviour that seemed to have survived from the old days was the pursuit of sex; and that old energy only seemed to return when he was trailing women on the dancefloor of the nearby club.

Padgham's role as engineer grew to that of producer as the sessions dragged on. He remembers some experimentation in the early stages of the album, but that in general David only betrayed excitement when he talked about his friend Iggy, who was at the sessions. 'David was talking about how he'd rescued Iggy. And I remember him telling lots of stories about him, like how they cut short his tour after Iggy had stamped on a girl's head and made her bite off her tongue.'

Padgham was at a loss to know the intentions behind *Tonight*; the most charitable explanation is that it was designed to make some money for his friend, for the album's nine tracks featured four Iggy credits, although the sole new song, 'Tumble and Twirl', was a confused assemblage, far from the glories of *Lust for Life*. But then, 'Tonight', the song Iggy and David had written for *Lust for Life*, was hardly recognisable, too; cut in a sanitised reggae style, with pristine drums and a warbling competition between David and guest star Tina Turner, both of them struggling to out-emote the other. The original's thrilling, shouted intro – 'I saw my baby, she was turning blue' – with its reference to a heroin overdose, was Bowdlerised: 'I didn't want to inflict it on her...' David explained to Charles Shaar Murray when it came time to promote the album. 'It's not necessarily something that she would agree to be part of.'

There is something sad, or deluded, as he sits in the Savoy with Murray, attempting to justify why he has emasculated a song he wrote just six years before; suddenly he sounds as if age or mainstream success has drained his ambition – and his hearing, for at one point he claims that the syruppy, phoned-in version of 'Tonight' 'still has that same barren feeling'. Most strikingly, the confidence and intensity of his normal conversation has ebbed away. In the old days, his music was always presented with a manifesto; now he utters tentative generalisations such as, 'The interesting thing about rock is that you never think that it's going to go on for much longer. Then you find that it has.' Just two years before, when he was acting in *The Elephant Man*, he had been filled with a sense of mission; now, there's a subdued, depressive undertone when he discusses his impact on society in the seventies, then tells Charlie Murray, 'I don't think I would ever contribute so aggressively again.'

In later years David would blame the recording, pleading that the album had 'great material that got simmered down to product level'. Yet more fundamental was David's refusal to choose collaborators who would challenge or inspire him and the loss of the key driver of his career to date – his appetite for risk, what his next collaborator, Julien Temple, describes as the 'appreciation of the randomness of things. It's a great artistic strength, if you're bold enough to follow it.'

As far as *Tonight* was concerned, Bowie's sense of risk, of the random, had ebbed away. Yet when it came to a new medium, the music video, David was energised, fired up that there was still much to learn. After seeing the work of Julien Temple – whom he'd searched out at a preview screening of the director's Sex Pistols documentary *The Great Rock 'n' Roll Swindle* back in 1980 – Bowie had done as consummate a job of charming and enthusing the director as he had with Nile Rodgers on *Let's Dance*. He opened up to him, talked about his philosophy: 'There is a real side of him which isn't confident. And then there is the dazzling superstar,' says the director. 'He can be quite a normal guy at times, with this amazing ability to transform into a glittering star. The charisma is not always there.'

It was this nervous, self-critical Bowie, the 'nerdy fan' persona that he displayed to Temple, who would be immortalised in the video *Jazzin' for Blue Jean*. Temple had played with the idea of two personae on some of his previous long-form videos, but David took the self-mockery further, splitting David Jones/Bowie into two characters. In the twenty-one-minute film, Bowie plays the geeky Vic – an artless cockney with an incessant, hopeless sales patter – who is attempting to impress the glacial Eve Ferret by taking her to meet rock star Screaming Lord Byron, David's other persona – a New Romantic concoction of silk and slap, haughty and unreachable, but helpless and isolated behind his painted sneer. Vic's efforts come to naught, and when Eve Ferret disappears with Screaming Lord Byron at the end of the evening, Vic shouts out an accusation that ran hilariously true: 'You conniving, randy, bogus, Oriental old queen! Your record sleeves are better than your songs!'

The shoot was intense, running seriously behind schedule; finally, dawn broke and they ran out of night for the final shots. As the sun comes up, David steps out of his Vic character, and complains to Julien about the ending in what Screaming Lord Bowie would describe as a Brechtian *Verfremdungseffekt* – played for laughs. 'It was when he worked up a new ending that I realised how good he was at responding to crises,' says Temple, 'and making spur of the moment decisions.'

The video would be regarded as a triumph, and its energy and sense of fun helped damp down the critical backlash to *Tonight*, which started out with promising sales, entered the UK charts at number one, and was certified platinum by the end of November. But by the spring, when it came time to record a video for the album's only other half-decent track, 'Loving the Alien', the zest he'd managed to summon up for his videos, if not his music, seemed to have dissipated, too.

Possessed of more self-awareness than most of his peers, Bowie would also be more acutely conscious of his failures. From the 1960s he had made a habit of reading all his own reviews, and cultivating writers and critics, but by the mid-eighties, he would exist in a bizarrely bipolar world – working mostly with unfailingly approving acolytes as he made his music, and then falling victim to the finely honed knives of critics once the music was unleashed. It was tough for a man who'd always been a critics' favourite to realise that, once he'd joined the mainstream with *Let's Dance* and *Tonight*, he was distinctly out of favour: the mainstream, the commercial, The Dame.

Bowie's nickname reflected some of the cynicism that was unleashed by his unashamed grab for mainstream success. Yet the attention David received from critics paled into insignificance compared to the onslaught of the tabloid press in the wake of a family tragedy.

David's half-brother Terry had remained at Cane Hill for long periods since David had last visited him, during filming for *The Hunger*. Since that time his isolation and depression had deepened until, on 27 December, 1984, he decided to end his life. Walking down to the local train station, Coulsdon South, he lay down on the rails, waiting for a train to approach before apparently changing his mind at the last moment. On 16 January, he took advantage of Cane Hill's shortage of staff, returned to the station, and once again placed his head on the rails. This time he did not lose his nerve.

Whatever anguish David felt, 'We probably can't imagine,' says his Beckenham friend, Mark Pritchett. But the family traumas reached a new intensity when David's aunt Pat, angry at both Peggy and David for not visiting Terry often enough, shared her anger with the *Daily Mirror* and then the *Sun*. 'I hope God forgives you, David, for this tragic rejection,' she told the newspaper. 'David turned his back on his brother when it would have been so easy for him to do so much. David cheered him up and promised to see him again, after a time. But he never did. This has caused a big rift in our family.'

Bowie decided not to attend the funeral, which became the culmination of a tabloid feeding frenzy. The note on David's bouquet, echoing Rutger Hauer's final soliloquy in *Bladerunner*, read: 'You've seen more things than we can imagine, but all these moments will be lost – like tears washed away by the rain. God bless you – David.'

The newspapers condemned him for not attending the funeral, too. Later, Pat would expand on her grievances via two *Sunday Times* reporters, Peter and Leni Gillman. The couple's biography of David, published the next year, would open with a graphic account of the family mental instability, catalogued mostly by Pat, and would close with Terry's suicide. In between, their gripping account – which rarely mentioned David's music except where it related to schizophrenia, gay sex, or the Burns family history – set out a portrait of an uncaring, manipulative monster. Some of David's confidants – notably Tony Visconti, whom David had last seen during the *Serious Moonlight* tour – spoke to the Gillmans for the book, and were hence judged accomplices in this assault on his privacy. Bowie would not speak to Tony for another fourteen years.

According to Ken Pitt, David's aunt Pat would come to bitterly regret her attack on David in the wake of Terry's death. 'She was never the same. It had a big effect on the whole family. It was very, very sad.'

Numbed by this family tragedy, seeking to escape the tabloid press, David stayed holed up in Switzerland for most of the spring of 1985. Around May, Julien Temple had a crew ready for a video shoot for 'Loving the Alien'. Bowie, the reliable showbiz trouper, did not turn up. When they finally met up there was no haughtiness or grand excuses: David told him he simply couldn't do it. 'He was very down. He was open about how he felt, about not feeling vibed up to be able to do the video.'

If David was in a mental tailspin, it would be fevered activity that pulled him out of it. By June, Temple had finally managed to obtain backing for

Absolute Beginners, his film based on Colin MacInness's 1958 novel. Temple pursued Bowie subtly for the role, but David proved an easy sell, enthused by the role of ad exec Vendice Partners. His character's name was a reference to Vance Packard, author of *The Hidden Persuaders*, the definitive fifties work on media manipulation – in fact, the movie encapsulated most of Bowie's obsessions, including the fifties, the birth of the youth culture that had liberated him, the notion of being British, rather than American, and also the advent of modern marketing, the 'branding' that David understood so intuitively. 'David was hugely into this, the simultaneous birth of the teenager, and the creation of a market,' says Temple. 'And like everything he does, there was total commitment.' Bowie learned to tap-dance for his main scene, which involved him frolicking round a huge typewriter, climbing an adman's phoney Everest, all set to his advertising anthem 'That's Motivation'.

It was when he had committed the first song to tape that he told Temple he'd come up with a second. 'He'd written "That's Motivation", which we needed. And he surprised me with "Absolute Beginners". He was surprised by it as well – it just kind of arrived.'

'Absolute Beginners' was Bowie's last great composition of the 1980s. Like his perfect songs of the early seventies, it arrived almost instantaneously. The song was an afterthought at an Abbey Road session arranged to demo 'That's Motivation'; short of a band, David had called up an A&R at EMI, Hugh Stanley Clarke, for suggestions. Clarke's nominees, including guitarist Kevin Armstrong, bassist Matthew Seligman and Attractions organist Steve Nieve, were instructed to turn up at Abbey Road for a session with a 'Mr X'.

The musicians had guessed Mr X's identity before the session started; they were all nervous, eager to please, and the sense of unreality was intensified by David's flirtatious affability. Kevin Armstrong would go on to work with Bowie for years, but this first session nearly ended in disaster. 'The only time I ever was with David Bowie that I saw him do anything with drugs was at that very first day. I don't know why he picked me, but he asked me to get him some coke halfway through the day. I rang a friend to see if he had any going – he rang me back an hour later to say he'd managed to find someone who helped him out: "You will never guess who I've got this coke from? Angie Bowie!" And I said, "You'll never guess who it's for – David Bowie!"'

A more experienced operator might have been more circumspect, but assuming his new boss would be amused, Armstrong told him, 'My mate is getting this coke from Angie!' Bowie's unruffled, cheery demeanour cracked. 'No, not that fucking witch! I hope she doesn't know who it's for?'

'No, no, I never told my friend,' lied Armstrong. 'Which was not true of course,' he says today. 'So I nearly had my marching orders there and then. We went on to work together for ten years so it's probably all right. And I never came across any reference to drugs from him ever again.'

In fact, David Bowie after a large toot of cocaine was not noticeably different to the Bowie Armstrong would get to know later. 'He was on sixty to eighty fags a day. He'd have a coffee machine and some Cuba Gold coffee delivered wherever he was and it would be constantly on the brew. Seriously, he'd be chucking down the coffee and fags – and it would always be pretty neurotic and manic around him. Also, it was my first experience of being in the orbit of someone so hugely famous – there's a kind of electrical crackle around them anyway.'

Fired up, Armstrong and the band laid down a demo of 'That's Motivation', and were left with an hour of studio time. David played Armstrong some chords and a few lines of a new song, listened attentively as Armstrong helped sketch out the arrangement, then they explained the song to the band – eight bars at a time, recording each section piece by piece. 'By not knowing the whole song, it totally forced you out of your comfort zone,' says bassist Matthew Seligman. 'It was an amazing technique, very art school.' In the opening bars Seligman was overcome by a joyous, 'Velvet Underground, "Sunday Morning" kind of feeling', and played an ebullient, melodic bass riff – 'It was the sound of me being happy.' He expected Bowie to comment that it was too intrusive; instead, it became an integral part of the intro. At one point in the session he arbitrarily changed key; Bowie changed key with him. It was almost telepathic: 'It felt like mind control – it was very powerful, this switched-on radar.'

The lyrics for 'Absolute Beginners' revolved around 'absolutely' – a buzz-word for the movie crew: 'It just seemed to be a word that everyone used a lot that year,' says Temple, 'maybe because Absolut vodka came out at that time and David just picked up on it.' Among the simplest of Bowie lyrics ever committed to tape, the words were scribbled down and recorded in chunks. 'He got an idea, and followed it without thinking too much,' says Armstrong. When they finished the demo, David was exuberant, thanking the musicians, as if they'd done him a huge favour. 'I feel like I felt when I finished "Heroes",' he told them.

Temple was 'blown away' by the demo. When the official version was recorded, only one extra touch was needed. Bowie said, 'I want a duet with a girl who sounds like a shop girl.' Armstrong piped up with the news that his sister worked at Dorothy Perkins; the twenty-two-year-old Janet Armstrong duly turned up at West Side for her first ever professional vocal session, which also happened to be David Bowie's last Top 5 single, when released in March 1986. A conventional but fabulous song, it offered a tantalising promise that *Tonight*'s creative block was only temporary.

Soon after the 'Absolute Beginners' demo, David called Armstrong. 'I'm doing a concert for Bob Geldof for charity. It's going to be a big deal. Do you want to help me out?' Armstrong agreed, as David continued, 'I've got this extra idea for a record to support it. Would you meet me at this film company in Soho at 10 o'clock and bring an acoustic?'

Armstrong arrived in Wardour Street at the appointed time. When David walked in, he was accompanied by Mick Jagger. The pair explained that they had planned a transatlantic duet for the upcoming concert but the delay caused by the satellite link made it impossible, so they'd decided to pre-record and video their number, a cover of Martha and the Vandellas' 'Dancing in the Street'.

When the band convened at Westside, they enjoyed a fascinating glimpse of Britain's two best-known rock singers at work. Bowie arrived first, with a copy of Springsteen's 'Born in the USA' and told the rhythm section to match that feel. Then Seligman and drummer Neil Conti felt a 'whirling dervish' presence behind them, as Jagger whisked in, with his fourteen-year-old daughter Jade in tow. Once the backing track was nailed, the ten or so people present watched the pair camping it up and competing as they recorded their ludicrously over-the-top vocals. The two old friends got on well, but their rivalry was obvious. 'My gut reaction was to feel a bit protective of David,' says Seligman. 'Mick was much more vocal, mouthy – more rockist. David was the smiling indulgent one, more good-natured about the whole thing.'

The 'big deal' charity show would of course turn out to be Live Aid, an infinitely bigger deal than anyone could have imagined; the event brought out a new, non-competitive side of David. It was the first time he'd worked with a younger band, now featuring keyboard player Thomas Dolby, and before the Wembley concert he bustled around like a mother hen, despite the fact he was busy filming at Elstree for another new project, the movie *Labyrinth*. Hearing that his sax player, Clare Hirst, had confessed to her local paper that she was nervous about the show, he phoned her up and reassured her. Then he sweetly requested if the band could all wear turquoise for the performance and asked Hirst if it would be OK if he grabbed her hand during 'Heroes'.

On the day, David was 'very up – it hit home, as it did for everyone what a great event this was', says Armstrong. David showed them the waistband of the *Young Americans* suit he was wearing, sharing his delight that, at nearly forty, he could still fit into it. The band drove by Stansfield Road on the way – a couple of them had lived in a squat there – and noticed the streets of Brixton were quiet, all the residents glued to their TVs. As he squeezed into Noel Edmonds' helicopter, David's hands were shaking, cigarettes constantly on the go – the pilots complained the smoke was obscuring the instrument panel. Otherwise, there was no sign of nerves.

Queen, according to posterity, stole the show, but on the day no one knew or cared. David had chosen one of the youngest, most under-rehearsed bands of his entire career and treated them as if they were doing him a favour, joshing them along, especially Seligman, whom David had nicknamed 'Brenda' in revenge for the bassist mentioning that 'Blue Jean' was boring. Before they hit the stage, the band heard him shout, 'Remember, no monitors for Brenda!'

There were flurries of nerves: David fluffed a line, introducing singer Tessa Niles as 'Theresa'; sax player Clare Hirst stood holding her hand out at the scheduled moment, like a lemon, as David danced around on the other end of the stage; Kevin Armstrong started 'Rebel Rebel' way too fast. Yet throughout, David's joy was infectious, pushing forward the band who were totally focused on remembering the songs they'd rehearsed exactly three times. Somehow, it was perfect, says Thomas Dolby. 'To my astonishment, I felt like I was on a magic carpet ride. These songs were like our teenage anthems – my fingers were just wafted along.'

Of every artist, Bowie was the most focused on pushing the cause, not himself, cutting short his set – which up till the penultimate rehearsal included 'Fascination' – to save time for a harrowing video of starving Ethiopian children, which raised donations to a new peak.

His fulsome tribute to the band – 'I'll be for ever in their debt' – was repeated off-stage after the performance, when they all hugged, over-come with emotion. Later he dropped in on the Royal Box, and cheekily asked Princess Diana, 'Will we be getting you up on stage for the grand finale?'

The spontaneity of Live Aid would help David's reputation more or less recover the momentum he'd lost with *Tonight*, but rather than attend to his own career, he spent much of that winter working with the man who'd become his best friend. Since setting up home with Suchi in New York, Iggy had demoed his own songs with ex-Pistol Steve Jones, anxious to self-start his own project. By October 1985, the pair had made an impressive set of demos; when Iggy tracked David down to send him the tapes, he was surprised to find David was making the kid's movie, *Labyrinth*, at Elstree. (Lambasted by critics, the film would eventually win Bowie a new generation of fans, rather like Ringo's efforts on *Thomas the Tank Engine*.) Practical as ever, David told Iggy, 'They're all midtempo, so you'll need some slow ones and some fast ones.' He volunteered to fill the gaps if Iggy and Suchi would join him and Coco on a working holiday into the New Year.

They spent some of their three-month jaunt on Mustique, where David had bought a holiday home, installing a small recording setup. Joey, now fifteen, came too; David was notoriously strict, demanding his son return home while the other rich kids stayed out partying. 'The other kids all made fun of Joey, because he had to be home at 10 o'clock,' says one friend. '[David] was very strict – but it worked for Joey. And of course a lot of those other kids ended up as cokeheads or junkies.'

After Mustique, there was skiing in Gstaad and an agreement to complete the album later in the spring. Meanwhile, David worked on promoting *Absolute Beginners*, which was released on 4 April, 1986. The film had been hatched with a media onslaught which helped attract the backing of UK production company Goldcrest, but ultimately brought a huge critical backlash. Temple's labour of love was vilified, becoming a celebrated box-office flop. As Temple's problems multiplied, Bowie was 'genuinely supportive. A lot of the problems we had brought on ourselves, [but] I'd invested a huge amount, psychically, in that movie. And he understood.'

A few weeks later, David was back helping Iggy recover from his own legacy of failure. Aided by Erdal Kizilcay, a local multi-instrumentalist who'd worked on the *Let's Dance* pre-production, they recorded Iggy's album in two weeks, starting at 10 o'clock each morning, Bowie, once more the punctual professional, scheduling each overdub with his clipboard. The album's standout song was 'Shades', with both words and music written by David, after he'd seen Iggy give Suchi a pair of sunglasses: 'He saw that situation and turned it around . . . made it one of those reformed-guy songs,' says Iggy. David was in the middle of a creative drought; now he gave what was, after 'Absolute Beginners', his best song of the late eighties to his friend. Kevin Armstrong arrived a few days in to add his guitar. Watching the pair together, he saw Bowie's behaviour as essentially selfless: 'I think he was genuinely saying, Iggy needs help here, and I'm the guy that can do it; I've done it before and I'll do it again.'

When the album was complete, David had his management company, Isolar, secure a deal with A&M. Nancy Jeffries, the A&R woman who signed the deal, remembers there was a hefty price tag attached, so that David could recover his costs. But having worked for RCA, she knew the value of the album. 'It was almost like the David Bowie record that you wished you'd had, but never got.' *Blah Blah Blah*, released in November 1986, would deliver Iggy's first ever Top 50 hit, and launch him on the road to something resembling a conventional career.

Iggy wasn't the only hero that David tried to champion over 1986. In June, he holed up in London's Edgware Road with his old manager, Leslie Conn, for a couple of days. After talking about Georgie Fame – whom Leslie had worked with, and David had imitated in the early sixties – they decided to resuscitate his career. David drew up a memo, offering to invest £100,000 in Georgie Fame, as part of a stable of artists to be produced by David, Bill Laswell and Clive Langer.

The plan of building up a production stable, building on Bowie's hugely successful but strangely underrated role as a producer, was an intriguing one. He'd produced career highlights for Iggy, Lou and Mott The Hoople, yet his production skills were rarely discussed – under-appreciated, almost. Where many producers worked on developing a trademark sound, his approach had always been psychological; vibing up musicians, easing the flow of ideas. Yet Bowie's move into mainstream production was to remain an intriguing might've-been, for by the autumn of 1986, he'd abandoned the idea and devoted himself to his own career. Outwardly, he remained unconcerned by the state of his reputation, but in private he'd mention that he was worried about his relationship with EMI. When he started his next recording project, he told his main collaborator, Erdal Kizilcay, 'let's keep it simple,' like the Iggy album. They didn't.

Recorded at Mountain and completed at New York's Record Plant, *Never Let Me Down* was neither as good nor as bad as *Tonight*. In his efforts to ensure the album was a hit, David worked out each song carefully with Erdal Kizilcay beforehand, thus excising any hint of the random. It featured no cod-reggae, nor any songs that, while derivative of his own work, were memorable, like 'Loving the Alien' had been. Instead, the album was filled to the brim with conventional music, lyrics and sounds. 'Never Let Me Down' was startlingly reminiscent of the opening section of John Lennon's 'Starting Over'; the same breathy counter-tenor delivery, confessional feel and a similar chord sequence. 'Glass Spider' was preposterous, and hence at least noticeable. The utter dearth of inspiration was epitomised by the sole cover version: Iggy's 'Bang Bang'. The original had been an act of desperation on Iggy's part when he'd been told by Arista to deliver a hit or leave the label. David's rendition of the plodding, predictable chord sequence and coke-addled lyrics represents the very nadir.

The reviews, when they came, were dreadful. That was not the main problem, for plenty of Bowie's contemporaries had made poor albums. More serious was the way that this album seemed to damn all his previous work by association. As *Rolling Stone*'s Steve Pond commented, '[Bowie] has reached a startling level of influence and status while making few genuinely groundbreaking records.'

The subsequent *Glass Spider* tour, based on the album's silliest track, would become notorious, a celebrated disaster in David Bowie's career. Such is the distaste in which it is held, that its one transcendent moment has been forgotten. It took place on the Platz Der Republik, Berlin, just north of Hansa Tonstudio 2, on 6 June, 1987.

David had dropped in to see his friend Edu Meyer, who was working on a session with David's band, two days before. 'He was still the same guy I remember from *Lust for Life*, still a worker.' The city was already filling with West Germans who'd made their way out to the isolated enclave of Berlin for the show: 'A big event for the whole country,' says Meyer, 'and the [East German] government was pretty upset that it was happening so close to the Wall.'

That night, David launched into 'Heroes' in the shade of the Wall, five minutes from where the song had been conceived, and realised the song was being redefined. 'As we got into it, we could hear the thousands of kids who had gathered on the other side, the Berlin side,' he says, 'all joining in [the song]. It was terribly emotional.' 'He let them do the singing,' says Edu Meyer, 'and the DDR government tried to get these people away from the Wall . . . but with no success.' Fifteen years later, when David played in Berlin, he suddenly became aware that many of the audience had been the voices he'd heard: 'the ones on the other side'.

It was one of the few happy moments on the tour. Previously, David had always chosen his key collaborators then left everything to them.

Now, he was becoming a control freak, fussing over every detail, always 'very very tense', says bassist Erdal Kizilcay. After the third date, Chip Monck, stage designer for The Rolling Stones, who'd been commissioned to build the huge glass spider prop that loomed over the stage, left the tour: 'I got the thing built and only saw the first few shows. That was enough.'

The contempt in which *Glass Spider* was held is often seen as being the product of hindsight, part of a reaction against the obese over-production of the late eighties; indeed, the tour was, according to press reports, the most successful of Bowie's career, out-grossing *Serious Moonlight*, with 3 million tickets sold over its eighty-six shows. But for the Bowie fans who'd seen his previous tours, the memory of the *Glass Spider* shows is still traumatic. Tony Horkins, then editor of *International Musician* magazine, was one of many who walked into Wembley Stadium and caught sight of the spider looming over the stage. 'It wasn't just that they were obviously trying too hard; it was that they hadn't spent the money to hit what they were aiming for. The spider looked pathetic.'

David was simply dwarfed by the ludicrous spectacle. '*Serious Moonlight* had been a big production – but it was about him, and his voice sounded great,' says Horkins. 'This looked like an am-dram production, very overblown, detached, and he was dwarfed by all these gimmicks. It didn't have any real soul.' The emptiness on display was embodied by the endless guitar masturbation contests between Carlos Alomar and David's old Bromley Tech friend, Peter Frampton, both competing to see who could play more notes in a second. Their juxtaposition of guitar gurning and drum machine-beats, lifted from Eddie Van Halen's work on *Thriller*, was five years out of date. The impression that this was an emotionally empty exercise in generating cash deepened with the announcement that Bowie's huge earnings were being further bloated by a Pepsi sponsorship deal; it was headlined by a predictably naff commercial in which David was joined by Tina Turner, with the duo camping around by a vending machine, yelping, 'puts my choice in my hand', to the tune of 'Modern Love'.

The empty virtuosity on display in London was a stark contrast to David's joyous Wembley show of just two years before. By the time the tour reached America, Erdal and Frampton were 'fed up. We just wanted to go home,' says Kizilcay. On several shows, David's voice gave out and Carlos had to step in. The energy with which David normally inspired his crew was gone – instead, he started blaming them for the poor reviews. When the tour finished in New Zealand, they torched the glass spider. 'We just put the thing in a field and set light to it. That was such a relief!' David acknowledged a couple of years later. In PR terms, the glass spider was a far bigger disaster than a Nazi salute.

Some versions of history cite *Glass Spider* as the beginning of a new high-tech touring vogue; in fact, Michael Jackson's hugely successful *Bad* tour of 1988 featured stripped-down staging, as did Prince's acclaimed *Sign o' the Times* tour of 1987. In the previous four years both young artists, as well as Madonna, had adopted David's fleet-of-foot style and made him look moribund and tired.

Yet, as ever, even the footnotes or failures in David Bowie's career would lodge in other musicians' consciousness. Over 2009 and 2010, U2 would tour their underwhelming *No Line on the Horizon* album, produced by Brian Eno. Hovering above the stage, in what was proclaimed the most lavish rock 'n' roll production of all time, was a huge claw.

20

It's My Life – So Fuck Off

David would joke, 'Why do David Bowie and Mick Jagger
both feel compelled to keep going out touring? It's laughable.'
We never came up with an answer.

Adrian Belew

By the end of 1987, David was spending little time mourning the fate of *Glass Spider*. He had something much more threatening on his mind – a lawsuit from a woman named Wanda Lee Nichols, who accused Bowie of sexually assaulting her in a Dallas hotel room, on 9 October, 1987.

As far as David's immediate social circle was concerned, if he had deep-seated worries about his career he kept them to himself, but he didn't conceal his worries about the Nichols lawsuit. 'It was a big deal,' says one friend. 'He's not invulnerable at all, it rattled the fuck out of him.' It wasn't so much the specific accusation – which in retrospect was bizarre, claiming that he'd bitten the woman and then mentioned he had Aids – so much as what it represented. He admitted to spending the night with Nichols but claimed the rest of her story was fantasy. From now on, whenever he was enjoying the traditional perk of his job in a hotel room, there was always the fear of another accusation and lengthy lawsuit.

Although a grand jury declined to indict him a month later, the accusation would hang over David for nearly three years before being dismissed. In the first few weeks that the ramifications of Nichols' accusations started to unfold, David found a much-needed confidante in the form of Sara Terry, press agent for *Glass Spider*. A journalist for the *Christian Science Monitor*, Terry had joined the tour for a break soon after finishing a gruelling project on child prostitutes and soldiers. She was a forthright, valued adviser, being, in the words of friend Eric Schermerhorn, 'cool, aggressive, subtle and intelligent – an alpha female just like Coco'.

Sara's husband, Reeves Gabrels, also dropped in on the tour; not as outgoing as his wife, he was, says his musician friend Kevin Armstrong, 'very quiet, kind, funny, shy, intellectual, one of those Americans with no mental barriers'. Reeves played guitar, and had studied at the prestigious Berklee College of Music, but had previously spent three years at art school. He'd never talked about his musical ambitions with David, who assumed he was a painter, but in the tour's final days, Sara slipped David a cassette tape of Gabrels' band, The Dark. After the tour, Sara resumed her work with the *Christian Science Monitor* and moved with Reeves to London. In January 1988, David checked out the tape and soon started recommending Gabrels for sessions. Then, in June, it turned out he needed a guitarist, too. All of a sudden, David Bowie was in a hurry again. 'It happened really fast,' says Gabrels. 'David called me, I went over to Switzerland and we had this music to do – in a weekend.'

The project was a collaboration with dance troupe La La La Human Steps; Reeves came up with an arrangement for 'Look Back in Anger', with an extended, dark, clipped instrumental passage: 'Because we'd only really talked about art before, when we did start working together all our reference points for sound were painterly or architectural. David was saying stuff like, "We should do something where the guitars are like flying buttresses and cathedrals."'

The first outward clue that Pepsi-sponsored, pre-planned Bowie had been laid aside in favour of art-house, improvised Bowie came in what was an obscure but, for fans, legendary performance at London's Dominion Theatre in July 1988. The nine-minute-long performance with the Quebec dance company was part of a benefit for the London ICA arts venue; Bowie learned his dance steps, in which he acted mainly as a foil to the lithe, muscular Louise Lecavalier, in two days. On the night, there was a genuine sense of danger and eroticism that had long been missing from his music, as Lecavalier leapt over him, or cradled him on her knees like a doll, while Gabrels, Armstrong and Erdal Kizilcay produced their twisted, gothic, drawn-out version of the old *Lodger* song. The show was a convincing reminder of David's talent for snatching something meaningful out of random strands.

Two weeks later, Gabrels went over to Lausanne for a weekend's visit. He ended up staying a month. 'Every day we'd drive down to Mountain

Studios in Montreux and just work on stuff. Then go back and have a meal. Then watch *Fawlty Towers* and go to sleep.'

In those two weeks during July 1988, the pair's discussion would lay the groundwork for David Bowie's next decade. The singer was open, intelligent enough to realise his predicament, and honest enough to acknowledge it. He told Gabrels that, in the wake of his huge deal with EMI, he'd felt obliged to deliver hits – 'and it was kind of killing him', says Gabrels. Together, they talked and talked, searching for the inspirations that turned David on to music in the first place. In that quest, to find that old sense of excitement, there came the plan for what would become the Tin Machine band project. 'If there was a plan, it was that David just wanted to make the music that he wanted to make,' says Gabrels. 'One cool thing was that we were listening to all the same stuff: Led Zeppelin bootlegs, Cream bootlegs, Hendrix bootlegs, Miles Davis' *Bitches Brew*, Coltrane, the Pixies, Sonic Youth, Glen Branca, Stravinsky, John Lee Hooker, Buddy Guy, Junior Wells and Muddy Waters. Put all that in a blender and you got Tin Machine.'

The pair's discussions started a matter of days before a chance meeting that summer, when David was launching a video of the *Glass Spider* tour. Iggy's ex-bassist Tony Sales saw David, walked up 'and surprised him. And a few weeks later we were in Switzerland doing *Tin Machine*.'

Today, Tony Sales cuts the same tall, cadaverously handsome figure that fans of *Lust for Life* and Tin Machine remember; he is calm and well groomed, with the reasoned air of someone who has gone through hell, and then recovery, which is exactly what happened after the Sales brothers split with Iggy. The way David Bowie had parted from most of his bands seems like a masterclass in sensitivity compared to how Iggy sacked the brothers who had underpinned his best solo album. According to Hunt Sales, Iggy delivered their marching orders with the words, 'You're like heroin – and I don't need you.' Soon afterwards, the brothers put together a twelve-piece soul band in LA, but on his way home after yet another crazed show, Tony ended up in Cedars Sinai hospital after crashing his car. 'They found me dead with a stick shift in my chest. I was in a coma for two and a half months. I almost died. And it ruined our Sales brothers thing.' During Tony's months in hospital, Iggy was conspicuous by his absence. David was the only celebrity friend who came to see him, asking, 'When can we get you on the road?'

The bassist's description of David as simply 'a friend' is at odds with the aloof, selfish figure remembered by predecessors like Trevor Bolder,

yet his account is not unique. The standard history of the formation of
Tin Machine is a Bowie-centred one, which involves him using them to
detonate a controlled explosion, demolishing the memory of his late
eighties hubris. Yet according to Sales, the urge to hang with his friends,
and help them, was just as powerful a motivation. Tony and his drummer brother, Hunt, arrived at Montreux Casino, hanging out and playing
for a week along with David, Reeves and producer Tim Palmer, before
the tiny group decided they needed a second guitarist. Kevin
Armstrong – then, like Tony Sales, attempting to rebuild his life, having
turned into a groupie-shaggin', drug-sniffin' rock-monster during his
last tour with Iggy Pop – answered the call and did a double-take as he
entered the huge room. The most significant clue to the psychological
make-up of the band was laid out in front of him, in the form of a line of
amplifiers – for Reeves, Tony, Armstrong and David – all facing a huge
podium in the middle of the room. On top of the podium, which was
scaled by means of a ladder, was Hunt Sales' drumkit, with its monstrous twenty-four-inch bass drum. With this kit, the feisty, funny, crazed
drummer could beat anyone into submission, without any electronic
assistance: 'He is the loudest drummer I have ever worked with in my
life,' says Kevin Armstrong. 'I almost went deaf within the first couple
of days. The power and the volume was simply superhuman.' Producer
Tim Palmer had carefully placed microphones around the studio to capture this massive sound, and on Armstrong's first day, they wrote and
recorded 'Heaven's in Here'.

Hunt Sales was the kind of person who, as Armstrong put its,
'consumes his own body weight in dangerous substances every day'.
Everyone around him 'loved his freedom and his naughtiness'. Tony, in
contrast, was now a born-again evangelist for the cause of teetotalism:
if David was standing nearby with a glass of wine in his hand, he would
administer a reproving lecture on the dangers of alcohol. Tony restrained
himself, however, in the case of his brother, figuring such arguments
would end in violence. An amazing musician, like his brother, Tony also
had to contend with a consequence of his car crash: memory lapses which
meant that at crucial points he'd sometimes forget chord sequences, which
the others had to shout in his ear.

Back in Berlin, when David had recorded with the Sales brothers and
Iggy, the cultural *leitmotif* had been expressionism, Fritz Lang and Das
Neue Sachlichkeit. In Montreux, eleven years later, the theme was Soupy
Sales: the foul-mouthed, sexist, undoubted comedy genius, who was
of course the inspiration for *The Simpsons*' Krusty the Clown, the kids'

entertainer with a filthy mind. During the Mountain recording sessions, the Sales sons would call their father on an international line and route the phone call through the studio monitors, while David, Hunt, Tony, Kevin and Reeves would fall over laughing to monstrously amplified jokes, such as:

What do 50,000 battered wives have in common?
They don't fuckin' listen!

More than anyone, Bowie deferred to Reeves; he praised his experimentation, his 'stunt' guitar, and he also loved his virtuosity, encouraging him to explore more extreme effects and sounds. Yet even as Bowie's lieutenant, there was little Gabrels could do to pull his rhythm section into line. When the Sales brothers joined, David decided this should be a proper band, run as a democracy. In reality, Gabrels thought, it was more like a shouting match.

The band's initial jam sessions at Montreux blended seamlessly into a recording project, with 'Heaven's in Here' recorded on the first day, then became semi-formalised with a move to Compass Point – a recording studio in the Bahamas, where David stayed in Robert Palmer's house near the beach. The sessions went on and on; not aimless, or desperate, just jams, with dozens of tracks reportedly recorded. Sean Lennon popped in during the school holiday with Joey, who was in the process of dropping out of Gordonstoun. Despite his schooling problems, Joey was a quiet, unspoilt kid, a fan of The Smiths – David claimed to be a fan, too, but Joey seemed unconvinced. It was hilarious for the band to watch their exchanges, to see a man they thought of as the coolest dad in the world trying to impress his son. Sean, too, was earnest, thoughtful, the opposite of a showbiz brat; it was in tribute to him that the band recorded their own version of John's 'Working Class Hero'.

The little community hanging around the beach was augmented by David's new girlfriend, Melissa Hurley, a dancer from the *Glass Spider* tour. The Sales brothers, rock 'n' rollers to their core, rarely talked to Melissa. Kevin Armstrong liked her: 'She was a genuinely kind, sweet person.' Just twenty two-years old, with a voluptuous, almost Italian figure and a mass of wavy dark brown hair, she was caring, not at all pushy. She also had a classic 1980s fashion sense which sat poorly with David's refined cool; she bought him hats or brightly coloured scarves which he would wear for a couple of days before managing to lose them. He, in turn, as a world citizen, and something of an art teacher *manqué*, loved showing her new locations, appreciating her delight; together, they seemed relaxed, almost child-like, and there was little surprise when, in May 1989, Melissa's parents announced that the couple had become engaged.

David's indulgence of his new girlfriend was charming; especially at the more ludicrous moments, such as when Melissa persuaded him to wear a thong, which he wore a couple of times on the beach, affecting indifference to his bandmates' sniggers. Another comic touch was the presence of hoary old British rockers Status Quo, working in the adjacent studio, always ready to give tuition in pool and table football. The unspoilt, carefree air owed something to the gossip that Coco, often a cause of tension between David and his musicians, had found love and was living with a lawyer in Los Angeles.

For one band member, though, the setting was not a tropical paradise. A week or two into the recordings, David walked over to Kevin Armstrong's beach hut and told him that Tin Machine had been conceived as a four-piece – they'd like to keep Armstrong on, but as a background musician. For the guitarist, the news was 'totally crushing'. Yet David's man-management was admittedly better than in the old days; he was honest and open about Armstrong's demotion, telling him they'd work together again after Tin Machine – which they did.

The Compass Point studio was in the most perfect location, with white sand and sparkling azure sea just moments away, and beautiful spartan beach huts for the musicians, but the studio's glory days had passed with the death in a car crash of manager and engineer Alex Sadkin, in 1987, and there were frequent power-cuts and technical problems. A few days into their stay there was a tropical rainstorm: the sky went black, with huge gobbets of rain beating on the tiny gaggle of buildings. In this gothic deluge, they recorded 'I Can't Read', a song of stark beauty, its throbbing bass and chaotic guitar reminiscent of UK band Joy Division – who had, of course, based their sound on Iggy's *The Idiot*, and in turn would influence emerging bands like Jane's Addiction. The song was one of several Tin Machine gems destined to be overlooked in the noise and chaos surrounding the band. Kevin Armstrong believes that was part of the plan: 'I thought some of the best work didn't make it to the first record. I think David was deliberately trying to go for a fucked-up sound. If it was too safe or polite, he'd dump it.' Some of the missing songs, like 'Now', based on the La La La Human Steps intro, would show up years later, in 'Now's' case as the title track of the *Outside* album. The exclusion of anything

Yael Brandeis Perry

Top: With producer Hugh Padgham (centre, in glasses), at Le Studio, Marin Heights, near Montreal, to record *Tonight*, David's move into white reggae – just as the smart money was moving out.

Kevin Armstrong

'Absolute Beginners': Bowie making his last great single of the 1980s at West Side Studios, June, 1985, written and arranged in a whirlwind with a new young band. When the session was finished he thanked them for doing him a favour.

Recording 'Dancing in the Street' with Mick Jagger, Kevin Armstrong (centre) and singer Helena Springs. Bowie was relaxed, Mick more 'vocal and mouthy', remembers one musician.

A quick cigarette with Freddie Mercury, backstage at Live Aid. Bowie looked after his nervous band like a mother hen during the day, devoting himself to the cause rather than his career.

Famously ludicrous, the *Glass Spider* tour marked the point at which Bowie (here flanked by Peter Frampton and Erdal Kizilcay) moved from being a relaxed delegator to a nervous control freak. Still, the Berlin show, on 6 June, 1987, was a triumph, sparking riots in East Berlin, while U2 would later lift some of Bowie's staging ideas. Right, he visits Hansa's Edu Meyer before the Berlin show.

Kevin Armstrong

Among friends: with girlfriend Melissa Hurley and new guitarist and confidant Reeves Gabrels, Compass Point, Nassau, late 1988, finalising Tin Machine's debut album.

Ebet Roberts/ Getty Images

'It never really gelled – it was a battle.' Tin Machine, February, 1989, with Reeves Gabrels (right) and the irrepressible Sales brothers – Tony on bass, Hunt on drums.

'I have never been so happy.' Bowie met Iman Abdul Majid on 14 October, 1990. He later mentioned that he started thinking of baby names that first evening.

A modest party, with only 17,000 guests, to celebrate David Bowie's fiftieth birthday, 9 January, 1997, at Madison Square Gardens; the music drew mainly on *Earthling*, the image – augmented with refurbished, all-American dental work – was state-of-the-art MTV.

Toby Melville/PA

'He came back dressed in *Hunky Dory* mode and played a full set of hits, every one was a winner.' Taking Glastonbury by storm, June, 2000, with a band which included old hand Earl Slick, David Bowie finally seemed reconciled with his own past.

Brian Rasic/Rex Features

David, in a kimono – with 'tiny Japanese slippers on his tiny feet' – greets Bono and Eno backstage at London's Royal Festival Hall after his recreation of *Low*, June, 2002.

Startraks Photo/Rex Features

'A mature singer, like Tony Bennett or Frank Sinatra.' A nervous Bowie returns after his heart attack, 8 September, 2005. The bandages and 'bruising' signalled his identification with the battered state of New Orleans; his voice was now grainy and world-weary, too.

WireImage

'It was an unusual relationship.' A rare public appearance in 2009, this time playing support to director son Duncan for *Moon*'s appearance at the Tribeca Film Festival, NYC, April, 2009.

'We'll see what's meant to be.' David Bowie's last tour, Los Angeles, 2003. Its final curtailment formed a *de facto* 'Houdini Escape' – a rationale for the retirement of which he'd long fantasised.

that sounded remotely conventional was designed to show anyone, however cloth-eared, that the David Bowie who made *Never Let Me Down* was history.

The public debut of Tin Machine was cooked up around a table at Compass Point: chatting, hanging out, they decided it would be good to play live. Later that night they walked up to the band playing a small bar in Nassau and asked if they could use their gear; forty or fifty stunned American tourists goggled at the spectacle, mouthing at each other, 'Is that who I think it is?' as the band played a short set featuring 'Heaven's in Here'. 'It was a mess, but it was a *huge* buzz,' says Armstrong, 'just to see the reaction of the crowd.' David loved the vibe, the raw excitement of what they all called 'the guerilla gig'; together, they decided that was how the band would proceed: a small gang, one for all, all for one.

This could never be a truly equal gang, of course. When the band finally started their club tour in New York, on 14 June, 1989, it was David Bowie who handed each of them $1000 to buy a Prada suit for the show. And when the reviews for the *Tin Machine* album appeared around its release on 22 May, 1989, it was naturally treated as another record by David Bowie, rather than the debut by a new outfit. The critical reaction was generally positive – Paul du Noyer of *Q* magazine called the album 'a more accessible sort of record than we're used to' – while fans were ecstatic at the prospect of seeing David Bowie play a club tour. They queued for two days for some of the European dates, at small venues like Amsterdam Paradiso and Kilburn's National Ballroom. David was buoyed up, revelling in the energy of the crowd and the sheer freedom. But there was tension, too; he was always nervous of fans. Kevin Armstrong had toured with Iggy in similar-sized venues, and noticed he had a talent for calming down any fans who were deranged or high; he could simply touch their shoulder, like a Vulcan death-grip, and they'd go all limp. David had never really worked in those circumstances; by the time he'd started attracting real crowds in his Ziggy days, he had his own security crew. Accosted by fans, he'd be polite, pleasant; if they were being too persistent he'd simply blank them, but he was always wary, never quite as relaxed amid the mayhem as Iggy.

The shows themselves were, 'crazed, and huge fun', says Armstrong; 'a blast', according to Tony Sales. But most proper bands gel as they play more shows. With Tin Machine, says Armstrong, 'there was no gelling. Musically, it never really gelled because it was simply a battle. Hunt and

Tony were the solidest part, then Reeves is utter chaos – although Reeves and Hunt did develop a rapport in the the end. But you never knew what was gonna happen – it was always on the edge. Then I was shouting the chords to Tony most nights, because his short-term memory is shot. You could hardly play the same song in the same way twice. It certainly wasn't comfortable for me.'

According to Iggy, David didn't get as good results out of his old rhythm section either: 'I have to say, when they were with me, they swung more.' And indeed, alongside the band *bonhomie*, there was a dull, dogmatic element to Tin Machine shows, demonstrated by songs like their plodding cover of 'Working Class Hero'. It was this worthiness, and the over-avoidance of the 'conventional' songs lamented by Kevin Armstrong, which meant the initially warm reception for *Tin Machine* – which hit number three in the UK, number twenty-eight in the US – soon petered out. The process was hastened by the release of lumpen singles like 'Under the God', backed with a workmanlike cover of Dylan's 'Maggie's Farm'. Democracy has its drawbacks. As Gabrels pointedly observes, 'Sometimes a benevolent dictatorshop can be a good thing.'

For David, though, there was a unique buzz about the band; he loved the Sales brothers' vibe, and Hunt's special craziness. Gabrels did, too, at first: 'They were like Dean Martin and Jerry Lewis,' he says. 'A handful. Then during Tin Machine they suddenly became like Cain and Abel. They made for a lot of extra tension, and entertainment – *if* you find tension entertaining.' One night in New York, Hunt had his manifesto tattoo'd on his back: in huge letters it read, 'It's My Life'. But that wasn't the complete manifesto – he'd planned to have the words 'so fuck off' inscribed underneath, but told his bandmates that the heavy Gothic lettering took so much work that he'd reached his pain threshold after the first three words.

The inescapable predicament of Tin Machine, of course, is that their democratic vision was a Utopia. Bowie would always be blamed for Gabrels' or the Sales brothers' artistic mistakes; equally, their ideas and inventions would be credited to him, too. EMI, meanwhile, had paid a huge advance for the David Bowie™ brand, not Tin Machine – which would soon cause financial problems. In the meantime, the man at the centre of these contradictions simply enjoyed the experience for what it was. 'I don't think David was frustrated at any point,' says Armstrong. 'Everyone was aware that he could just whip this magic carpet away but while it was there you can't avoid letting the Sales brothers do their thing, because they are very powerful people.'

David's relaxed attitude about Tin Machine's internal conflicts was understandable, given he always had Brand Bowie to fall back on. Even as the band booked their tiny club gigs in the spring of 1989, Isolar and Bill Zysblat, now Bowie's business manager, were pencilling in stadiums across the world for a full year later, while David was also preparing for the re-release of his RCA albums.

In 1989, most record companies had hoovered up maximum profits for minimal effort from fans who were switching from vinyl to CD. The Beatles and Stones' CD reissues were both a notorious mess; Bowie's re-mastering of his album catalogue, in comparison, was first-rate. He selected CD specialists Rykodisc to master the albums and release them in Europe, while EMI licensed them in America. The new editions were a masterclass in CD releases, incorporating rarities and superb packaging, while a *Sound + Vision* boxset made up a kind of alternative greatest hits, comprising outtakes or alternate versions. If there was any contradiction in the fact that one of the world's most forward-thinking artists was one of the first to re-market his own history, it was overlooked, given that he did it so much better than his peers. The election of Bill Clinton as American president in January 1993 would soon mark the accession of the baby boomers to power. This generation – Bowie fans among them – had more disposable income than any of their predecessors. Experts like David and Bill Zysblat – who would soon lead the way in promoting stadium tours with his company RZO, maximising their financial returns – were there to help them spend it.

David had discussed the notion of a greatest hits stadium tour with Reeves Gabrels within the first few months of Tin Machine's existence. But the guitarist believed 'it didn't feel like my place to do it'. Appearing on stage with David for a greatest hits tour would also make Tin Machine look like a mere side-project, so Gabrels suggested a musician he knew and respected, who also had a link with Bowie's back catalogue: *Lodger* guitarist Adrian Belew.

Perfectly organised, impeccably choreographed – by Édouard Lock of La La La Human Steps – and presented with state-of-the-art video technology, *Sound + Vision* was another groundbreaking tour. An unadorned set was flanked by a huge screen showing video footage, much of it a giant moving image of David himself, with which the real singer would interact. Marketed as the first and last time David would do a 'Greatest Hits' set, the tour marked a period when ten of his reissued albums all entered the British charts. What would effectively be Bowie's last grand-standing stadium tour was, says musical director Adrian Belew, 'sensational' for both the musicians and the crowd. 'We'd walk out and start playing "ground control to Major Tom", and it would overwhelm you, this emotional feeling, then there's the video, the lights and all these huge images floating around – it would absolutely give you the chills.'

After eighteen years of touring, though, live shows felt anything but sensational for David Bowie, the artist who as a teenager had told his manager he hated 'ballrooms and the kids'. Several times during the *Sound + Vision* tour, which ran from 4 March to 29 September, 1990, David would ask his MD, 'Why do David Bowie and Mick Jagger both feel compelled to keep going out touring? Why do we do this? It's laughable.' The topic was raised several times, 'but there was no resolving it', says Belew.

David had once again deployed all his charm when he called Belew, even suggesting using Adrian's own band: drummer Mick Hodges and Rick Fox on keyboards. For Belew it was like 'a dream come true, to bring my band, childhood friends on tour I was like a kid with a handful of candy.'

For bassist Erdal Kizilcay, though, the tour was 'horrible'. There was a simple reason for the conflicting account; it depended whether you were in front of, or behind the screen. For the stripped-down visuals, it turned out Belew would be Bowie's main foil; the other three would remain invisible: 'It was devastating for them when they heard,' says Belew. 'They get to play with Bowie – and nobody can see them.'

For Erdal Kizilcay, a sponsorship deal arranged for the opening dates in Canada exemplified the seemingly intractable problem of David's desire both for cult status and mainstream income. David had attracted derision for accepting the Pepsi dollar in 1987. Labatt's sponsorship of the opening Canadian leg of the new tour was more damaging. Proclaimed an industry breakthrough by the agency that brokered it, the deal included a gap for the sponsor's message in the set, which fatally sapped away its momentum. 'It was horrible,' says Erdal Kizilcay, 'people left the venue – and didn't come back again. I don't know how much money he got for it but it blew up the highest point of the concert, the middle fifteen minutes. You'd come back and have to start warming up the people again, and it was, No way.'

Belew doesn't remember the sponsorship slot as the main problem; instead, the design of a clear metal stage, with amplifiers hidden underneath, together with the four-man line-up, meant the music would always come a distant second to the innovative visuals. 'I was fairly disappointed musically throughout the tour, with myself and what we were able to do. We were under severe restraint with a small band – how do you play "Young Americans" without a saxophone? Mike, Rick and I had just come from a club tour where the sound is warm and everyone can hear you . . . here for us it sounded metallic, the guitar sound was thin. I wish I could have done a much better job.'

Despite the technical frustrations, David and Adrian were in good spirits throughout most of the tour; for the backstage boys, despite getting to use Chrysler CEO Lee Iacocca's private jet for several dates, and the plush hotels, it was boring. During the performance, keyboardist Rick Fox was often restricted to simply pressing a button to play a sample or sequence; hence he'd munch on a sandwich or a burger if he was feeling peckish, mid-set. Then one night, Erdal saw David make a gesture in the middle of 'The Jean Genie', and thought he was being signalled to emerge from behind the curtain, which he did. Then: 'David shouted at me, "Get off!" It was weird.'

As the band sat on the plane at the end of the show, David 'yelled and yelled' at Erdal, says Belew, 'and a quiet came over everyone. We just sat there on the plane. It was horrible.'

It was a one-off incident, but it showed how, for all the musicians, 'You start with a lot of excitement and enthusiasm, then gradually you wear down,' says Belew. 'But that time with Erdal was the only scene – which is pretty good for a group of forty-five people travelling around the world.'

David himself made a good fist of enjoying the tour – he was more fun to be around than in 1978, and took Belew out for a memorable night in Paris, where he and Mick Jagger attempted to out-camp each other on the dancefloor, in that distinctive blend of friendship and schoolboy rivalry. Throughout, he'd vibe up Adrian, worked at stretching him as a musician, while trying to discuss ways he himself could tour and keep it from being routine. He didn't complain, but it was obviously hard work for him, although the band did not quite believe his widely publicised statement that this would be the last time he'd play his hits live; rather, it seemed a good marketing ploy. David had introduced a telephone poll, asking fans to nominate their favourite songs for inclusion in the set, and as the tour reached Europe, the *NME* launched a campaign to lobby for the inclusion of 'The Laughing Gnome'; he was unphased by their cheekiness (although, sadly, they never played the song). Even as the tour rumbled on through Europe before its conclusion in South America, he remained much less stressed than on the 1978 tour:

joking throughout, talking about Marlon Brando, singing Beatles songs.

During the second half of the tour, it was obvious David was having problems with Melissa; it added to his rapport with Belew, with whom he'd chat about his problems – his openness, the fact he was still having girl troubles at forty-three, was endearing. The band liked Melissa – 'She was a great person, but maybe not strong enough for David,' says Erdal, who'd also seen her occasionally in Switzerland – but for the later European dates she sat on the bus by herself. Then she was gone. David was gracious about the split, commenting he'd worried it was becoming an 'older men, younger girl situation' and describing her as 'such a wonderful, lovely, vibrant girl'. Some years later, Melissa married Patrick Cassidy, brother of seventies teen heartthrob David.

For the last few dates, in South America, there was no room for the staging, so half the crew were absent; together with an undercurrent of violence from the police, it made for an oddly anti-climactic finish for David's last huge stadium tour. After the last date, David said he'd give Adrian a call – 'And here we are nineteen years later!' says the guitarist. 'But he's a fun person to be around. I miss him.'

Whatever the backstage frustrations, the end of the *Sound + Vision* tour marked a life-changing encounter for David, one whose significance he realised a couple of weeks after the final date at Buenos Aires' River Plate Stadium on 29 September, 1990. A hairdresser friend, Teddy Antolin, had arranged a blind date for David, on 4 October. Later, David would comment it was love at sight, although in fact he been introduced to his date three or four times before, at the theatre and backstage at his LA show in May.

Iman Mohamed Abdulmajid was an eighteen-year-old political science major at Nairobi University when wildlife photographer Peter Beard, a friend of the writer Isak Dinesen, happened to spot her in May 1975; she eventually agreed to her first photoshoot in return for having her tuition fees paid, and caused a sensation on her arrival in New York when she signed with the prestigious Wilhelmina Models agency. Iman worked closely with Thierry Mugler, and became a muse for Yves Saint-Laurent. She established herself in the pre-supermodel era, when her main counterparts, says *Marie Claire*'s then-Beauty Director, Emma Bannister, were, 'Christie Brinkley, of "Uptown Girl" fame, and Carol Alt – real American cheese. So Iman really stood out – she was striking, strong and African.'

Iman finally became a household face, if not a household name, through an advert for Tia Maria: she smoulders and smiles briefly, her cheeks striped in fluorescent green – a true world citizen selling ersatz exoticism and, by most accounts, reviving the brand. At her peak, her earning were exceeding $2 million a year, but by 1989 she decided she had outstayed her welcome on the modelling scene.

Nearly everyone who's met Iman describes her using words similar to guitarist Eric Schermerhorn, who says, 'She was very nice, quieter than you'd think – and also not as tall as you'd think.' Iman was attracted to David straight away, but later said she truly fell in love when she found he adored reading to people, just like her father – who was the Somali ambassador to Saudi Arabia before his country was wracked by war – and was good at doing funny voices. As for David, he later said he started thinking of children's names the night they met.

The couple spent a few months together in LA, where they both owned houses, followed by an idyllic six-week trip up and down the Italian coast. If Iman had ever wondered what it would be like being married to a rock 'n' roller, she got a true taste of it that summer. After rehearsals in St Mâlo and Dublin, Tin Machine hit the road for another tour on 15 August, 1991, and continued playing, almost night after night, all the way through to the final show at Tokyo's Budokan in February, 1992. Together with the first Tin Machine tour, and his huge stadium jaunt, it would be David's longest period on the road since his Spiders days. Iman would travel with David for many of the shows in America and Europe.

By the time the second Tin Machine tour came round, Kevin Armstrong was booked elsewhere; Eric Schermerhorn, a friend of Reeves Gabrels from Boston, took his place. Seeing the band chemistry up close, he was amazed to see how laid-back Bowie was. But he also realised what it was like for the singer, with three opinionated, boisterous musicians in constant competition. Hunt Sales was a brilliant drummer; the hedonistic swagger of his drum intro to 'Lust for Life' would earn decades' worth of royalty checks for both Iggy and Bowie. Schermerhorn found Hunt the most vibrant character in the band, but the most troublesome. It was obvious that David shared his opinion: 'I think he watched Hunt self-destruct and I think it angered him, in that he was trying to help him. I think Hunt had a lot of resentment for his brother and David. Stay out of my business. It's my life – so fuck off.'

Schermerhorn, as a neutral party, got to hear everybody's complaints. 'I was close to Hunt because nobody else was. I was the in-between guy with everybody. Between all three of them they would come to me telling me all different things. I wanted to keep it all running smoothly because I liked them all.' Gabrels, meanwhile, had the thankless role of band manager: 'The good news, and the bad news, was I was the guy who looked at the books every week with the tour manager and the office, keeping an eye on the money – so I was keeping the Sales brothers from renting limousines and the band from getting charged for David wanting a bigger hotel room because Iman was coming to visit, things like that. My sideburns actually went grey in three months on that tour.'

David remained generally oblivious of the band's internal disputes. Only upcoming shows in the bigger cities worried him – he was surprisingly nervous, and gave better performances at the smaller venues. Even twenty-five years into his career, he still followed his press coverage too closely, but was relaxed about the increasingly vociferous critical drubbings the band were now receiving: 'He understood it happens with everyone,' say Gabrels, 'that it cycles.'

It was not just the critics who were unimpressed. After promising early numbers for the Tin Machine debut, sales had tailed off rapidly, with none of its singles cracking the Top 40. EMI baulked at the prospect of another Tin Machine album; the band signed instead to Polygram offshoot Victory, the brainchild of Phil Carson, who'd worked with Led Zep at Atlantic. Ultimately, the public was as unenthusiastic as EMI; *Tin Machine II* boasted some wonderful songs, like Bowie and the Sales brothers' translucently beautiful 'Goodybe Mr. Ed', and Gabrels' 'Shopping for Girls' but, like the live dates, it didn't quite gel. For Gabrels, the experience was frustrating: 'I would have had one less Hunt Sales vocal on the record,' but David seemed unconcerned. For him, playing and touring with Tin Machine allowed him to act like a 'normal bloke', says Eric Schermerhorn. 'He'd be blown away by the most mundane things. One time in Minneapolis walking into a pawn shop, with loads of used radios and beat boxes, he bought a used boom box for $65. He was, "This is great!" It was like he'd never done that stuff.'

Travelling with a band – as opposed to with a bunch of employees, as on the *Sound + Vision* tour – brought out a side of him often hidden under The Dame's snootiness. He was surprisingly open, trying to round up his bandmates for trips to local junk stores or museums – mates to keep him company and share the view; he was often emotional, especially after the occasional raid on his hotel minibar, and for a man who'd been so ruthless with himself, and his musicians, there were odd, nostalgic notes. His bandmates noticed how he seemed to keep and catalogue everything: drumsticks, clothing, guitar picks. The collecting demonstrated his odd relationship with his own past: often he'd be reluctant to talk about old works, yet once he started you often couldn't stop him – then he'd reveal how many old features on himself he'd read, how many errors he wanted to correct.

Much of the apparent contradiction was explained by the fact he was still a record nerd, who treasured the albums he'd bought thirty years ago from Medhurst's or Dobell's. He didn't want to play 'Space Oddity' every night until he was an old man; yet he needed his own records to slot alongside those of Little Richard and Iggy Pop in some *High Fidelity*-style ranking of the rock 'n' roll greats. Later that year he'd venture to Llangynwyd in South Wales, telling locals he was researching the genealogy of the Jones family. It was not a mid-life crisis, but there was an overwhelming urge to work out how he'd got here, and what his legacy would be.

Over the autumn of 1991 that occasional vulnerability alternated with skittish excitement: mainly because he planned to ask Iman to marry him. He put the question twice, both times in Paris, around 29 October – the first on the Seine, to the strains of 'April in Paris'; the second at the Paris L'Olympia, where he repeated his proposal on stage, in French, then played some saxophone as his fans cheered. It could have been hokey, 'but he was pretty amazing', says Schermerhorn.

It was just a couple of weeks later, in November 1992, that Bowie found himself in Brixton: looking out through the windows at Stansfield Road, wondering how life would have turned out if he'd been a shipping clerk or an accountant, crying. Then at the show at the Brixton Academy – David's childhood cinema – that evening, Hunt Sales hogged the mic for at least two songs too many, and a third of the audience left before the end.

The journey with Tin Machine had been idyllic, in a fucked-up way, but it was coming to an end. 'I remember once in the back of the bus, talking with the whole band and him saying, "Listen you guys, I'm getting older,"' says Schermerhorn. 'I heard David say, "I don't want to be doing this for ever. I want to make one more record." He didn't want to fuck around.'

In public, David remained strongly committed to Tin Machine; he said at the beginning of the project that they'd produce three albums, and there was no sign of his reneging. But out in Japan, he gently asked Schermerhorn what he was planning to do next and offered to make a few calls for him. Soon, Schermerhorn would help Iggy Pop craft his last great record, 1994's *American Caesar*; an album partly inspired by David's suggestion that Iggy start reading history books. 'They were amazing, complementary characters. They would each ask me about the other. It's amazing: each one wants what the other has got. Maybe Iggy was the better front man. But David was a better boss – he wanted people to succeed after they've worked with him. He didn't have to help me, but he did.'

The tour ended at the Budokan on 17 February, 1992. For the Sales brothers there were no regrets, says Tony, who ascribes much of the reaction to the band as down to fans' conservatism. 'People like the excitement of something different, but if you try to change, it terrifies them and they can't accept it.' Gabrels believes the project achieved David's aims, if not the band's. 'Tin Machine fell on the grenade of not just *Glass Spider* but *Never Let Me Down* and *Tonight*. I think the intentions were good at the start and then . . . it got sidetracked.'

Reeves Gabrels was one of many people who, during their time with David, debated the nature of fame: like gold, or diamonds, it was seen as precious, but its inherent value was impossible to determine. Reeves' conclusion was that it was 'a pile of shit'; David, for all his contradictions, was addicted to it. Even if he abhorred the intrusions of the media, his insecurities demanded he court them, for his public persona – how he was perceived – was now an intrinsic part of his own self-image. Thus the most personal, anguished emotions were both something to be concealed and to be displayed – most famously at the memorial concert for Freddie Mercury, which took place a few weeks after the close of the Tin Machine tour, on 20 April, 1992.

The show was a strange mix, reflecting Queen's quixotically diverse fan base: from heavy metallers like Guns N' Roses, through to Liz Taylor and Liza Minnelli. David showed an effortless understanding of the event; for if Freddie wasn't a truly close friend, their careers were closely intertwined, as two of the songs performed that night, 'All the Young Dudes' – a favourite of Brian May's – and 'Under Pressure' illustrated. David looked composed and impossibly well groomed in mint-green suit and Action Man hair, next to Annie Lennox, who was seemingly made-up as Pris, the 'pleasure model' replicant from *Bladerunner*, and nuzzled provocatively against his cheek at the song's climax.

The night's real resonance would come from the presence of Mick Ronson, a man who'd been as crucial an influence on the sound of Queen as David himself; David's one-time lieutenant had been diagnosed with inoperable liver cancer the previous August. Yet even the unflappable Ronson looked uncomfortable when, at the close of

'Heroes', David knelt on one knee and narrated the Lord's Prayer. The press reaction ranged from supportive to ridicule. Few commented on what an old-fashioned figure he cut alongside Annie Lennox, who could have been him twenty years earlier.

Just four days after the Wembley show, David married Iman in a private civil ceremony in Montreux; once more, David's simultaneous yearning for privacy and publicity was reflected by the public celebration at the American Church of St James in Florence which followed. The nuptials were celebrated in a twenty-three-page *Hello!* magazine cover story. David wore white tie; Iman a Herve Leger oyster dress with train. Joey was best man, Geoff MacCormack read Psalm 121, and Peggy had her photo taken with Bono. Yoko Ono and Brian Eno were among the guests. There were many flashes of humour in the accompanying interview, as well as instances of history being rewritten: 'I don't think I ever really had what we could call a proper marriage,' he says, of his days with Angie. There was a conventional, happy air, as if he were grateful finally to put aside his days of androgyny and transcending moral codes, and start over.

While many of the sentiments were standard *Hello!* fare – David's comments on how his friend Thierry Mugler had done 'a delightful job' of designing his suit – there were many moments of insight, more than in some of the more probing interviews to which David had been subjected. His open statement that, while he is not formally religious, 'God plays a very important part in my life,' as well as his admission that he spent his first few weeks with Iman worried that his 'silly sense of humour' might put her off, were both illuminating demonstrations of how, in his forties, he was happy to admit to the strong streak of conventionality that had always run through him.

If the wedding was memorable, the album that marked it would be generally forgotten – continuing Bowie's unhappy recent tradition of attempting for commercial crossover and failing. David felt 'pressured' into recruiting Nile Rodgers as producer for this next work, says Reeves Gabrels. Rodgers had gotten over his resentment that, in the wake of *Let's Dance*'s huge sales, David had barely mentioned its producer. He found, though, that he and Bowie had different intentions for this new album right from the start: 'I literally said, "David, let's kick *Let's Dance* in the ass,"' says Rodgers. 'He said, "No, it's impossible. We can't do that." "What do you mean we can't?" "I don't know."'

Reeves Gabrels, meanwhile, felt 'we'd put all this effort into trying to get rid of the stuff that followed *Let's Dance* to change expectations and allow David to be an artist again. So I was irritated by the notion, but, for whatever reason, they decided to do it.' David, in turn, had an entirely different agenda, according to Nile Rodgers. 'He made that record to mark his wedding. That's what he told me. I kept thinking, Well "Let's Dance" and "China Girl" would have played fine at a wedding.'

Black Tie White Noise betrayed the mix of motives behind it; taken on its own merits, as a snapshot of influences, it made sense, was endearing even, with its backstory of the wedding, the LA riots, even, in 'Don't Let Me Down & Down', a song written by a Mauritanian princess and rendered both in the Indonesian language and a Brixton patois. The album was launched with the usual fanfare, a collective sigh of relief from the critical community that David had apparently terminated his Tin Machine experimentation, as well as extensive promotion by David's new record company, Savage, an ambitious start-up business who paid a reported $3.4 million for the record in order to establish their credibility – a deal which ultimately ruined the company, which declared itself bankrupt in December 1993 amid a flurry of lawsuits.

David was relaxed and playful during the sessions; there were many flashes of his old brilliance. When Nile was about to record his guitar solo for the twitchy, insistent 'Miracle Goodnight', David used one of his trademark, left-field instructions. '"Imagine the fifties never existed," he told me. I went, "Wow, now we're in some nebulous era because if the fifties hadn't happened there would be no Jeff Beck and Hendrix." It was a great direction.' Gabrels, meanwhile, contributed most of his guitar work when Nile was filming the *The Tonight Show* in California, working on several songs including 'You've Been Around' and a cover of Cream's 'I Feel Free' – a song that David had lately revived with Tin Machine. Bowie recorded the song, he mentioned later, in tribute to Terry, and the Cream show at the Bromel Club that they had attended together; a second song, 'Jump They Say', addressed his ex-brother more directly.

'I Feel Free' was shrouded in two layers of loss. There had been regular exchanges between Bowie and the ailing Mick Ronson throughout the year; David had sent several songs for the album Ronson was struggling to complete, and had publicly complimented Mick's production of Morrissey's *Your Arsenal*. The new version of 'I Feel Free' was essentially complete before Ronson arrived in the studio to contribute his signature sound; Gabrels' solo was wiped to make way for his predecessor. 'It wasn't sad – it was simply great to play with him and to have him around,' says Nile Rodgers. 'Mick just did it and it was cool.'

Ronson's presence on *Black Tie White Noise* helped generate a flurry of press on the album's release in April 1993; whereas David had been careful to avoid the role of elder statesman in the eighties, he bowed to the inevitable in the early nineties, a time when the influence of Ziggy Stardust was at its peak thanks to Britpop pioneers Suede: the partnership of Bernard Butler's muscular guitar and singer Brett Anderson's feyness closely mirrored the Ronson/Bowie relationship.

Interviewed with Anderson for the *NME* in March, David was genial, relaxed, effortlessly taking on the mantle of founding father of Britpop – which, in most fundamental respects, he deserved, for various phases of his own career had indeed made their mark on The Smiths, Suede and Blur. The *NME* story helped generate a sense that David was back to making personal, rather than corporate albums: the intensity of 'Jump They Say' powered the single to number nine in the UK charts, while *Black Tie White Noise* debuted at number one in the UK.

The album's sales were a powerful vindication of Bowie's scorched-earth policy with Tin Machine, and seemed also to show him fitting neatly into the nineties, while acknowledging his own past – influences like Mick and Terry – with a new honesty. Mick Ronson's death, on 30 April, emphasised the passing of an era. Yet its aftermath showed that not all of David's demons had been exorcised.

Shortly after Ronson's death, David paid a fulsome tribute to his best-known lieutenant: 'He was really up there in the so-called hierarchy with the great guitar players . . . superb, absolutely superb.'

There had been no formal reconciliation after their seventies split, for one was not really needed – 'I've got no complaints, why would I?' Ronson told this writer in 1989 – but Bowie's relationship with the guitarist who had, more than any other musician, powered him to fame, remained troubled. The issue flared up at Ronson's memorial concert at the Hammersmith Odeon the following April, an event at which Bowie was conspicuously absent.

Trevor Bolder, Bowie's Spiders bassist and Ronson's old friend, was told, 'He had a couple of issues with some people on the bill and he didn't want to get involved.' Bolder also heard that David was worried about playing to a small crowd. 'Fair enough. It's sad you have to worry about [such] things.' Others involved in the event, like Suzi Fussey-Ronson, ask, 'If he felt that the event wasn't big enough for him, why couldn't he have made a video, to at least say something?'

Quizzed on this subject in 1998, Bowie responded: 'The truth is I was not convinced by the motivations of this event but, frankly, I prefer to

stay silent.' Many of David's fans questioned *his* motivations – especially considering his presence at Freddie Mercury's memorial. Perhaps
the rivalry between Bowie and Ronson survived the guitarist's death.
For instance, in his otherwise illuminating contributions to Mick Rock's
book, *Moonage Daydream*, Bowie comments, 'Another of Mick's singu-
lar abilities . . . was the ability to take a hook line that I might whistle
or play badly and make it sing – we worked well together because of
this talent of his as an interpreter.' Suzi Ronson was one of many who
were offended by Bowie's condescending attitude: 'Like David had
arranged all his bloody solos. I spent $500 on that book and sent it
back, saying I was disgusted. Mick Rock and I didn't speak for a while
after that.'

Ken Scott, the producer who witnessed their collaboration, agrees
there were indeed instances where David was very specific indeed about
some instrumental passages – '"Moonage Daydream" in particular' –
but as for the suggestion that David humming Mick's solos to him was
their normal practice, 'I wouldn't agree. No. That's not the way I remember it.' The frostiness between the Bowie and Ronson camps was
maintained with David's reference in the same book to Suzi Fussey,
Ronson's wife and David's long-serving personal assistant, as 'a local
hairdresser in Bromley or Beckenham'. There were, obviously, parts of
David's past with which he was not quite at peace.

Bowie's belated, ungracious comments on Ronson were counter-
productive: a case of The Dame doth protest too much, suggesting that
David was more aware than he cared to admit how integral Ronson had
been to his breakthrough. Certainly, the negligible long-term impact of
Black Tie White Noise – a pleasant, competent album which soon vanished
from human consciousness along with the record company that released
it – seemed to show how reliant David was on a musical foil; a Ronson
or a Brian Eno whom he could feed off, who made his music gel. Without
one, he seemed to be locked into a cycle of diminishing returns.

But that foil, that source of inspiration, didn't *have* to be a musician;
for in the case of David Bowie's best album in nearly a decade, a rushed
commission done on a tight budget, the vital spark came from a
relatively obscure novel about a Bromley childhood, which was turned
into a film by the BBC.

The genesis of the project that would re-ignite Bowie's creativity came
in the closing minutes of a Q&A with one of David's favourite magazines, *Interview*, famously founded by Andy Warhol in 1969. As so often,

the magazine sent a celebrated name to interview the month's cover star, and the choice of writer Hanif Kureishi was particularly astute: the novelist, like David, was a Bromley boy and a fellow ex-student of Bromley Tech. In the closing moments of the encounter, Kureishi mentioned the BBC were planning a TV version of his 1990 novel, *Buddha of Suburbia*, based on Kureishi's own upbringing in south-east London. Cheekily, Kureishi asked if David would contribute the soundtrack. Instantly, David agreed. The pair were huddled over a mixing desk at Mountain Studios just a few days later.

The recording fell into two sections: the first a more conventional soundtrack, written against a video of the shows. Kureishi dropped in to observe, overawed by the fact his own work was being screened over a mixing desk, 'dotted with dozens of buttons, levers and swinging gauges', and later by the fact that David, noticing a couple of pieces changed the mood of key scenes, quickly rewrote them. Then, most of the themes used to soundtrack the drama were extended into a full Bowie album. *Buddha of Suburbia*, like so many of Bowie's triumphs, from *The Idiot* to 'Absolute Beginners', benefited from its rushed creation. 'Something happened for that album,' says Erdal Kizilcay. 'There wasn't a big budget, David explained the story before we started. It was a challenge, it was a small budget, but David just said, "Let's go, let's do it," and everything worked.'

Throughout the 1990s, countless music critics remember that, every time a new David Bowie album was biked into the office, it would be preceded by a PR's guarantee that, 'It's his best since *Scary Monsters*.' Probably the only album sent over without such blandishments, it was the one most worthy of them; in its modest way, the *Buddha of Suburbia* album was a perfect evocation, not just of Kureishi's youth, but of his fellow Bromley boy, now aged forty-six.

There were plenty of nostalgic moments in the *Buddha* album, but perhaps its most pervasive connection with its own life was that, like all his best works, it was made without thinking too much – moments snatched out of the ether. Bowie and Kizilcay worked alongside each other, Bowie using the instrumentalist as a kind of one-man sound library. They'd work from 10 a.m. until 8 o'clock at night – joking, eating burgers, playing records by Prince or Nine Inch Nails to get them into the mood. A fair amount of the time, they'd talk about Turkey; Erdal was a cultural transplant in Switzerland, like Hanif Kureishi was in Bromley – as was David, the kid who'd once fondly imagined himself 'the English Elvis'.

A couple of songs had been sketched out on demo – notably the subtle but anthemic 'Strangers When We Meet', which David had attempted with Reeves during the *Black Tie White Noise* sessions – but most of them were put together as first takes. They'd discuss an idea or chord sequence and Erdal would say, 'I'll try it.' Then David would laugh, 'Don't try it – play it!' Erdal's own life journey was absorbed into the work, a huge amount of which was his improvisation – for instance, the gloriously meandering 'South Horizon', in which Kizilcay's simple trumpet motif, swinging drums and busy bass duel with the piano of Mike Garson, who'd just reappeared on the scene and overdubbed his part on the other side of the Atlantic.

Yet if the musicianship was Erdal's, the driving force was David: 'He is just a master – he knows exactly what he wants. I was like his hands, his musical hands.' Even the more electro tracks – heavily influenced by the newly emergent Underworld – were tougher and more south London than the glossy sheen of *White Tie*'s dance songs. 'The Mysteries' was based on an Austrian classical work, sampled and reversed, rather like *Low*'s 'Subterraneans'. Fragments of the lyrics were straightforward autobiography, mostly the title track, which mentions Plaistow Grove, by the railway tracks; Terry, too, is invoked through the words *'ouvre le chien'*, a quote from David's 1970 song dedicated to his brother, 'All the Madmen'.

The album sneaked out in Britain in November 1993, almost unnoticed (it would wait another two years for a US release on BMG) although the title track reached number thirty-five in the UK singles chart. It was the best David Bowie album in a decade, and the first in twenty-two years to entirely miss the charts. Its creator, the man always focused on success, seemed not only unconcerned, says his collaborator, Erdal Kizilcay, 'He was very happy.'

21

The Heart's Filthy Lesson

I've got to think of myself as the luckiest guy – Robert Johnson
only had one album's worth of work as his legacy.

David Bowie

By 1994, David had apparently expended almost as much energy in transforming himself into an underground artist as he had in transforming himself into a star. Yet no one could have possibly confused his lifestyle with that of a musician struggling to make ends meet. David and Iman largely divided their time between Los Angeles, Lausanne and Mustique, where he retained an immaculately groomed house, furnished in the airbrushed ethnic style purveyed by the most expensive international interior designers. There, he posed for *Architectural Digest* magazine atop an antique Indian mahogany lounger. 'My ambition,' he told writer William Buckley, 'is to make music so incredibly uncompromised that I will have absolutely no audience left whatsoever – and then I'll able to spend the entire year on the island.'

The comments were partly a reflection of the Bowie sense of humour, but there was a serious core to the sentiment. Over the late nineties, a string of worthy, arty projects – a one-man show of twenty years' worth of paintings at a gallery on London's Cork Street in 1995 and a position on the editorial board of *Modern Painters* magazine a year later – gave the impression that he was simply a rich hobbyist. It wasn't true, though. In reality, his compulsion to keep busy couldn't be kept in check for ever, and within months of this statement, he was planning one of the most extreme recording experiences of his career – an art project, but one he would struggle to keep uncompromised.

Mike Garson was the restlessly inventive pianist who had transformed *Aladdin Sane*, and last played with David on *Young Americans*. Like many musicians decades into their career, he'd wondered if he could match the creativity of his youth. In March 1994, he started his first complete album with David in twenty years, with those doubts nagging at him. 'Personally, I didn't think I could really meet the mark or come up to the standard that I had set on *Aladdin Sane*. I was thinking, Could I top that? I was a little doubtful. But there was this great affinity and rapport. I still remember thinking to myself, This is special. It was a gem, to me.'

The inspiration for the new project came from David's chats with Brian Eno at his wedding. Eno was, of course, hot property as a producer thanks to his work on U2's electrifying *Achtung Baby*, an album steeped in the sound of Bowie, Eno and – it needs stressing – Tony Visconti's experiments in Berlin. Once they'd decided to work together, their collaboration started to take shape through what was, in 1994, the most high-tech of methods. Reeves Gabrels first heard about the planned album just after he'd completed a tour with Free's Paul Rodgers. He walked into a hotel rooom in Oklahoma City with the strains of 'All Right Now' ringing in his head and saw a fax from Eno lying on the floor. Soon fax machines around the world were spooling out apparently impossible concepts and intractable questions: 'One idea that David and Brian were trying to figure out was almost like a Charles Ives thing where you have two songs playing simultaneously then have them suddenly link up where the same word, beat, everything was right on the same spot: a mathematical problem.'

In essence, the work harked back to David's first trip to America, when he'd discovered the music of outsiders like Iggy Pop, the Legendary Stardust Cowboy and the fake Lou Reed. Hoping to tap a similar source in their quest to record the most extreme music of their careers, Bowie and Eno ventured, in January 1994, to the Gugging Hospital near Vienna, where psychiatrist Leo Navratil had assembled a group of patients who would become known as Outsider artists. In 1981, Navratil opened a formal Haus der Künstler (house of artists) within the hospital, where these artists could live and work as a community. Bowie told *Interview* magazine later, 'Some of them don't even do [their art] as an expression of themselves; they do it because their work is them. Their motivation for painting and sculpting comes from a different place than that of the average artist who's sane on society's terms.'

Interviewer Ingrid Sischy was sensitive enough not to ask the obvious question: whether David Bowie's half-brother might have benefited from a similarly enlightened regime, rather than the depressing, under-staffed confines of Cane Hill. Unsurprisingly, David and Eno were 'both very affected by the experience' of visiting the Haus der Künstler.

In some way the album sessions, which started in March 1994, were like a replay of the Berlin days; for Garson it was a throw-back to Philadelphia and *Young Americans*, his last full album outing with Bowie. The two had been reunited after a chance remark by writer Jérome Soligny, who happened to mention that the pianist had quit Scientology. Partly inspired by the news that Garson was no longer a parson, Bowie called him a few days later to overdub piano to *Buddha*. But for their first meeting in a studio in nearly twenty years, there was no nostalgia, says Garson: 'He just settles into it and that's all that exists at that moment in time. If I was to meet him tomorrow I'd have to come in as a fresh artist – none of the things from the past would mean anything.'

Today, Garson expresses no regret at his two-decade separation from David; rather there is an admiration for David's immersion in the present. 'We would sit down every morning when we got in the studio, push RECORD and just play and play and play. It was a wonderful experiment and it turned into great music. There were times when David and Brian would play us tracks through the headphones; we'd be listening to a Marvin Gaye song and improvising against it, then they'd take that away and mess around with what we got from that based on how we were influenced by that piece. I thought that was brilliant.'

Reeves Gabrels arrived in Lausanne roughly a week before the album sessions to write, and just to hang out. In this new context, he realised how David might have eight hours set aside, six of which would be spent talking: 'but all of that informs the two hours when the flash happens'. The sessions were consciously arranged as an art happening. Each musician had his own corner in the studio; when David wasn't setting up their head space, talking to them and making suggestions, he stood at an easel, sketching the band in charcoals. He constructed his lyrics using a randomising programme on his Apple Powerbook to recreate the old cut-up technique he'd used on *Diamond Dogs*. As in Berlin, he was using words for their sounds and associations, rather than a linear narrative.

Eno had prepared role cards for the participants, aimed at forcing them out of stock ideas and responses. At times, Garson remembers Eno holding up cards signalling chord changes and being ignored by the Reeves-Garson-Kizilcay trio: 'Erdal was incredible, like a one-man jazz-rock fusion ensemble, all filtered through his growing up in Turkey. He was like, "I don't get this shit, what is this shit?" He would ultimately play incredibly well.'

In this new atmosphere, Kizilcay, who'd worked on Bowie sessions since the pre-production for *Let's Dance*, felt uncomfortable. He missed the musical intimacy of the *Buddha* sessions and he was not a fan of Brian Eno's Oblique Strategies, in which each musician was assigned a character: 'He wrote me something like that I was an Arabic Sheik and I wanted to marry this guy's daughter – so I needed to show him I can play psychedelic, arabesque funk. But I don't need a letter to play Oriental stuff!'

Gabrels was more receptive: 'Mine was, "You're on the third moon of Jupiter and you're the house band." I liked that. What was funny was I would sometimes play that game in my head anyway.' Garson's card read, 'You are the morale booster of a small ragtag terrorist operation. You must keep spirits up at all costs.' Bowie, when he wasn't sketching, was 'a town crier in a society where the media networks have tumbled down'.

For Garson, this was a powerful experience: 'There was a camera, too. Hours of it every day just running, fixed cameras on each of us. So they knew it was special on some level. Then David doing charcoals of everybody as we're improvising was almost like another instrumentalist playing, part of the creation.' All of the musicians remember the genesis of certain key songs, including 'The Heart's Filthy Lesson', as dating from this period, with over thirty-five hours of songs that evolved over the sessions. When complete, the work was edited into two CD's worth of material, titled *Leon*. Brian Eno, in particular, was keen to release the results as a black label 'with no name on it', says Gabrels: 'Let it leak that it was David Bowie but put it out as a completely separate entity, like Prince's *Black Album*. Use it as a work of art and also something that creates interest for the next project.'

As they laboured in the smoke-fogged studio at Mountain, with both Bowie and Gabrels chain-smoking one Marlboro after another, the way ahead seemed clear. For David, there was an obvious artist on whom to model himself: Scott Walker, the man who had turned him on to Jacques Brel and whose career he had followed for twenty years now, since hearing the singer in Lesley Duncan's room at Redington Road. According to Gabrels, 'Scott Walker was still one of David's heroes,' and the small group of musicians saw their project in a similar uncompromising vein to Scott's more challenging works.

But near completion of the album, David encountered exactly the same problems finding a sympathetic record company that had plagued

Scott Walker. The best prospect was Virgin America, now owned by EMI; according to Gabrels, it was on their persuasion that David reworked the album over January 1995, mostly at the Hit Factory in New York. Carlos Alomar returned to contribute sublime rhythm guitar to 'I Have Not Been to Oxford Town'. Over the same period, they introduced another version of 'Strangers When We Meet', 'Thru These Architect's Eyes' and 'Hallo Spaceboy', which originated from a Reeves' ambient tune called 'Moondust'.

Soon after the New York sessions, Kevin Armstrong got a call to turn up at West Side studios in London; his own song, 'Now', recorded for the first Tin Machine album but left in the vault, was reworked as the title track of *Outside*; Armstrong also added guitar to 'The Heart's Filthy Lesson' and 'Thru These Architect's Eyes'. The songs' dark, gothic atmosphere was offset by the breezy presence of Sabrina Guinness, heiress and ex-girlfriend of Prince Charles. Guinness had recently returned from Hollywood and was setting up a video workshop for deprived kids, who filmed the sessions. Brian Eno agreed to a taped interview with the children, the intellectual guru turned total sweetheart: 'He was absolutely charming with them,' says Armstrong; the kids, in turn, added their voices to 'The Heart's Filthy Lesson'.

That song caused one of the first artistic disagreements between Gabrels and his boss, showing how hard it could be for a musician who was simply an employee. After recording the first version, Bowie had second thoughts and re-recorded his vocals with new lyrics – based on the theme of English landscape painters. Gabrels voiced his reservations: 'Maybe I was too critical, so he said, "Why don't you go away and come back in two hours?"' says Gabrels. 'I came back and heard it and said, "David, that's nice and all – but it's kind of destroyed the essence of the song, don't you think?" And he just waved his hand, "Fine, we'll just move on." "No no, David, I don't mean to hurt you." "No, forget it, we'll just go to another track. We'll come back to that next month."'

The pair never discussed the subject again, but when it came to the mix, David had reverted back to the original. The final version eventually ended up in a celebrated slot over the end titles to David Fincher's twisted serial-killer movie, *Se7en* – perhaps a treatise on English landscape artists would not have done the trick in that setting.

It was, of course, typical of the entertainment industry that David and Brian had started the project inspired by an artistic community who were blissfully heedless of commercial pressures, and then had to rework their initial concept to get a record deal. Yet the album would soon undergo a second reworking at David's hands, intended to restore the art-house element he thought had been lost. Over 1995, he added spoken-word recordings, reshaping the album into a concept piece based on a surreal murder story he'd written for *Q* magazine in late 1994 called 'The Diary of Nathan Adler': what Bowie called a 'non-linear gothic drama hyper-cycle'. The plot revolved around the murder and dismemberment of fourteen-year-old runaway Baby Grace Blue, her body parts destined for a Damien Hirst-esque artwork, with Bowie's Nathan Adler providing a Philip Marlowe-style voiceover in a dodgy Brooklyn accent.

Challenging, complex, often thrilling, over-long and – in the spoken segues – undoubtedly self-indulgent, *1.Outside* finally made it to the record shops on 25 September, 1995, eighteen months after the first Montreux sessions. Its release met with a deluge of media attention, most of it effusive – 'bold and fascinating' said Tom Doyle of *Q* – although dissenters, like the *San Francisco Examiner*, proclaimed it 'pretentious and nearly tuneless'.

In what would soon prove a habit, Bowie chose to lead with an uncompromising single – 'The Heart's Filthy Lesson' – accompanied by a deliberately provocative video directed by Sam Bayer, also responsible for Nirvana's 'Smells Like Teen Spirit'. The video was a magnificently squelchy snuff-movie assemblage, whose cabinet of freaks and sepia styling echoed the video for Nine Inch Nails' 'Closer' – which was famously screened on MTV with 'Scene Removed' placards to denote the cuts. As was surely intended, MTV duly refused to screen Bowie's promo, which was later broadcast in edited form, and the single limped to ninety-two in the US, thirty-five in the UK.

Bayer's video – the MTV kids with body piercings and tattoos assembling a Minotaur from spare body parts – embodied the mid-nineties aesthetic so perfectly as to suggest that Bowie was merely jumping on a fashionable bandwagon. If anyone had form for that crime, it was he. Yet, in fairness, artists like Smashing Pumpkins, Marilyn Manson, Nine Inch Nails and of course Nirvana, who had recorded their limpid version of 'Man Who Sold the World' back in November, 1993, all took elements of their dense, claustrophobic sound from Bowie. In any case, Bowie's incursion into the MTV alternative scene was aimed more at getting his groove back, than in pursuit of commercial success.

Even as Bowie's music started to pass out of youth culture, as a father and forty-something he seemed to have a more profound understanding of it. In 1971, he'd predicted a post-sexual society, throwing together a youth manifesto that was, in retrospect, half-baked. In the 1990s, many of his pronouncements about art provoked sniffiness, with adjectives like 'portentous' being directed at him by interviewers such as British writer Chris Roberts. Yet in retrospect, Roberts realised the insight behind some apparently throwaway comments. When the two met in 1995, Bowie predicted a 'non-linear' society, telling him, 'I think that we as a culture embrace confusion. We're happy to recombine information, we take event horizons incredibly fast. The generations – and I *can* use that plurally now – underneath me have an ability to scan information much quicker than my lot, and don't necessarily look for the depth that maybe we would.'

In a couple of sentences, he'd summed up how the information society was starting to change, anticipating how people would consume media over the forthcoming decades. Within that interpretation though, there was the unmistakable implication that in the coming years, the cultural impact of a single pop star, however famous, would be limited. The manifesto was becoming more modest.

The impact of *Outside*, too, was limited, and not just for reasons of cultural change; the narrative segments, in particular, would become unbearably irritating on repeated listening, and in subsequent years the album would fall out of favour. Yet two decades later, when albums are indeed being consumed in non-linear fashion, shuffled on iTunes with the irritating portions removed, *Outside* is being seen in a different light, according to pianist Mike Garson, who has lately become convinced that the album is a career highlight. 'I remember thinking, This is quite a special album – because it was a little far out. Maybe people wouldn't get it for a long time but recently I've had a lot of calls and emails – I have a feeling that people are starting to get it.'

When *Outside* was being recorded, Bowie had played down his affinity with younger bands like Nine Inch Nails, saying that his major influence was the Swiss industrialists The Young Gods. But when it came time to promote *Outside* on the road, Bowie chose to explicitly link himself with NIN front man Trent Reznor, touring on a joint bill in a deliberately challenging move which left him open to trend-hopping jibes and even hostile reactions.

Bowie's band now sported a new rhythm section of drummer Zachary Alford and bassist Gail Ann Dorsey, with George Simms, last seen on the *Serious Moonlight* tour, on backing vocals; Peter Schwartz was selected as musical director so David wouldn't have a 'favourite child' among Carlos, Reeves or Garson: all previous incumbents. The tour opened on 14 September, 1995, in Hartford, Connecticut, winding up in LA in late October. Nine Inch Nails' set included Bowie's 'Scary Monsters' and 'Subterraneans'; Bowie joined them for 'Reptile' and 'Hurt'.

Mike Garson: 'I thought that was a brilliant move. We were standing on the side of the stage every night and watched them play their set. I was intrigued. In the middle of the show, when Nine Inch Nails were going off, our band would come on, David would sing "Hurt" and Trent Reznor would sing on the David Bowie song and it was amazing.'

For Reznor, the experience was thrilling, but intimidating. Sometimes he'd find himself hoping that Bowie wouldn't be there when he walked into the dressing room, so he wouldn't have to talk to him. 'Not that I didn't like him. But I felt like I had to impress him. I had to impress his band. I couldn't just let my hair down.'

Reeves remembers: 'It was a cool idea but also hard work because we would have to front-load our set with the up stuff because we'd be coming off the Nine Inch Nails encore. Also we did a meld where Carlos and I would join Nine Inch Nails. It was a tough one; some of the Nails crowd would leave when we came on, then our crowd would come in from the lobby. It made us work really hard – in a good way.'

In November, the band hit the UK, with Morrissey replacing NIN. The UK leg started with a four-night run at Wembley. The tour was a prime example of an older artist refusing to play his greatest hits – although 'Look Back in Anger', 'Scary Monsters' and 'Teenage Wildlife' were all delivered in ruthlessly efficient versions – and met with the predictable response. If there were any Phil Collins fans in the audience, taking the stage to Philip Glass's 'Some Air' and opening with 'The Motel' was an admirably effective method of dispersing them. Morrissey left the UK tour after the first ten dates, taking offence at Bowie's suggestion their sets should overlap, like they had done on his American tour. Morrissey was not as accommodating as Trent Reznor of a move 'which deprives people of saying goodbye to me', he asserted later, adding for good measure, 'He's a business, you know. He's not really a person.'

On 19 February, 1996, as the European leg of the tour came to a close, there was a rather more fulsome tribute from Tony Blair, Labour Party leader, who hailed David as 'an innovator' as he presented him with a Brit award for Lifetime Achievement. The future world statesman was six years younger than David, who later commented he'd only turned up at the awards ceremony to perform his current single, 'Hallo

Spaceboy' – if so, the tactic worked, for the Pet Shop Boys' remix of the song entered the UK charts a fortnight later at number twelve.

The success of 'Hallo Spaceboy' was a welcome vindication in a year in which David's public, and the critics, gave his new material a generally grudging reception. His own enthusiasm, though, was fired up to a new peak, for after a short break in the spring the band – stripped down to Gabrels, Garson, Alford and Gail Ann Dorsey, whose vocals on a superb version of 'Under Pressure' were now a staple of the set – returned to Europe for festival dates in June and July. It was just a couple of days after the band had returned home that David called Gabrels to tell him he'd booked Philip Glass's studio in New York, for a fortnight later.

'That summer was the end of *Outside* and beginning of *Earthling*,' says Gabrels. 'I had written about six tracks, more like electronic stuff, on my laptop. I was trying to write without guitar at that point because we'd been crossing paths with bands like Underworld and The Prodigy.' The sessions would be the most intense and untroubled of David's 1990s: the band called the studio The Clubhouse, and visitors included David Lynch and Lou Reed, with whom David had now made his peace. Inspired by the sounds they'd heard over the summer – Bowie was an Underworld fan, Gabrels favoured The Prodigy – the team made a conscious decision to abandon tradition, says the guitarist. 'I felt everybody was looking around them, musically, and thought, Fuck, it's the end of the millennium and we're still playing like we're in The Rolling Stones. We've got to get on this otherwise people are gonna look back at us and say we were lame.'

Rather than playing conventional electric guitar, Gabrels used a Roland processor, which digitally modelled different guitar sounds; the entire album was recorded on hard disk, rather than tape, allowing vocals or instruments to be cut and pasted within a song. As they excitedly explored this new world, their guide was Mark Plati, who'd been working at Looking Glass Studios since 1991. Tutored in the bass guitar by Duke Ellington's nephew William at Indiana University, Plati moved to New York in 1987 and engineered, programmed and played at Arthur Baker's Shakedown Studios while also filling the same role for superstar DJ Junior Vasquez. Plati had helped Gabrels craft the samples used for the summer dates, and over the three weeks in which they made the album, he became its co-producer, making music out of bits of sonic 'junk' – old tracks or samples that he and Reeves found around the studio.

Working with Brian Eno, David had gone through complex psycho-logical techniques to bypass writer's block; for *Earthling*, simply using a computer did much the same thing. The songs arrived quickly: lyrics assembled on Post-It notes, decisions made on the fly, vocals recorded first or second take, notably 'Little Wonder', where they ended up using the original guide vocal. Approaching his fifties, David's voice and writing sounded fresh, revitalised – there were many echoes of his youth, a Tony Newley inflection in 'Little Wonder', or a trace of 'Letter to Hermione' in 'Dead Man Walking', which also featured the simple two-note guitar riff Jimmy Page had shown him at IBC studios with The Manish Boys, three decades earlier.

If it came easy, though, *Earthling* didn't stay the course. By its release in January 1997, drum 'n' bass, and Bowie's main obsession, Underworld, were both mainstream phenomena; although many reviews of the time praised the rejuvenated songwriting, the album was doomed to be consigned to history as another exercise in apparent bandwagon-jumping. Even the title, *Earthling*, seemed crassly self-referential, while the Alexander McQueen Union Jack frock coat looked like an attempt to cash in on Britpop, which was the talk of the spring. Yet despite the air of dad at the disco, the passion was real, and inspired Bowie and Gabrels to sneak to events like that summer's Phoenix Festival, playing as the Tao Jones Index before their main set.

When David celebrated his fiftieth birthday at a packed Madison Square Garden on 8 January, 1997, the line-up seemed carefully chosen to emphasise the birthday boy's cutting-edge credentials. Fans like the Smashing Pumpkins, The Cure's Robert Smith, Black Francis from The Pixies and the Foo Fighters' Dave Grohl were there to duet on better-known songs, but his own set was dominated by material from his last two albums; Lou Reed – 'the King of New York', as David fulsomely introduced him – was the only contemporary, joining him for 'Queen Bitch' and 'Waiting for the Man'. Only towards the end, after crowd and band had sung him Happy Birthday, did he run through 'Under Pressure' and 'Heroes' and then closed the evening with a beautifully simple 'Space Oddity'.

It was a powerful ceremony, a convincing testament to his musical impact; but over the same period that the exacting preparations for the show had been going on, a more intimate package was being assembled. For months before, Iman had been calling up friends – some of whom hadn't seen David for years – to ask them to contribute an artwork to be bound into a book, each contribution marking a moment of their life with this supposedly cold, calculating individual. The work, a collection of drawings and writing, was supremely moving, according to those who have seen it, an unaffected tribute to a man who is simply, as boyhood friend Geoff MacCormack puts it, 'very funny – a good mate'. Friends from Bromley, Berlin and New York contributed – Iman charmed each of them, discovering new stories about her husband. Only Iggy, according to friends, didn't contribute.

For many of David's peers, hitting the age of fifty was a dark moment; a few, like Keith Richards, relished emulating heroes like John Lee Hooker and playing long into the good night. For Iggy, just three months younger than David, his fiftieth year on the planet was a time to split with his wife Suchi and embark on a crazed affair with an Argentinian girl, who inspired his crisis-ridden *Avenue B* album. David, though, seemed idyllically happy with Iman, telling friends and even people he bumped into casually – on a plane or in an airport shuttle – how getting married was the best thing that ever happened to him: the part of him that was utterly conventional seemed to have gained dominance.

One gleaming signpost of this conventionality were the perfect white teeth he now sported. The disappearance of his slightly crooked, overlapping fangs in favour of even, Hollywood-style crowns would later become the subject of a hilariously sleazy British TV show, *Celebrity Surgery*, featuring several Bowie acolytes, all of whom thought they were contributing to a conventional documentary. The snippet is now a YouTube classic, studded with poignant comments from fans, mourning the departure of his iconic English gnashers. The teeth completed a style makeover that also included a small, alternative-rock goatee and the body art applied in Kyoto in 1992, by a tattooist popular with the organised crime syndicate, the Yakuza: a figure riding a dolphin, overlaid with a Japanese serenity prayer and Iman's name in Japanese Kanji characters, on his left calf. (Iman reciprocated with a Bowie knife above her right ankle.)

There was something about David's well-groomed, 'alternative' appearance that looked distinctly airbrushed and American: the product of spending more time with New York's fashion and music crowd. (Iman disliked the Lausanne house, which the couple put up for sale the following year.) The couple loved the city, and in the following years could often be seen huddled, deep in conversation, in cafés nearby their condo at 708, Broadway. Still, he remained distinctly British, for Iman brought out his playful, funny side, and loved the ever-present dry humour. Many a New York waiter would be caught out by his little jokes, handing him a hot rolled towel before he ordered, only for Bowie to look at it quizzically and ask, 'Is it dead?' Even the occasional toot of cocaine was consigned to the past; now he rarely drank to excess, and while he cut a cool rug in his frock coat for that summer's tour, he was content to leave Reeves Gabrels to check out the dance culture with which he'd aligned himself: 'He couldn't really go to raves – nor was he inclined to, being, at that point, sober for a long time.'

Gabrels and Bowie had as close a musical relationship as any of those between Bowie and a fellow musician, all the more complex because the guitarist was from a younger generation, someone who'd grown up on Bowie's music. Gabrels would teeter between waves of euphoria at working with a childhood hero, and frustration at dealing with Bowie's business organisation and niggles about percentage breakdowns on songwriting credits, which seemed to crop up around that time. Many of Bowie's musicians cite him as among their best employers – 'I'm his biggest fan, in that respect,' says Carlos Alomar – but others found dealing with Isolar consistently unpleasant. Bowie's management gave some collaborators, like Erdal Kizilcay, the impression he should take the percentage on offer and count himself lucky. The Bowie camp had a point – after all, any musician working with David was practically guaranteed an overnight transformation of their financial fortunes – but such arguments were especially hard to stomach in the late nineties, at a time when David was gaining new fame, not for music, but for the money he was fast accumulating.

'Bowie Bonds', the controversial means by which David raised 55 million dollars against revenues from his back catalogue, would cause a sensation within the music industry. The bonds – securities issued against Bowie's future royalties for the next ten years – would also make a star of David Pullman. The man most associated with the Bowie Bond, Pullman would, at age thirty-nine, be named as one of *Time* magazine's 100 Innovators, and go on to package similar deals for other musicians. Soon he was being celebrated in profiles across the world's press, while the most convincing testament to the fame of the bond phenomenon arrived in 2001, in the shape of a thriller, *Something Wild*, in which novelist Linda Davies wove a complex plot around the issue of Bowie Bonds; 'Linda's book gives readers a look at how exciting this industry can be,' gushed Pullman, in a press release around its launch.

Bowie banked $55 million from the deal – £39 million at 1997 sterling rates – some of which was reportedly used to pay British taxes. However, David wanted the money for quite another reason: to buy back his own music.

When David had first negotiated his split from Tony Defries in March, 1975, his ex-manager retained a percentage of all the music David recorded, right through to 1982. This percentage was on a sliding scale – reportedly a full 50 per cent of Bowie's share on the pre-1975 releases, and less thereafter – but the money was due in perpetuity. Defries retained co-ownership of the masters – and even retained the right, he claimed, to issue further Bowie recordings; a right he exploited from the early nineties, with the release of the *Santa Monica 72* live album in 1994, plus other albums based on BBC and Astronettes sessions. By the mid-nineties, Isolar opened negotiations with their predecessor for Bowie to finally buy out his rights. The talks, according to Defries' friends, were amicable: David's people told Defries' people he wanted the assets 'to pass on to his children'. None of the parties involved has ever confirmed how much of David's $55 million went to Defries, but some of those peripherally involved suggest it was at least half. If so, Tony Defries made over $27 million; an impressive return for the £500,000 it had cost him to buy Bowie's masters from Laurence Myers, back in the summer of 1972.

Over subsequent years, the notion of Bowie Bonds would be raised again and again, often with the implication that David, like Mick Jagger, was obsessed with money: a lower-middle-class boy wanting to make up for childhood austerity. Few commented on the fact that, at the age of fifty, he was paying tens of millions to reclaim his own life's work. Following the transaction, Tony Defries bought an impressive estate in Virginia and – on top of his considerable existing assets – now had tens of millions to invest, a practice in which he'd always been an expert. David had purchased his own past.

If the motivations for Bowie seeking another $55 million were misunderstood, the furore signalled a period when his name was invariably connected with commerce. The implications of Bowie Bonds were closely followed within the financial industry, although the gloss was taken off them by a series of lawsuits between Pullman and various other parties, arguing over who had invented the bonds. The final verdict indicated that the inspiration for the bonds came not from financial wiz-kid David Pullman, but from David's own business manager, Bill Zysblat. The controversy around the issue would never subside. Lamont Dozier, the acclaimed Motown songwriter, would later sue the advisers who worked on his own bond issue; in the wake of EMI's financial problems, Bowie Bonds were downgraded by Moody's, the leading credit ratings agency, to one notch above junk grade in 2004.

Since the days when he had kept a close eye on finances on the *Serious Moonlight* tour, Bill Zysblat – who also worked for the Stones – had become David's key adviser. In the wake of the excitement generated by the Bowie Bonds, Zysblat would also plan a Bowie Bank – an idea that was eventually dropped after problems with the bank chosen to operate the scheme – and, in the summer of 1998, announce that he was going to create an internet provider called BowieNet.

Over the past few years, David had become as fired up by the internet as he was by art and music: 'He was right at the forefront, and it made sense he would be,' says Thomas Dolby, Bowie's Live Aid keyboard player. Dolby had moved to America's West Coast to launch an internet start-up company, and Bowie had shared his excitement with him. 'It was a hedonistic thing – of being in the moment, of getting a thrill, a rush out of what he was experiencing.' Dolby had lived through a similar arc, of seeing contemporaries like David Byrne progress from hanging out at the Mudd Club to exploring the medium of video. 'These were the lightning rods for creativity. And he was very fired up – what he was seeing was a return to a grass roots movement. He could have a ringside seat, and be in control, do spontaneous things and get instant feedback.'

Bowie's life would be mapped out online for at least the next decade; yet his influence went beyond his own site, or his own music. According to some industry insiders, he was mapping out the very future of the world wide web. Technology writer John Naughton later cited Bowie as a 'leading futurologist', the originator of some of the 'most perceptive observations anyone's ever made about our networked world'. In the late nineties, Bowie saw the web's potential for building new communities; yet he also spotted the long-term implications for copyright, predicting how authorship and intellectual property would become endangered. Most presciently, in 2002 he suggested that music 'is going to become like running water or electricity', anticipating the rise of streaming services like Spotify. Bowie would always stop short of describing himself as any kind of visionary – his opinions on the evolution of modern culture were usually confined to promotional interviews. But his perceptiveness inspired Naughton to comment, in 2010, 'If you want to know the future, ask a musician.'

By January 1998, David was promoting the launch of his own websites, davidbowie.com and bowieart.com, and on 1 September an internet provider, BowieNet (subscription fee $19.95 per month). One of the staff at Outside, his PR company, remembers that the launch was 'one of the most stressful things I can remember, there would be webcasts with him, Boy George, Visconti – and he absolutely loved it'. The obsession – David would also drop in on his own chatrooms; his handle 'sailor' – was also recreational; he'd spend hours trawling the world wide web, or looking for bargains on eBay.

Over the same year that the Bowie brand was launched online, the man himself was launched as an independent digital entity, too. Towards the end of 1998, David called Reeves Gabrels over to London to join him and Iman at a meeting with a computer game company, Eidos. The developer needed not only a soundtrack, 'They wanted David, Iman and me to be a character in a game,' says Gabrels. 'So we started talking about how to do it, set up in a hotel room and started writing.' The resultant game, *Omikron*, was a cult classic, albeit no mainstream success, but 'Survive', the main song Bowie and Gabrels crafted for the game, was a gem, simple and unaffected, almost *Scary Monsters* in vibe, without any of the over-complexity and over-thinking that otherwise seemed synonymous with nineties Bowie.

During that most multimedia of years, it was perhaps fitting that a meeting which would have a profound effect on his future work was hatched as a result of a kids' cartoon. David had been asked to contribute a song to the *Rugrats* movie (also featuring Iggy), and called Tony Visconti to produce the vaguely retro song, 'Safe'. As he took the call, Visconti's eyes 'welled up. I hadn't realised how much I missed him.' Sadly, the song wouldn't make the film, for the scene featuring it was cut. But their relationship had been rekindled.

As one friendship was being patched up, another was coming to its term. The *Omikron* project expanded into a full-blown album, first called *The Dreamer*, later renamed *Hours*, which was started in Bermuda, where David and Iman now had a holiday home. In search of a low-key, emotional feel, Bowie and Reeves reverted to conventional one-on-one songwriting methods. According to Reeves, he'd originally intended two of the songs, 'The Pretty Things Are Going to Hell' and 'Survive', for his own solo album. Throughout, his guitar work was tasteful, less exhibitionist than before: 'I'm not sort of Jackson Pollocking my way through it, it's more Norman Rockwell.'

After the aggression and exuberance of its predecessors, *Hours* was widely interpreted as a reflection on mortality. There is a distinct world-weariness about songs such as 'Thursday's Child', exacerbated by David's Nick Cave-influenced vocal; at other points, particularly 'The Dreamers', Scott Walker comes to the fore, in what is one of David's more vocally self-effacing albums. The instrumentation, too, was conventional, predictable at times, in what seemed to be a 'genre-free' album, as if in conscious over-reaction to its predecessor. The best songs, notably 'Seven', and 'Thursday's Child', were potential masterpieces, but their predictable, occasionally plodding arrangements suggested that David's assured instinct for picking the right setting had deserted him. As if to confirm this, the sleeve, always an intrinsic part of the appeal of Bowie albums, was a mess: despite being crafted by noted San Francisco collagist Rex Ray, it was a hammy mix of designer clutter and mawk-ishness, with its photo of the long-haired Bowie cradling his short-haired alter-ego, as if in a deposition from the cross.

For most listeners, the autumnal mood was taken as Bowie reflecting on his life. In his talks with Reeves, David told him, 'It was autobio-graphical but it wasn't his biography, it was someone close to him. There was some discussion about whether he was writing from my point of view. I don't know. The end was nigh. I knew I needed to go, it just took a long time to figure out how.'

Gabrels had helped lead Bowie out of the creative cul-de-sac of the late eighties, but both parties sensed it was time to move on. Mark Plati, the computer wizard behind *Earthling*, had now moved into a more con-ventional role as bassist, a change essentially initiated by Reeves. Gabrels had thus prepared his own replacement. There was no falling out, says the guitarist: 'I was basically burning out. A lot of it didn't have to do with David as much as with time away from home, time on the road and just dealing with some of the people around him. I thought it was amicable.'

In his later years, David was sometimes remarkably gracious about his previous collaborators; this was certainly the case with Reeves, to whom David would often publicly express his gratitude. Still, the pair soon fell out of touch: 'I think it got misinterpreted over time – Coco got in there after I left,' says Reeves. 'I was no saint either at the end, but my crimes were entirely personal. I was trying to make my way home at that point– literally! I felt like if I had stayed I was going to become everything I disliked in musicians I had known – bitter and twisted – or I was gonna die because I would be so miserable I would just drug myself to death. I just knew I was done with that. There were also personal complications because I was having a child with David's wardrobe mistress. That played into their hands as a source of shit-stirring.' Gabrels' last appearance with Bowie would be at the VH1 *Storytellers* performance, filmed in August 1999. (It was a good, slightly nostalgic show, with Bowie sharing some hilarious anecdotes, such as the time when, in Ziggy guise, he discovered he was expected to use the dressing-room sink as a urinal. 'My dear man, I can't piss in the sink!' he protested. 'Son,' the promoter replied, 'if it's good enough for Shirley Bassey, it's good enough for you.')

While *Hours* was undistinguished, its marketing was world-class. The build-up to its 4 October release featured a 'cyber song contest', offering fans the chance to contribute four lines of lyric to one song. Bowie's website unveiled the album cover one section at a time, strip-tease style, while announcing the album would be available as a download before its CD release: another first for an established artist. And if this wasn't sufficient media saturation, in the run-up to release, 'Heroes' blared out regularly from British TV screens in a £8.5 million campaign for CGU Insurance, which, the ad agency announced, 'focuses on the consumer as "hero" for taking responsibility for the financial future'. The promotion, and the fans' genuine affection for the more traditional, unvarnished Bowie, helped the album to number five in the UK charts. American sales were disappointing, however; at number forty-seven it was his worst solo chart performance since *Ziggy Stardust*.

But as the century ebbed to its close, there was welcome vindication from the *Sun*, whose readers voted him the biggest star of the twentieth century, beating Michael Jackson and Liam Gallagher; in a *Q* magazine poll of the 'Greatest Star of the Century', he pipped Madonna to come sixth, after Lennon, McCartney, Cobain, Dylan and Elvis. On Christmas Eve that year, he spent two and a half hours chatting with 19,000 fans on an intermittent internet feed, thanking the kids who mentioned their parents thought him a bad influence, promising new sessions with Tony Visconti, throwing in a good joke every line or two, mentioning his son was standing by with a saucepan and explaining that the Christmas tree had been decorated, 'but our balls keep tending to fall off'. It had been a good half-century.

The fresh new decade was a good one, too. David and Iman had been trying for a child since the late nineties, resorting to IVF, Iman said later, and undergoing two unsuccessful bouts before conceiving naturally. The pair announced Iman's pregnancy on 13 February, 2000, monopolising headlines worldwide. (The competition for cheesiest headline was won

by music365.com, whose story read 'Nappy Ch-ch-changes . . .'.) Iman
later told *Jet* magazine she'd used an old African technique to get pregnant; holding a borrowed baby, kindly supplied by Christie Brinkley,
during a *Vogue* shoot the previous September.

Of all the regrets that David ever voiced in public, the fact that his son
had had such an irregular upbringing was the one he mentioned most
often. After leaving Gordonstoun, Joey had worked briefly with handi-
capped kids in Switzerland, and at the Jim Henson puppet workshop–
a connection he'd made during his dad's work on *Labyrinth* – before
winning a scholarship to the College of Wooster in Ohio to study
Philosophy. Once there, he started using his given first name, Duncan. In
1999, David had suggested Duncan accompany him to the shoot for
Tony Scott's TV series of *The Hunger*; Scott became a mentor to Duncan,
inspiring a love affair with cinema. In February 2000, the *Daily Mail*
trumpeted the news that the 'quiet and polite' Duncan had enrolled at
Covent Garden's International Film School.

From the beginning of 2000, David knew there would be parallels
with the summer that Duncan had been born, for Glastonbury organiser
Michael Eavis had called before Christmas, asking him to return to the
festival, twenty-nine years after his first appearance there. The spring
was dominated by the preparations, with Earl Slick returning to the
fold, joining Plati, Gail Ann Dorsey, drummer Sterling Campbell and
backing singers Holly Palmer and Emm Grynner. There were three warm-
up shows in New York, one of which was cancelled, as his voice gave
out. Perhaps for that reason, David was conspicuously nervous before
his Sunday night slot at the festival, on 25 June.

BBC executive producer Mark Cooper oversaw the live coverage,
and remembers, 'He took the place by storm. He came back dressed in
Hunky Dory mode and played a set full of hits, every one was a winner.'
The performance was fabulous; only one factor stopped the set being
the live broadcast of the year: 'They [David's management] told us they
would only let us broadcast six songs. I wept. It was such a stonking
set, he had the whole crowd eating out of his hand. And it was painful
to come off it.' Rather like musicians who describe encounters where
David played the Angel and Coco played the Devil, the BBC executives
were struck by the contrast between David's cheery demeanour and
the difficult, almost miserly attitude of his organisation when it came
to broadcasting the show. 'I always thought of Bowie as someone good
at hoarding his past,' says one of them, 'paying it out a bit at a time. Like
Scrooge.' Cooper, meanwhile, saw the performance as a life-changing

event, which should have been shared more widely: 'An artist can be reborn with a performance like that, get another ten years in their career. He's earned the right to deliver things on his terms, but I think it was a mistake. Because this was the moment.'

There was another nod to 1971 two days later, with a show at the BBC Radio Theatre, which echoed the show at which he'd premiered the newly written 'Kooks'. Then, back in New York, he started sessions on the sixties-themed album that he'd trailed in the December webcast. Named *Toy*, the proposed album was inspired by one of his first great songs, 'Let Me Sleep Beside You': 'place your ragged doll with all your toys and things and deeds'. With Mark Plati overseeing, they cut a terrific version, imbued with the spirit of Mick Wayne, who'd played on the BBC version – the Hull guitarist, Ronson's predecessor, had died in a house fire in June 1994, his work forgotten. Tony Visconti, whose inspirational arrangement for the song had marked his debut collaboration with Bowie, was called in for some of the sessions, in which David delved deeply into his own back pages, to re-record Ziggy-era numbers such as the jewel-like 'Shadow Man': a near-masterpiece, this obscure, forgotten work illustrated the quality and breadth of the song catalogue he'd built up over thirty-five years.

Though they'd been working hard, there was the most welcome interruption to the sessions on 15 August, 2000, with the birth of Alexandria Zahra Jones at Mount Sinai Hospital in New York. David and Iman celebrated the event in the now obligatory cover feature in *Hello!*, sharing with the public their bliss, their fantasies of later having a boy they could name Stenton, after David's father, and the universal frustration with builders, whose delays prevented their move to their bigger, new apartment in Chelsea, New York, in time for the birth. Iman mentioned that David was doing his share of nappy changes for Alexandria – her name inspired by the ancient Greco-Egyptian seat of culture. The notion of a multimedia superstar dealing with such down-to-earth routines was heart-warming, but apparently the novelty wore off, for three years later, in bloke-ish mode, he announced, 'I don't do nappies.'

A year after Alexandria's birth, David was still describing his main job as 'daddyfying', his excitement at the new experience just as all-consuming as the obsessions of his youth. His work schedule was light; there was a short break filming a hilarious, self-parodic cameo for Ben Stiller's film *Zoolander*, plus more frustrating weeks spent wrestling with problems over the completed *Toy* album – in June David mentioned 'scheduling conflicts' with EMI/Virgin. In reality, this was a terminal falling-out, triggered by managerial conflicts within the company. He was uncon-cerned by the hassles, as far as anyone could tell; instead, he seemed to have settled in to life in New York. The public perception was of him as a culture buff, always visiting the ballet or a new exhibition, or hanging out with local musos like Moby or Lou Reed, all of which he did. But he was just as happy Googling randomly in 'the bunker' – his computer and work room – waking up at 6 a.m. and dealing with emails before taking Lexi for a walk around SoHo or Greenwich Village in her buggy, or sitting chatting to Iman over a bowl of pasta by a restaurant window, the two of them smiling graciously if they happened to be interrupted by a fan.

In his first few years as a New Yorker, he still considered moving back London; it was a part of who he was. But over the next couple of years he came to detest British celebrity culture, the prospect of having to endure 'having a camera lens stuck in either my face or my wife and child's face every morning'. He had reverted to much the same sentiments he'd expressed in 1980, the feeling that New York was the perfect place to wander, seek out interesting book or antique shops, pick up the urban buzz without being hassled. Only once did he venture out publicly that spring, to Carnegie Hall for the Tibet House Benefit on 26 February, 2001. Together on-stage for the first time since The Hype, he and Tony Visconti played an extraordinary version of 'Silly Boy Blue'. When they'd recorded it together in December 1966, it had disappeared without trace, prompt-ing thoughts of giving up music; now the pair were backed by Philip Glass on piano and Moby on guitar, and led the enraptured crowd in a chant of 'Chime chime chime' in tribute to the monk David had gone to see at the Tibet Centre.

The sense that, as a new father, David was becoming reconciled to his own past deepened in the aftermath of his mother's death. Margaret Mary Jones' passing was announced on 2 April, and for David had come 'out of the blue'. Several faces from his youth were at the funeral, includ-ing Ken Pitt and Pat Antoniou, the aunt who had so publicly accused David of callousness to his half-brother, prolonging the feuds that had blighted the Burns family for half a century. When David saw her, he 'walked straight over, threw his arms around her', says Ken Pitt, the one man who had stayed in touch with all the various disconnected branches of the family. 'He was absolutely wonderful.'

A ghost had been laid to rest, but others would remain. On 11 May, Freddie Buretti died of cancer in Paris. David had kept nearly all the cos-tumes Freddie had made for him. And the problems with *Toy* deepened during the summer; the record would be a casualty of Mariah Carey's legendarily disastrous album, *Glitter*, which sold so badly that Virgin were forced to pay a reported $19 million to terminate her contract early; Nancy Berry, who had signed Bowie as well as Carey, was fired. But even before the album's fate was sealed, David was planning its replacement. In June, he came to stay with Tony Visconti and his new girlfriend at their 'humble', draughty, wooden, three-storey apartment in suburban West Nyack, New York. The pair worked on songs together in Tony's loft, just as they had in the Haddon Hall basement, only this time they would cut and paste ideas using Pro Tools software, rather than Mark Pritchett's Revox. On their second day, Tony took David to see Allaire, a beautiful wood-lined recording studio set in the Catskill Mountains: it felt like a finely crafted Edwardian yacht, with panoramic views over the reservoir that quenches New York City. The moment David stepped in the room, he said later, 'I knew exactly what lyrics I was to write – although I didn't yet know what the words themselves were.'

When they started recording, David brought his 'little family', who stayed in a tiny house in the grounds some of the time, and there he remained, until the album was essentially finished. One morning, he got up around five, as was his habit, looked out of the windows and saw two deer grazing below the field, in the fresh light of the rising sun. In the distance a car was driving slowly past the reservoir, and then words started streaming out of him and tears ran down his face. The song was 'Heathen': 'I didn't like writing it. There was something so ominous and final about it.' The lyrics read as if taking leave of a lover; but the object he addresses is life.

The song was indeed bleak, but throughout the *Heathen* album, there is a visceral connection with the world David saw around him, and an almost loving engagement with his craft. (Later, he'd enumerate all the instruments he played in the sessions, including his Stylophone and Brian Eno's old EMS synth.)

For the past two decades, Bowie had wrestled with that worry about whether, in his later years, he could ever 'contribute so aggressively' again. In the relaxed, almost spiritual atmosphere of Allaire, he had found his answer, for a renewed confidence and passion pervades each of the songs. There was a luminous simplicity about most of the material that evoked *Hunky Dory*; but where *Hunky Dory* speaks of rebirth, of the shiny and new, *Heathen* displays a hard-won confidence in a life that's been well lived, like beautifully worn leather – the quirky, almost baby voice on 'A Better Future'; drifting, dark, drum loops on 'The Angels Have Gone'; impassioned singing, reminiscent of 'Heroes', on 'Slow Burn'. Perhaps there wasn't the visceral thrill of the twenty- and thirty-something Bowie, but there was nonetheless the sense that this was a classic album, one that didn't suffer by comparison with *Scary Monsters*.

Many of the reviews of the album were coloured by the knowledge that Bowie and Visconti were still out in the Catskills on 9/11; David was talking to Iman, who was back in the apartment, on the phone as she saw the second plane hit. When David returned to Manhattan, there was an ominous gap in the familiar view from the kitchen window; Iman realised that many of the men who used to greet her and Lexi as she wheeled the buggy by the local Fire Department station a couple of blocks away were probably dead. It would cement the family's relationship with the city; David headlined October's Concert for New York and would talk no more of moving back to London. But for all the fear and anxiety David sensed in the air, convinced there would be a further attack, he was infectiously optimistic, recounting Lexi's babywords verbatim to friends, reading her books, telling those around him how lucky he was.

The sense of event around the release of *Heathen* in June 2002 was palpable – the presence of Tony Visconti seemed to fire up fans far more than an internet marketing campaign. The excitement was stoked up by a show at New York's Roseland Ballroom, and then his appearance at the culmination of his own Meltdown Season at London's Royal Festival Hall. The series had been controversial – or rather 'disappointingly unadventurous', according to the London *Evening Standard* – for his involvement as curator was patchy, with his attention diverted by negotiations with new record company Sony. Yet the closing night was a sensation, mostly for the performance of *Low*, in its entirety, followed by *Heathen*. Mark Plati had prepared by listening through the original Hansa and Château multitracks: massive, long-obsolete reels of two-inch tape, which had to be baked in an oven to stop them crumbling into dust; he crafted individual mixes which he gave to each band member, as a kind of karaoke version of the album. The show was 'genuinely overwhelming, people did recognise the magnitude of the event', says Glenn Max, who had struggled to put the festival together. As the band launched into 'Always Crashing in the Same Car', the audience took to their feet, and pretty much stayed there. The only problem with the show was that by the close of *Low*, the audience were drained: 'It had been so dazzling, you almost needed a two-hour run around the block to recover,' says Max, but then the band came out again, David changed from his Thin White Duke shirt and waistcoat to a white silk suit for a gripping rendition of *Heathen*.

When the applause died down, Bono and Brian Eno were among those queueing for admission to the tiny dressing room; this event alone was great theatre – David looking spent but cool as a cucumber, dressed in a kimono, 'with little Japanese slippers on his tiny Japanese feet', remembers Max Glenn. When David introduced Brian Eno to Mark Plati, he told him, 'This is the man responsible for all of this.' Thinking Bowie meant he was the architect of the Queen Elizabeth Hall, Plati pointed at the ceiling and murmured, 'Nice job!'

For both the album and the tour that promoted it, there was a consensus in the coverage: that this was an artist who, if not at the peak of his own giddy career, was still producing work that towered over most of his younger rivals. And with the fevered activity, he said, 'I'm very confident and trusting in my abilities right now.' The old sense of having to rush that had driven him through the 1970s was renewed. Back then, the impetus came from youthful ambition; now it came from what seemed an excessive sense of his own mortality: 'I've got to think of myself as the luckiest guy,' he said that summer, 'Robert Johnson only had one album's worth of work as his legacy.' After smoking obsessively, trying brand after brand for forty years, he'd managed to cut down to a minimum now he was a father again.

The *Heathen* tour concluded in late October 2002, marked by shows in each of New York's five boroughs, but David was thinking of new songs even as he settled back into his daily routine of walks and reading sessions with Lexi, visits to Iman at the 7th Avenue office of her cosmetics company, or his three-times-a-week boxing sessions at a nearby gym.

After a couple of days pre-production in November, he and Visconti were ready to start work again in January. This time they recorded in New York, at Looking Glass, but in a smaller studio, which gave a more constrained, urban feel 'to capture the angst of NYC', says Visconti. He and David worked closely together, making decisions quickly; there was a matter-of-factness about the recording, much of it using David's touring band. Mike Garson, like Chuck Hammer and Dominic Muldowney before him, was struck by how intuitive their musical relationship was: 'I worked with perfect love with Tony Visconti. He's an incredible guy.'

Throughout his life, David had developed his unrivalled genius for getting the best out of musicians; in just two songs, 'The Loneliest Guy' and 'Bring Me the Disco King', he seemed to reach into Garson to inspire something new. The latter track, with Garson's minimal, milky chords underpinned by a drum loop saved from *Heathen*, was as fine as anything they'd recorded together in the last thirty years. 'You promised me the ending would be clear,' David sang, in a voice rendered cloudy by four decades of Gitanes and Marlboros; after twenty-eight albums, he was still constructing songs that were fiercely understated, yet would yield up new secrets with repeated listens.

From The Spiders onwards, one of the most frequently voiced accusations about David's work was that he exploited his musicians and influences – that he was really a curator, not a creator. But as Garson attests, he had a practised, effective and indeed almost mystical ability to inspire them to create something entirely new: 'Somehow his being-ness and his essence pulls out the best,' says the pianist. 'He might give you little guidances but never says do this or do that. Just by his space I always tend to play my best stuff, to contribute every aspect of my playing. I don't think I would have come up with those solos had he not been there.'

Garson, in his own way, summarises all the issues of how David conjured up music from his musicians. In his early days, the word 'vampiric' was used more than once to describe how he benefited from other musicians' creativity. Yet, in reality, he rarely took from them – he inspired them, as Garson points out, to summon up ideas that would never have existed without him. In these years, David Bowie was always modest about the achievements to which he laid claim; but he was demonstrably correct when he told Livewire.com: 'To not be modest about it, you'll find that with only a couple of exceptions, most of the musicians that I've worked with have done their best work by far with me. I can shine a light on their own strengths. Get them to a place they would never have gotten to on their own.' This was a bold claim, but as Garson and others attest, it was true. He didn't take. He gave.

Tony Visconti thought that David looked tired when he next saw him. *Reality* was released, to a warm response, on 15 September, 2003, and by October David had embarked on his biggest tour of the last five years. In retrospect, the portents had been stacking up for months, but at the time, the tour was thrilling: 'We didn't sit on our laurels – at one point we had sixty or seventy songs in our repertoire,' says Garson. 'He would call things out from nowhere sometimes and we would just play them in front of 3,000 people. It was pretty brave.' Yet on 12 November, the Toulouse show was cancelled as David contracted laryngitis; two days later, they resumed, only for the first leg of the US tour to be delayed by a week when he came down with influenza. Come January he was back on the road again, but tragedy struck on 6 May, 2004, in Miami, with the night's performance cancelled after a lighting engineer fell to his death. Then on 18 June, his outdoor show in Oslo was interrupted when a female fan throw a lollipop that lodged momentarily in the socket of his left eye. For a few moments his composure deserted him as he demanded to know who had thrown the object – then, relaxing, he warned them, 'I've only got one good eye, you know,' before telling them he planned to retaliate by making the concert extra long. Five nights later, David cut short his set after fifteen songs in Prague, complaining of what felt like a trapped nerve in his shoulder. He played one more show, at the Hurricane Festival in Scheessel, Germany, on Saturday 25 June, before collapsing backstage in agony.

For the next nine days, BowieNet would trail the message that the tour had been cancelled 'due to continuing pain and discomfort from a trapped/pinched nerve'. Only when David was back in New York, on 8 July, did his US publicist announce that he had undergone emergency angioplasty surgery for a blocked artery. Two days later, press reports quoted a tour insider who asserted that David had suffered a heart attack backstage, and had undergone surgery the night of his collapse: 'The heart surgery wasn't routine. It was a lot more serious than anyone is letting on.' David's friends would later be told that the procedure involved stents – spring-like mesh tubes fitted inside an artery to keep it open – a less invasive alternative to heart bypass surgery, which happened to be a speciality of the Klinik St Georg in Hamburg, where he was rushed after the Scheessel show.

On 28 July, David was photographed walking around the streets of New York City's Chinatown. Wearing a stetson and a green T-shirt, he shook hand with well-wishers, then stepped into a health food shop to stock up on tea and a variety of ancient Chinese remedies. One year later, Iman told friends that David was still busy with writing and recording: 'We're not retiring people,' she said.

22

The Houdini Mechanism

The thing I remember was a sense of wanting to escape: to parachute out, to find a strategy that would give a glorious exit. That was what he was looking for. A stunning escape mechanism – a Houdini escape from pop stardom.

Julien Temple

Wasn't he brave? To do what he did?

George Underwood

A liens are immortal; that was what fans continued to believe in the months that followed David's heart attack, punctuated by tantalising glimpses of the man in the audience for shows by Gail Ann Dorsey, Arcade Fire and the occasional red-carpet event. It was over a year later – 8 September, 2005 – before David stepped once more into the limelight, an event fraught with nerves, emotion and warmth.

The rehearsal for the Condé Nast Fashion Rocks show, organised in aid of the Hurricane Katrina victims, was nerve-racking. Bowie had not met up with Mike Garson, his sole accompanist, until their rehearsal the afternoon of the performance. When they ran through the song, various performers and crew were busy around Radio City Music Hall. Then, as Garson rippled into the opening chords at the rehearsal, he realised, 'Everybody who was performing that night was listening – you could hear a pin drop'. 'Life on Mars?', the song that had been gifted to the twenty-three-year-old Bowie on the bus to Lewisham, sounded radically different from any previous version.

Garson had first played the song with David on his New York debut thirty-two years before, but at the Fashion Rocks performance that evening he was more nervous than he could ever remember, his feet and knees shaking as he sat down at the grand piano and Alicia Keys announced, 'My good friend, David Bowie.' The pitch of the song had been shifted down all the way from F to B; the new key was tricky, unfamiliar, 'and if I screwed up, it would almost inevitably make him screw up. There was no one else to cover up. No safety net.'

David was even more tentative; he was out of practice, almost a little scared: 'You have a heart problem, you've got to be wondering to yourself, "Am I gonna drop dead on-stage?"' says Garson. 'Anything could go through the mind – you've had a rough period, you don't know if that's gonna happen again.' Yet for Garson, as Bowie settled slowly into the song in front of an enthralled audience, there was something magical about the moment: the fact that their rendition was on the edge and vulnerable gave it a new depth. 'It was poignant and nostalgic. It was magical – one of the deepest things we've done, with factors that go beyond the laws of music; rhythm, harmony, melody and intonation and all that. It was a deeper thing. Almost more of a spiritual experience.'

The sight of David walking up to the mike-stand, nervously clutching it almost as if for comfort, was affecting and – as the camera panned to show him wearing high-water pants, showing bare ankles, with a bandaged wrist and black eye – faintly ludicrous. With the pitch at which David sang lowered by half an octave, there was a sense of the changing of the seasons, from spring to fall. The song had originally been delivered by a young buck, a snotty challenge to Sinatra. Tonight, even in the lower key, that glorious octave leap up to 'Mars' that had launched a career was no longer effortless and transcendent; it spoke of pain. David Bowie was not facing down the Chairman of the Board; he was following in his footsteps. 'He came out as a mature singer that night, like Tony Bennett or Frank Sinatra: someone with presence. A gentleman in his fifties who was not about to try and do something that a twenty-year-old would. It was phenomenal,' says Garson.

There were countless resonances in those moments. The high-water pants, the bandage and black eye make-up reflected many ludicrous outfits of the past. Yet its reference to Louisiana's flooded, battered state also reached back to the aura around New Orleans, where Little Richard had recorded those first songs that electrified the boy from Bromley. In the flicker of doubt so plainly evident as he hit the high note on 'Mars' – or what was once a high note – it became obvious this was a great, profound Bowie performance: the first in years that boasted the on-the-edge danger – the omnipresent fear that 'it could have fallen apart', as Garson puts it – that characterised his career.

Yet it was also the first David Bowie performance in which the boyish radiance, the charisma that had so entranced Ken Pitt during Bowie's rendition of a Judy Garland song in 1965, had plainly faded away. That radiance had become a platform on which a mediocre musician had built his acknowledged genius. Now, as he sang the haunting melody that marked his debut as a great songwriter, all most people noticed was the fragility of his voice and the solidity of his frame.

The spectacle of David Bowie, older gentleman, was one that his fans found hard to contemplate. Over subsequent days, and months, as still photos and then videos – the kind of view behind the gilded curtain that would have been unthinkable in the MainMan era – spread around the world wide web – where Bowie fans lived – the reactions ranged from affection and sympathy to horror and ridicule: 'He's a mess,' was one of the kinder opinions. 'He looks a bit . . . dead,' states YouTube commenter Lindadox, before adding insult to injury: '[and] the hair isn't quite working for him'.

Over the next year, occasional flurries of activity encouraged some observers to liken this quiet period to the pregnant pause that followed *Scary Monsters*. There were more guest appearances: '(She Can) Do That', co-written with trance pioneer Brian Transeau for the abysmal *Top Gun*-wannabe movie *Stealth*, a guest vocal on Kashmir's *The Cynic*, plus backing vocals for TV on the Radio, the Brooklyn band who, throughout 2005 and 2006, would notice his appreciative, expensively suited presence at the side of the stage for their every show in NYC. Then in September, David guested on Courtney Pine's Radio 2 show, and when the saxophonist asked if he was working on a project, told him, 'Yeah, I've started writing already and . . . er . . . it looks pretty weird, so I'm happy.' A few weeks later he signed up to play Nikolai Tesla, his finest movie role in years, for Christopher Nolan's *The Prestige* – which depicted two rival magicians, each obsessed with staging the most glamorous, shocking disappearing act.

Still, the next major outing was not until 2006, in a tribute to Britain's most celebrated, most reclusive rock casualty, Syd Barrett. David Gilmour was playing London's Albert Hall on 29 May, and had just sailed through a complete performance of his recent soft-rock solo album, *On an Island*, when the audience were jarred out of their slumbers with the words, 'I'd like to announce Mr David Bowie!' Syd's famous fan– elegantly dressed, spookily reminiscent of actor John Hurt – paused momentarily at the rapturous applause, and almost shyly was heard to voice the words, 'I hope I warrant that.' For the crowd, it was an 'extraordinary, unexpected, real pinch-yourself moment', according to audience member Ian Gittins. There were nostalgic flashes of that London voice – 'almost East End' – whose whimsy, style and above all Englishness had been inspired by the Pink Floyd singer – who was to die of diabetes just a few weeks later, in July. At the end of the year, Gilmour and Bowie's version of 'Arnold Layne' was released on single and download, and would crack the UK Top 20.

Yet, over the weeks that the news and photos of David's appearance at the Albert Hall spread, so did quotes from an off-the-cuff exchange at a *Vanity Fair* party that same month: 'I'm fed up with the industry,' he told Jada Yuan. 'And I've been fed up for quite some time... Just don't participate. I'm taking a year off – no touring, no albums. I go for a walk every morning, and I watch a ton of movies. One day, I watched three Woody Allen movies in a row.' On 5 June came the news that Bowie would guest in what turned out to be a hilarious edition of comedian Ricky Gervais's *Extras*. Gervais's humour had always traded on embarrassment, the agonising silence that follows an attempted joke or insight; here, Bowie brilliantly parodies his own image as a stoney-faced manipulator, mercilessly mocking the 'little fat man' who attempts to bond with him, recruiting the crowd around him for a singalong. 'The Little Fat Man (with the Pug-Nosed Face)' would be the most significant new Bowie song of an entire half-decade. Distressingly, fans noted, David now seemed to confine himself to walk-on roles, with the occasional sighting at fashion-related events – there was another tantalising guest appearance at New York City's Black Ball benefit that November, again backed by Mike Garson, and duetting with Alicia Keys on 'Changes'.

Even David's virtual appearances were becoming infrequent. Since 2005, the updates in his BowieNet journal had become more desultory, before, on 5 October, 2006, David Bowie penned the most enthusiastic entry in years: 'Yesterday I got to be a character on – tan-tara – *SpongeBob SquarePants*. We, the family, are thrilled. Nothing else need happen this year, well, this week anyway.' And nothing else did. For in January 2007 came the news that a planned live date, which would close a Bowie-curated Highline festival the following May, had been quietly cancelled. In place of the Bowie show was a live rendition of 'The Fat Little Man' with Ricky Gervais and then ... nothing.

*

As David Bowie disappeared from the music scene, the assumption that this was the calm before a new burst of activity was natural, given what had been a prodigious work rate in the previous forty years. The off-the-cuff remark – 'just don't participate' – surely represented a passing disenchantment. The prospect of a permanent retirement seemed unthinkable – except that retirement was an option for which David had been longing, for at least twenty years.

It was in the lull after *Tonight* that Bowie had first shared a yearning for an escape with director Julien Temple, who points out: 'He does always appear very vibed up. But maybe he's not underneath.'

Over that period Temple had accompanied the singer to Brixton Carnival, watching his minders clearing a path ahead of him, witnessing the problems of 'that bubble life'. Watching David work over three separate phases of his career, the director saw the biggest problem David had to contend with was the 'gruelling nature of reinvention. The huge creative surge required to do that again and again. It takes its toll, psychically – and that's beyond the normal clichés of fame. The pressures of stardom do take their toll – even on David, who may not appear as overwhelmed by them as others.'

In their conversations over 1987 and 1989, Bowie had shared with Temple a desire to 'escape: to parachute out, to find a strategy that would give a glorious exit'. Over those years, of course, Bowie's career was sliding into a creative downward spiral. The reception of *Never Let Me Down*, and the debacle of *Glass Spider*, had delayed Bowie's fantasy of going out with 'a real, stunning escape mechanism – a kind of Houdini escape from pop stardom.'

For well over a decade, at least part of David Bowie had still been seeking to make that glorious exit, that one grandiose explosion behind which he could disappear. Ultimately, mortality provided its own less glamorous escape mechanism. And as one of David's friends points out, 'If you were in hospital after a heart scare, would you be wishing you'd spent more time flogging yourself on tour? Or would you be wishing you could spend more time with your five-year-old?'

In the meantime, those around David moved on. Today, Coco is back from California and works with David fairly closely once more. Having devoted decades of her life to caring for him, she has duties that are now less stressful. She now has time to walk around Manhattan, with a dog that keeps her company.

Iggy Pop reunited with his Stooges, to be fêted at festivals around the world, but by the late nineties David had lost touch with the man who more than anyone had benefited from his help. Asked about their friendship by writer Robert Phoenix, David acknowledged, 'I probably shouldn't talk about it,' while admitting, 'We have drifted away from each other.' The problem was a simple clash of egos: 'Jimmy,' he said, had come to resent the fact that 'he couldn't do a fucking article without my name being mentioned'. Over recent years, Iggy repaired his relationships with Stooges guitarists Ron Asheton and James Williamson, with whom he had fallen out spectacularly. Yet there is still a certain reserve when he discusses David, a man with whom he was indisputably closer. According to one close mutual friend of the two, 'I think in any close friendship you can use the word "love" – and in many friendships you'll see that one person loves the other more than the other loves him or her. I believe David loved Jim more than Jim loved David. And, in the end, I think Jim found he could manage without him.' Three months younger than David, Iggy continues to tour with the reformed Stooges. He looks frail in person, with a noticeable limp, but still hits the stage with the joyous energy of a spring lamb.

The career of Tony Defries, the man who more than anyone benefited from Bowie's success, was as eventful as that of his one-time employee. After falling out with his next management charge, John 'Cougar' Mellencamp, Defries steered the troubled early career of Sandy Dillon, was involved in inconclusive negotiations to manage Madonna, invested in a steel plant, and recently claimed to have patented a new means of converting solar energy into electricity. In August 2007, he announced the imminent publication of an autobiography, but six months later the book was abandoned as news leaked that Defries had lost $22 million in a Cayman Islands tax haven, set up by the Swiss Bank Julius Baer. That spring, the IRS started tracing Defries' contacts, investigating whether he'd paid tax on the huge sum; over the same period, lawyers working for Griffin Music, to whom he'd sold rights for several Bowie rarities and live albums in the early nineties, were in pursuit, as rumours spread that the Svengali had abandoned his estate in Virginia and disappeared to Europe. In 2009, he appeared to have resolved his legal disputes and returned to the USA; but the $22 million, a huge proportion of the money David Bowie had paid to reclaim the most fertile period of his creativity, had apparently disappeared for ever.

More repercussions of the troubled relationship between Bowie and MainMan rumbled on: in 2009, five years after Bowie Bonds were downgraded by credit rating agency Moody's to one notch above junk grade, headlines around the world read, 'Is Bowie to blame for the credit crunch?' BBC journalist Evan Davis claimed the global financial meltdown was caused by bankers who took their cues from David Bowie; seeing him securitise his future income, they followed his lead with their mortgage business, with disastrous results. (Subsequently, other financial experts surfaced to ridicule the charge.) Bowie's own financial fortunes are thought to have declined gently in the recession; in 1997, *Business Age* magazine estimated his wealth at $917 million, although this is regarded by most financial experts as an exaggeration; a recent survey by the *Sunday Times* put his wealth at £100 million. In 2012, his back catalogue will be available for licence once more, outside EMI, and many fans hope to see more of what is thought to be the most intriguing set of unreleased recordings of audio and video outtakes of any major recording artist.

Yet there was one person, in the early years of the twenty-first century, whose career was taking shape even as David Bowie let his own lie fallow. In November 2004, Duncan Jones painstakingly recreated the England of 1979 – a world he had known only briefly – for a commercial celebrating the twenty-fifth anniversary of McCain's Oven Chips. His first press interview didn't even mention his father's identity; by the time he'd been recruited by ad guru Trevor Beattie and attracted the gimlet-eyed glare of the *Daily Mail* for the 'lesbian kiss outrage' of his 2006 TV commercial for fashion brand French Connection, a few reports mentioned his parentage. Then in 2009, Duncan Jones elegantly stepped out into the world's media to publicise his thoughtful, lovingly crafted debut movie, *Moon*.

Duncan's interviews provided a revealing insight into the life of David Bowie, father: there were stories of how they'd worked on stopframe animation together, and of David bringing home his bootleg videos of *Star Wars*. There was also evidence of how David had kept a tasteful distance to avoid overshadowing his son. (Bill Zysblat, David's business manager, was credited as executive producer on the film, but there was no mention of Mr Jones senior.) It is probably unfair to note the presence of the words 'I think' in Duncan's description of his upbringing: 'I think we always loved each other, but he was travelling and working a lot, and I was in his custody, so it was . . . tricky, because obviously there were people who would look after me, but a lot of the time he might not be around. So it was an unusual relationship.'

David had often voiced his guilt over his son's unsettled childhood; but there was some vindication of the way he'd nudged his son towards the cinema in the overwhelming positive reaction to *Moon*, which was made for the unthinkably tiny budget of $5m, grossed $6m within the first nine weeks of release, and picked up two international awards before finally clinching Duncan a BAFTA award for Most Promising Newcomer in February 2010. Jones politely dismissed suggestions that his modest science-fiction gem had been influenced by his dad's 'Space Oddity' (or indeed Kubrick's *2001*), citing instead later influences such as *Silent Running* and *Bladerunner*. But there was plenty of resonance with his father's work. The isolation and loneliness of the sole protagonist, Sam Bell, evokes the lonely childhood of Duncan Jones and the isolation of his father. More profoundly, Bell takes solace in sculpting a church out of balsa: an image that echoed Merrick's cardboard church, or the 'cathedral made of matchsticks' which David had eulogised in one of his *Heathen* interviews as a symbol of the British amateur tradition – that compulsion to perfect a job, whether or not anyone will see it. Lastly, Bell is imprisoned in a cycle of rebirth, wearing out each new manifestation of himself until finally he manages to achieve, as Bowie never did, his 'Houdini escape'.

David's appearance with Duncan at the Sundance Film Festival on 23 January, 2009, was a surprise event, fleeting, but perfectly timed; remaining in front of the camera long enough to ensure a flurry of press for the movie, David, dressed in grey, let his son do the talking. At a Q&A after the screening, Duncan thanked his father for giving him 'the time to work out what I wanted to do – because it's taken me a while'.

Together with an appearance alongside Iman for *Moon*'s debut at New York's Tribeca Film Festival in April, this would be Bowie's only media outing of the year; by 2010, Iman would generally appear on red carpets solo, until David turned up in a tux and black scarf for his wife's acceptance of her 'Fashion Icon' award. And every few months there would be a new reissue: the DVD based on his VH1 *Storytellers* appearance, ten years after it was recorded; a fortieth-anniversary edition of the *Space Oddity* album, complete with an iPhone app, allowing fans to mix their own version of David's debut hit; and later, the announcement of an illustrated book of Bowie artefacts.

For the fans, Bowie's continuing absence seemed an almost unforgivable desertion. Day by day, fewer of them pay the $60-a-year subscription fee to BowieNet, while the bowieart website closed down entirely in 2008. The faithful huddle together on the net, their numbers diminishing. Despite the continuing reissues of his classic works, there would be a growing consensus among fans and business figures that this man is not maintaining his work; that it's like a grand estate with weeds sprouting in the garden and paint flaking from the window frames. What could he possibly be doing that was more important than attending to them?

'It is the wrong way round,' says George Underwood, as he pours coffee into a china mug decorated with one of his serene, slightly sinister paintings and places a couple of lemon curd biscuits on a plate. Yesterday George celebrated his sixty-first birthday with the aid of a giant hamper of Fortnum & Mason delicacies sent by his schoolfriend and ex-bandmate. Today, we sip coffee and sample some of the hamper's goodies, as George describes his 1958 trip to the Isle of Wight with a ukulele and a washboard bass in the back of the van, of cocky letters sent to millionaires, and of the times his best mate shot him looks 'like daggers' because he'd scored his own record deal with Mickie Most, who groomed him for success, advising him on the music business and driving him around the West End in his Roller.

For many fellow pupils from Bromley, or kids who'd hang around The King Bees, George – good-looking, outgoing – was the boy most likely to. Yet his career in music was impressive but short. After one single with Mickie Most something happened: 'I will never know what caused it, but the men in white coats came to take me away.' Confined to hospital for three months, he would never know if someone had slipped a tab of acid in his drink, or some other random stimulus had triggered his breakdown. A promising career was over. It was, he says, 'a blessing in disguise. Because I don't think I'd be sitting here talking to you. I would have said yes to everything – and ended up dead somewhere.'

David, his friend once more, would eventually secure the success he craved. George, over the same period, established himself as an artist and illustrator, crafting dozens of record and book covers, for David, Marc Bolan and countless others. Today, sitting in his elegant, airy north London house, his artworks studded throughout like jewels, there is still a kind of wonder for what his friend achieved. Not for the money, or the fame, but simply, 'Wasn't he brave? To do what he did?'

Yet with the admiration, there's a sense of what David missed out on: the family life, all the little tokens of which surround us, the photos, the well-worn objects that signal a well-worn life. For a moment, I feel pity for Underwood's friend. And then George mentions how David has lived his life 'the wrong way round'. How the twenty-year-old who loved kids is finally getting the chance to spend time with his own, as a sixty-year-old. A few weeks later, I find other old friends whom David has started calling again, to tell them of his nine-year-old daughter, as if what she's up to is more interesting than his current business. Often he'll open a phone call by putting Lexi on the phone for a chat. As if there just might be a legacy more important than the hundreds of songs known to remain in the Bowie vault.

In the meantime, the music is not static. Every new generation of musicians, whether aimed at the stadium or the college circuit, takes some part of Bowie's legacy as a template. As Echo and the Bunnymen's Ian McCulloch, a leader of the generation of musicians that followed him in the 1970s, puts it, 'He changed the face of music. And the world. Everybody's got mad hair or mad clothes now – when he kicked off in 1973 it was rare. I was twelve when "Starman" came out, and it connected with me in a way that no other record ever had. I was still impressionable and naive – and at that moment I knew exactly what I wanted to do.'

Generations since have experienced similar epiphanies. Bowie has been derided for billing himself as a cult artist, a seemingly ludicrous claim for someone who has scored so many Top 10 singles, yet there is a truth in this, for his music continues to speak to outsiders, those who are either on the edge, or wish to go there. For Black Francis of the Pixies, whose music would define the nineties so-called alternative rock scene, it was the Bowie of *Low*, *"Heroes"* and *The Idiot* that called to him: 'It was so brave'. That sentiment occurs again and again: 'He showed no fear,' says Nicolas Godin of Air, who discovered the same trio of albums while training as an architect in Versailles. The French band's 'humble' career was inspired by the example of how Bowie mixed electronics and rock, but Godin stresses that Bowie's influence goes far beyond this: 'He's the total artist – the look, the voice, the talent to compose, the stage presence. The beauty. Nobody is like that any more. Everybody is reachable; he was unreachable.'

So many other artists have picked up on aspects of Bowie's work, from Madonna to Lady Gaga, Radiohead to Momus – the enigmatic Scots musician who laments that 'I was lucky, as a teenager, to have someone like that to latch on to. Bowie wasn't just a rock star in the seventies – he was an exemplary creative animal. He took influences from so many sources: from Kabuki, from Jean Genet and William Burroughs, from the New York Downtown art scene, from Die Brücke, and so on. Because of his influence, musicians could take their cue from other artforms. I saw an interview with him where he said he thought he might have been a good teacher if he hadn't been a rock star, because he loves introducing people to cultural things and seeing their excitement. And I thought, Well, you've been both!'

Philip Glass, a composer, friend and interpreter of Bowie, also laments what now seems like an all-too-brief period when popular music and experimentation co-existed. 'What Bowie and Eno were trying to do was to redefine certain parameters in pop music. To work less in terms of formula and to work in a more experimental fashion. The idea was that pop music had an artform to it; it wasn't always commercial music, it didn't always have to be entertainment music, those people could work in another mode. It was this funny world of art rock, which has since disappeared. But it was a beautiful moment for a while.'

John Lennon, the man who acted almost as an elder brother to David Bowie, occasionally complained how the world always wanted more from his band. The Beatles made eleven albums together, he'd tell people: 'What more could you want?' As David Bowie wanders around New York, watching his daughter grow up, he's entitled to share Lennon's sentiment. Yet even those who worked with David in the past can't help sharing the fans' longing – that once again, this man will free the music that will otherwise stay locked within. 'I'm waiting,' says Mike Garson, his longest-serving accompanist. 'The magic is not in the air right now. We're in a little bit of a slump so maybe in a couple of years he'll start hearing the next thing.

Still, there remains the uncertainty of that elusive alchemy. Can the man who transformed himself perform that magic again?

'If he's not feeling it, who knows?' says Garson. 'Sometimes an artist knows when to cool it. Why do something if you're not feeling it or hearing it? We'll see what's meant to be.'

A SELECTED DISCOGRAPHY

David Bowie ★★

Recorded: November 1966 – February 1967; Decca Studios, West Hampstead, London.
Released: Deram, 1 June, 1967.
Chart Peak: – (UK); – (US).
Key Personnel: Derek 'Dek' Fearnley (bs, arrangements); John Eager (dms); Derek Boyes (kbds, early songs only); plus session musicians unknown.
Producer: Mike Vernon.

Nineteen-year-old David Bowie had bowled over Decca executives, who were convinced of his genius. This first studio album provides convincing evidence of the fact – in everything but the songs. The sheer breadth and ambition of the material – from the kooky sci-fi epic 'We Are Hungry Men', to the earnest, Lionel Bart-ish 'When I Live My Dream'; the playfully sinister 'Uncle Arthur' to the disturbingly psychotic 'Please Mr. Gravedigger' (which references the Myra Hindley murders) – is staggering, even today. His confidence in the studio was, in retrospect, astounding, but the young Bowie lacked the skills to realise his lofty ambitions and it's only the more conventional material, such as 'When I Live My Dream' or the single 'The Laughing Gnome', which succeeds on its own terms. Yet although later derided, this quirky album established Bowie's reputation amid a small crowd of London faces. More crucially still, it gave him his first experience of using the studio like a giant sketch pad, a technique which would become fundamental to his career.

•••

David Bowie ★★★
aka *Space Oddity* (UK 1972 re-release); *Man of Words/Man of Music* (US).

Recorded: June – September 1969; Trident Studios, London.
Released: Philips/Mercury, November 1969.
Chart Peak: 17 (UK); – (US.
Key Personnel: Mick Wayne, Tim Renwick (gtr); John 'Honk' Lodge (bs); John Cambridge (dms); Keith Christmas (acoustic gtr).
Producer: Tony Visconti.

A failure of an album that betrayed its creator's lack of confidence, Bowie's second release was almost an afterthought to his obvious breakthrough song, 'Space

Oddity' – its style and song selections arranged by committee. Predictably, perhaps, it therefore never quite transcends its obvious influences and limitations to become a coherent statement in its own right. Yet in the larger context of David's career, it has many moments of charm, for the very reason that it is unconsidered and confused. 'Letter to Hermione' is gorgeously gauche, while 'Cygnet Committee' is a grandiose construction which shows David attempting to piece together a philosophy and style – and failing. Only 'Space Oddity' truly transcends its intentions.

●●●

The Man Who Sold the World ★★★★

Recorded: April – May 1970; Trident and Advision Studios, London.
Released: Mercury, November 1970 (US); Philips, April 1971 (UK).
Chart Peak: 26 (UK); 105 (US). Both on RCA re-release.
Key Personnel: Mick Ronson (gtr); Tony Visconti (bs); Mick 'Woody' Woodmansey (dms); Ralph Mace (Moog synthesiser).
Producer: Tony Visconti.

Bowie's first truly gripping work, *The Man Who Sold the World* is dark in sound and tone. Crucially it took collaborators – fellow artists, even – to fashion David Bowie's sound for him, and engineer Ken Scott confirms that Tony Visconti and Mick Ronson laboured on their own for much of the album. Yet, for all that, the spark that fires up this album was Bowie's: in framing the concept and delegating crucial tasks, he inspired his collaborators to surpass anything they achieved on their own (Ronson, Visconti and Woodmansey's work as Ronno would be famously dull). However erratic his involvement, the album's sense of unease – the disturbing unreality of the title track, the twisting visions of 'Width of a Circle', or the child-like empathy of 'All the Madmen'– derives entirely from Bowie, who seems most himself when he relies most on others.

●●●

Hunky Dory ★★★★★

Recorded: July 1971; Trident Studios, London.
Released: RCA, December 1971.
Chart Peak: 3 (UK); 93 (US).
Key Personnel: Mick Ronson (gtr); Trevor Bolder (bs); Mick 'Woody' Woodmansey (dms); Rick Wakeman (pno).
Producers: Ken Scott and David Bowie.

The opening salvo of the majestic trio of albums that launched the Bowie legend was understated compared to its successors. While there were plenty of out-there moments – the campness of 'Queen Bitch', the louche tribute to Andy Warhol, and the enigmatic 'The Bewlay Brothers' – in the main, *Hunky Dory*'s appeal was subtle, deriving mainly from the faultless effervescence of the writing. Above all, there is an infectious love of life and a sure-footed sense of destiny: 'Oh! You Pretty Things' slogan, 'make way for the homo superior', is self-aggrandising, a camp joke and a manifesto for a kooky philosophy.

Hunky Dory is as crucial a part of Bowie's cultural legacy as its better-known successor, for where *Ziggy*, in essence, involved donning a quilted catsuit, *Hunky Dory* was based on self-transformation and positive visualisation. *Ziggy*'s songs are skilled and knowing, *Hunky Dory*'s are translucently innocent and effortless: 'Oh! You Pretty Things' was inspired by a dream; 'Life On Mars?' arrived on a bus trip to Lewisham; 'Kooks' was arranged and recorded within days of Duncan's birth. The arrangement and playing, too, is instinctive but faultless, the product both of Mick Ronson's unrivalled musicality and of Bowie's motivational skills. The tributes to Warhol, Dylan and Lou Reed are both naive *and* cynical; by paying them fealty, Bowie also gives himself licence to assimilate them. Lastly, 'Changes' would be the manifesto that energised Bowie and all around him; matching a luscious McCartney-style melody with a powerful Lennon-style message, it would only graze the charts but, crucially, would energise a tiny group of believers, who helped their 'golden boy' ascend to fame over the months that followed.

● ● ●

The Rise and Fall of Ziggy Stardust and the Spiders From Mars ★★★★★

Recorded: November 1971 – January 1972; Trident Studios, London.
Released: RCA, June 1972.
Chart Peak: 5 (UK); 75 (US).
Key Personnel: Mick Ronson (gtr); Tony Visconti (bs); Trevor Bolder (bs); Mick 'Woody' Woodmansey (dms).
Producers: Ken Scott and David Bowie.

If *Hunky Dory* came from the heart, *Ziggy* came from the head. The constituent elements were being assembled as early as January, 1971, when David wrote the magnificent, pile-driving 'Moonage Daydream' a few days after first hearing an Iggy record. Other crucial blocks were hoisted into place right up to the final days of recording, with the title track and breakthrough single 'Starman' written well into the sessions. Inspired by Iggy and fifties rocker Vince Taylor, *Ziggy* was rather polite in comparison: its songs more precise and both delivery and production arguably over-refined. (Only the Santa Monica bootleg, an underrated influence on seventies punk that was officially released in 2008, demonstrates the power of The Spiders in their prime.) Instead, it's the drama of the ideas that give the album its power, opening and closing with two magnificent ballads, 'Five Years' and 'Rock 'n' Roll Suicide', and taking the listener on an exhausting emotional rollercoaster in between. The songs function perfectly as rock 'n' roll, with Mick Ronson's guitar the electricity that brings each finely crafted chord sequence to life, so perfectly that they'd inspire a generation of rock bands – even Iggy and his Stooges, who lifted 'Suffragette City's' central chord change for their punk anthem 'Search and Destroy'. Yet they also stand apart from rock 'n'roll, which gives them a wider power, for *Ziggy* works overall as a drama which demands suspension of disbelief from each of us, and hence makes us all participants. Even today, it's a thrill to be part of the action.

●●●

Aladdin Sane   ★★★★★

Recorded: October 1972; RCA, NYC. December 1972 and January 1973; Trident, London.
Released: RCA, April 1973.
Chart Peak: 1 (UK), 17 (US).
Key Personnel: Mick Ronson (gtr); Trevor Bolder (bs); Mick 'Woody' Woodmansey (dms); Mike Garson (pno); Ken Fordham, Brian Wilshaw (sax).
Producers: Ken Scott and David Bowie.

Both slicker *and* sketchier than its predecessor, *Aladdin Sane* is in some ways a more convincing document on the nature of fame and show business than *Ziggy* – its flakiness adds authenticity. The strained, edgy cover of 'Let's Spend the Night Together' is shallow, yet glamorous; 'The Jean Genie', too, is outrageously slick, a magnificently flagrant rip-off of The Yardbirds. Yet the album's great songs are cavernous in their depth, with Mike Garson's rippling piano evoking decadence or oblivion in haunting songs like 'Aladdin Sane' or 'Time', while Ronson and Bolder's musicianship is devastatingly sophisticated, most notably on 'Lady Grinning Soul'. The personal dramas being played out add to the edginess: 'The Prettiest Star' is a re-statement of David's paean to Angie, recorded just as he decided his marriage was doomed, while arguments over Woody's drumming on 'Panic in Detroit' helped inspire the termination of The Spiders, just as they were at their peak.

●●●

Pin Ups   ★★

Recorded: July – August 1973; Château D'Hérouville, France.
Released: RCA, October 1973.
Chart Peak: 1 (UK); 23 (US).
Key Personnel: Mick Ronson (gtr etc.); Trevor Bolder (bs); Aynsley Dunbar (dms); Mike Garson (pno); Ken Fordham (sax); Geoff MacCormack (perc, backing vox).
Producers: Ken Scott and David Bowie.

Recorded in a race to beat Bryan Ferry's covers album, *Pin Ups* was an odd mixture of nostalgia and cynicism. Mick Ronson had mixed feelings about his imminent solo career, Trevor Bolder and Ken Scott were completely estranged, while David affected indifference to the power struggles around him. *Pin Ups* was therefore nostalgic not only for the good times of sixties London (some of it seen through the eyes of a Yank – Scott Richardson – who helped choose the tracks), but for The Spiders themselves. The album itself is both a Warholian display of appropriation – featuring songs like The Who's 'Anyway, Anyhow, Anywhere', that Bowie had already used once with The Lower Third – and a demonstration of Bowie the unabashed fan. For Americans, the album represented a brilliantly decadent collection of garage-band nuggets; for many Brits, the covers were predictable, insipid and watered down, with the frenzied teenage angst of songs like The Easybeats' 'Friday On My Mind' reworked into turgid, platform-booted camp. Unashamedly exploitative, intermittently vital, the album fell well short of brilliance except in one respect: it was a devastating 'so what?' riposte to those who claimed that Bowie's music was merely a cynical reworking of The Who, The Kinks and The Yardbirds.

●●●

Diamond Dogs   ★★★★

Recorded: December 1973 – January 1974; Olympic Studios, London and Studio L, Hilversum, The Netherlands.
Released: RCA, April 1974.
Chart Peak: 1 (UK); 5 (US).
Key Personnel: Herbie Flowers (bs); David Bowie, Alan Parker (gtr); Aynsley Dunbar, Tony Newman (dms);
Producer: David Bowie (Tony Visconti oversees mix).

Bowie's depiction of a future dystopia was messy and sprawling, inspired by George Orwell's *1984*, but also permeated with the paranoia now besetting his friends and colleagues. Previous sessions had been focused and compact; *Diamond Dogs* – once the nucleus had been assembled around Blue Mink musicians Flowers, Parker and Newman – was confused, with overdubs layered on messily and Spiders bassist Trevor Bolder called in – perhaps out of desperation – to help salvage one song. Bowie's songwriting changed, too: the melodic inventiveness and rolling chord sequences he'd first harnessed on *Hunky Dory* disappeared; instead there's a new concentration on texture, simple rock chord sequences and swaggering rhythms heavily influenced by The Rolling Stones, whom Bowie aimed to knock off their pedestal. Adding to the mess, there was confusion about the credits, and the catchy 'Rebel Rebel' stands out like a sore thumb alongside the resonant 'Sweet Thing' and the bizarre, hellish funk of '1984'. Overall, the album is a beautiful mess, its confused mêlée every bit as appropriate as *Ziggy*'s finely honed choreography.

•••

David Live ★

Recorded: 8–12 July 1974; Tower Theatre, Philadelphia, PA.
Released: RCA, October 1974.
Chart Peak: 2 (UK); 8 (US).
Key Personnel: Earl Slick (gtr); Mike Garson (pno); Herbie Flowers (bs); Tony Newman (dms); David Sanborn (sax); Richard Grando (baritone sax); Pablo Rosario (perc); Geoff MacCormack, Gui Andrisano (backing vox).
Producer: Tony Visconti

The old-school showbiz element of Bowie's career was never more evident than in MainMan's revival of the neglected tradition of covers and live albums, designed primarily to keep the corporate presses rolling. Widely lambasted on release, *David Live* does indeed show his music coarsened, with overcooked backing and over-emoted singing replacing the electrifying joy of, say, The Spiders' Santa Monica bootleg. The album is not totally devoid of charm – Sanborn's sax interlacing with the 'All the Young Dudes' chorus; the shuffling undercurrent of drums and bass on 'Rebel Rebel' – but the album highlight, 'Here Today, Gone Tomorrow', is perhaps the ultimate indictment. In this setting, it sounds stripped down and affecting, but one listen to the Ohio Players' jewel-like original reminds us how lumpen the Bowie machine has become.

•••

Young Americans ★★★★

Recorded: August 1974; Sigma Sound, Philadelphia, PA. January 1975; Electric Lady, NYC.
Released: RCA, March 1975.
Chart Peak: 2 (UK); 9 (US).
Key Personnel: Carlos Alomar (gtr); Willie Weeks (bs); Andy Newmark (dms); Mike Garson (pno); David Sanborn (sax); Larry Washington (conga); Pablo Rosario (perc); Ava Cherry, Luther Vandross, Robin Clark, Anthony Hinton, Diane Sumler, Geoff MacCormak (backing vox). 'Fame' and 'Across the Universe' musicians include Earl Slick, John Lennon (gtr); Emir Kason (bs); Dennis Davis (dms).
Producer: Tony Visconti.

The commercial success of *Young Americans* was so overwhelming, the stylistic makeover so complete, that it has become a set-piece, an exemplar of an artist often typecast as manipulative, or cold-blooded. Yet the opposite is the case: the genesis of *Young Americans* was instinctive, born of a fan's enthusiasm, and the album was recorded on the hoof, like the material that inspired it. The rushed recording adds an edge and adrenalin readily audible on the title track, a splicing of brittle funk with Springsteen-style lyrical imagery, that, given more gloss, would have sounded trite. 'Can You Hear Me?' and 'Fascination', too, are entrancing, sketched out quickly. The album's high and low points were similarly rushed: 'Fame', recorded in New York, is an impressionistic assemblage that, with its unvarying central chord sequence and riff adapted from The Rascals' 'Jungle Walk', anticipated the sampling culture of the eighties and nineties; 'Across the Universe', the other last-minute addition, is a cloying example of Bowie's new, over-emoted, yodelling singing style, partly inspired by Bryan Ferry; worse still, it bumped off 'It's Gonna Be Me' – a superb showpiece for Bowie's voice. Sketchy and inconsistent from today's perspective, in 1975 the album restored the momentum lost by the unconvincing *David Live*, while the impressionistic working methods pioneered here would underpin Bowie's career through the rest of the decade – and more.

●●●

Station to Station   ★★★★★

Recorded: November 1975; Cherokee and Record Plant Studios, Los Angeles, CA.
Released: RCA, January 1976.
Chart Peak: 5 (UK); 3 (US).
Key Personnel: Carlos Alomar, Earl Slick (gtr); Dennis Davis (dms); George Murray (bs); Roy Bittan (pno); Geoff MacCormack (backing vox).
Producers: David Bowie and Harry Maslin.

The key turning point in Bowie's recording career, *Station to Station* marked the transition from conventional songs, written on the piano or guitar and recorded at breakneck speed, to slabs of sound constructed entirely in the studio. Even those songs sketched out before Bowie arrived at Cherokee, such as 'Golden Years', were transformed within it – all of its key elements worked up while the studio clock was running.

Most accounts depict Bowie undergoing some kind of cocaine-induced breakdown during the end of 1975; his psychological trauma was indeed extreme, but during the sessions even drug buddies like Glenn Hughes noted he was in full command of the studio. Given that Bowie himself has little memory of this time, we will never get a more coherent picture of his mental state than in the contents of this album. The title track is obsessive, megalomaniacal, yearning for spiritual clarity yet oddly muso (the churning rhythms and heavy textures were inspired by Jethro Tull); the catchy, mildly deranged 'TVC 15' – its vocal interjections obviously influenced by The Yardbirds' 'Good Morning Little Schoolgirl' – was a comical take on Bowie's recent months spent watching grainy Second World War footage over and over; while the magnificent, sensitive 'Golden Years' also reflects Bowie's ability to surface from a cocaine jag and dispense insightful career advice or a hilariously deadpan joke. Although the melodicism of *Hunky Dory* was by now a thing of the past, *Station to Station* is packed with invention –

a bizarre blending of spritely and monumental themes – and marks the point at which David Bowie moved from pop musician to phenomenon.

●●●

Low ★★★★★

Recorded: September – early October 1976; Château D'Hérouville, Paris. Overdubbed and mixed Hansa Studio 2, Berlin.
Released: RCA, January 1977.
Chart Peak: 2 (UK); 11 (US).
Key Personnel: Brian Eno (vocals, kbds and treatments); Carlos Alomar, Ricky Gardiner (gtr); Dennis Davis (dms); George Murray (bs); Roy Young (pno, organ).
Producers: David Bowie and Tony Visconti.

Its title was a reference both to being low profile, and to David's mental state – beset by marital and management problems. Yet those troubles were offset by the thrill of a new beginning, and an album that was dismissed by many on release as inhuman and inaccessible stands today as joyous, uplifting and optimistic. The glacial beauty of Brian Eno's EMS synthesiser, which dominates side two, is balanced by the zest and humanity of side one. Bowie's voice is rendered naked and unaffected, with many songs enlivened by distinctive soul references – for instance, the melody from 'Stand By Me' that echoes 'Always Crashing in the Same Car'. As if to help orientate the listener, the album follows an impeccable internal logic, with concise, up-tempo instrumentals bookending side one, which was chockfull of catchy melodies and rhythms, to contrast with the icy languor of side two. As Bowie intended, this is great art, but it's great pop music, too.

●●●

"Heroes" ★★★★★

Recorded: May 1977; Hansa Studio 2, Berlin.
Released: RCA, October 1977.
Chart Peak: 3 (UK); 35 (US).
Key Personnel: Carlos Alomar, Robert Fripp (gtr); Dennis Davis (dms); George Murray (bs); Brian Eno (synths etc.).
Producers: David Bowie and Tony Visconti.

The only album of Bowie's 'Berlin trilogy' to be recorded entirely in the city – at Hansa's capacious Studio 2 – *"Heroes"* was a tougher, heavier album than its predecessor, with chunkier rhythms overlaid by Robert Fripp's audacious guitar work, all recorded in two days flat. Bowie's own lyrics and singing were freer: the most intuitive, improvised and simple of his career. The songs, meanwhile, were assembled in almost random fashion from odd snippets, then lovingly overlaid, with odd little melodies – a marimba here, a koto there – emerging on every new listen. Although the album is less funky and more Germanic than *Low*, the key figure alongside Bowie and Eno is Carlos Alomar, whose inventive, infectious guitar melodies underpin most of the songs – most notably the title track, where he powers the music on even as Robert Fripp's guitar soars above and Bowie's voice, totally without artifice, cranks up the emotional temperature. His simplest, most affecting and most memorable song, the title track sounds timeless today but was out of time in 1977, only reaching number twenty-four in the UK singles charts.

•••

Stage   ★★

Recorded: April – May 1978; The Spectrum, Philadelphia, PA, Providence Civic Centre, Providence, RI, and Boston Garden, Boston, MA.
Released: RCA, September 1978.
Chart Peak: 5 (UK); 44 (US).
Key Personnel: Carlos Alomar, Adrian Belew (gtr); Dennis Davis (dms and perc); George Murray (bs); Simon House (vln); Sean Mayes (pno); Roger Powell (kbds and synth).

An impressive memento of a challenging, innovative tour, *Stage* still sounds bravely unconventional today; its finest moments, rather than the expected crowd-pleasers, are the glacial and uncompromising 'Warszawa' or the spiky, off-kilter 'Breaking Glass'. In isolation, the Ziggy-era tracks falter, sorely lacking the muscularity of the original versions, but Bowie's voice, at least, is mostly flawless, undiminished.

•••

Lodger   ★★★★

Recorded: September 1978 and March 1979; Mountain Studios, Montreux, Switzerland, and Record Plant, NYC.
Released: RCA, May 1979.
Chart Peak: 4 (UK); 20 (US).
Key Personnel: Carlos Alomar, Adrian Belew (gtr); Dennis Davis (dms); George Murray (bs); Brian Eno (synths etc.); Simon House (vln); Sean Mayes (pno); Roger Powell (synth).
Producers: David Bowie and Tony Visconti.

Both more conventional and more intellectual than its predecessors, *Lodger* was denoted the last of Bowie's Berlin trilogy (or 'triptych', as he termed it) but is distinct both in mood and method – and disappointing in comparison. The singing is mannered – self-conscious yelps on 'Red Money', Bowie channelling David

Byrne channelling Bowie on 'DJ' and an alarmingly literal Scott Walker imitation on 'Look Back in Anger' – the songs more conventional and the recording process dryer, in every sense of the term. Still, once preconceptions are abandoned, the album is studded with delights. It's quirky rather than emotional, with delicious detailing: the fairground Arabic lilt of 'Yassassin', the unassumingly romantic theme of 'Fantastic Voyage', the constant tension between the plain, almost predictable chord sequences and the random guitar and vocal explosions scattered throughout. Although *Lodger* would never equal the emotional impact of *Low* or *"Heroes"*, it nonetheless defined the sound of eighties art rock, and echoes of its spiky, New Wave quirkiness can still be heard today.

•••

Scary Monsters . . . and Super Creeps   ★★★★★

Recorded: February 1980; Record Plant, NYC. April 1980; Good Earth, London.
Released: RCA, September 1980.
Chart Peak: 3 (UK); 12 (US).
Key Personnel: Carlos Alomar, Robert Fripp (gtr); Chuck Hammer (synth gtr); Dennis Davis (dms); George Murray (bs); Roy Bittan (pno); plus Pete Townshend (gtr); Andy Clarke (synth).
Producers: David Bowie and Tony Visconti

Recorded during yet another frenzy of activity, as Bowie re-explored New York and prepared for *The Elephant Man*, *Scary Monsters* was a kind of organised pop version of *Lodger*. The endless experimentation favoured by Brian Eno was abandoned; instead, Bowie stalked the sessions with a clipboard, ticking off items on a to-do list, for songs that were mostly sketched out in advance. The material was almost old-fashioned in Bowie terms: 'Up the Hill Backwards' evokes both Bill Withers' 'Lean On Me' and *Young Americans*; 'Ashes to Ashes' features the old-school musical bridge ('the shriek of nothing is killing me') used in classic Bowie songs from The Lower Third's 'Can't Help Thinking About Me' to 'China Girl'. Self-references abound: 'Teenage Wildlife' addresses Bowie's influence on the world over the classic two-chord change of 'Heroes', while, of course, Major Tom pops up once more on 'Ashes to Ashes' – an almost impossibly sophisticated assemblage adorned by the guitar synth of Chuck Hammer, who noted the almost telepathic bond between Bowie and Tony Visconti as they seized on musical ideas and honed the sound, intuitively. The dense, tough, rock-meets-funk backing was hugely influential – listen to Blur, The Strokes, or dozens of art-rock bands for evidence – and represents Bowie's most versatile band, ever, at their very peak. A few months later, they'd all be looking for new jobs.

•••

Baal ★★★★

Recorded: September 1981; Hansa Studio 2, Berlin.
Released: RCA, February 1982 (vinyl or download).
Chart Peak: 29 (UK); – (US).
Key Personnel: Dominic Muldowney (gtr, arrangements). Main backing comes from Berlin session musicians headed by percussionist Sherry Bertram.
Producer: Tony Visconti.

The blinkered overview of Bowie's career is that his last great album was *Scary Monsters*, yet this contract-filler – recorded in two rushed days in Berlin – is, in its own way, a masterpiece. The setting of Brecht's songs is small-scale, almost domestic, with most of David's vocals dropped in during a single afternoon. The result is a masterclass in singing and an album that is always intriguing. On first impression it seems polite and formal, but on better acquaintance, it is as great an evocation of Bowie's Berlin years as *"Heroes"*, for it preserves magnificently the last echoes of Brecht's adopted city.

•••

Let's Dance ★★★★

Recorded: December 1982; Power Station, NYC.
Released: EMI, April 1983.
Chart Peak: 1 (UK); 4 (US).
Key Personnel: Stevie Ray Vaughan, Nile Rodgers (gtr); Carmine Rojas, Bernard Edwards (bs); Rob Sabino (kbds); Tony Thompson, Omar Hakim (dms).
Producers: David Bowie and Nile Rodgers.

Vilified in the decades after its release, partly because it signalled the rise of mainstream Bowie, it is arguable that *Let's Dance* is one of his most underrated albums. It was certainly one of his most influential, for its luxurious, minimal sound, dominated by Tony Thompson's swinging drums, stripped-down R&B horns and tough but exhibitionist guitar, would become a template for the late eighties. It's fair, too, to comment that it launched the era of form over function for Bowie, as well as his followers: with just eight tracks, including old collaborations with Iggy Pop and Giorgio Moroder and a cover of 'Criminal World', written by arty New Wavers Metro, he was plainly short of good songs. But not of great ones, for the title track – which, according to producer Nile Rodgers started life as a folksy Byrds-style ditty – and the impeccably infectious 'Modern Love' were a pinnacle of eighties pop. 'China Girl', too, is a sumptuously pimped-out version of the dark, gothic original, completing the irresistible opening trio of songs which announced Bowie's ascension to the mainstream. Other songs – 'Without You', 'Ricochet', 'Criminal World' – are an assemblage of pleasant noises and pass the time nicely, 'Shake It' is dull and 'Cat People' desecrates the memory of a Bowie classic – it was lost until exhumed by Tarantino for *Inglorious Basterds*. While not a Great Album, *Let's Dance* is at least a Great Eighties Album.

●●●

Tonight ★

Recorded: May – June 1984; Le Studio, Morin Heights, Canada.
Released: EMI, September 1984.
Chart Peak: 1 (UK); 11 (US).
Key Personnel: Carlos Alomar (gtr); Derek Bramble (bs); Carmine Rojas (bs); Omar Hakim (dms).
Producers: David Bowie, Derek Bramble and Hugh Padgham.

In retrospect, every failing of *Tonight* had been evident in Bowie's career to date: a rushed recording, shameless lifting of ideas, overwrought vocals, undistinguished songs and excessive reliance on sidemen. But on *Tonight*, they came together all at once, in a perfect storm of mediocrity.

The prime example of *Tonight*'s failure is its best song, 'Loving the Alien': a decent, subtle tune, it also represented a crucial loss of confidence, for whereas previously Bowie had taken his stylistic cues from the underground, here he sources from the mainstream – the chorused guitar sounds from The Police, the vocal 'ah ahs' from Laurie Anderson and the marimbas from The Thompson Twins. The three Iggy songs were likewise decent enough, but were reworked as leaden white reggae. Worse still, the warbling vocal style, apparently influenced by Bryan Ferry, plumbs new depths on 'Tonight' and 'God Only Knows', which with its clumsy, predictable arrangement sounds like a pub singer punting for wedding and bar mitzvah jobs – two decades on, he'd reinvented The Kon-Rads. As one of his musicians once commented, David Bowie was known for 'stealing from the best'. Now the self-proclaimed tasteful thief was finally pilloried for taking something worthless.

●●●

Never Let Me Down ★

Recorded: Circa December 1986; Mountain, Montreux, Switzerland, and Power Station, NYC.
Released: EMI, April 1987.
Chart Peak: 6 (UK); 34 (US).
Key Personnel: Carlos Alomar, Peter Frampton (gtr); Erdal Kizilcay (bs, dms, kbds etc.); Carmine Roja (bs); Phillipe Saisse (pno, kbds).
Producers: David Bowie and David Richards.

Often in Bowie's career, preconceptions and received wisdom are wrong;

however, the 1980s consensus that *Never Let Me Down* stinks still holds good today. Bereft of inspiration, fantasising of one last hit to provide a glorious exit, Bowie abandoned the intuitive, impressionistic approach to recording he'd used for a decade and prepared meticulously. Perhaps it was lack of confidence that inspired his bizarre vocal mimicry: on the title song he copies John Lennon, on 'Day-In Day-Out' it's Prince, 'Bang Bang' is a cover of Iggy Pop copying Billy Idol, while the laughably slushy 'Zeroes' sounds like a Michael Jackson reject: Bowie had gone from Heroes to Zeroes in just a decade.

More confused even than his Deram debut, the album was a strange throwback to David Jones, the teenager who'd mimicked his idols for Shel Talmy. As with those earliest efforts, the results were not so much awful as forgettable. The album seemed to indicate a man in the grip of a midlife crisis, adrift without talented sidemen – but for the fact that, over the same period, he'd bashed out superb songs for director Julien Temple and friend Iggy Pop.

● ● ●

Tin Machine ★ ★

Recorded: August 1988 – 1989; Mountain, Montreux, Switzerland, and Compass Point, Nassau, CA.
Released: EMI, May 1989.
Chart Peak: 3(UK); 28 (US).
Key Personnel: Reeves Gabrels (gtr); Tony Sales (bs); Hunt Sales (dms); Kevin Armstrong (gtr, kbds).
Producers: Tin Machine and Tim Palmer.

Tin Machine's debut was mostly greeted with relief and enthusiasm by fans and critics, grateful for another album that, like *Low* or *Station to Station*, offered elements of challenge and mystery. The feelings of gratitude eventually evaporated, with the very same material criticised as pompous, dogmatic and dull. The worst Tin Machine songs did indeed deserve that description – many were assemblages of blues clichés, while the cover of 'Working Class Hero' is turgid and monotonous. All the same, some of the material was Bowie's best in years: 'Prisoner of Love', obviously Pixies-influenced, still sound fresh today; 'Run' is haunting despite its resemblance to 'Don't Fear the Reaper', while 'I Can't Read' is simply spellbinding – Bowie's most emotionally affecting song of the decade. Outside of those gems, though, the album is hard to love – which was quite possibly Bowie's intention, for the band apparently worked on more commercial, memorable songs which never made the final edit, presumably because Tin Machine were designed primarily as a scorched-earth policy to wipe out the memory of eighties Bowie.

● ● ●

Tin Machine II ★

Recorded: October 1989 and March 1991; Studio 301, Sydney, and A&M, Los Angeles, CA.
Released: Victory, September 1991.
Chart Peak: 23 (UK); 126 (US).
Key Personnel: Reeves Gabrels (gtr); Tony Sales (bs); Hunt Sales (dms).
Producers: Tin Machine, Tim Palmer and Hugh Padgham.

Released as the enthusiasm for Tin Machine was already fading outside diehard fans, *Tin Machine II* exhibited exactly the same virtues and drawbacks as its predecessors – each of them magnified. Most of the album was prosaic, predictable rock 'n' roll, and if anyone was bored by the bluesy jams of the first album, they could hardly be enthused by hearing Hunt Sales, an excellent drummer, display his mediocre abilities as a singer – twice! 'Goodbye Mr. Ed', on the other hand, was a beautiful song, destined to become a lost classic.

●●●

Black Tie White Noise ★★

Recorded: 1992; Mountain, Montreux, Switzerland, and 38Fresh and Hit Factory, NYC.
Released: Savage Records, April 1993.
Chart Peak: 1 (UK); 39 (US).
Key Personnel: Pugi Bell, Sterling Campbell (dms); Barry Campbell, John Regan (bs); Nile Rodgers (gtr); Richard Hilton, Philippe Saisse, Richard Tee (kbds); plus guests including Lester Bowie (tpt), Mick Ronson (gtr, 'I Feel Free'), Mike Garson (pno, 'Looking For Lester').
Producers: David Bowie and Nile Rodgers.

Bowie's most commercially successful album for years saw him being fêted by a new generation of fans and featured on the cover of youth-oriented magazines alongside young guns like Britpop pioneers Suede. Songs like the tough, edgy 'Jump They Say', devoted to half-brother Terry, or the stripped-down, taut 'Miracle Goodnight' – which featured the welcome return of Bowie on sax – further heightened the sense of renaissance. But there were plenty of cloying moments, too, such as the cutesy 'Don't Let Me Down & Down' – featuring David singing in a kind of Brixton Caribbean patois – and the general over-polite, airbrushed sheen of the album means that, when it disappeared from the shelves following the bankruptcy of record label Savage, few bemoaned its passing.

●●●

The Buddha of Suburbia ★★★★

Recorded: circa September 1993; Mountain, Montreux, Switzerland.
Released: Universal, December 1993.
Chart Peak: 87 (UK); – (US).
Key Personnel: Erdal Kizilcay (gts, bs, kbds, tpt etc.); David Richards (programming etc.); Mike Garson (pno); Lenny Kravitz (gtr).
Producer: David Bowie and David Richards.

A rushed recording, assembled as an expanded version of the themes Bowie and multi-instrumentalist Erdal Kizilcay had conjured up for Hanif Kureishi's BBC film, *The Buddha of Suburbia* featured much the same collection of dance beats and melodies as *Black Tie White Noise*. It demonstrated what could be achieved by lack of time and lack of expectations, for it is throughout a far more gripping album than its predecessor. The title song is conventional – shimmering guitars and mid-paced drum machine – but displays a beguiling simplicity long absent from Bowie's work; it's shot through with the loneliness of suburbia and kicks into action with a vintage, impassioned middle eight. Other songs – notably 'Strangers When We Meet' – are his catchiest material in years, but never overblown, while there is experimentation aplenty in the form of grandiose or disturbing tracks like 'Sex and the Church' and 'South Horizon', as well as the welcome return of pianist Mike Garson. Undoubtedly Bowie's best album in nearly a decade, it was given a low-key, belated release by Universal, limped out on to the schedules and disappeared without trace.

•••

1. Outside ★★★

Recorded: March – November 1994; Mountain, Montreux, Switzerland, and West Side, London. January 1995; Hit Factory, NYC.
Released: ISO/Virgin, September 1995.
Chart Peak: 8 (UK); 21 (US).
Key Personnel: Reeves Gabrels (gtr); Brian Eno (synths, treatments); Erdal Kizilcay (bs); Mike Garson (pno); Sterling Campbell (dms); plus Carlos Alomar, Kevin Armstrong (gtr) and Joey Barron (dms).
Producers: David Bowie, Brian Eno and David Richards.

Bowie's long-awaited reunion with Eno is a fascinating curate's egg, developed over drawn-out sessions which featured Bowie painting and the musicians each allotted bizarre roles – with much of the action filmed by underprivileged kids. It features the best of Bowie – the courage, the ability to spur musicians on to new creative heights – and the worst – namely over-thinking, weighing his material down with too many ideas. The album is packed with significant songs – the hard-bitten, ominous 'The Heart's Filthy Lesson', 'Thru These Architect's Eyes' and 'I

Have Not Been to Oxford Town' – but as a musical experience it's hampered by a ludicrous voiceover and the sense that its maker was simply trying too hard.

●●●

Earthling ★★

Recorded: 1996; Looking Glass Studios, NYC.
Released: BMG, February 1997.
Chart Peak: 6 (UK); 39 (US).
Key Personnel: Reeves Gabrels (gtr, synth, programming); Mark Plati (programming etc.); Mike Garson (pno); Gail Ann Dorsey (bs); Zachary Alford (dms, perc).
Producers: David Bowie, Reeves Gabrels and Mark Plati.

Bowie would be mocked as a 'dad at the disco' for this collection of mostly drum 'n' bass tracks, but there is a rush of excitement in the opening moments which banishes cynicism: 'Little Wonder' features the return of cheeky, cockney Bowie, its agile, sweet melody perfectly offset by crunchy guitar and clattering drum machine – like *Outside*'s 'Hallo Spaceboy', it's a classic which stands outside of style. But the trick soon wears thin. Despite some innovative structures, like the slightly loopy 'Looking for Satellites', and ruthlessly efficient rock songs like 'Dead Man Walking', the album soon develops into a drearily repetitive loop, each chorus followed by two bars of chattering drums and then a heavy guitar riff. As a whole, the album is conservative and formulaic – even the self-referential title and Union Jack cover seemed to indicate a jaded palate. Those faults would have been forgivable had the album been released two years earlier; its appearance just as the nineties drum 'n' bass craze was subsiding suggested Bowie was content to surf on someone else's wave, rather than making his own.

●●●

Hours ★★

Recorded: April 1999; Seaview Studios, Bermuda, and Looking Glass, NYC.
Released: ISO/Virgin International, October 1999.
Chart Peak: 5 (UK); 47 (US).
Key Personnel: Reeves Gabrels (gtr); Mark Plati (bs); Mike Levesque and Sterling Campbell (dms); Holly Palmer (backing vox, 'Thursday's Child').
Producers: David Bowie and Reeves Gabrels.

Refreshingly unadorned, sometimes hauntingly intimate, *Hours* abandoned the high-tech cut and paste of its predecessor for a production that was distinctly downhome – indeed, too much so, for the real David Bowie is surely to be found more in gloss and the artifice, than in dress-down introspection. Although some material was thin – 'What's Really Happening?', for instance, a collaboration with fan Alex Grant, featuring a melody lifted from 'You Keep Me Hanging On' – songs like 'Seven' and 'Thursday's Child' were finely crafted – beautiful, even – but the distinctive Bowie voice that he'd rediscovered on *Earthling* was gone, to be replaced mainly with a Nick Cave-ish throaty baritone. The third in a string of stylistic about-turns, the album once again suggested a return to the teenage Bowie struggling to find a unique voice – and rather like *Space Oddity*, *Hours*, for all its finely crafted moments, ended up being less than the sum of its parts.

•••

Heathen ★★★★

Recorded: Mostly August – September 2001; Allaire Studios, New York State, and Looking Glass, NYC.
Released: ISO/Columbia, June 2002.
Chart Peak: 5 (UK); 14 (US).
Key Personnel: Tony Visconti (bs); Matt Chamberlain (dms); David Torn (gtr); plus guests including Pete Townshend and Dave Grohl.
Producers: David Bowie and Tony Visconti.

Bowie's long-awaited reunion with Tony Visconti was almost unassuming; gone were the intense sonic textures, overlayered production and the sense that Bowie had tried too hard. In its place was simple, unassuming songwriting, a sense of clarity – and, above all, that wonderful voice, a glory pretty much absent since *Baal*, Bowie's last work with Tony Visconti. On first listening, songs like 'Slip Away' and 'Everyone Says Hi' perhaps sound unadventurous, too tasteful and luxurious, with their smooth fretless bass and luscious strings – but they have that niggling sense of unease that draw the listener back in. 'Sunday' and 'Heathen', with their spiralling, disturbing instrumentation, are enchanting, intriguing dramas, showcasing the immense potential of Bowie's reunion with his best-known producer.

•••

Reality ★★★

Recorded: January 2003, Looking Glass, NYC.
Released: ISO/Columbia, September 2003.
Chart Peak: 3 (UK); 29 (US).
Key Personnel: Gerry Leonard, Earl Slick, David Torn (gtr); Mark Plati (bs); Sterling Campbell (dms); Mike Garson (pno).
Producers: David Bowie and Tony Visconti.

Thirty years on from the albums that made his name, *Reality* shows Bowie as the consummate professional. The angst and paranoia is seemingly consigned to the past, in favour of a reassuringly familiar edginess: 'Pablo Picasso' is, as you'd guess, quintessential art rock, 'The Modern Lovers' meets Bob Dylan; the throbbing 'She'll Drive the Big Car' is vaguely reminiscent of 'Ashes to Ashes'; 'Days' is a conventional, confessional love song ('all you gave, you gave for free . . . I gave nothing in return'). It's all intriguing, but faintly familiar – the outsider has finally come in from the cold. Yet there is still darkness in this heart, above all on the magnificent 'Bring Me the Disco King': Mike Garson's majestic piano echoes into the distance, Bowie's voice is foregrounded, more prominent than on any previous recordings, revealing new depths of experience and musicality. It holds out an intriguing prospect – that rather than simply revisit his past, like so many of his peers, David Bowie retains the potential to conjure up pleasures as yet unknown.

Unless specifically referenced otherwise, all sources refer to the author's own interviews. A full list of interviewees follows at the end of this section. I've endeavoured to acknowledge every significant quote and fact presented in this book; in time I will post more background information – deleted scenes, alternate takes, but hopefully no corrections – at www.trynka.com.

1 When I'm Five

Opening paragraph is based on interview with Eric Schermerhorn. Description of Brixton draws on recollections from Roger Bolden, who lived at 7, Stansfield Road, David West, Linda Stagg, Sue Larner, Linda McCartney, Barbara Gray, Suzanne Goldschmitt and Val Wilmer (who lived nearby in Streatham, and would later become a key expert on Caribbean culture in Brixton). The problems for mothers attempting to buy nappies and candles around December 1947 were recorded by Florence Speed, Grace Golden and Judy Haines for their Mass-Observation diaries, and were quoted in David Kynaston's *Austerity Britain* (Bloomsbury, 2007), a superb depiction of this largely forgotten era, which was complemented by Dominic Sandbrook's *Never Had it So Good* (Abacus, 2006) and Peter Hennessy's *Having it So Good* (Allen Lane, 2006).

Information on the Jones family's tenure in Brixton comes from electoral records in Lambeth Archives. Background information on David's family comes from Ken Pitt's *Bowie: The Pitt Report*, and Peter and Leni Gillman's *Alias David Bowie*, both of which drew on interviews with Pat Antoniou; information on Haywood Jones' Barnardo's career was supplied by Dorothy Howes at the charity; helpful recollections of Peggy were provided by her friend Aubrey Goodchild.

Early Bromley and Burnt Ash memories: Max Batten, John Barrance, Richard Comben, Susan Hill, Gill Hymas, Jan Powling, Peter Prickett; ex-Bromley Tech pupils and friends who all offered helpful insights include Mike Bassett, Chris Britton, Nick Brooks, Peter Davidson, Greg D'Souza, John Edmonds, Pete Goodchild, Cary Granger, John Kendall, Len Outridge, Colin Ovenden, Brian Payne, Howard Phillips, Alan Reader, Andy Twiner, Adrian White and Keith Wilkinson. David's *Quatermass* recollections, and later quotes on his early record-ing-buying habits, come from his 2006 'Nokia Music Recommenders' story. 'Everyone finds empathy in a nutty family' is from David's 1976 *Playboy* interview with Cameron Crowe. The conclusion in the final paragraph that George Underwood, rather than David, was the 'Boy Most Likely To' comes from many Bromley kids who remember *his* presence on the stage, rather than David's; as yet another contemporary, Roger Bevan, puts it, 'George was the singer, we all remember his Elvis impressions and *everyone* reckoned he was going to be big.'

2 'Numero Uno, Mate!'

Main sources include George Underwood, who was interviewed for a *MOJO* feature on the recording of 'Liza Jane', Geoff MacCormack, Dorothy Bass, Les Conn, David Hadfield and Dick Taylor. Quotes on David's job at Nevin D. Hirst from Mat Snow's interview for *Q*, 1995. David's recollections of hanging out with Marc Bolan from are Paul Du Noyer's *MOJO* interview, July 2002. This interview, and Du Noyer's later thoughts and insightful comments, can be found at his website, www.pauldunoyer.com. The date of The King Bees' public debut, and other details, come from John Bloom's *It's No Sin to Make a Profit* (W.H. Allen, 1970). Special thanks to Dorothy Bass, whose diary of those early days was hugely helpful in pinning down The King Bees' live dates, and who has recorded a typical week in a Bromley teen's life as follows: Monday: R&B at the Bromley Court Hotel or the Marquee; Tuesday: R&B at the 100 Club; Wednesday: R&B/Jazz at the Court or Folk at the Star & Garter (Bromley High Street); Thursday: R&B at the Marquee or Trad at the Court; Friday: R&B at the Bell or the Court or Folk at Catford Bridge (presumably a pub in Catford); Saturday: Modern Jazz at the Marquee.

3 Thinking About Me

The Manish Boys section relies on recollections from band members Bob Solly, Paul Rodriguez, Woolf Byrne, Johnny Flux and Mick Whitehead; special thanks to Bob and Woolf for the access to their diaries and cuttings. Lower Third interviewees were Denis Taylor and Graham Rivens. Special thanks to Kenny Bell, who invited me to a Pinot Grigio-fuelled Denmark Street reunion which featured many key figures of that era, including Mike Berry, Terry King and Simon White. Terry King and John Singer provided invaluable insights into the background of Ralph Horton; other key interviewees were Shel Talmy, Wayne Bardell, Kenney Jones, Jeff Dexter and Tony Hatch. Information on Marc Bolan's early career is from Mark Paytress' wonderful book *Bolan: The Rise and Fall of a 20th Century Superstar* (Omnibus, 2006).

4 Laughing Gnome

Principal sources, in addition to those detailed for the previous chapter, are Ken Pitt, Hugh Mendl, Mike Vernon, Tony Hall, Derek 'Dek' Fearnley, John 'Hutch' Hutchinson, Alan Mair, Tom Parker and Neil Slaven. Most dates quoted come from Ken Pitt's paperwork and Decca records. Special thanks to The Riot Squad, one of the most mysterious bands ever to play behind David; I was treated to an impromptu Squad reunion with Bob Flag, George Butcher and Del Roll in an

Essex pub, which gave me a wonderful insight into those carefree, zany days. Thanks to Paolo Hewitt, Jeff Dexter and Graham Marsh for sharing their thoughts on Mod, and Marcus Gray for sharing his insights into the Deram/Essex connection, and also pointing out the Ian Brady and Myra Hindley references in 'Please Mr. Gravedigger'.

5 I Wish Something Would Happen

Principal interviewees: Chris Welch, Ken Pitt, Hugh Mendl, Tony Visconti, Steve Chapman, Lindsay Kemp, Mick Farren, Gordon Rose, Michael Garrett, Jeff Dexter, Vernon Dewhurst, Ray Stevenson, John Hutchinson. The story of how David discovered Jacques Brel via Lesley Duncan comes from David's 'Nokia Recommends: Sounds of My Universe' interview (although David doesn't mention Lesley by name). David's 'he got all snitty' quote about Marc Bolan is from Paul Du Noyer's Bowie interview, MOJO, July 2002; David's description of Terry's schizophrenic fit during the Cream show at the Bromel Club comes from his NME interview, March 1993.

6 Check Ignition

Main sources: Ray Stevenson, Keith Christmas, Alan Mair, Tony Visconti, Calvin Mark Lee, Simon Hayes, Mark Pritchett, Angie Bowie, Terry Cox, John Cambridge, Tim Renwick, Gron Kelly, Olav Wyper, David Bebbington, Jeff Griffin. The account of how the Philips album was recorded cross-references the memories of Cambridge, Renwick, Christmas and Tony Visconti. The author's own interview with Gus Dudgeon has been greatly improved with a transcript of a longer, more detailed interview conducted by Fred Dellar in March 1978. Bowie fans will notice I don't mention Tony Visconti's anecdote about how Mick Ronson attended the final overdubs for the Philips album, principally because Visconti believed Cambridge had brought Mick to the session – and John is adamant that he did not.

7 All The Madmen

Opening description is based mainly on interviews with Mark Pritchett, whose mother Donna was housekeeper at Haddon Hall. The description of Pitt's visit to the session for 'The Prettiest Star' derives from my interview with David Bebbington, cross-referenced with Tony Visconti; Bebbington also attended the Arts Lab session at which David first mentioned his half-brother, Terry. Early history of Mick Ronson is based on accounts by Keith Herd – who recorded The Rats' first sessions – Rats bassist Keith Cheesman, Rats drummer John Cambridge and Ronno bassist Trevor Bolder. Other sources for the chapter include Jeff Griffin, Ray Stevenson, Laurence Myers, Olav Wyper and Ken Scott – whose account is crucial because it confirms Visconti's suggestions that he and Ronson were solely responsible for major sections of The Man Who Sold the World. Lastly, Mick Farren's contention that David quoted Kahlil Gibran or Nietzsche on the basis of reading book jackets is confirmed by Dai Davies, who spent many late nights discussing philosophy with David the following year.

8 Kooks

Main interviews for this chapter: Bob Grace, Bill Harry, Anya Wilson, Herbie Flowers, Henry Spinetti, Robin McBride, Ron Oberman, John Mendelssohn, Ken Scott, Trevor Bolder, Leee Childers, Tony Zanetta and Robin Mayhew. Much of the information on Tony Defries comes from David Thompson, who collaborated with Tony on an abandoned autobiography; his information was augmented by interviews with Laurence Myers – who is often written out of the story – and Olav Wyper. Tony Visconti's account of his dealings with Tony Defries come from his book, *Bowie, Bolan and the Brooklyn Boy* (HarperCollins, 2007); Angie Bowie's description of Zowie's birth is based on her account in *Backstage Passes*. Details of how David's new deal left him with an obligation to Essex Music – ultimately settled with several *Scary Monsters* songs, including 'Up the Hill Backwards' – were provided by Simon Platz. The story of David meeting Doug Yule and thinking he was Lou Reed was described in *Record Collector* magazine, September 2001. Robert Kensell, a Sombrero regular, gave a great account of the club. Special thanks to Mark Pritchett, who provided unique insights into Bowie's songwriting during the most crucial period of his career. Evidence that David initially intended to book Herbie Flowers and Tim Renwick for his 'Kooks' BBC session came from Jeff Griffin, who has a booking sheet dated just one week earlier, which names them in the band line-up, replaced by the future Spiders at the last moment.

9 Over the Rainbow

Main sources for David and Defries' trip to RCA are Danny Fields, Iggy Pop, Lisa Robinson and Tony Zanetta. Throughout this period, Tony Zanetta is an excellent, objective source, and I'm grateful to him for subjecting to perhaps a dozen interviews. Zanetta and Henry Edwards' book *Stardust* (Michael Joseph, 1986) has been widely criticised – by Nicholas Pegg, among others – but while its coverage of the other eras is flaky, it gives a brilliant overview of the MainMan years. For the run-up to the 'I'm gay and I always have been' *Melody Maker* interview, Dai Davies – perhaps David's closest, most objective confidant of the period – was an inexhaustible, definitive source of insights. It was also Dai Davies, as one of those dealing closely with Ronson, who points out that his misgivings about The Spiders' makeover were more about muso credibility than homophobia in Hull (which of course did, and does, exist). The fact that 'Somewhere Over the Rainbow' was also plagiarised for 'The White Cliffs of Dover' was first pointed out by musicologists interviewed for a Radio 4 documentary in October 2009, dedicated to the wartime anthem (incidentally, there are no bluebirds over Dover). Barry Bethes quote courtesy of Mike Berry. Other interviews: Leee Childers, Tom Parker, Kris Needs, Will Palin, Trevor Bolder, Ken Scott, Mark Pritchett, Robin Mayhew, Jeff Dexter, Dave Marsh, Herbie Flowers, Suzi Fussey, Matthew Fisher, Lindsay Kemp. Spider Special recipe is courtesy of Will Palin. Ian Hunter interview is courtesy of Kris Needs. David Bowie wrote about The Legendary Stardust Cowboy and Vince Taylor, one inspiration for Ziggy, in the edition of *MOJO* which he guest-edited in July 2002; David's account of the creation of the Ziggy jumpsuits comes from *Moonage Daydream: The Life and Times of Ziggy Stardust* by Bowie and Mick Rock (Palazzo, 2005).

10 Battle Cries and Champagne

The account of the Cleveland aftershow, the writing of 'The Jean Genie' and the problems recording 'Panic in Detroit' come from Trevor Bolder. Main sources are as for the previous chapter, with the addition of Scott Richardson, James Williamson, John 'Hutch' Hutchinson and Ava Cherry. Descriptions of David's boat trip, and attendance at the Bruce Springsteen show, are described by Geoff MacCormack in his book *From Station to Station* (Genesis, 2007). Special thanks to Rodney Bingenheimer for putting me in touch with six of the Rodney's English Disco regulars, including Kathy Heller, Nancy McCrado and Lori Madox. The effects of Scientology on the MainMan organisation were described primarily by Trevor Bolder and Robin Mayhew. The Iggy quote about 'rolling my eyes' comes from Cliff Jones' interview with Iggy in 1996. (Iggy was always much more polite about his ex-buddy during my interviews with him.) David's 'highly symbolic' quote, illustrating just how early his marriage seemed doomed, comes from Mick Rock's *Moonage Daydream*. Ian Hunter's 'holding up well' observations about Bowie, and some other dates, come from his excellent *Diary of a Rock 'n' Roll Star*. Additional research on this chapter, specifically the Mike Garson interview, is by one-time Mott The Hoople fanclub organiser, Kris Needs.

11 Star

Descriptions of the US routine are based on interviews with Bolder, Zanetta, Mayhew, Fussey, Davies and Hutchinson, augmented with dates and references from Zanetta's *Stardust*, MacCormack's *Station to Station* and Mick Rock's *Moonage Daydream*. Details of The Spiders' attempts to sign to Columbia are based on Trevor Bolder's account; David's seduction of Lulu, with Angie Bowie in pursuit, was witnessed by John Hutchinson, and recently confirmed by Lulu in her autobiography *I Don't Want to Fight* (Time Warner, 2003). Other sources include interviewees from the previous chapter, plus Ken Scott, Scott Richardson, Jayne County, Mark Pritchett, Hugh Attwooll and Ava Cherry. Descriptions of the interior of Oakley Street come from its decorators, Mick Gillah, Chris Goodchild and Aubrey Goodchild.

12 The Changing isn't Free

David's relationship with Mick Jagger was sketched out primarily by Ava Cherry, Scott Richardson and the pair's agent, Maggie Abbott. *Diamond Dogs* description, and especially the genesis of 'Rebel Rebel', comes from Alan Parker and Herbie Flowers. Especial thanks to the ever-diplomatic Herbie for an objective view of a controversy which has fascinated musicians for years, including Nile Rodgers, who points out, 'I could never believe it was David played that guitar.' Other sources are as for the previous chapter, plus Wayne Bardell, Keith Christmas and Carlos Alomar. The Apollo dates were supplied by the Frank Schiffman Apollo Theatre Collection – thanks to Christine S. Windheuser of the NMAH Archives Center.

David went to at least two Apollo shows, one around 18 September, with comic Frankyln Ajaye, The Spinners and The Temptations. Richard Pryor and The Main Ingredient shared a bill on 26 April with Inner Voices, who were out on prison leave. The archives contain brief assessments of each performance: Richard Pryor, still to achieve widespread fame on *Saturday Night Live*, is pronounced: 'Dirty, dirty! But funny, funny! Absolute control of audience . . . Excellent!' Descriptions of Norman Fisher come from Ava Cherry, Cherry Vanilla and David's recollections on 'Nokia Recommenders'. David's Nuremberg-influenced lighting scheme was recalled by Mark Pritchett. Other details of New York in 1974 come from *The Ossie Clark Diaries* (Bloomsbury, 1998). David's soul record collection was detailed by Geoff MacCormack, Ava Cherry and Harvey Kubernick.

13 Make Me Break Down and Cry

Key sources include Ava Cherry, Tony Zanetta, Carlos Alomar, Tony Visconti, Iggy Pop and May Pang. Details of Bowie's position as 'employee' of MainMan come from his contract dated 31 March, 1972. Terry O'Neill's account of David's meeting with Liz Taylor conflicts with Zanetta's version, which is that Liz Taylor first met David when she arrived at a rehearsal. Zanetta's version is in *Stardust*, p276. Description of the Hyatt Regency bust relies on MacCormack's account in *Station to Station*. Reports of Iggy's reunion with David come from Ron Asheton, and others, interviewed for the author's biography of Iggy, *Open Up and Bleed* (Sphere, 2008). Sources for the recording of 'Fame' are Carlos Alomar (who mentions here, for the first time to my knowledge, how David played a key guitar riff on the song), Eddie Kramer and May Pang. Carlos Alomar does not remember Lennon singing 'Shame, Shame, Shame'; however, May Pang contends that 'I was the only one not on drugs and that's what happened.' Her version is supported by the fact that the song's descending melody, first heard at 3.01, is essentially identical to 'Shame, Shame, Shame's' chorus. The simplest explanation is that David heard John singing the line, but Carlos didn't. Thanks to Keith Badman, author of *The Beatles After the Break Up* (Omnibus Press, 1999) who pinned down Paul's arrival in New York as 10 January, and places the 'Fame' session as circa 15–20 January. Defries' share of Bowie's work up to 1982 was first uncovered by the Gillmans, who had access to MainMain paperwork and put the relevant date as 30 September, 1982. However, David's original contract, as mentioned above, dates from 31 March, 1982.

14 White Stains

Main sources: Ava Cherry, Maggie Abbott, Cherry Vanilla, Geoff MacCormack, Glenn Hughes, Earl Slick, Iggy Pop, James Williamson, Carlos Alomar, Ben Edmonds. For this chapter, I owe a huge debt to writer Rob Hughes, who shared all the interview transcripts for his excellent *Uncut* article on *The Man Who Fell to Earth*. This helped give me a vital sense of the wider context behind the movie; it was vital, too, for Roeg and Litvinoff's accounts of what happened to Bowie's soundtrack for the movie. All the quotes from Candy Clark, Nicholas Roeg and Si Litvinoff come from Rob's transcripts. Thanks also to Joel McIver, Glenn Hughes' biographer, for sharing information and putting me in touch with

Glenn. Slash quote is from *Slash: The Autobiography* (Harper, 2008). Paul Buckmaster quotes come from his interview with David Buckley in the *MOJO* Bowie birthday special, January 2007.

Thanks to Gary Lachman for providing extensive background information on Bowie and the occult. The obvious influence of Trevor Ravenscroft's *The Spear of Destiny* and other texts, and Bowie's avowed interest in Gnosticism, has inspired a huge amount of sometimes hilarious background reading. The net is a good place to investigate these theories. One amusing fantasist, contacted by this author and quoted widely elsewhere, claimed to have intimate knowledge of Bowie's early involvement with characters like Stephen Ward and other members of the Profumo circle. Disappointingly, such conspiracy theorists omit facts that could shore up their batty fantasies. Some of Bowie's key works are in fact intimately connected with a line of occult power running across London – mapped by Nazi theorists – which led to Omphalos, the spiritual centre of the British Empire, according to the London Psychogeographical Society. 'Space Oddity' was first recorded in Deptford Creek, on this line of power – where Christopher Marlowe was allegedly sacrificed by dark forces involving the magician John Dee – and *Ziggy Stardust* was rehearsed nearby in Greenwich, or Omphalos, itself. The line of power also bisects Bromley Road. I hope an expert will investigate this subject more deeply.

More seriously, there is a brilliant analysis of the concepts invoked in *Station to Station* by the late Ian MacDonald, reprinted in *The People's Music* (Pimlico, 2003). Gary Lachman explores the 1960s history of the occult in *Turn Off Your Mind: The Mystic Sixties and the Dark Side of the Age of Aquarius* (Sidgwick & Jackson, 2002).

Information on David's involvement with Wally Elmlark comes from Cherry Vanilla, who goes on to say that after writing down the telephone number, David promised he'd produce Cherry's next album. 'Bowie said, "I'll be in New York in a week I'll see you then." I was floating around on cloud nine – Bowie's going to produce my record! The next week I'm at Norman Fisher's and Norman gave this party for Bowie . . . the top of the fireplace was all white with coke. I walked up to David and said, "When are we going to talk about the record?" He said something to me in German, turned away and I didn't see him again for years.'

Deep Purple live dates come from http://www.deeppurpleliveindex.com/.

15 Ghosts in the Echo Chambers

Main interviews: Andrew Kent, Iggy Pop, Carlos Alomar, Laurent Thibault, Pierre Calamel, Marc Zermati, Philippe Auliac, Roy Young, Tony Visconti, Angie Bowie, Kuelan Nguyen, Phil Palmer, Eduard Meyer. David's intention to record with Iggy at Musicland was first mentioned in Iggy's interview with *Punk Magazine* in March 1976. My thanks to Christophe Geudin, who interviewed Laurent Thibault for *Recording Musicien* magazine, exchanged ideas with me and helped me make several breakthroughs in understanding *The Idiot*. Bowie's confused communications with Michael Rother were first revealed in Tobias Rüther's *Helden: David Bowie und Berlin* (Rogner und Bernhard, 2008). Brian Eno quotes are from Stephen

Dalton's *Uncut* interview, more background on Eno comes from *On Some Faraway Beach: The Life and Times of Brian Eno* by David Sheppard and Eno's insightful interview with Ian MacDonald, *NME*, November 1977.

16 Helden

Opening section is based on an interview with Tony Visconti; the description of a typical day in Berlin comes from Iggy Pop, augmented by the recollections of Edu Meyer, one of the recipients of Bowie and Iggy's surprise visits. Main interviews: Angie Bowie, Edu Meyer, Hunt Sales, Tony Sales, Esther Friedmann, Ricky Gardiner, Kris Needs, Carlos Alomar. David's quotes on 'the sense of yearning for a future we knew would never come to pass' are from *Uncut*. Thanks to David Sheppard for sharing his thoughts on this period in Eno's artistic life; Eno's quotes are from Ian MacDonald's *NME* interview. The section covering Bowie's appearance on *Marc* derives from interviews with Keith Altham, Jeff Dexter, Chris Welch and Cliff Wright. Information on Marc's fatal car crash comes from Mark Paytress's research.

17 I Am Not a Freak

Main sources for David's later days in Berlin are Edu Meyer, Esther Friedmann and Klaus Krüger. *Stage* and *Lodger* sources: Adrian Belew, Carlos Alomar, Simon House and Tony Visconti, augmented by Sean Mayes' *We Can Be Heroes: Life On Tour with David Bowie*. *Just a Gigolo* background was aided by Michael Watt's feature for *Melody Maker*, February 1978. The Lou Reed encounter is based primarily on Chuck Hammer's recollections. Other interviewees: Barry Andrews, Steve Strange. Primary *Elephant Man* interviews: Ken Ruta, Jeanette Landis. The description of David's reaction to John Lennon's murder comes primarily from May Pang.

18 Snapshot of a Brain

Duncan Jones talked about his front-room viewing sessions of *Star Wars* in the *New York Times*, 3 June, 2009. David's bodyguard and stalker-avoiding routine were described by Kevin Armstrong and others. David's 'I've gotten closer to her' quote about Peggy comes from his interview with Timothy White, *Musician*, May 1983. Figures for Mitchelson's divorce settlement for Angie come *Ladies' Man: The Life and Trials of Marvin Mitchelson* by John A. Jenkins (St Martin's Press, 1992); Angie's comment that David 'used his millions to poison Zowie against me' comes from the *Daily Mail*, which has featured Angie many times over the years; David's 'As much insight into the human condition as a walnut' quote comes from the same source. Brian May's 'It was hard because you had four very precocious boys' quote comes from Mark Blake's interview for the *MOJO* Special of 2008. The *Baal* section derives from interviews with Louis Marks and Dominic Muldowney, plus John Willett's fascinating essay, 'Brecht for the Media', 1982. Jeremy Thomas and Ryuichi Sakamoto quotes come from the 'Making of . . .' documentary on the special edition of *Merry Christmas Mr Lawrence*. Other interviews: Esther Friedmann, Carol Clerk, Tommy Shannon, Gary Lachman, Nile Rodgers, Gary Gersh, Hugh Stanley-Clarke.

19 On the Other Side

Principal interviews: Tommy Shannon, Frank Simms, Earl Slick, Charles Shaar Murray, Hugh Padgham, Julien Temple, Kevin Armstrong, Matthew Seligman, Clare Hirst, Thomas Dolby, Iggy Pop, Nancy Jeffries, Erdal Kizilcay, Edu Meyer, Tony Horkins. Bowiedownunder.com had a fascinating, useful account of the filming of the 'Let's Dance' and 'China Girl' videos. Thanks to David Buckley, who put me in touch with Hugh Padgham and whose Bowie biography, *Strange Fascination* (Virgin, 1999), gives a superb account of the making of *Tonight*. For *Open Up and Bleed*, I believed the assurances of Iggy's management that David's tale of Iggy stamping on a fan's head was apocryphal; now, thanks to Ed Hunter and Noel Tepper, we know the fan was Lucille Reed of Poughkeepsie, who won a settlement from Iggy's lawyers. Most of the quotes from Pat Antoniou come from pieces in the *Sun* and the *Daily Mirror*, throughout spring 1985, accessed via the British Library at Colindale. Records of David's plans to set up his own production stable with Bill Laswell came from paperwork in the possession of Les Conn.

20 It's My Life – So Fuck Off

Principal interviews: Kevin Armstrong, Reeves Gabrels, Tony Sales, Hunt Sales, Eric Schermerhorn, Adrian Belew, Erdal Kizilcay, Emma Bannister, Nile Rodgers. Much of the information on David and Iman's first meeting comes from (where else?) *Hello!* magazine. The story of David's trip to Wales first appeared in the *South Wales Echo*, September 1992. David's quote, 'the truth is I was not convinced by the motivations behind this event', comes from *Rock Et Folk* magazine, December 1998. Interviews around the Mick Ronson tribute include Suzi Ronson, Trevor Bolder and Ken Scott. Ronson's quote comes from an interview I did with him for *International Musician* magazine in February 1989, in which it was obvious he was a little sniffy about Bowie – but had no complaints. In the same interview, Ronson and I discussed whether David's switch to a deeper, more baritone voice was influenced by Iggy. Ronson's conclusion was 'Sound like Iggy? He wanted to *be* Iggy!' Hanif Kureishi tells his own story of The Buddha of Suburbia at hanifkureishi.com. His site also contains his 1999 story, 'Strangers When We Meet'.

21 The Heart's Filthy Lesson

This chapter would not have been possible without the inspiration, help and persistence of Kris Needs, who did the bulk of the research on the *Outside* sessions, and conducted the detailed, insightful interviews with Reeves Gabrels, Mike Garson and Mark Plati. Other sources for this chapter: Kevin Armstrong, Erdal Kizilcay, Tony Visconti (augmented with material from *The Brooklyn Boy*), Carlos Alomar, Thomas Dolby, Mark Cooper, Max Glenn. The background on Bowie Bonds is sourced primarily from court records and judgements in the Pullman v. Prudential and Zysblat case, decided in favour of the latter by Supreme Court judge Ira Gammerman in judgement 600772/01, July 2003. Duncan Jones' career was summarised in, among others, the *New York Times*, June 2009. Over the period in question, David's webchats at wwww.davidbowie.com provide consistent, often hilarious insights into his family life and music. Bowie's account of the making of *Heathen* comes from his excellent interview for *Livewire*, 16 June, 2002.

22 The Houdini Principle
The title of this chapter, and much of the reasoning, derives from Julien Temple's conversations with David early in 1985. Bowie fans will also recognise a resonance with his intriguing performance as Nikolai Tesla in Christopher Nolan's *The Prestige* – a movie whose title and plot revolve around the notion of making a magnificent exit. Fan quotes are posted on the YouTube video of the Fashion Rocks Show, 8 September, 2005. The 'pregnant pause' theory was advanced by, among others, Nicholas Pegg in the *MOJO* Special of 2007; the announcement both of Bowie's appearance at Highline, and his cancellation, appeared on davidbowie.com. David confided his estrangement from Iggy to Robert Phoenix on gettingit.com, October 1999. Details of Defries' disastrous investment in the Cayman Islands was reported on wikileaks, 3 March, 2008. Information on Defries' planned autobiography *Gods and Gangsters*, come from his press release of 2008. Duncan Jones' quote about his relationship with his father comes from the *Daily Telegraph*, 14 July, 2009. Ian McCulloch quote from *MOJO*, issue 100. Other interviews: Julien Temple, Mike Garson, Ian Gittins, George Underwood, Momus, Charles Francis, Nicolas Godin.

General Sources
UK chart positions are sourced throughout from *The Q Encyclopedia of Rock Stars*; US positions from *Billboard*. I also used the index of UK chart runs at polyhex.com. My invaluable source for the various brands of cigarettes favoured by Bowie over the years was Jarvis Cocker's interview with David for *The Big Issue*, December 1997. Bowienet.com, bowiewonderworld.com, 5years.com, bowiegoldenyears.com, teenagewildlife.com and www.illustrated-db-discography.nl were invaluable throughout.

Background Reading
All written sources used in the book are cited within the notes. The following books made for invaluable Bowie background reading and reference.

Alias David Bowie, Peter and Leni Gillman (Hodder & Stoughton, 1986)
Backstage Passes: Life on the Wild Side With David Bowie, Angie Bowie with Patrick Carr (Orion, 1993)
Bowie, Jerry Hopkins (Macmillan, 1985)
Bowie: The Pitt Report, Ken Pitt (Omnibus, 1985)
The Complete David Bowie, Nicholas Pegg (Reynolds & Hearn, 2000)

The Dark Stuff: Selected Writings on Rock Music 1972–1993, Nick Kent (Penguin, 1994)
David Bowie: A Chronology, Kevin Cann (Vermilion, 1983)
David Bowie: Moonage Daydream, David Thompson (Plexus, 1989)
Diary of a Rock 'n' Roll Star, Ian Hunter (IMP, 1996)
Free Spirit, Angie Bowie (Mushroom, 1981)
Johnny Thunders: In Cold Blood, Nina Antonia (Jungle, 1997)
The Life and Death of Andy Warhol, Victor Bockris (Bantam, 1989)
Lou Reed: The Biography, Victor Bockris (Hutchinson, 1994)
Low, Hugo Wilcken (Continuum, 2005)
Mick Ronson: The Spider with the Platinum Hair, Weird and Gilly (IMP, 2003)
New York Rocker, Gary Valentine (Sidgwick & Jackson, 2002)
On Some Faraway Beach: The Life and Times of Brian Eno, David Sheppard (Orion, 2008)
The Q Encyclopedia of Rock Stars (Dorling Kindersley, 1996)
Rebel Heart, Bebe Buell (St Martin's Press, 2001)
Strange Fascination: David Bowie The Definitive Story, David Buckley (Virgin, 1999)
We Can be Heroes: Life on Tour with David Bowie, Sean Mayes (IMP, 1999)
Wonderland Avenue: Tales of Glamour and Excess, Danny Sugerman (William Morrow & Co, 1989)

All magazines and periodicals quoted within the text are detailed in the notes. The principal magazines used for background reading include *Billboard*, *Circus*, *Creem*, *Disc*, *East Village Other*, *Denim Delinquent*, *End Times*, *Entertainment World*, *Evo*, *Fifth Estate*, *Fusion*, *Gay Power*, *Goldmine*, *GQ*, *Guitarist*, *International Musician*, *Jazz & Pop*, *Q*, *Melody Maker*, *MOJO*, *Motorbooty*, *Motor City Rock and Roll News*, *NME*, *Pavilion*, *Phonograph Record Magazine*, *Record Mirror*, *Record World*, *Rock Scene*, *Rolling Stone*, *Sounds*, *Stereo Review*, *Strange Things*, *The Guitar Magazine*, *Trouser Press*, *Variety*, *Village Voice*, *Wire*, *Zig Zag*. Copies of *The Times*, *The Sunday Times*, the *Sun* and the *Daily Mirror* were all accessed courtesy of the British Library reading rooms. Thanks to *Q*, *MOJO*, Johnny Black, Fred Dellar and Richard Morton Jack for use of their archives.

ACKNOWLEDGEMENTS

As ever, my deepest thanks go to Julian Alexander, an oasis of calm and good sense in a changing world, as well as a rigorous commentator in the earliest days of this project. Thanks also to my US agent, Sarah Lazin, for her acumen and encouragement.

I also count myself very lucky to work with Antonia Hodgson and John Parsley, of Little, Brown UK and US respectively. Both of them shared complementary, multiple, sustained insights, without which this would not have been the same book. They were also good company, and I look forward to another Bowie tour into the nether regions of Soho (and his personal life) soon.

Others deserving of thanks are probably too many to mention, but a brief list would include Martin Aston, Louis Barfe, Mark Blake, Tony Beasty, Kenny Bell, Johnny Black, Romain Blondel, Billy Bragg, Anne Bourgeois-Vignon, Dave Burrluck, Chris Charlesworth, Fred Dellar, Peter Doggett, Roger Dopson, Richard England, Miles Evans, Eve Fegyveres, Carl Ferris, Marcus Fuhrmann, Ken Garner, Debra Geddes, Pat Gilbert, Marcus Gray, Paul Guimaraes, Sue Harris, Paulo Hewitt, Graham Marsh, Martin Hopewell, Laurie Hornsby, Dorothy Howes, Jim Irvin, Leonora Jackaman, Graham Johnson, Kieron Jones, Ashley Kahn, Terry King, Colin MacKenzie, Spencer Leigh, Ian Muir, John Myer, Kris Needs, Mark Paytress, Christopher Porter, John Reed, Carlton Sandercock, Josh Saunders, Joe Smith, Mat Snow, Bob Solly, Michael Stimson, Dave Thompson, Geoff Travis, Gerald Wallis, Dorian Wathen, Cliff Watkins, David Wells, Marc Zermati. Thanks also to all the staff at *MOJO* magazine, especially Mark Blake, Jenny Bulley, Danny Eccleston, Phil Alexander, Ian Harrison and Andrew Male for their help and forbearance. Not to forget Chris Ingham – MOJO's 'Doctor Rock' – for sharing thoughts on Bowie's songwriting.

People who offered help with the Iggy book, which also proved pivotal in this book, include Christophe Geudin, who helped me locate Laurent Thibault, and Tony Zanetta, whose patience seemed inexhaustible. Thanks, once more, to my schoolmate Nick Hunter, the only fifteen-year-old kid I knew who had a copy of Bowie's Santa Monica bootleg, from which we worked out our own (dreadful) version of 'Waiting for the Man'. David Buckley was a confidant on my Iggy book, who should have been a rival on this book, but was as helpful and generous with his insights as ever. Kat Johnson, both on this book and *Open Up and Bleed*, did a heroic job of helping with transcription. Most profoundly, my everlasting thanks and appreciation to Lucy and Curtis; as mentioned at the Trafalgar Tavern, in the last ditch I will always think of you.

Thanks to all my interviewees for sharing their time and insights. They are: Maggie Abbott, Carlos Alomar, Keith Altham, Keith Andrew, Barry Andrews, Bernie Andrews, Annie Apple, Kevin Armstrong, Ron Asheton, Hugh Attwooll, Philippe Auliac, Jim Avery, Emma Bannister, Wayne Bardell, John Barrance, Mike Bassett, Max Batten, David Bebbington, Kenny Bell, Adrian Belew, Mike Berry, Rodney Bingenheimer, Roger Bolden, Trevor Bolder, Angie Bowie, Stephen Braine, Chris Britton, Nick Brooks, Bebe Buell, Rodney Burbeck, George Butcher, Woolf Byrne, Pierre Calamel, John Cale, John Cambridge, Steve Chapman, Keith Cheesman, Ava Cherry, Leee Childers, Keith Christmas, Carol Clerk, Richard Comben, Les Conn, Mark Cooper, Jayne County, Terry Cox, Sydney Curtis, Peter Davidson, Dai Davies, Vernon Dewhurst, Jeff Dexter, Wolfgang Diebeling, Thomas Dolby, Bryan Drew, Greg D'Souza, Gus Dudgeon, Ben Edmonds, John Edmonds, John Edward (Johnny Flux), Robin Eggar, Mick Farren, Hermione Farthingale, Derek 'Dek' Fearnley, Danny Fields, Matthew Fisher, Bob Flag, Herbie Flowers, Kim Fowley, Charles Francis, Esther Friedmann, Reeves Gabrels, Michael Garrett, Mike Garson, Gary Gersh, Mick Gillah, Dana Gillespie, Ian Gittins, Max Glenn, Nicolas Godin, Suzanne Goldschmitt, Aubrey and Chris Goodchild, Bob Grace, Cary Granger, Shaun Greenfield, Barbara Gray, Jeff Griffin, Tony Hall, David Hadfield, Bill Harry, Tony Hatch, Simon Hayes, Kathy Heller, Keith Herd, Susan Hill, Clare Hirst, Gill Hymas, Chuck Hammer, Tony Horkins, Simon House, Glenn Hughes, John 'Hutch' Hutchinson, Norman Ingram, Nancy Jeffries, Kenney Jones, Graham Kelly, Lindsay Kemp, John Kendall, Robert Kensell, Andrew Kent, Terry King, Erdal Kizilcay, Eddie Kramer, Klaus Krüger, Harvey Kubernick, Gary Lachman, Jeanette Landis, Sue Larner, Calvin Mark Lee, Suzanne Liritis, Dorothy Bass Macedo, Lori Madox, Alan Mair, Louis Marks, Dave Marsh, Glenn Max, Linda McCartney, Nancy McCrado, Geoff MacCormack, Robin McBride, Robin Mayhew, John Mendelssohn, Hugh Mendl, Eduard Meyer, Momus, Dominic Muldowney, Charles Shaar Murray, Laurence Myers, Kuelan Nguyen, Kris Needs, Ron Oberman, Len Outridge, Colin Ovenden, Hugh Padgham, Will Palin, Phil Palmer, May Pang, Alan Parker, Tom Parker, Brian Payne, Les Payne, Howard Phillips, Ken Pitt, Mark Plati, Simon Platz, Iggy Pop, Jan Powling, Peter Prickett, Mark Pritchett, Alan Reader, Tim Renwick, Scott Richardson, Graham Rivens, Lisa Robinson, Nile Rodgers, Paul Rodriguez, Derek 'Del' Roll, Suzi Ronson, Gordon Rose, Michael Rother, Ken Ruta, Hunt Sales, Tony Sales, Carlton Sandercock, Eric Schermerhorn, Ken Scott, Matthew Seligman, Tommy Shannon, Harry Shapiro, Frank Simms, John Singer, Neil Slaven, Earl Slick, Bob Solly, Henry Spinetti, Linda Stagg, Hugh Stanley-Clarke, Ray Stevenson, David Stopps, Steve Strange, Shel Talmy, Denis Taylor, Dick Taylor, Julien Temple, Laurent Thibault, Dave Thompson, Andy Twiner,

Diana Udall, George Underwood, Mike Vernon, Tony Visconti, Chris Welch, David West, Adrian White, Simon White, Mick Whitehead, Keith Wilkinson, James Williamson, Val Wilmer, Anya Wilson, Jonathan Wingate, Cliff Wright, Olav Wyper, Roy Young, Tony Zanetta, Marc Zermati.

Sadly, since I started work on this book and its predecessor, *Open Up and Bleed*, the following interviewees have passed away: Ron Asheton, Les Conn, Hugh Attwooll, Carol Clerk, Hugh Mendl, Louis Marks, Will Palin and Derek 'Dek' Fearnley. All of them were enthralling raconteurs; I will miss speaking to them again, as I will Ian MacDonald, always one of the most thought-provoking writers on *MOJO*, and Mick Ronson, who was unfailingly tolerant with me as a star-struck, novice writer.

INDEX